# Supervisory Management

## SEVENTH EDITION

P.W. Betts

Mte , PhD, FInstAM(Adv Dip), FIMgt, MCIM

**FINANCIAL TIMES**

Prentice Hall

An imprint of **Pearson Education**

Harlow, England · London · New York · Reading, Massachusetts · San Francisco
Toronto · Don Mills, Ontario · Sydney · Tokyo · Singapore · Hong Kong · Seoul
Taipei · Cape Town · Madrid · Mexico City · Amsterdam · Munich · Paris · Milan

**Pearson Education Limited**
Edinburgh Gate
Harlow
Essex CM20 2JE
England

and Associated Companies throughout the world

*Visit us on the world wide web at:*
http://www.pearsoneduc.com

First to fifth editions published as *Supervisory Studies:*
*A Managerial Perspective*
Sixth edition published as *Supervisory Management* by Pitman
Publishing, 1993
Seventh edition published by Pearson Education Limited, 2000

ISBN 0 582 41877-1

**British Library Cataloguing-in-Publication Data**

A catalogue record for this book is available from the British Library.

10  9  8  7  6  5  4  3  2
05  04  03  02  01

Set by 35 in 10/12pt Sabon and News Gothic
Produced by Pearson Education Asia Pte Ltd
Printed in Singapore (COS)

# Contents

# Contents

# Preface

This book has been revised to incorporate the latest features of modern thought, views, concepts, theories, practices and techniques. The theme remains unchanged: to provide a complete coverage of the important factors of supervision, which include areas of knowledge that are essential for the effective development of supervisory skills; experience factors that affect competences; comprehensive details of supervisory skills, including development techniques, essential features, problems, and the effects of social and technological changes; an examination of management standards within the context of supervision; and the use of competences, their nature, depth, levels, applications and transitory nature.

The text is written for those who are actively engaged in supervising and for those who are training to qualify in the art of supervision. Supervising is similar to all other arts: the use of science and disciplines learned through books is basically essential, but achieving desired results demands experience and a creative flair.

Supervising permeates all levels of business activity – from the top executive who supervises senior managers to the shop-floor supervisor or office supervisor who directs and controls employees. Consequently, effective supervision is the key to the successful operation and survival of any organisation. This feature applies provided other factors are taken into consideration, such as bungling governments, intransigent trade unions, competition from countries with high technologies and very low pay levels, and power blocs.

The text has been designed to include most of the topics in schemes offered by institutions associated with the development of a more highly skilled workforce. Their programmes which are included are the Certificate in Supervisory Management offered by the National Examining Board for Supervision and Management (NEBSM); the NEBSM Introductory Award in Supervisory Management; the NEBSM/SNVQ in Supervisory Management, Levels 3 and 4, developed by the Management Charter Initiative (MCI); BTEC National Certificate in Business Studies; BTEC GNVQ Advanced Level; MCI Management Levels 3 and 4 for practising managers and supervisors; and the Certificate of the Institute of Supervisory Management.

The book will also be useful for individuals who are undertaking programmes for BTEC Higher Diplomas, the Diploma in Management Studies, management modules in courses at universities, short management courses, and open learning in supervision and management.

Studying supervision in depth may be approached in many different ways. This book attempts to divide the major features into three logical parts. Although it treats them separately, in practice they are interrelated and integrated. Part One introduces the various aspects of supervision; organisation of work; group activity and teamwork; supervision in industry and business; and the principles, practice and role of management. Part Two concentrates on human relations; motivation; behaviour; leadership, power and influence; many aspects of communication; and various other personnel aspects. Part Three examines the nature of control, along with setting standards, production control, total quality control, financial and cost control, and the administration features of productivity. Questions and case studies are provided at the end of each chapter. Appropriate projects are at the end of each part.

The priority study should be social and moral responsibilities. Perhaps this might motivate supervisors and managers to undertake more intensive training in knowledge and skills. Neglecting social and moral responsibilities may cause distress in many forms, typically insolvency, bankruptcy, tempting employees towards criminal behaviour, harassment, bullying and using fear techniques. However, a balanced scene would include the segment of outstanding performers. Unfortunately, they are in short supply and are often overshadowed by the 'unmentionables' who achieve notoriety and give the profession a bad name.

Legislation in this text provides only a brief guide. There is no intention of recommending, providing complete details, or indicating courses of action. Legislation is complex, extensive, often ambiguous and sometimes has hidden meanings. Consequently, there is a strong recommendation not to become involved in any arguments on legislation. This could lead to serious implications later on. The best possible advice for the supervisor is to seek professional help whenever problems arise concerning the law.

Much material is based on theories, hypotheses, principles, practices, concepts, views and prejudices. The supervisor should know the meaning of these terms and relate them to the material before arriving at conclusions. The limitations of research should also be recognised.

The most important features of supervisory management are included in this book, but all the information of use to the practising supervisor is beyond one volume. Continual study is essential. Anyone who has read this book is assured of a sound base to build on.

# Acknowledgements

I sincerely appreciate the advice and experiences offered freely by my friends. Also, I gratefully acknowledge the assistance given by the Management Charter Initiative, the Health and Safety Executive, DfEE, DTI, the National Institute of Industrial Psychology, ACAS, HMSO Publications Centre, IBM (UK) plc, and the British Standards Institution. I am also indebted to the editorial staff of Pearson Education for their patience and guidance. Finally a special thanks to my wife Rosalinde, who has always listened tolerantly to discussions, critically commented and offered valued advice.

# PART ONE

# Building and maintaining an efficient organisational structure

# 1

# The supervisor

## Introduction

Throughout history groups of people have been subjected to supervision. Today the supervisor remains as an important factor in organisations. No doubt many individuals accept this but detest ineffective supervisors.

Competent supervision is essential to improve profitability – a vital requirement for a company to survive in a competitive world market. Such competence is reached by developing the art of supervising, which means using managerial knowledge in all its forms, applying appropriate skills, and fully utilising them in real situations to achieve objectives.

Human characteristics remain a powerful factor in productivity despite the introduction of new techniques and new technologies. Unfortunately, most people and groups seem to reduce their effectiveness as employees unless they are persuaded to adopt more favourable behaviour. This tendency applies regardless of age, education level, intellect, the activity, organisational level and the situation. Moreover, people also possess important features which need encouraging and developing. Here the supervisor operates as a catalyst, a coach or a counsellor to ensure fully their capabilities.

## Importance of training

Many supervisors are poorly trained, neglected by management, usually blamed for unproductive employees, and resented by trade union representatives.

Unfortunately, many managers do not fully understand the supervisor's role. Consequently, this creates weak support and causes poor relations between supervisors, employees and trade unions. Indeed UK managers fall below standards set in other developed countries. This fault increases the burden on supervisors who must adapt to difficult situations, aggravated now by the accelerating challenge of implementing information technology and other technologies.

## Definitions of a supervisor

There are many definitions of a supervisor due to variations in either traditional or modern viewpoints, and the degree of emphasis on current trends. All views tend to conflict when organisational structures, supervisory roles, and relationships with managers are discussed.

Fundamental features are the five organisational categories which have to be considered:

- supervisors
- managers
- specialists
- supervision
- management

The first three are job titles, whereas the last two are organisational terms. These appear in the following sections and are related to organisational and operating problems in later chapters. Various views, trends, distinguishing features, similarities and differences, which help to clarify role definitions and categories, are now discussed.

# The traditional view

From the traditional viewpoint, a supervisor is any person who is given authority and responsibility for planning and controlling the work of a group through close contact.

In the broad sense, this definition means supervisors may be delegated the authority to deal with the following aspects:

- engagement, transfer, reprimand and dismissal of staff under their control
- staff grievances
- staff discipline
- quantity and quality of output
- recommendations to management

In the narrow sense it may include anyone who directs the work of others by:

- giving instructions on operations
- co-ordinating specialist departments
- recommending courses of action to management

This classical approach is commonplace, fits the traditional, formal organisation's method of operation, and conforms to many organisational principles described in the next chapter.

## THE MODERN VIEW

The modern view is based upon acceptance of supervisors as a part of management and as managers, but the term 'supervisor' remains. Typical definitions from this viewpoint are:

- The supervisor is the key front-line manager, the person who can make or break top management plans (NEBSM definition).
- The supervisor is any manager who controls non-managerial subordinates and is wholly accountable for their work.
- Supervisors, managers and any others who are responsible for the work of other people, at any level and in any type of organisation, should regard themselves as managers.

# Current trends

Current trends are emerging as new techniques and improvements in technologies are used to assist companies in countering the growth of world competition. Also the need for full utilisation of each individual is more recognised now. Such trends give rise to the following aspects.

## EFFECTS OF NEW TECHNIQUES

The use of certain techniques is changing the emphasis on particular supervisory roles and creating new approaches towards employees. These techniques (described in later chapters) include autonomous work groups, empowerment, just-in-time (JIT) and a total quality culture.

The employee may be urged or forced to take more responsibility, to be more conscientious and work to higher standards of quality. However, basic human problems are seldom solved by urging or pressurising employees, or by introducing new techniques. Such techniques are fundamentally tools and are not necessarily motivators or replacements for supervisors and managers. Although adopting new techniques is essential, the full implications should not be forgotten.

## THE COLLABORATIVE APPROACH

The collaborative approach concentrates on stimulating employee help and involvement by using interpersonal and conceptual skills more effectively (Chapter 2). Coaching employees who are established in autonomous teams is an important supervisory role. Such coaching, in collaborative management terms, means close control is removed and replaced with a rapport (a communication relationship). Team members recognise the supervisor as a facilitator, catalyst or counsellor. They feel free to discuss their strengths and weaknesses when they feel the need and to seek help with their problems and decisions. However, giving advice or answers is reduced if replaced with prompting, offering information and generally being helpful. Thus employees are cultivated to think for themselves, discover lessons in time, and they are encouraged to develop.

An employee-centred culture is supported, the supervisor becomes a part of the team, and collaboration is expected by employees. The main aspects of coaching skills are discussed in Chapter 12 from the motivational viewpoint, and in

Chapter 19 considering development and adjusting to changes more rapidly. Counselling is covered in Chapter 15.

## EFFECTS OF INFORMATION TECHNOLOGY

Information technology (IT) can seldom eliminate all the wide range of supervisory roles. Certainly IT is effective in improving communication, and in improving and increasing operating data, but its use in attempting to modify employee behaviour is debatable. Clearly, IT applications change the emphasis on some supervisory roles, others may disappear, and new ones may emerge. However, the strong need for supervising remains.

## COMPUTER NETWORKS

More powerful computer networks have given senior management the opportunity either to remove whole layers of middle management (Chapter 2), or to reduce middle managers' authority. These networks, for example, help to simplify problems by presenting data and graphics quickly for control and co-ordination; assisting in planning; identifying critical data immediately; and providing summarised data for calculating costs, times and resources required.

A further opportunity occurs by empowering all employees (Chapter 10) to contribute fully. This means establishing an organisational climate where they feel obliged to use their initiative, offer ideas and use their inventiveness. Furthermore, employees receive appropriate authority and the opportunity to develop more power, while managers relinquish some authority and act more as facilitators. Naturally, appropriate rewards for employees' efforts are an essential feature.

Many specialists such as accountants and stock controllers have faced redundancy since much of their work can be done more cheaply and accurately by machine.

## RELATIONS BETWEEN SUPERVISORS AND SENIOR MANAGERS

Computer networks have also brought senior management much closer to supervisors and employees when middle managers are made redundant, or their authority is reduced. Often the outcome is direct relationships between supervisors and senior managers. This implies that the concept of an organisational hierarchy (Chapter 3) is now partially redundant. Furthermore, some individuals are able to manage and control themselves up to a point where supervision takes over to ensure correct communication, appropriate co-ordination and overall control. Also the computer-literate people remaining after lay-offs emerge with new roles, new career patterns and more mobility.

Clearly this continual restructuring process creates opportunities for well-trained supervisors as more computer-illiterate individuals retire or become redundant, and networking improves. Consequently, supervisory development programmes should be a part of top management's strategy.

## EFFECTS OF OVERSEAS COMPETITION

Overseas competition and its effects are discussed in Chapter 6. However, for the supervisor there are three major aspects which are changing the industrial and business scene.

### Management training and development

The urgent need to improve supervisory and managerial performance is now more recognised. Training and development programmes are increasing, alongside a background of research, development and promotion of national management standards. These standards are promoted by the Management Charter Initiative and recognised by the National Council for Vocational Qualifications (NCVQ). NVQ was established to ensure the right kind of qualification is available for all occupations. The award at higher level relates to specialist and supervisory jobs. Competence in knowledge, skills, understanding and ability in application is included.

### Total quality control

Critics have claimed that the UK is notorious for poor-quality goods and services. To overcome this situation many companies now have adopted the intention to change employees' attitude – with no exceptions – to feeling totally responsible for quality (Chapter 27).

Total quality means adopting 'quality' as a philosophy. The aim is continually to satisfy customer requirements by attending to all aspects of customer relations – not just the product or service.

Customers are now more discerning, more demanding and more cautious buyers. Therefore a successful company must provide the best product or service in terms of value for money; ensure all employees fully understand this philosophy when dealing with customers; while managers are actively engaged in testing the market and adjusting to change.

### Productivity improvement programmes

Usually productivity refers to the operational performance of the workforce, but overall productivity includes all employees, supervisors and managers. This often involves the supervisor in trying to improve the effectiveness of all main functions, especially administration. Various cost reduction concepts may be encountered (Chapter 30) which treat costing systems as a continuing updating process of preventive measures.

# Distinguishing features

Despite variations in defining the role of a supervisor, five role relationships remain. These distinguish more clearly the following differences between a supervisor and a manager in organisational thinking.

## TECHNICIAN LEVEL

Usually a three-tier organisational structure may be identified:

1  Higher technology
2  Technology
3  Technical levels

In the first tier a specialist controls the technological specialists; in the second tier these technological specialists control a range of technicians; and in the third tier technicians control the operators and clerical staff.

## SECTOR MEMBERSHIP

Supervisory sector membership extends to all organisational levels since all managers and supervisors have a group for which they are responsible. A distinguishing feature for supervisors, however, is non-membership of the management sector. This is clearly marked by differences in salary, working conditions, status and perks. Although this demarcation conflicts with modern definitions, in practice it is apparent to everyone.

## RESTRICTED POLICY INTERPRETATION

Simplified, top management makes policy; middle management broadly interprets policy; while lower management (including supervisors) is restricted to narrow interpretations, which ensure the day-to-day running of sections conforms with overall policy. However, computer networks and closer relationships between supervisors and senior managers ensure broader interpretations at supervisory level.

## DECISION MAKING

Senior managers make strategic decisions, which have a broad effect on topics such as marketing, products and services, growth, finance, organisational structure, public relations and personnel. Middle managers make tactical decisions to implement the strategies through the use of resources, allocation of duties, and various means of control.

Works supervisors make operational decisions (more on a day-to-day basis) involving, say, synchronising production, stock control, labour and machine utilisation, and adjustments to the production schedule; while office supervisors make similar decisions on administrative aspects.

## WORKLOAD LIMITATION

Critical variables affecting the load or stress on a supervisory or managerial job determine the appropriate level and grading. Typical features are the degree of similar tasks in jobs performed by subordinates, complexity of planning and control, proximity of subordinates to each other, complexity of tasks performed, and the degree of supervision imposed by subordinates' maturity and training levels.

Theoretically, as complexity of features increases, the education, training, qualifications and experience will increase. These variables should determine the category and suitability of the individual for that category. Unfortunately, this may not always occur in practice, especially if selection procedures are faulty.

# Similarities and differences

To clarify the definitions discussed and avoid blurring later, the similarities between supervisors and managers are outlined first followed by the main differences.

## SIMILARITIES

- They are responsible for the work of other people.
- They use similar principles, practices and techniques (managerial knowledge or science) and develop an art (the know-how) to achieve results.
- Some of their roles coincide, typically leader, liaison work, various communication activities, handling disturbances and negotiator.
- They conform to loose definitions of management such as the art of dealing with people; the art of getting things done through people; and to forecast, plan, organise, command, co-ordinate and control.

## DIFFERENCES

- Additional managerial roles are mainly figurehead, entrepreneur, resource allocator, and providing technological expertise.
- Managers are involved in long-term direction and control of employees as well as short-term activities.
- Managers conform to comprehensive definitions emphasising policy, strategy, entrepreneurial activities, overall direction and control, and technological and specialisms expertise.

- Senior managers make strategic decisions; middle managers make tactical decisions; supervisors make operational decisions.

# Range of supervisory jobs

No two supervisory jobs are exactly alike. Two apparently similar supervisory jobs may be very different, depending on such factors as status, company size, the product, the type of company and its structure, relationships between management, supervision, trade unions and operators, production tempo, growth problems, staffing, and the use of specialists.

This variation in supervisory jobs depends mainly upon the range of duties, the complexity of each duty, and the particular level of supervision. It is most important to understand the level of supervision.

The many levels of supervision can be grouped in a number of ways, depending on such factors as titles, salary, number of employees controlled, or degree of authority and responsibility. Grouping based on the last two factors, for example, can be further divided into four sub-groups: primary group supervision, section supervision, department supervision, and works and administration supervision. These are discussed below. In most cases a supervisor will fit into one of these groups. Generally all four levels are seen in medium and large companies whereas in the small firm only the second and last would operate.

## PRIMARY GROUP SUPERVISION

Primary group supervision includes chief clerks, leading hands and chargehands who are responsible for supervising small groups. This cluster (generally 6 to 12) forms a primary working group headed by a primary group leader.

## SECTION SUPERVISION

Section supervision generally includes about six primary group leaders headed by a section supervisor, junior foreman, assistant foreman or office supervisor. A section supervisor rarely does any manual work, instead authority and responsibility are generally restricted to allocating duties, ensuring smooth workflow by co-ordinating the activities of the primary group leaders and dealing with the day-to-day running of the section.

## DEPARTMENT SUPERVISION

A control group of about six sections is headed by a foreman, department supervisor or department superintendent. General responsibility for the department includes planning and controlling the work.

## WORKS AND ADMINISTRATION SUPERVISION

All senior supervisors come under works and administration. There are many titles in use, including general foreman, senior foreman, production foreman, shop supervisor, shop superintendent and office manager. Whatever the title, the job carries substantial authority and responsibility for effectively controlling the six to eight departments which generally make up the shop, works or office.

# Relations with employees

In general terms, the difference between employees and their supervisors is that employees perform their own work using their technical knowledge manually; whereas supervisors control the work of others using their technical knowledge theoretically, combined with supervisory techniques.

In modern terms the supervisor should concentrate more on developing the co-operation and direct involvement of employees who, it is hoped, will behave more responsibly and feel committed as a result. Emphasis is placed on teamwork, coaching, participation, autonomy and flexibility – key factors that allow employees to work within much wider limits. Indeed, to be successful, the supervisor must adopt roles associated strongly with co-ordination, advice, adaptability and associated specialisms.

## MATURE DISCUSSION

Often logical changes are not acceptable to employees through their fear of the consequences such as less autonomy or redundancy. This apprehension may be reduced by discussion in advance, divulging plans, noting responses and suggestions, and endeavouring to gain support. Without ample discussion the supervisor risks ridicule. The usual accusations are discourtesy, ignorance, lack of understanding, and having no idea of employees' capabilities and experience.

The old saying still applies: Treat adults as children and they will behave like them; treat them as idiots and they will behave like them; treat them as dogs and they may bite.

# Basic elements of supervision

The three basic elements, which are the titles of the three parts in this book, contain many aspects that demand appropriate techniques. Some of these techniques are used instinctively by applying good sense; others demand training and practice. Applying the right principles at the right time needs something more than knowledge alone because the basic elements must interact closely, although they are outlined independently.

A representative sample of ten supervisory activities is given for each basic element in Fig. 1.1. These activities or duties are interdependent in practice. For instance, no decision should be made on data and theory alone; the human factor must be considered, along with control features operating in a given situation. Finding and maintaining the right balance is difficult, time-consuming and often frustrating. Furthermore, particular techniques demand more emphasis on certain elements.

# Responsibilities of a supervisor

A supervisor is responsible for subordinates, the activities and the workplace where he or she is given formal authority to control. Within this overall definition, the finer points of responsibility that make possible the performance of the job should now emerge.

One way of thinking about these responsibilities is to examine again the list of duties given under each basic element and to summarise them in a list of responsibilities:

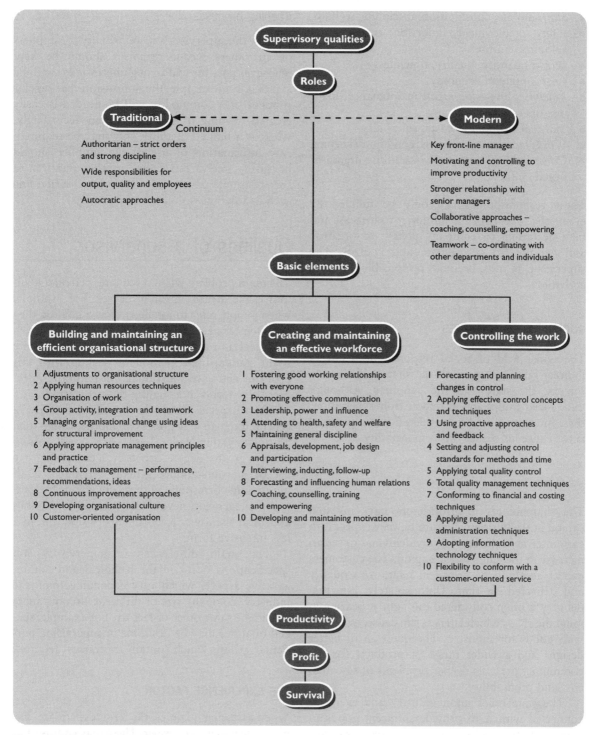

**Figure 1.1** Roles and basic elements of supervision
Roles vary from traditional to modern approaches and may appear in practice at any point along the continuum. The three basic elements interact although portrayed independently. A representative sample is shown of ten major activities for each basic element. Particular techniques demand more emphasis on certain elements.

- *Staff*: morale, consultation, discipline, welfare, safety, employment, induction, training, developing, culture
- *Work*: quantity, quality, timeliness
- *Cost*: optimum economy
- *Machines and equipment*: maintenance, loading, operation
- *Materials*: supplies, waste, suitability
- *Workplace*: layout, tidiness, good housekeeping
- *Co-ordinating with other sections*: organisational culture

These responsibilities can only be fulfilled by giving the supervisor the authority to forecast and plan according to company policy, to organise and execute, to co-ordinate and control. The supervisor, in turn, becomes responsible for these activities.

### SOCIAL RESPONSIBILITIES

The wider field of social responsibilities covers indirect relationships with the shareholders, customers, the state and the suppliers. Although these social groups appear remote from supervision, their interests must be considered if a supervisor is to realise his or her full responsibility.

### Value for money

The shareholders or proprietors have invested capital in the business. Naturally, they expect it to earn interest in the form of dividend and to see an increase in the value of the capital. The customers expect goods to be priced in relation to quality and delivered on time. Unfortunately, punctual delivery is often considered too lightly, bearing in mind the chaos which lateness can cause, especially with goods for industry. The question of better designs and a wider range of products for the community presents deeper problems of research, cost and profitability.

The state relies upon industry and everyone connected with it to provide sufficient goods to export and to supply the home market. Economic stability is vital to everyone; success depends largely upon the best use of capital and the effectiveness of the workforce.

### Keeping promises

Finally, the supervisor's responsibility to suppliers or customers means promises should be kept whenever possible and wrong impressions carefully avoided. For example, the impression that regular supplies of a commodity will be needed is easily created, leading a supplier to plan accordingly, whereas a limited quantity only may be required. Any information of use to the supplier should be given freely, especially on the question of specifications which may be unnecessarily fine such as tolerances, finish and packing.

## Qualities of a supervisor

The main problem when discussing personal qualities is the measurement of degree. For example, when people refer to intelligence as a quality, they use such terms as average, reasonable, high level, low level and average level. Unfortunately, there is no standardised method of dealing with this problem and each individual will naturally interpret these terms in a slightly different way.

Two aspects should be appreciated. First, a general foreman may possess no more qualities than a primary group leader, but he or she will possess them in greater degree. Secondly, a comprehensive list of an outstanding general foreman's qualities would correspond with specifications for general management; nevertheless, the same qualities appear at the lower levels of supervision, but in a less intensive form.

The main differences in supervisory job specifications occur in the technical and administrative aspects which vary depending upon the industry, company size or different circumstances within the same office or factory. For example, special qualities may be desirable in supervising particular groups which contain an unusual feature.

### THE EXPERIENCE FACTOR

When assessing qualities, the term 'experience' has many meanings to consider. These may confuse and cause misunderstandings. Caution is needed when relating an individual's assessment or assumed capabilities to experience. Three features which attempt to explain experience are the meanings, associated terms, and learning through experience.

## Meanings of experience

The meanings which are directly connected with supervision are:

- actual observation of, or practical acquaintance with, facts or events
- knowledge or skill resulting from actual observation
- an event that affects an individual

There are many more definitions but these are related to different topics.

## Associated terms

Associated terms cause difficulties because they are often used loosely when applied to experience:

- discover information
- trial and error to arrive at a conclusion
- enlightenment on a subject
- acquaintance or familiarity with an event
- tolerance
- skilfulness or style
- receive an impression (or a feel) of an event

Considering these terms, discussion on a person's experience may easily lead to wrong conclusions.

## Learning through experience

The degree of learning through experience depends upon:

- the breadth and complexity of problems and situations encountered
- the role played by the person at the time
- recognising mistakes
- the accuracy and guidance of others
- effective use of the lessons learned

## Problems

Assessments should take into account the following problems:

- Being able to judge by means other than discussion.

- Experience quoted in years is an inaccurate indication of its worth. For example, many similar experiences are of little value, compared with a variety of experiences.
- Complacency or carelessness developed through experience, compared with recognising the importance of sensitive awareness and caution.
- Human weaknesses mean there are many dangers. Typical examples are cynicism, inaccurate perception, refusing to listen to people's opinions and their experiences, relying on experience alone, and avoiding other means of learning.

Apart from repetition, experience is an important feature of improving supervisory skills and developing the art of management.

## ESSENTIAL QUALITIES

There are five essential qualities. They are discussed below, but not in order of importance as each job demands a different mix of all these requirements.

- drive
- leadership
- intelligence
- skills and knowledge
- character

## DRIVE

The basic need for vitality, energy and enthusiasm is good health. Physical and mental fatigues impair judgement and are demoralising for subordinates who need to be impressed by the supervisor's example and vigour. Making the best use of time and energy requires careful planning. Whenever possible, nervous energy should be conserved by avoiding over-excitement and bursts of stop-gap measures. An even spread of effort sustained over long periods is desirable for good performance, which can then be expected from others. This sustained effort or drive demands self-discipline and conscientiousness in the face of outside distractions and the general pace of living.

## LEADERSHIP

A good leader is an outstanding member of the group who gets along easily with people and has above-average competence. Leadership is difficult to define accurately; its intangible qualities cannot be learned, yet they are easily recognisable.

Naturally, ability is not enough. Previous environment, which moulds personality and character, should provide a balanced background for an individual to feel at ease, socialise easily with many types of people and sense the ability to supervise well. Some people, of course, manage to overcome an unhappy past, while others who have been more fortunate fail to make the grade.

### Essential features

Good leaders tend to demonstrate the following features:

- Set high standards of performance and clear objectives for themselves and for employees.
- Avoid three demoralising factors: complacency, blaming others, and disparaging remarks.
- Mix easily with everyone by understanding them and using clear and constructive methods of solving everyday problems.
- Appreciate their own strengths and weaknesses, using errors to foster new ideas and celebrating successful performance when employees excel.
- Know they are not always more skilful or more intelligent than their subordinates.
- Recognise their authority and responsibilities for the development of employees and effective control by feeding back performance results.
- Be sufficiently far-sighted to see potential problems before they arise.
- Ensure that communicating information is successful by checking that employees understand the reasons for change and management's actions.
- Encourage continuous improvement in all aspects of the organisation by welcoming changes, rewarding new ideas and keeping in close contact with each employee.
- Endeavour to be courteous, understanding and self-controlled, to ensure their actions agree with their words.

This abbreviated list illustrates some of the key aspects which have a strong impact on employee performance.

### Management's task

An important management task is to create conditions under which leaders become effective but, at the same time, to avoid development of a situation where leaders struggle for power among each other. If the well-known rat race is allowed, subordinates suffer and the organisation is badly affected. Given the opportunity and the right conditions, the leader pushes people beyond their normal capabilities. This leads to a higher level of effectiveness and increased work satisfaction.

## INTELLIGENCE

Most supervisory jobs require average intelligence, which is similar to the general level of intelligence found among skilled operators and clerks. Some people expect supervisors to be more intelligent than their subordinates, which is naturally desirable.

A high level of intelligence is essential in some supervisory jobs where technical and administrative problems are intricate and demanding. However, many supervisory jobs contain a disproportionate amount of routine work which would soon frustrate the highly intelligent person.

In reality, supervisors need the following intellectual capabilities:

- shrewdness, judgement, an acute mind and good sense
- quick-witted, able to distinguish major and minor problems, and apportion sufficient time to deal with each problem
- ability to decide whether permanent or temporary arrangements are needed
- understand clearly the many and varied written and spoken instructions
- able to pass on information clearly to various types of subordinates

## SKILLS AND KNOWLEDGE

Three main skills are distinguishable: technical, interpersonal and conceptual. They apply to all managerial and supervisory jobs but the ratios between them depend on the organisational level.

As top levels are approached, technical skills tend to decrease, interpersonal skills should remain the same, and conceptual skills should increase. Understandably, collaborative philosophies demand more emphasis on interpersonal and conceptual skills for supervisors. These two skills are major supervisory assets, rated above many other qualities such as IQ, knowledge and job skills. To achieve high performance levels there needs to be a crucial appreciation of the total organisation and the total involvement of employees.

## Technical skills

An inherent part of any supervisory job is technical competence. Supervisors need a sound knowledge of every operation or process under their control to be able to recognise and eliminate common faults, wastage and any dangerous practices. Practical and theoretical knowledge plus varied experience help to command respect and help others.

To train successfully, supervisors should illustrate:

- Why a job should be done, consequently the criteria used for the job are seen to be correct.
- How it should be done, to demonstrate the proper use of all the knowledge (or data) available.
- A willingness to seek contributions from the trainee, who may be innovative and who may be able to offer suggestions through his or her own knowledge or ideas.
- A questioning approach to discover any problems which are bothering trainees.

Supervisors do not necessarily have to be the best operator in the group, but certainly they should not be the worst.

A reasonable elementary education and further education are essential. Technical skills are learned relatively quickly by repetition and are specific to particular activities. They are classified by referring to an established management principle or methodology and are measurable. Implementation and appraisal are learned through practice. A general definition is the capability to apply knowledge, experience, techniques and methods to perform specific tasks with the aid of appropriate machines and equipment.

## Interpersonal skills

Often called human skills or interactive skills, interpersonal skills use motivational and behaviourist techniques to extract higher performance. They stimulate ideas, concentrate on needs and goals, and encourage participation. A selection of such skills would include developing teams, improving human relations, motivating, leading, effectively communicating, and training and developing employees.

A general definition is the capability and judgement to work with employees and to utilise fully their talents through leadership and various behavioural theories. Usually they take a long time to develop since learning and experience are needed, along with patience, perseverance and tolerance.

Sound interpersonal relationships are viewed occasionally as difficult to achieve because of cultural and subcultural factors. These vary widely between countries, areas within countries and with company size. Although some variations in managerial behaviour patterns are noticeable between countries, organisational structuring mostly follows logical patterns that dominate managerial development and induce similar managerial behaviour patterns. On a broader basis, interpersonal skills are also applied between management and suppliers, customers, the community and the government.

## Conceptual skills

Abstract in nature, conceptual skills are drawn from knowledge and experience over a long period. For further development, the opportunity to gain insight into corporate activities and problems is essential.

Conceptual skills concentrate on broader issues, corporate and organisational planning and policy, and systems. Collectively, a definition is the capability to act in accordance with the objectives of the company as a whole. Unfortunately, conflict often exists between the objectives visualised by the group or section and those of the corporate whole.

The development of thought processes and intuition which improve conceptual skills requires specialised training, perseverance and close examination of experiences. The mental process of attempting to visualise the future includes not only using data available and experiences, but also utilising many aids such as checklists, systems, procedures, statistical frameworks, and models. Such forecasting does not rely upon trends or data, but more upon intuition to identify important relevant features and mentally classifying events into significant areas that have causal connections.

Making better decisions and coping with difficulties should be in line with the total organisational scene or corporate whole. This relies heavily on posing searching questions using the normal why, when, where and how approaches (as in work study) and conceptualising or visualising outcomes.

In practice, typical observations show there is more reliance on asking searching questions and less on detailed knowledge as senior levels are approached. Also, the more rapid the change, the more reliance there is on experience to seek appropriate solutions. The real difficulty is knowing the right questions to ask.

Unfortunately, asking questions is restricted to discovering information. This technique does not necessarily provide solutions and is certainly not constructive or creative. To create change rather than simply forecasting change is a demanding task involving many modern techniques to improve conceptual skills (Chapter 8).

### CHARACTER

Nobody possesses all the qualities of character in the ideal supervisor. A compromise is inevitable and the choice will be governed by the particular circumstances.

Some of the important qualities are honesty, trustworthiness, a strict sense of fairness and justice, integrity, wholeness, uprightness and soundness. A stable personality is essential for an even temper, steadiness and reliability. A direct, open and positive approach is desirable, giving due consideration to all parties when dealing with problems and grievances. Cheerfulness and enthusiasm, coupled with a sense of humour, provide the right type of industrial atmosphere.

In brief, supervisors must possess something besides technical competence, which clearly places them above their particular group. Someone without higher intellect may still shine by having more drive or inherent qualities of leadership. A person displaying strength of character, who bubbles over with activity, can make up for other faults.

Each particular combination of qualities suits certain groups in particular work situations. Thus, one person stands out in a group and, provided his or her outlook is reasonably aligned with management policy and not objectionable, he or she is a likely choice.

## Suitability for supervision

The transition from technical or administrative work to supervision may be difficult for some people. They might have a strong interest in specialist activities but a weak interest in supervising and teamwork. Supervising means acquiring managerial knowledge, developing many new skills, and coping with new roles. These basic interests need self-examination to find out whether personal strengths coincide. If they do not agree, the transition could be stressful and frustrating.

### WORKING EFFECTIVELY

Apart from other aspects, effective working means ensuring that personal preferences and demands of the job coincide. Considerable thought and self-analysis are essential before choosing a career path to supervision and management. Typical indications to explore are the different work preferences available; the authority, responsibility and duties of each job in the organisation; the range of organisational functions, roles, principles and practices, and business activities; and a careful self-analysis, which may involve help from others.

## Selection of supervisors

Careful and fair selection of supervisors is often overlooked by management. Promotions from the shop floor and appointments in the lower levels of supervision are viewed very critically by operatives who are often directly affected.

Poor selection may destroy the efforts of previous supervisors who have managed to improve the organisational climate. Overlooked employees may feel frustrated and suspicious of management if the appointed individual is obviously unsuitable. The working harmony of the group or groups may be upset and resentment tends to spread like a disease – in all directions. The disgruntled individuals, who may have a legitimate complaint, mention the injustice to everyone and a sense of frustration may develop throughout the company.

## SOME OBSERVATIONS ON SELECTION

Before considering the methods of selection, here are some circumstances that affect selection. A common fault among supervisors is to stop the promotion of individuals because they are considered to be indispensable in their present positions, even though they are eminently suitable for promotion. Sometimes the supervisor cannot be bothered to train a replacement and the easiest remedy is deliberately to penalise a person's chances of promotion, often forcing the person to seek employment elsewhere.

Some superiors who are able to influence promotion, or who actually select the individual, allow unimportant incidents to dominate their impressions or opinions of subordinates. Typical examples are a heated discussion at the company's Christmas dinner or failing to acknowledge the general manager in the high street. Such trivial misdemeanours are sometimes held against a person for years. In some cases, even the suspicion of a wrongdoing is sufficient reason to bypass an individual. A true understanding of reality makes due allowance for human errors. A wiser and fairer way is to give people the benefit of the doubt.

### Type suited to management

Managers' opinions on the type of supervisor required are diverse and vary with company size. The manager in a small concern may demand a yes-man who carries out orders to the letter; while in a large firm the opposite type may be required, typically one who shows initiative, makes decisions and has a powerful personality. Some managers prefer the outsider with new ideas; others favour internal promotion. No two managers agree entirely on the qualities they seek for a particular position, consequently a compromise is necessary.

### Temperament

Naturally there are many different temperaments which suit a supervisory role, but a certain temperament may suit a particular post. Certainly important general attributes are a stable disposition, reliability and thoroughness. Being able to control emotions in variable circumstances helps when dealing with employees who may exhibit instability or immaturity at times.

Appropriate judgement, perception, sensitivity and intuitiveness are features that highlight potential effective supervisors. There has been extensive research to determine the best ratios between these four features in a particular post.

## METHODS OF SELECTION

The methods of selection are divided into two groups to show the importance of using scientific methods.

### Unsubstantiated methods

Unsubstantiated methods are methods that do not allow for systematic selection and result in the detrimental effects of poor selection upon employees and the company. These methods do not necessarily imply spontaneous selection – some are planned well in advance. Selection is not based on true grounds but on such grounds as:

- favouritism, promoting friends and relatives
- length of service or age seniority
- high standard of skill alone
- haphazard recommendations by a supervisor
- chance, through stop-gap arrangements – someone being in the right place at the right time

### Scientific methods

A scientific method is any method that attempts to reduce the possibility of error. The aim is to find the best person available for each vacancy.

Consequently, all employees initially have an equal opportunity and those with ability have good prospects of promotion which will not depend upon influence and favouritism. The essential requirements for any scheme with these aims are:

- Planning by estimating the vacancies that are likely to occur.
- Preparing a job specification by listing all the main requirements of the vacancy.
- Advertising internally and externally with the understanding that promotion from within will always take precedence where suitable internal applicants are available.
- Investigating carefully all employees as promotion prospects.
- Interviewing all candidates who are likely to be suitable. These should be conducted by skilled, objective interviewers and supplemented by appropriate tests.
- Choosing finally or approval by top management or a selected panel.

### The advantages

Scientific choice, although not perfect, has obvious advantages. Many factors that may have been omitted are now included in the job specification, there is less chance of potential supervisors being overlooked, better assessment of individuals is now assured, and unbiased selection is more likely.

Frankness and open dealings are needed to make the scheme acceptable. Any queries should be discussed openly. Every applicant should be fully informed of proceedings and the unsuccessful candidates must be told in confidence why they failed.

A fair scheme must be seen to be fair by everyone. This smooths the way for the new supervisor who may have to face special problems if he or she comes from the group to be supervised. Such a change may be stressful and it will help the person to adjust quickly if everyone accepts the selection was fair.

## Training and development

Governments and companies in the UK have neglected training and development for over a

century. Insurmountable problems face supervisors and managers unless training is taken seriously. Even when many difficulties are overcome without training, managers never know *why* they succeeded. Conversely, when they fail they are unable to analyse accurately why these failures happened and so discover their weaknesses.

Training means learning information and skills for the present job. Development involves learning not only for the present job but also for future jobs and possible promotion opportunities. This difference in emphasis illustrates the importance of continually updating knowledge and skills to maintain effectiveness and provide ample opportunity for mental growth.

## Informal training

Most supervisors learn their jobs by actually doing them, making mistakes and avoiding recurrences as a result of these experiences. Although this system of trial and error is considered to be an essential part of training, practical experience must be supplemented by formal training to form a sound framework for future action.

Working with an effective supervisor is an invaluable experience, but to gain full benefit a knowledge of the basic elements of supervision helps considerably. Techniques are built up through the experiences of many supervisors and specialists who have spent years studying supervision. These should be learned and integrated with informal training.

## Formal training

Many of the half million supervisors in this country have not received any formal training, although various courses have been on offer for a number of years. Any successful training scheme must have suitable training facilities, the right syllabus, appropriate lecturers and back-up staff, and strong support from management who should ensure adequate follow-up and assessment after the course.

Although managers often agree that some form of supervisory training is essential and show enthusiasm when the matter is discussed, few seem prepared to take any practical steps in this direction. Some managers say either supervisors cannot be spared or they are too busy to make the arrangements. Others ignore the facilities offered, possibly because they think the subject is unimportant or perhaps they fear the supervisor, after training, may know more than the superior.

## CASE METHOD OF TRAINING

Case studies are given at the end of each chapter. The case method of training provides a theme for discussion in a group or for a supervisor to relate theory to his or her practical experiences. Cases provide material for problem solving and decision making in technical and human situations, and give a supervisor the opportunity to develop an insight into why organisations succeed or fail.

The situations in a case study are intentionally incomplete. Consequently, it is possible to imagine the overall situation by using inferences, intuition and value judgements. These may be related to a supervisor's own working environment and for him or her to appreciate there is no single or correct answer.

Certain fundamental guidelines apply:

1 Read the case completely and make notes of items that come to mind.
2 Develop a feeling for the situation and try to gain a full understanding of the requirements.
3 Read the case again and relate each person mentioned to others and the situation. Make appropriate notes on the sequence of events.
4 Draw up a rough profile of each person involved. Note any personal bias and any issues that were not immediately obvious before.
5 List any information not available which is considered to be important. Verify the facts that have emerged with evidence given, avoiding any assumptions.
6 Attempt to determine the real issues and their significance. Refer them to theory and practical experience.
7 Relate the issues to the questions and identify the possible courses of action and answers.
8 Plan the answers, bearing in mind various viewpoints and using appropriate diagrams.

Essential requirements for solving case studies include problem solving, planning and decision making (Chapter 8).

## THE MANAGEMENT CHARTER INITIATIVE

In 1987 a number of surveys revealed that the average UK manager received only about one day's formal training each year, one-third had received no training since starting work, and four-fifths possessed no professional qualification or a degree. To counter this situation, the Management Charter Initiative (MCI) was founded in 1988 by leading industrial concerns with the support of the government, the CBI and the Institute of Management. The aim is to encourage the competence-based approach to management development which focuses on whether managers can actually do their jobs, regardless of their qualifications or lack of them. Managers are assessed against national standards and are only trained and developed in areas of incompetence.

## COMPETENCE

The Training Agency defines competence as the ability to perform activities within an occupational area to levels of performance expected in employment. A two-part model outlines the competence standards reached by effective managers and the underlying personal abilities and skills required to achieve them.

These standards include managing people, operations, finance and information. Personal competencies include displaying self-confidence, taking initiative and coping with stress. All have been known for a long time, but relating the model directly to performance is a new development. The model may be used in many ways and should form the basis for programmes offered by management institutions. A clear distinction is made between courses about knowledge and analysis, and those related to competent performance.

Other views on competence are an ability to do a task, a capability to do a particular job, and the capacity to perform to a set standard. Accordingly, being competent may mean adequately qualified, legally qualified, or proven to be capable to perform a task or a job.

These definitions raise many questions involving the depth of competence, levels of competence, management standards to measure competence, assessing competence, the nature of competence, and behavioural and skills competencies. The answers to these questions help to determine the level of management when standards are applied.

## Depth of competence

Considering the vast range of supervisory and managerial jobs, there are various depths of competence which apply to appropriate levels or development stages. The four main features that may be distinguished are the individual, knowledge, skills and experience.

The personal qualities of the individual are an important feature; they involve intelligence level, mental and physical health, charisma and flair. The depth of knowledge will depend upon the person's ability and capability to absorb information and relate it effectively to management. Skills development depends upon perseverance, flair and charisma. Experience depends upon opportunities, capability and simulated or actual situations.

## Levels of competence

If related to typical organisations, competence levels would refer to senior management, middle management and supervisory management. But, as many employees can confirm, this is an illusion. The well-known Peter principle (bosses rise to their level of incompetence in bureaucracies) rests on this myth and is supported by many notorious cases of malpractice and ineptness by managers.

## The MCI management standards

The MCI management standards are arranged in logical sequence to cover every aspect of management at every level in an organisation. Seven key roles are each divided into a number of units. Within each key role a unit summary describes the relevance to a particular job. Within each unit, elements describe the requirements, together with performance criteria.

The standards allow a person to judge their competence in an objective manner by seeing how their performance matches up to the national criteria. The MCI (0207 872 9000) provides free development materials: 'Right first time guides', 'Good practice in action' and an information pack.

## Assessing competence

Competence assessments are usually divided into two categories:

- *The traditional approach*: This recognises knowledge and skills which are achieved though standardised inputs of study, practising skills, and workshop training. Testing competence is usually through tests away from the actual workplace.
- *The MCI approach*: This recognises studying, practising skills, and simulated or actual practice. Individuals assess themselves to note development and problem areas. The problem areas receive special treatment and assessments are based on evidence from the workplace or work-related simulations.

Various views on assessment tend to concentrate on the difficulty of assessing competence without personal bias or the vagueness of determining capability in different situations.

## The nature of competence

Certain observations clearly indicate the transitory nature of competence. Competence today does not guarantee competence tomorrow or next week. This factor highlights the feature relating to the particular individual. Unfortunately, a person may change slowly or quickly for many reasons, such as the effect of domestic problems, changes in mental or physical health, and stressful situations. Nevertheless, aspiring to higher levels of competence is essential regardless of difficulties and setbacks. Career progress depends partly on this factor, and perseverance usually reaps rewards eventually.

## BEHAVIOURAL AND SKILLS COMPETENCIES

There is an important distinction between behavioural competencies and skills competencies. In total, behavioural competencies may be crudely interpreted or witnessed on the basis that appropriate behaviour leads to effective performance. Considering the generic nature of behaviour, there are many attributes that make up behaviour. This implies there are various behavioural patterns and levels which will still lead to effectiveness in any occupation.

Typical factors in any behavioural pattern witnessed by anyone with sufficient expertise would include:

- *Personal characteristics*: attitudes, values, temperament and perception.
- *Motivation process*: needs, drives, and observable behaviour which might lead to a goal.
- *Expertise*: experience, knowledge, behavioural skills and good sense.
- *Motivation level*: reinforcement, performance-related pay, the group, the job itself, participation and organisation culture.

### Features

A person's behaviour is unique in any situation. Extensive but incomplete knowledge exists on behaviour. There are many interpretations of witnessed behaviour which are subjective, often inaccurate, and subject to change after analysing the behaviour. A typical error is to link behaviour with common sense.

Clearly, there is a multitude of competencies. The idea that any person exists who possesses all of them is a myth. Probably the vital factors in assessments or interviews are being aware of all the competencies, being able to place them in some order of importance, and achieving a compromise with the individual.

### GENERAL SKILLS COMPETENCIES

General skills competencies may be viewed as tools or techniques which are necessary for the performance of a particular task or job. Often they need several behavioural competencies to develop, they are relatively easier to learn, but they use applied technical, technological or procedural knowledge. A typical example is customer contact: apart from knowledge and experience of the product, the employee may need to present information graphically or statistically, and communicate effectively with the customer.

# Development

Development clearly depends on a person's ambition and potential, and the seriousness of a company's development programme. Long-term investment is essential in any human resources development scheme, consequently arrangements must be made and time allowed for supervisors to learn on the job. The process is continuous and progressive, with appropriate changes being made to job content and challenges being presented. Ample opportunity should be given for self-development, initiative and creativity.

### COMPREHENSIVE DEVELOPMENT SCHEMES

Apart from publishing them directly within the organisation, schemes are easily recognised. Indications are follow-up on training, assessing individual requirements, appropriate coaching and advice, discussing future roles and organisational objectives, stressing conceptual skills development, organisational change, environmental aspects and long-term planning.

Understandably the degree of competence required is subjective and subject to various opinions by observers. Therefore to some extent the whole process of developing competencies is challenging and debatable. Certainly the degree of competence is fixed by the structural level in the organisation, whereas competencies are determined by the key requirements in the particular job (including roles) and the associated team.

### The main process

Seven phases illustrate the main process:

1 *Conduct an initial follow-up programme*: All education, training and development courses should be examined by the superior with the supervisor to assess his or her strengths and weaknesses.
2 *Seek agreement on competency*: Discuss and agree the competencies required, including

technical and technological knowledge, interpersonal skills, conceptual skills, and outlook.

3  *Relate competencies to performance*: Connect the competencies with the basic elements of supervision (Fig. 1.1), and ensure complete coverage.

4  *Assess present performance levels*: Attempt to assess present performance levels with the ideal situation; seek opinions from superior and employees.

5  *Test competencies*: Try out envisaged improvements in skills, behaviour and practices; note the effects.

6  *Continue to practise competencies*: Use various situations to try out improvements; where possible consolidate and clarify ideas.

7  *Ongoing development*: Establish a programme and use the improvements and new ideas as they emerge.

### Underlying features

Underlying the competencies (within which standards are set) are six basic features: health, education, ability, drive, character and temperament. These features determine an individual's capability to reach various levels of performance.

Competencies may be divided in many ways. A suggested approach is in line with the qualities of a supervisor described earlier. They are illustrated in Fig. 1.2, which provides a detailed model of probable competencies.

# Self-development

Often self-development is encouraged by companies to supplement formal development programmes. This philosophy recognises people with drive who are sufficiently motivated to undertake self-managed development and improve their competency level. Furthermore, changing roles are more frequent now as people adopt serial careers involving new skills. Training schemes become more difficult to prescribe in these circumstances.

Usually there is considerable data already available for the supervisor to make a start and there are many opportunities to study through various organisations. Also the human resource department may offer time off, financial help, facilities and advice.

## A SELF-DEVELOPMENT APPROACH

A logical approach should use sound training and development practices outlined in Chapter 19. Also there is the question of appropriate education to consider if such practices are above the requirement level. Naturally this aspect will have to be solved by undertaking educational courses before proceeding further.

The following four-phase guide clarifies the main points and ensures a thorough coverage of the important areas.

### Phase 1: Gather information

1  Collect data from appraisals and ongoing control sessions.

2  Conduct a self-analysis as detailed in Chapter 13.

3  Compile a personal record (Chapter 13) by using individual thoughts and ideas, data from appraisals, and advice from friends.

4  Diagnose strengths and weaknesses by examining situations and problems from previous difficulties.

5  Prepare a summary of achievements in present and previous jobs.

6  List qualifications, experience and obvious areas of inexperience.

### Phase 2: Identify learning style

The learning process section in Chapter 19 should enable the supervisor to classify his or her learning style and use accordingly.

### Phase 3: Prepare a programme

1  Draw up a suitable framework in logical sequence to accommodate the information from phase 1. Allow spaces to record development plans for control purposes.

2  Outline a timetable to suit personal requirements and areas of development. These will depend

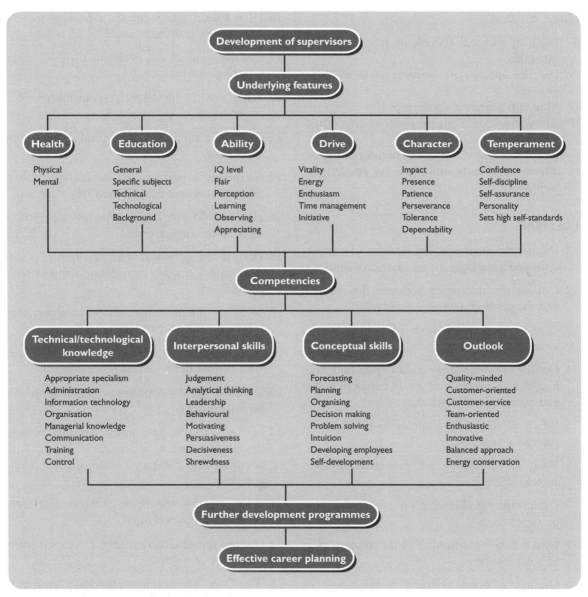

**Figure 1.2** Development of supervisors
A suggested model of the main competencies and underlying features associated with supervisory development. Choice of competencies depends upon the particular supervisor's roles and the job. Each competence contains theory and practical applications, divided into appropriate aspects. For example, behavioural skill contains many skills such as counselling, coaching, teamwork, selection interviewing, improving relationships, communicating and appraisals.

on the objectives in mind, suitably divided into knowledge requirements, skills and principles.
3 Check on the programme by examining the roles, authority, responsibilities and duties of the present job, and note any discrepancies.
4 Revise item 1 as appropriate.
5 Consider future career plans. Determine whether there is adequate coverage in the timetable and revise if necessary.
6 Consider the facilities, etc., offered by the human resource department and maintain flexibility to allow for changed circumstances.

*Phase 4: Learning*

1  Begin in a logical fashion by referring to the timetable.
2  Use the appropriate learning style wherever possible.
3  Maintain a strict control record.
4  Always seek opinions on progress from trustworthy friends.
5  Remember to be flexible, persevere, ignore adverse comments, and use every opportunity to practice.

## QUESTIONS

1  Discuss the distinguishing features of a supervisor and a manager in organisational thinking.

2  Outline the difference between the training and the development of a supervisor.

3  Give a detailed definition of the traditional view of a supervisor.

4  Outline the range of supervisory jobs under the headings of supervisory levels, range of duties and complexity of each duty.

5  What are the likely qualities to be seen in a successful supervisor?

6  What are meant by interpersonal and conceptual skills?

7  Outline the possible effects of computerisation on supervisors.

8  Give a detailed definition of the modern view of a supervisor.

9  Outline a good training programme for supervisors.

10  How would you judge the effectiveness of a supervisory training course?

11  Discuss some of the problems involved when selecting supervisors.

12  What are the probable responsibilities of a supervisor?

13  Describe a suitable code of conduct for a new supervisor.

14  An inherent part of any supervisory job is technical competence. Discuss this statement.

15  How would you decide whether a person is suitable for supervision?

16  Discuss the proposal that experience is difficult to assess when considering a supervisor's capabilities.

17  What are the probable changes in supervisory roles over the past twenty years?

18  How important is self-development compared with formal development programmes?

19  Outline a self-development programme suitable for supervisors.

20  In your opinion how much emphasis should be placed on a supervisor's behavioural competencies compared with general skills competencies?

21  What are the underlying features and competencies for supervisors?

22  Discuss the observation that a competence is transitory in nature.

23  What are management standards and how may they be applied to supervisors?

Having attended a course on supervision it was very clear to Jane, a supervisor for twenty years, that it was impossible to implement many of the practices that had been explained. She was convinced that management would not agree to the changes she had in mind and that her superior would certainly not co-operate.

Gradually she became more frustrated by this assumption until, one day, an incident occurred that caused her to lose her temper. This was a further complaint from her staff that the employees in the sales department nearby were allowed to come and go as they pleased. She stormed into the sales manager's office and complained in very strong terms. Fortunately the sales manager was an understanding man and, after explaining adequately *why* some of his staff had to work odd hours, he suggested that there should be more liaison between the two departments. Jane readily agreed, having calmed down, and maintained that she had always thought that a liaison committee was essential for good communication and alignment of objectives but she was sure her boss would not hear of it. To her amazement, her boss responded positively to the idea. Indeed, she reproached Jane for not being more forthcoming before.

*How much blame could be attributed to the training course, management, the superior and Jane in these circumstances?*

John Cummings, 36, had worked for Newland Techniques Ltd for six years. His supervisor was transferred and John, as senior, became the new supervisor.

He muddled his way through the week feeling thoroughly incompetent. After a month, to his surprise, his superior mentioned that she thought John had settled down well in his new job.

Whenever there were queries, John simply contacted the specialist departments concerned and waited for answers, which he then implemented. He used the same technique with the shop steward when decisions were needed, passing the problems over to his superior.

After six months two changes occurred: his superior retired and the company lost one of its major contracts. His new superior, about the same age as John, soon made it clear there would be no buck-passing and that John would be taking full responsibility in future for a number of duties that he listed.

After a fortnight, John was severely disciplined for not controlling his section properly. John was confused. He has no idea what else to do but give in his notice.

*What factors contributed to John's downfall? Also, what advice could John receive from an experienced supervisor?*

# 2

# Background: the development of supervision

## The changing role of the supervisor

Up to the twentieth century, industry was usually considered to be degrading and dirty by the middle and upper classes. Economists concentrated on political economics and business aspects but they ignored management as a subject. Owners and managers thought managing was an art and training was unnecessary. Their main preoccupations were technological changes, accounts and prices. Consequently, supervisors were very powerful, hiring and firing as they wished and receiving little interference from owners so long as profits were acceptable. People were treated as a commodity concept which meant they were bought and sold in the employment market and the human element was ignored. Trade unions were struggling to survive and employees were working long hours for low wages in poor working conditions.

During the twentieth century new supervisory roles have emerged and been modified as industrial and economic situations changed. These changes have mainly been due to organised conflict between employees and owners, increased competition between countries, two world wars that demanded higher output and revolutionised technologies, productivity problems, the impact of information technology, and the growing importance of organisational culture.

This collective pressure encouraged the introduction of various concepts by management pioneers. This caused a growing emphasis on scientific research into behaviour, improved education and training in some countries, and increased interest in productivity and design. These features affected supervisory roles since they naturally coincided with developments and phases of management thinking. The recognisable phases are:

- autocratic management
- semi-autocratic management
- constitutional management
- contingency management
- collaborative management
- holistic management

## Autocratic management

During the Middle Ages, supervision through force was commonplace, both for free and slave labour. Output was probably very low and life was cheap. This barbaric use of labour died slowly – slaves were still being used in the British Empire even as late as 1833.

## Semi-autocratic management

From about 1500 to 1940 a more subtle form of supervision developed by applying dismissal, which could mean near-starvation for the worker and his family. Supervisors faced similar treatment as the labour market outpaced industrial growth. The outcome was low wages, cheating, and the truck system where workers were paid in goods instead of money, or in money but they were forced to buy their provisions in the employers' shops. This ill-treatment eventually led to organised conflict early in the nineteenth century. By 1940 the bargaining power of the trade unions had substantially strengthened.

At the beginning of the twentieth century, F.W. Taylor launched new techniques in the USA to foster closer co-operation between management and workers. He also functionalised many of the foreman's duties. These methods were successful at first and extensively used to increase production. In Britain, Taylor's teaching was mainly ignored. By 1924 the American managers had realised that in practice the proposed innovations were not reaching the visualised targets. This generated further research in human relations which revealed new important factors, including group spirit, self-discipline, participation and the concept of a social system in the organisation.

# Constitutional management

The critical war situation in 1940 demanded about four times the existing output from industry. Working overtime did not provide the complete answer to the problem, so other ways were attempted. These included improving working conditions, introducing welfare officers and establishing joint production committees.

Disruptions were experienced through go-slows and unofficial strikes. Gradually management realised that the first steps towards maximum efficiency were only possible when human resources and machine operations were treated as equally important. Close consultation between the government and trade unions led to many trade union leaders and officials entering government departments. Wages were guaranteed and claims were settled at a national level between the unions and employers' associations.

## THE UNITARY FRAMEWORK

A new era started in the mid-1940s and continued throughout the 1950s. During this period the unions gathered strength and consolidated, the government co-operated and consulted, and employers gradually changed their attitude towards employees.

The concept of a fundamental common interest existing between all groups within a society was slowly recognised. Management, however, was viewed as the best qualified to pursue these common interests. Opposition from employees was considered to be irrational and misguided, and organised by troublemakers or politically motivated fanatics. Supervisors gradually absorbed the ideas of consultation, more emphasis was placed on human relations and loyalty, and the 'one-big happy family' approach appeared.

This concept is often known as the *unitary framework* and at national level it includes the idea of acting within the common interest. Thus any person or any organisation who is construed to be acting against it is considered to be holding the country to ransom, or acting in a subversive manner.

# Democratic management

In the 1960s it became increasingly obvious that employees were not responding to the unitary framework. Management was forced to recognise the existence of a variety of different and conflicting interests. Compromise was assumed to be the answer, which meant the employee had to surrender autonomy and recognise some rights of management, while management recognised employees' rights to organise, loyally oppose, and bargain over procedures and financial rewards.

This *pluralist* approach, benign in character, became the basis for dealing with industrial relations issues. For the supervisor it meant a change in persuasive techniques, the use of logical argument, even more emphasis on good personal relationships, and the encouragement of a free exchange of information.

# Contingency management

In the 1970s several fundamental working assumptions became more acceptable. The pluralist framework became suspect and was replaced with the *radical framework*. Further research led to the *systems approach*, which gained support and resulted in the development of *contingency theory*.

## THE RADICAL FRAMEWORK

Pluralism failed to account adequately for the marked inequalities and unfair opportunities in society. Various fundamental social issues remained, such as an unequal distribution of wealth and a lack of a principled basis for income. Among many other criticisms, pluralism wrongly assumed a stable balance of power between employers and employees. Consequently, the *radical framework* became more acceptable on the basis of its analytical power, *not* its political emphasis.

### The approach

Briefly, the approach goes to the roots of issues and analyses contradictions in social, economic and political structures. Moreover, it locates internal tensions and strains within systems that tend to lead to collapse or adaptation by those who wish to retain basic features. For example, in a culture where freedom, independence, choice and autonomy are important values, conflict is inevitable when most employees are in a work situation that does not agree with these cultural expectations.

From this analysis, conflict is fundamental, has to be expected and taken into account. Co-operation, however, is also fundamental in society and industry. Herein lies the basic problem of supervision and management, and the difficulty of revising organisation design to avoid narrow tasks and to develop the humanising of jobs.

## THE SYSTEMS APPROACH

In addition to the social aspects, research revealed the importance of technical and economic factors in achieving organisational effectiveness. Consequently, new theories viewed organisations as complex systems of individuals, tasks and technology that interacted with, and were part of, a larger environment. Collectively these concepts became known as an *open system* (Fig. 2.1).

Briefly, the systems approach analyses activities to see how they communicate with, and relate to, each other; and how they are controlled. Essentially, systems are groups of parts that are dynamically combined and interrelated into a purposeful whole. In other words, to be effective any collection of activities with a common objective should ensure each activity is recognised as having an effect on all other activities, especially when any changes occur.

This simple explanation becomes complex when an organisation is examined. For example, it is pointless for marketing to accept orders that production cannot manufacture. Therefore marketing activities affect production and finance, and their effectiveness depends on relating them to other activities to ensure co-ordination. Activities that ignore this approach establish boundaries which isolate, cause communication and control problems, and defeat co-ordination.

Expanded further, interrelationships operate through complex communication networks that self-regulate (control mechanisms) and adapt to internal and external environmental changes. Networks are examined in Chapter 14, self-regulation in Chapter 23 (and homeostasis in Chapter 9), and environmental aspects in Chapters 3 and 6.

## THE CONTINGENCY APPROACH

Emerging out of systems theory, the contingency approach determines organisation design and management style for a particular situation. It relies upon finding the best combination or compromise, considering the existing or forecasted conditions associated with human skills, technological aspects and the external environment.

This situational approach to management uses all the previous approaches but in the right combination and proportions depending upon circumstances. The supervisor must be knowledgeable, adaptable and able to cope with boundaries problems. Key supervisory roles emerge: achieving co-ordination, encouraging participation, developing group autonomy, recognising situational changes and rapidly adapting to them.

Although the contingency approach is more flexible, changing approaches based upon the situation may confuse employees and appear to be inconsistent or insincere. Therefore, explaining the reasons for decisions is important. Indeed, an essential requirement is to maintain certain principles to satisfy moral difficulties and ethics, regardless of the situation.

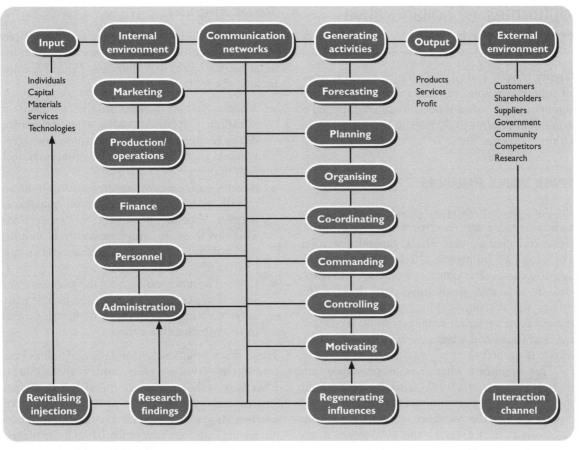

**Figure 2.1** A simplified open system of management
The restricted framework illustrates an open system. Each activity and specialism affects all activities and specialisms through complex communication networks. They self-regulate control and adapt to internal and external environments.

# Collaborative management

In the late 1980s productivity difficulties continued. In the USA four features were experienced: over twenty years of increasingly strong competition from certain countries, unfavourable economic circumstances, degrees of recession, and technological changes. Poor productivity was attributed to an increasing resentment from employees caused by the continued imbalance between technical and interpersonal or conceptual skills exercised by supervisors.

Proposed restructuring and some actual restructuring have emphasised supervisory role changes. These are based upon introducing or strongly reinforcing existing human resource management.

This means managing is concentrated on stimulating employee help and involvement. The term 'collaboration' is used to emphasise working jointly and co-operating with employees.

## INTERPERSONAL AND CONCEPTUAL SKILLS

Supervisory skills should be balanced to pursue this collaborative philosophy and to cope with the effects on employees of technological change. Since about 1960 writers have expressed concern over the neglect of interpersonal and conceptual skills. Decades ago research findings verified the urgent need to develop these skills, but only recently have the full implications been highlighted through large discrepancies in productivity between competing countries.

# Outcomes of collaborative management

The two main features of change now prevalent in supervisory roles are more direct contact with senior managers and modern coaching applied to autonomous teams to develop an employee-centred culture (Chapter 1).

## FEWER MIDDLE MANAGERS

Introducing technologies, especially information technology, is a serious error without appropriate structural change that alters supervisory roles. For example, information technology has made desktop computers commonplace, therefore ample data is available at all managerial levels. This affects the decision-making process and allows direct access by senior managers to all levels during operations and when information or specialist advice is needed.

This significant change is all-pervading and invites drastic structural reform. Apart from overcoming many communication problems, the change queries the relevance of middle managers as *information processors* and as *linkages* in the organisation. Computerised procedures and systems further reduce the need for finding, processing and transferring information to other levels, which until now were the province of the middle manager.

### The delayering process

Already whole layers of middle managers are being removed from many companies. Inevitably supervisors assume these roles since they are next in line. They give information direct to senior levels, hierarchical protocol seems to disappear, and new relationships emerge, especially involving information procedures and systems. Consequently, the organisational pyramid is flattened, which simplifies the structure and pushes more power towards the supervisory level. One outstanding example was British Petroleum's 1990 management reduction where eleven levels were reduced to five.

### The remaining roles

Bearing in mind certain organisation principles (Chapter 3) some middle management roles remain despite recent developments. Typical features include the following:

- Middle managers are usually involved in interpretive decision making when structuring decisions are received from senior managers, whereas supervisors deal with situational decision making.
- Middle managers are expected to communicate or talk with the workforce on all managerial matters affecting them, via the supervisors. This involves an employee-centred culture, national culture and an organisational culture (discussed soon).
- Upward communication from the workforce and supervisors usually flows through middle managers who apply a sifting and sorting process to smooth communication.

These three points raise fundamental issues concerning supervisory roles and responsibilities. Also there is the question of imbalance in the pay structure and the effect on promotion prospects where a large gap appears in the organisation. An interesting feature is how potential senior managers gain experience if middle management levels are entirely removed.

The following important features complete the survey of collaborative management. These are:

- The concept of culture.
- Employee-centred culture which involves empowerment, guidelines, and managerial and supervisory roles.
- National culture which includes research on this feature.
- Organisational culture (OC) which includes types, fundamental features, company policy, fear generation techniques and the development of cultural concepts.

## THE CONCEPT OF CULTURE

Culture is usually considered as a complex series of characteristics which may be related to nations, political bodies, families, groups of people, and an individual. Consequently, the subject should be treated with caution and needs to be developed from initial stages through to various ways of identifying culture. Here are the main features:

- definitions of culture
- cultural change
- managing culture
- objectives
- essential requirements
- typical examples of programmes

### Definitions of culture

Dictionary definitions may be summarised as improvement by mental or physical training; intellectual development; and a particular form, stage or type of intellectual development or civilisation. Hence the idea that 'cultural' relates to culture of mind or manners.

Unfortunately, culture is often not defined in terms of *what* it is, rather than *how* it operates in practice. Examples are customary ways of doing things, or in organisational concepts, 'the way we do things here'. This concept is often expanded to describe the amount of attention to detail, approaches to the job, how newcomers are inducted, and attitudes towards new technologies and innovation. In other words, mainly operating policy and methods.

Considering the ambiguity and vagueness of these definitions, any study of culture may reveal a pseudo, apparent or real culture. Determining which one is accurate may be guesswork.

### Cultural change

Any culture is subjected to many influences that cause change in an individual's characteristics. These may be related to people's education, attitudes, wants, beliefs, general outlook and norms. There are many forms of influence whose strength may depend on the prevailing situation and appropriate timing.

Influence may be applied by a political body, the educational system, the advertising media, propaganda by a leader, and company policy at local level. Consequently, culture is determined by political power, democratic will of a group, or the revised educational level within a group or individual.

### Managing culture

Managing culture means developing and reinforcing a proposed culture in the organisation that assumes the change will improve productivity. To achieve this change often involves extensive study and alteration to management style, management behaviour, the organisational climate, and attempts to alter attitudes, beliefs and values. These will all coincide with aims, strategies and tactics used to reach the company's objectives. In addition, there is emphasis on:

- Maintaining and reinforcing the favourable factors of the prevailing culture.
- Demonstrating the advantages for the workforce through their improved commitment.
- Ensuring that managers and supervisors adapt to the changes.
- Encouraging the workforce to co-operate when operating procedures and systems, and when setting standards.

Clearly the supervisor should be consulted at the initial stages of any proposed changes and be closely involved in the operational stages of introducing changes.

### Objectives

Management hopes to promote a better understanding of the organisation and to gain the commitment of the workforce. These outcomes should be achieved by creating a more positive organisational climate which outlines the behaviour needed to reach the objectives. A fundamental requirement is structuring an ideology that guides senior management on how to adopt and implement appropriate strategies, and how to formulate policies which will improve the culture. Effective communication and sincerity are vital factors.

### Essential requirements

To adopt, reinforce and maintain cultural changes demands careful analysis, diagnosis, application and prognosis. This comprehensive requirement means adopting a logical approach:

- Analyse the prevailing culture by assessing features such as values, norms, attitudes, beliefs, artefacts, climate and management style. The analysis must be conducted vigorously by using surveys, examining feedback, interviewing and group discussions.

- Plan a programme to achieve the envisaged changes, based upon visualising how commitment is possible.
- Take various forms of action to demonstrate sincerity, to explain the changes, and to indicate the objectives and advantages to the workforce.
- Continue with analysis and feedback.
- Adjust to faults and failures.
- Adopt an ongoing series of adaptations as the opportunities occur.

The co-operation and co-ordination of changes demand conscientious adjustments by managers and supervisors. Success usually depends upon senior managers, who are probably forced to make drastic changes in their attitude towards the workforce, to avoid actions that will irritate or infuriate the workforce, and to show sincerely their commitment to an improved culture.

Furthermore, effective communication is essential and demanding on most organisational levels where it is often ineffectual and misleading. Finally, it is fatal to expect the workforce to adapt without installing relevant improvements in rewards, education and training schemes, and managerial behaviour and style. Equally fatal is scheming to change a culture through insincerity, ignoring human behaviour and distrust.

### Typical examples

Programmes to change a culture may include the following topics:

- Ensuring that all contacts with customers or clients are conducted on the basis of a quality service.
- Demonstrating the importance of mutual interdependence of *all* employees.
- Improving communication at all organisational levels, with emphasis on *why* actions are taken and *how* the actions are based on improving the organisational climate.
- Ensuring that everyone accepts the need for applying information technology to maintain market share.

- Attempting to show the vital requirement for continuous improvement programmes to survive strong competition.

## EMPLOYEE-CENTRED CULTURE

The second feature of the middle management roles listed earlier directly involves employees who are recognised as being strongly affected by national and organisational cultures (discussed shortly). Creating cultural change is essential so that managers may work jointly with employees (collaboration) and be supportive. This feature extends to coaching (Chapters 12 and 19) by encouraging, tolerating, training and developing, providing appropriate assistance and fostering mutual respect.

Collaborative philosophy is often thrust upon top management when its vital nature is recognised. Previously, strong competition forced companies to streamline the workforce, introduce technological changes in production, and encourage employees to be more committed through various devices such as co-partnership, profit-sharing schemes and shareholding opportunities. However, these encouragements alone are insufficient to create the productive potential of the remaining workforce. Supervisors must play the crucial role of building up employee commitment to the company and achieving more involvement from them.

Attempting to develop an employee-centred culture is a complex process which involves collaborative and empowerment philosophies, and ultimately holistic management. Figure 2.2 illustrates the overall application.

### Empowerment

Nowadays collaboration and supportiveness is seen to be the only sensible way to achieve high productivity levels already enjoyed by communities and companies elsewhere. This is possible by using a modern approach called empowerment. Employees are made responsible for their own actions by giving them the appropriate authority to apply discretion and make decisions concerning their work.

Such productive potential gives employees the opportunity to:

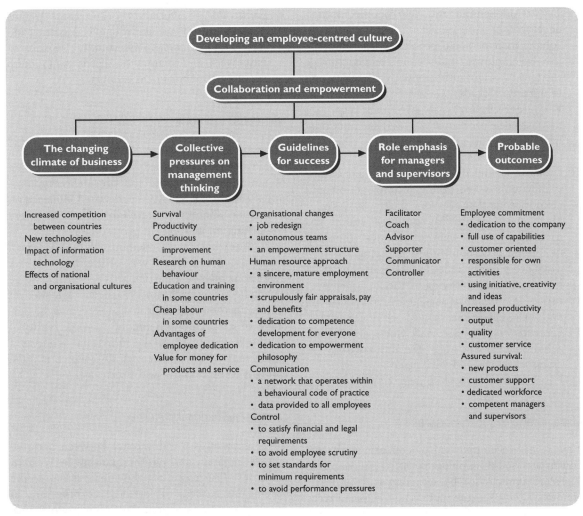

**Figure 2.2** Developing an employee-centred culture
Collaboration and empowerment (and ultimately holism) are essential in attempts to introduce an employee-centred culture.

- use initiative
- develop a feeling of ownership over their jobs
- provide power to satisfy customer quality
- fully participate and achieve high fulfilment at work

### Essential guidelines

The following points summarise an employee-centred culture and the empowerment approach:

1 Recognise and heed the influence of national and organisational cultures.

2 Encourage and help people to develop, and be tolerant when errors occur by discussing and trying to help.
3 Always find time to gain employees' confidence by being understanding, ready to listen sympathetically, and ensuring people feel they can express their true feelings in confidence and without fear.
4 Be responsive to human difficulties and provide appropriate assistance.
5 Seek ideas and contributions; give due credit.
6 Demonstrate genuine trust and confidence.

7 Try to understand and help people in their development and self-development, and in solving their personal problems.

8 Involve employees in discussion and encourage them to use their authority with discretion and in making decisions.

9 Encourage employees to give quick responses to customer problems, cut across functional boundaries, and take opportunities whenever they occur.

10 Create a feeling that a certain amount of risk is inevitable when taking prompt action and acknowledge that everyone makes mistakes.

11 Have strict regard for business ethics and managerial ethics; only fools believe they can be unethical without others knowing.

12 Take every opportunity to emphasise eliminating waste and improving methods.

13 Ensure that organisational goals are understood and seek suggestions or ideas to revise goals.

14 Persuade employees to talk freely about their achievements and use the information to assess strengths and weaknesses.

15 Foster mutual respect at every opportunity.

### Managerial and supervisory roles

New roles are emphasised to conform with empowerment and the employee-centred philosophies. They are summarised below along with abbreviated descriptions. Note that certain classical roles remain to ensure structural effectiveness, but with reduced influence.

- *Facilitator*: to promote the philosophies, encourage, and ensure ethics are maintained.
- *Coach*: to be available when needed, accept risk and errors, encourage discussions, and foster autonomous teamwork.
- *Advisor*: to ensure concepts are understood and followed by emphasising survival, accepting human difficulties, recommending training and development, and promoting ways to avoid waste and to improve methods.
- *Supporter*: to gain everyone's confidence and understanding, and to avoid fear.
- *Communicator*: to operate a behavioural communication network and ensure data reaches all employees.

- *Controller*: to steer all procedures and systems towards satisfying essential financial, costing and legal requirements, to avoid undue scrutiny of employees, and to apply standards as minimum requirements not norm ceilings.

## NATIONAL CULTURE

Strongly associated with the introduction of an employee-centred culture is the underrated effect of national culture and the prevalent organisational culture (OC). Their deep-seated influence on behaviour should be carefully assessed before embarking on adaptation programmes.

Culture has many meanings. Simplified in a national context, it is a way of life, but complex definitions include a particular type, form or stage of intellectual development; all the knowledge, beliefs, customs and skills in a society; and the outcome of a specific and unique history. National culture is ingrained in the individual who, as a result, may be in conflict with OC, which is often thought to be shallow and short-term.

### Contrasting national cultures

Often debated is the difference between national culture in Japan and national culture in Western countries. The reason for the debate is due to the spectacular success of Japanese corporations in world markets, compared with poor performance by their US and UK counterparts. This may be attributed *partly* to Japan's national culture, which strongly influences many aspects of its organisational culture and contrasts sharply with Western approaches.

Briefly, Japanese culture assumes unavoidable interdependency and the primacy of the group. The outcome is emphasis on traditionalism, loyalty, co-operation, obligation, respect for authority, conformity and self-restraint.

Motivation appears to hinge on the individual being accepted by the group, therefore any action that may disgrace the group must be avoided. In this way, a company is a strong community or family, not simply an economic unit. Strong social relationships and group loyalty engender high motivation.

Observers often claim that Western culture clearly contrasts markedly with Japan. The bureaucratic characteristic of the West tends to dominate and causes many organisational problems. However, many aspects of Japanese organisational culture have been adopted by the West, with varying degree of success.

## Research on national culture

In 1980 Professor Geert Hofstede conducted extensive research in forty countries on national culture, its effects on employees, and the role and character of leadership. He grouped differences in values and behaviour into four main measures:

- individualism/collectivism
- power/distance
- uncertainty avoidance
- masculinity/femininity

The main cultural aspects and their association with particular countries are now briefly given.

### Individualism/collectivism

Individualism is the degree of personal choice, freedom and challenges allowed at work, whereas collectivism is a tight social framework which provides security in return for loyalty.

Individualism is preferred in Europe and the USA, where self-determination is a strong cultural characteristic. Less well-developed countries tend to prefer collectivism. The Japanese feel the will of the group should decide beliefs and behaviour.

### Power/distance

Power is interpreted as a measure of the degree to which less powerful employees are prepared to accept the unequal distribution of power. High power/distance accepts low involvement in decision making, typically seen in India and the Philippines. Low power/distance refers to participative management where employees have a say, typically seen in Denmark and Israel.

### Uncertainty avoidance

Uncertainty avoidance (UA) is the extent to which people will tolerate ambiguity and uncertainty, and the degree to which they will seek more career stability. Stability includes rejecting unconventional behaviour and encouraging clear, formal rules. Germany and Austria have high UA, along with Japan, Greece and Portugal, where lifetime employment is a traditional characteristic. Low UA is seen in the USA, Hong Kong, Denmark and Singapore, where high job mobility is typical.

### Masculinity/femininity

Masculinity is interpreted as the extent that dominant values emphasise assertiveness and acquisition of money and goods, while displaying little concern for people. Femininity is interpreted as the extent that dominant values emphasise human relationships, concern for others and the quality of life. High masculinity is seen in Japan and to a lesser extent in the UK. Femininity is noticeable in Sweden and Denmark. In Japan the combination of high masculinity and high UA seems to produce high motivation where quality circles successfully achieve high quality.

## Other cultural influences

Apart from Hofstede's four variables, there are other cultural issues which particularly affect leadership behaviour when two countries are involved in a business or company.

### Countries with a different culture

Often a company setting up a concern in another country will force its home culture on to the other country's concern. This is known as an ethnocentric approach.

### Ignoring national cultural boundaries

Ignoring national cultural boundaries, often known as a geocentric approach, relies on the reputation of the home company. This is achieved by advertising and offering the identical product and quality of service anywhere in the world. Some companies have been very successful in adopting this approach.

### Acceptance of the local culture

The polyconcentric approach applies where a home company allows the local culture to be adopted by a subsidiary in another country. A flexible organisation is arranged to provide facilities which react favourably to local conditions.

## ORGANISATIONAL CULTURE

A behavioural definition of organisational culture (OC) involves two aspects: the common assumptions of employees in the company relating to beliefs, customs, values and norms; and the common behavioural patterns relating to strategy, tactics, operations, applications of management principles, communication and leadership practices. This complex definition may be simplified as the way the organisation operates, or the way things are done. These definitions imply that either culture is determined by management or it just happens in a haphazard way. Determined culture is an essential part of competent management whereas haphazard culture is a recipe for disaster.

The concept of OC is also seen as a co-ordinating mechanism, which includes social interaction, norms, rules and regulations, acceptable physical and ethical conduct, and the degree of group cohesiveness associated with interpersonal and group relations. Important features of this concept and OC in general are the effects of company policy, the development of cultural concepts, the impact of fashionable theories which attempt to change OC, and attempts to assess OC.

Organisational culture is interpreted in many different ways. E.H. Schein assumes OC involves assumptions, beliefs, values, rituals, myths and languages. He suggests OC has three layers:

- Artefacts and creations which can be seen, but seldom interpreted; examples are furnishings and decor.
- Values or things that are important to the workforce.
- People make basic assumptions that guide or influence their behaviour.

Considering this interpretation, there are varying strengths of OC. A weak culture may mean the values of the organisation are not shared by the workforce, whereas a strong culture is more influential on behaviour.

### Contributory factors

Usually OC evolves slowly and imperceptibly. Often the workforce may be unaware of its existence. If an employee is asked about the company's culture, the immediate reply might be any of these: rule by fear, jobs for the boys, somewhere to work without hassle, or good working conditions. However, OC should indicate how people feel about their jobs by examining people's perceptions, assessing the leaders and how they operate, feelings on how work should be performed, and attitudes on a variety of organisational topics. Certain factors have an effect on OC:

- Company policy and the strategies adopted, which are interpreted by employees as values to follow to remain in favour.
- Personnel policy in all its forms, which involves operating procedures in an attempt to secure competent employees.
- Particular emphasis on education, training and development of the workforce, and human resource techniques to demonstrate sincere appreciation and acknowledgement of their importance.

But they may not immediately affect OC. Particular circumstances might force certain measures to compensate for inertia. These include empowering employees, promotion programmes for those with appropriate attitudes, introducing newcomers with modern ideas, and genuine financial and non-financial incentives to encourage new approaches.

### Types of organisational culture

Building up or changing OC is usually a long process; the time depends on the type already existing. The types explained below should be related to motivation (Chapter 11) and further aspects of motivation (Chapter 12). The significance of each type is an important factor in motivation psychology and motivation techniques. The immediately recognisable types are autocratic, bureaucratic, teamwork and individualistic.

### Autocratic type

In an autocratic organisation the power is centralised and its influence is felt throughout. Employees might feel suppressed, lack motivation and refuse to co-operate fully.

### Bureacratic type

In a bureaucratic organisation a person's power is determined by their position in the organisational structure (Chapter 3). Rules and procedures within a group of functions are usually rigid.

### Teamwork type

A teamwork organisation is arranged according to the tasks and objectives allocated to the groups. The culture avoids individual power and rigid rules, and it encourages flexibility, freedom and appropriate rewards.

### Individualistic type

An individualistic organisation has pronounced characteristics: individuals only serve the interest of those in the organisation; there are no formal distinguishable hierarchies except by mutual consent; and usually the organisation is not profit motivated.

### An alternative classification

A different approach to classifying types of organisational culture is given by Charles Handy. He visualises four types: power, role, task and person. One type could dominate the whole organisation, or different types could exist in various sections of a company. Handy sees a culture emerging in various situations such as historical circumstances, the local environment, prevailing technology, and the human needs and wants within an organisation. Consequently, he feels any culture is no better than the others.

### Power culture

A power culture is autocratic and easily recognisable, especially in the small business. Usually there are few rules and procedures. Often there are no committees. Decisions are either made by the senior person or by a few managers who rigidly apply the precedents. Changes may occur rapidly but not necessarily competently.

### Role culture

A role culture corresponds to the bureaucratic type in the earlier classification. There are formal roles, strict procedures, and clear rules for settling disputes. Security and predictability usually prevail but the structure is rigid and reacts slowly to change.

### Task culture

A task culture identifies jobs and projects; it may be seen in matrix organisations. Similar to teamwork, there is no individual dominant leader, and members concentrate on a collective task. Therefore flexibility and change apply, along with high satisfaction and group cohesion.

### Person culture

A person culture applies in an organisation which exists to serve the people within it. Typical examples are seen in professional companies offering, say, consultancy.

### Fundamental features

In practice there are usually two forms of OC: the unconcealed assumptions and the hidden operational framework. The open approach is obviously preferable and highlights managerial philosophy. The disguised approach is unplanned and usually the result of inept management. Both may be seen operating together.

There are many examples of drastic OC transformations in companies, brought about by privatisation, takeovers and mergers. Probably new values are created but the old disguised approach may continue until management adopts a new philosophy which is acceptable to employees. Many management strategies have been used to change OC to suit market conditions. Typical approaches are process re-engineering, total quality management (TQM) and human resource management systems.

### Effects of company policy

Often overlooked by owners and senior managers is the effect their policies have on OC. Such company culture is often assessed by employees through top management's attitudes towards status, ethical conduct, values and moral codes. The grapevine soon reveals 'behind the scenes behaviour' and typical indicators are:

- Salary increases and perks inconsistent with pronouncements for employees.
- Appointing people obviously unsuitable for the job.

- Degree of concern for the external environment, such as ignoring the effects of pollution and effluents.
- Manipulation of the law when dealing with injuries to employees, redundancies, takeovers, mergers, and cases involving the private individual and the community.

## Fear generation techniques

Surprisingly, a form of semi-autocratic management still persists, even in large companies. The traditional techniques were to create fear through the effects of dismissal when unemployment meant near starvation, and using bad practices to maintain control. Now some approaches are more subtle, but equally effective and harmful to organisation culture. Examples are:

- *Bullying*: shouting and blustering to browbeat employees.
- *Vagueness*: communicating in such a way that employees are confused or uncertain of the intention.
- *Poor communication*: to generate stress and irritation.
- *Off-hand treatment*: to upset and bewilder.
- *Victimising*: to suppress both free speech and rocking the boat. This is achieved by creating examples of known offenders who are treated badly by picking on them for redundancy, withholding extra perks at early retirement or retirement, and allocating unsavoury tasks.
- *Veiled threats*: making ambiguous remarks which have obvious hidden implications.

There are many more examples of these techniques which are familiar to employees. They cause feelings of distress, pity and justified hatred. The polite labels for managers who use these techniques are little Hitlers, tyrants, rogues and clowns.

## Development of cultural concepts

Effective structuring of a particular organisation hinges on the degree of management competency and the cultural background of its employees. Managers need the capability to adjust and work effectively within the established OC, and to initiate and co-ordinate cultural change.

Views differ on the depth of OC and the possibility of changing it rapidly. Certainly the complex process involves development of managers, supervisors and all employees to a point where OC evolves to a more advanced form. One view sees OC as essentially shallow and short-term; consequently, manipulation of management styles and human resource management have greater impact while national culture is subordinated.

## The productivity factor

The obvious reason for emphasis on OC is the hope that 'improvements' will mean higher productivity. However, this assumption does not always agree with reasearch. Strong OC assumes high performance because there should be a firm relationship between OC and company strategy and policy. Furthermore, there should be more commitment from the workforce. However, some research has revealed that a participative OC yielded better results compared with those who omitted the concept. K.S. Cameron and S.J. Freeman thought there was no difference between strong and weak cultures.

Regardless of research, there are usually acceptable advantages through 'improving' OC. These are expressed as:

- Employee behaviour is improved.
- The expected behaviour of the workforce may be assessed more accurately.
- Employees feel more committed to a shared value arrangement which demonstrates common objectives.
- Productivity improves in many companies.

## Fashionable theories

Managers may seek short cuts to success by adopting new theories that claim to solve cultural problems. However, OC is mainly determined by the situation which the company inflicts on employees. Whether managers have the power to influence OC by changing techniques is debatable.

The use of fashionable theories is encouraged by consultants, business magazines and management courses at colleges. All are useful management tools provided they are in capable hands and used in the right circumstances. Often criticised when they fail to produce forecasted results, they are not necessarily inappropriate; it depends partly on the particular organisation structure. Typical theories often quoted are management by objectives, merit rating, critical path analysis, organisation development and quality circles. All are excellent but often condemned for the wrong reasons.

## Essential empowerment features

Empowering employees successfully depends partly on convincing people through OC that they *are* able to contribute far more than is traditionally believed. Therefore, all procedures should demonstrate such sincerity by ensuring there is a mature, trusting theme. Some examples are serious responses and open encouragement to recommended changes through suggestions schemes and proposals at meetings; a communication network that operates within a behavioural code of practice, not a rigid, cold line of command; appraisals, pay schemes and benefits are scrupulously fair and not benefiting particular sectors at the expense of others; using monitoring employees and control procedures to satisfy legal and financial requirements, taking care not to give the impression that the aim is to scrutinise the individuals unduly; indicating clearly that establishing standards is to ensure minimum requirements for operational effectiveness, not for the purpose of applying pressure on performance levels.

## Qualitative assessments

The role of OC and how it influences behaviour are important features which need assessing. Often inexplicable employee reactions may be attributed to cultural conflicts at organisational and national levels, but being able to understand and assess culture is a difficult task. These difficulties also explain the behaviour of some supervisors. Intuition, responses by employees and self-examination of the supervisor's own feelings all help. The assessment's qualitative nature remains and must be treated with caution.

# Holistic management

The term 'holism' means a tendency in nature to form *wholes* that are more than the sum of the parts, by ordered grouping. This is based on the theory that the fundamental principle of the universe is the creation of complete and self-contained systems from the atom upwards. Such power sharing related to an organisation means using this principle in employee relationships. Support and commitment from employees is gained by establishing an organisational environment where *all* members thrive as individuals. This ultimate concept implies a highly developed workforce where everyone is able to use fully his or her capabilities.

## THE BACKGROUND

In the early 1990s the concept of collaborative management and its real implications continued to grow. A realisation began to emerge that employees do not fully respond to collaborative management ideas unless *all* managers (especially senior managers) undergo a drastic change in outlook. This 'change' (or holistic shift) means a manager is no longer the boss but 'first among equals'. Although a manager's particular competence is essential, employees will not be convinced or whole-hearted about collaboration unless the organisation culture, with all its codes, is consistent with holism.

In other words, secretive, unethical, immoral codes of conduct by certain managers who work against a successful, collective organisational culture will undermine ultimate collaboration. Furthermore, a 'competent' manager must be competent in all senses, including codes which generate maximum favourable impact on employees. A manager, regardless of expertise, must be highly respected not despised.

## ESSENTIAL REQUIREMENTS

The holistic style of managing and supervising depends upon a number of essential requirements. If they are not established, holism no longer applies. The use of another style automatically takes over. Usually this would be a collaborative style if management is seriously considering holism, until the following requirements are satisfied.

### Managerial strategy

Senior management is geared to operating revised systems with all their holistic implications. These include moral and environmental codes of conduct which are consistent and comprehensive, as well as operating effective ongoing competence development programmes for everyone.

### Managers and supervisors

Attending development programmes is required to ensure the strategy is interpreted correctly by introducing, updating and operating all the holistic tactical manoeuvres. These programmes are designed to create a strong desire among employees to improve and fully contribute.

### Members of the organisation

All employees are able to contribute fully. This is achieved by engaging suitable members who may be educated, trained and developed to appropriate standards where they are able to thrive as individuals. Each member knows his or her roles, clearly understands the direction of the business, and knows how the strategy is achieved through tactical means.

### The organisational culture

All the modern concepts of human resource management are in place and operating successfully. Any deficiency is immediately rectified.

### Market orientation

Maximum customer satisfaction dominates and is supported by all modern research devices. Continuous adjustment automatically occurs as information is processed and distributed.

The role of everyone in the organisation is to provide feedback on all information received from customers. Such feedback is only meaningful if a customer orientation philosophy is achieved by management. This involves employees in understanding completely the essential contributions they make to improving relationships with customers (Chapter 4).

## SUMMARY OF UNDERLYING ASSUMPTIONS

The important assumptions are:

- effective selection programmes
- application of human resource principles
- a senior executive team dedicated to the concept
- stringent regular appraisals plus appropriate adjustments
- a well-meaning redundancy, termination and early retirement policy
- effective application of the critical organisation principles
- competent managers and supervisors
- an ongoing competency development programme at all levels

## PROBABLE DIFFICULTIES

In practice the underlying assumptions (or some of them) are often incomplete or non-existent, or not accepted by senior management. Attempting to launch holistic management in these circumstances involves costly, comprehensive, innovative programmes to correct the problems. Any scheme is a long-term project; it is time-consuming, and includes drastic changes in the organisation and its members. Adopting holism demands courage, tenacity and capital. However, the final outcome is a dynamic business.

# Supervisors' and managers' tasks

Although theoretical definitions of supervisors and managers are clear, the distinction in practice is frequently obscured. There is a natural tendency to overlap; this is partly from necessity, where managers may show a close personal interest to achieve co-operation, and partly from lack of management training. Moreover, supervisors are inclined to avoid essential detail and concentrate on forward planning; whereas managers are often seen to be keen on attending to detail, because of the need to compensate for their lack of drive, vision and decision-making ability (Chapter 7). Consequently, supervisors and managers have very different views of each other's jobs.

Attempts to overcome this diversity of opinion have included retraining managers, completely removing the supervisory level, and encouraging collaboration at the interface between supervisors and managers to develop mutual tolerance.

Another factor is the supervisor's organisational background. For example, if a supervisor were promoted from the shop floor or office, the tendency would be to feel a strong link with previous peers but a weaker bond with management; thus behaviour as a manager may be more difficult. However, starting a job as a junior manager would probably mean a weak link with operators or clerks, but a strong link with management. Thus it may be easier to act as a junior manager but more difficult to relate to employees.

## IMPROVING RELATIONSHIPS

In both instances the void between managers and employees is clearly marked and somehow interface difficulties have to be tackled. Bringing the two sides together involves various techniques. Three typical approaches are collaboration, retraining and the classless concept.

### The collaborative approach

Collaboration means sharing problem solving and decision making, and communicating views and ideas on an equal footing. The aims must be clear:

- to close up the structure
- to analyse and arrive at more acceptable approaches
- to improve relationships generally

### The retraining approach

The retraining approach means developing both parties to understand the two environments thoroughly – the management sphere and the working sphere. Forgetting traditions, changing basic attitudes and ideologies, and achieving co-operation are a part of the programme.

### The classless approach

The classless approach attempts to remove the variety of class structure models in organisations.

Many countries are proud of their 'classless' society. In the UK many managers seem to be proud of belonging to a seemingly different class, are pre-occupied with status, and intent on widening rather than closing the gap. Senior managers even consider themselves to be upper-class. Seldom do managers see themselves as part of the proletariat, although they are employed by the company (except the owner-managers). Supervisors seem to feel the divide is a level above them.

The damage to relationships often involves mental, and sometimes physical, reactions against those who think themselves above everyone else.

## QUESTIONS

1 What are the main guidelines the supervisor should follow to build up employee commitment and to accomplish more employee involvement?

2 Explain the concept of organisational culture and its effects on behaviour.

3 Discuss the effects of inconsistencies in company policy on organisational culture.

4 Outline the collaborative, retraining and classless approaches to improving relationships between managers and employees.

5 Discuss the effect of rapid change in information technology on the role of the supervisor.

6 What are the main factors that cause supervisory role changes?

7 How may the decline in union power affect the supervisor's role?

8 A common interest exists for all people in an organisation. How would you attempt to convince an employee that this statement is true?

9 Explain the difference between unitary, pluralistic and radical approaches.

10 Examine the systems approach and its effect on key supervisory roles and the organisation.

11 Outline the main phases in management thinking that have affected the supervisor.

12 An employee-centred culture is essential to exploit the productive potential of a working force. Discuss this statement.

13 Explain the collaborative approach and its importance in a modern organisation.

14 The supervisor's job is easier in a classless society. On what grounds would you agree or disagree with this statement?

15 Discuss the importance of empowerment in a modern progressive company.

16 Maximum customer satisfaction depends on modern market research. Discuss this statement considering the modern role of the workforce.

17 What are the essential features of empowment?

18 Fear generation techniques are the favourite tools of many mangers to achieve co-operation. Discuss this statement.

19 Outline the essential requirements of holistic management.

20 Consider the main difficulties confronting a company if holistic management is to be introduced.

21 Outline the main fear generation techniques usually encountered in many organisations.

## CASE STUDY

Punddit Ltd was holding its monthly senior executives meeting. The sales director mentioned he had heard about empowerment and its advantages when applied to workgroups in the factory. The works director said he has been reading about automated work teams and their success in the USA over the past five years. The personnel director was apprehensive, considering the organisation culture in the factory. After discussion the managing director decided to try a pilot scheme as he was not altogether convinced that it was suitable for the company considering its previous record of productivity.

From ten groups in workshop A, three were chosen and training schemes established according to the requirements learned from a management magazine. The three supervisors were appraised and developed for their new roles.

Training was completed and after one year a thorough appraisal of the scheme was conducted by personnel. The main result was the low output and quality ratings of all three compared with the other seven groups.

The three supervisors were interviewed separately. Each one gave a similar story: they had not been able to overcome suspicion of the scheme, there was antagonism within the group, and a strong resistance to taking over authority and extra responsibilities with no pay increases or extra bonuses to compensate.

*Discuss the possible reasons for the scheme failing. Why should all three groups perform badly apart from the excuses given concerning pay?*

## CASE STUDY

'I know all about these new-fangled ideas of supervising but so far as I'm concerned it's heads down and do a fair day's work for a fair day's pay, then we'll see better results', stressed Janet, seated at the coffee table with two other fellow supervisors.

Elsie reacted. 'That's OK for you; I've got teenagers to cope with and if I don't give them freedom to have a chat and a giggle they would go round the bend working those blasted terminals eight hours a day!'

'You're too nice to them, Elsie', complained Paul. 'What you don't realise is that my people are distracted by your people chatting away and walking around. Concentration is lost and up go the errors.'

'There, you see', exclaimed Janet, 'Give them an inch and they cause nothing but trouble. We've got the upper hand now with high unemployment and it's up to us to take advantage of it.'

'That's a joke, Janet! Your productivity figures are worse than ours', cracked Elsie.

*Are there any clear-cut answers to these problems and what could management do about this situation?*

# 3

# Organisation of work

## Organisational design

An organisation is not an organism that responds and reacts biologically. Consequently, there are difficulties in designing an organisation to cope effectively with growth, contraction, new technologies and environmental changes. Construction of an ideal organisation is not possible, therefore a compromise relies on supervisors' and employees' capabilities to adapt and to understand structural problems. As Peter Drucker asserted in 1955, 'The best managers are those who think through organisational dilemmas'. Success also depends upon managers whose role is to assess results of changes, consider organisational design techniques and adjust accordingly.

### VIEWPOINTS

Many specialists claim that organisational design has only a partial effect on productivity. However, they also feel that successfully applying behavioural knowledge and motivators depends partly upon various structural aspects of organisation. These are discussed from two viewpoints. First, from the strategic viewpoint of treating the organisation as a whole, which is consistent with modern systems theory and holism. Second, from the tactical viewpoint which includes many features such as structuring, problem areas, organisation criteria, integration difficulties, organisation theory, critical organisational principles, co-ordination, overcoming structural faults, practical steps towards improving the organisation, organisational behaviour, organisational development and structural designs.

## Organisational structuring

The ideal organisation achieves its objectives by structuring and restructuring in such a way that maximum effectiveness is drawn from its members – the employees. This goal should not be superseded by other supplementary objectives often encountered when powerful individuals, or groups, structure organisations to suit their own personal requirements.

The term 'organisation' in this context means structuring activities into operational groups, each of which contains employees who are allocated roles and duties, and given varying degrees of authority and responsibility. In brief, the formal organisation.

### THE SOCIAL UNIT

The way people behave within the organisation is a product of their job description and events which directly affect them during their initial period at work (induction). In other words, they are affected by the economic system (their job) and by the social system (interaction with others), which create expectation of the roles they should undertake. This twofold effect explains why no two people see the organisation in exactly the same way and why the informal organisation is so important.

Formal and informal structures are intertwined and often indistinguishable. Thus organisation is a purposeful social unit. The implications are each employee possesses a slightly different mental make-up; their attitudes towards events bias their view of the organisation structure; their reasons for staying in their job vary; and they possess differing expectations of roles they and others should play.

## Problem areas

Certain fundamental difficulties must be overcome to accomplish maximum effectiveness. From the list below, probably the three most important considerations are the customer, organisational culture, and innovation.

- Formal organisations are structured to conform to an established set of traditional principles that do not allow sufficiently for social interaction and modern technologies.
- So far there is no workable way of restructuring to suit the modern employee and to replace completely the outdated traditional organisation concept.
- Although incomplete, there is sufficient evidence to show how people and groups behave in organisations, and where there is room for improvement.
- Organisational change is often traumatic, expensive and sometimes disastrous at present. This causes some inertia from owners and managers to adopt sound ideas.
- Some managers feel, and through experience know, many popular behavioural theories do not necessarily conform to industrial reality and are not easily installed.
- As organisations grow they tend to become more complex and inward-looking, therefore they should be kept as simple as possible and seek to promote customer contact.
- Incompetent management creates organisational rigidity. In-built flexibility, however, ensures that innovation is made easier. This is a vital factor which should mean cultural change is continuous, and work is fulfilling and enjoyable.
- Treating an organisation as an end in itself ignores both customer wants and the need to search constantly for high quality products and services.
- Neglecting the cultural impact of applying managerial or organisational techniques on employees invites disaster.

- Short-term gearing of an organisational structure is commonplace. Short-term *and* long-term thinking is needed to satisfy customers' wants now and in the future.

## Organisational criteria

There are certain essential requirements for high productivity to satisfy the customer and the community. In some respects these requirements are conflicting but this is mainly due to imbalances between economic and social factors. Balance may be attained when each requirement is allowed to find its own determinable level through the operation of political, technological, economic and social interaction. Figure 3.1 illustrates the criteria and essential factors.

### JOB DESIGN

Designing the job to suit the individual is a complex subject which is discussed as a motivating feature in Chapter 12 and as an employment topic in Chapter 17. Essential features are:

- synchronisation with other jobs
- integration with the organisation
- solving problems of values, pacing, repetitiveness and unreal objectives
- fostering role participation
- using critical organisational principles
- arranging adequate rewards

### SELECTION

This sensitive area is closely watched and judged by all employees. The three criteria are:

- Manpower planning to ensure current and future human resources are carefully assessed. This plan should provide an accurate profile of the individual required.
- Use of specialists for interviewing. The supervisor should ensure coverage of the technical aspects and the personnel manager should check details and assess personal qualities.
- The adoption of a high moral code by management, e.g. avoidance of nepotism.

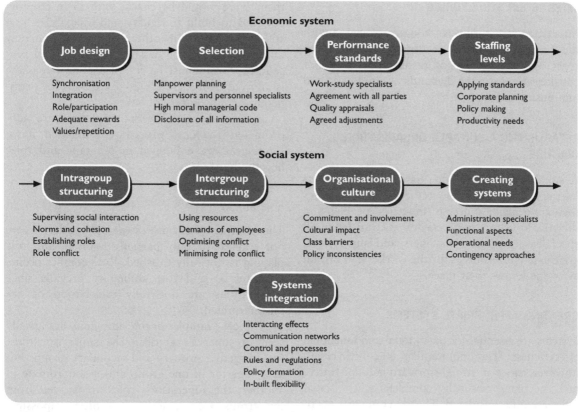

**Figure 3.1** Structuring an organisation: some useful criteria
Certain essential requirements must be considered for behavioural balance and to achieve high productivity. Standards are judged by employees and are accepted as essential. Each factor finds its own determinable level through political, technological, economic and social interaction.

## ESTABLISHING SUITABLE PERFORMANCE STANDARDS

Acceptable performance standards are difficult to achieve because they must be agreed by management, employees and trade unions. Conflict may arise here. For example, if work study specialists are employed, they have the capability to accurately assess performance standards for quality and working rate, but their findings may not be acceptable to everyone.

## APPROPRIATE STAFFING LEVELS

Staffing decisions are hazardous because the performance standards may be contested. Indeed manpower planning is never easy and mistakes or enforced corrections might have disastrous consequences affecting corporate planning and policy making.

## INTRAGROUP STRUCTURING

Group formation and development are discussed in Chapter 5. The success of this process depends upon supervising social interaction, the development of cohesion, norm formation, the establishment of roles, and the correct use of power. A thorough understanding of group activity is essential. This knowledge provides an appreciation of the effects of intragroup changes, the importance of teamwork and self-regulating or autonomous groups, and ways of resolving conflict.

## INTERGROUP STRUCTURING

Intergroup structuring is strongly associated with the functional aspects of organisation and the most appropriate use of resources. The major considerations are the demands of employees and minimising conflict.

## ESTABLISHING A SUITABLE ORGANISATIONAL CULTURE

A suitable culture is often associated with class barriers and human resource concepts. Together they are a major source of industrial problems in the UK. In Germany no classes exist; in Japan all specialists, including managers and supervisors, are treated as resources for the workers; in Britain everyone knows their place.

## CREATING APPROPRIATE SYSTEMS

Systems are essential for operational and functional effectiveness. The requirement is controversial, however, since a straightforward administrative task becomes absurdly complex when social interaction is considered. This dynamic process of systems integration, through communication networks and control processes, introduces contingency approaches where refinements absorb a variety of the behavioural aspects already discussed.

## INTEGRATION OF THE CRITERIA

Although complete integration is an unreachable objective, it should not be ignored. All changes in the above requirements must be treated carefully since they interact and affect each other. Any changes should be made with integration in mind and they should contribute positively in this direction.

### Integration difficulties

A common dilemma appears when all the roles and tasks are allocated, groups formed and functions structured. This is because communication networks must be established to achieve co-ordination, which means designing forms, establishing rules, regulating control mechanisms, and so on. Without

them there would be chaos; with them employees tend to build in rigidity and inflexibility that stifles initiative. In other words, bureaucracy takes over: everyone must conform to rigid procedures, forms must be completed, no bypassing is allowed, and there are no exceptions for extraneous circumstances.

In this situation overall objectives are subordinated to local procedure-dominated aims. Employees are entangled in red tape and roles become blurred.

### Role stress

This blurring effect causes stress as expectations are not realised or only partially realised, and role playing is not fully satisfied. Role conflict occurs (Chapter 5) and role ambiguity prevails since expectations are not fully understood or are misinterpreted.

Typical examples of role ambiguity are usually seen in supervisory jobs. The supervisor must bond together primary and secondary groups but as a superior in one group and a subordinate in another; the supervisor's roles are viewed from two fronts. Consequently, it is often impossible to please management and subordinates as both groups expect the supervisor's support.

A further example is the secretary who feels a loyalty to the boss and to the company. When the secretary discovers the boss is falsifying petty cash claims, he or she suffers uncertainty – torn between a supportive role for the boss and a protective role towards the company.

An outline of organisation theory now follows, which is complex but essential for supervisors. Supervisors must know which type of organisation they are involved in as the expectations of management will vary accordingly. Furthermore, when organisational changes are proposed or occur, supervisors should understand their significance in the job and know how to adjust.

# Organisation theory

Organisations were first studied thousands of years ago. Many complex and diverse theories exist mainly due to changes in organisation size and number and the increased complexity of technologies this century. Recognition of dependency among various organisational activities is now an important feature. Such dependency could mean increased harmony, solidarity and support for the concern. Members often resent dependency and react against each other. New theories have emerged to counteract this tendency.

A selection of theories has been chosen here to illustrate the main schools of thought and to provide matters of interest to the supervisor. A school of thought incorporates similar basic principles, doctrines and working methods on a particular subject; these are offered by specialists, writers and practising managers.

## TRADITIONAL THOUGHT

Classical approaches are cold, impersonal and mechanistic. They follow a systematic pattern: establishing all the tasks required, designing a structure to accommodate them, achieving co-ordination mainly through supervision, communicating through the line of command, and controlling by holding everyone accountable for the work performed. Many principles were established but some are severely criticised on grounds of poor behavioural sensitivity, contradictions, and lack of evidence to prove they are universal truths.

Within traditional thought is the classical school of organisation and management. There are several approaches which include scientific management, bureaucratic management, and fundamental aspects of organisation and management.

### Scientific management

The American F.W. Taylor is the acknowledged father of scientific management. His concepts are based upon using scientific principles, fostering harmony and co-operation, and creating highly efficient employees. He believed employees are motivated by offering high material reward. In 1911 he developed new techniques which were successful at the time and widely practised in the USA. These were based upon:

- close supervision
- establishing time study techniques

- efficient methods of working
- standard working conditions
- setting high targets to stretch employees
- relating wages to productivity

Taylor had several famous followers. F.B. and L. Gilbreth carried out important research on the principles of motion economy (Chapter 25), and H.L. Gantt developed a versatile chart (Chapter 26) that can be adapted to any control system where a number of functions are allied to the time factor.

### Bureaucratic management

Bureaucratic management was introduced by the German sociologist Max Weber and is well known for its operating problems. He believed bureaucracy was the most efficient organisational structure because he thought it could easily cope with external change, was logical and self-perpetuating. His work is mentioned in Chapter 4.

### Fundamental aspects of organisation and management

In 1916 the French mining engineer H. Fayol concentrated on managerial aspects that should apply in any organisation. These were planning, organising, co-ordinating, commanding and controlling. They are discussed along with other management functions in Chapter 7. Also he tabulated a number of organisational principles and listed the main business activities as finance, technical, commercial, security and management.

## TRANSITIONARY CONCEPTS

Transitionary concepts recognise that organisations are essentially dynamic due to the human element. Therefore many control mechanisms and relationships exist. A dynamic base implies there is feedback into the organisational process, typically methods of communicating, participating, decision making, problem solving, planning and motivating.

This *cybernetic* trend (Chapter 23) leads to open systems and management science. The human relations movement emerged from these ideas which were strongly influenced by the Great

Depression of 1929 in the USA, the rise of trade unions and the Hawthorne studies of 1924.

The Depression, it is claimed, was partly due to human relations problems. During this period the organised labour movement grew as managers often exploited the workforce; and research by Elton Mayo and his team at the Hawthorne plant in the USA (Chapter 10) highlighted the vital need for participation, self-discipline and the right type of supervisory climate.

## BALANCE THEORY

The concept of organisational equilibrium or balance emphasises the importance of an employee actually deciding to participate. This overall decision is based upon two features or considerations: a decision to join the organisation, remain employed or withdraw; and a decision to participate which is influenced by inducements to stay and by the contributions offered from the individual. Balance is determined through these two features which ideally should equate.

In practice there is a continual struggle to achieve equilibrium through favourable interaction. The outcome draws attention to motivation and the many favourable and unfavourable factors affecting it. If the right balance is achieved and maintained, the individual will stay. Peter Drucker in 1967 emphasised this aspect, 'If an organisation cannot hold or attract people it is doomed'.

## ROLE THEORY

The organisation is viewed as a number of role performers who are co-ordinated by a role system. Each person adopts roles through certain expectations from others and from themselves. Roles interact with each other and so continuity or co-ordination is achieved. Their importance in association with group activity is discussed in Chapter 5.

## THE SYSTEMS APPROACH

The systems approach sees organisations as systems of elements (or parts or activities), each contributing to the operation and each being dependent on other aspects of the system for its own requirements. These elements are interdependent, interrelated and self-adjusting to pressures or disturbances that upset aims.

Systems are commonplace everywhere, especially in the social, physical and biological worlds. A system is generally described as an organised or complex whole: a combination of parts that form a unitary whole. Two types of systems approach are recognised: closed and open.

### Closed systems approach

The closed systems approach originates from traditional organisation theory. It is based upon physical sciences, is applicable to mechanistic systems, is self-contained and adopts highly rationalistic approaches. The external environment, including economic, technological, governmental and other factors, is ignored. As expected, this inherent tendency moves the system towards equilibrium and maximum entropy. In other words, it runs down.

### Open systems approach

The open systems approach adapts continually to the changing external and internal environments by revising subsystems within its structure. The dynamic process causes changes in all the critical features such as goals, values, chosen technologies, the organisational structure itself, psychosocial aspects and managerial aspects.

The maintenance process is an essential part. It constructs and maintains the staffing establishment, buildings and plant. Consequently, the manufacturing (or servicing) process can function more easily to change the inputs of materials into finished products.

In total, inputs include all managers and employees, all physical resources and all financial resources. Outputs include not only finished products but also services offered, the efficiency and effectiveness of the system and, if successful, improved remuneration for managers, employees and shareholders. A typical basic model of an open system is shown in Fig. 3.2.

The complete process embraces all aspects of productivity, including the organisational structure and attendant features, the total working force in terms of creativity, motivational factors,

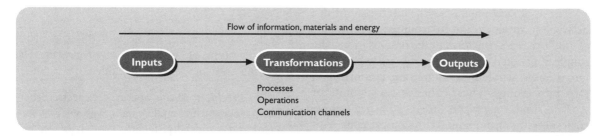

**Figure 3.2** A model of an open system
The system continually interacts with its environment and reaches a steady state which allows for the recycling process.

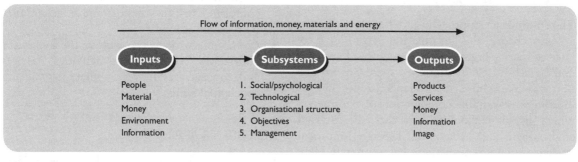

**Figure 3.3** A structured sociotechnical system
The subsystems interact and are interdependent; they provide a structured and integrated form in which human activities are surrounded by technologies.

managerial competence, all control devices, and philosophies. Such coverage offers many obvious advantages considering its holistic approach, meaning the complete concern is grouped to form more than the sum of the parts. Thus, critical aspects are constantly considered: causes and effects are transformed into models to analyse problems, situations and possible decisions; all influences are included; proposed changes are analysed to note their effects on other parts of the organisation; and all inputs and outputs are carefully related.

## Criticisms

Although all factors are considered, it is often claimed that few specific proposals emerge to guide managerial behaviour. Unfortunately, managers must still choose courses of action since the systems approach is abstract; it is idealistic not definite, or it lacks practical applications considering particular human considerations.

Besides technological skills, these decisions involve interpersonal and conceptual skills that are unique to the situation. Many other considerations apply outside the capability of systems theory. Typical examples are the degree of centralisation, taking into account individual relationships and motivational aspects, plus to some extent communication difficulties and cultural aspects.

## A SOCIOTECHNICAL SYSTEM

A structured sociotechnical system is an open system; its characteristics were determined by the work of E.L. Trist and his associates at the Tavistock Institute. The concept is based upon the consideration that any production system needs both a technological organisation and a work organisation. Figure 3.3 illustrates the format which transforms inputs by structuring and integrating employees' activities, surrounded by technologies.

The approach emphasises the interrelationships between technology, the environment, sentiments of employees and the form of the organisation. The simple, individual elements of a job are recombined into a larger whole by assigning the reconstituted jobs into groups. Thus, cohesive social units of workers and supervisors are established which correspond to meaningful technological units with reasonable autonomy and responsibility for the total job.

## THE CONTINGENCY APPROACH

The contingency approach is a refinement of open systems theory and information technology related to specific organisational structures. Lawrence and Lorsch in 1967 maintained there was no one best way to organise since it depends upon choosing the most suitable combination of parameters which include technological factors, the external environment and behavioural aspects. Empirical evidence supports this situational approach. Here is one important contribution among several.

### Production technology

Joan Woodward studied one hundred British companies, classifying them according to their production technological environment:

- unit and small batch
- large batch and mass
- process

The organisational structure, human relations and status were examined. A direct relationship between them and technical advance was discovered.

Interesting features related to the three groups were span of control for first-line supervision: 21–30, 41–50 and 11–20 respectively; levels of management were 3, 4 and 6; and the numbers reporting to a top executive were 4, 7 and 10. In unit production there were small, intimate groups, considerable participation, permissiveness and flexibility in job interrelationships; in mass or batch production there were clear-cut duties, line/staff conflict and poor industrial relations; in process production there were good interpersonal relations and little conflict or stress.

### Supervisory roles

Clearly the supervisor's role will differ depending on the type of production environment. The following tendencies are noticeable:

- *Unit production*: the operator expects leadership, pace setting, quality standards, general control and, especially, technical advice from the supervisor.
- *Batch production*: the supervisor tends to be a disciplinarian or undertakes a more task-oriented role. He or she expects operators to complete work to schedule and in accordance with specifications.
- *Continuous process production*: the supervisor undertakes co-ordination activities, advises and concentrates more on interpersonal and conceptual skills.

## THE ORGANIC APPROACH

The ultimate effects of approaches moving away from traditional or mechanistic thought are forms of organic organisation that emphasise a much looser structure. Lines of command and communication channels are flexible and aided by computer networks. The structure still exists for obvious reasons, but seasoned employees appreciate this and use the flexibility to full advantage in using initiative and creativity, and solving problems. Empowerment is an essential feature and adapting to rapid change is easier.

### The sociocultural adaptive system

Within organic approaches are complex adaptive systems which are assumed to govern society. A typical example is the sociocultural adaptive system. In brief, the principles are based on tension, or stresses and strains, which cause people to try always to live beyond their means and react accordingly.

This open system is capable of changing organisational structures by constantly adapting to tension as an organic entity in its own right. Consequently, there is always a state of flux and it may be similar to the process of natural selection or the law of effect (Chapter 12).

# Critical organisational principles

## CENTRALISATION

Inevitably a designer must consider the amount of authority to be retained at the apex, how much to delegate throughout the structure and how this spread should be arranged. These considerations determine the number of managers who will be able to commit resources and by how much.

If the spread is wide and deep, a highly decentralised organisation is evident. If commitment of various resources rests with only a few at the top, the organisation is obviously highly centralised.

Various spreads may be seen in practice. Generally, as the organisation grows, there is increasing decentralisation and specialisation, accompanied by more rules and procedures. Decentralisation offers less overload at the top, more rapid decisions, more flexibility throughout, more accountability for budgets, and improved conditions for motivation and participation. There are difficulties, however, such as increased probability of control and communication failure, inaccurate alignment of objectives, inconsistency of behaviour towards outsiders, and the need for a higher number of capable managers.

## AUTHORITY LEVELS

Considering the span of control, production and marketing complexity, and management style, probably the size of the concern automatically determines the number of authority levels. Usually this is the case, but there are choices open to the designer. Certainly the small organisation tends to have fewer levels (about three or four), is centralised and has a wide span of control. This flat type of structure may cause behavioural problems if managers and supervisors have insufficient time to spend with individuals and groups. Nevertheless there should be better communication and improved co-ordination.

In the large concern, a tall structure is normal, authority is decentralised, there is a high degree of specialisation and span of control tends to be narrow. Above a certain size there seems to be pressure to maintain the same number of levels at around seven or eight. The effects of more

powerful computer networks and empowerment on authority levels are now noticeable.

## SPAN OF CONTROL

Span of control dates back to Henri Fayol in approximately 1906; it means the number of subordinates reporting to a supervisor. Various theorists have attempted to place precise figures on the minimum, optimum and maximum span. Graicunas propounded a mathematical formula to provide the exact number by calculating the number of social relationships involved. L. Urwick stated that, at the most, six subordinates are sufficient if their work interlocks. More recent surveys have shown considerable variation – from ten up to eighty.

Experiments with spans have tended to prove that reductions do not necessarily improve performance and have raised many questions. Some examples are:

- *Which subordinates should be included?* There is no simple answer, considering staff officers, the varying width of close control and the influence of co-ordinating devices.
- *Should the supervisor's capability be considered?* It seems that some supervisors effectively control a large number easily.
- *Should the subordinate's capability be considered?* Some employees are self-disciplined and self-controlled, therefore they require very little supervision and co-operate without aid.

Clearly the choice of span is complex and demands careful analysis in each situation.

## CORRESPONDING AUTHORITY AND RESPONSIBILITY

Any supervisor who is given responsibility for a task should receive commensurate authority. Although obvious, in practice it is not unusual for supervisors to be held accountable for certain activities without having sufficient authority to influence them.

According to L. Urwick, smooth working at all levels depends on authority and responsibility having the same boundaries and extent, and being equal. Unfortunately, many committees are allocated authority that tends to cut across this principle, as do staff and matrix concepts discussed in the next chapter.

## DELEGATION

Delegation has stood the test of time but is probably the most difficult to apply in practice. Many supervisors fail because they tend to take on too much work, even when capable help is available. This often occurs because courage, trust in subordinates and delicate control are lacking.

An adequate definition of delegation is the assignment of tasks or jobs to subordinates who are given the authority to make decisions related to the work.

The procedure for delegating is simple. However, having sufficient faith in subordinates depends on the supervisor's basic philosophy towards people; see McGregor's Theory X and Theory Y (Chapter 11).

### Advantages of delegating

Appropriate delegation indicates clearly to superiors the capability of the supervisor because the following aspects are recognised:

- Delegation is an essential part of competent supervision.
- Concentrating on more complex work and priorities develops higher capabilities.
- Promotion prospects are higher as capabilities improve.
- Employees are developed and motivated, so full use is made of their particular knowledge and skills.
- The section achieves increased overall effectiveness.

### Main difficulties

There are many difficulties which tend to make supervisors avoid effective delegation. Some of them demand strict self-discipline and perseverance; others may be insoluble due to political, trade union and managerial pressures. The main difficulties are:

- inadequate training of employees
- non-cooperative employees

- rigid job specifications blindly applied
- a fear that employees' performance of delegated tasks will demonstrate the inadequacies of the supervisor
- the supervisor is incapable of releasing tasks for various reasons:
  - low opinions of subordinates
  - fear of errors
  - creating an impression of being overworked
  - liking the lower grade tasks
  - avoiding more complex tasks
- poor time management which does not allow for delegation procedures

### Balancing workloads

A supervisor should not waste valuable time on routine or simple matters and straightforward decision making, which should be made at the lowest level consistent with capability. The aim should be to spread work more evenly, based upon capability, appropriate levels and fair workloads.

Properly arranged, people will have opportunities to develop, gain experience and practise co-ordinated responsibility. Thus the subordinate is always responsible for doing the job while the supervisor is responsible for seeing it done. Delegation is an important feature of time management (Chapter 8).

### Inspection

Since the supervisor remains responsible, the natural consequence of delegation is inspection. Control of work is lost without it, hence the saying, Inspection is the corollary of delegation. The object is to check on the work without destroying initiative and causing resentment. Initiative is a vital ingredient for expanding capability. How to inspect and encourage initiative requires experience and judgement. A saying worth remembering during inspection is, People with average intelligence are very sensitive whilst those of above-average intelligence are extremely sensitive.

A superior who shows an interest in the work can give much pleasure and satisfaction to the subordinate. In this manner the art of unobtrusive inspection is developed where checking comes through the normal course of contact. The idea is to keep all operations running smoothly; pinpointing any unsatisfactory work is only a halfway stage, it needs to be followed by action. Both are delicate operations because people's feelings are involved. Tactless treatment is likely to have repercussions later, although they may be disguised and seemingly unconnected.

### Procedure for delegating

1 Make a list of all the tasks to be performed, including those which are neglected or omitted through lack of time.
2 Mark each one on an 'importance' basis and rearrange in descending order of importance.
3 Allocate time for each task. Accuracy is unimportant so long as an estimate is made to provide a rough guide.
4 Decide how much can be coped with by oneself, starting from the top, and draw a line across the list at this point.
5 Make sure each subordinate is assessed for his or her capabilities and always give the benefit of the doubt where necessary.
6 Allocate tasks below the line to subordinates, as appropriate to their capabilities. Explain carefully the authority given, why it is necessary, the quality required, and the timetable. Agree with the subordinate that he or she is capable of doing the work. If not arrange for suitable training.
7 Follow up by checking progress as required, give constructive criticism if requested, and coach and counsel when difficulties are encountered.
8 Rearrange if vital, but remember it takes people some time to expand and adjust. A fair trial is essential.

Methodical approaches such as those outlined above make the supervisor's task less burdensome.

### Effective delegation

Apart from the procedure for delegating, remember the following essential features that highlight competence:

● Recognise that responsibility for seeing the task or job is completed properly remains with the supervisor.

● Avoid delegating disagreeable tasks which are obviously the province of the supervisor.
● Plan well in advance and include goals and timetabling; ensure all resources are available; give clear instructions and obtain agreement.
● Recognise that difficulties will arise and deal with them quickly.
● Accept that performance levels may not be ideal; always praise if appropriate but criticise in private.

## UNITY OF COMMAND

The phrase 'unity of command' was coined by H. Fayol in 1906, who firmly believed in its critical nature. The principle states that each employee should be responsible to and receive orders from only one superior. From the employee's viewpoint it makes good sense; from the superior's viewpoint it avoids divided loyalty and is a discouragement to the tactic of playing one manager against another. Structurally it seems sound but is not in line with modern situational concepts.

The trend is to move away from the principle when using matrix concepts discussed soon and in the next chapter, and it seems to be reverting to F.W. Taylor's idea in 1900 of functional foremanship. This old concept allowed a worker to be responsible to eight foremen, each specialising in one particular function such as speed boss, repair boss, gang boss and inspection boss.

## SPECIALISATION

The natural tendency to specialise is obvious considering the vast amounts of knowledge, skill and experience required in any main or subsidiary function within an organisation. Marketing, production, finance, research and development, to name a few, are so specialised now that it is beyond one person's capabilities to cope successfully with more than one element. Indeed, in practice it is often beyond some managers to cope with one effectively.

Specialisation is essential. It does cause difficulties but they do not negate the concept, they simply indicate lack of co-ordination or communication failures.

A further feature involves technologies that are undergoing rapid change and affecting organisations in traumatic ways. Two related specialisms in this area are information technology and management science.

## Information technology

The increasing importance of information technology probably influences the structure in two ways. Information processing systems are complex and demanding on managerial specialisms and expertise, so more emphasis on the administrative function is inevitable. Information systems assume organisations are open systems that cope with external environmental uncertainty and work-related tasks uncertainty.

The degree of uncertainty depends upon information that is not available to managers. Reducing this uncertainty depends upon using information technology more effectively. Peter Drucker makes the point: 'You can usually get all the figures except those you need.'

Clearly an organisation should be structured to cater for this situation. Without due regard for information technology, a concern soon lags behind and eventually fails. Furthermore, the critical reliance on information for some parts of the organisation has to be recognised and adjustments made accordingly.

Certain fundamental changes are already apparent and modern organisations are adapting rapidly to them. Here are some obvious examples: to be effective there must be a match between information processing needs and the internal capacity to provide them; the degree of uncertainty varies in each organisation sector; some organisations are able to adapt more easily than others, but for all organisations the time factor is becoming increasingly important as new concerns enter markets.

## Management science

A brief look at the quantitative approach or management science indicates its place in organisation design and the need to consider management practice.

A modern supervisor uses various management techniques that employ mathematical techniques and operational research. Although the use of higher mathematics is helpful as an aid in decision making, planning and control, the importance of behavioural science remains and should be seen in perspective. Nevertheless, organisational designs cannot be constructed effectively without due consideration for this factor which hinges on high technology in the administrative fields and permeates all organisational aspects.

## STRUCTURAL HEIGHT

Structural height is included here since it is closely related to delegation, span of control and authority levels. The tall form is designed by narrowing span of control, increasing authority levels and implies the maximising of delegation. The flat form is achieved by reversing the process (Fig. 3.4).

Tall forms encourage close control and strong discipline, similar to the bureaucratic model which is notoriously tall. Modern theorists are critical of this approach because it supports McGregor's Theory X (Chapter 11) and employees naturally react against close control.

In theory, flat forms have shorter lines of communication; allow for modern control; provide for increased delegation which devolves responsibility and decision making, and facilitates job enrichment; and conform more to Theory Y with its distinct advantage in managing the modern employee.

This delayering process (or flattening) induces many role changes which affect top managers and lower management levels. Top managers will concentrate more on cultural features and skills, as well as stimulating enthusiasm and ensuring organisational balance. Lower management levels will be absorbed with interpersonal and conceptual skills; they will be highly customer-oriented.

However, some observations show that paperwork does not necessarily decrease but personal contact improves (as may be expected). Also there is more use of information technology through e-mail, control systems and computer networks; this speeds up access to information but it does not necessarily improve targeting. Time spent at

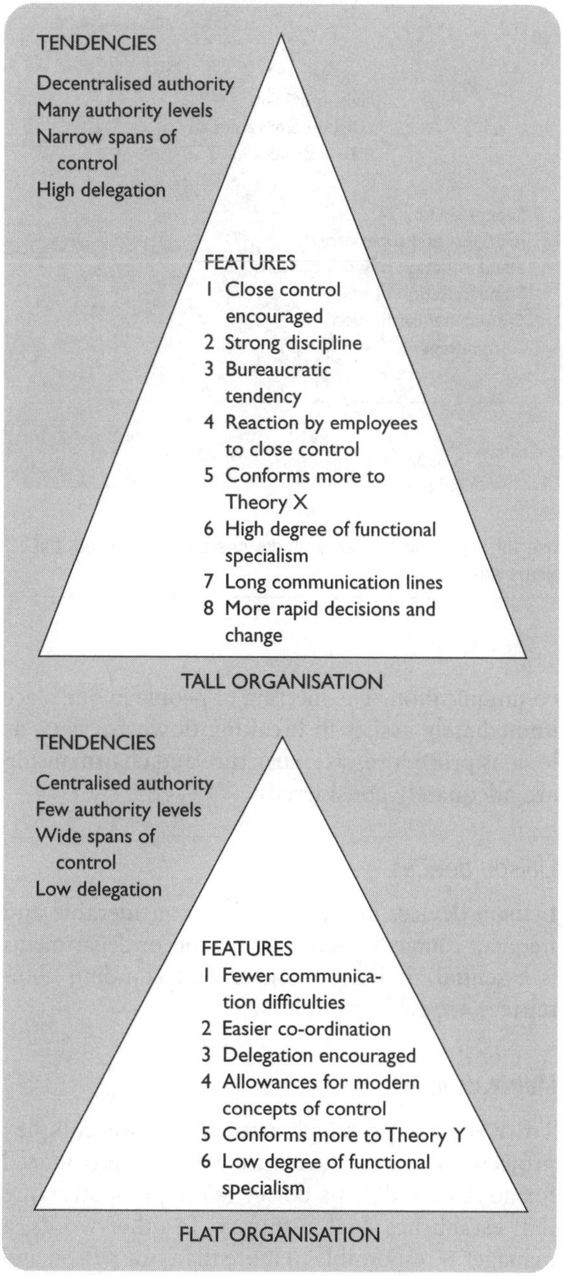

TENDENCIES

Decentralised authority
Many authority levels
Narrow spans of
   control
High delegation

FEATURES
1 Close control
   encouraged
2 Strong discipline
3 Bureaucratic
   tendency
4 Reaction by employees
   to close control
5 Conforms more to
   Theory X
6 High degree of functional
   specialism
7 Long communication lines
8 More rapid decisions and
   change

TALL ORGANISATION

TENDENCIES

Centralised authority
Few authority levels
Wide spans of
   control
Low delegation

FEATURES
1 Fewer communica-
   tion difficulties
2 Easier co-ordination
3 Delegation encouraged
4 Allowances for modern
   concepts of control
5 Conforms more to Theory Y
6 Low degree of functional
   specialism

FLAT ORGANISATION

**Figure 3.4** Structural height of an organisation
The tall form is designed by narrowing the span of control,
increasing authority levels and, by implication, maximising
delegation. The flat form is achieved by reversing the
process. Height depends mainly on size, management style,
nature of business and production technology.

meetings seems to increase but there is a danger of authority not matching accountability, and communicating long-term objectives continues to be neglected.

# Co-ordination

Dividing work into tasks and allocating them to employees immediately causes communication problems when employees attempt to perform their duties successfully. Unlike a situation where there is no division of labour or specialisation (as in the case of the sole proprietor), employees rely heavily on various linking means and devices to overcome co-ordination difficulties. The amount of attention paid to this aspect partly determines design effectiveness. Employees soon feel isolated and like machines if behavioural means of linking them are neglected.

Co-ordination in this context means the outcome of successfully applying all the communication methods and devices needed to link everyone. Neglecting even one employee may easily cause many operating difficulties. A thorough plan is needed that gives special consideration to the human aspects as well as the mechanics of the work environment. A graphical representation is given in Fig. 3.5.

## LINKAGE DEVICES

### Direct linkages

Each employee is able to contact his or her co-worker and achieve co-ordination by informal discussion. The concept also applies to managers.

### Supervision

Allocating authority to an individual who supervises a group should include giving him or her responsibility for the work undertaken. Thus the supervisor establishes links with each subordinate, issues instructions, monitors results, discusses problems, listens to grievances and elicits ideas. This supervisory process will naturally occur at all levels of authority.

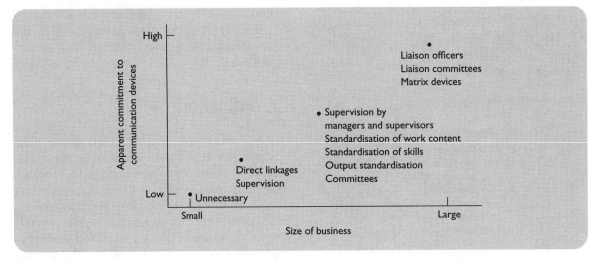

**Figure 3.5** Communication devices: a graphical representation
Devices seem to develop in phases as communication difficulties arise through growth. Ideally all devices should be used, but time and expense work against this concept until co-ordination problems arise.

### Standardisation of work content

Through establishing standards of work content, each employee knows what is expected by following concise instructions. Depending on the degree of specialisation, a certain amount of flexibility may be built in to allow for job enrichment.

### Standardisation of skills

Standardisation of skills makes it possible to train employees so that management will know exactly how they will respond in certain situations. It is useful when organisations are decentralised among many sites and it is really an alternative to following detailed instructions.

### Output standardisation

If the expected results of any procedure or system are made known, everyone realises their objectives and the anticipated quality of performance. This concept applies not only to production but also to all functions and authority levels.

### Committees

Committees are all the various meetings that may be arranged to improve human relations and communication. The meeting of people in one place immediately assists in breaking down barriers, as long as procedure, size, structure and chairmanship are adequately considered.

### Liaison devices

Liaison devices are useful when considerable and frequent contact between two people or departments is essential. A liaison officer and standing committees are two examples.

### Matrix devices

To overcome problems associated with complex projects, a matrix structure may be introduced for a set period. This device is a type of structure that establishes dual authority. In other words, a manager is responsible to more than one person and the chain of authority splits at convenient points to accommodate this requirement. Unity of command is abandoned and line managers are equally and jointly responsible for the same decision. This temporary device forces managers to co-operate and reconcile difficulties between them, thus achieving co-ordination. A permanent form is also used when interdependencies between managers have a fixed nature (Chapter 4).

# Overcoming structural faults

Structural faults are mainly caused by poor initial organisation design, growth or contraction, internal and external changes, and product or service changes. Faults may be grouped under the following headings:

- poor planning
- vague structural relationships
- poor delegation
- vague authority
- poor communication
- reluctance to participate
- vague objectives

Overcoming these faults requires effective design planning, achieved by using information feedback and managerial expertise. L. Urwick summarised it like this: 'Lack of organisation design is illogical, cruel, wasteful and inefficient'. However, there are two main limitations: allowing for the complexity of human relationships and constructing sufficient flexibility to compensate for individual creativity, discretion, capabilities, likes and dislikes.

## THE INFORMAL STRUCTURE

An informal structure is an unofficial structure beyond formal control; it consists of many different relationships such as tea break groups, various sports groups, an amateur dramatics group, or a winemaking group. Any joint personal activity qualifies but there is no conscious joint organisational purpose, although a group may unknowingly contribute to organisational objectives.

The informal organisation may overcome many structural faults because its own structure is generally small, fluid and flexible. Apart from group members in a particular section, members are often spread among many departments. Through their close relationships, they are easily able to overcome formal structural boundaries, ignore bureaucratic operations and reduce role stress; consequently, the organisation works more smoothly. Improved communication is also achieved through the grapevine.

The informal organisation is complex and difficult to assess. Unless there is a thorough knowledge of the formal organisation and a continuous effort to communicate closely with the informal structure, there will be poor decision making and lack of sensitive control. Classic examples of informal structures are illustrated in the Hawthorne studies (Chapter 10).

Informal groups satisfy the social needs of employees by developing a culture, a communication system and social control. These overcome many formal organisation faults and reduce frustration.

### The supervisor's role

An essential requirement is to work through and with informal groups. This role assures that co-operation is increased, resistance to any proposed changes is reduced, and the grapevine is used effectively. Furthermore, structural faults become apparent. Close contact with informal groups soon reveals structural faults, provided the supervisor thoroughly understands formal structures. This information is vital for managers who are planning design changes.

The supervisor should maintain all communication lines to provide the smooth working of formal and informal structures. Furthermore, the different viewpoints of subordinates and managers should be understood. Subordinates may think in terms of wages, stability of employment, conditions and participation; managers may think in terms of cost, flexibility, output and productivity. Such conflicting views inevitably mean some instructions will be unpopular and demanding on the supervisor's ability to compromise and reconcile differences.

Certain deficiencies outlined below indicate problem areas, although isolating the organisation as the cause is often complex. The supervisor must eliminate other possible causes before arriving at definite conclusions.

## INDICATIONS OF FAULTS

Apart from other main aspects of management and supervision that may contribute towards faulty operational activities, certain deficiencies highlight structural problems whereas others are harder to diagnose easily. Where two or more aspects appear to be at fault, or where there is an overlap, these points are clarified in other chapters. Here are some typical problem areas.

### Low productivity

Low productivity can be the result of one or more of the following:

- believing employees in other departments have an easier life, coming and going as they please
- decisions appearing to be wrong or unnecessary
- lack of standardised rules and regulations to suit the situation
- little or no opportunity for advancement and achievement
- lack of opportunity to make decisions affecting work
- too many managers and supervisors but not enough workers
- overloads of paperwork and petty procedures
- obvious signs of low morale

### Poor communication

This is discernible when:

- essential information always seems to be missing in emergencies
- conflicting reports arrive from various parts of the organisation
- there is an overactive and unreliable grapevine
- information received is often incomplete and inaccurate

### Excessive conflict

This is evident when:

- employees behave in an aggressive manner beyond normal expectations
- there are conflicting goals that are not aligned with objectives
- managers are seen to be working *against* each other
- there is a general state of uncertainty

### Poor co-ordination

This is indicated when:

- there is lack of teamwork at all levels
- individuals are working in isolation or out of step with each other
- there is a lack of liaison devices
- supervisors and managers seem reluctant to discuss problems and consult

### Weak control

This is detectable when:

- there are no clearly defined work programmes and directives
- everyone appears to be at cross-purposes with no well-defined priorities

### Low innovation

This is apparent when:

- there are no project teams or committees or meetings to exploit situations
- employees are unsure of what is expected from them, to whom they are accountable and how they are appraised
- no attempts are made to explore or utilise people's ideas

### Poor delegation

This has the following effects:

- managers and supervisors are always overloaded with work
- there seems to be no time for solving problems and making decisions by studying the situation thoroughly
- employees feel frustrated and powerless to help

### REMOVING THE FAULTS

The many problems already listed are obvious deficiencies which should be considered by the supervisor during daily activities. Overcoming some of these faults is partly possible by using principles which minimise their effects and lead to more effective systems. The main principles which the supervisor could use are now outlined in accordance with the aspects mentioned above.

## Improving productivity

- Providing improved communication to overcome false beliefs about others in the organisation, so that everyone feels they can perform well without prejudice towards those they think are slacking.
- Establishing standards which employees should not fall below to maintain an acceptable minimum performance level.
- Providing principles to follow whenever possible rather than rigid rules to obey without question.

## Improving communication

- Arranging channels so that information passes quickly to vital points for immediate response.
- Establishing training to ensure employees are proactive so that information is not missing in emergencies.
- Ensuring that information channels are always open to provide as much information as possible to avoid excessive grapevine activity.

## Reducing conflict

- Providing employees with accurate objectives and clear aims.
- Promoting effective communication channels between management, trade unions and employees.
- Arranging regular meetings to ensure programmes and projects are aligned.

## Improving co-ordination

- Checking that aims and objectives are clearly understood.
- Adjusting aims and objectives as required.
- Providing regular feedback at all levels.
- Using feedback to improve co-ordination.

## Improving control

- Arranging for cost-effective control; abandoning controls with no purpose or controls that are uneconomic to operate.
- Correcting deviations more rapidly.

- Careful checking to revise controls to meet new demands.
- Ensuring customers receive priority by arranging controls accordingly.
- Designing systems so employees in close contact with customers receive information quickly and have priority.

## Promoting innovation

- Designing all procedures to accept creativeness and imagination.
- Encouraging employees to take calculated risks within the boundaries of good sense.
- Introducing empowerment programmes and teamwork whenever possible.
- Rewarding innovative suggestions.

## Improving delegation

- Enforcing appropriate training and development programmes.
- Checking regularly to ensure employees are not overloaded or overstressed.
- Appraising employees to ensure delegated duties are working and not needing counselling.

## RESTRICTIONS

Although the importance of organisation design has been stressed, it is only one aspect of many that contribute towards success. Structural changes cannot easily solve internal political wrangles on many subjects among managers and among employees. Indeed, managers will not quickly alter their views and operating methods through such changes. Neither will employees see the firm in a different light if they hold strong radical views on matters such as giving up autonomy, receiving unequal financial reward or generally feeling exploited at work.

Beyond the field of formal organisation design are correct corporate planning and tactical planning, appropriate education and training schemes, sincere participation schemes, appropriate control of political influences, an overall innovative culture, and allowing for the changing concept of work and work ethics.

# Improving organisation

The following principles are now summarised to help the supervisor during day-to-day activities. They should be accepted as a more detailed summary in conjunction with the section on removing faults.

Clearly there are certain aspects which appear as rules to satisfy legal and financial requirements. Formal rules often do not allow sufficiently for social interaction and modern technologies. Consequently, they should be followed with some flexibility to avoid reaction. Where appropriate, regular checks and action should be taken.

1 The overall objective and purpose of each part of the organisation must be known by everyone.
2 Know each person's capabilities and encourage innovation.
3 Orders must be final and concise.
4 Do not spend, or allow subordinates to spend, too much time on enjoyable tasks at the expense of distasteful or mundane ones.
5 Always welcome suggestions and ideas.
6 Reports must be conscientiously completed.
7 Reports must be used and kept up to date.
8 Plan carefully with the objective in mind.
9 Policy, rules and regulations should be known by every employee.
10 There should be a place for everything and everything should be in its place.
11 Each employee's responsibilities must be clearly defined and known to him or her.
12 The authority conferred upon an employee must correspond with the given responsibilities.
13 Any changes in responsibility should be made known to everyone concerned.
14 Each employee should be responsible to, and receive instructions from, only one superior. However, see unity of command and trends earlier in this chapter.
15 All duties and instructions must be clearly defined and consistent with a person's capabilities.
16 The formal line of command must run from top to bottom of the organisation. However, see matrix structures (Chapter 4) and collaborative concepts (Chapter 5).
17 A supervisor should not control more than five or six subordinate supervisors who, in turn, should not control more than twelve staff. However, see span of control (earlier in this chapter) and group activity (Chapter 5).
18 Excessive overloading of work will impair efficiency.
19 Delegate lower grade work and spread the workload evenly.
20 Provide a continuous supply of replacements to ensure continuity.
21 Full use of specialisation should be made of people, machines, equipment and processes.
22 Encourage self-discipline.
23 Try to be scrupulously fair and just at all times.
24 Critical words to individuals must always be given in private.
25 Any queries regarding organisation should be carefully investigated and settled quickly.
26 Remember the key factor of customer orientation.

## PROCEDURE

A sound practice is to write down information on the organisation under the supervisor's control rather than to rely upon memory. The overall position is often clearer on paper because the proportioning of the workload, possible improvements and any deficiencies can be seen more easily. Here is a simple method of assessing and improving an organisation:

- *Job specification*: Note all the duties and responsibilities of each subordinate, elaborating if desired to include skill required, mental effort, physical needs, working conditions and any other relevant factors.
- *Process chart*: Draw a diagram in flow chart form from the beginning to the end of the process or procedure, using information from the job specifications.
- *Organisation chart*: Draw a diagram showing the lines of authority and responsibility, using titles instead of names. Remember to indicate status by using some form of code where misinterpretations might otherwise occur.

This method may be supplemented to suit particular requirements. The important point is to put something down on paper which can be rearranged and improved as a continuing process.

This task is made easier by using the following two approaches.

- *A functional diagram*: Draw up a form listing the functions and subfunctions down the left-hand side and the subordinates across the top in columns, thus making a space available for each function to be allocated to an individual. Better grouping of functions is immediately apparent when the form is completed. An outline of functional analysis and appropriate diagrams is given in Chapter 17 in connection with job evaluation and the need to analyse jobs when a concern is growing rapidly.
- *An ideal organisation chart*: Draw the chart with all the improvements which are considered desirable; consequently, when opportunities occur to make changes they may be made with a definite plan in mind.

# Organisational behaviour

The study of behaviour in organisations is vital to understand why people do not behave as expected. Organisational behaviour (OB) is essentially a multidisciplinary approach involving material from many subjects: sociology, psychology, anthropology, economics, humanities, law and medicine. OB is not a discipline nor a function, but it attempts to relate their disciplines and findings to the reality of organisations.

Macro OB is concerned with formal organisations, including structures. Micro OB deals with individuals, informal organisations and small groups. OB seems to indicate that decisions which ignore the deeper social and psychological patterns within human nature will result in exactly the opposite of what is intended. Clearly this pattern is an important consideration when planning organisational redesign.

# Organisational development

The urgent need to revise organisation because of constantly changing pressures is often covered by the process of organisational development (OD). This is a systematic planned method of managing change by using specialised techniques which audit the existing organisation to assess whether it meets operational needs.

The techniques examine communication; assess employees' knowledge of objectives, systems and procedures; analyse problem solving and decision making; and determine the capability of managers to respond to change.

OD may be implemented in many ways. Typical arrangements are to appoint an experienced individual within the company, or to use an external consultant periodically. After surveys there may be proposals to:

- restructure communication
- revise motivational and empowerment techniques
- programme education, training and development courses
- restructure departments, sections, or teams
- introduce specific courses for tackling organisation redesign

## THE PROCESS

Various means of operating OD are available. The pattern follows a logical scheme by investigating any resistance to change, identifying the areas for change, introducing changes, and reinforcing the changes by ensuring employees' behaviour is modified to feel commitment.

## CONCEPTS

Several famous social scientists have designed various models; they include K. Lewin, W.G. Bennis, P.R. Laurence and W.L. French (see the bibliography). Many specialists have offered a variety of opinions on how to reach organisational effectiveness and listed the important factors that govern success. Four examples are given below to indicate the breadth of the problem and the wide range of ideas on offer, along with the debates that often occur when ideas are discussed.

### A learning organisation

C. Handy suggested a learning organisation, which provides a formal approach to asking questions, seeking out theories, testing them, and reflecting upon the answers. Some of the questions would be:

- How does the organisation plan to achieve effectiveness?
- What type of organisation is envisaged?
- What reputation does the organisation hope to achieve?
- What are the strengths and weaknesses of the organisation?

## Managing change

Rosabeth M. Kanter emphasised that managers must be 'change masters' to help and guide the organisation to exploit and triumph over change. She also mentions it is not how responsibilities are divided which is important but how individuals can pull together to pursue new opportunities.

## Focus on performance

J. Katzenbach and D. Smith suggest the high performing organisations focus on performance and the teams that deliver it. There should be a strong and balanced performance ethic which includes the provision of superior value for customers.

## Operate as networks

R. Pascale suggested among other ideas that organisations should operate as networks rather than hierarchies. Managers should be used as facilitators with employees being empowered to initiate improvements and change, thus commitment is encouraged.

## CONCLUSIONS

The works of these authors should be studied to gain a full understanding of their ideas. Only a limited choice is given above. All concepts need careful analysis, including such topics as cost, upheaval, education and training, and culture. Clearly there are no easy answers and each organisation has its own peculiarities that demand special consideration.

## QUESTIONS

1 Describe the ideal organisation.

2 Outline the main problem areas likely to be encountered in an organisation.

3 List organisational criteria.

4 What is meant by integration difficulties in an organisation?

5 Carefully explain the systems approach.

6 Outline the results of Joan Woodward's study on types of production.

7 Discuss the importance of span of control and delegation.

8 Outline a procedure for delegating.

9 Write an essay on information technology.

10 Discuss the role of the supervisor as a co-ordinator.

11 Give a brief description of the main linkage devices that could be used to improve co-ordination.

12 What is meant by natural grouping?

13 An open system continually interacts with its environment. Discuss the significance of this statement.

14 Describe a structured sociotechnical system.

15 What organisational changes are likely to occur when a company decides to flatten the organisation structure?

16 Describe organisational behaviour and its approach.

17 What is meant by the organic approach?

18 Explain how the organisational development process manages change.

19 Consider how the supervisor should use the informal structure in an organisation.

20 List the main principles a supervisor could use to minimise the effect of structural faults in an organisation.

At a meeting of senior managers the managing director raised the subject of creativity. He thought it was sadly neglected in the organisation and employees were not coming forward with ideas. The human resource manager insisted that employees were always having ideas for improvement which they mentioned during interviews or counselling. Apparently the ideas were not taken up, or not divulged to higher levels, or not mentioned at all.

The managing director retorted that it's the fault of the managers and supervisors for not using the ideas. He added that people do not seem to be approaching him with ideas either. The human resource manager thought there were much deeper problems that needed to be tackled.

*Comment on the probable situation that exists in the organisation.*

Ruth Remply was worried about the way the staff kept referring to the poor organisation. Every time something went wrong they would make the same remark, 'It's the organisation – that's the trouble with this place'.

As supervisor, she was being subjected to considerable scrutiny by management. She maintained that the cause of poor returns from her department was due to delays in orders being supplied, but management seemed to have other ideas.

At a recent meeting with management she was asked whether she kept any records of the delays. She replied that she had not bothered as nothing would be done about it anyway.

*Comment on the remark made by the staff. What should the supervisor do to rectify the situation?*

# 4

# Functional aspects of organisation

## Introduction

The accurate presentation of organisational design to illustrate how work is organised in a company resolves many difficulties. These may involve areas of ambiguity, confusion over authority and accountability, lines of command, horizontal and vertical linkages, any joint responsibilities, and probable roles. Each position in the organisation should be accompanied by a job specification (Chapter 17). The main features which clarify the situation are:

- organisation charts
- structural designs
- functional specialisation

## Organisation charts

Diagrams that illustrate the positions of everyone in the organisation, and their jobs or departments, are usually called organisation charts. They show more clearly authority and accountability. These formal positions are coupled by lines and arrows indicating communication points. They are arranged in various patterns to suit relationships. In other words, a chart is a pictorial presentation of group responsibilities, relationships that exist between groups, and a planned pattern of work.

Charting has two obvious advantages: (1) superior–subordinate relationships clearly show, among other factors, essential reporting features; and (2) relationships between employees in a group are highlighted to show a clear understanding of team spirit. Producing charts is always worthwhile since the process often indicates inconsistencies and complexities which may be avoided. All members will see more clearly where they fit and match with others, and their unique position in the organisation. Operational difficulties may appear, such as overloading a certain individual and identifying overlaps and gaps.

### CHARACTERISICS: THE MAIN HIGHLIGHTS

- Only formal relationships are shown. Informal relationships always exist between individuals and these bring the organisation to life through many emerging roles.
- A chart is usually only accurate at the time of origin. Changing circumstances force alterations, therefore updating is essential.
- True relationships between individuals are not possible in diagrammatic form.
- A chart does not indicate the actual organisational structure. This may ignore certain principles, incorporate various weaknesses involving personality problems, and contain inaccurate job descriptions.
- A chart is restricted to indicating relationships only within a particular company. Any company has certain peculiarities involving people and the business. Consequently, the concept of a *typical chart* should be avoided.
- A chart should always be examined in conjunction with job descriptions. Everyone should understand the significance of flexible working arrangements and avoid rigid interpretations.

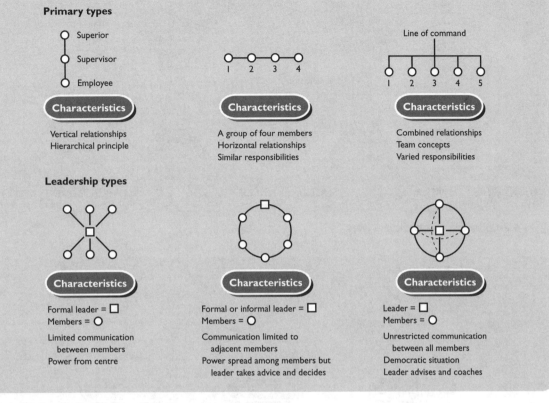

**Primary types**

Superior
Supervisor
Employee

**Characteristics**

Vertical relationships
Hierarchical principle

1  2  3  4

**Characteristics**

A group of four members
Horizontal relationships
Similar responsibilities

Line of command

1  2  3  4  5

**Characteristics**

Combined relationships
Team concepts
Varied responsibilities

**Leadership types**

**Characteristics**

Formal leader = □
Members = ○

Limited communication
between members
Power from centre

**Characteristics**

Formal or informal leader = □
Members = ○

Communication limited to
adjacent members
Power spread among members but
leader takes advice and decides

**Characteristics**

Leader = □
Members = ○

Unrestricted communication
between all members
Democratic situation
Leader advises and coaches

***Figure 4.1*** Organisation charts: primary types and leadership types

- A chart is naturally restricted to two dimensions, whereas in practice structures are multidimensional.

## EXAMPLES OF ORGANISATION CHARTS

Organisation charts may be divided into primary, leadership, pictorial and ad hoc types; they are illustrated in Figs 4.1, 4.2 and 4.3. The types are self-explanatory and should be interpreted considering formal communication networks (Fig. 14.1) and informal communication flow lines (Fig. 14.2) together with the next section on structural designs.

These pictorial presentations may be identified with power, centralisation, communication networks and communication restrictions. A chart may be restricted to a section, a department or a division, or it may represent the whole company. But an organisational structure is more complex

than a chart; there are limitations to how the chart represents collective and individual responsibilities and indirect relationships.

## BUREAUCRATIC AND ORGANIC FORMS

### Bureaucratic forms

Primary, leadership and pictorial charts are bureaucratic or mechanistic. They rely upon formalisation of behaviour to achieve co-ordination, and they differ according to the circumstances. Their working environment usually has a high degree of certainty, and rules and regulations can apply without unduly upsetting relationships.

Such mechanistic forms depend mainly upon whether behaviour and operating conditions are predetermined or predictable. In other words, standardisation can be applied with confidence in stable situations.

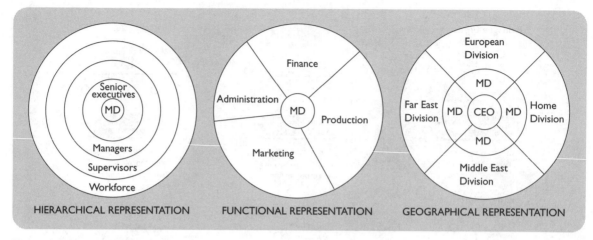

**Figure 4.2** Organisation charts: pictorial types

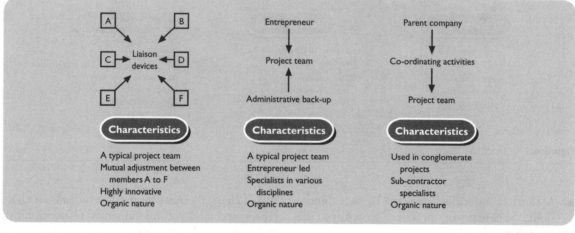

**Figure 4.3** Organisation charts: ad hoc types

## Organic forms

Other situations demand high innovation and rapid adaptation to survive. They are identified as organic and operate in environmental uncertainty. The ad hoc types in Fig. 4.3 are essentially organic. They are flexible and informal, and they are committed to a particular task or project. Various liaison devices may be used to co-ordinate each member's contributions and ideas. Specialists or members mutually adjust, so high innovation is possible.

Some companies deliberately encourage organic structures within the organisation as a whole. Others may have difficulty in avoiding them, even when attempts are made to install more formal structures. The main characteristics are:

- Members are chosen to contribute their specialised knowledge and experience.
- Projects are created by the need for solutions to complex difficulties or problems.
- Interaction and adjustment are made possible by the informal operating arrangements.
- All members should feel committed to the project.
- Administrative back-up is needed to provide information and advice as required.
- A member's status or rank is unimportant
- Expertise, initiative and experience are vital features of an inividual's capabilities to contribute.

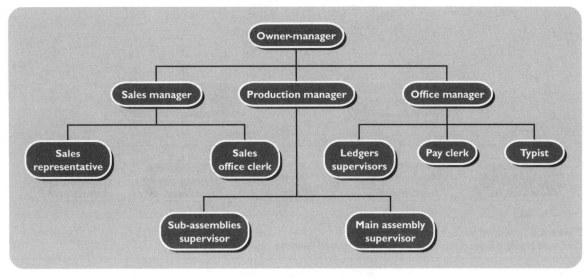

***Figure* 4.4** A basic line structure is the first stage of growth from a one-person business

# Structural designs

Many organisations are in a state of tension because of the need to differentiate or specialise and to integrate. Reducing this tension to acceptable limits involves consideration of eight main features.

- specialisation of roles and the degree to which this should be followed in practice
- whether to centralise or decentralise the main managerial skills, including planning, controlling, problem solving and, especially, decision making
- how many authority levels are thought to be necessary, considering span of control and information technology
- how much discretion to allow at each level
- the degree of standardisation to satisfy legal and financial requirements
- consideration of the appropriate balance between formality and informality
- rapid adaptations to change which include more flexibility in the lines of command and communication channels
- emphasising an organic approach where status is reduced and employees feel free to group together to solve problems and are encouraged to show initiative

The use of principles already mentioned restricts the designer to some extent, since he or she is forced into using a limited range of viable structures.

### THE BASIC STRUCTURE

An example of a simple structure is given in Fig. 4.4. This line-type organisation represents the first stage of growth from the 'one-man' business or sole proprietor, and incorporates the engagement of a manager to be responsible for, say, marketing or accounts. Usually a power culture exists where a single authority or a small group makes decisions because there are few rules and generally no committees.

### THE LINE/FUNCTIONAL STRUCTURE

As functional specialists are needed in personnel or purchasing, the structure is modified accordingly.

### THE MODIFIED LINE/FUNCTIONAL STRUCTURE

Continued growth soon causes overloads. They are solved by introducing staff officers (Fig. 4.5). They ease the load on the managing director because they represent him or her in specified areas, ensuring policies and decisions are interpreted

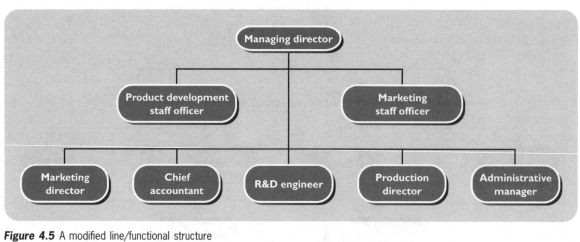

**Figure 4.5** A modified line/functional structure
Continued growth causes overloads in certain areas, solved by introducing staff officers.

correctly. They may assume various titles such as staff manager, personal assistant or assistant to the managing director.

## THE BUREAUCRATIC MODEL

This famous structure represents a rational form for companies and it uses the basic principles of organisation. However, it possesses other characteristics which distinguish it markedly:

- *Division of labour*: This concept implies the use of authority, power and boundary limitations to jobs.
- *The hierarchy*: This principle is rigidly applied, thus each lower post is under the supervision and control of a higher one.
- *Abstract rules*: The rational approach insists on a complete set of formal rules and regulations. They are applied rigidly to ensure conformity, co-ordination of effort, continuity and stability.
- *Impersonal relationships*: The concept of an ideal rationality means a manager should possess a spirit of formal impersonality. In other words, he or she should operate without hatred or passion, which implies without affection or enthusiasm.
- *Promotion*: This usually depends upon seniority and achievement.
- *A role culture*: This operates through formal roles and procedures. It provides security but is rigid and slow to change.

## Criticisms

Most people have experienced bureaucracy and know the irritating effects of red tape. The usual criticisms include inhuman approaches to employees and outsiders; the emergence of the pompous, self-important official; managers lacking in technical competence; arbitrary and silly rules and regulations; an undercover informal organisation; and conflicting roles. Two popular laws are often quoted in bureaucracies:

- *Parkinson's law*: bureaucratic staff increase in number in inverse proportion to the amount of work carried out.
- *The Peter principle*: managers tend to rise to their level of incompetence in bureaucracies.

## The development factor

The critics of bureaucracy accept that organisations tend to go through early stages of development where bureaucratic rules, etc., help the company to survive. However, as the company develops, bureaucracy becomes a fatal menace and hinders survival.

Development depends upon reducing the characteristics of bureaucracy, often a difficult task. There is no hope of change from bureaucracy unless modern concepts of motivation and control are established and believed in by senior management. Unfortunately, the managers responsible for early

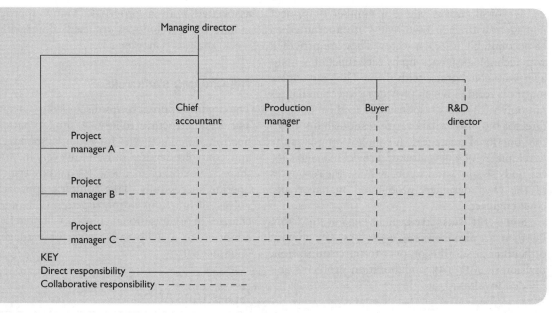

**Figure 4.6** A typical matrix structure
A permanent form of matrix structure is useful when interdependencies are fixed between managers. The project managers not only have direct responsibility to the managing director but also collaborative responsibility to all the functional managers. Theoretically this device forces managers to co-operate and reconcile differences between them, thus achieving co-ordination.

development through bureaucratic techniques are usually still employed and often they naturally have reservations about the transition.

## Warning signs

Reaction to bureaucracy and the need for change is usually obvious. Employees make their feelings known in many ways. Typical signs are:

- violating rules and regulations
- bypassing authority whenever the opportunity occurs
- increased grapevine activity
- establishing more informal communication channels
- making excuses for not seeking permission to take action
- increasing resentment of status, separate dining rooms, biased perks
- causing control difficulties and making excuses for not maintaining official records
- open suspicion of management and a corresponding reduction in morale

## MODIFIED SPECIALISATION STRUCTURES

Apart from the basic line/functional structure which operates by grouping together common activities, there are three other forms of grouping:

- on a geographical basis, often seen in transport companies
- by product, which lends itself to companies that produce a number of different articles
- by forming divisions

Forming divisions is particularly useful in large concerns where several different articles are produced: the head office retains key functions such as corporate planning, finance and personnel policy; the divisions operate in a functional role for each article.

## MATRIX MODELS

The temporary type of matrix structure was explained in Chapter 3 as a means of achieving co-ordination. A permanent form (Fig. 4.6) is also useful when interdependence between managers is of a fixed nature.

A typical case is where a number of project managers with their own teams are appointed to be accountable for each sector. They are provided with technological back-up by each functional manager who collaborates with them. Thus a complex matrix is formed which provides project managers not only with direct responsibility to the managing director but also collaborative responsibility to all the functional managers. A simple example is the development of a new aircraft. Project managers for the body, engine, and so on, will use the resources of the chief designer, production manager and chief engineer.

Some criticisms have been levelled at this form, but there are also many success stories. The obvious difficulties are confusion over resource allocation, division of authority, collaboration problems and divided loyalties.

### Task culture

A task culture develops where all members concentrate on completing the collective task. Consequently, in general there is no dominant leader, rapid changes are easier, and there is high job satisfaction. Being more flexible and more informal, matrix styles suit trends towards decentralisation, more delegation and increased personal accountability. Understandably they create administration difficulties unless the trend to centralise administration is followed and information technology is exploited in the process.

### Project management concepts

There are other forms besides using project managers within a matrix structure. These may establish a project manager to examine a specific subject. Other organisation members from various functions relevant to the project may be used by the project manager. Furthermore, a permanent project manager may be appointed with the authority to select a suitable team for each assignment allocated by senior management.

In a large company a project manager may control a section that deals with requests for projects and conducts investigations. Typical projects are to examine the time to complete a service or programme, and to consider ancillary activities

associated with a proposal. Many appropriate management techniques are used, along with network analysis (Chapter 23).

## THE ORGANIC STRUCTURE

The organic approach was discussed in Chapter 3. The basic structure follows a similar pattern to line/functional activities for essential management and control purposes only. However, in practice there is flexibility to allow for empowerment to operate successfully. This complex approach involves all functions in job redesign (Chapter 17), changes in organisational culture (Chapter 12) and adoption of a deliberative style of management (Chapter 10).

# Specialisation

An easily recognised process is to group together similar activities. The usual method is by functional specialisation:

- marketing
- production/operations
- finance
- administration
- human resources
- distribution

Collectively they form a number of main functions within which are found technical and technological expertise.

The advantages are the people associated with a similar activity relate to each other easily, they see promotional opportunities clearly and a strong common interest develops. Unfortunately, this interest may also be a disadvantage if conflict, misunderstandings and poor co-operation occur between functions.

## OUTSOURCING

Highly specialised activities may be sub-contracted or contracted-out in circumstances where in-house facilities are not able to compete. An outside contractor may have the advantages of more economic use of capital equipment and expertise. Consequently, a better service at lower cost may be offered. Typical examples are share registration and facilities management. Various contractors are available and the most appropriate one may be chosen on the basis of price, quality, convenience and the range of services on offer.

# Conceptual skills development

Supervisors should acquire a knowledge of all the activities in a company. This enables them to develop conceptual skills for the purposes of more effective organisational planning, policy development and systems development. Thus they can apply their influence over wider fields (Chapter 13) and deal more effectively with the difficulties arising from specialisation.

# Orientations towards the market

Of particular importance are the relationships developed by everyone with customers. There are four approaches:

- market orientation
- sales orientation
- product orientation
- production orientation

## MARKET ORIENTATION

This technique concentrates on customers' wants and is often called the marketing concept. The total organisation is geared up to marketing and the customer forms the basis for corporate planning. Apart from marketing personnel, many people throughout the organisation become involved in marketing activities since the customer is rightly considered to be of prime importance and everything must be done to achieve the maximum degree of customer satisfaction.

### Corporate responsibility

Putting the customer first has always been the operating principle of the marketing department. Extending this philosophy to corporate level, where everyone is committed to this approach, demands a major change in attitudes for many personnel. There is no doubt that the introduction of a marketing culture increases marketing effectiveness. However, the lead must come from the top and supervisors have a strong role to play in planning based upon marketing strategies and forecasting.

## SALES ORIENTATION

Sales orientation means concentrating on positive selling to persuade people to buy. Thus selling skills are paramount compared with the wants of the buyer. Some insurance companies use this technique.

## PRODUCT ORIENTATION

The quality of the product is considered supreme. Product orientation relies on the manufacturer knowing exactly what the customer requires, having expertise in designing and developing the product, and being able to protect adequately the ideas. Classic examples are the Waterman fountain pen, the IBM golfball typewriter, the Filofax personal organiser and the Tupperware kitchen container.

## PRODUCTION ORIENTATION

In production orientation the dominant strands are production effectiveness, distribution and price. A good example is Japanese cars.

# Orientations towards the customer

The relationships with customers are of prime importance. Probably this aspect is neglected in many companies for many reasons. There is a need for a clear policy from the board on customer contact and its implications. Unfortunately, the tendency is to treat the customer as a source of income, a statistic or a nuisance. Enlightened companies generate an organisation which is geared to customer priority. This approach is demanding on the following features.

## THE PHILOSOPHY

The board demonstrates a philosophy that concentrates on five points:

- All managers and employees should accept that the customer comes first.
- The organisation is structured to ensure that bureaucratic tendencies are banned and all functional activities are arranged to provide the maximum opportunities for employees to relate effectively with customers.
- The product or service is aligned to customer requirements.
- Every opportunity is seized to sell customers both the product and the company.
- Every customer must be treated as an individual *not* a burden on the company.

## TRAINING ON CUSTOMER ORIENTATION

Unfortunately, many managers and employees do not understand the significance of customer orientation. To overcome this fault, a training programme should be aligned to include:

- consulting everyone in the organisation to assess the attitude towards customers
- assessing the capability to relate effectively to customers
- arranging for training where necessary to ensure a complete understanding of:
  - customer orientation
  - development of conceptual and interactive skills
  - development of human behaviour
  - communicating customer information to appropriate people
  - how the organisation functions within the concept of customer relationships

## SELECTION

Often selection does not include the question of customer awareness and tends to concentrate on the technical aspects of the job. This should be corrected by a careful analysis of feelings towards the customer, the degree of empathy with people, and any tendency to ignore this aspect.

## THE CUSTOMER

Most customers are particularly sensitive towards recognising a company's attitude and the perception of employees and managers towards them in general. These feelings are generated by direct and indirect contact, the reaction of employees when they try to be helpful, and any attempt by employees to consult rather than conducting one-sided discussions.

Customers like to give opinions which may be helpful. Most people with a complaint are placated when employees listen sympathetically and try to be helpful rather than off-hand.

## ESSENTIAL EMPLOYEE CONTRIBUTIONS

To summarise, everyone in the organisation should ensure that the following major points *always* apply when dealing with customers:

1. Be positive, shoulder blame and do not offer excuses.
2. Act as quickly as possible to deal with the complaint or query.
3. Keep the customer informed if there is a delay.
4. Show due care and sensitivity, avoiding any sign of complacency or off-hand treatment.
5. Attend to detail – the customer expects full treatment, not the major issue alone.

# Main functions

Functional departmentation divides an organisation into its major activities: marketing, production/operations, finance, administration, personnel (or human resources) and distribution. Figure 4.7 shows a functional departmentation for a medium-sized company. Although functional departmentation is probably the most common, there are other kinds. Some very large companies use product departmentation, where the organisation is divided into self-contained product groups. Geographical departmentation creates a network of activities to substantiate a regional structure.

Remember that main functions emerge from numerous technical specialisms; seldom can one person cover two or more of these activities. Nevertheless, specialisms once considered as bounded are

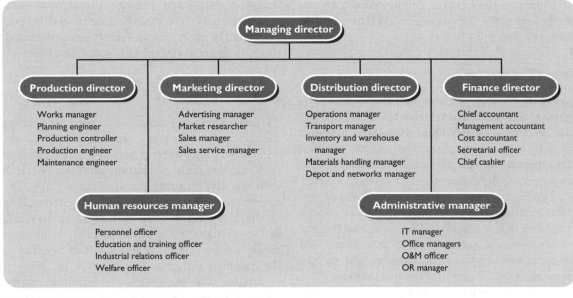

**Figure 4.7** Probable functions within a medium-sized company

nowadays treated using flow processes, which form a total supply chain throughout the organisation. Artificial boundaries must be subordinated to processes and not hinder them in any way. A typical example is logistics applied to the distribution concept (see below).

# Marketing

Marketing aims to provide the right quality product at the right price, on time and with high quality after-sales service. This all-embracing philosophy applies to the marketing department and everyone in the organisation. Thus existing and potential customers should be at the centre of all strategic discussions, policy and decision making.

Marketing is essentially a creative activity which attempts to satisfy customer wants profitably. The implications are a strategic policy that copes with rapid change, a flexible outward-looking organisation, employment of people with innovative talents, and decision making pushed towards the closest customer contact points.

## MAJOR THRUSTS OF MARKETING

Three major activities are essential:

- creating and maintaining customer satisfaction and loyalty
- developing an innovative organisation
- encouraging an appropriate organisational culture

If successful the customer will come back for more, provided the innovative organisation includes effective customer research. This must feed technological research (production) with information which is used and not subordinated to the egos of designers, technologists, ergonomists and value analysts. There is little doubt that retaining existing customers is much easier than finding new ones.

The organisational culture is often totally inadequate to cope with this task. Here are some typical attitudes: the customer is a necessary evil; the customer never comes first; the customer is not taken seriously by senior managers. Employees feel embarrassed when customers complain, and motivation suffers as a result. Changing the organisational culture to exhibit a serious commitment to customer care is the job of top management. Within this concept the importance of communication should be recognised. Especially important is developing the art of listening (Chapter 15). This topic is essential for everyone in the organisation since customer contact is generally extensive and all opportunities should be taken to provide sufficient feedback.

Here is a brief survey of the main activities of marketing; the structures do vary depending on company size and product.

## MARKET RESEARCH

Specialists conduct research into the current sales of other companies and visualise the future market. Outside groups or individual consultants may also be used for this purpose. The market research department collects, analyses and communicates the data to other departments.

Typical data items include a breakdown of products on offer, where they may be obtained, prices, their uses in households, complaints, suggestions for improvement, and the class of customers. Many sources of information are available and statisticians analyse and interpret the information.

Marketing strategy is determined and a programme developed that includes resource locations, processes involved, the final profile of the product, demand forecasts, and pricing.

## ADVERTISING

The object is to inform prospective customers about products and to illustrate their benefits. The advertising department is concerned with the design of the packaging, sales promotion displays, exhibitions, and distribution of circulars. Critical decisions are made on the choice of media.

## SALES

Often a sales manager will be responsible for a number of sales representatives who regularly visit wholesalers and shops to promote the product. Closely associated with this activity is the sales office. Here sales documents are prepared and processed, including orders, invoices, quotations and estimates. A separate estimating department is needed where products vary with requirements.

## WAREHOUSING AND DISTRIBUTION

Storage of finished goods and distribution are important features of an essential customer service since deliveries should conform to the promises made by sales staff. People are easily irritated when delays occur, often through production hold-ups. Some may even cancel the order and become vindictive if they are severely inconvenienced. Production strikes may easily lose sales.

## AFTER-SALES SERVICE

Typical after-sales problems are misunderstanding the instructions for use of a product, difficulty in use, quality not matching requirements, and immediate or developing faults. Such complaints must be dealt with quickly, thoroughly and diplomatically. The customer will soon tell friends and relatives if he or she is not entirely satisfied, and this may lead to the company losing potential sales. Some companies compensate by giving a gift or voucher to the customer who has complained.

Liaison with market research is important. To illustrate, even seemingly clear assembly instructions are often difficult for a customer to understand. This causes frustration, dissatisfaction and possibly damage to the product. Often the reason is that technical staff have written the instructions without checking first that non-technical people will be able to understand them.

## THE MARKETING MIX

Marketing strategy is based on the marketing mix, defined as a blend of controllable variables that may be used to achieve an objective in the market. The four variables are easily remembered as the four Ps: product, price, promotion and place. Each subdivides as follows:

- *Product*: quality, variety, brand name, packaging, warranty, style, service, etc.
- *Price*: gross, net, discounts, credit terms, etc.
- *Promotion*: advertising, sales promotion, sales force, etc.
- *Place*: distribution channels, transport, national/local coverage, stocks, etc.

Choosing the most appropriate marketing mix to suit the proposed market demands expertise. The right balance is difficult to achieve in terms of the product to be offered, the right price, allocation of funds, type of promotion, and the choice of distribution. Timing is also critical.

Market situations change rapidly; a new product may emerge or a competing product may withdraw. Proper use of the marketing mix allows for speedy changes in plans, but there are limits. Often manufacturing and distribution cannot easily change overnight; revised sales campaigns have to be funded; and selling space in the media has to be booked well in advance.

# Production and operations

Production exists to convert raw materials and components into finished goods to satisfy the wants of customers. A typical sequence of activities starts with prospective customers who provide information through market research. This information is passed to research and development (R&D). Here any pure and applied research, design and development work are completed. Next prototypes are produced and, if approved, they pass to the pre-production stage, which simulates actual production conditions. If a successful product is manufactured, feedback is requested from potential customers. Eventually production commences after discussions, modifications and further trials.

In most situations the production transformation process described above applies equally to operations in the service industries such as retailing, insurance, warehousing and transport. The well-established production techniques may be applied successfully, and the interaction between operations and the customer remains vitally important.

Modern production philosophy relies on the customers deciding their requirements, not the production designers deciding in isolation. All production specialists involved in shaping the finished product need to work closely with the customer to be sure they know clearly the user's requirements and customer trends. Leaving these aspects to the marketing department alone is inviting product failure. The criterion is creating product value as perceived by the customer.

## PRODUCTION ORGANISATION

Various major activities are identifiable in any manufacturing organisation. Understandably there will be different types of structure depending on the type of product, degree of mechanisation and automation, emphasis on quality, complexity of R&D, financial importance of purchasing and maintenance, and the expertise of production personnel.

An example below covers the subfunctions usually encountered. The works manager or production manager is at the apex. Beneath this person may be a production planner, production controller, production engineer and maintenance engineer. All their responsibilities are now described.

### Works manager

In some organisations the works manager is responsible for the manufacturing processes. He or she reports to the production manager, who is also responsible for the other subfunctions.

### Production planning and control manager

Production planning is often divided into two. It covers planning, scheduling, stores control, purchasing, works orders, progress, and quality control. In large companies some activities are so big and important that separate managers are appointed, together with appropriate staff.

### Production engineer

The role of the production engineer may be seen in various activities and is often divided among several specialists, e.g. R&D, quality control (often shared with other functions), work study and value analysis. An R&D manager and work study manager may be appointed in the large company. They report either to the production engineer or direct to the production manager.

### Maintenance engineer

There is no recognised level for the maintenance engineer; they might be responsible to the production manager or the works manager. Their responsibilities often cover machines, equipment, plant, buildings, services and R&D requirement. Being responsible direct to the production manager avoids any undue influence by a particular section. The role is demanding since all production sections need to be operational to achieve objectives.

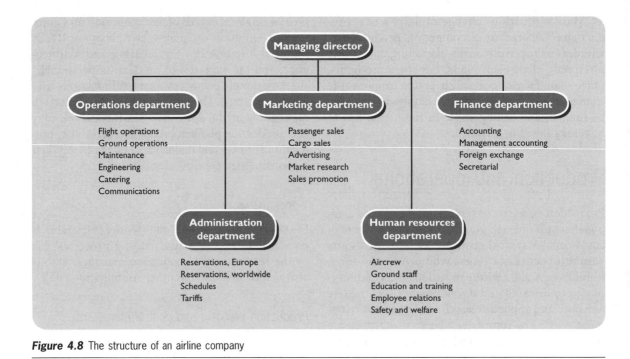

***Figure 4.8*** The structure of an airline company

## CONFLICT WITH MARKETING

Although an organisation may have a marketing department and support its activities, situations often arise which cause conflict between production and marketing. Production employees may see marketing employees arriving late and not conforming to rules that are essential to a smooth-running production department. This may cause friction unless production staff appreciate that sales people may have to see customers late into the evening.

A further example is where a sales representative on commission is forced to take an order for delivery in seven days, knowing the amount cannot be manufactured in under fourteen. This creates a major problem for production and probably excessive costs to produce on time or near the promised delivery date, for which production staff cannot see any benefit.

## SERVICE INDUSTRIES

Although the concepts of manufacturing also apply here, there are some additional unique concepts. The term 'operations management' is used in service industries but its importance and purpose remain unchanged.

Most operational systems interact directly with the customer. This feature emphasises the marketing function and often a sales orientation. A typical example is the financial services industry. Two extra concepts may be identified: compliance and portfolio management. Under legislation, a compliance officer must be appointed who ensures that a comprehensive compliance monitoring programme is undertaken and conforms to the requirements of the Personal Investment Authority (PIA). There are heavy penalties if any of the PIA requirements are ignored, or not strictly adhered to, by all company personnel. Portfolio management is an activity where funds are managed on behalf of clients to produce the required returns in terms of income and/or capital growth.

### Functional departments

Within each particular service industry there are certain specialist departments. A typical organisation for a direct service company may be arranged as in Fig. 4.8. An example would be a department store where typical major functions could be:

- *Merchandising*: buying arranged by product line, and may include budgeting, merchandise control, sales promotion and the sales force
- *Finance*: financial management, credit control, cash control and accounting
- *General management*: supplies, customer service, deliveries, warehousing and store protection
- *Publicity*: advertising, display, media, and public relations

# Finance

All the financial and accounting activities in an organisation are included in the finance function. It involves everyone in accepting responsibility for monetary aspects, regardless of any particular specialism. Typical subfunctions are:

- *Financial management*: taking care of working capital, capital projects and financial provision
- *Financial accounting*: making daily records of all asset and liability transactions
- *Cost accounting*: determining the cost of all activities
- *Management accounting*: giving data to managers for planning, controlling and decision-making activities

## FINANCIAL MANAGEMENT

Short-term finance for each period and long-term finance for fixed assets are covered by financial management. Sources of cash internally and externally, the justification of expenditure and the feasibility of funds required, are all debated. Projects are carefully appraised and alternative sources of funds are reviewed to choose the most economic device. Thus the balance sheet is managed and various sources of funds are constantly monitored.

## FINANCIAL ACCOUNTING

Financial accounting centralises managers' requests for funds and external demands from various creditors. Information is also provided to outside parties such as the Inland Revenue, the Registrar of Companies and the shareholders.

All revenue and expenditure are carefully recorded and analysed to provide the trading position at any time and to give any particular information required by managers. A typical broad coverage would include fixed, current and other assets; current and long-term liabilities; income and expenditure on a daily basis; and manufacturing, trading and profit and loss accounts.

## COST ACCOUNTING

The cost accountant is responsible for providing information on total expenditure for a single item or a group of items or a particular activity. Data are collected from all sources and collated. This activity is very demanding since a clear knowledge of the organisation and its multiple activities is needed to ensure all expenditure is included.

## MANAGEMENT ACCOUNTING

The management accountant is responsible for decision making and control accounting. Various accounting techniques are applied which provide managers with sufficient information. The job demands expertise in both accountancy knowledge and the business to provide relevant information, partly through interpretation and partly through appropriate statistical devices.

Control accounting of this nature means providing data at set intervals in a standard format, along with variances or deviations from previous reports. Thus managers may see more easily the need for any corrective action.

## CONFLICT SITUATIONS

Often production and marketing employees view finance staff as parasites because their role is not understood. Furthermore, senior staff may view the financial function as a retarding influence since both departments always seem to need more funds than are readily available. From a corporate viewpoint, the difficult task of allocating funds to functions is sometimes seen to favour one function at the expense of another.

A finance director may assume too much power if there is no other senior executive who is capable of effectively balancing funds between functions.

When this occurs there is a risk that awareness of functional problems and their effects is not fully appreciated. Enmity and frustration inevitably develop.

# Administration

Administration is concerned with procedures to communicate information; paperwork handling by data capture, information retrieval, processing and recording data; and the effective use of staff involved in these activities. Administration permeates all departments.

If administration is dispersed, its true cost may be difficult to assess. Furthermore, enormous savings are possible by having centralised administration. As information technology continues to advance, the need for a specialist becomes imperative to structure effective systems and to relieve specialists in other functions of this responsibility. In medium-sized companies the finance manager may undertake this role.

### TYPICAL SUBFUNCTIONS

Typical subfunctions relate to particular specialisms which are constantly evolving because of advances in information technology. Expertise is essential to ensure the free flow of information through networks in the organisation, to satisfy the demands for more information, to determine information requirements and forms of presentation, and to interpret data more accurately.

Professional individuals are developing within narrow spheres and becoming recognised as information technologists in their own right. They are often known as electronic data processing (EDP) or IT managers, corporate planners, long-range forecasters, communication officers, liaison officers, cyberneticists (associated with operational research (OR)), economic intelligence officers, organisation and methods (O&M) managers, management services managers, chief systems analysts, network managers and telecommunication managers.

### INFORMATION TECHNOLOGY

Information technology (IT) includes the following aspects:

- collecting, analysing, recording and distributing sufficient appropriate information to all organisation sectors
- operating within a suitable timescale and using the most appropriate statistical form for data according to each manager's and supervisor's capability
- providing them with appropriate back-up to solve problems, make decisions and improve anticipating skills in pursuing, adjusting and setting the company's objectives

The emerging problems date back to when people first found ways of communicating with each other. Now problems exist in more sophisticated forms due to discoveries in other technological fields, resulting in advanced computers and associated machines and equipment.

### The effects of IT

Information technology is the prime mover of change and practically every job will be affected eventually. Computers (especially personal computers) have revolutionised systems and organisational structures, and have created new skills. Managerial and supervisory roles are changing as networks provide direct access to massive information stores.

The use of integrated systems is essential to provide full benefit and remove old functional barriers. Nevertheless, functional specialists remain, although they now incorporate modern wider viewpoints which are vital for corporate success.

Drucker stresses that computers only hold quantifiable data but accuracy still depends on the human being inputting the information. Unfortunately, external events are often in qualitative form, so they are incapable of immediate quantification, which is when the information is most needed. Furthermore, external events are changes in trends, not the trends themselves. If they were trends then managing would be easy; visualising and perceiving what is going to happen would not be necessary.

The effective use of IT involves a number of complex features, namely a knowledge of information science, software, hardware, equipment suppliers, networking, databases and open systems.

Apart from operating the equipment, the supervisor should be aware of the following important aspects. Read them in conjunction with production control computer systems (Chapter 26) and managing business information (Chapter 30).

## SOFTWARE

Software packages and their user manuals contain lots of jargon words which hinder people's understanding. Software is simply program support to operate the computer so that a series of tasks with various applications can be used. Typical functions are storage and retrieval of customer data, fact finding and analysis, visual graphic analysis (VGA), standardised letters, diary for appointments, reports and accounts, income and expenditure, and 'what if' scenarios which allow the user to propose changes and note the effects calculated.

Computer programs are plentiful; some even design new programs, but many suffer with quirks. Three essential points should be noted: the need for correct input information; the computer is fallible; and nothing can be effectively planned without efficient information.

Sometimes software packages are not suitable for particular needs. In these cases programmers are available to write bespoke packages, but there is always a risk they may not be available later to solve problems.

## HARDWARE

After choosing the right software, a reputable supplier is found to advise and provide an appropriate computer and peripheral equipment such as hard disk stores and a printer. Reliability and possible breakdowns are important issues but there are fault-tolerant computers available where every module is duplicated so that one failure switches a mirror module into the system.

The Data Protection Act 1984 (Chapter 22) should be remembered since all data users must register with the Data Protection Agency.

## NETWORKS

Networking is transferring information between data users by linking computers. These networks can share hard disks and printers, and the information is available to many users with workstations. Large savings are possible since information files can be shared by all users and updated only once. Also, everyone receives the same information and the use of an electronic mail (e-mail) facility improves communication. Some disadvantages are that special software packages and extra random access memories (RAMs) are needed, security may be difficult, and networks need to be managed.

Networking imposes more reliance on informal groupings of peers (supervisors) of different departments and sections at the same level, and less on hierarchical relationships. This linkage provides access to more rapid and accurate information, the increased adaptation of new ideas, and higher motivation. The risk when relationships are fluid is confusion about commitment and responsibilities. Also, such operations rely on mutual respect and confidence, which may be lacking.

### Major developments

Networking is a constantly developing and improving field. The joining of computing with telephony has provided computer networks all connected together, known as the Internet. On a global scale any computer may be coupled with another, which gives users of the Internet access to enormous amounts of data. Many services are available and private networks (intranets) provide LAN and WAN.

Local area networks (LANs) link a number of computers. They share software and hardware, typically sharing programs, data files, disk drives and printers. This type of network is controlled by a file server – a hard disk machine holding programs and files for use as required.

Usually a LAN links computers in the same office block. Two LANs in adjacent buildings would be connected by a bridge, which synchronises the networks. Two incompatible LANs can be linked by a gateway, which modifies and synchronises. LANs can also be connected with a WAN, usually by a telephone link.

Wide area networks (WANs) are on a larger scale than LANs and link several sites or countries via the telephone system. A WAN gives users access to other companies' data banks, allows transmission between companies and provides a linkage for e-mail.

### The network manager

The network manager is responsible for all the hi-tech services at various sites, such as telex, fax, videoconferencing, facsimile printing, telephony and the network installation. He or she maintains the network, upgrades it if required, controls the files and programs, and distributes rapid reports on status changes and costs.

The network manager should provide information on business databases which are available on subscription and provide online external sources of information. An increasing range of databases are on offer, including up-to-date information on such topics as trading companies, sales prospects, legal aspects, marketing and research data.

### Network providers

Significant savings may be obtained by communicating electronically between companies in some industries, typically insurance services where correct information and efficient service are essential. However, problems may arise through incompatibility of software and hardware. The answer is to use a network provider (NP) who enables one computer to communicate with others via one route – a telephone call. There are five major NPs, including British Telecom (BTIS) and AT&T/Iste (Inview). At present they charge the service companies; for example, an insurance broker may seek quotations from four insurance companies free of charge.

### ORGANISATION AND METHODS

Work study is equally important in the factory and in the office. The term 'organisation and methods', used for clerical work study, tends to take second place through so much concentration on the technology of office automation. Although high capability to store, analyse and produce information is essential, due thought to why, how, when and where the information is used is vital. Unless organisation and methods (O&M) is given sufficient emphasis, the probability is low use of information, high administration costs and inefficient systems and procedures. The O&M manager should be responsible for studying the objectives and needs of clerical operations, designing the best systems and procedures, and recommending the most suitable equipment.

# Human resources

The purposes of the human resource (HR) function are to create and administer a human resource strategy, to utilise human resources in the most effective way, and to emphasise the importance of the human aspects of management. These purposes imply a philosophy of attracting and maintaining an effective complement of employees by concentrating on two fields: human resource management and personnel management.

### HUMAN RESOURCE MANAGEMENT

This is a long-term, proactive, strategic role where employees are treated as a valuable resource which demands their maximum utilisation. Inherent in this process is the creation of strong employee commitment and self-control, and high trust by management and employees. The main activities are:

- Forecasting future demand for employees by analysing current human resources, assessing probable changes in the organisation, reconciling the forecast with management, and determining policy.
- Estimating the future supply of human resources by conducting research, and assessing internal development schemes, turnover and external supplies.
- Planning development programmes, estimating costs and seeking approval from management.
- Studying internal and external environmental influences, considering their effects on human resources.
- Studying organisational culture and behaviour by diagnosing changes in group behaviour, foreseeing possible problems, and considering strategies and tactics to cope with these problems.
- Liaising with the personnel department.

## PERSONNEL MANAGEMENT

Personnel management aims to administer the short-term aspects of HR by managing employment negotiations, pay structures, industrial relations, education and training, health and safety, and general welfare services. The role is reactive, relies upon controls, is inclined to be mechanistic, bureaucratic and centralised, and tends to emphasise minimising costs.

A competent personnel manager is a good communicator, really understands people, and ensures personnel staff understand their role and react quickly to problems and queries. In the small company, supervisors and managers adopt this function without the aid of a specialist. Furthermore, these individuals in larger companies are obviously more closely involved in some aspects of personnel management. One view is this overlap is wasteful and removes too much responsibility from the line.

## TYPICAL ACTIVITIES OF A PERSONNEL DEPARTMENT

### Employment

The employment activity should begin by considering the job itself. Surveys of existing and proposed jobs are needed to plan and to draw up accurate descriptions of requirements.

Further aspects associated with this activity are liaising with the sources of prospective employees; updating a knowledge of terms and conditions of employment; understanding existing and proposed legislation affecting personnel; conducting interviews for engagement, transfer, termination and dismissal; operating a procedure for any employee movement; maintaining accurate personnel records; preparing personnel statistics; attending committees associated with personnel; overseeing an induction procedure for new employees; and operating manpower planning.

### Remuneration

The remuneration activity provides accurate information on wages and salaries for the pay section of the accounts department. The wages and salaries structure should be administered fairly by careful application of pay scales, merit rating schemes and bonus schemes. Any changes in remuneration must be properly authorised. Assessment of pay in similar industries and consultation with unions and work study engineers concerning pay rates also form an important part of this process.

### Education and training

Procedures for training new employees and schemes to improve employees' capabilities are essential. The aims are to increase productivity, increase employees' pay through improved performance, and to promote from within wherever possible.

Such training includes schemes for managers, supervisors, instructors, apprentices, transferees and newcomers. Encouragement of further education involves the use of internal training schemes, projects and programs of Training and Enterprise Councils (TECs), colleges and evening institutes. This activity also covers the maintenance of records showing attainments, the publication of information on training opportunities, circulation of educational publications and company magazines, organising any special lectures, training in safety, operating suggestion schemes, and conforming to appropriate legislation.

### Industrial relations (or employee relations)

Industrial relations involves mediating, negotiating and conciliating between employees' trade unions and management. The essential requirements are a thorough knowledge of collective agreements, conciliation and arbitration procedure, company policy and rules, and current legislation. The aims are to maintain and improve joint consultation, fostering good relationships and making full use of joint committees.

Liaison with unions should include ensuring personnel policy is clearly understood and that all procedures within the policy are fairly conducted. These procedures include wage negotiations, complaints and grievances, apprenticeship and other training schemes, application of rules and regulations, dismissals and transfers, redundancy, social activities and general conditions of employment.

### Health and safety

Attending to work-related illness, stress-related sickness, and safety is a demanding task. If neglected they cause distress and heavy costs. Essential requirements are a knowledge of current legislation and EC directives, recording and statistical analysis of sickness and injuries, issuing regulations to all employees, updating ergonomic aspects, and protecting the environment. Typical activities include arranging accident prevention meetings, publicising health and safety measures, inspecting workshops and offices, minimising fire risks, and promoting regular exercise.

### Welfare

Welfare services and facilities are an important consideration for potential employees and for retaining existing employees. The wide breadth of this subject includes the social responsibilities of management and supervision, acceptable standards, working conditions, workplace design, equal opportunities, modern job design, physical and psychological harassment, and workplace counselling. To safeguard employees' interests and to improve their general position in the community involves the study of extensive legislation, creating many social facilities, and establishing and maintaining control features.

### PERSONNEL POLICY

Ideally there should be a clear, written personnel policy which is fully supported by management. The personnel manager is responsible for maintaining and interpreting the policy. Here is an example of a typical personnel policy:

- To promote fairness and justice to all employees irrespective of status, position, sex or race.
- To provide a fair system of adequate wages and salaries which compare favourably with other companies.
- To operate a merit scheme which compensates those employees who achieve increased effectiveness.
- To allow all employees to develop their own capabilities fully.

- To recognise the needs of employees, their desires for job satisfaction, and to consult them when any changes affecting them are contemplated.
- To provide suitable education, training and development facilities; this enables employees to progress and have equal opportunity in applying for vacancies within the company.
- To operate personnel selection based upon placing individuals in the work situation most suitable for their requirements.
- To provide working conditions which satisfy all the health, safety and welfare legislative requirements.
- To help employees whenever possible with domestic and industrial problems.
- To provide and encourage social activities as considered desirable by employees and which are of mutual benefit to them and the company.
- To operate fair procedures for settling disputes and grievances quickly, and to provide joint consultation facilities.
- To conduct all activities between management and employees in a friendly and co-operative spirit.

### Personnel's reputation

Underlying personnel policy there are essential requirements which determine the personnel department's reputation:

- A comprehensive personnel package should be given to all newcomers immediately they join the company.
- There should be rapid follow-up procedures for newcomers, to ensure there are no problems or misapprehensions.
- Ensure all newcomers and existing employees promptly receive any updated procedures.
- Avoid irritating features such as being slow to respond to requests, passing the buck, giving out-of-date information, and adopting off-putting attitudes.

# Distribution

Although originally treated as a logistics concept, the distribution function has grown into a line management activity with a number of subfunctions which must be integrated to be effective. Clearly it cuts across other functions such as production and marketing, since by definition, managing logistics means creating a total supply chain from planning the acquisition of materials, through the chain of purchasing, stores control, materials and product handling, packaging, warehousing, distribution of finished goods, and point of sale.

The co-ordination of these distribution activities is usually called logistics management, which liaises with production and marketing in a business strategy to create an effective customer service.

The use of logistics involves many techniques which are associated with the art of moving, storing and supplying materials and products, or the managing of commercial supplies. These techniques include just-in-time, dynamic channel selection, materials resource planning, and distribution requirements planning. Effective control depends heavily on the use of information technology and employees to provide accurate data between vital points in the total supply chain.

In traditional organisational formats, this activity was split between production and marketing, with possibly a separate function in say transport if it formed an expensive part of the total operation. Indeed various procedures were planned and controlled by administration and finance departments. Consequently, the overall cost of distribution and its effectiveness, in total, remained hidden.

## QUESTIONS

1 Discuss the change in emphasis from personnel to human resources management.

2 Do you agree that customer requirements should always be given priority? Explain your answer.

3 O&M should precede any contemplated changes in computerised systems. Discuss this statement.

4 Explain the meaning of power, role and task cultures in an organisation.

5 Outline the major aims of the marketing function.

6 Discuss ways of reducing tension to acceptable limits in an organisation.

7 Consider the advantages and disadvantages of a bureaucratic model.

8 What are the advantages and disadvantages of using a matrix structure?

9 Consider possible conflict between production and marketing.

10 Outline the financial function.

11 Discuss the importance of the administration function.

12 What is the purpose of the personnel function?

13 Discuss how the activities of a personnel department affect the activities of the supervisor.

14 Consider the various ways in which a personnel manager could help a supervisor.

15 What is the main aim of developing conceptual skills?

Alec and his wife decided they would buy a videotape recorder at a local store rather than renewing their rental scheme. Alec thought he could install the machine easily and they took it home with them. To his surprise it would not perform according to the instructions which were perfectly clear. His wife was irritated because the salesman had offered a free installation.

Alec telephoned and made an appointment for a service engineer to call the following week, which was the earliest possible time. Apparently the machine was faulty and the engineer removed it, saying he would give them a ring.

After two weeks Alec decided to telephone the store but was told by the operator they were very busy and would deal with it soon. After another week Alec called at the store, saw the stores manager and demanded a new machine. The manager was sympathetic but would not agree to the demand. He said he would chase the service department and that was the best he could do. Alec was very annoyed and told him it was the last time he would deal with the store. The manager said there was nothing he could do about it.

*What are the inherent organisational problems in this store? Write an account of the possible procedures the members of staff concerned should follow when dealing with a customer.*

The company operates flexitime and staff are allowed to take appropriate time off based on set hours and a clocking system. Angela manages to save several days every few weeks but she insists on taking time off at busy periods or when difficult jobs are arising. This conduct is noticed by her colleagues, who complain to the supervisor.

Her appraisal interview coincides with the complaints and the supervisor raises the question with her. She denies the accusations and says she always works overtime when they are busy. She also thinks her promotion to senior clerk is overdue and would like to know why she is being overlooked.

*Explain how you would treat this situation.*

Amanda Pouton was convinced that the personnel department of Latham Contacts Ltd, a large company, was an unnecessary financial burden.

'I seem to spend half my time on personnel matters', she was saying to Ted, a fellow supervisor. 'I can't imagine what they all get up to every day when most of the personnel work is done by us'.

Ted agreed. 'Did you hear of that car rental firm in the States who sacked all the personnel staff and had an "employment person" for every 300 employees? She did all the essential personnel tasks and they saved a fortune.'

'Yes, I did hear about that. The comical thing about it was that the president of the company insisted these people should never meet, otherwise they would immediately form another personnel department!'

*Consider this case in the light of all the activities undertaken by a personnel department. Would Amanda's estimate of time spent on personnel work be an exaggeration?*

# 5

# Group activity and teamwork

## Introduction

The urge to belong to and be accepted by a group is commonplace. In companies, group membership helps to compensate for poor organisational design, which may ignore people's desire to be creative, does not allow them to do something worthwhile, and avoids giving them appropriate recognition.

Group cohesiveness can be very strong, although membership may range from enjoyment down to discomfort. A member may even go against natural desires to work well if the group's attitude is negative.

A firm aim for managers and supervisors is to align group objectives with organisational objectives. Indeed, if group dynamics are understood and applied correctly, synergy improves, favourable group norms develop and, with training, creativeness is encouraged.

The effect of national and organisational cultures on each person was mentioned in Chapter 2. This feature should be related to group activity when considering social interaction, norms and regulations, acceptable physical and ethical conduct, and group cohesiveness.

### GROUPS

A traditional group is a number of people clustered together to perform various tasks. These are allocated to them in accordance with a set of instructions. Each person tends to be insular or indifferent to the rest of the group and does not act as a team member regarding input, how the group operates, its development and its capability to create power.

In practice, many different types of group exist with varying degrees of development into a crude team. Some groups even maintain their identity as a 'group' but they may be sophisticated teams. This applies particularly to autonomous workgroups, a group subjected to empowerment, project groups and working parties.

### GROUP ACTIVITY

Group activity is divided into the basic group and the developed group. The basic group is a crude cluster of individuals who may be in conflict, competitive or hostile, but not necessarily in accordance with an effective organisational culture. Each person may have selfish aims, be insufficiently educated and trained, and lack the support of sound formal leadership with productivity in mind. Distinct patterns of behaviour exist which are attributed to intergroup dynamics. These patterns may eventually lead to the creation of a team if intergroup activity is successful.

The developed group has followed a team formation process that starts with bringing individuals together to form a group, continues with interaction between the individuals, development of the group into a team, and ends with power development.

To clarify this process, the next section covers group formation and team development; then comes an examination of group dynamics which involves synergy, autonomous workgroups and empowerment. The chapter continues with examining conflict and co-ordination; recognisable activity; resolving unhealthy conflict and team building, essential at all levels. Chapter 7 looks at teams for management levels. Certainly the development of autonomous workgroups is considered vital in improving human relations (Chapter 10) and in motivational concepts (Chapter 12).

# Group formation

The success of group formation depends upon the following:

- interaction
- development of cohesion
- norm formation
- roles
- correct use of power

Figure 5.1 outlines the main features which are now discussed.

## SOCIAL INTERACTION

A complex interacting structure exists in any organisation. Establishing formal groups invariably leads to restructuring into informal groups and social groups, although the original groups retain their identity. Within a group, members influence each other in many ways. Conversations on various subjects affect their opinions and expectations. Fairness and justice are important criteria when decisions affecting the group are examined. If logical and acceptable, then rational behaviour follows; if not, emotional reactions occur.

### Joining a group

An individual may change favourably or adversely when he or she joins a group, depending on previous circumstances. Before, that person may have felt insecure and restricted in outlook, thoughts and actions, and unable to exercise individuality. In the group he or she may feel a new power, possibly lose some individuality, and responsibilities may change. The new member may influence the group's culture; other members will develop expectations of him or her which will largely govern the roles the individual will play.

### Social activities

Encouraging group pride is possible by providing adequate accommodation and financial support for social activities. Although some managers have been disappointed at the lack of enthusiasm or wavering interest in such schemes, no doubt they should look elsewhere for the cause rather than blaming employees. Workers in Japan spend more leisure time together; they identify strongly with each other and the company. In the UK many social and sports schemes fail to attract sufficient support from employees.

There should be more personal identification and more satisfaction if employees suggest the facilities needed and organise the activities. Managers should actively support the proposed programmes but possibly not take any part in controlling them.

Supervisors should be active and enthusiastic. Although they may not necessarily be keen on sport themselves, they can often recommend certain employees whom they know have a flair for sport and other interests. This recreational sphere allows supervisors to gain a better understanding of subordinates outside the working environment.

There are many opportunities open for sports and social clubs to represent their company in the outside community. Examples are joining local sports leagues, assisting in charitable work, taking part in parades, and holding joint dances with other companies. All are ways of fostering group spirit and enabling employees to appreciate their role in the community.

### Group conditioning

Most members conform to a group's conditioning process to such an extent that their behaviour changes and their beliefs apparently change. However, usually members resent changing to suit a group's needs and may revert quickly. People who avoid group pressure are often ignored by other members; if they attempt to protest too strongly to their superior they are considered to be troublemakers.

Individuals are more likely to conform under certain conditions and there are many notorious

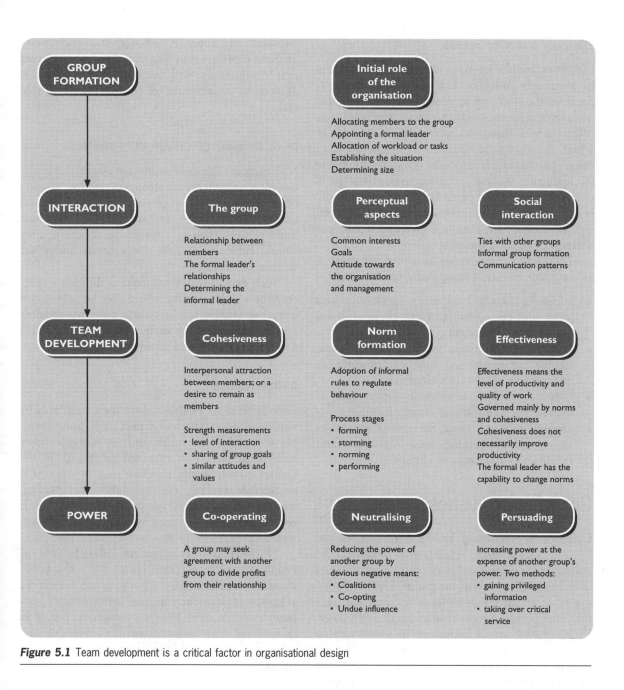

**Figure 5.1** Team development is a critical factor in organisational design

examples where excessive group pressure has forced people to ignore moral codes. The usual excuses after appalling behaviour are 'I was only obeying orders' and 'Others were doing it so I followed suit, knowing it was wrong'.

Typical situations in industry that encourage conformity are:

- strong interaction among group members
- moderate group pressure, rather than severe
- standing alone – with no support from other members
- an unstable or uncertain work environment
- insecurity – the need for support from the group
- group membership is valued highly by outsiders

### Efficiency and effectiveness

Efficiency should improve as everyone conforms to a group's influence and teamwork emerges, provided the objectives agree with the organisation's objectives. However, effectiveness depends upon other factors discussed later. Rigid conformity which suppresses the so-called troublemaker may cause imbalance. It depends upon whether the troublemaker is simply causing disruptions or is over-enthusiastic and partly frustrated when his or her sound ideas and initiative are ignored. The usual sign of an inept superior is if the troublemaker is accused of rocking the boat.

There are various means of achieving balance as a prelude to introducing autonomous teams:

- Superiors should encourage criticisms and ideas, and be tolerant towards those who are not always subservient.
- Demonstrate to group members that a questioning approach and any contribution to improve the group are welcomed.
- Indicate clearly that extreme suppression of members is harmful and creates insularity.
- Demonstrate the need for group norms to be revised to maintain their usefulness and validity as circumstances change.

# Group cohesiveness

Cohesion is determined by the degree of mutual respect, liking each other, group spirit, the amount of interpersonal attraction, and the need to retain membership of the group. The basic feeling of safety in numbers leads to some satisfaction and increased individual strength and power. Each member needs assistance in some way to do his or her own job, and some tasks require members' collaboration. Certain basic needs are satisfied by the group and there is ample opportunity for social interaction. Feelings of solidarity and increased security are fostered but they may be false in reality.

No doubt high cohesiveness improves member relationships, a more pleasant atmosphere is created, and co-operation is more likely. However, it does not mean that group productivity will automatically improve, although the productivity of some members may increase. Evidence suggests that productivity will improve if the group is allowed to concentrate on completing the whole task.

## DEVELOPMENT OF GROUP COHESIVENESS

Management's sincere support is essential. Fundamental requirements are strong interaction, sharing of objectives, and alignment of attitudes and values. Contributory factors are that members must possess various interests in common, they should fulfil social and safety needs and resist adverse pressures.

Such demands in total make it difficult to perceive how cohesiveness would ever be achieved if it were not for protection against poor management and for strong feelings of distrust. Cohesion in this case negates increased motivation.

## GROUP NORMS

Groups tend to establish their own standards of workload. One type will expect each group member to produce so much and no more; another will easily exceed an expected workload. In the former group, strong pressure may be applied if a member exceeds the standards set (norms), whereas in the latter increasing productivity is encouraged and pressure is applied to perform well to save group pride.

Norms may also be set for social behaviour. Penalties may be severe if social and work behaviour norms are broken. Ideally, group norms are aligned with company norms. Unfortunately, differences often exist because the group perceives its own interests do not coincide. Leadership and other means are used in attempting to improve the situation.

## NORM CHARACTERISTICS

The supervisor perceives what are taken to be group norms by witnessing a group member's behaviour, which may not coincide with the person's actual feelings or thoughts. Such norms are important to the person as they are a part of being a member of the group, but some latitude is noticeable. Consequently, a range of acceptable behaviour is permitted by the group within the limits imposed.

## NORM FORMATION

Norm formation may be identified as a gradual development which passes through various stages and short cuts. The development involves four main stages: (1) the *forming* process, when the new group seeks information, analyses, orientates and relies upon the leader; (2) the *storming* process, when internal conflict and emotional disturbances occur; (3) the *norming* process, when conflicts are resolved, co-operation is established and norms emerge; (4) the *performing* process, when teamwork is recognised, roles appear and informal problems are solved.

Short cuts may be easily recognised. They include a critical incident which has a profound effect on the group; an explicit statement from management or the supervisor which is taken seriously by the group; a situation which warrants an obvious standard; a strong preference by an influential group member; an ambiguous situation which bothers the group and justifies classification; an embarrassing or emotional problem which can be solved by setting a norm; revising a norm if a developing situation warrants it, such as a trusted supervisor possibly being transferred; and any undue tension which threatens to break up the group.

## NORM CHANGES

If a supervisor notes norm changes and attempts to discuss why and how they are enforced, he or she should be able to diagnose more easily any problems within the group. Although this is difficult, there are indications. Norms tend to cluster around certain aspects of behaviour which immediately arouse concern in the members. Also they are associated with personal relationships such as particular pairs going to the cloakroom, eating lunch and taking tea breaks. Sometimes behaviour does not match norms, therefore true norms remain undisclosed.

# Roles

Each employee plays a particular role related to his or her job description and position within the group. The difference between holding a job and performing a role within that job depends upon norms and rights governing the person's eventual behaviour pattern.

In the theatre an actor plays a part but their role onstage is far more than simply playing that part. Therefore a role relates to how the job is performed, whereas the job involves duties, authority and responsibilities.

Roles are determined by expectations from superiors, peers and subordinates and by the job holder's own expectations, whereas the job is officially designated with appropriate duties. In other words, employees' expectations relate to roles but employees' demands relate to duties.

## ROLE COMPETENCE

Any individual is subjected to continuous role innovation through the learning process. Refusal to accept such innovation through perception or personality difficulties generally amounts to unacceptable behaviour.

Problems of perception may have their cause in motivation level, previous experience, attitudes, values not conforming to those of the group, or a mixture of these. Roles that are unacceptable must be revised to gain social acceptance. If the roles are seen to be acceptable then reinforcement (Chapter 12) influences them and they are repeated in future coinciding interactions. Usually the individual will constantly probe contacts to assess where their role and level of competence are approved or rejected.

## FORMAL AND INFORMAL ROLES

Typical formal roles are committee membership, chairmanship, secretary, functional advisor, departmental representative and liaison activities.

Informal roles coincide with personality, knowledge and skills. Some examples are proposing ideas, developing ideas, criticising ideas, supporting proposals, displaying antagonism, disagreeing, testing, acting passively, generating enthusiasm, seeking help, disrupting, introducing humour, and demanding orientation.

## TYPICAL EMPLOYEE ROLES

An employee might assume different roles in different situations – there is no established pattern. Some examples are short-circuiting procedures to hasten job completion, the good Samaritan, perpetual willingness to help solve problems, going by the rule book, the yes-man, the questioning type, the maverick, the lone wolf, the rule evader and the fairness seeker.

Inevitably some roles conflict with each other. For example, the trade union representative may be forced to take a stance that conflicts with his or her role as a loyal employee. Frustration develops as attempts to overcome barriers fail.

# Group power

Solidarity and cohesiveness in a group increase its ability to influence other individuals and groups. This may improve group effectiveness but not necessarily organisational effectiveness. It depends on the group's objectives. Methods to gain power are diverse and devious. Three main ways are co-operating, neutralising and persuading.

## CO-OPERATING

Two groups seek an agreement where both benefit in some way. They may guarantee behavioural stability or agree to divide the profits arising from their relationship.

## NEUTRALISING

Three ways are possible:

- adopting coalitions
- co-opting other group members
- exercising undue influence

Coalition means joining up with one or more groups, which greatly reduces opposition from an isolated group. Co-opting is commonplace and occurs when a member is invited to participate in another group's activities. This move often effectively neutralises the opposition's criticism since one of its own members is involved. Undue influence is achieved by lobbying. Although effective in committee work, it may adversely affect decision making.

## PERSUADING

Often called theft of power, there are two forms of persuading. First, by gaining access to privileged information which is denied to other groups and is of great benefit when competing for resources; thus a group can present a superior case. Second, by taking over critical services, a group may dominate if it can withhold or delay a service to another group that relies on it to achieve objectives.

# Group dynamics

The study of group formation and development has illustrated the complexity of group activity. Within this subject is group dynamics which studies in depth the forces that are operating. These include the concept of synergy, roles, competition between groups and within groups, power and teamwork, all of which are discussed throughout the chapter.

## SYNERGY

Synergy assumes that the collective output of a group exceeds the aggregate of the members' individual outputs. In other words, synergy is often described as 'two plus two equals five'. However, certain requirements are essential for success:

- avoidance of personality clashes
- keeping irritations to a minimum
- careful structuring to achieve a reasonably small group size
- encouragement of ideas, innovation and power
- coaching to draw out talents
- effective communication to provide ample information, improved problem solving and joint decision making
- strong interdependence
- an effective informal leader

# Autonomous workgroups

Autonomous workgroups are mentioned again since various techniques may be applied. One way is to group work tasks to form a logical whole task which is performed with minimal interference. Another way is the group technology approach: machines or desks are grouped together based on their contribution to the product or service, not on work similarity. Examples are grouping workers together to make a diesel engine injector or part of a carburettor. The work is so arranged that higher integration and more job satisfaction are achieved through increased autonomy and productive co-operation.

Those who are more instrumentally oriented (financial rewards), do not necessarily welcome such job redesign. Others see it as another management ploy to extract more work for no extra pay. Finding the best fit for technological and social factors is difficult for management to determine. This work orientation problem is illustrated in Fig. 5.2.

## FORMING AUTONOMOUS WORKGROUPS

Successful formation of autonomous groups relies not only on the process outlined in the previous section but also on a number of factors. These are the careful choice of team members, appropriate development, clear objectives, limitations, empowerment, the encouragement of free speech and new ideas, selection by the group of an informal leader, and the supervisor or coach. A simplified block diagram of an autonomous working group programme is illustrated in Fig. 5.3. The main aspects are now discussed.

## SELECTING A TEAM

Unfortunately, some employees do not always work well together. Therefore choice of team members must depend on compatibility where each person is willing to work within a team, is prepared to share common goals, and is reliable. However, this idea of teamwork and its requirements is subject to group conditioning discussed earlier. Also, to achieve effectiveness, it is often argued that some team members who do not conform to rigid group requirements are equally essential. These people may be wayward to some extent. However, they are often enthusiastic and creative, so they have to be tolerated.

## THE LEADER

Probably the leader will be selected by the group and be expected to work alongside other members. The fundamental requirements are enthusiasm, being able to take responsibility along with commensurate authority, applying democratic principles, and being accepted by each member. A close relationship with the supervisor or coach is essential to maintain communication, development of the team, and general liaison.

## DEVELOPMENT

Giving employees more responsibility, more power and expecting them to apply self-discipline and self-control without appropriate development and back-up is a naive move and it invites disaster. Careful analysis of capability needs to be coupled with coaching and full management support.

## CLEAR OBJECTIVES

Members must know what is expected from them. Their objectives should be realistic and established in such a way that teamwork becomes essential. Indeed their acceptance of the commitment is a vital part of the process.

**Figure 5.2** A work orientation graph
The extreme concepts of high instrumentality and high self-fulfilment are for illustration only. Most jobs contain an element of both concepts.

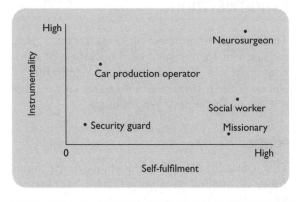

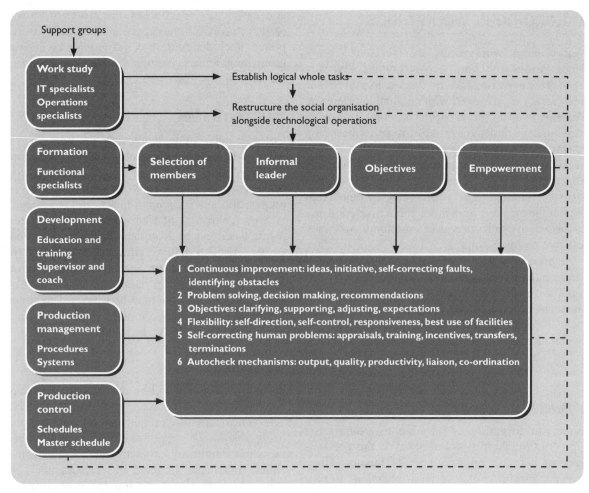

**Figure 5.3** A simplified autonomous workgroup programme
Support groups determine the structure, aid its development and inject essential adjustments. Successful achievement of autonomy creates a working team which operates with minimal interference consistent with overall co-ordination.

## LIMITATIONS

Clearly a group cannot be allowed to work with complete freedom. There must be co-ordination with other groups, alignment of objectives, appraisals, and coaching to keep within the boundaries of overall plans and processes. This is achieved by clarifying roles and rules, designating authority and responsibility, applying systems and procedures within the framework of administration and production, and establishing the hierarchy where appraisals and coaching are arranged.

# Empowerment

The concept of empowering employees is a basic requirement for the successful operation of autonomous teams. To understand the significance of empowerment, there are three terms to consider: power, authority and responsibility.

## POWER

This is usually defined as the ability to get things done; it implies capability. There are various methods of developing power (Chapter 13). Power is also described as the ability to instigate or incite group activity. Such power may be exerted in many different ways such as:

- using force (or coercion) which dominates and achieves obedience through fear
- applying a strong personality
- using subtle means to gain support
- aligning beliefs and values within the group to gain acceptance as a leader
- satisfying the wants of the group
- claiming the right of power through seniority and experience

## AUTHORITY

This is conferred by management. It gives the person the right to require action from others or to take appropriate action within the boundaries of responsibility for undertaking various tasks outlined in a particular job. Therefore authority power, in this sense, is a form of empowerment.

## RESPONSIBILITY

This means being accountable for certain tasks. It implies that a person should receive commensurate authority to enable him or her to influence or adjust those tasks within the terms of such responsibility.

## EMPOWERMENT IN PRACTICE

Bearing the above three terms in mind, empowerment means giving the person the opportunity to develop power by providing appropriate authority and responsibility for particular tasks, and ensuring there is either existing capability or a development plan to achieve such capability.

Empowerment also implies certain opportunities: to have freedom of speech, to exploit new ideas, to use all the strengths available and to overcome any weaknesses. The process should allow more discretion and quicker responses to problems. Therefore there is more risk of mistakes (but this is accepted), employees are more exposed when errors occur, and managers' and supervisors' control is reduced. However, initiative and imagination are increased, there should be alignment of effort and morale improvement. Naturally there are some people who do not want more power while others are corrupted by power.

### The supervisor or coach

There are two opposing views on the need for a supervisor or coach. One view sees the supervisor as superfluous because all the basic elements of supervision are incorporated in the team. This arrangement is possible but unlikely when all the essential features of autonomous teams are considered:

- Ideal autonomous teams do not need a supervisor or coach because each member is highly trained.
- The personnel department operates effective education and training schemes, and counselling, which maintain the development of each member as changes occur.
- Effective computerised systems, procedures and communication networks are maintained and updated as required.
- New ideas flow freely and are carefully examined before being incorporated.
- The team is self-disciplined, self-sufficient and self-controlled.
- Competent management receives and responds to all vital feedback, and it ensures co-ordination.
- Everyone is customer-oriented.
- The competent informal leader within the team is able to cope with all the problems, liaising constantly with the personnel department to solve all the staffing difficulties that arise daily.

### The vital factor

Clearly this ideal organisation does not exist and cannot exist at present. The opposing view to the entirely self-sufficient autonomous team sees the supervisor or coach remaining as the vital link who deals with all the elements shown in Fig. 1.1 and helps to achieve an increased degree of effectiveness. The tasks of the coach are outlined in Chapter 19.

Developing an empowering culture with clear organisational objectives is a challenge for the supervisor, who needs comprehensive training for

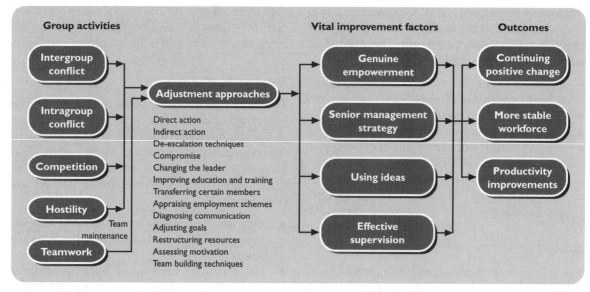

**Figure 5.4** Group activities: an overview
Many types of activity are seen in practice. A multitude of disrupting influences and causes of conflict exist in any organisation.

success. Also the use of empowerment workshops for managers, supervisors and employees is a fundamental feature to ensure that cultural change will occur eventually.

# Conflict and co-ordination

Conflict and co-ordination cover important concepts affecting conflict, recognising the situation, attempting to understand intra- and intergroup activity, and methods of removing unhealthy conflict to achieve co-ordination. The first factor is to analyse the differences.

## CONFLICT, COMPETITIVENESS AND HOSTILITY

Recognising the differences between conflict, competition and hostility demands careful diagnosis. If the diagnosis is correct, the chosen approach to resolve difficulties will avoid disasters. Figure 5.4 illustrates an overall scene of business situations involving these topics.

### Conflict

There are many general meanings of 'conflict'. Within a group or between groups, a useful business definition is to treat conflict as degrees of incompatibility, a struggle to achieve a purpose, and a clashing of opposed principles. Note how these meanings avoid the use of hatred or rivalry.

### Competition

To distinguish competition it could be treated as a contest, friendly rivalry, imitation, or perhaps jealousy.

### Hostility

The term 'hostility' entails more aggression, belligerence or pugnacity. Usually it is defined as enmity, hatred, unfriendliness, or a state of warfare. Internationally, conflict and hostility are often treated as identical situations.

## TYPES OF CONFLICT

These are distinguished by the number of people involved:

- interorganisational
- intergroup
- intragroup
- between individuals

They are easily identified by referring to the definition of conflict, but each one demands a different approach to resolve conflict without destroying it to an unhealthy level.

## TYPES OF COMPETITION

There are important differences between types. Healthy competitiveness is encouraged where contests and rivalry are seen to be generating ideas and improvements. However, there might be unhealthy competition when jealousy or imitating are seen to be degenerating into unfriendly or negative behaviour.

## TYPES OF HOSTILITY

These involve clashes for many reasons. They may involve people's beliefs and values, organisational and managerial insecurity, inadequate communication, perceived inequality, and class and status problems. They are all dangerous, lead to disastrous situations and cause considerable distress.

# Recognisable activity

An understanding of activity within the three areas – conflict, competition and hostility – is an essential requirement before proceeding to approaches that attempt to deal with situations.

## INTERGROUP ACTIVITY

To achieve co-ordination, the supervisor must understand and influence intergroup activity. Success depends on understanding conflict, diagnosing the causes, appreciating the changes that occur when conflict is reduced, and recognising the tactics and strategies that groups adopt in different situations.

A broad view of intergroup activity is interaction between individuals from different groups. Consequently, interpersonal conflict, intragroup conflict and organisational conflict are included.

## CONFLICT EFFECTS

Organisational conflict is inevitable due to personality clashes and incompatible pressures or influences. Each member has certain roles, objectives and responsibilities which may be frustrated by others who induce barriers and do not co-operate.

There are many outcomes. Constructively used, conflict may create a more dynamic group which is creative, solves problems more easily, makes better decisions and is generally more productive.

Unfortunately, many adverse effects are seen such as high mental stress, un-cooperative group behaviour, misalignment of goals between the group and the organisation, various stages of group disintegration, irrational and illogical conduct, and communication breakdowns.

## COMPETITION BETWEEN GROUPS

A useful introduction to this subject is to examine the classical work of Sherif in 1953. Although the survey was conducted at a boys' camp in the USA, it clearly illustrates the problems. Two groups were formed and deliberately arranged to encourage separate identities. Boys having no particular ties with each other were chosen for each group. They soon integrated, however, and the climate changed from play-oriented to work-oriented, leadership became more autocratic and the group became highly structured with considerable conformity and loyalty.

Each group gradually began to view the other as the enemy which induced hostility and reduced communication. This situation caused negative, stereotyped opinions (Fig. 5.5).

Understandably, other factors should be considered when relating Sherif's work to companies, typically economic and market conditions, the external environment and the existing organisation structure. Two aspects emerge (1) the states of differentiation, which include specialisation, attitudes and managerial behaviour; (2) integration in the structure, which is the degree of collaboration between departments.

## CAUSES OF INTERGROUP CONFLICT

An important feature of Sherif's study is the strong indication of several causes. These are communication problems through differences in work orientation, co-ordination difficulties through task

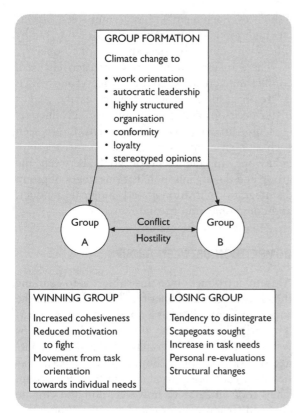

**Figure 5.5** Sherif's survey of intergroup activity in a US boys' camp
Two groups were formed and deliberately arranged to encourage separate identities. Each group gradually began to view the other as the enemy; hostility increased; both the winning group and the losing group demonstrated particular tendencies; there were advantages and disadvantages of success and failure.

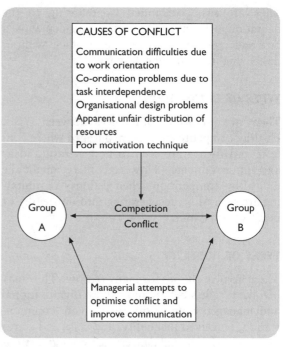

**Figure 5.6** Causes of intergroup conflict
The outcome of Sherif's study indicated several causes of conflict. The supervisor must accept the philosophy that conflict is healthy and inevitable; he or she must diagnose the causes, establish rules that optimise, and resolve high conflicts by adopting appropriate techniques.

interdependence, organisational design problems, apparent unfair distribution of resources, and poor motivation techniques. Figure 5.6 illustrates the situation.

Recent research has revealed further causes of conflict:

- different frames of reference which affect members of a group by influencing perception and interpretation of events
- being forced to compete for limited resources
- general lack of organisational co-ordination
- different interpretation of goals and organisational aims
- misplaced loyalty to group members which conflicts with loyalty to the department or company

### Reducing intergroup conflict

Possible approaches include:

- ensuring that frames of reference coincide
- adapting a fair method of allocating limited resources
- improving co-ordination through using matrix structures and enhancing social interaction
- attempting to reduce role stress (Chapter 13)
- exchanging members between groups, and varying tasks

### INTRAGROUP ACTIVITY

The usual changes within a group during intergroup conflict are:

- increased cohesiveness
- more autocratic leadership to create high responsiveness
- increased structural rigidity
- more concern for high performance
- stronger loyalty towards the group
- discouragement of external social interaction
- strong control and punishment for deviation from norms
- increased formal climate
- improved co-ordination
- allocation of specific responsibilities

## Intragroup conflict

Intragroup conflict may occur for various reasons such as some members not conforming with expected norms, personality clashes, difficulties with new technologies, perception problems, communication difficulties, bullying, rigid outlooks, poor working conditions, low wage levels, and job insecurity. The symptoms are low output, high absenteeism, lateness, general ill-feeling and an increasing number of grievances. Resolving intragroup conflict may involve changing the group leader, improving training, or transferring some members.

## The teams concept

Successful intragroup activity creates a team where all members voluntarily co-ordinate their work, correctly interpret their roles, and are interdependent. Many characteristics distinguish a team from unsuccessful groups. Some examples are:

- acceptance of the leader who represents the team and strongly supports it
- strong social interaction and mutual support
- high group cohesion
- acceptance of group norms
- strong team spirit which allows for role interchange, support for each member by encouraging and helping out, and ensuring fair workloads
- high output levels and quality work

All teams are groups, but all groups are not teams. Team spirit must be maintained and constantly developed through democratic leadership where

fairness and justice are paramount, firm support is essential, new ideas are generated and used, and synergy is created.

## HOSTILE ACTIVITY

Conflict causes changes in perception, attitude and behaviour, both within groups and between groups. Favourable changes may occur if conflict is reduced to an optimal level since this achieves higher productivity and improved relationships.

However, high conflict levels cause enmity and sometimes vicious behaviour. Examples are sports where players use verbal abuse and even physical violence against each other, a referee or a spectator, especially if money is at stake.

## Observable changes in group relations

When hostility rises beyond sensible levels between groups the tendencies are:

- a decrease in communication
- perception distortion
- less interaction
- overemphasis of enmity
- personal or group goals often overriding company goals
- a reduction in problem-solving and decision-making orientation, leading to an emotional win-or-lose orientation

Classical examples in the UK are some negotiations between trade unions and companies.

# Resolving unhealthy conflict

There are many ways to resolve unhealthy conflict, but choosing the appropriate one may be difficult. This may depend upon contingencies, the environment, the technology and the needs of individuals, groups and tasks. The first step is to attempt a diagnosis of the conflict. The second step is to choose a course of action, based upon that diagnosis.

## DIAGNOSE THE CONFLICT

Attempt to encourage the group members to list their points of view or ideas. When completed, examine each one by introducing the evidence or justification, but avoiding any emotional arguments, criticisms of other views, or negative thinking. Ask each member to consider any possibilities that may prove to be a positive contribution towards each idea. List the findings for each view and examine carefully any similarities. Usually the emotion or conflict element is reduced. Members see other viewpoints, good and bad points emerge, and possibilities of agreement become apparent.

## COURSES OF ACTION

Courses of action include direct action, indirect action, de-escalation techniques, compromise and team building.

## DIRECT ACTION

One approach is to redesign the structure at the trouble spot. Reducing task interdependence and clarifying task responsibilities is possible, but building in joint work responsibilities may cause more conflict. Usually the aim is to create self-contained workgroups with sufficient resources. A controversial approach is to bring together both groups and allow them to sort out difficulties with a minimum of guidance. A fundamental requirement is to have a feel for the situation and to act accordingly.

### Power and influence

Undertaking this approach should not be attempted unless the supervisor feels confident to exert sufficient power or influence. You should read Chapter 13 before considering direct action.

## INDIRECT ACTION

One indirect action is to impose a rule which will delay an upheaval and allow time for investigation. Another is to wait and see if the issue disperses naturally. Both methods are useful if a minor issue is believed to be hiding a deeper problem.

### The dangers

Indirect action is valid if there is insufficient information available immediately to resolve the situation in a logical and acceptable manner.

However, it should not be used as an excuse to avoid solving the problem; invariably the trouble will occur again, probably with increased emotional reactions.

## DE-ESCALATION TECHNIQUES

These are attempts to defuse, deflect or smooth over conflict. Skilful discussion may convince the group that the issue is of minor consequence or that essentially both parties' views are similar. This delaying tactic allows tempers to cool and gives the group time to reconsider more logically.

## COMPROMISE

Compromise may work if mature groups are involved. Bargaining is a popular means, although it is criticised because of lack of openness and an absence of genuine problem solving. Another means is to increase contact or communication between warring groups so that stereotyped views disperse. However, one view sees increased interaction as providing more opportunity to reinforce negative views. Structuring the interaction to avoid sensitive areas is one answer.

### Negotiation

Negotiating skills are discussed in Chapter 20. Read it carefully before attempting to compromise. One view is that resolving conflict is on a sliding scale from an unacceptable solution, through an acceptable compromise, to an ideal solution. This means the aim is to move carefully towards the ideal but to understand the nature of compromise.

# Team building

There are two approaches to team building. One is for existing teams performing an established number of tasks. The other is for teams formed to execute a set purpose, e.g. a project team or an interdepartmental working party.

## EXISTING TEAMS

The supervisor will usually be involved with existing teams. The approach is to concentrate on the following aspects: emphasising the achievement of certain objectives by using techniques for problem solving, decision making and goal setting; developing and maintaining interpersonal relationships within the group; coaching and counselling to improve the organisational culture; interpreting rules; and dealing with empowerment difficulties.

## The competent team

The outcome of development by the supervisor should be:

- sound and enjoyable communication between members
- a continuous improvement philosophy
- capability to overcome difficult problems
- encouraging each other to improve performance and to improve capability
- high morale, stability and strong cohesiveness

## Procedural factors

Procedural factors are inclined to follow set patterns as inevitable changes occur which tend to upset the team. Briefly, the first sign is a reaction which is noticed or brought to the supervisor's attention. In an effective organisation the need for change is communicated and discussed. Alternatively, the supervisor will have to explain and present a logical case for the team to adjust. This demands trust and willingness to accept the situation.

If accepted and the team is sufficiently developed, the members diagnose and make action plans to reach a revised objective. Finally, taking action according to plans should lead to more effective performance. Such team building is more complex in practice and demanding on the supervisor's time.

## The team leader

Training the team leader involves courses in:

- coaching and counselling
- self-confidence in the leader and in team members
- understanding group dynamics
- team development
- techniques for adjusting difficulties
- human relations
- observation techniques

## Leadership qualities

The classic role conforms to adaptive leadership within contingency theories described in Chapter 13. The development of leadership skills is essential before any team will recognise the leader, have trust, and be willing to confide.

## SET-PURPOSE TEAMS

Teams created for a set purpose are involved in establishing objectives; dealing with special problems as they arise concerning resources, employees and finance; and attempting to resolve them as the work develops. Relationships and communication need special attention considering the diversity of team members and their locations. Some flexibility is needed as roles become firmer and more clearly defined.

## QUESTIONS

1 Outline the process of group formation; indicate the importance of interaction, development and power.

2 Are there likely to be any effects on group cohesiveness when people of differing national cultures are brought together? Explain your answer.

3 Should there be any change in a person's role competence through additional education and training? Give a reasoned answer considering the effect on the person if his or her roles were previously rejected by the group.

4 Define group cohesiveness.

5 Give reasons why group objectives may differ from organisational objectives.

6 Explain social interaction in a group.

7 Why are informal groups formed?

8 Explain norm formation.

9 Why should a person change when joining a group?

10 What are the likely advantages of forming autonomous workgroups?

11 Discuss the importance of formal and informal roles.

12 How may a group develop power?

13 Discuss the constructive use of conflict.

14 What are the main causes of intergroup conflict?

15 Outline the main approaches to resolving conflict.

16 Discuss the importance of teamwork.

17 Outline an autonomous workgroup development programme.

18 Outline a team development process.

19 How may team maintenance be achieved?

20 Discuss the possible disrupting influences within a workgroup.

21 How would you recognise an effective team?

22 Discuss the main types of conflict occurring in an organisation.

23 What approaches are available to resolve unhealthy conflict?

## CASE STUDY

Five assembly workers were mainly left to their own devices. Brown, their supervisor, was applying pressure to make them increase their output, but how they achieved it was left to the group. The following comments were overheard by the supervisor.

Jim:    I haven't so much energy now at my age. I'm working as hard as I can, but I know I'm holding you others up.

Ken:    I can easily do more work but Jim slows me down. We don't want to get Jim into trouble do we.

Ivor:    I try to help Jim out whenever I can, but I have to be careful that Brown doesn't see me.

Sid:    I haven't got enough to do in this set-up, but I haven't got the skill to help Jim. Why can't Brown see what the trouble is?

Harry:    I'm like Sid. I could rearrange this assembly easily and we would all be happier, but what's the use, Brown's on an easy number and couldn't care less about us.

Comment on the supervisor's attitude and his handling of the group. Consider why the group are left to their own devices but make no attempt to change the working arrangements.

## CASE STUDY

The output at Sunturn Ltd is continually being disrupted by faulty workmanship at the components manufacture stage where five groups are employed before final assembly. Costs are rising sharply as more employees are switched to replacing the faulty components.

Frank Jones, the works manager, decides to adopt the concept of semi-autonomous groups, holds a meeting with the five supervisors and tells them to start the new programme in six weeks' time. It consists of job rotation within each group and each worker is responsible for checking quality. Appropriate arrangements are made to commence training immediately.

To Frank's surprise, next morning two groups have downed tools and refuse to continue work unless he drops the new scheme. The two supervisors concerned report to him and are puzzled as their groups have the best record for output and quality. Frank cannot understand the situation, 'I expected your groups to welcome the idea. It's in their own interests considering the others are causing the problem'. The supervisors cannot offer any explanation.

Comment on the behaviour of the two groups and discuss Frank's method of introducing the new scheme. How could the situation be rectified now?

## CASE STUDY

Ralph, unemployed for a year, is pleased to be starting work again at his old factory where business has picked up. He worked in main assembly before, but this time his job is in goods inwards. His job is to locate parts and deliver them to the counter. After a while he realises that the computer files are incorrect and often finds parts that are supposedly out of stock.

Other people in the group are annoyed when they are told by the fitters, 'Not you, where's Ralph? He always manages to find what we want'. Soon Ralph is shunned, excluded from the usual lunch time chats and tea break get-togethers and generally ignored.

The chief storekeeper notices and asks Ralph for an explanation. 'I don't know why they're giving me the cold shoulder. I pull my weight, manage to find parts apparently out-of-stock and the fitters seem happy. I know what it's like on bonus in main assembly when you're held up for spares.'

'Ah', is all the chief storekeeper says and walks away.

A week later Gloria, one of the goods inwards employees who always has plenty to say, approaches Ralph. 'Look, mate, you don't seem to get the message. Unless you work like the rest of us you're in dead trouble.'

Ralph loses his temper. 'I don't give a damn for you lot. You haven't worked in main assembly – I have. You're just a lazy lot who don't care for anyone or anything!'

*Comment on the goods inwards group. As chief storekeeper how would you have tackled the problem? Also, are there any fundamental organisational difficulties apparent from this case?*

# 6

# Industry and business

## Introduction

Employees are now far more aware of the economic, political and social forces that affect them directly and indirectly. Consequently, the supervisor must accept these pressures, know how they affect outlooks and be able to discuss them rationally with colleagues.

These forces are often subject to misconceptions and bewilderment. Many related topics tend to interact with each other and cause conflicting views which are constantly expressed through the media.

Due to its long history, traditional practices and unique culture, British industry is complex and difficult to visualise clearly. Unfortunately, comprehensive coverage is not possible in this chapter. Certain subjects have been chosen for discussion that arouse differing views and which are of general interest. They include:

- the industrial structure
- historical features
- the 1990s
- the government
- environmental forces
- green issues
- effective economies
- business structure
- human assets
- the European Union

## The industrial structure

The main items of interest are scarce resources, opportunity costs, interdependence, structural change, growth of the service sector, trading blocs and business strategy.

### SCARCE RESOURCES

Resources are *scarce* when related to their number of uses. The two main types are physical and natural resources, and human resources. Such scarcity exists due to lack of availability and people's insatiable wants. Some resources are irreplaceable, such as certain minerals which cannot be created when resources are finished. Another factor is the effect on some resources when fumes are released into the atmosphere. Also skilled labour may be a problem unless there are adequate training programmes.

### OPPORTUNITY COSTS

A resource used to produce an item can only be used once. Therefore, a sacrifice is made because that resource cannot be used to make something else. Consequently, the real cost (or opportunity cost) is the next best use for that resource. A country that uses its resources to make armaments cannot use these resources to improve its infrastructure. A farmer may decide to grow wheat rather than potatoes, so the opportunity cost of the wheat is the potatoes.

### INTERDEPENDENCE

There is a constant state of flux (or flow of change) between organisations and the environment. Slow changes occur in some activities whereas rapid changes occur in others. This continuum of slow to rapid change makes decisions difficult unless careful assessments ensure an awareness of situations. Hence the importance of creativity and ideas, and actually using them as changes occur.

## STRUCTURAL CHANGE

From about 1960 an important trend has developed; it is called deindustrialisation. Manufacturing jobs have slumped but service jobs have boomed. Also self-employment has grown, along with more small companies. Consequently, if the standard of living does not drop it means there is a decline in the importance of industry. However, production has continued to increase, there is more variety, new models are replacing old ones more rapidly, and the standard of living has actually increased.

Such deindustrialisation means manufacturing has improved in terms of smaller-sized establishments, quality of product, effectiveness, and in response to environmental dangers. Now nearly every country has a reduced workforce in industry and an increased number in services.

There are many explanations for deindustrialisation in a country. Typical reasons are discovery of a natural resource; reduced competitiveness which results in fewer exports and more imports, causing major problems; competition from low wage countries; a high value of the currency; high interest rates coupled with low productivity levels relative to other countries.

## THE SERVICE SECTOR

The service sector continues to grow and its effectiveness is a key factor in raising living standards. The reasons for growth are usually attributed to a higher proportion of incomes spent on services when a country becomes richer and productivity improvements are more difficult within the service sector. A more involved reason is that as countries become richer they use their money to invest in manufacturing in other developing countries; the rewards are profit, dividends and interest on investments, which are then spent on leisure activities.

## TRADING BLOCS

Trading blocs also have a powerful effect on structural change. There are now three main blocs:

- the European Union
- the North American Free Trade Area (USA, Canada and Mexico)
- Japan and the Association of South-East Asian Nations (ASEAN)

Although the blocs have some restrictions on imports, on the whole they are not very restrictive. They are rapidly developing and using new technologies, which is causing concern in countries outside the blocs.

### China

The demand from China for various commodities, especially scrap metal, has increased drastically. There are 1.2 billion consumers in the world's fastest-growing marketplace. China has an enormous production capability and offers cheaper manufacture compared with many countries previously noted for their low costs. Some famous companies are already investing and operating in China. There are problems such as local corruption and possible political instability. However, the country offers spectacular opportunities.

## BUSINESS STRATEGY

Structural change places a particular burden on the role of senior managers. They must determine strategy for the business and revise it based upon many factors. This decision-making process at strategic level depends partly upon the aims of the business.

A selection of the aims is:

- to provide the owners and shareholders with appropriate financial rewards
- to maximise or optimise profit
- to provide the community with a quality product or service at an appropriate price
- to maximise sales
- to protect the business by operating in many markets
- to determine how to promote rapid growth

Note how strategic decisions are restricted to ensuring there is a clear purpose to guide tactical decision making. Strategic questions are mainly associated with the following factors:

- the long-term direction of the organisation
- the determination of organisational change
- the range of organisational activities
- the human aspects, considering values, expectations, ethics and moral conduct
- the external and internal environment
- all the available resources of use to the organisation

There are many wide-ranging questions to be answered for each one of these items before sensible decisions are possible. Indeed the interaction between the items and the financial implications are major considerations and demand expertise of a high order for senior managers.

# Historical features

The UK was in a unique position during the eighteenth century, a time of great industrial change and expansion. The UK had many natural advantages:

- climate
- geographical position
- harbours
- navigable rivers
- supplies of coal and iron

These were supplemented by political and financial stability. Industry gradually developed and the outcome was the Industrial Revolution.

The emergence of the UK as a superpower because of the Industrial Revolution and the impetus for the revolution itself, were due to those with drive, initiative, inventiveness and business acumen. They had unrestricted opportunities to develop the country and many main industries emerged: textiles, coal, iron, steel and engineering, including railways and canals. New machinery, new techniques and improved communication and transport created large-scale production.

## THE RELATIVE DECLINE

According to some records, the relative decline started around 1880 and was accelerated by two world wars. Many causes have been proposed. Certainly, during the UK's rise to power, self-sufficiency was replaced by entering world markets and integrating with other countries' economies. Thus the development of the USA and Germany, and their emergence as successful competitors weakened the home economy.

Unfortunately, previous success caused complacency and naive notions, and profits were steered away from industry. Eventually, the outcome was antiquated plant and machinery, less superior products compared with others available, failure to exploit new ideas and the spread of a general industrial malaise across the country.

## WORLD WAR II

Typical situations in World War II illustrate other difficulties. Even during this critical period, the UK's performance was poor. The term 'British disease' already existed despite government propaganda to the contrary at the time. The so-called magnificent war effort was fictitious. Output compared with Germany was 80 per cent for aircraft and machine tool industries, 84 per cent for coal and 70 per cent for aero-engines.

The British machine tool industry could not cope with demand from wartime factories. The USA supplied enormous quantities to fill the gap, whereas Germany tooled most of her factories herself.

Research and development scientists who invented many famous technological devices were often not familiar with production requirements. Consequently, there were many delays and much reliance on supplies of American components.

### Education and training

In 1939 education and training in the UK was deplorable and well behind that of Germany and the USA. Typical examples in the UK are:

- no management or business schools
- 700 graduate engineers a year compared with 1900 in Germany plus 2000 qualified practical engineers
- 20 000 in part-time further education, compared with 1.8 million in Germany

### Strikes and stoppages

Strikes and stoppages were commonplace and increased year by year during the war. Walkouts often seemed to be for trivial reasons. There were strikes in coal mines, the unions strongly resisted the introduction of new technologies in the aircraft industry, and there were countless arguments and disruptions over staffing levels. A typical example was in the shipping industry: the union insisted that a riveter's mate, who otherwise would be redundant, should remain on full pay and watch over a riveter when hand riveting was replaced by pneumatic riveting.

## EARLY POST-WAR HISTORY

The end of World War II marked a drastic change in the financial position of the UK. Before the war it had enjoyed a long reputation as a creditor nation, mainly because of flourishing export markets. The cost of the war had meant selling many foreign investments and severe restrictions on exports, so the UK entered a precarious phase of financial instability.

Debts amounted to £3500 million and these were blocked by the government. Aid from the USA included a loan of about £1000 million, which was soon spent. This was followed by a gift of goods valued at nearly £1500 million under the Marshall Plan, as part of a scheme of assistance to many European nations, including West Germany and Italy.

The urgent need to increase exports was thrust upon industry under changed conditions where:

- the workforce had become highly organised and fully employed
- greater spending power existed in the home market, which tended to distract from exporting
- extensive government influence over many aspects of industry had increased

## HALF-TIME BRITAIN (1950–79)

World trade boomed in the late forties and early fifties and tended to hide the UK's industrial problems. In the late fifties the country was dubbed 'Half-time Britain', when performance was compared with other successful countries. Clearly the weaknesses were persisting and especially noticeable compared with Japan. Government finance and industry were unable to work together to exploit

technological changes, and there was a lack of long-term planning.

Stagnation continued in the sixties and seventies. During the period 1955–1973, productivity (output per person per year) in manufacturing industry grew at about 3.2 per cent compared with about 5 per cent in West Germany, France, Belgium, Italy and the Netherlands. The cumulative effect was substantial. Real earnings grew at an average rate of 2.0 per cent in the UK, 8.1 per cent in Japan, 6.2 per cent in Italy, 4.5 per cent in West Germany, and 4.3 per cent in France.

The trend was clear, although complete analysis would include other factors, typically output trends, investment, profitability and exchange rates.

By 1979 there was industrial turmoil and unions were very powerful. In 1979 strikes cost about 27.5 million working days; this dropped to 759 000 in 1991.

## NEW POLICIES (1981–90)

The government started a programme of radical changes which included labour legislation to reduce the power of the trade unions. Traditional industrial practices were slowly abandoned, government support increased and more confidence developed. Redundancy programmes and plant closures reduced overstaffing of the workforce and obsolete practices. Efficiency improved as some countries were experiencing recession, but high unemployment and lethargic management remained.

Further changes included privatisation and adopting the rule of market forces, but much of industry was left without the skills or the resources to compete overseas. Industry started to apply new management practices, including corporate aggression and quality circles, but with little success.

The government's policy of creating a property-owning and share-owning democracy encouraged a spending spree. Cheap loans and tax cuts caused a balance of payments crisis, wage and price inflation, and an increase in imports. Drastic steps to reduce inflation were undertaken. Other countries continued to exploit markets, notably Japan and West Germany, while the UK failed to take advantage of microelectronics, information technology and other technologies.

## Productivity in the 1980s

At least the radical changes had caused output per person in the 1980s to grow faster than any other leading country, except Japan. This was in marked contrast to previous decades when the UK almost invariably lagged behind. Here are some average annual percentage changes for manufacturing industry:

1960–70  UK = 3.0  G7 average = 4.5
1970–80  UK = 1.6  G7 average = 3.3
1980–88  UK = 5.2  G7 average = 3.6

The G7 countries are the USA, the UK, France, Germany, Japan, Italy and Canada. Now Russia has been included to create the G8. This striking improvement had been sustained through the years of continued growth, indicating a fundamental change in performance.

# The 1990s

By 1990 Japan and Germany were economically strong, East and West Germany were reunited, the USSR had collapsed, the USA was the remaining superpower, the Middle East was politically unstable, and the EC (now EU) pondered the Single European Market, concepts of federalism and a single currency.

In the UK a paradox exists. World status and power is declining but this is accompanied by rising material wealth – most people are better off than they were in 1900. Also, a well-known fault is prevalent: many know how to improve the economy but are powerless, whereas those who are able to take action refuse to participate.

Four main features of this era are now considered: debatable issues, fundamental weaknesses, competing overseas, and positive aspects of the UK economy. These topics naturally tend to overlap. (The external issues associated with the Single European Market are covered later.) Finally the UK recession and recovery are discussed.

## DEBATABLE ISSUES

According to professional scholars, there are important issues which are debatable. Briefly these are:

- Economic policy, including monetary policy and federalism.
- The welfare state (or social democratic state), which is a valuable social service but has restricted the capability to create wealth to finance it.
- A deadlocked political system.
- An anti-industrial political culture, created by the culture of the ruling class and the culture of the labour movement. The probable outcomes are enforced egalitarianism which discourages entrepreneurial activity; fewer rewards for enterprise and responsibility; hostility towards profits; and the weakening of economic management, self-reliance and initiative.

## FUNDAMENTAL WEAKNESSES IN THE ECONOMY

- Underinvestment in research and development; education and training of the workforce and management; and equipment.
- Poor attitudes created by status, lack of participation and collaboration, distribution of wealth, class (the Establishment) and militant trade unions. These have caused low mutual forbearance.
- Poor quality products sustained by low workforce skills and a slow application of design and technology.
- Feebleness in the boardrooms, evidenced by corporate disasters and decisions that upset the workforce and local community.
- Incompetent management, although some improvements have been noticed. Tax cuts and other fiscal and non-fiscal advantages have rewarded managers who have not performed any better than before.
- Competitive potential weakened by cutting back jobs, products and plant to raise productivity.
- Complacency everywhere, and little awareness of the need for rapid and radical change.
- Narrowing manufacturing base, which seems to indicate too much reliance on imported goods and an expanding service industry to compensate.
- False idea that a service-led economy allows a reduction in manufacturing without creating problems.
- Lack of internal competition caused by mergers and protectionist policies. These ignore the idea

that the greater the number of competitors, the greater the national competitive advantage.

- Lack of a sound knowledge base or a firm market share to compete in world markets.
- Incorrect type of education and training. Apparently too many people believe they are able to fulfil a destiny that is below their capacity.
- Workers who price themselves out of a job while managers let them do it. In other words, inflationary pay settlements.
- Inadequate government, which ignores the business cycle and is incapable of effectively managing the economy.
- Banks and industry influenced by strong short-term pressures to perform at the expense of long-term planning.

## COMPETING OVERSEAS

According to a cross-section of specialists, the following major requirements are essential if the UK is to become internationally competitive:

- A government which uses effectively outstanding specialists in all economic operations; conducts consistent, sound, long-term policies to control inflation; and encourages industrial growth.
- A financial system which is brought into line with European policies (especially in Germany) to promote and provide long-term monetary investment programmes.
- A new financial strategy which is aligned with a revised financial system (see above).
- A marketing strategy which uses specialists and reorientates attitudes to product quality, customer care, delivery dates and after-sales service.
- An upgraded workforce created by locating, engaging and training suitable employees to a high performance level. This includes encouraging participation and giving more responsibility, upgrading teamwork and creating conscientious employees, and giving due regard to their health, safety and welfare.
- The workforce, trade unions and management should recognise the eventual commonality of interest in survival, work closely together, ignore outdated pressure groups, and have due regard for all human assets.

- A lean production base which closes unproductive plants, relieves older workers of excessive stress if they cannot adapt, reduces inventories, invests in automation and new technologies, and adopts cost-cutting measures in all functions to improve effectiveness.
- A national education and training system geared to the needs of industry.
- Improved rewards for workers which include adequate payments to highly capable people, a fair distribution of rewards, and avoidance of excessive rewards which cause resentment.
- Industry is seen as respectable. This involves a revised image which emphasises its vital nature and attracts high quality individuals.
- Heavy investment programmes in new technologies.
- Full utilisation of all current technologies in manufacturing and administrative functions.

## POSITIVE ASPECTS OF THE UK ECONOMY

One view is that an economic revolution has occurred already through government policy in the 1980s. This view is based upon the changes in a number of economic factors:

- Productivity improvements are continuing.
- Inflation is now low.
- The workforce is now disciplined to a low inflation economy.
- Industrial disputes are infrequent; this encourages a high inflow of overseas investment.
- The population is now geared to reducing debt and increasing savings.
- Privatisation of nationalised industries has been very successful.
- The housing boom has collapsed through high interest rates and recession, but is slowly recovering. This has resulted in treating ownership as a lifelong investment (not speculation) and routeing funds to the equity market.
- Export confidence has improved. According to some indicators, there are good or excellent expectations of orders for about 60 per cent of exporting companies. Nevertheless, the 'tiger economies' of Asia-Pacific seem to pose the greatest threat to the competitiveness of British exports.

Taking into account all factors, it could be argued that recovery may be easier when world recession eases compared with the situation in the 1970s, provided there is no reversal of these favourable aspects. Other views claim that industry has suffered too severely from the measures used to bring about these changes.

## THE UK RECESSION AND RECOVERY

The UK economy is slowly recovering from the 1990–92 recession. Unlike the previous two recessions (1974–75 and 1980–81), which were due to sharp increases in crude oil prices and were worldwide, the 1990–92 recession was attributed to a period of unsustainably fast growth in the UK during the late 1980s.

A recession may be defined in many ways. The usual convention is when two or more consecutive quarters of falling output occur. However, if the economy grew strongly beforehand, the effect may be slight; therefore judgement is needed in deciding whether it is a full recession. Another way is to adopt a situation where the output level is below its long-term trend, but this may imply that a recession often occurs and could include times when the economy is growing fast.

During the 1990–92 recession firms shed labour more quickly. Employment fell and unemployment rose ahead of the decline in output, compared with the previous two recessions. Unemployment usually tends to lag behind recovery and continues to rise. But in the 1990–92 recession there seems to have been an improved labour market performance, which may mean a more flexible labour market, considering trade union reform and an increase in part-time employees.

### Recovery

Recovery has been difficult because of a worldwide recession. In Europe the German reunification caused an economic slowdown as Germany raised interest rates to pay for money invested in the poorer East German sector.

In the UK, recovery seems to be established as consumer spending and exports increase. Interest rates are now low and there is a strong growth of real disposable income which increases spending power. A lower exchange rate and falling wage costs have contributed to an improvement in competitiveness abroad.

### The productivity factor

According to one recent survey by management consultants McKinsey, the UK is still on half-time, compared with foreign rivals. This situation is despite productivity improvements. Labour productivity in the UK automotive industry is 50 per cent below Japan's; US hotel productivity is twice the UKs; and the UK telecom sector achieved only 55 per cent of best-in-class performance.

It seems that UK companies are un-coordinated and slow to react to customer requirements. The McKinsey study showed that overall UK labour productivity was 73 per cent of the US level.

# The government

The two main issues of government control often discussed are the extent of its role in industry and the degree of influence exerted on industry.

The government's role may be viewed as removing defects of the marketing system by introducing more planning and control of resources, or being limited to supplying public goods and improving the market system. Public goods benefit everyone, typically national defence, the police force and the judiciary. This role is important since the market system has inherent weaknesses and is unable to deliver certain types of goods.

The extended government influence today really amounts to the state assuming, in many respects, the function of top management of industry. By means of budgets, the demand for goods and services can be varied, growth adjusted, inflation checked and modernisation programmes encouraged. Government investment schemes also play a very important part in the economy.

The main topics of particular interest in this area are now discussed. They include the private and public sectors, nationalised industries and privatisation, wider share ownership, monetary policy, economic operations, information technology, and manpower development.

## THE PRIVATE SECTOR

In a mixed economy the private sector comprises privately owned companies independent of the government. They represent about 70 per cent of commercial firms and about 50 per cent of the economy.

To survive in free enterprise, a firm must make a profit so that supply becomes adjustable to price changes. Although profit is a debatable topic, it is certainly essential to finance growth, replace obsolescent and obsolete equipment, and compensate investors. The amount of profit which should be made is inevitably subject to fierce argument.

### Private Finance Initiative

In 1992 the government launched the Private Finance Initiative, the aim being to involve the private sector in financing and managing services and projects which were previously the government's responsibility. This scheme provides the opportunity for private sector skills and expertise to improve public services and so give better value to the taxpayer. Included are infrastructure projects, the prison service and patient care.

The government has sought to contract out services which could be more efficiently provided by the private sector. This means the public sector is changing from being a supplier of services to being a consumer of services.

Justification lies in the previous poor performance of the public sector's projects, considering design, construction, cost and time. Designs are often overelaborate or overengineered in the public sector, and there is little concern for striking a balance between costs, return and risk. Furthermore, there are construction risks where a balance between quality and future expenditure on maintenance and usage is neglected.

There are two essential requirements: the private sector must genuinely accept risk; and value for money must be demonstrated for any expenditure by the public sector. About ninety projects have been completed, are under way or are being considered. Typical examples are the Channel Tunnel, the Dartford River Crossing and the Severn River Crossing.

## THE PUBLIC SECTOR AND GOVERNMENT

Owned by the state and under government control, the public sector and government employ about 7 million people and they include nationalised industries, governmental and local authority services, and various agencies. These institutions are established to protect the public interest. Typical justifications are natural monopolies, high capital requirements, social essentials, natural rights, general safety and national importance.

### Structures

The government authorises and is responsible for the structural organisations. Distinct forms are the Civil Service, local and regional authorities, public corporations, nationalised industries, licensed monopoly and joint ownership.

### Monopolies

The Monopolies and Restrictive Practices Act 1948 was passed to counter certain business practices thought to be against the public interest. By definition, public interest covers efficient production, sufficient output and appropriate prices to meet demand at home and overseas.

The Monopolies Commission investigates, analyses and reports on industries where a few large firms dominate the market through assumed collusion. The government may refer a case to the commission and, after receiving a report, the minister responsible decides whether any action is necessary.

### Viewpoints on monopoly control

One view sees control as directly conflicting with the concept that the market is self-regulating and automatically achieves maximum efficiency. Another view supports compulsory intervention by stopping or preventing any firm from dominating the market regardless of the situation. Anti-trust legislation in the USA is based on this concept but has proved difficult to enforce.

More competition has been encouraged in the UK recently. UK legislation aims to improve efficiency by preventing overseas control of key industries, assisting in maintaining competitiveness overseas, taking advantage of economies of scale, and supporting more rationalisation.

## Mergers

Under the Monopolies and Mergers Act 1965, the Department of Trade and Industry (DTI) can refer any merger or proposed merger to the Monopolies Commission provided a monopoly is considered to be strengthened or a monopoly created and assets exceed £5 million.

Some companies are deterred by the knowledge that the proposed merger will be referred to the commission. Others pursue proposals if initially refused by persevering with new schemes.

Substantial evidence on the benefits of mergers is often difficult to obtain. Typical justifications are to improve efficiency and effectiveness, in particular to take advantage of the increase in size to pursue research and development projects; use the particular expertise of managers in both concerns; create more marketing outlets and so compete more effectively against overseas concerns.

## Restrictive trade practices

Abolishing or curtailing restrictive trade practices is a vital part of making markets more competitive. In recent years there has been growing evidence of evading legislation by failing to register agreements and by careful drafting of some agreements, although they have anticompetitive effects. Also, an increasing number of unobjectionable agreements are being caught by existing legislation.

The present system is similar to the situation established in the 1950s and consists of 1976 legislation: the Restrictive Trade Practices Act, the Resale Prices Act and the Restrictive Practices Court Act. Proposed new legislation will overcome the present flaw of action being directed against the form of agreements rather than their effect. It will apply to all sectors of the economy, including the professions; deal more effectively with agreements that damage competition; reduce unnecessary administrative burdens on firms; and make UK law compatible with the current approach in the EU.

## The public sector borrowing requirement

The public sector borrowing requirement (PSBR) is the main measure of the difference between income and expenditure of the public sector, which includes central government, local authorities and public corporations. The PSBR has been highlighted recently since borrowing in 1994 rose to £50 billion and is projected to fall to £2 billion by 1999. If public spending exceeds revenue from taxes and other sources, the public sector becomes a net borrower.

Central government expenditure is met by tax and other revenue, borrowing through government stock issues and National Savings, or running down the stock of liquid assets. Public corporations expenditure is met by borrowing from central government, and market and overseas borrowing. Local authorities expenditure is met by council tax and other income, and borrowing from central government.

During recessions the PSBR tends to increase as expenditure rises on benefits to the unemployed and tax revenues fall. During recovery the revenues, spending and profits increase with higher levels of earnings. The government aims to restore sound public finances which help sustainable recovery. Keeping interest rates low, restraining expenditure and increasing taxes are all part of a complex process which seems to be easy, but forecasting economic (and political) side effects is difficult.

## NATIONALISED INDUSTRIES AND PRIVATISATION

The drive to nationalise after World War II was mainly ideological and sometimes due to industrial unrest, abuse of a natural monopoly and trade union influence. Many major industries were nationalised by 1977. They represented by then about 8 per cent of the labour force, 11 per cent of total output and 20 per cent of total gross investment in fixed capital.

Government intervention in this extreme form has been subjected to continual political controversy. One view sees nationalisation as beneficial because it stops a small group of capitalists from dominating society's interests. An opposing view sees nationalisation as detrimental because it concentrates economic power within one enterprise, considering it better to disperse this among private firms.

## Nationalisation problems

Often nationalised industries (NIs) have not performed in accordance with their main advocates' ideas. In some cases they have fallen below the levels achieved by their counterparts in private enterprise. Typical criticisms are that many constitutional problems arise: the concept of monopoly and its faults persists; a tendency to be subsidised if losses occur, thus leading to complacency and lack of market discipline; industrial relations have not improved; a 'take it or leave it' outlook; and overcaution in decision making develop.

## Privatisation

Due to the problems mentioned and the many criticisms of NIs, the new government of 1979 decided to return them to the private sector. The main aims of privatisation are to remove government influence, encourage wider share ownership, expose concerns to capital market disciplines, improve prospects for competition, and subject monopoly power to detailed regulation.

## WIDER SHARE OWNERSHIP

Privatisations and other share issues have led to an increase in the number of people buying company shares. About 25 per cent of the public now hold shares in at least one company, but the proportion of UK equities held directly by the public has fallen. Shareholder power still remains with large financial institutions.

To encourage wider share ownership (WSO) the government launched personal equity plans (PEPs) in 1987, which offered exemption from capital gains and from income tax normally levied on dividends. PEPs have not been very successful, but employers' share schemes have been popular. About 2 million workers currently hold such shares or share options, but they only account for 1 per cent of the total equity market. The government also supports employee share ownership plans (ESOPs); corporation tax relief is available for any contributions made to ESOP trusts meeting certain conditions. From 6 April 1999 PEPs have been superseded by Individual Savings Accounts (ISA).

## Apprehensions

The main barriers to WSO becoming more widespread are failure to appreciate the benefits of share ownership, poor knowledge, unfavourable tax treatment, high transaction costs, scarce information on buying and selling shares, and the belief that shares are a risky investment. Indeed some people save to meet particular future expenditure. Consequently, security and convenience are obviously important considerations, while asset appreciation and dividends are considered less important.

## Benefits

The tangible advantages are that equities consistently give higher rates of return in terms of capital growth and income, compared with many other investments. Rewards are higher than cash deposits and gilts, and they have outpaced inflation over the longer term.

Share ownership should enhance motivation because the employee possesses a personal stake in the business. Indeed there should be more interest in industry, which should lead to a better understanding of the mutual benefits of improving performance. Also, many companies feel individual investors give more loyal support compared with institutions governed by fund managers who, allegedly, have a traditional reputation for investing in the short term.

## Legislation

The Financial Services Act 1986 was introduced to protect both the investor and the integrity of financial markets. Financial services are offered by insurance brokers, insurance companies, commercial banks, building societies, and stockbrokers. Enormous sums are involved considering about 10 million people directly own shares, over 5 million own a personal pension, and 60 per cent of households have at least one life assurance policy. Heavy fines have been imposed on some concerns who have not complied with legislation. The regulations are constantly being strengthened to overcome misconduct.

## MONETARY AND FISCAL POLICY

The government only has a limited control over its economy. By deciding on a fiscal policy (the difference between expenditure and taxation), and a monetary policy (the level and rate of the money supply), it is assumed the correct combination of all the policy instruments will achieve full employment, stable prices and strong, sustainable economic growth.

Unfortunately, other complex factors upset economic management: complete control of public spending is not possible; monetary policy alone cannot decide on the circulation rate and quantity of money; the economic behaviour of consumers, producers and other agents tends not to conform with predictions; and it takes a long time to obtain information, decipher it and calculate its meaning. In these circumstances fine-tuning an economy is not feasible.

### Key principles

Certainly the government sets a framework for policy rather than reacting to every external development. Typically there are five key principles:

- to help establish the right economic climate for the private sector to thrive, since growth is generated in this way
- to keep inflation low, which is vital for competitiveness
- to achieve a high and stable employment level
- to increase the role of the private sector by abandoning unnecessary regulations and establishing competitive and open markets, thus increasing the long-term growth rate of supply performance of the economy
- to avoid balance of payments difficulties

Unfortunately, any one of these factors affects the performance of the others. However, various governments have tried differing approaches but without successfully achieving all five factors.

Under one inept government in 1975 inflation peaked at about 25 per cent and the general price level tripled between 1968 and 1979. This meant £1 in 1968 was worth only 30 pence in 1979. A new government succeeded in reducing inflation to about 6 per cent from 1982 to 1990 and about 4 per cent in 1991; then prices stabilised.

## ECONOMIC OPERATIONS

The government has taken a leading part in promoting 'structural adjustment'. This means improving the capability of individuals, enterprises and institutions to respond to change by exploiting new opportunities and moving away from declining sectors. The Organisation for Economic Co-operation and Development (OECD) conducted a study which showed industrial countries do not adapt as quickly as they might because their economies are overregulated and overprotected. This situation indicates that 'structural adjustment' should be promoted vigorously.

The OECD's report showed economies work best when allowed to operate freely with the minimum of government interference. Markets are hindered by interventions that distort price signals or reduce competition.

### Relaxing controls

In the 1980s many overseas governments substantially opened up their economies to market forces but more remains to be done. The UK government removed many controls, including those on prices, dividends and pay. Incentives were improved by reducing income tax rates and raising tax thresholds. Several taxes were removed, including investment income surcharge and national insurance surcharge. Individual ownership of property and wider share ownership were encouraged, especially through privatisation programmes and share option schemes. Finally, the liberalisation of financial markets was encouraged.

## INFORMATION TECHNOLOGY

The government seems to be fully committed to the use of information technology (IT), promoting computers integrated with advanced telecommunication and office systems. Government departments have strategic plans to cope with the changing roles of technology, considering cost benefits and value for money. Top-level committees discuss the use of IT, accompanied by the Central Computer and Telecommunications Agency (CCTA). IT is treated as a resource with no intrinsic value and, like all resources, its values lies with competent management.

In industry the poor management of IT resources is well known. Measuring intangible benefits like competitive advantage and quality is often ignored. According to some surveys, companies even now remain reluctant to install comprehensive systems and they do not value IT highly. Nevertheless, IT has dramatically changed the way information is made available, processed and distributed within a company. Consequently, if IT is properly applied, the quality, access and delivery of information can improve problem solving and decision making, which is a distinct advantage in any organisation.

# Manpower development

Governments have made many attempts to solve the acute problem of skill shortages. These include establishing training boards under the Industrial Training Act 1964, setting up the Manpower Services Commission (MSC) under the Employment and Training Act 1974, renaming the MSC the Training Commission (TC) in 1987, renaming the TC the Training Agency (TA), renaming the TA the Training Enterprise and Education Directorate (TEED) and in 1990 launching Training and Enterprise Councils (TECs).

A summary of the present situation is given below and includes the Management Charter Initiative, TECs, Training Standards, and the National Vocational Qualification.

### THE MANAGEMENT CHARTER INITIATIVE

In 1988 this independent body was established by employers and backed by the government. The Management Charter Initiative (MCI) is the operating arm of the National Forum for Management Education and Development. The aim is to promote management development, particularly competence-based management development, for the benefit of organisations and individuals. MCI works with Business Links, TECs and industry training organisations, together with the awarding bodies and providers of management development training.

### TECs

The creation of about eighty TECs marked a change in structuring by adopting a network of employer-led councils, based mainly on the experience of Germany and the USA. Thus, local chief executives from industry comprise two-thirds of the membership of TEC boards and they decide how best to meet local labour needs. These boards are also expected to launch a coherent strategy for small business support and to liaise with other government schemes such as Employment Training and Youth Training.

In 1995 the government established the Employment Select Committee to enquire into the activities of TECs because of adverse reports. During 1994 South Thames TEC was in financial difficulties despite receiving £42 million a year in public money, while Essex TEC appeared to have conflicts of interest which caused many scathing comments. It seems that about £1.8 billion a year is spent by TECs which is about one pence in the pound on income tax.

### TRAINING STANDARDS

Training standards are promoted by a business-led body called Investors in People UK (IIP). These standards are linked to the business needs of companies and are assessed by the IIP. The so-called standard was developed by the government and is promoted by TECs and local enterprise companies. An employer may be 'recognised' if there is a public commitment to employee development, if regular reviews of training and development needs are undertaken, and if there is evaluation of the effectiveness of training.

### THE NATIONAL VOCATIONAL QUALIFICATION

In 1986 the National Council for Vocational Qualifications (NCVQ) was established to ensure the right kind of qualification is available for all occupations. The aim is to provide a comprehensive, flexible and relevant system of qualifications which is responsive to current and future needs of industry and commerce. This is achieved by vetting and classifying all the vocational certificates awarded, so creating national standards.

The NCVQ gives an accreditation (NVQ) to any qualification issued by a professional body, provided the award satisfies certain criteria. A National Vocational Qualification (NVQ) is a statement of the competence in skills, knowledge, understanding and ability in application needed for entry into a particular area of employment.

# Environmental forces

The competent manager responds to and interacts with the internal environment and the complex external environment. He or she conforms to the open system approach by forecasting and planning changes to account for these influences. The main considerations are:

- cultural
- ethical
- legal
- political
- economic
- technological

Their relationship to a company is complicated and there are many effects. These include opportunities and constraints, the provision of people and capital, and the creation of legal and moral rights. All are complementary, all businesses are affected and, of course, businesses in turn affect the external environment.

## THE EXTERNAL CULTURAL ENVIRONMENT

The external cultural environment covers the attitudes of people along with their degrees of intelligence, levels of education, wants and desires, expectations, beliefs and customs. Understandably a strong connection exists between cultural, ethical and political external environments. The ethical aspect includes acceptable and practical standards of behaviour, which are also often included in, or considered to be part of, the social or cultural environment. Similarly, political and legal aspects are closely connected since political influences conform to some extent with social demands and beliefs, and legislation is the outcome of social pressures and difficulties.

## THE EXTERNAL ETHICAL ENVIRONMENT

Ethical behaviour is seen as fair and just conduct, which is often supported by legislation, beliefs and moral codes. Everyone should benefit from high ethical codes and behaviour, provided all conform to them. The important features are mutual respect, individual integrity and contributing to society. Unfortunately, business ethics often fall short of ideals, typically disregarding ecology, treating employees poorly, engaging in fraudulent activities and taking advantage of customers in various ways.

### Corporate responsibility

The terms 'corporate responsibility' and 'business ethics' are interchangeable, but they are not the same as personal morality. Corporate responsibility implies that a code of conduct (or behaviour) exists in a company. However, it is not necessarily practised, although it is considered by some specialists to be an important feature of competitiveness.

## THE EXTERNAL LEGAL ENVIRONMENT

Companies should conform to legislation which is mainly aimed at protecting society. The government attempts to regulate and constrain business by adopting regulations and passing laws. These are designed to protect individuals, enforce contracts, protect property rights and control the behaviour of owners, managers and employees. Ignorance of legislation is no excuse, therefore managers often use specialists to interpret the law and recommend appropriate courses of action. Nevertheless, there are many cases of abuse and manipulation of laws by companies.

## THE EXTERNAL POLITICAL ENVIRONMENT

The political environment within the UK is notorious for policy turnabouts as failures occur and social pressures and beliefs change. This unpredictable behaviour by government is often caused by patriotic fervour, disillusionment and fluctuating support for various political parties. Therefore, perceiving changes is ultimately guesswork, although survival many depend upon it.

*European Union government*

Electors can choose Euro MPs (MEPs). The UK has 87 MEPs in a parliament of 567. The European Parliament meets in Strasbourg where European matters are discussed, including any legislation being suggested or changed.

## THE EXTERNAL ECONOMIC ENVIRONMENT

This feature embraces customers, productivity, capital, inflation levels, labour, entrepreneurs, managers, and government's fiscal and tax policies. Here are the important points:

- The importance of customers and their wants is fundamental, but assessing the market is difficult since so many factors rapidly alter the situation. Typical examples are changing tastes, demand for higher quality, substitute products, and an increasing range of products.
- Availability of capital and the level of interest rates.
- Availability, quality (educational level and skills) and price of labour. These three features are affected by many influences such as recession, inflation, immigration policy, demographic trends, the education system and degree of support from government, trade union pressures and the political party in power.
- Inflation naturally affects price levels, which affect the input and output of a company, including importing and exporting difficulties.
- Productivity levels are affected by national culture, trade union policies, managerial effectiveness, banking policies related to loans, and capital investment. This vital feature determines general economic growth, exporting success, wealth creation and standard of living.
- Availability of high quality managers and entrepreneurs is of major economic importance. Unless the school and higher education system is geared up to supply appropriate numbers, disastrous effects are inescapable. Similarly, industry and business must be sufficiently attractive to highly qualified people and be thought of as providing worthwhile careers, not solely dirty occupations.
- The effects of government's fiscal and tax policies are immediately apparent in credit availability, interest rates on loans, and various taxes on businesses. Poor judgement by government on the effects of such policies may lead to recession and general industrial chaos.

## THE EXTERNAL TECHNOLOGICAL ENVIRONMENT

The external technological environment covers information on methods of work, inventions, techniques, outcomes of research into design, machines, computers, tools, materials, services, and so on. An obvious statement is that technology cannot be ignored and is vital for survival. Surprisingly many companies do not embrace technological advance, ignore new ideas taken up successfully by other countries, and eventually collapse. Using technology correctly achieves higher productivity, higher living standards and a wider range of products.

# Green issues

In recent years the dangers of environmental pollution have become universally recognised. However, responses by different countries have varied, as have scientists' predictions. Certainly the evidence is taken seriously in the USA and Europe, and the green revolution is now slowly spreading worldwide.

The USA has seen the establishment of the Environmental Protection Agency, the Clean Air and Clean Water Acts, Greenpeace and Friends of the Earth. The EU has issued various directives and established the European Environment Agency (EEA) to verify data and supply objective, reliable, comparative environmental information at EU level. Other interested countries may also participate. A particular EC directive in 1997 extended the existing regulations on *environmental assessment*. Originally the potentially significant environmental effects of development were identified, assessed and taken into account when a planning decision was made regarding the development. Now the results may be adopted to lessen the potential environmental impacts which are identified so that considerations for the environment are included earlier in the development process before planning commences.

In the UK the Environment Protection Act 1990 established a new regime called Integrated Pollution Control. This applies to prescribed industrial, commercial and other processes. Local authorities are legalised to control air emissions and insist on processes that produce less pollution. HMSO (now the Stationery Office) has issued a wide range of publications on environmental issues.

## ENVIRONMENTAL RESPONSIBILITIES

Clearly companies face many problems, typically the cost of changes, profitability, legislative pressures, and competition from companies who do not comply with environmental regulations.

Furthermore, the launching of ethical and green investment contracts shows that some investors feel business should have a conscience as well as a commercial strategy. A green corporate image is also important for recruitment programmes since enlightened graduates and women returning to employment may favour conscientious companies.

The vast range of environmental issues usually divides into five headings: the ozone layer, waste management, transport, energy efficiency and purchasing policies. Each one includes many factors. Within companies there are green agendas, which may include no smoking, dining-room cleanliness, recycling waste, office cleaning, air conditioning, and many other aspects amounting to controlling or eliminating sick building syndrome.

Finally, individuals should feel they can play their part. Some examples are using bottle banks, controlling hazardous waste and abandoning local pollution.

# Effective economies

Effective economies are here restricted to five major topics:

- the key task
- the economic system
- types of economy
- the financial system
- national commercial banks

## THE KEY TASK

The main economic difficulties encountered by all countries involve three major factors: scarcity, choice and supply. Attempts to economise effectively must take them into account because inevitably resources are limited; allocating them involves choice; and supply depends upon demand and related price, along with cost of production. Three questions emerge from this key task:

- What to produce?
- How to produce?
- Who should benefit from the goods?

Any country must attempt to answer these questions and, in so doing, has to choose a method or system to operate the economy. The final choice depends mainly upon political power, attitudes, aims, tradition and culture. In brief, the questions involve consumption, production and distribution, which are now discussed.

### Effective consumption

Effective consumption depends upon placing wants in priority order by considering society and the nation, and satisfying them accordingly. Decisions are influenced by individuals and companies who may act selfishly; the government, which considers national problems; and other countries, which exert political or physical pressures.

### Effective production

The full utilisation of each company is essential. Consideration must be given to suitability for manufacturing the product, all work study aspects, appropriate location of site, upgrading production by using new technologies and modern designs, and applying economic services.

### Effective distribution

Effective distribution covers the distribution of wealth, equality, status, ownership, freedom of choice, political outlook, distribution of income, profits, idealistic concepts, and culture. Most people resent situations that are obviously unfairly biased against them. Such resentment retards mutual understanding with those who are more privileged, and affects the degree of co-operation at work.

However, people in an advanced society usually recognise that capital must be raised to produce and sustain the flow of manufactured goods. This situation is accepted as capitalism in the economic sense. Resentment stems from the political argument as to who owns the capital and the land. This is capitalism in the political sense: owners are rewarded regardless of whether they do any work, and workers are rewarded for labour performed. To avoid political upheaval, an acceptable balance between the two is vital and must be maintained as workers adjust their attitudes.

## Mutual trust

To achieve mutual forbearance or patience with each other is often narrowly interpreted as per-suading employees to co-operate by applying many techniques associated with motivation and human resources management. Broader interpretations include governmental action to create a fairer society, and reducing the Establishment's power to resist obvious benefits for everyone.

Unfortunately, there is strong resistance to accepting an organisation as a social fabrication, not a biological organism. Employees do not auto-matically act and react to internal and external forces; they expect equal rights before accepting mutual trust and fully co-operating.

## THE ECONOMIC SYSTEM

The national economy may be visualised as a systems model. A *simple model* would see organ-isations using people, machines and materials to create goods and services. If demand is above the available stock, then organisations will increase production. Prices may rise through scarcity, and unemployment falls as more jobs become avail-able. Conversely, if supply is above demand then unsold stock forces organisations to reduce the workforce, fewer machines will be purchased and prices will fall.

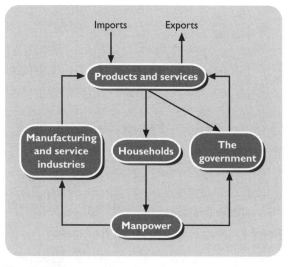

**Figure 6.1** An open economic system

A more *complex model* introduces organisations and households. Households provide manpower and funds, and receive incomes to spend on goods produced by organisations, provided their wants coincide with the goods on offer. However, the government and international activities must be added. The government buys and sells goods too, and trading between countries involves importing and exporting goods and services. Figure 6.1 illus-trates this open system.

## TYPES OF ECONOMY

Various methods have evolved in attempts to economise. Two opposing major systems are a *planned economy* operated by the state and a *market economy* where the price mechanism operates through private enterprise. Within these extremes are different combinations of both, col-lectively known as a *mixed economy*.

Any economy has market and non-market sectors, which implies that no extreme type of planned or market economy is possible in practice. Figure 6.2 illustrates a continuum from planned economy to market economy. A country may move in either direction along the continuum; its position depends on its current situation such as a change in government, war or a variety of economic difficulties.

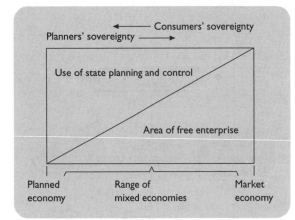

**Figure 6.2** A continuum from planned economies to market economies
A country may move in either direction along the continuum; its position depends upon the current economic situation and may be affected by war or a change in government.

## THE FINANCIAL SYSTEM

A common claim is that the UK financial system is the most important reason for economic decline. Apparently, specialists know reform is vital but the Establishment resists because it benefits from a system which provides fees and careers. The Oxford Dictionary definition of *Establishment* is 'a social group exercising authority or influence, and generally seeking to resist changes'.

## NATIONAL COMMERCIAL BANKS

Before about 1875, British industry received similar financial support to that of Japan and Germany today, then a drastic change occurred. The reasons for the change were complex. International competition increased, together with expensive technological change; local banking networks which existed before could not cope with higher demands, and some collapsed.

The eventual outcome was the formation of national commercial banks whose policies were to provide short-term credit and finance for commerce, not for investment. The role of *risk money* was undertaken by the stock market, consequently investor nervousness developed. In other words,

there was no confidence between companies, bankers and investors. The overall effects are the insensitive treatment of customers, a risk-averse outlook, and investment mainly in safe projects.

### Insensitive treatment

High street banks have been criticised by the Office of Fair Trading (OFT) for their insensitive, high-handed treatment of small business customers. Many complaints to the OFT have included hidden or opaque charging, lack of notice about changes, a failure to act upon informal agreements with clients, and not passing on lower interest charges in spite of cuts in base rates.

### A risk-aversive outlook

The largest 115 companies in the UK pay dividends which are twice and sometimes three times that of their German counterparts, and they have risk-averse corporate strategies to maintain profit and dividend growth. Indeed the capital market drives business strategies and internal organisation, not the needs of the product market. Therefore cost minimisation, risk aversion and stable results are highlighted, whereas elsewhere internal accounting systems are geared to showing increases in market share and growth. Consequently, investment in the UK is geared to sound and predictable returns, and biased against investing in proposals with uncertain returns.

### Investment mainly in safe projects

Although there have been high increases in investment, it has been channelled into low risk areas, typically financial services, hotels, property, communications and distribution. All these areas are usually protected from international competition, they possess property as collateral and they support large amounts of short-term debt.

In less predictable income areas, typically manufacturing, investment is unpopular because of long-term requirements such as essential heavy expenditure on research and development, and technologies. British banks prefer short-term debts whereas Japanese and German banks extend loans into the long term. The outcome is obvious: British banks will not support in crises; strategic projects are severely restricted; and undue caution is practised.

## PROPOSED REFORMS

There are many proposed reforms and all are well known, but according to the experts, there is no possibility of change. The main reforms to stop continued decline are in line with Japanese and German systems. Some of them are to decentralise commercial banks into their regional constituents, change company law, tax short-term capital gains, rediscount industrial loans through the Bank of England, launch a public investment credit bank, and establish sound lending criteria.

# Business structure

The thousands of industrial companies in the UK vary in structure as well as in size. The six main types of business range from the sole proprietor to the nationalised industry.

## SOLE PROPRIETOR

Sole proprietor is the oldest type of business and is still quite common, especially among retailers, craft specialists and farmers. The proprietor provides his or her own capital, raised either by savings or borrowed from relations and friends. The proprietor is liable for all debts, is responsible only to himself or herself, and profits do not have to be shared. The accounts remain private and are not publicly available.

## PARTNERSHIPS

The common form of partnership consists of two or more individuals who agree to establish a business and who generally share responsibilities and profits. The total number of partners is limited to twenty (except solicitors, accountants and stockbrokers) under the Companies Acts 1948–89. The Limited Partnership Act 1907 allows individuals to form a partnership under which a partner's liability is limited, but such a partner is not allowed to participate in the concern's management.

The partners finance the business; profits or losses are shared according to an agreed proportion. Managing the business is arranged between the partners; some may be sleeping partners, meaning they do not participate. Like sole proprietors, partners are not legally required to publish accounts. Typical examples of partnerships occur in professional occupations such as barristers, solicitors and accountants; also in many small businesses.

## LIMITED COMPANIES

The principle of limited liability means investors are liable for the company's debts only up to the amount invested in fully paid-up shares in the company. This system, legalised in the original Companies Act 1856, has encouraged industry to develop at a phenomenal rate. Large amounts of capital can be raised and companies may expand more easily by raising further sums of money.

Under the Companies Acts, companies may be public or private. Both must have at least two members and be registered. A public company must end its name with 'public limited company', more commonly seen as PLC; its memorandum and articles of association must state it is a public company; and its minimum issued share capital must be at least £50 000, of which 25 per cent and all premiums are paid up. Any company not complying with these provisions is automatically private and is prohibited from offering its shares to the public.

A proportion of the profits is generally distributed to shareholders as dividends. Losses are borne by the concern, although obviously the shareholders suffer eventually. A board of directors is appointed to manage the concern; the board is responsible to the shareholders.

Private limited companies often appear in retailing, the building trade and clothing. Local family businesses are commonly organised this way. Public limited companies are corporations which raise capital from the public, therefore large sums may be obtained. They are generally large concerns capable of developing into enormous worldwide organisations.

## MULTINATIONAL COMPANIES

These large companies appear in many forms, such as worldwide organisations owned by British companies operating overseas (Shell, Hanson, Rank), jointly controlled companies in several countries (Unilever), and British subsidiaries of foreign companies (IBM UK, Ford and Nestlé UK). These companies are powerful, difficult to control by governments, may have critical effects on an economy, often suffer with large-scale problems, and usually apply different philosophies to suit local conditions.

## CO-OPERATIVE SOCIETIES

The co-operative movement in production has not grown, mainly because the employees provide the capital and elect their own managers from within. The restriction in raising capital and the problem of locating effective managers has resulted in the establishment of only twenty-seven concerns which are members of the Co-operative Production Federation. The main lines of production are footwear and clothing; the bulk of output is distributed to co-operative societies.

Consumers' co-operative societies are still popular, with a membership of about 12 million, but the movement is declining. Each member is a customer who may invest up to £1000 in the particular society, he or she has only one vote, and interest on the investment is at a fixed rate. Any individual may join or leave whenever he or she wishes and there is no maximum number of shareholders. Management is elected by members and the accounts must be published. Services offered include banking, insurance, travel, funeral arrangements and DIY stores. The societies apply ethical principles, are democratically organised, and support the Labour Party, sponsoring fourteen MPs.

Attempts by Labour governments to establish co-operatives following threatened closures have encountered many economic difficulties. Examples are the Kirkby Manufacturing and Engineering Company, Triumph Ltd at Meriden and the Scottish Daily News. These co-operatives have been severely criticised, mainly on the grounds that practically all declining industries suffer from misguided enthusiasm caused by added strains on an already faltering spirit. The result is often a further decline, which tends to increase in speed. Other criticisms include the inference that backing, in various forms, is insufficient and too late.

Supporters of co-operatives claim that, given a viable situation, the principle of co-ownership avoids the innate conflict between the usual two sides, owner and employee, and provides a firm basis for operating industrial democracy successfully.

## MUNICIPAL UNDERTAKINGS

The functions of local authorities are governed by various legal acts. The services vary depending upon the type of authority and may include education, police, lighting, refuse collection, road maintenance, swimming baths, theatres and fire services. Income is from the government, miscellaneous receipts and local residents. The government operates an inspection scheme to ensure standards are maintained and to ensure the authority meets its statutory responsibilities.

## STATE UNDERTAKINGS

Various organisations exist with different working arrangements:

- Public corporations, such as the Post Office, Bank of England and the former Girobank. They receive capital and are responsible to the government.
- Trading concerns controlled by the Treasury, such as the Stationery Office.
- Service concerns who do not receive a direct fee from the public, such as the Arts Council, the BBC and NHS hospitals.
- National security, such as the armed forces and Customs and Excise.

## NON-PROFIT-MAKING CONCERNS

Non-profit-making concerns exist through subscriptions by members who have the use of facilities such as a social building, a cricket ground or tennis courts. The concerns may make a surplus which is shared among members, held in reserve, or used to maintain or expand the facilities.

# Human assets

Pushing managers towards a philosophy of 'people matter most' seems to be a dominating trend today. Whether every level of industrial society adopts this philosophy sincerely is debatable. Unemployment and the reduction of trade union power may have persuaded managers to feel they now have the right and the opportunity to manage as they wish. Nevertheless, many managers are slowly realising that giving their human assets priority is rewarding. The main features of this trend (discussed below) are manpower, the occupational structure, demographic change, autonomous groups, empowerment, social trends, comparative management and management development.

## MANPOWER

There is a severe shortage of well-educated, skilled industrial employees, although there is a surplus of well-qualified people for professional services. Suggestions to rectify the situation include improving the literacy and numeracy of young people, developing strong vocational skills, increasing the number of people with managerial and financial skills, and increasing the number of students at universities.

Many models for action are available from the USA, Japan and various European countries. All specialists agree that productivity is directly related to the knowledge and skills of the workforce and that a drastic improvement in the education system of the UK is vital.

## OCCUPATIONAL STRUCTURE

Changes in the occupational structure are partly due to the growth of the service sector, the declining primary and secondary industries, a heavy decline in unskilled jobs, and redundancies which have led to a large number of retraining programmes. The demand has increased for trained skilled workers, competent managers and technicians, consequently education and training programmes are urgently needed to make up this shortfall.

*Table 6.1* UK population statistics, 1971–2001 (000s)

| Age | 1971 | 1981 | 1988 | 1991 | 2001 |
|---|---|---|---|---|---|
| 0–14 | 13 470 | 11 602 | 10 760 | 11 054 | 12 041 |
| 15–24 | 8 144 | 9 019 | 8 978 | 8 203 | 7 198 |
| 25–44 | 13 482 | 14 784 | 16 239 | 16 849 | 16 932 |
| 45–64 | 13 423 | 12 475 | 12 204 | 12 390 | 13 844 |
| over 64 | 7 409 | 8 472 | 8 883 | 9 038 | 9 187 |
| Total | 55 928 | 56 352 | 57 065 | 57 553 | 59 201 |

*Source*: Annual Abstract of Statistics

## DEMOGRAPHIC CHANGE

The UK population statistics shown in Table 6.1 cover the period from 1971 until 1991 and are then projected forward until 2001. The decline in numbers for the late teenage and early twenties age group has forced changes in recruitment programmes in companies. Difficulty in recruiting sufficient numbers of school leavers has already resulted in employers trying to attract unemployed women and people from other age groups. As the decline continues further, changes in training, policy, organisation of work and career structures are inevitable. Being able to attract and retain a skilled workforce will be a major problem.

## AUTONOMOUS GROUPS

Lessons are now being learned from overseas competitors, research and previous UK industrial catastrophes. Furthermore, technologies are influencing and encouraging the formation of autonomous groups joined by various matrix models.

This trend is noticeable in large firms and means that classical organisational structures are discounted, but not completely, to be replaced by closely co-ordinated groups in loose structures held together by modern IT. Typical management jargon for these groups includes self-directed teams, autonomous and semi-autonomous teams, empowered teams, self-disciplined teams, multifunctional teams, flexible-working teams, and collaborative interdepartmental (and intradepartmental) teams.

## EMPOWERMENT

The philosophy of empowerment extends to all employees, managers and supervisors. The assumption is that everyone has the ability and capability to contribute far more. This may be achieved by allowing people to make decisions traditionally taken by levels above, introducing more flexibility and responsibility through the increase of authority, and encouraging risks and high commitment (Chapters 5 and 10).

## SOCIAL TRENDS

The effects of IT, changing education programmes and new cultures are more noticeable now in people's changing attitudes, wants, beliefs and general outlook. New behavioural patterns are emerging which indicate that in the future people will be more interested in self-development and will be looking for a more balanced life. This trend amounts to expecting more dignity and more respect, not being pushed around easily. Thus fraternal rather than paternal management of employees is inevitable. Managers will be severely stretched to cater for these demands, but they will certainly be in difficulties if they ignore them.

## COMPARATIVE MANAGEMENT

Comparative management is discussed further in Chapter 8, under cultural and environmental differences. But note how claims are made that management science is universal, although management philosophy tends to vary from country to country. This variance is critical, it seems, since countries like Japan and Germany investing in the UK find the workforce is willing to accept their ways, and the companies they establish thrive.

### The Japanese philosophy

Reports indicate that the Japanese approach works well in the UK:

- establishing a new approach to industrial relations by stressing dialogue and co-operation rather than concentrating on differences and confrontation

- insisting on a day's work for a day's pay
- sole bargaining rights with one trade union
- applying one uniform status for everyone – one canteen, using first names, open-plan offices, standard hours for office and shop-floor employees, common pension scheme, similar sick pay and holidays, and similar clothing to avoid status symbols such as suits
- general concern for welfare
- open communication and employee involvement in decision making
- a five-minute daily briefing on the previous day's work with any comments noted and used
- a monthly meeting of an advisory board; minutes are circulated and reactions and ideas presented at the next meeting; representatives from all groups sit on this board
- establishing teams, encouraging team spirit and assigning tasks and targets
- persistence in the use of sound techniques, with a strong drive to succeed
- ensuring everyone feels personally responsible for the success of the company by entrusting people with responsibility for the quality of their work and making them an integral part of the organisation

Japanese industrial philosophy is also worth noting:

- customer care
- new product development
- careful targeting of international markets
- concern for product reliability

### The German industrial philosophy

In Germany one analysis reveals a strong commitment to three main approaches:

- productivity
- quality and service criteria
- sound personnel management practices

### The US philosophy

America also invests in the UK. Here are some notable US approaches:

- a unitary framework is common among managers

- emphasis on free enterprise, self-interest and individualism
- the use of changing market conditions to hire and fire
- encouraging competition and the use of market mechanisms to allocate resources

### Japanese influence

Certainly America has been influenced by Japanese manufacturing processes, and Japanese companies have established hundreds of 'transplant' factories in the USA where American workers have been adapted to their ways. However, some transplants are not highly successful, especially where strict rules are applied and some intimidation and surveillance are used to enforce company loyalty. Furthermore, it seems that some American managers do not adapt easily in terms of commitment to the company and the new collegiate style of management which emphasises an organic link with managers and workers.

### Main factors affecting management

Certain differences within countries seem to determine managerial approaches. These differences include the following:

- *The community*: culture, work ethics, class systems, religion, attitudes towards industry, accumulation of wealth, role of women, lifestyles, and traditional outlook.
- *Natural resources*: underlying wealth such as oil, gas, coal, other minerals and fertile land.
- *Technologies*: nuclear power, computers, engineering, aerospace, machine tools and equipment.
- *Educational system*: modern approaches, degree of investment, and accurate forecasting of industrial requirements.
- *Business structures*: average size, forms of ownership, organisational factors, and modern equipment.
- *Legal system*: laws relating to business such as contract, health and safety, monopolies and insider dealing, as well as the degree of faith in the system.

- *The economy*: stage of development, growth or decline, government influence and competence, conditions, and size of home or collective market.

## MANAGEMENT DEVELOPMENT

A competent managerial force is critical to economic growth and development. Management know-how is essential for the effective use of all resources and for the adaptation of all external environmental factors.

The need for effective management development is recognised outside industry, but there are many views on how it should be achieved. Within industry the general disregard for training and developing managers continues, probably because ineffective managers do not attempt to read about modern management and new techniques, and they generally resist change. Indeed they often have difficulty in understanding marketing, the need for modern products and processes, and in communicating successfully overseas.

### The Handy Report

In 1987 Professor C. Handy and his colleagues produced a report on the training of British managers and their counterparts abroad. The findings were that most managers elsewhere (especially Germany, Japan and the USA) possess a higher standard of education.

Handy's suggestions to rectify the situation reinforce many specialists' views which have been ignored over the years. A brief summary of the proposals is given below:

- a wider, longer education base
- work experience during education
- a framework for early business education
- articles of management linked with the first stage of management development
- five days annually for off-the-job training
- leading companies to set trends
- mechanisms for co-operation between business schools and companies
- official statistics on management development
- encouragement of individual learning
- companies should seek good recruits and give them early responsibility.

# The European Union

The European Union (EU), previously EC and EEC, now has fifteen member states. Austria, Sweden, Finland, France, Germany, the UK, Italy, Spain, Netherlands, Denmark, Belgium, Luxembourg, Portugal, Greece and Ireland. The EU has the power to spend money in its own right and has an annual budget (about £39 billion) financed by revenue from the member states.

The main expenditure items are agricultural price support (over 50 per cent), a regional development fund that promotes the economically less favoured regions (about 10 per cent), training and employment projects (about 7 per cent), and grants to farmers for modernisation and environmentally beneficial projects (about 4 per cent). Smaller amounts are spent on administration, research and investment, a social fund, and other agricultural and fisheries funds.

The EU continues to grow. Other countries interested in joining are Turkey, Poland, Hungary, Czechoslovakia and Norway. There are contradictions in policy – the integration of economic, political, legal and security aspects is problematical – and there are complex enlargement difficulties.

## THE TREATY OF ROME

A number of articles were contained in the Treaty of Rome 1957, of which the UK became a member in 1972. Their direct implications are being calculated and involve many initiatives related to the objectives of the EU. These objectives include an economic and social union, allowing free movement of people, goods and capital by removing national barriers, and establishing common policies. The key sectors are designed to provide equal opportunities, social and economic progress, and continuing improvement of living and working conditions.

## MAJOR ISSUES

Major issues are the impact on member states, agreement on the objectives, and the speed and degree of social and economic integration. There are five aspects to consider. They continue to be strongly debated since views differ markedly.

## The structure

Compromises between the opposing viewpoints on structure will eventually emerge. Certainly, a well-integrated EU is seen by many specialists as essential to the achievement of harmonisation and greater power. Here are the two structural outcomes envisaged by the main protagonists:

- A loose federation of countries with coinciding policies and strong links but with separate sovereignty. Parliament, government and courts in the UK, for example, would be supreme, not subordinated to a 'super state'. Also, a single, common currency and unified legislative system would be resisted.
- One large state with a common currency, one central bank, and a unified legislative system. A European Parliament and common courts led by the European Commission would control all activities.

## A large economic unit or bloc

A powerful argument for this cites the worldwide trend towards large economic blocs or units that dominate markets and wield enormous power. Small, isolated countries face survival problems as these large units grow further and squeeze them economically, unless they are in a unique situation where the obvious difficulties do not apply to them.

## The Maastricht treaty

The Maastricht treaty was signed in 1991 to satisfy widespread pressures (notably by Germany and France) to form a 'United States of Europe' which would speak with unity in world councils. The aim is to organise relations between member states and create an ever closer union among the people. The complex document refers to twenty-nine policies, political union, economic and monetary union, the Social Chapter, institutional changes, and subsidiarity. The 135-page treaty is published by the Stationery Office (telephone 0117 926 4306).

## The Social Chapter

The objectives of the Social Chapter are:

- the promotion of employment and job creation
- improved living and working conditions
- proper social protection
- dialogue between management and labour
- the development of human resources

The legislative proposals amount to a social action programme of about fifty proposals. Typical sensitive areas are working conditions, protection levels for part-time and temporary workers, working hours and rest periods, night work, protection at work of pregnant women, National Insurance contributions and employee consultation.

## European Monetary Union

Member states agreed to form an Exchange Rate Mechanism (ERM) in 1978. This would reduce fluctuations in members' currencies if they chose to join. In 1999 exchange rates were fixed between the euro and the currencies of the eleven countries joining in the first wave. A three-year period of adaptation has been arranged, then the euro will be circulated and the old currencies withdrawn. The new Euro-zone will account for about 20 per cent of the world's output. If all countries were to join, the Euro-zone would include 380 million people and a GDP of about £16 trillion.

**The UK's situation**

The Maastricht treaty included among its objectives a process and timetable for moving towards European Monetary Union (EMU). The treaty also recognised the right for the UK to decide whether to join the final stage of establishing the single currency. Various complex views are expressed which cover the advantages and disadvantages of joining. Certainly there has been a rapid integration of European economies during the past twenty-five years. The development and competitiveness of the European economy is a relevant and crucial factor for the UK. There are obvious signs of interdependency and mergers.

## THE LEGISLATION AND JUDGEMENTS

Legislative procedure is divided into three institutions. There is also the European Court of Justice.

- The European Commission makes proposals.
- The European Parliament gives opinions and proposes amendments.
- The Council of Ministers makes decisions.

## The European Commission

The European Commission has seventeen members appointed by the governments of the member states. It proposes policy and legislation, implements EU decisions and initiates action against member states who do not comply with EU rules.

## The European Parliament

The European Parliament (EP) consists of 567 members who are elected every five years from the member states. It is consulted on draft legislation, proposes amendments and gives formal opinions. Along with the Council of Ministers, it is responsible for establishing the EU budget.

## The Council of Ministers

The Council of Ministers, often known as the European Council, adopts legislation on the basis of proposals from the European Commission. Councils are attended by relevant ministers from the fifteen member states to discuss topics such as fishing rights, sport and trade. They are accountable to their own parliaments and represent their national interests. The ministers take decisions in three ways, dependent on the subject:

- unanimous agreement
- qualified majority voting (based on population size of the country represented)
- a simple majority vote.

Decisions must be unanimous on important issues for national governments. The presidency of the Council of Ministers is held in rotation every six months. The president sets the agenda and chairs the meetings.

## The European Court of Justice

Judgements of the European Court of Justice (ECJ) are binding in each member state. The ECJ rules

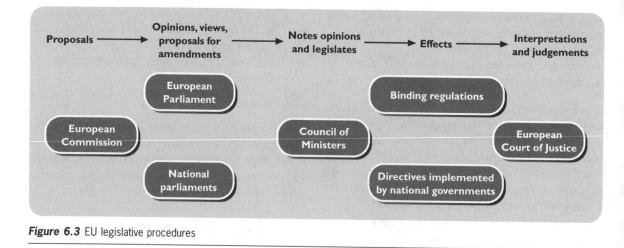

**Figure 6.3** EU legislative procedures

on the interpretation and application of EU laws and has fifteen judges, one from each member state. If a member state fails to implement an EC directive or regulation, the European Commission may apply to the ECJ for infraction proceedings to commence.

### Court of Auditors

The Court of Auditors audits the EU budgets and should help to detect and prevent fraud and waste.

### Types of legislation

- *Regulations* have a binding legal effect. A regulation prevails when it conflicts with an existing national law.
- *Directives* state the result to be achieved within a defined period, but leave the method of implementation to national governments. If a directive is not duly implemented within the timescale, there are provisions to enforce it, although there is no legal force.
- *Decisions* are binding on those to whom they are addressed, whether they be individuals, companies or member states. If financial obligations are involved, they are enforceable in national courts.
- *Recommendations and opinions* state the view of the institution issuing them, but they are not binding.

### Legislative procedure

The legislative procedure is complex and involves the European Commission, the European Parliament, national parliaments, the Council of Ministers, and the European Court of Justice. A simplified diagram of the procedure is given in Fig. 6.3.

### THE SINGLE EUROPEAN MARKET

A major step was taken in 1985 when the heads of governments of countries belonging to the then EC committed themselves to completing the Single Market programme by 1992. This objective was fixed to eliminate the existing tariff and quota barriers and other technical barriers between states so that free movement of goods would become a reality.

The Single Market is defined as an area without internal frontiers in which the free movement of goods, people, services and capital is ensured in accordance with the provisions of the Treaty of Rome. The benefits claimed are:

- a broader choice of goods and services
- assured quality and safety requirements as guidelines become legally binding
- theoretically more employment
- qualifications standardised
- cheaper travel facilities
- removal of routine customs controls

The EU is now extended by including European Free Trade Association (EFTA) countries: Iceland,

Liechtenstein, Norway and Switzerland. This forms the European Economic Area, consisting of 375 million consumers and representing about 40 per cent of world trade.

## THE ENTERPRISE INITIATIVE

To persuade businesses to take full advantage of the Single Market, the DTI launched the Enterprise Initiative in 1988. This vast programme is a self-help package which provides a valuable source of information and expert resources. Experts are available to help in marketing, design, quality manufacturing systems, business planning, financial and information systems, and export planning. They also assist in linking companies with universities, help to solve technical problems and provide access to collaborative research projects. Support services include overseas market data, company information on registration, design testing, patents and trademarks, small firms assistance and business development assistance.

## EUROPEAN HIGH TECHNOLOGY

There is a crucial need for member states to continue developing collaborative research and to improve the capability of bringing new products on to the market since these are essential features of selling competitive products overseas.

Some companies are already strong and there are encouraging signs in others. Examples are the aerospace industry, where the Airbus consortium has successfully produced an aircraft to counter US dominance; nuclear energy, where European fast reactor technology equals the world leaders, Japan and Russia; the software industry, which is beginning to link up into larger groups; weapons systems, where there are heavy export programmes; materials technology, where development projects are part of aerospace programmes; pharmaceuticals, chemicals and biotechnology, all of which are in a strong position and poised for further development.

Collaboration in all its forms provides a unique opportunity for EU industries to become world competitors and face up firmly to competition from the USA, Japan and China. Abandoning all the national barriers to protect local industries in member states has been a fundamental problem which should be overcome eventually.

### Probable effects of collaboration

- Increased awareness and use of management practices and philosophies adapted from more successful countries.
- More co-operation between companies as the advantages of collaboration and large units emerge.
- Increased mobility of specialists, entrepreneurs and managers.
- Some management and development courses improved and centralised.
- Less successful companies may respond more readily to change by adapting to methods used by more successful concerns.

## EUROPEAN MANAGEMENT: MAIN CHARACTERISTICS

- American management practices are accepted.
- Functional specialism is recognised and pursued through subject-based career development.
- Companies enjoy limited liability and ownership is separated from control of large enterprises.
- Large concerns tend to decentralise, establishing divisions and subsidiaries.

## QUESTIONS

1 Illustrate the main features in an open economic system.

2 What is meant by structural change?

3 Outline the main items of interest within the industrial structure when discussing this subject with employees.

4 Explain the term 'business strategy' and comment on its effect on employees.

5 Give your opinion on the role of the Management Charter Initiative.

6 What are the major issues often debated on the European Union?

7 Discuss the possible effects of collaboration between countries within the EU.

8 Explain the probable opportunities and challenges for the UK in the Single Market.

9 List the fundamental weaknesses in the UK economy.

10 Give your opinion on wider share ownership.

11 Outline the external environmental influences that a competent manager must take into consideration.

12 Discuss the problems probably faced by companies on green issues.

13 A competent managerial force is critical to economic growth and development. Write an essay discussing this statement.

14 Why is it essential for a company to achieve high productivity?

15 What effect can government policy have on industry?

16 Discuss the UK's major economic difficulties.

17 What is meant by a mixed economy?

18 Explain the possible adverse effects of monopolies and mergers.

19 List the likely effects if an industry does not keep pace with changing technologies.

20 What are the main topics you would raise with an employee who feels that doing as little as possible for as much money as possible is a sensible approach?

21 Human assets are of prime importance in any company. Discuss this statement.

22 Why is exporting so important to the UK economy?

## CASE STUDY

A long-established company with a good reputation had offered a superior product and accessories. There were 140 employees who felt secure as the company had strong export markets in Europe and the USA. To everyones' surprise, the managing director announced 40 redundancies in the department manufacturing the product. A cheaper product from the Far East was being imported and large quantities were immediately available.

Six months later there were many customer complaints and faulty products were being returned for servicing. Sales dropped and the time and cost of servicing caused a heavy drain on profits. Labour turnover increased and finding suitable replacements became a major problem. The four remaining supervisors were severely stressed as the workforce was disgruntled and often refused to co-operate. Employees were openly resistant to proposals and several suspensions had made no difference to the situation.

*From the employees' viewpoint, is it possible for management to salvage the situation?*

Durajuice Ltd, a company specialising in producing cartons of apple juice for the hotel and catering industry, runs into strong competition, mainly because it is more expensive and partly because of a new product that maintains a better flavour.

At the factory the situation deteriorates when management is trying to maintain costs. The union insists on a wage rise well beyond the cost-of-living increase. Management refuses to agree to it, a strike lasts for three weeks, and eventually ends in a compromise: payment of the asking wage and a productivity deal. The outcome is a further loss of business, caused by delivery delays and no price reduction.

After two months there is no response to higher productivity commitments and profit deteriorates; the union presses for a further wage rise. Management decides to renew negotiations with a firm in Germany for a licence to produce an automatic juice dispenser. If successful the deal would mean that 35 per cent of the employees would have to be made redundant, but survival would be assured and the price could be lowered. Meanwhile, the production supervisors are taken to task for not being able to improve productivity.

The excuses given by the employees are that the managers are inefficient and they do not put in a good day's work. The supervisors are reluctant to take up the case with the works manager, who spends two afternoons a week playing golf with the managing director.

One morning a rumour circulates that the dispenser may be produced in Germany.

*What are the courses of action open to the supervisors when they meet together?*

# 7

# Managerial roles

## Introduction

Over a long period of time, management thinking has undergone various changes that coincide with the changing role of the supervisor. Nowadays there are many approaches to management which affect the teaching, analysis, and study of management theory and science. A careful study of the various approaches reveals confusion over the meanings of terms, differing definitions, the degree of abandonment of early management thought, misunderstandings, and rivalry between management experts.

### DEFINITIONS

- *Functional specialists*: Professional people with technical or technological expertise in such functions as accountancy, marketing, engineering, brewing, electronics, and biochemistry. Problems arise when a functional specialist is appointed to a management post. He or she has high capability in the specialism but might have low capability in management.
- *Managerial roles*: A personal assessment made by the manager of the activities which he or she feels are expected in the job. Usually there is some overlap with management principles. This aspect is dealt with later.
- *Management principles and practice*: A general guide to action or activities using fundamental truths as a basis of reasoning. These principles are outlined later and they are used to develop management skills.
- *Management skills*: These skills underlie and permeate management principles because their

development through repetition and adjustment creates increased capability.
- *Management functions*: Modes of action or activity that fulfil the purpose of management. Although these functions are usually aligned with management principles, there is some overlap with managerial roles.
- *Key business activities*: These are the technical, commercial, financial, accounting, security and managerial activities which are vital aspects seen in most firms. Key business activities include many management topics discussed in this book.

The supervisor should be able to distinguish clearly these six approaches, especially when considering the roles he or she feels are important within the context of a supervisory job. Figure 7.1 is a simplified diagram illustrating the difference between managerial roles and the associated activities of functional specialists, management principles and practice, management skills, management functions and key business activities. It also outlines the related factors which integrate the roles.

## The main features of management

The main features of management include the approaches just described which cover organisational aspects, managerial roles and functions, and key business activities.

What managers and supervisors actually do (in terms of roles, principles and practice) is an input

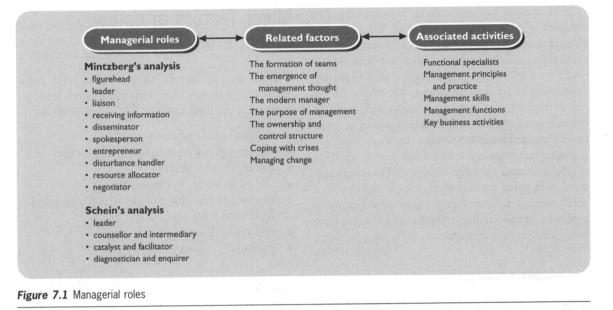

*Figure 7.1* Managerial roles

activity – it is the actions they undertake. What managers do is *not* an output assessment or the achievement of results. Therefore, when results are known, it is possible to relate input with output and arrive at a measure of efficiency, but not necessarily a measure of effectiveness.

A high measure of efficiency may easily relate to input and output both being low if there is an emphasis on, say, reducing costs and solving problems; whereas effectiveness is measured by an increase in profits, and a degree of change to ensure stability now and in the long term.

## MANAGERIAL ROLES

According to Professor H. Mintzberg of McGill University, managers perform a number of roles:

- figurehead – social activities and ceremonial duties, acting as the company's representative
- leader
- liaison – communicating internally and externally
- receiving information on operations
- disseminator – passing information to subordinates
- spokesperson – passing information externally
- entrepreneur – risk taker
- disturbance handler
- resource allocator
- negotiator – dealing with individuals and groups

Clearly there are similarities with some managerial principles (forecasting, planning, etc.), but Mintzberg claims that the usual way of classifying managerial functions (implying principles) is folklore. Nevertheless, some of the roles are not purely managerial.

Professor E. Schein analysed managerial roles as:

- leader
- counsellor and intermediary
- catalyst and facilitator
- diagnostician and enquirer

Certainly such roles indicate features outside the principles of management.

## DEFINITION OF A MANAGERIAL ROLE

Employees' roles are discussed in Chapter 5 (related to group activities); supervisors' roles are discussed in Chapters 2, 3 and 27 (related to development, organisation and quality culture). These discussions cover role theory, role stress, role compliance, formal and informal roles, and situational problems.

The Schein and Mintzberg lists indicate the complexity of attempting to define a managerial role. In broad terms it means how a manager (or supervisor) sees his or her behaviour which is governed by a self-contained pattern based upon the position held by the individual. Therefore such a role includes his or her actual behaviour, how the behaviour ought to be, and the responses or reactions expected from employees. In other words, it is a personal assessment based upon an evaluation of the job and its requirements. Thus management principles are included, which amount to a total managerial job based upon perceptions of authority, responsibility, obligations and acceptable behaviour in the organisation.

## MANAGEMENT FUNCTIONS

Management functions are often interpreted as the major part of a manager's duties, or as fields of managerial activity, or the main principles of management. Functions differ from roles. Roles may be viewed as a personal assessment of managerial activities, whereas business activities are associated with the manager's capability to perform successfully.

The main functions (or principles) are forecasting, planning, organising, co-ordinating, commanding, controlling and motivating. Each of these functions is described in detail in the next chapter. This approach emphasises the managerial process and leadership. In practice, managers use a number of principles or functions at any one time as each plan reaches various stages of development.

## KEY BUSINESS ACTIVITIES

Certain activities are essential. Henri Fayol recognised six key features which represent individuals' capabilities to perform successfully. These are:

- *Technical*: production or service
- *Commercial*: distribution and purchasing
- *Financial*: obtaining capital and using it effectively
- *Accounting*: providing accurate financial information
- *Security*: safeguarding assets
- *Managerial*: forecasting, planning, etc.

# Major factors affecting managerial roles

Certain major factors affect managerial roles. Their integrating effect with associated activities creates co-ordination (Fig. 7.1). They include:

- the formation of teams
- the emergence of management thought
- the modern manager
- the purpose of management
- the ownership and control structure related to directors' roles and policy
- coping with crises
- managing change

## TEAMS

Group activity was examined in Chapter 5 in relation to employees. In this chapter group activity is related to teams of managers, teams of supervisors, and teams of representatives of staff and operators.

The formation of a team and roles within a team determine its effectiveness. Fundamental issues are whether each person feels he or she is a true member, whether membership is blurred by poor relationships, low cohesiveness, and lack of co-operation. Each team's contribution may be outstanding if techniques of problem solving (Chapter 8) are adapted to teamwork.

### Natural formation

The natural formation of teams occurs at various structural levels. Typical examples are a senior management team headed by the managing director; various function teams headed by the marketing manager or the finance manager; various subfunction teams headed by appropriate specialists; and various lower management teams headed by supervisors.

### Scientific formation

The scientific formation of teams improves communication, since new ideas and essential feedback are provided when representatives are appointed on teams above their operational level.

The creation of autonomous teams and responsive team structures involving empowerment severely affects managerial roles and imposes new stresses on the manager and supervisor. Indeed the need for cross-functional operations and sophisticated teams to appreciate such activities is essential. They demand comprehensive education and training programmes, the creation of new outlooks, and continual improvement of each team member's capability.

## THE EMERGENCE OF MANAGEMENT THOUGHT

As empires grew and clashed, it became clear that managers were needed to achieve effective group effort. Major contributions towards management thought, however, did not appear until the twentieth century. Many management theory pioneers emerged from different countries, each one being influenced to a degree by local conditions. Many theories, principles and techniques have been proposed in the textbooks. After testing and refining, they eventually formed the basis of an operational discipline that emphasises a systems approach. This concept absorbs situations and contingencies, and recognises the logical social aim of making a surplus.

### The vital human factor

Competent managers now know that relying on a sound framework of theory and principles is preferable to relying on trial and error and limited experience. Nevertheless, major advances in management thought have only occurred since World War II. The main reasons for this delay were that for centuries industry has been regarded as dirty and degrading; economists were preoccupied with political economy and other aspects of business; political theorists thought mainly about policy making at national and international levels; and managers tended to concentrate on technology and accounts.

The change in emphasis and thinking is due to a realisation by specialists that the human factor is vital if an effective organisation is to cope with severe competition, rapid technological change and free trade. Some experts think competent managers should use this important foundation to develop their roles, but others think the time would be better spent learning thoroughly modern thought and practice.

## THE MODERN MANAGER

A competent manager is thoroughly educated and trained in management. Expanded a little, this means the manager:

- has genuine sensitivity towards people of all groups
- appreciates all the difficulties facing industry
- is fully aware of external aspects and knows how to cope with them
- understands and copes with the innovations of information technology
- works towards modern organisation structuring (more power to the periphery)
- applies human resources techniques
- establishes the right organisational culture, together with a customer-oriented philosophy
- manages time effectively

Even this short list illustrates the need for individuals with high ability, good sense and strong character.

According to Drucker, an effective manager seriously affects the ability of the organisation to perform. The implications of this statement are that a manager is one who gets the right things done, which means working effectively on the right things.

The modern manager creates wealth and values people within the company and outside, with consideration for their wants, desires and general welfare. An important feature or role is counselling.

### Counselling

Individuals and groups need considerable support due to the pattern of social life in domestic situations and at work. Anxiety and apparently irreconcilable problems invariably affect performance, attitudes and morale. The manager's role in these circumstances extends to advice, guidance or recommendations. This role may be proactive where appraisals indicate likely problems, or reactive where an employee seeks guidance on difficulties at work or at home.

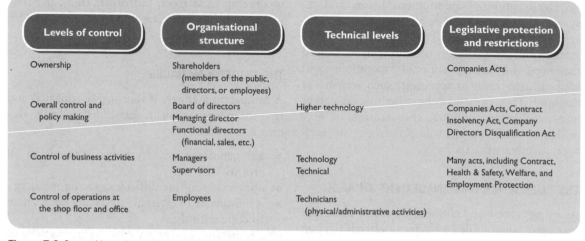

| Levels of control | Organisational structure | Technical levels | Legislative protection and restrictions |
|---|---|---|---|
| Ownership | Shareholders (members of the public, directors, or employees) | | Companies Acts |
| Overall control and policy making | Board of directors Managing director Functional directors (financial, sales, etc.) | Higher technology | Companies Acts, Contract Insolvency Act, Company Directors Disqualification Act |
| Control of business activities | Managers Supervisors | Technology Technical | Many acts, including Contract, Health & Safety, Welfare, and Employment Protection |
| Control of operations at the shop floor and office | Employees | Technicians (physical/administrative activities) | |

**Figure 7.2** Ownership and control structures: joint stock companies

The manager may feel incompetent when dealing with these situations, which may sometimes be complex. Then the manager should recommend consultation with a specialist. Remember that problems may seem trivial to others but they are vital to the individual. Some cases are difficult to disentangle when only one side of the story is told, especially in domestic crises. These might be referred to the statutory or voluntary agencies.

Here are some basic guidelines for managers or supervisors when counselling:

- Keep an open mind; do not attempt to impose an opinion.
- Develop the art of listening sympathetically.
- Avoid getting involved by taking sides.
- Attempt to summarise objectively by seeking agreement on points.
- Point out significant factors and leave the individual to suggest an answer.
- Usually the answer is more logical than expected and this may ensure implementation by the person.

### THE PURPOSE OF MANAGEMENT

Management's purpose is to protect the owner's interests by steering the company along channels that lead to sound goals. This will at least enhance and preferably ensure the company's future existence. To survive in the long run, management must build a reputation for the company of supplying goods or services of good quality at reasonable prices. In other words, the company offers value for money. Profitability in these conditions means management's purpose includes increasing productivity to a high standard of effectiveness. Thus, owners, consumers, the community and the country benefit, but not at the expense of one particular group.

### Protecting and conserving the external environment

A company's reputation also depends upon management's regard for environmental issues. The universal green revolution has created moral and legal obligations which cannot be ignored. Topics include radiation, waste disposal, effluent, pesticides, greenhouse gas emissions and nature conservation.

# Ownership and control structure

To provide a cohesive structure at the top of an organisation, a pattern similar to Fig. 7.2 is established in limited companies, which are the major part of British industry. The shareholders own a limited company. They may be members of the public (either directly or indirectly through various institutions), directors or employees of the company.

Under the Finance Act 1978, schemes for extending the ownership of a company's shares to its employees have been encouraged through tax advantages. The Finance Act 1987 launched a further encouragement, the personal equity plan (PEP). Subsequent Finance Acts have modified the schemes and, in 1991, included equities quoted in any recognised EU member state.

Some public limited companies (PLCs) are controlled by a small group of shareholders. By issuing non-voting shares, this small group will continue to control an expanding company with no change in the balance of power. Shareholders are also discussed in Chapter 28.

## BOARD OF DIRECTORS

Although ownership is vested in shareholders who may be spread throughout the country and abroad, control is delegated to the board of directors. They formulate and approve policy, and comply with legislation designed to protect shareholders' interests.

Such legislation includes the Companies Acts 1948–89, which require directors to disclose financial and non-financial information in the annual report and accounts. Furthermore, public listed or quoted companies must comply with Stock Exchange requirements, often more onerous than those in the statutes.

The size of the board varies. It may consist of full-time directors and working directors; there may also be part-time directors who sit on more than one board. Members are usually chosen for their ability and sometimes for their influence. Often they hold shares in the company but under the Companies Acts their holdings must be disclosed in the company's annual reports.

The managing director is elected by the board and normally holds the position of chairperson of the board. Company policy is conveyed to the senior executives and policy proposals are presented to the board for formal approval.

## A DIRECTOR

A director is appointed to manage the affairs of a company in accordance with its *articles of association* and the law generally. Should a supervisor be approached, which is not unusual, a safe policy is to seek professional advice. Every company director has a personal responsibility to ensure certain statutory documents are delivered to the Registrar of Companies, as and when required by the Companies Act. This includes accounts (usually only for limited companies), annual returns, and notice of change of directors or secretaries.

Failure to conform with requirements may incur civil penalties and criminal proceedings. Alternatively, the registrar could assume the company is no longer in business and strike it off the register. This serious step means the assets immediately pass to the Crown and may only be changed through court action.

The Companies Act 1989 requires directors to have a personal responsibility for making information known about the capital structure, management and activities of their companies, both to the members of the company and the general public. Also, in the event of liquidation the directors must provide the liquidator with a statement of affairs and co-operate.

Legally a director is either formally appointed or is anyone who undertakes the role. Alternative titles are a governor or a manager but a court may decide that, regardless of the title, it remains the role of a director.

Under the Employment Protection (Consolidation) Act 1978, a director has the obligation to ensure that each employee has a written statement of the terms of employment, within eight weeks of commencement. A director also has an obligation to ensure that employees have a safe working environment, outlined in the Health and Safety at Work Act 1974 and various EC directives.

Two other acts of importance are the Insolvency Act 1986 and the Company Directors Disqualification Act 1986. This legislation includes two important points:

- Personal liability to contribute to the company's debts in insolvency situations where wrongful trading applies. This means a company has gone into insolvent liquidation (assets being insufficient to pay liabilities, including debts) but the director knew, or ought to have known, before winding up commenced that there were no reasonable prospects of avoiding insolvent liquidation. Typical possible steps would have been immediate cessation of trading or appointment of an administrator to run the business until it was sold. The director must make a personal contribution to the company's assets if wrongful trading is proved and the liquidator makes an application to court.

- The court can issue a disqualification order against the director as well as a declaration of personal liability. The maximum period is fifteen years. During that time, if he or she manages a company, personal liability applies for debts and liabilities; and there is a criminal penalty. The Companies Registration Office maintains a register of disqualified people, which can be inspected. Disqualification may also apply if the director's conduct is shown to be unfit and if there is persistent default in filing legislative requirements.

### Expected capabilities of a director

Wrongful trading is associated with liability for negligent mismanagement. The court must determine the expected standard of conduct of a reasonably diligent person. This means the general ability, skills, knowledge and experience expected from a director. Liability applies if the level of capability is considered to be below the expected standard of conduct, although the director may have done his or her best.

# The importance of policy

Company policy is a guide or principle for the use of managers and supervisors. This enables them to reach objectives by following a set, broad pattern of behaviour.

Policies are intentionally widely defined to allow for individual interpretation in situations that require judgement and initiative. A rigid interpretation destroys policy and turns it into a narrow rule that dispenses with the human approach. A rule has its own place at a lower level in the organisation where policy is interpreted into detailed principles, followed by even more detailed rules for operational purposes.

Policy should be positive and lasting. Detailed principles and rules, in turn, must be more flexible for adaptation to rapidly changing situations. To summarise, a rule is intended to be interpreted in the same way all the time whereas a policy allows for discretion in application.

## POLICY MAKING

Policy making may take two forms. Multi-stage policy making commences with suggestions well down in the organisation structure. Someone has an idea and discusses it with others, who then pass on proposals or information to their superiors and so on, until definite suggestions reach the managing director. He or she, in turn, receives many suggestions from other sources, all of which are eventually moulded into proposals which are placed before the board of directors. The board, after due discussion, may formally approve or disapprove the proposed policy. In two-stage policy making, a proposal from the managing director is given approval by the board.

## FIVE POLICY REQUIREMENTS

### Acceptability

Policy should be acceptable to everyone. This is increasingly important considering the persistence of employees who want to know why policy is made or changed. Adequate reasons must be forthcoming and management ought to provide supervisors with sufficient information to satisfy queries. Withholding information creates gossip and speculation. This may be disastrous since it causes increased friction between management and employees, upsets relationships because of general suspicion, and lowers morale.

### Communicated to everyone

There should be no exceptions in communicating policy to employees. In the large company a group can easily be overlooked, so a number of channels should be used. Convincing people they were unintentionally overlooked is not an easy task, unless there are excellent relationships.

### Genuine application

Often management declares a policy for prestige reasons, such as publicity, and then fails to put the policy into practice. Management's policy, in these circumstances, is to ignore the declared policies. Such complete lack of wisdom is difficult to understand; not one employee is deceived and the word gradually spreads to all interested outsiders. Some managers use 'policy' in a negative way, making it an excuse for not carrying out some course of action. In this case policy does not appear in writing and is often made immediately to suit the circumstances. Another bad practice is wording policy in such a vague way that it can be distorted to fit in with any course of action at the time.

### Balanced interpretation

Supervisors who rigidly conform to principles – without due regard for the human situation – would be correctly interpreting policy in their own minds. Something more than correctness is needed in a human society; all the factors, when weighed carefully, might well provide a more balanced interpretation that would not match up with the narrow correct one. Therein lies the art of supervision, which is in no way an abuse of policy.

### Alignment with the objective

All policies should follow parallel courses on a broad front towards the objective. If they cross or oppose, a collective effort is lost and confusion develops. Misunderstandings are often the cause of the problem rather than faults in the stated policy. This danger highlights the need for a careful check that ambiguity or lack of understanding is not occurring at other levels.

### FIELDS OF POLICY

Fields of policy usually divide into three forms or stages in the organisation: (1) the overall policy (or top policy) governing a sense of belonging for everyone; (2) a policy for each function to clarify responsibilities and to identify collaboration with other functions; and (3) departmental policy to provide essential detail but allowing for flexibility. Here is a brief outline.

### Top policy

Broad policy, which indicates the general course the company takes, is usually the one that people have in mind as 'top policy'. Policy making should be a collective effort and this concept must be communicated to employees to develop a greater sense of belonging. The scheme applies equally in the following two fields.

### Functional policy

A breakdown of principles for each function (based upon top policy) forms the next logical step. Functional policy is the responsibility of the appropriate senior executive such as the sales manager, the works manager or the development engineer.

### Departmental policy

More detailed principles are formulated in departmental policy. These principles ensure that everyone who is much nearer to the actual operations is able to work within more closely defined limits. There should be a correspondingly smaller chance of misunderstanding. Some flexibility is needed which enables principles to become guides rather than hard and fast rules. In this sense, departmental supervisors are actually policy makers within their own sphere and they are responsible for the effectiveness of such policies.

# Coping with crises

Unfortunately, situations arise which force managers and supervisors to make urgent, critical decisions. These pressures may be internal or external, sudden, foreseeable but ignored, or a gradual build-up of events which eventually reaches breaking point.

Crises often involve conflict situations where a manager or supervisor must decide on how to respond by analysing motives, intentions, expectations and tactics. If there is a sound case to react to the crisis, there should be a good chance of success. The degree of force to use should be in line with the importance of the objective.

## USING LOGIC IN A CRISIS

Often time has run out for planning, consequently the individual has to resort to logic. The danger of this practice is that instant action may be fatal. Whenever possible, use of delaying tactics may be worthwhile to gain time to think. If time allows try to adopt the following procedure:

- Keep cool and coldly assess the crisis, using what, where, how, why and when techniques.
- Establish a contingency plan.
- Use other people who may be able to help.
- Carefully assess the crisis as it develops further and take appropriate action if it is going out of control.
- Avoid fringe problems that cloud the main issue.
- Launch the plan and monitor results.
- Revise as necessary and take corrective action.

## COMPETENCE IN A CRISIS

Dealing with crises is much easier for competent individuals, and their capability is invaluable at these times. They are recognisable immediately and senior management usually makes full use of their talents. In some companies these people are given authority to act wherever a crisis occurs.

# Managing change

Company survival usually depends upon management's capability to exploit change and employees' acceptance of change. For these reasons, managers and employees should thoroughly understand change and its eventual advantages.

Today changes are accelerating as new technologies become available. They create new skills, new methods of control, and increased discretion for employees. As a result, new problems appear in many forms, typically redundancy, terminations, increased stress, and empowerment difficulties. The complexity of managing change is illustrated in Fig. 7.3.

## EVENTS THAT TRIGGER CHANGE

Change may be viewed as any event which causes a substitution or succession of one element in place of another. This event may take many forms:

- sociological changes
- an invention
- an increase or decrease in any resource, e.g. products, labour, capital
- changes in legislation, locally or abroad
- environmental alterations, e.g. serious fires
- political moves, e.g. fiscal or monetary changes
- market changes affecting consumer choice and taste, supply and demand patterns
- opportunities to improve the organisation through technological improvements

# Categorising change

There are various ways of classifying or categorising events that cause change. These categories are usually termed control factors (controllable and uncontrollable), forecasting factors (foreseeable and unforeseeable) and planning factors.

## CONTROL FACTORS

- *Controllable factors*: Many internal events may be manipulated or managed effectively. This mainly depends upon sufficient information being available through sound communication. If the cause is an external event, this may be controllable provided there is an element of influence that may be applied by management.
- *Uncontrollable factors*: Uncontrollable factors are external events that cause pressures which cannot be influenced by management.

## FORECASTING FACTORS

- *Foreseeable*: The use of research and experience in all its forms provides information that can be analysed and used for forecasting.
- *Unforeseeable*: Unexpected events that defy prediction, such as unusual economic changes and environmental catastrophes.

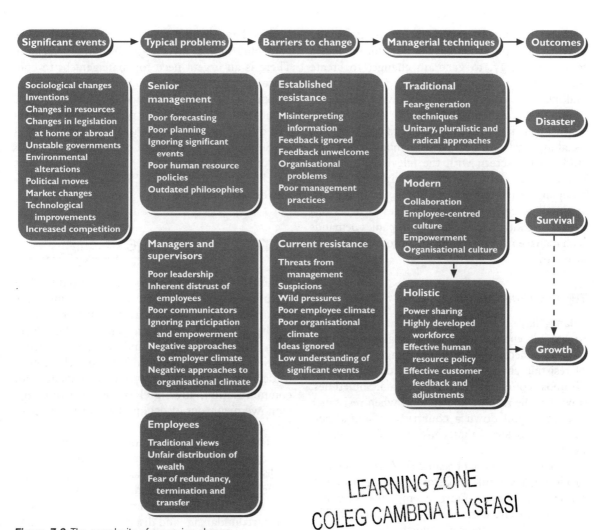

**Figure 7.3** The complexity of managing change

## PLANNING FACTORS

Planning factors are essentially internal changes created by managers and supervisors through the application of appropriate sills. Obviously plans must follow recognised principles and employees need to be fully committed. There are two aspects.

- *Creating change*: The application of skills through the use of foreseeable events, experience and planned programmes or projects.
- *Planning control techniques*: These are used to suit situations where planned control features are introduced to cope with new internal events which are causing problems.

## INFORMATION AND COMMUNICATION

The key activities in recognising the need for change are obviously obtaining information and communicating it to appropriate sectors in the organisation. These vital factors only become effective, first, when they are treated equally with other resources such as people, machines, materials, and capital; and second, when competent individuals manage change.

In management terms, information is usually interpreted as the availability of data for managers to create energy, to generate change, to create power, and to aid problem solving and decision making. The difficulties are knowing where to obtain the information and how to obtain it.

Insufficient information leads to disaster. The usual analogies are steering a car blindfolded, and studying the screen with the television switched off. Unfortunately, there are many cases where companies have followed a similar fatal pattern.

Intelligence in the armed forces is a serious matter. Treating intelligence in companies demands high management skills and an appropriate strategy at board level.

### THE NEED FOR CHANGE

Change has no boundaries: if one nation refuses to exploit change for various reasons, another nation immediately takes advantage. The result of resisting change on moral, political and other grounds is often not fully appreciated. Sometimes, however, the result *is* understood when resistance is used to pull down a country's economic performance to levels that cause unrest and create political situations.

Change is essential because there is no point in producing unsaleable goods or providing unwanted services. Trying to improve employee performance in these circumstances is a waste of time. The aim must be to improve worthwhile employee performance.

### RECESSIONS AND AFTERMATH

Recessions either force some companies out of business or create rationalisation programmes to survive. They cause particular problems associated with inept management, overambitious growth projects and inadequate profit targets. Consequently, recessions may accelerate mergers, contraction, expansion and severe structural changes. Severe structural changes often involve redundancies, early retirements, and terminations for those with poor performance records.

Change to overcome recessions is usually a painful process for many employees and supervisors. Indeed senior managers have to be replaced if they have insufficient vision and knowledge. New philosophies involving everyone are essential. There is an urgent need for management to convince each person that change is not simply a discipline but a means of survival. Also everyone should be involved, typically through empowerment and other motivation techniques.

Survival in the aftermath of a recession depends not only on adopting new technologies, but also on changing all employees' views and using employees effectively.

# Barriers to change

Although employees' behaviour is affected by their culture and beliefs, there are many other important factors which affect behaviour and resistance to change. These factors are generally thought to stem from inept senior and middle managers. Barriers to change therefore have to include poor leadership, inherent distrust of management, poor communication, low level of participation and empowerment, out-of-date philosophies, and poor human resources policies.

There are often well-founded suspicions of management. Even now firms exist where obvious faults are prevalent. Typical examples are employees being treated as uneducated; absence of pay scales; scandalous programmes involving terminations, redundancies and discipline; extremely high salaries paid to senior executives; and poor industrial relations policies involving unacceptable changes which create strong reactions.

Unfortunately, most managers are exceptionally good at creating barriers to change and upsetting the workforce. Even now fear-generation techniques are still used (Chapter 2). Managers could not achieve more negative reactions from employees if they spent a lifetime training for the task.

### ESTABLISHING THE RIGHT CLIMATE

The management employee plays many roles. They are an economic resource. They are also a professional within a system of power and authority, and within a social group. Properly conducting these roles helps to establish a climate of trust and mutual understanding of the harsh reality of change and its implications. Unfortunately, employees are adversely affected by three features: traditional views handed down to them from previous generations, the distribution of wealth, and educational levels. They all detract from managerial efforts.

### Influencing the climate

One strong criticism often levelled at British managers is they seem to place less value on change, innovation and professionalism compared with their American counterparts. There are many other faults which also affect their acceptance of change. Eleven major topics over which a manager has influence are listed below and are well worth studying:

- effective recruitment, including sound selection techniques
- removing nepotism and favouritism
- abandoning the hierarchy of rights involving unfair perks and unearned financial gain
- improving standards of behaviour by setting a good example
- installing modern technologies to keep abreast of change
- enforcing high ethical conduct with specific reference to sexual harassment and any unfair treatment
- establishing sound career development programmes with an appropriate pay structure
- sincerely supporting socialisation projects
- creating mutual trust and avoiding fear-generation techniques
- encouraging new ideas, using them and adequately rewarding contributions
- creating an education and training scheme to improve the capability of employees to contribute

### Environmental influences

Internal and external environmental influences have an overspill effect on productivity. They may cause managerial resistance to change which must be overcome by establishing a climate where managers respond automatically to pressures and changes.

Managers should accept that their efforts will be affected by these influences, which are a part of both the sociological structure and political life. In turn they will meet resistance from employees. This takes two forms: established resistance and current resistance. The ideal is to avoid resistance of whatever kind by adopting modern management techniques already described, but this is a lengthy process.

# Discouraging established resistance

## MAJOR TECHNIQUES

### Familiarisation

Spend time with employees and attempt to develop their awareness and understanding of change and its effects. Employees invariably misinterpret information they receive if they do not understand its implications to the company and themselves. Generally this means the change is treated as a threat.

### Feedback on views

Obtain as much feedback as possible on employees' reactions to information. Careful analysis is essential to find out (1) why views are biased; (2) why more information and discussions were neglected if views were based on ignorance; and (3) the possible organisational difficulties that give rise to the situation.

### Positive action

Recognise that discussion and passing information are inevitably insufficient. Negative views are generally based upon deeper organisational problems and poor managerial practices. These difficulties must be traced, analysed and corrected as opportunities arise.

## COUNTERACTION TECHNIQUES

Choosing the appropriate technique depends upon capability, the environmental situation and the philosophy senior management is attempting to develop. Often all techniques may be seen operating in various parts of the company. Degrees of success are difficult to analyse. Techniques tend to align with styles of leadership. Starting with abdication, the pattern develops to include autocratic or domineering rule, selling proposals by various forms of persuasion, consultation, and finally, participation.

## AVOIDING CURRENT RESISTANCE

Theoretically, the removal of all the threats and suspicions which appear in employees' minds solves the problem. Unfortunately, managers are never in full control of all the pressures that create threat. Often wild pressures cause most of the problems. Much can be done, however, to minimise the effects and, in the case of controllable pressures, to avoid threat completely.

### Main approaches

Application of sound management skills is obviously the answer to avoid current resistance. The main features strongly associated are:

- to examine the complexity of co-operation
- to create a better climate
- to discuss openly innovation and the risks if it is ignored
- to recognise the controversial aspects of change related to technology, culture and social structure
- to discuss possible industrial trends and their effects if they are ignored.

### The underlying difficulty

Changes often create threats to employees, typically risks of permanent or temporary unemployment. These risks are reduced if the economy improves by establishing new industries and increasing production. However, this is small consolation to those declared redundant, especially in later stages of life; hence the importance of state social and welfare schemes.

# Ongoing change

Continual survival implies a policy of ongoing change which means everyone in the organisation is committed to updating all the activities. Especially important are research, development, production and marketing. These must keep abreast with competition, technologies and customer wants.

## FUNDAMENTAL MANAGEMENT REQUIREMENTS

- Review all activities; this should be treated as one of the roles for all managers and supervisors.
- Introduce innovation flexibility as a part of everyone's job.
- Adopt periodic centralised reviews to discover weak areas and compensate with revised objectives.
- Check on the organisational climate (as indicated earlier) and adjust if necessary.
- Ensure that managerial professionalism is being maintained by checking on internal and external environmental influences and adjusting if there is any sign of managerial resistance to change.
- Discourage any established resistance from employees by using the techniques previously mentioned.
- Involve key employees at all stages of change and accept any reasonable proposals.
- Always emphasise the benefits of introducing change by disclosing all the information (within the limits of industrial security) without delay; this should include plans, progress, modifications, changes in competitors' companies, and changes in customers' wants, based upon research.
- Whenever adverse rumours develop, explain the truth in detail to employees by using various means to satisfy any misapprehensions; remember to check later.

## ORGANISATIONAL DEVELOPMENT

Organisational development (OD) for ensuring ongoing change was described in Chapter 3.

Closely associated with the process is thorough understanding of organisational behaviour (OB), which is essential before any changes are introduced.

## QUESTIONS

1 What are the essential characteristics of a competent manager?

2 Explain the managerial roles approach and list the roles, according to Mintzberg.

3 Discuss the key business activities, according to Fayol.

4 What are the disadvantages of relying on trial and error and limited experience when supervising?

5 Define the terms management team, supervisory team and business team.

6 What is the prime purpose of management?

7 Discuss the term 'managerial activities'.

8 Discuss the responsibilities of management to shareholders, to the community and to the employee.

9 Carefully explain the term 'company policy' and state the essential requirements of a policy.

10 Describe the various fields of policy encountered in a business.

11 Why is managing change essential in any company?

12 List ten topics that, in your opinion, managers should concentrate on to reduce employee distrust.

13 How would you attempt to reduce resistance to change from employees?

14 The formation and roles within teams determine the degree of organisational effectiveness. Discuss this statement.

15 List the managerial roles and associated activities.

16 Why is counselling considered to be so important to employees?

17 Outline some basic guidelines when counselling employees.

18 Discuss how the supervisor should deal with crises.

19 What are the main causes of a crisis in a section?

20 Discuss the events that often trigger change.

21 How may the right climate be established to cope with change?

22 What are the fundamental requirements to encourage change?

23 Discuss the importance of ongoing change in an organisation.

---

## CASE STUDY

At a supervisors' meeting, James suggested the managing director should visit each section and make himself known to the employees. Apparently the managing director often managed to introduce himself to visitors touring the factory and preferred if possible to deal with any complaints from customers.

The other supervisors agreed with the idea since it was well known that employees and supervisors felt cut off from the levels of organisation above them. Indeed one supervisor thought the senior managers should also show themselves occasionally. A memo was drafted and sent to the managing director.

Some weeks later the chairman read out a reply from the managing director; it said he would like to attend the next supervisors' meeting to discuss the proposal. The surprised supervisors were confused and wondered how to proceed in view of the complete change of attitude. One supervisor mentioned they had not said anything about it to the works manager.

*Comment on the managing director's decision and his probable views of the organisation. Consider the items to be included in the next supervisors' meeting and any further action they should take before the next meeting.*

A college lecturer visits a company that has already sent all of its supervisors on a part-time one-year course over the past few years. Walking round the offices with the managing director and renewing acquaintances, she is appalled to discover that no changes have taken place.

The principles of ergonomics have been ignored; simple faults are still evident, such as bad lighting, poor layouts, no regard for motion economy, no safety provisions and poor seating arrangements.

Remembering the excellent projects on work study that had been submitted by the supervisors there, she was puzzled and disappointed.

At the end of the visit she poses the usual question about recruitment and receives the following reply from the managing director: 'No, I'm sorry, Madeleine, we're not sending our replacement supervisors on courses any more. As you know times are bad and we have to cut costs wherever possible. We look at every penny these days'.

*Give the possible reasons for the failure of the training programme.*

Andrew was a newly appointed trained supervisor. He was confronted with a situation where the three other supervisors seemed to sit back and allow the sections to run themselves. The general atmosphere was relaxed and cordial between sections. Discipline appeared to be non-existent.

Andrew found this way of operating difficult to accept and, after a few weeks, decided to see his boss. He explained and thought that, although the workloads were completed on time, there was overmanning according to his calculations.

To his surprise the manager scowled, sat back and said, 'So you want to rock the boat and upset everyone? You'll cause a lot of trouble with the supervisors and staff but at the end of the day will it be worthwhile?'

Andrew reacted, 'Yes, I think it will in the long run. It's soul-destroying to work in a department that's out of step with the rest of the organisation!'

*What can be done in this situation where Andrew obviously lacks his manager's support? If you were Andrew, would you consider discussing the problem with the other supervisors?*

# 8

# Principles and practice of management

## The validity of management principles

There is always some concern over how principles are formed and developed, and their validity in management and supervision. Unless the background is known, there can be little confidence in applying principles, apart from the use of blind faith.

The study of management has been based upon the assumption that an underlying science exists which explains phenomena (occurrences and perceptions). Logically, therefore, management science is the search for knowledge; when discovered it is classified through scientific method (Chapter 9); the relationships between variables and limits are distinguished; and underlying principles are established.

Scientific method, in total, means finding facts through observations of events and things, verifying their accuracy through further observations, classifying and analysing the facts to discover causal relationships which are thought to be true. However, opinions differ because the use of scientific method to find principles does not imply there is an absolute truth. Further research and analysis may modify the findings, consequently conjecture or guesses are often proposed. There is a strong belief that management, involving social sciences, is an inexact science because it deals with complex phenomena which remain a mystery.

To be realistic, the knowledge already discovered should be used and not discarded, although it is incomplete. Principles should be treated as fundamental truths based upon the present state of scientific research. There are three relevant terms to explain. One way of packaging the terms and contributions to make some sense is to think of each one as a part of total management.

- *Management science*: This is a quantitative approach to management. It includes management techniques which use mathematical techniques and operational research. Higher mathematics in decision making, planning and control are also used.
- *The practice of management*: This is a means of improving management skills by using management principles as a basis for further development. According to Peter Drucker, 'Management is a practice rather than a science, so there are no precise solutions; as with treating an illness, what matters is that the patient recovers, not whether the doctor is right'.
- *The art of management*: This is the practical application of management science; the use of knack and imaginative skill.

## Cultural and environmental differences

A current aspect causing concern is the effect of cultural and environmental differences on management science. Research on this topic is called comparative management. It entails analysis of management in different environments and looks at why enterprises show different results in various countries. Investigations indicate that management philosophy tends to vary in different countries, but organisation structuring and growth rely on logical, recognised practices for success.

Management philosophy is broader than management science because it covers ultimate reality, human perception and beliefs, ethics (or moral philosophy) and the conduct of life. Thus cultural and environmental variations place an extra strain on relationships when managers and supervisors are faced with a multiracial workforce.

Management philosophy is recognisable by the way business practice (or cultural outlook) is adopted. One way is to allow an organisational culture to happen or evolve with no guidance. Another way is to operate a comprehensive strategy which is consciously planned or preferred in the organisation. This strategy incorporates a distinct orientation towards the market (Chapter 4). In modern practice this is a market orientation where all organisational activities are geared to satisfying customers' wants. Evolution without guidance may be disastrous, but it is not unusual.

A sound strategy attempts to change behaviour patterns which do not coincide with the philosophy. Aspects that are examined include the way business is conducted, ways of dealing with people, values, norms and beliefs. After analysis new programmes are arranged to guide everyone towards the intended outlook.

Philosophy may be seen as idealism, humanising, materialism and practical approaches; culture may be viewed as the degree of sophistication and refinement, knowledge, and teaching in a community or organisation.

In this chapter a universal application of management principles and practice is assumed. It begins by discussing major principles, the application of managerial skills and the skills cycle. Next come management–supervisor relations, with particular reference to pressures and demands on managers, the present state of management and how the supervisor should make allowances for managers. Finally, it looks at making the best use of available time.

## Principles of management

All principles of management may be grouped to fit conveniently into seven main management functions:

- forecasting
- planning
- organising
- co-ordinating
- commanding
- controlling
- motivating

L. Urwick published in 1943 a logical arrangement of these principles in his book *Elements of Administration*. They remain essential; most managers continue to neglect some of them and many behave as though they have never heard of their existence. Some even believe and boast that common sense (Chapter 9) is sufficient to manage, much to the amusement of surrounding employees.

Remember the importance of collaborative management (Chapter 2) applied to commanding and controlling when reading these two principles.

Peter Drucker believes there are five basic principles: setting objectives, organising, motivating and communicating, establishing measurements of performance, and developing people. When associated with the seven management principles, three divisions are apparent. First, set the objectives; this is done by forecasting, planning, organising, motivating and communicating. Second, establish measurements of performance; this is extensive and includes controlling in all its forms (Part Three) and especially work study (Chapters 24 and 25). Third, develop the people; this is a complex process involving motivation, education and training, and human resources development programmes.

## Forecasting

Forecasting is often recognised as being essential but unpredictable for many reasons. The five main aspects to consider are the process of prediction, the unknown factor, major guidelines, research problems and the creativity factor.

### PREDICTIONS

Assuming there is sufficient information available to make a prediction, the individual must now find a place where it is possible to think without undue distraction. When located, he or she should marshal thoughts logically and try to visualise or predict future happenings. Some people call this process intelligent guesswork, luck or being psychic.

## THE UNKNOWN FACTOR

Unfortunately, a forecast is often arrived at with very little information and in difficult circumstances, hence the phrase 'muddling through'. The unknown factor (the missing information) must be taken into account to maintain balance. Consider the serious punters who attempt to marshal as many facts as possible on the horses in a race. To lessen the odds, they take everything into consideration, including factors such as the weather and injuries, which make the results unpredictable with any accuracy.

## MAJOR GUIDELINES

In the above circumstances there are certain guidelines to follow that minimise the risk of error:

- Use all sources of information and attempt to assess accuracy.
- Gain the maximum amount of information possible in the time available.
- Work in surroundings conducive to thought.
- Take account of the unknown factor.
- Do not rely on trends.
- Consider all the possible avenues or alternatives.
- Avoid being dogmatic; emphasise what may happen rather than what will happen.

## RESEARCH

The problems of research are sometimes insurmountable because of high expense, the time factor, and the uncertainty of decision making to explore the appropriate fields. The results of research may be unproductive through lack of sufficient background information, and not recognising their significance at the time. Nevertheless, research is vital for a successful business. A simplified way of examining research is to consider searches and experiments. These highlight the use of information.

### Searches

The value of constant investigation is usually recognised. Attempts to investigate become difficult in practice through lack of time. People who are under pressure at work must make decisions based upon less and less information, with the inevitable consequences. However, the sight of everyone working at high pitch pleases rather than bothers some managers. If managers are overworked, it is their own fault for not delegating; but there is a limit if top management restricts staff to smaller numbers than are really adequate. Some managers, too, are unable to assess work content accurately, even after research has been conducted and the information is presented to them. Take care to distinguish between two main aspects:

- *Searching with known objectives in mind*: seeking information on obvious missing areas or 'objects'. This straightforward process is attempting to uncover information leading to a source which is known to exist. There is no creativity involved.
- *Searching unknown areas*: seeking causes of problems or questionable activities. This complex process usually demands far more thought and creativeness.

The information gathered may now be analysed, data produced from the analysis, and various techniques applied (Chapter 2). The following minor principles should be intrinsic to any searches:

- *Cause and effect*: a belief that effects can be traced back to particular causes, which is the motivator when pursuing investigations back to sources.
- *Comprehension*: the results must be measurable and presented in an understandable form to be of practical use in forecasting.
- *Intelligent observation*: studying an activity requires a certain degree of awareness and appropriate background knowledge for intelligent interpretation to be possible.
- *Recognition and analysis*: following from intelligent observation, the recognition of similarities is essential when analysing the information and knowing how to proceed to the next stage of investigation.

| Creativity | Generating creativity | Extracting ideas | Innovating |
|---|---|---|---|
| Many ideas already in existence<br>Ideas not divulged | Establish a favourable<br>   organisational climate<br>Provide time to think<br>   and daydream<br>Provide time to develop<br>   flexible opinions<br>Encourage inquisitiveness<br>Allow new approaches<br>   regardless of possible errors<br>Use empowerment<br>Use thought techniques | Develop informality<br>Seek advice and views<br>Couple activities with objectives<br>Use empowerment sensibly<br>Search<br>Experiment<br>Discuss and allow freewheeling | Use the ideas<br>Experiment<br>Analyse<br>Conduct research and<br>   development<br>Forecast<br>Organise and co-ordinate |

**Figure 8.1** The creativity factor

### Experiments

Experiments use existing basic information and the outcome of searches. There are two main areas:

- *Known objectives*: these experiments use trial and error, follow established scientific techniques, or rely on ideas.
- *Unknown fields*: these experiments use existing techniques and often discoveries are made, such as penicillin. Note the *object* already existed; it was not invented. Experiments may rely on chance alone.

## The creativity factor

Forecasting has been achieved if a new situation or a change can be imagined. This is the vital feature which guarantees survival, provided the process moves to the planning stage. Accelerating the change can then begin. Figure 8.1 illustrates the creativity factor and its vital processes.

### ACCELERATING CHANGE: THREE PHASES

#### Phase 1: Creating

A fundamental requirement is to develop an organisational climate that encourages creativity. One view is that most employees already possess new ideas on how to improve their jobs and the organisation. Creating should use the outcomes of searches and experiments to avoid duplication.

The two main areas that demand perseverance are:

- creating a unique or revolutionary object
- creating a new technique or new mode of operation

#### Phase 2: Extracting the ideas

Using techniques to encourage employees to divulge their ideas which remain hidden for many reasons.

#### Phase 3: Innovating

Implementing the new ideas is a key factor. Without innovation the whole process of accelerating change will collapse.

### ENCOURAGING CREATIVITY

Although many new ideas already exist, generating further ideas is a healthy process that uplifts employees to higher performance levels. The principle of problem solving relies heavily on various methods to aid this process. These methods are based upon creative thinking (see below). At this stage there are certain ways the supervisor can use to encourage creativity:

- Allow employees time to daydream and use their imagination on situations. This helps the brain to freewheel, although many managers would deplore seeing an 'idle' employee.

- Allow time for flexible opinions to emerge in discussions and so avoid rapid judgements. Unfortunately, the time factor often intervenes.
- Encourage inquisitiveness and searching questions. This develops a more favourable attitude towards contributing ideas on any aspect which seems different and apparently unrelated until probed more deeply.
- Demonstrate the courage to try new approaches regardless of possible errors. This accelerates the feeling of respect and initiative. Also the approach may lead to a breakthrough later if a critical examination is used to study the outcomes of the new situation.
- Use empowerment and ensure the team structure remains flexible and buoyant.

## EXTRACTING THE IDEAS

There are many approaches for extracting ideas; the choice depends on the particular situation in an organisation. Here are the essentials:

- Ensure the relationship with employees is conducive to open discussion and a friendly atmosphere where formality is neutralised.
- Ask for advice, seek to involve employees, and do not ridicule even the silliest ideas.
- Try to focus attention on coupling activities with objectives and how to achieve them without emphasising existing problems and situations.
- Use the empowerment concept to show reliance and respect for the authority and responsibilities placed on employees, but do not attempt to pressurise for answers.

## INNOVATING

The importance of innovating is demonstrated in the case of the Dual Cyclone vacuum cleaner invented by J. Dyson. The Dyson cleaner is more efficient than conventional cleaners because it has no dustbag to become clogged up. It uses a high speed vortex of air to whizz dirt particles towards the rim of a cylindrical collector and it continues to perform at the same level when conventional vacuum cleaners have become clogged. The machine has swept the market, proved the fallibility of brands, and J. Dyson is now a millionaire. Here are the features which illustrate these concepts:

- *Information* was known of companies that use systems of spinning airflow, minicyclones, to produce orderly paint droplets.
- *Experiments* showed that performance dropped as the dustbag filled in conventional cleaners.
- *Creativeness* produced an idea from the information and experiments.
- *Innovation* combined the paint technology with a standard vacuum cleaner to produce a revolutionary machine, after five thousand prototypes.
- *Forecasting* predicted that removal of the obvious fault of standard vacuum cleaners would sell and prove the fallibility of standard brands.

The importance of forecasting is often overlooked, especially when related to production planning and total lead time (Chapter 26) where the initial sector contains forecasts for procurement and processing time before a customer's order is received and produced. This forecasted sector (or risk sector) has high potential for considerable cost-reduction programmes by using logistics (Chapter 30).

# Planning

After forecasting, the next step is to determine the targets or objectives and plan a way to reach these goals.

All industrial activities must be examined considering available resources so that plans will be realistic. The good planner will be thinking along lines of economy, which implies his or her designs are simple, standardised with due allowance for changes, and weighted for each item depending upon its importance to the plan.

Scientific control is not possible unless a plan is based upon a timescale. Planning on this broad front means deciding what shall be done, where, when, how and by whom. It involves not only re-adjustment of objectives as new information flows in, but also revision of policies, programmes, budgets, systems, organisation and controls.

Top management's task is strategic planning of overall policies, objectives, finance and control. This is implemented by managers or senior supervisors who are responsible for tactical planning of how the objectives are to be achieved in the time given.

Supervisors then plan, on a short- or medium-term basis, the actual achievement of broad plans using the resources available. This is process planning, involving scheduling, progressing, controlling and motivating employees.

The fourth and final phase must logically end with the shop floor or office where employees plan their work (task planning) to complete the jobs allocated to them within the established time limits.

# Organising and co-ordinating

Organising means arranging for everything to be at the right place, at the right time, consequently work may continue according to the plan. Co-ordinating means ensuring all the formal activities of the concern are combined to form a balanced, effective organisation. Three phases that lead to co-ordination:

- Planning includes organisation design, or establishing the structure.
- Staffing is completed under the aspect of command.
- Aligning everyone's efforts is the eventual effect of co-ordination.

When employees agree to co-operate and naturally participate, management will be able to co-ordinate successfully. An underlying condition is the ability to lead and motivate people. It is pointless for management to complain that employees will not co-operate; the solution is within management's hands to create the right conditions that encourage and promote co-ordination.

Co-ordination is achieved if all the activities are arranged and adjusted in time and situation to ensure smooth economical running and progress towards objectives. Smooth economical operation is an all-embracing term which includes the absence of selfish interests, the balancing of units and adherence to plans.

The achievement of balance begins with the co-ordination of main activities or functions by the managing director, and continues through to the level of supervisors who co-ordinate the activities of sections (or departments) with other sections. Balance is made possible by allowing unrestricted input of both information and production

assemblies from those who supply the section, and unrestricted output to the receiving sections in turn. If the chain of movement is broken, production is off-balance and the co-ordinating effect ceases. In this sense, co-ordinating is an intentional active principle.

# Commanding

Commanding (or directing) means giving orders, issuing instructions and deciding when and how subordinates should carry out the work.

Maintaining command includes making decisions about the relative priority of the jobs needing to be done and ensuring discipline is kept at a reasonable level, consistent with good working arrangements. Effective leadership is essential for commanding and motivating.

Although organisation and co-ordination are discussed together because all the principles of organisation are used to achieve co-ordination, in practice command must appear between the two for the following reasons.

When the design and planning stages are completed, the next step is to appoint competent staff to the positions drawn up in the organisational plan. Upon completion of staffing, when the individuals are assigned to their jobs and given appropriate duties, authority and responsibilities, they will immediately start to issue instructions. Command becomes operational at this point and its effectiveness will depend upon the ability of managers and supervisors to raise morale by fair and just treatment and to lead in the right direction. Here are the guiding principles for achieving effective command. They are discussed in Part Two.

### ALIGNMENT OF INTEREST

All effort must be directed towards the general interest. Self-interest must take second place, otherwise command has failed.

### STAFFING

Staffing means appointing managers of the right calibre, consistent with company policy.

## MORALE

The critical test of command is unmistakably the general feeling of all employees (including majority and minority groups) towards management and the company. Because much ill-feeling and friction are possible between the two sides (management and employees), it takes courage and faith to carry out a long-term programme for morale improvement. A permanent change in management's attitude is essential, otherwise relationships will deteriorate rapidly again.

Apart from sensing morale by the atmosphere, variations can be measured through productivity; the amount of information flowing to the top; the number of mistakes, complaints, grievances and strikes; wastage; labour turnover; and the degree of co-operation.

The causes of low morale are usually poor leadership; very little fairness and justice in all aspects of industrial life, which includes wages, promotion and working conditions; no chance to display initiative and participate; no satisfaction from the job; and no feeling of importance.

## ADEQUATE PAYMENTS AND APPROPRIATE PENALTIES

Adequate payments and appropriate penalties should be second nature to the competent manager. Fairness and justice are essential to maintain a good reputation. Any attempt to show favour to one person results in antagonising the rest. Where it is obviously essential to deviate from the rule, the reason must be made known whenever possible, if the circumstances are not already common knowledge.

## ACTIVE PARTICIPATION

People must be allowed to expand their capabilities by using their initiative, criticising and making suggestions openly with no fear of rebuff. In these conditions they feel more important and develop enthusiasm and drive in response to the progressive atmosphere. The manager must use the ideas by displaying a positive approach and only resorting to rejection in exceptional circumstances. Such rejection demands a logical reason and careful explanations to avoid demotivation.

# Controlling

The principle of controlling implies conforming to legislative and financial requirements and maintaining systems and procedures that provide accurate information on time to various levels of management. This form of control may appear to be bureaucratic in the sense of conforming to rigid requirement. However, flexible control for empowerment purposes may be achieved provided there is a responsible attitude towards basic control requirements and an emphasis on improving the processes. The danger of misusing control flexibility to distort information and deviating funds is often present.

The principle of control means checking performance and taking action to remedy deviations from the plan, which involves a constant vigil on all stages of the work and the costs incurred.

Effective control demands (1) full knowledge of the plans and instructions to start; (2) accurate feedback on operations and results; (3) a common measure to gauge the amount of deviation from the plan; and (4) positive action to correct the deviations. (This subject is detailed in Part Three.) Such scientific control is a very demanding and continuous process.

The managing director gives the board of directors control information to check on broad policy and programmes, generally from the financial viewpoint. Management accountancy techniques and all the financial control systems connected with them provide the machinery for control throughout the company.

For production and operations supervisors and specialists obtain their control figures from information about labour, machines, quality, throughput and output. Similarly, managers obtain their control statistics from information on operations and administration, including sales in cash and quantity, and all the distribution expenses. All the information prepared must be worthwhile, providing figures at an economic cost for some positive purpose.

# Motivating

Each managerial activity depends on all the others; this makes it difficult to think about a particular activity in isolation. Managing is a combined operation which demands a wide, balanced, human outlook. This should be tempered by the use of a multitude of major and minor principles.

Probably motivation – the inner force that stirs people from lethargic attitudes into dynamic action – is the most neglected aspect of management. Furthermore, employees are irritated and depressed by half-hearted attempts to improve the situation; they naturally fail to respond to fresh encouragement, and the blame is nearly always laid unfairly on them. Successful motivation of employees requires a complete change in the outlook of most managers who are either unenthusiastic, or too cynical, or too set in their ways to change. To overcome management's faults and misconceptions, long-term programmes are needed, although results are sometimes not seen for a few years.

The strong tie between motivation and co-ordination is apparent when the principles involved are considered. These include:

- job enrichment programmes
- constant communication to everyone of all relevant information concerning the business
- encouragement of participation and self-discipline
- ambitious education and training schemes
- joint consultation
- personnel counselling
- fair schemes of pay, work and welfare
- a sincere management

## The skills cycle

Underlying and often permeating the principles described above are certain basic management skills which also apply to supervisors. By appropriate training it is possible to improve these skills through practice and adjustment. The development of each skill also depends upon the degree of education in certain disciplines or knowledge areas.

Naturally there is a tendency for the disciplines to overlap into more than one skill, and in actual operation the dividing line between some of the skills becomes blurred. Figure 8.2 indicates these skills in sector form to show the cycle effect, which operates in a clockwise sequence when logical thought is applied to the work processes in any situation. The diagram also indicates some ways of checking on the supervisor's performance as he or she develops. During the working day, the supervisor will have to cope with many situations and people, which means several of these cycles are operating at any one time.

Figure 8.2 may also be used to break down certain principles into component skills. For example, the skills associated with control are to establish suitable standards, to check performance and to make decisions that correct the deviations. A further use is to locate operating faults. For example, the tendency for some supervisors is to think that so long as employees have been told what is required of them, the essential motivating factor has been provided. 'I told them what to do but they didn't do it' is a very common saying in industry. Two skills are, in fact, necessary: action to achieve the plan, which is the communicating skill; followed by the motivating skill, which will decide whether the employees will actually do anything once they know what is required.

## Planning and the supervisor

Any person who controls a labour force, regardless of its size, must plan so far as can be foreseen. Employees expect to work to a set plan and schedule, and be controlled according to the plan and changing circumstances. Absence of planning produces chaos where the work is being done. Consequently, individuals work from crisis to crisis, frustration develops and productivity is reduced to a minimum.

The supervisor must allocate time for planning in sufficient detail to satisfy the requirements of subordinates and production. Time spent on planning is never wasted, provided the supervisor is reasonably proficient at the task. The extra thought should result in more accurate and detailed plans, with less risk of overlooking possible difficulties. There is more likelihood, therefore, of the plan succeeding.

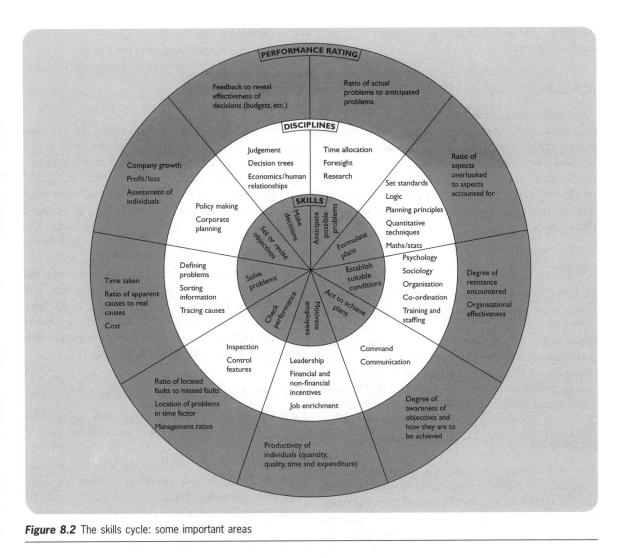

**Figure 8.2** The skills cycle: some important areas

## PLANNING SUPERVISORY ACTIVITIES

Most supervisory activities lend themselves to planning, and this leads to more effective supervision. A cross-section of the main aspects is given below.

### Production and operations

A large range of separate plans makes up the overall plan for production. Machine capacity, labour utilisation, scheduling workloads, supplies of materials, provision for tools and equipment, safety devices, batch quantities, and all other resources are planned and combined to form the production plan (Chapter 26).

Within this plan, the supervisor's section generally forms only a part of total production, which means co-ordination with other sections is of primary importance. He or she must allow for this factor and be able to accept work according to overall production, supply work in sequence to the next section, and be prepared to help in emergencies.

In the majority of situations, this production process applies equally to operations in the service industries. Well-established production techniques may be applied, and the interaction between operations and the customer remains vitally important.

## Objectives

Any objectives must be intelligently planned to fit into a timescale that takes account of the performance capabilities. Establishing unrealistic targets is a waste of time. Progress must be controlled and adjustments made as required. The total collapse of efforts to reach specified objectives is bad for morale; planning with too much optimism should therefore be avoided.

## Control

Effective control does not happen by chance. A plan of the particular activity must be drawn up on a time, cost, quality or quantity basis, or some other form of standard for measuring results. Variances from the plan are now apparent by reference to the data, and control is possible by taking appropriate action (Chapter 23). Planning and control must always be complementary.

## Organisation

The importance of planning associated with organisation has been stressed in Chapter 3. Careful planning avoids haphazard growth, rigidity and disregard for organisational principles. Working towards the ideal organisation and making wise changes when opportunities occur, are both made easier by conforming to a plan.

## Work study

The introduction of work study is simplified by planning a careful explanation to employees. The programme may include posters, literature, personal letters, films and introductory talks. Thus work study can be introduced with a minimum of disruption. Planning the work to be studied may be based upon sectors with the following characteristics; further information is given in Chapters 24 and 25.

- causing hold-ups
- expensive to operate
- creating trouble spots
- relatively high labour turnover areas
- identified for a contemplated increase in output

## Communication

Communication may be improved by gaining experience in running the particular section and by a plan of methods, routes and check systems. Suitable improvements may be planned to eliminate weak spots. A simple plan would begin with an assessment of each communication between supervisor and subordinates. Its importance, the time factor, the cost and the confidentiality factor would all be revealed. This information will indicate the best means of communication from the methods available for each kind of message. The objective is to ensure the right person receives the right message at the right time, and interprets it in the right way. (All aspects of communication are discussed in Chapters 14, 15 and 16.)

## The daily routine

It is important to plan the way each day will be spent. Certain daily tasks cannot be neglected and, unless the supervisor plans the day, or week, there is a risk of overlooking a vital activity. Simple checklists are useful reminders of daily and periodic tasks which otherwise may easily be forgotten. More elaborate activities that extend over long periods may be charted on the wall by using a time base across the top of a sheet and an activity base down the left-hand side to form a grid. Each square may be either ticked or used to enter details if on a larger scale. Pending jobs may be similarly progressed or listed; use a pending tray or file for the paperwork.

In conjunction with delegation, the supervisor should plan to offload duties as the opportunities occur and use the freed time for more important tasks which have been neglected. (Time management is discussed in detail later in this chapter.)

## Health and safety

Reducing the accident rate and promoting health depend upon detailed planning by management and the supervisor. Planning for safety is an integral part of reducing accidents to a minimum by making machinery and equipment less hazardous and promoting the right attitudes towards safety. The supervisor's social responsibility cannot be fulfilled unless he or she plans to prevent accidents rather than wait for them to happen and then reduce the risk. (Chapter 21 covers health and safety, and Chapter 22 covers welfare.)

## Maintenance

Planned maintenance is similar in some ways to planned safety. Time and cost may be cut by planning the maintenance of machines to reduce the risk of breakdown. Ensure smooth output flow by replacing limited-life components and assemblies before a breakdown occurs. (Maintenance is discussed as an aspect of cost reduction in Chapter 30.)

## Training

Training must be treated seriously as a planned activity to improve productivity by introducing better methods and safer ways of working to reduce fatigue and frustration. Planned training includes induction training schemes, training employees to use new machines as obsolescent models are superseded, training newcomers at weak points where hold-ups are occurring or are likely to occur, and making hazardous operations safer by increasing the skill of the employee (Chapter 19).

## Motivation

Everything mentioned above about management and motivation applies also at supervisory level. All factors which affect motivation closely interact; therefore the approach must be on a broad front for employees to develop their capabilities and enthusiasm simultaneously. The plan should be long term and sustained in application. New techniques of leadership and supervision, group activity, organisation, human relations and job satisfaction are essentially long-term projects and have a sustained effect, whereas financial incentives are short term and often short-lived as motivators (Chapters 11, 12 and 13).

## Human relations

The supervisor who plans successfully also improves relationships with subordinates. They have more faith in a leader who defines objectives, plans carefully and shows command of the situation. Morale will rise as schemes develop and employees benefit from effective plans (Chapters 9 and 10).

# A guide to better planning

The topics so far only indicate some of the many activities which must be planned by the supervisor. Savings in time and nervous energy are possible by planning an activity. Some guides to better planning are now listed, followed by the characteristics of a sound plan, SWOT analysis and APACS.

## MAIN GUIDES

- Planning must not be postponed. Planning is hard work, but tasks become even harder without it.
- Planning must not be selfish. Remember the part played by the section within the organisation; co-operative and co-ordinative elements are essential in plans.
- Always plan within a realistic timescale. Effective control depends upon measurement of work or a project within a period. Furthermore, employees tend to work within periods related to output, which means they work to time targets.
- Marshal as much information as possible. Remember to include employees, machines, materials and other resources. Use up-to-date information and all available resources.
- Aim to provide as much detail as possible. There is less chance of overlooking important points and more chance of work conforming to plan if there is thorough coverage.
- Ask for opinions and ideas. Many individuals have something to contribute towards a sound plan; ask now and avoid adverse criticisms later.

- Clearly define the problem or objective. Before planning begins, look at the whole project and break it down into its constituent parts to ensure full coverage and to provide a working scheme.
- Try to be creative. A sound workable and economic plan is the outcome of something more than logical marshalling of information into a set routine. Certain intangible qualities must be forced into activity within the supervisor's mind. He or she must be imaginative and creative, exercise judgement and perception, and yet retain an objective, critical approach to the problem.
- Have the courage to stand by the plan.
- Check and revise the plan as circumstances change.

## CHARACTERISTICS OF A SOUND PLAN

A sound plan is:

- economic, within the financial capabilities of the concern
- workable, considering the resources available
- thorough, allowing for most contingencies
- balanced, to blend with other plans
- resilient, to cope with unforeseen changes
- worthwhile, fulfils a desirable purpose
- attractive, creates interest among all who are concerned
- detailed, to establish adequate procedures
- timely, to obtain maximum benefit
- impersonal, avoids personal prejudices

## SWOT ANALYSIS

Originally SWOT analysis was developed by Harvard Business School in 1974. At that time its main use concentrated on corporate planning. Now SWOT has become a popular technique at all organisational levels. The supervisor should find the analysis useful at departmental and sectional level, and at individual level.

SWOT extends to planning, problem solving, decision making, case studies and projects. The initials stand for analysing strengths, weaknesses, opportunities and threats. Studying situations or organisations under these headings and com-

pleting the information in four boxes forces an analysis of the situation from diverse viewpoints. Consequently, a more comprehensive base of knowledge about how the company works provides opportunities to build on the company's strengths, minimise its weaknesses, take advantage of opportunities and allow for external environmental difficulties.

The extent of SWOT may be gained by examining some examples. A cross-section of popular uses includes examples at strategic level for a production company and a service company, the use of an outside survey, research in market strategy, and a case at individual level.

## STRATEGIC SWOT: A PRODUCTION COMPANY

A company should examine and consider the key actions to achieve overall objectives through adopting particular policies. Deciding on these important strategies involves considering current performance and the external environment.

### Strengths and weaknesses

Such topics as output and productivity, market share, investment programmes, and human resources would be included among many others. These would be divided into strengths and weaknesses. For example, the need to automate is recognised and a continuing programme is operating (a strength), but financial costs are escalating and causing problems as delays are caused though lack of funds (a weakness).

### Opportunities and threats

Appraising the external environment involves assessing the likely effects of new technologies, developing overseas competition, political unrest, and national economic problems. These are divided into opportunities and threats as viewed by senior managers. For example, an overseas country may flood the market with a cheaper product and cause reduced sales in the company. Although the reason may be cheap labour costs compared with the home company, it remains a key issue for survival.

## Alternative strategies

From the above analysis, a list of alternative actions will be drawn up to outline a corporate plan. Typical strategies may be to improve quality, cut profit margins, bargain for financial help, launch new lines, increase advertising, and possible mergers.

## STRATEGIC SWOT: A SERVICE COMPANY

The owner of a small estate agency has two offices in nearby villages. He conducted research on the basis of SWOT and summarised his findings below.

| | |
|---|---|
| *Strengths* (+) | Excellent reputation |
| | Quality service |
| | Client oriented |
| *Weaknesses* (−) | Limited outlets |
| | Liquidity problems |
| | Locating experienced staff |
| | Limited profits |
| *Opportunities* (+) | Opening new branches |
| | Expanding existing premises |
| | Entering property development |
| *Threats* (−) | Possibility of new agents opening |
| | New legislation restricting operations |
| | High interest rates |
| | Risk of recession |

## Possible plans

- Open new premises and risk a recession plus adverse new legislation.
- Enter the property development market and raise a loan, risking short-term problems but enjoying long-term gains.
- Merge with another local agent to secure increased stability and possibly higher profits.

## EMPLOYEE RELATIONS

Outside surveys can be used to identify more easily the strengths and weaknesses of personnel policy and the opportunities and threats of the external business environment. In the case of strikes and stoppages, the opinion of outside specialists may reveal the cause or causes of employee relations problems which were not apparent before.

## RESEARCH IN MARKET STRATEGIES

Research in market strategies is primarily concerned with diagnosis and prognosis. Consequently, typical questions to answer are:

- Has the company reached a particular stage envisaged previously?
- How has this stage been achieved?
- What are the objectives or revised objectives envisaged?

Internal research might show the outcome of these questions as:

- *Strengths*: a unique product; excellent reputation; sound management.
- *Weaknesses*: a small company; limited production therefore mainly manual work; a limited market; low overall profits; limited capital.
- *Opportunities*: redesigning the product to satisfy a larger market; designing a new product incorporating the unique features in the existing product.
- *Threats*: cost of machinery and equipment to increase production; risk of competition from overseas; locating suitable operatives.

This analysis should indicate various strategies on the market, pricing, training and loans. The supervisor should be able to relate this analysis to local production or administrative problems by adopting a similar diagnosis-and-prognosis approach. Knowing strengths and weaknesses reduces the risk of errors and decision making should improve.

## INDIVIDUAL SWOT

SWOT is a useful aid to individual career planning. A haphazard approach to career problems may be avoided by adopting the techniques to cover the four important factors. Although a personal opinion cannot be ignored, the exercise is worthwhile and the analysis may be discussed with family or friends to seek wider views. An example is given below to indicate some essential features. However, this should be augmented to suit the individual's personal ideas.

- *Strengths*: sociable; conscientious; good planner; ambitious.
- *Weaknesses*: inexperienced; suffers with inertia; lateness; unqualified.
- *Opportunities*: vacancies in the North at cheaper locations; encouragement from a friend who moved to the North; increased promotion prospects in the North; better training schemes.
- *Threats*: local family ties; leaving clubs and friends; increased family costs soon; heavy mortgage.

*Four possible plans*

- Move to a new job and break local ties.
- Change to a new job and stay in lodgings during the week.
- Stay in present job and study for a qualification.
- Stay in present job and demonstrate conscientiousness by arriving on time, studying and working harder.

### REVIEWING STRENGTHS AND WEAKNESSES

Changes will naturally continue after an analysis. Consequently, the supervisor should adopt a programme to check periodically whether strengths and weaknesses should be revised. Changes may occur as decisions become effective or ineffective; there may be unintentional changes; or the original diagnosis may have been faulty.

### REVIEWING OPPORTUNITIES AND THREATS

Unfortunately, opportunities and threats are usually based partly on predictions, forecasting or assumptions. So as the additional real situations emerge, it is essential to revise and continue with prognosis. Typical examples are changing interest rates, new technologies appearing, and sudden industrial unrest.

### APACS

A practical application of SWOT, APACS provides a logical framework for study; the letters stand for adaptive planning and control sequence. There are eight steps:

- State objectives.
- Appraise SWOT.
- Specify activities involved.
- Evaluate courses of action.
- Forecast results of alternative actions.
- Implement the chosen plan.
- Assess outcomes.
- Modify accordingly.

# Problem solving

Problems and choices are met in all supervisory and managerial activities. These must be dealt with as reputations are built or ruined on individual performance. Supervisors often automatically establish standards for a vast number of control aspects connected with problem solving without fully realising the implications to their subordinates. Human behaviour is a typical example where supervisors expect a particular code of conduct in many different situations. They are faced with a problem when a standard is violated, and control is lost if they fail to investigate, find the cause and make a decision.

Often many managers do not even realise there is a problem to be solved. Unfortunately, problems do not solve themselves effectively, although some managers will openly admit they believe that if a problem is left for a sufficient length of time it will solve itself. Such managers have not bothered to check on the results of this negative approach, which ultimately brands them as ineffectual.

### TYPES OF PROBLEMS

*Dynamic problems*

Dynamic problems have reached operational conditions. Standards for the activities are set, activities measured, and deviations from the standard are noted. If the deviation is adverse, an investigation may commence to solve the problem.

Such problems must be actively solved. The art of recognising and carefully defining problems should be developed. The causes of faults may be more effectively located by looking at common factors and isolating the unusual aspects within those factors. In this way the trouble may be tracked down by means of a logical step-by-step approach (see below).

Dynamic problems originate from many sources and all must be considered. Unfortunately, some sources are obscure such as the effects of a bullying manager, non-disclosure of customer complaints, and fear-induced employees who fail to reveal information. Sometimes a supervisor may feel there is a problem without having any specific knowledge; careful probing for information is probably the best way to pursue these hunches.

### Static problems

Static problems occur when standards are set but activities cannot commence because of an obstacle. The reasons for this dilemma vary. Three categories are apparent:

- The sudden appearance of an obstacle which did not exist before. In this case the cause of the problem is the obstacle, the problem is solved and a decision is needed to remove it.
- The discovery of an obstacle which was missed at the forecasting and planning stages.
- An existing obstacle which has already been reported but has still to be removed.

Apart from problem-solving techniques, there are important features which need a thorough investigation. This applies in circumstances where the static problem was due to the activities of other departments or sections.

### STANDARDS

Employees also apply their own standards to many aspects connected with their job. One operator may switch off a machine immediately a fault is suspected, whereas another may wait until a more obvious sign appears. This range of standards among individuals becomes important in problem solving. One operator may report that a machine failed to start when switched on, whereas a second may state that when the machine was switched on a smell of burning was noticed. Precise description

by the second operator immediately narrows down the cause of the fault.

### Using standards

In a broad sense, the use of standards for gathering information should not be ignored. The approach to obtaining facts as they appear should be made on a basis of comparison to find a common factor or an isolating component within that factor. A line of machines may be powered from the same electricity point; if one machine suddenly stops, the fault may be isolated to a particular section if the basis of comparison is applied by stating whether the other machines continue to run. Investigating a problem in this way helps to isolate areas quickly where the cause is likely to be found.

The use of standard practice or standard set-ups is common to many facets of industrial activity. Here are some examples:

- *Use of raw material in batches*: if faulty work appears, it may be isolated to a particular batch which is below standard.
- *Planned maintenance programmes*: when a machine develops a fault, it may be possible to trace it to the last maintenance job.
- *Shift work*: a mistake may be isolated to a particular shift or shift changeover.

### METHODS OF SOLVING PROBLEMS

The many problem-solving methods may be divided into two groups:

- *An individual activity*: one person solves a problem through intuition or the use of a technique.
- *A group activity*: people are brought together to solve a problem.

Both dynamic approaches automatically develop the people and the organisation. Consequently, they learn to improve their problem-solving techniques and they recognise the problems or issues confronting an organisation. However, any method demands several fundamental requirements:

- sufficient knowledge and experience to cope with the complexity of the problem

- sufficient capability to recognise the breadth of the problem related to solutions and their overall effects
- recognition of the learning situation and its use to develop the individual
- implementation of the solution to avoid frustration

Here are the main approaches; some methods demand professional help.

- intuition
- analytical thinking
- creative thinking
- brainstorming
- lateral thinking
- synectics
- morphological analysis

## Intuition

Apparently simple and rapid, intuition is essential when coping with common daily problems. The cause is often immediately clear. Consequently, simple and complex problems may be solved effectively in this manner by the experienced supervisor. The obvious danger lies in not appreciating the whole problem because of a lack of experience and knowledge, and jumping to conclusions. Automatic problem solving of this nature may also be dangerous when a recurring problem – normally having a standard cause – suddenly occurs through a new cause not foreseen at the time. But considering the time factor, full use of this method is essential.

Using intuition, current experience, or ad hoc rules of thumb to solve problems is also termed heuristics. A heuristic system applies tentative solutions and is subject to alteration as the situation changes. Heuristics is therefore useful when problems are vague, which is not unusual.

## Analytical thinking

Logical deduction is often used to avoid the dangers of intuitive thinking. The approach is to arrive at an indisputable solution by analysing known information. Fundamentally, there must be a unique answer which is predictable; the assumption is that the problem has only one

solution. For example, if 240 working hours were lost in the assembly section last month, 25 per cent of which were due to absenteeism and 10 per cent through sickness, the losses in hours are 60 and 24 respectively. However, if the question is how to cut down the high absenteeism rate, there are many answers. Imagination is needed, which means it is a creative problem.

## Creative thinking

Creativity usually means the ability and power to produce new ideas, whereas innovation refers to the use of these ideas. Creative thought is essential if ways, events or ideas that were previously unrelated must now be related to arrive at an answer to a problem.

Apart from relying on the creative individual, there are several techniques which may be used to improve the use of creative thinking. They tend to concentrate on group interaction or individual action (see below). Popular methods have been introduced by E. de Bono; among them are parallel thinking and lateral thinking (see below).

## The creative individual

Unfortunately, the creativity of many managers, supervisors and employees is probably a neglected asset. Most people are creative, but the degree of capability obviously varies among them. New ideas are vital and people should be encouraged to be creative. However, care is needed in implementing the ideas (innovating) to avoid conflict with established policies and procedures.

Highly creative people are easily recognised. Usually they are capable of independent judgement, they are inquisitive, enthusiastic about problem solving, detest conformity, and are generally discontented with an unchanged situation.

## Brainstorming

The use of groups in creative thinking was developed in the 1930s. The techniques usually conform to a number of basic concepts which concentrate on breaking down the inhibiting barriers to creativity. Typical examples are to suspend judgement on other people's ideas; to allow everyone to 'freewheel' so that any ideas are proposed, regardless of whether they make sense; to produce as many ideas as possible; and to cross-fertilise all the ideas if something new emerges.

The main barriers to creative thinking are a tendency to think there is only one answer, to restrict thinking within a narrow self-imposed framework, to give answers that sound reasonable, to allow obvious statements to go unchallenged, and to worry too much about looking a fool.

In 1957 a related approach called brainstorming was introduced by A.F. Osborne. This debatable popular technique is based upon the idea associated with value analysis (Chapter 27) and is a quick way of extracting a large number of ideas. However, research findings are conflicting; typical evidence includes the following:

- Groups produce more and better solutions to problems than do individuals, provided the groups have similar competence.
- Sometimes group membership inhibits and constricts creativity.
- Groups (unlike individuals) continue to produce ideas indefinitely.
- Individuals who work alone under brainstorming rules produce many more ideas than do groups.

Certainly people are more likely to co-operate when changes occur if they have participated. Furthermore, the technique is useful to develop interpersonal relationships and it is easily adapted to most problems. A successful brainstorming session depends upon the group leader, the experience of the groups and appropriate use of the basic concepts mentioned above.

## Lateral thinking

Lateral thinking was designed by E. de Bono to help the mind escape from vertical thinking, which uses habitual mind patterns learned at school. Lateral thinking uses various techniques which challenge preconceptions and reject yes/no thinking. They are easily learned and convert people into a new way of thinking creatively.

Although there are two types of thought processes (vertical and lateral), do not assume they will lead to different outcomes. Both are important and E. de Bono's book *Lateral Thinking* (1980) should be studied to understand thoroughly the techniques. Here are some of the essential features:

- Avoid assumptions and dominant ideas; they are self-imposed and may be incorrect.
- Seek as many choices as possible for solving a problem; do not reject ideas because they seem irrelevant.
- Abandon ingrained attitudes and preconceived ideas; allow thoughts to expand fully in the mind.

## Synectics

Synectics is a complex series of techniques used in imaginative problem solving; it should really be practised with the aid of authorised practitioners. The body of knowledge is considerable as the techniques have been developed over a long period.

Originally called the Gordon technique (after its originator W.J. Gordon), synectics relies on careful selection of the team members who are suitable for the particular task. This often involves the entire organisation and an experienced group leader who excludes from discussions full details of the problem. The approach claims to prevent premature solutions, overcomes 'right-brain' thinking and involves sophisticated group behaviour.

## Morphological analysis

Morphological analysis is based on a series of dimensions. These dimensions are examined relative to each other and to the possible elements within each dimension. The analysis is complex and demands a considerable amount of preparation. A typical example is to use two dimensions such as products and markets. Elements for each dimension are listed and combinations are established to trigger off ideas.

## A LOGICAL APPROACH

1 *Set standards*: establish standards for as many activities as possible; in other words, set appropriate sights.

2  *Measure activities*: measure actual results against established standards to highlight deviations.

3  *Assess deviations*: a deviation may be favourable or adverse and demand different treatment:

   - *Favourable*: this is a situation (not a problem); nevertheless, the cause should be traced and identified for revising standards and increasing effectiveness.
   - *Adverse*: this is a problem which is detrimental to the plan, so the cause must be located and decisions made.

4  *Carefully define the problem*: a complete, detailed description of the problem is essential.

5  *Investigate*: there are three aspects to this:

   - *Judge the time factor*: the supervisor generally has to work within a timescale.
   - *Search for information*: haphazard, intermittent fact-finding is unsatisfactory, but often inevitable; try to build up a system so that information flows in a continuous process.
   - *Evaluate the information*: learn to distinguish between facts, inferences and value judgements (see next section).

6  *Analyse and establish the cause*: draw up a detailed analysis from the information available, look for indications leading to the source, and establish the cause, thus solving the problem; successful elimination of the cause or avoiding a recurrence depends upon making a correct decision.

## EVALUATING INFORMATION

When assessing information the items of prime importance are the source and the number of mouths that have passed on the information. The reliability of the source and the distortion factor – as information passes from one person to the next – cannot be ignored. The well-known game of Chinese whispers – making up a sentence and passing it round in a group of say ten people – often produces bewildering results, bearing no relationship to the original sentence. This may happen, to some extent, in the workplace. The only sure way to be certain something is a fact is to see it at first hand; unfortunately, there is seldom time and it is often impracticable.

### Facts, inferences and value judgements

A further confusing point is the inability of some people to distinguish between facts, inferences and value judgements. Each one has its usefulness, but the danger lies in mistaking one for another.

Here is a typical example of the three: two people decide to walk from A to B along a street that is often very congested with traffic. The lamp posts are a standard distance apart and, as the two people walk at a set pace, one takes the time between lamp posts and calculates their speed as $2^{1}/_{2}$ mph. This is a fact. From the calculated speed a further reckoning indicates they should arrive at B five minutes earlier than they intended. This is an inference because any number of situations may arise which will affect their estimated time of arrival, therefore it is a conclusion or deduction from a given fact. One then says to the other, 'It is quicker to walk along this road these days because the traffic is so congested'. This is a value judgement because it is an opinion based upon a series of events that have not been accurately measured or analysed.

### The human factor

If the cause of a problem is traced back to an individual, a new problem emerges. Naturally the seriousness of the original problem will determine the next step. There must be consideration for the circumstances, the individual's record, any recent changes in behaviour or the job, and any known domestic problems. Clearly counselling (Chapter 15) is essential by the supervisor and possibly by personnel.

# Decision making

Effective decision making depends upon many factors involving knowledge, experience, background, training and development, and the environment. When making a decision, these factors are influenced by the supervisor's views on the principles to apply and the industrial situation. The degree of decisiveness must also include weighing conflicting influences such as the objective, ruthlessness, fair treatment of employees, profit and costs.

There must be an evaluation of all the relevant features such as financial considerations, budgets, political aspects of the organisation, critical implications and company policy.

Choosing between different courses of action is often tempered by conflicting groups such as superiors, subordinates and peers. There is the frustration of realising one group will be pleased while other groups may be unhappy and reactionary. Decision making is an exceptionally difficult process but its successful application determines the supervisor's status and reputation.

## A NINE-STAGE APPROACH

1 *List the criteria*: There are always principles and standards to consider which will determine the order of priority when deciding on the objective.
2 *Assess all the criteria*: Assessment is mainly intelligent guesswork based upon the possible courses of action and their effect on individuals, general effectiveness and the inevitable desired results.
3 *Establish priorities*: This is a personal matter in which good sense is essential. Choice must depend to some extent on morale and the prevailing industrial atmosphere.
4 *Determine the objective*: A worthwhile exercise is to consider carefully the main features of the objective and to write a comprehensive description.
5 *List the various courses of action*: A number of courses usually appear while studying how to reach the objective.
6 *Weigh the influences involved*: Weighing is a difficult task which includes many influences discussed later. These include social, cultural, ethical, racial, legal, and political aspects. Fundamental features are the individuals who will be involved, costs, undesirable after-effects, and morale.
7 *Choose a course of action*: This critical stage determines the capability of the supervisor. All the facets of decision making are involved which are considered on the basis of experience and intuition. Theoretically choice is made by careful and objective consideration of the various alternatives which are appropriately

weighted. However, the decision which is most beneficial for the supervisor and the company may be influenced by other evaluations.
8 Set standards to check after-effects.
9 Follow up and revise if necessary.

## EXPERIENCE AND INTUITION

Experience in a particular job is a useful asset because it should lead to enhanced intuition in decision making. Such intuition is also linked with perception (Chapter 9) but it should not replace a logical approach where analysis or considering alternatives is an important step. Intuition is not entirely guesswork or a gut feeling, part of the process is the development of good sense where knowledge and experience play a vital role.

A sensible use of mature intuition improves decision making since it provides a broader base for considering alternatives and, in urgent situations, indicates quickly a more accurate course of action. Furthermore, it may indicate three important factors: invalid or inaccurate information, the insincerity or sincerity of individuals, and a deeper understanding of the organisation and its culture. Indeed, with practice and assessment, intuition may provide more insight, highlight the key issues and indicate opportunities.

## TYPES OF DECISION

Clearly the type of decision is an important feature. There are three main types, based upon their direct effect on employees:

- low grade decisions
- high grade decisions
- emergency decisions

### Low grade decisions

Low grade decisions are routine, such as cleaning programmes and garden maintenance. They are predictable and usually acceptable to employees, so no consultation is needed. But if they directly affect employees, as in the cases of holiday arrangements and rest periods, then consultation and acceptance are essential.

### High grade decisions

High grade decisions demand specialised knowledge and heavy expenditure. Careful evaluation is essential but employee consultation is usually pointless. However, high grade decisions such as pay, overtime rates, working methods and automation obviously need consultation and acceptance.

### Emergency decisions

Emergency decisions appear in a crisis where, for example, a manager has not made a decision on time or in the case of fire. The supervisor must be ready to act immediately without consultation or hesitation. Procrastination may mean heavy losses. Strength of character is established in these circumstances.

### The time factor

The time available must be assessed alongside the type of decision. When an individual makes a decision the time factor is usually rapid. However, if the decision is critical but not an emergency, a group may be used which usually slows down the process and is time-consuming. Delays are often caused by discussions on the criteria, which are generally conflicting among group members. Determining the appropriate criteria in high grade decisions is often controversial and compromises are inevitable.

## DISCRETIONARY LIMITS

The number of authority levels in the organisation determines the degree of decision making allowed. Typical discretionary limits are easily identified as they will usually be based upon job titles and organisational levels. Strategic levels include top management to make policy and senior management to make structuring decisions. Tactical levels include middle managers to make interpretative decisions and supervisors to make situational decisions.

## SOCIAL ASPECTS

Companies are now expected to make decisions based upon social considerations (Chapter 6), but often social issues are vague and only become involved when all aspects are included. Difficulties often arise over interpreting legislation, monopolies and their effects; satisfying all cultural factors; and conflicts between ensuring the company's survival and providing requirements to satisfy social trends.

Arguably there could be decisions that would conflict with shallow social factors but are fundamentally sound and would benefit society as a whole. However, excessive appropriations of revenue at the expense of society are obviously suspect. They may even warrant state intervention to reduce misuse of such economic power.

## ETHICAL CONSIDERATIONS

When ethics are involved the supervisor may often be confronted with difficult decisions associated with conflicting loyalties and cultural conflict. Ethics are essentially subjective personal feelings about human behaviour. Everyone behaves within a certain code of moral conduct. Situations arise continually where decisions are tempered by ethical considerations, especially when legality, bribery, theft, loyalty and confidentiality are encountered. Such dilemmas cause frustration, stress and often upset relationships within the hierarchy.

Resolving ethical issues depends upon many circumstances such as acceptable practices in certain countries and companies; the flexibility of individual moral codes; rigid interpretation or adjusting to each case; and acting within the best interests of the company, employees, managers or society.

## LEGAL ASPECTS

Considering the wide range and complexity of legislation, whenever there is doubt consult a specialist. Apart from laws affecting the main topics discussed in other chapters, there are many general laws affecting management. These include contract, tort, company formation, debt collecting, business ownership, consumer protection, credit agency, fair trading compensation, and negligence. Considering the enormous mass of detail and ambiguity, an appropriate textbook is helpful but it should not be relied upon if the supervisor is directly involved.

## POLITICAL ASPECTS

A logical decision-making process may not take into account the external environment and cultural features. Unless explanations, participation at the early planning phases, and consultation are generally employed, internal political problems may arise. Although sharing the decision-making process minimises the effects of beliefs, prejudices and attitudes that may upset outcomes, there are limits beyond which personal responsibility is weakened.

## LOCATING INFORMATION

The telephone can be used to provide much information to help with decision making by accessing online databases (ODBs) and viewdata. ODBs are systems that hold computerised information. They are located worldwide and use the international telephone network. Over three thousand ODBs are available and they cover many subjects. Searching is fast and accessing is easy. Host organisations advise on the equipment required to use ODBs and provide passwords to access the system. Some organisations charge a subscription whereas others charge on a time basis, the cost being shown on the screen at the end of a session.

Viewdata is another system employing two-way communication. The user needs an acoustic coupler or modem, and a computer. Central computers store information that can be accessed through a keyboard. Prestel is a public viewdata system, and Topic was introduced by the Stock Exchange to give up-to-the-second financial information to subscribers.

These systems provide excellent facilities for keeping up to date, essential in a business world of rapid change and increasing complexity. The supervisor should identify sectors where help and advice are needed, look for relevant details, and be prepared to accept new ideas and techniques where appropriate.

## DEFERRING DECISIONS

It often appears that managers are deliberately sidestepping decisions, or they fail to notice a decision is needed and then they make excuses.

The reasons for this odd behaviour are generally that decision making is a stressful process and the decision is immediately identified to that particular manager. Also, there are political problems, ineptness, and often timing difficulties. The supervisor should try to identify the reason if a decision is refused and use this information to plan a suitable tactic.

If the manager suggests raising the subject at the next committee meeting, the reasons could be insecurity, political, or simply avoiding the issue. Should the decision be thrown back to the supervisor, record the fact somewhere since presumably the type of decision was identified by the manager. If the decision is high grade and imperative, the supervisor should think carefully about taking appropriate action by approaching the manager's superiors; and he or she should tell this to the manager. Sometimes this approach triggers action.

A similar procedure may be followed if other delaying tactics are employed, typically having no time available, losing temper, implying there are political reasons when there are not, confusing the issue, or not admitting a decision is needed.

To avoid delay, always try to ensure sufficient information is provided when the manager is approached and remember to consider other schemes in operation which may conflict with a positive decision.

# Relations with management

The extra pressures and heavy responsibilities on managers must be recognised. To appreciate the real situation, the present state of management is now examined, followed by proposals on how to make allowances for managers in the circumstances.

## PRESENT STATE OF MANAGEMENT

In the UK there are some outstanding managers whose success is known worldwide, but the remaining majority are often accused of being poor managers. According to reports, many are not educated and trained in management, lack drive and initiative, and cause more problems than they solve.

### Indications of incompetence

Without large-scale surveys, indicators are:

- The poor performance of many companies.
- State of the economy.
- Ignoring outstanding research findings and discoveries which are eventually exploited overseas.
- Poor individual managerial performance compared with counterparts in other countries.
- Inability to avoid and resolve disputes successfully.
- Never-ending accounts of personal experiences from employees, trade unions and customers.

### The causes

Here are some of the reasons given by experts. Many of them have a self-perpetuating effect on managerial selection.

- Raw graduates are selected then given no further training.
- Recruiters are impressed by people with the right education (public schooling).
- Recruiters follow poor selection procedures.
- Recruiters are content to employ the 'right' people who mix well with existing management.
- It is assumed an effective functional specialist will make a good manager.
- Possession of the 'right' social background is overvalued.
- Recruiters are deceived by ruthless people who use devious means.
- Nepotistic recruiters employ their friends and relations.
- People are promoted according to age, length of service or seniority.
- Some people possess a particular characteristic that overimpresses.
- Some people are afraid of others with management qualifications.
- Some people are overimpressed by graduates from certain universities.
- Industry fails to attract high calibre individuals because it is generally considered a dirty occupation.
- The management education system lacks financial and physical support.

## ADVERSE PRESSURES

Some argue there are conditions that are outside the control of managers but others say effective managers should be able to instigate change. Here are four conditions that are often quoted:

- trying to cope with employees whose national culture or attitude is non-cooperative
- fighting militant trade unions whose selfish aim is to justify their own existence to members by ignoring the national and local effects of their actions
- relying on inadequate supervisors
- trying to combat situations created by poor governmental actions and policies

## MAKING ALLOWANCES FOR MANAGERS

To avoid severe frustration, the supervisor must make allowances for managers. Unfortunately, individuals (including supervisors) usually expect high standards of performance from their superiors but allow their subordinates some latitude.

### Main approaches

1 *Be sympathetic*: demonstrate an understanding of problems faced by superiors and the difficulties they meet in solving them.
2 *Be mature*: show tolerance in any circumstances. Eventually mutual tolerance may emerge as the superior recognises the advantages of this kind of relationship.
3 *Set an example*: always maintain due dignity. Expect a negative reaction in any situation where the superior is feeling insecure, fearful, confused or inadequate. Be ready for rudeness, off-hand treatment and sarcasm, but try to avoid showing contempt.
4 *Be diplomatic*: use your knowledge and point out tactfully other ways of dealing with situations and solving problems. Ensure the superior thinks your suggestions are his or her own ideas and so avoid time-wasting arguments.
5 *Expect strange treatment*: calculate ways of counteracting it. A few common examples are:
    - When the compulsive talker has difficulty in listening, try interposing and ask a question on the subject you wish to discuss;

surprise might be the response but a reply is also possible.

- When the manager keeps you waiting as a way to demonstrate status, try saying, 'Excuse me please, I'll come back later when you're not so busy'.
- When the 'atmosphere creator' causes a reaction before discussion starts, try withdrawing and telephone or send a memo.
- When the Establishment snob intensely dislikes anyone beneath his or her status and ignores you, try avoiding confrontations – you are wasting your time.
- When the intellectual snob corrects your grammar but misses the message, try a memo.

# Time management

Making the best use of precious time is obvious, but unfortunately this essential practice is often ignored. Unless time is carefully planned and controlled, and self-discipline applied, the result is crisis management and poor performance.

Time should be viewed as a scarce resource; more time is simply not available since once passed it cannot return and each person has the same amount; consequently, its effective use is a distinct advantage. Time management is essentially a discipline but it should not become an obsession where a stressful state develops.

Although chronological time is nearly constant, the individual's experience of time varies depending upon whether he or she is experiencing uninteresting or interesting activities. Furthermore, people often seem to seek ways of wasting time rather than trying to find ways of making full use of it.

From the financial viewpoint, the use of time is, firstly, an investment generally based upon the *number of employees × the number of hours they are paid*, and secondly, an income considering the *number of employees × the number of hours worked productively*. From the human resource viewpoint, appropriate time is essential to cope successfully with all the employment activities and to equate it with productivity. Consequently, time management should include how the supervisor uses employees' time as well as his or her own time. Indeed it becomes a vital feature of control, considering autonomous teams and the use of time by their leaders.

Two main features of time management are:

- Learn management and organisation principles, supervisory roles, communication techniques and work study (outlined in various chapters).
- Use a logical approach to make the best use of time.

# A four-step logical approach

### CONDUCT INITIAL CHECKS

- List the aims of the job either from the job specification, or based upon experience, or seek help from the superior.
- Record roles and activities; determine the main tasks and measure the time taken for each one during the working day.
- Establish priorities; find out the importance of each activity in terms of its vital nature and how long it takes to complete.
- List omitted tasks; try to determine the tasks that should have been done but were neglected through lack of time.
- Rearrange items from the above three points to form a comprehensive structure.

### ASSESS ESSENTIAL ASPECTS

- Carefully examine the job specification and update if considered necessary.
- Determine the main objectives.
- Check priorities.
- Clarify responsibilities.
- Roughly assess the level of performance.
- Develop a personal plan.

### CLARIFY THE OBJECTIVES

- List the main objectives of the job, including initial checks and any further information.
- Identify any personal objectives.
- Calculate key results areas and the key tasks involved; these are the main activities which determine whether aims are achieved.

| WORK SCHEDULE | | | | |
|---|---|---|---|---|
| Day ......................... | | Date ......................... | | |
| Activity | Priority T/M/L | Delegate? | Info required | Completed |
| | | | | |

Figure 8.3 A supervisor's daily work schedule: T/M/L = top/medium/low

- Determine priorities.
- Reconcile the qualitative and quantitative aspects.

**APPLY PRINCIPLES AND TECHNIQUES**

Apart from the management principles already discussed in this chapter, there are the following important aspects.

*Establishing key results areas*

Key results areas are the vital parts of the job which make a large impact and achieve highly productive results. A well-known generalisation is that one-fifth of the work produces four-fifths of the results, or that four-fifths of the work only yields one-fifth of the results. Within these areas there are various levels of priorities:

- *Top priority*: urgent and essential work to avoid delay or to produce change.
- *Medium priority*: essential work with longer deadlines (these become top priority as deadlines approach and should not be allowed to accumulate).
- *Low priority*: non-essential work which can be delayed, destroyed if redundant, or delegated.

Objective assessments of priorities are important since personal preferences often dominate.

*Daily scheduling*

The degree of detail and timetabling of a schedule varies depending upon the type of supervisory job. In these circumstances it is only possible to produce a guide which highlights the main features; it should be used accordingly.

*Listing activities*

A typical work schedule is shown in Fig. 8.3. The main points are:

- Check outstanding items and review from the previous day.
- Include new items forecasted for the day.
- Allow for contingencies.
- Bear in mind delegation.
- Remember priorities.
- Remember key results areas.

*Timetabling*

Ideally a time log should be maintained, but activities often tend to build up and working under

**TIMETABLE**

| Outstanding priorities | Top ............................................................................................................... |
| | Medium ............................................................................................................ |
| | Low ................................................................................................................. |

| Estimated start | Estimated finish | Actual time | Item | Delay time | Reason | Action |
|---|---|---|---|---|---|---|
| | | | | | | |

| Total time | Hours | Minutes | Percentage | Action |
|---|---|---|---|---|
| Worked Delays Productive | | | | |

*Figure 8.4* A framework for a supervisor's timetable

pressure seldom allows for this luxury. At least remember the following points:

- Try to work within a time frame.
- Attempt to assess a time for each activity.
- Allow for incidents occurring with employees and for crises.
- Guessing is better than avoiding an assessment.

A further luxury for the few is timetabling some hours (either by arranging not to be disturbed, or moving to a quiet area) when working on an activity that needs uninterrupted concentration.

The biggest problem with timetabling is interruptions that are unavoidable. It is possible to reduce the time by various means such as avoiding gossip and personal difficulties; making an excuse to break off discussions when the reason is clear; and summarising as soon as possible. A typical framework for a supervisor's timetable is shown in Fig. 8.4.

## Telephone calls

Telephone calls may take up to 15 per cent of a supervisor's time and can be time-wasters unless properly controlled. Making the best use of the telephone demands skilful handling of calls, which includes diplomacy, various time-saving techniques, and careful planning.

## Incoming calls

Time may be reduced by:

- quickly recognising the reason for the call
- assessing its priority and if necessary relocating the caller or delegating to a subordinate
- giving the caller time to explain and respond to questions
- trying to assess any agitation and responding accordingly if it is a customer with a complaint (Chapter 10)
- always addressing the caller by name

- as soon as the answer to a query is clear, notifying, making sure it is understood, and closing diplomatically

### Outgoing calls

- Use a quick-reference diary of telephone numbers and update regularly.
- If the person is not available do not hold on.
- Plan the call – information required or to be given.
- Note the information as it is received.
- Close the conversation quickly and diplomatically; typical techniques are:
  - Must go now, the operator is flashing me.
  - Pleasant to talk with you again, will ring you soon.
  - One final point I should mention . . .
  - We must meet again soon.
- Check when times are most convenient to call people and make a note.
- If long-distance calls, announce your location immediately and this should encourage a rapid response; keep the time to a minimum.

### Using diaries

Examine the range of diaries available to record information. There are elaborate personal organisers with refills, which include a diary, addresses, references, a notebook and subject tabs; electronic organisers with many facilities; and simple diaries which are often adequate. Avoid overcomplex systems, choose one to suit the needs of the job and choose large formats to avoid running out of space.

### Delegating

Apply the principles outlined in Chapter 3.

### Avoiding time-wasters

Activities that waste time are usually glaring since they irritate. Some examples of good practice are:

- Apply self-discipline; avoid unnecessary social calls, wandering around aimlessly, interrupting people for a chat simply to waste time, being easily distracted, spending excessive amounts of time with visitors, and setting impossible deadlines.
- Be businesslike by noting all important items, filing documents and updating records regularly, and maintaining a tidy area.
- Constantly check those employees who are difficult and likely to have potential grievances and personal problems; build up sound relationships since time spent ahead of a crisis is always worthwhile.
- Do not shirk unpleasant tasks such as troublesome telephone calls, difficult projects, risky actions, and reprimanding; deferring action generally leads to an increased amount of time required to solve the problem.
- Strictly control irrelevant or mundane activities which tend to build up; paperwork should be dealt with as soon as possible, else it should be filed, scrapped or delegated.
- Regulate personal activities, typically private telephone calls, lengthy frequent visits to the cloakroom, taking unofficial smoking breaks, and extending tea and lunch breaks; these activities are often the cause of adverse criticism.
- Complain strongly if there is uneven workflow from other departments.
- Take firm action immediately if workflow delays which cause extra work are occurring within the department.
- Try to avoid needless switching from one activity to another, concentrating on completing one task before moving on to the next.
- Take action immediately when information – quantity and quality – is not available to avoid similar problems recurring.
- Attempt to restrict interruptions by diplomatically establishing periods for discussion with subordinates.
- Determine quiet and busy periods and plan particular tasks accordingly, such as creative work and activities that require concentration.
- Choose appropriate times to contact others when they are able to devote sufficient time to the task.
- Do not rely on memory, write everything down immediately, record notes in the appropriate places later if necessary.

### Using communication effectively

Apart from the information in Chapters 14, 15 and 16, some important points are:

- Ensure communications with subordinates and superiors are clear and understood.
- Conduct all meetings effectively to avoid unnecessary debate, checking beforehand they are essential and justifying the presence of those who attend.
- Always listen attentively and write down important points.
- Choose times to interrupt carefully and so avoid loss of concentration.
- Liaise with other sections to check that work is not duplicated.
- Seek out all sources of information and advice.
- Progress outstanding requirements.

### Developing good management–supervisor relations

Remember to make allowances, as mentioned in the previous section. Attempt to manage and manipulate the superior; aim to avoid spending needless amounts of time with him or her. Avoid accepting more work unless there is sufficient time given to the consequences, such as work time, employees available, the budget, resources, some existing tasks being neglected, and so on.

### Controlling time management

Monitoring the activities helps to ensure the objectives are met and should incorporate adjustments as opportunities allow and circumstances occur (Chapter 23).

Remember that attempting to control by an open-loop system means omitting feedback of results which is obviously disastrous. Time management problems can only be solved by careful control, self-discipline and perseverance. A closed-loop control system is essential, whereby feedback on performance (measured outputs) allows the supervisor to adjust operations. Thus to achieve an objective, divergencies between the planned and resultant activity may be rectified. With time management the use of computer networks shortens the feedback process and many adjustments become automatic. An example is a computer program that notes when stock is drawn, calculates a new stock balance and compares with the minimum stock level for reordering purposes.

### QUESTIONS

1 How can a supervisor delegate and still retain effective leadership?

2 Outline the various phases of planning.

3 Why does the supervisor have to make allowances for managers?

4 Discuss fully any two principles of management.

5 Describe the activities of forecasting and planning.

6 What supervisory activities lend themselves to planning?

7 Advise a new supervisor how to plan effectively.

8 What are the characteristics of a sound plan?

9 Outline the main principles of a command.

10 Describe the main approaches to improving management–supervisor relations.

11 Discuss the political, social, ethical and legal aspects of decision making.

12 Why is decision making so important when supervising?

13 Briefly outline the practical steps that are essential to good decision making.

14 Describe the principles you would bear in mind when conducting research.

15 Discuss the phases that lead to successful co-ordination.

16 What are the essential requirements for effective control?

17 Outline a logical approach to problem solving.

18 What are the main management skills?

19 Outline a logical approach to time management.

20 Discuss the skills cycle and how it operates in practice.

21 Draw up a supervisor's typical daily work schedule.

22 Draw up a diagram which could be used as a timetable for supervisory activities.

23 Why is the creativity factor considered to be an important role for the supervisor?

24 How do you encourage creativity?

25 Discuss the difference between innovating and creativity.

26 Outline the main aspects of forecasting and comment on the likely difficulties to be encountered.

27 How do you plan to create change?

28 Why is lateral thinking so important in problem solving?

29 Discuss a typical approach to decision making which covers the main features.

30 Experience and intuition are often thought of as useful assets in decision making. Explain their uses and limitations.

31 How would you identify time-wasters?

32 Discuss the two main types of problems likely to occur when controlling a section?

## CASE STUDY

Johnson was a senior supervisor, responsible for seven supervisors in the sales office. He always seemed to be overloaded with work and flustered. Members of staff thought he received lack of support from the supervisors who took advantage of his inability to cope. Johnson collapsed one day and retired through ill-health.

Marple, an existing supervisor, was promoted. He knew the problem that Johnson had failed to solve and delegated appropriate authority to the supervisors below him. They resisted strongly and caused heated discussions without making any attempt to conform to the new arrangements.

Marple could not understand why his job enrichment technique had failed and decided to ask for the personnel manager's advice.

*What were the basic organisational faults in these circumstances? Consider the possible advice from the personnel manager. What action could the marketing director take when this situation was reported to him.*

## CASE STUDY

'Every time I come up with an idea it's turned down and for no good reason that I can see.' Charles said this in a loud voice in the dining room and the supervisor overhead him. Andrew who was sitting at the same table said he had received the same treatment and had given up suggesting improvements. Eric said, 'It's about time something's done about it. Now we've got shares in the company it's affecting our dividend'. Rachel chimed in, 'Well, I can't complain. I suggested cutting out that base and got £100!' Charles retorted, 'It's the personnel department. They decide and I expect you received preferential treatment because you're a woman and they daren't say no!'

*Outline the possible problems in this case and suggest how improvements could be made.*

Laura's manager has a habit of walking around her office and speaking with the word processor operators as they are working. Laura has been a supervisor for three months and is still uncertain of herself. One morning, after one of these casual inspections, she walks around the office and is infuriated to see that Adrian, one of her best operators, is working on material that has nothing to do with his job.

'What's the idea? We don't allow private work – you know that. Pack it up at once!'

Adrian is livid. 'I'm fed up with this dump. First the boss comes round and says "Type this for me", now you tell me to pack it up. This is the third time I've typed things for him!'

Laura is taken aback but recovers quickly and says, 'I'm sorry, Adrian, I had no idea. Leave the typing with me'.

Adrian immediately calms down and duly hands over the work.

*Now that Laura is committed, what choices are open to her?*

# Suggested projects for Part One

## Project 1
- Attempt to assess the productivity level in your establishment by surveying the main aspects which affect it.
- Draw up a list and write an account of the prevailing conditions under each factor.
- Make recommendations for improving the situation.

## Project 2
Conduct a survey on the organisation of the production department in your company and suggest suitable improvements. Draw diagrams of the existing organisation and the proposed organisation. Tabulate the principles which you consider to be misapplied, the proposed changes and the human problems which are likely to occur during the changeover.

## Project 3
- Conduct a detailed survey on the authority, responsibilities and duties of two managers and two supervisors in your company.
- Attempt to assess the main differences between management and supervision by conducting your investigation within a framework suitable for this purpose.
- Draw up a suitable documentation of your findings and give a careful, detailed description of the main differences between the managers' and supervisors' jobs under investigation.

## Project 4
- Conduct a survey on how supervisors or managers make decisions. The co-operation and assistance of individual superiors will be necessary in preparing a detailed report on the procedures they adopt in various circumstances to arrive at decisions.
- Attempt to tabulate your findings in logical sequence and grouped under various methods. Give an account of your conclusions and recommendations.

## Project 5
- Trace the price alterations of products in your company and attempt to find out why the changes were introduced.
- Tabulate the price changes and dates and list the possible causes for each change, together with any explanations and your findings.
- Attempt to draw conclusions from your investigation.

## Project 6
Study the organisation of the stores, including the layout, stores control system and the efficiency of the service. Attempt to plan improvements considering the economic factors involved.

## Project 7
Trace the growth of your company over the past thirty years and attempt to discover the main causes of its present pattern.

## Project 8
Examine and analyse the authority, responsibilities and duties of three clerks and assess the critical areas of their jobs. Draw up a programme to incorporate empowerment into their roles and outline the probable training requirements to ensure each one's effectiveness.

**Project 9**

Conduct a survey to establish a list of employees who have contact with customers. Telephone conversations, correspondence and face-to-face contact should be included. Interview these employees to assess their attitudes towards customers and note any training they have received to improve employee–customer relationships. If appropriate, suggest any features which should be improved.

**Project 10**

Select two supervisors who seem overloaded with work and persuade them to agree to a study of the main aspects of their jobs and the time spent on each one. During the study try to assess areas where effective time management would improve performance and any areas where delegation is obviously needed.

# PART TWO

# Creating an effective workforce

# 9

# Trying to understand people

## Introduction

Knowing how to treat people successfully depends upon understanding them and understanding oneself. Despite research a complete understanding of both these factors is not possible so far. Managers have difficulty in assessing employees' behaviour, while employees often see managers' behaviour as amusing or insensitive. On a global level, lack of understanding causes wars, hatred and tension.

### THE PROBLEM

This century an enormous amount of literature and evidence on management and people has accumulated from practical research. Many theories have emerged; some have been strongly disputed while others have been successfully applied. However, many questions remain unanswered.

In view of this problem the chapter starts with an outline of the way research is conducted. This study of human behaviour and the way theories are formed is followed by the major features of disciplines which attempt to characterise the human being.

## Research methodology

Any scientific research attempts to conform with a number of criteria. These include precise definitions, objective data collection, a systematic and cumulative approach, and the disclosure of the research procedures. Unlike the physical or biological sciences there is no exact science of behaviour for the following reasons:

- People cannot be controlled or treated like physical elements (chemicals, etc.).
- Individual variations are extensive.
- Behaviour differs according to the internal and external environment.
- Research findings are basically deduced or inferred and limited to suggested truths.
- Conducting experiments is difficult for three main reasons: the interactive effect between the subject and the particular situation, all the intervening variables, and the resultant false situation if the subject is isolated.
- Complete truths or facts are elusive since the inferences are restricted to a finite number of observations.

### SCIENTIFIC METHOD

The scientific method is used to reduce the risk of arriving at incorrect conclusions about human behaviour. The five main steps are:

1. Establish a hypothesis – an assertion that a statement or line of reasoning is true or false. This is based upon intuition and data that are limited to personal capability and the availability of information respectively.
2. Test the validity of the hypothesis by observing behaviour or using experiments.
3. Adjust the hypothesis considering the results, bearing in mind the effects of the immediate environment, external and internal influences, and any unusual circumstances.
4. Continue the investigation using the revised hypothesis and adjusting again as new evidence is received.

5 Draw conclusions, bearing in mind the unpredictability and irrationality of people.

## Hypotheses and theories

A hypothesis (used in scientific method) means a starting point for further observation from known facts or data, and is a basis for reasoning without assuming it is true or false. Whereas a theory is a supposition or system of ideas that attempts to explain something, such as the behaviour of an individual or an occurrence. It is often based on general principles or phenomena, and may be speculative, abstract or a collection of propositions.

## BEHAVIOURAL SCIENCE

Behavioural science covers many disciplines, including psychology, sociology and anthropology. Although scientific methods are used, methodological and validation problems remain. Completely reliable theories are not available at present because concepts are often contested and abandoned as research continues. The main areas of interest for supervisors are:

- basic physiological behaviour – limited here to examining the human brain, sensation, and homeostasis
- individual variation – noticeable through the input of senses, stages of growth, intelligence, and the use of common sense
- mental features – personality, human characteristics, attitudes, temperament and emotion
- basic mental processes – perception, mental levels and mental experience
- sociology of work
- class and status
- breakdowns in relationships
- social influences in general
- the stress factor

Information on these areas is derived from experiments, surveys and the case method, which is a thorough study and analysis of one or several employees over a long period. These disciplines are subjected to techniques such as the scientific method, logic and formulation of hypotheses and theories. The main features are now outlined to show their weak and strong points.

# Basic physiological behaviour

Basic physiological behaviour is governed by the brain through sensation and homeostasis. These three aspects of major interest are now discussed.

## THE HUMAN BRAIN

The brain seems to possess an infinite capacity to assimilate information: it constantly seeks data during consciousness, clarifying and tabulating it for future use. This peculiarity, coupled with its capabilities, means it naturally functions to acquire knowledge and use it effectively, given the opportunity and the right conditions. This learning process develops a vast range of skills by using various muscles and nervous systems. Such a valuable tendency is often overlooked.

A further aspect is the absurd way the brain will arrive at reciprocal answers unless the individual learns appropriate disciplines. Examples are bragging to impress, shouting to make a point, and grossly exaggerating. Generally they have the opposite to the desired effect on individuals who are subjected to these faulty techniques.

## Higher and lower centres

The brain and nervous system combined are similar to a telephone exchange, sending out and receiving messages to and from all parts of the body. Simplified, the brain has two levels. All mental activity is a continuous interaction between the two.

- The lower centres are where primitive emotions are felt, the viscera (internal organs such as the heart, liver, etc.) are controlled and simple actions are initiated.
- The higher centres partially control the lower centres.

To illustrate, touching a very hot object immediately sends a message via the sensory nerves in the spinal cord to the lower centres of the brain. They return a message through the motor nerves (dealing with movement) that cause the hand to jerk back. This movement may be inhibited by the higher centres, which develop through complex mental processes and partially govern behaviour.

Such control applies equally to all emotional situations, typically anger and crying.

The lower centres are often described by psychologists as the unconscious mind and the higher centres as the conscious mind. They help to explain the variance in behaviour which is found in such areas as motivation, boredom, fatigue and rest.

### The human mind

Within the brain there exists a mental world of thoughts, ideas, feelings and self-awareness. Various sensations are experienced, typically many different emotions; the ability to recognise, recall and play back previous events; thought processes relating to images and words; and being aware of activity within and outside the brain.

Such complexity is bewildering. Many explanations have been offered and related to biological and evolutionary concepts. Often emphasised are the effects on life and the brain of seasonal changes over millions of years and the creation of speech and language.

The paranormal powers of the mind are also often mentioned. These include telepathy, clairvoyance, precognition and psychokinesis (the power to move physical objects). However, there is no convincing evidence that satisfies all investigators. Certainly the majority of people do not exhibit any such powers considering that casinos, horseracing, lotteries and football pools still flourish.

### SENSATION

The five common senses are vision, hearing, touch, taste and smell. There are other senses which provide information on pressure, pain and temperature within the body; the position of limbs; tension in muscles; and the position of the head to maintain balance. Without senses there is no perception or understanding of the surrounding environment. However, sensation does not completely influence perception (see below). The perceptual process is also affected by past experiences, learning, and the way sensory data is presented.

### HOMEOSTASIS

The human body is an open system (Chapter 3) – it is continually subjected to a changing external environment. Controlling these changes internally is called homeostasis. The process buffers and neutralises external stimuli by means of biophysical and biochemical processes.

This control process, often called the systems approach, is the basis of modern organisation theory, new management practices, modern economics and cybernetics. The process is related to the individual (homeostasis) and the organisation (open systems approach). The organisation cannot come to life without people who obviously have an impact, it can survive without particular individuals, and adaptations are possible by changing people's roles to overcome setbacks.

# Individual variation

Each person is different from all others in many ways. These differences are mainly noticeable through the input of senses which distinguish physical appearance, the stages of growth, the level of intelligence and the approach to common sense. Growth and intelligence are in the province of differential psychology. The aims are to find better ways of measuring the strength of traits so that people may be educated and trained more effectively and be given more appropriate jobs.

### INPUT OF SENSES

One glance at a person is usually sufficient to see that he or she is different from other people, twins excepted. Over a longer period of observation people are seen to think and react slightly differently from each other in similar situations. Each person has inherited and developed certain mental qualities and feelings as he or she experiences life. Consequently, the supervisor must treat each person as an individual to achieve a sound relationship.

### Limitations of observation

True recognition of an individual involves knowing many facets of his or her nature which are difficult to perceive at the workplace. Only one side of the person is seen, whereas there will be many additional outside interests which affect his or her outlook. Family ties, religion, politics, hobbies and sports all influence the person's general attitudes. There is also an unlimited range of traits in people, such as greed, dishonesty, kindness, carelessness, perseverance and patience. Everyone is subjected to many pressures which often confuse and irritate. This may lead to distorted thinking and a tendency to keep people at a distance.

Sympathetic observation and treatment help to reduce the mental barriers, although not many people will allow someone to get too close. Hence a 'mask' is always worn which conceals an individual's true feelings in daily contact with others.

## STAGES OF GROWTH

What happens in the very early stages of life governs attitudes to some extent, traits, character and general outlook. This forms the basis of the well-known saying that people are products of their environment, as well as the view that environmental and educational problems are the responsibility of the community.

Basic attitudes are formed in the first five years. Habits are established and attitudes develop towards parents and other close relatives. These attitudes tend to become models that are used later in dealing with people outside the family. If attitudes work successfully for the child, they gradually become traits which are the core of his or her personality. Examples are aggressiveness, gentleness, greediness, independence, capability, activity, noisiness and cruelty.

Complex phases occur in the sixth and subsequent years. Conscience, personality, repression of emotions and other features continue to develop.

## INTELLIGENCE

Three typical meanings of intelligence are mental ability, quickness of understanding and the capacity to use intellect effectively. Alternatively, intelligence means using the mental processes of thinking, appreciating, learning, observing, reasoning or problem solving, and perception. Views on intelligence are subjective and variable. They are often based upon various observations or interpretations involving such topics as mechanical aptitude, numerical capability, rapid speech, flair such as playing a musical instrument or writing, effective public speaking, accurately visualising complex processes or phenomena, and high creativity.

### Intelligence testing

Considering all the attributes involved and the many interpretations, the concept of intelligence testing (or the intelligence quotient) is debatable. Here are some typical opinions:

- *Against testing*: Improvements are possible by practising the tests; validating results is not scientific; findings are not valuable compared with many other important attributes; extensive general education can improve results; and test conditions may intimidate some people.
- *For testing*: Apparently scientific and genetically sound; practising tests does not make a significant difference; identifies high ability for further development; does not discriminate against race, class, nationality or income; and identifies low ability, therefore indicates job suitability.

## COMMON SENSE

Some people possess so-called high intelligence but seem to lack sound common sense. Perhaps this is simply forgetfulness or carelessness. Maybe common sense is a flair as it partly involves a certain sensitivity towards people's feelings, the human race and the community.

Most people make adverse comments about an individual's common sense although there may be insufficient information on the particular situation to warrant an opinion; or they make a favourable comment based upon their knowledge of the problem and its solution, that has an obvious answer. In most cases the key point is knowledge or information available at the time. Therefore this term should be used with caution since it is often misunderstood, misused and misinterpreted. Also when further information is revealed the accusation of poor common sense may become invalid.

Certainly the term is widely used but it has many meanings: an obvious choice, an obvious course of action, accurate reasoning, rational reasoning, a trait, sanity, intelligence, a logical application of knowledge, instinct and a practical approach. Views vary widely: common sense is uncommon; a decision may be sound common sense to one observer but poor common sense to another; everybody has a good measure of common sense. Victor Hugo claimed that common sense was acquired in spite of, not because of, education; Albert Einstein defined it as the collection of prejudices people have accrued by the age of 18; a judge stated, 'common sense says . . .' (apparently he sees common sense as agreeing with his particular thoughts). Clearly it seems very difficult to define, measure and use common sense as a factor for selection.

Supervisors and managers are often accused of having poor common sense. However, the real reasons for an error (apart from lack of information or poor information) may be disguised; there could be an emotional bias, lack of experience, insufficient education and training, undue influence, low intelligence, forgetfulness and faulty reasoning. Claims are made that managing is common sense but these are not substantiated by explaining why such claims seem to invalidate all the disciplines of management science.

# Recognising mental features

Substantial knowledge and experience of mental features are essential before a supervisor can accurately note behaviour and analyse findings. Suitable allowances for employees have to be made when they behave in certain ways that do not coincide with their usual personality or attitudes. The supervisor should avoid categorising people based upon his or her own particular values, outlook, likes, dislikes and shortcomings.

Developing recognition skill may be divided into the study of personality, human characteristics, attitudes, temperament and emotion. Equally important are the basic mental processes in the next section, where perception, mental levels and mental experience are explained.

# Personality

Simply described, personality is a collection of attributes observed in the individual. Each one varies in strength and is seen as a habit or mode of behaviour. These habit patterns develop in sequence with maturity and are seen as responses to various stimuli. Any definition includes certain features. First, a person behaves in a consistent and enduring way from situation to situation. Consequently, behaviour is predictable in certain situations: if shy today he or she will probably be shy tomorrow. Second, there seems to be a system operating that produces a style of behaviour. Third, each person is unique in his or her behaviour pattern. People are predictable in some situations, unpredictable in other ways, undergo change as they develop and continually gain experience.

## THE HIDDEN PERSONALITY

As relationships between two people develop, more self-disclosure and feedback occur which reveal aspects of personality hidden before. This natural process is explained by the Johari window, a technique for improving perception through the reduction of stereotyping and individual biases.

The theoretical window has three parts to awareness of personality: open, blind (or hidden) and unknown. The open part illustrates a person's own awareness of his or her personality that is obvious to others. The blind part illustrates a person's hidden part of his or her personality that might be apparent to others since it compromises attitudes and feelings in the subconscious which tend to manifest themselves through behaviour. The unknown part remains hidden to both parties, nevertheless it influences behaviour.

Naturally a person is reticent at a first meeting, therefore the open part of the window is small. As the relationship grows the open part increases and the blind part decreases, thus revealing a more definite recognition of personality. Clearly the supervisor should develop a relationship to assess the reasons for behaviour and attitudes through personality problems.

## PERSONALITY THEORY

There is no universally accepted personality theory although many are on offer. Theories have been dominated by Freud's psychoanalytic ideas, followed by various contributors who concentrate mainly on approaches to personality types and traits. Three famous examples are given below.

## FREUD

According to Sigmund Freud (1856–1939) many factors of personality and behaviour do not conform to rational expectations since they originate from unconscious motivation. Thus inexplicable feelings such as aversions, revulsions, petty fears and obsessions are caused by the consequences of experiences at an early age. These are assimilated into the unconscious mind and influence emotions and behaviour.

Freud believed in the conflict view of behaviour or personality, which is created by three interrelated but often conflicting psychoanalytical concepts: the id, the ego and the superego. The ego concept is especially important since it relates to transactional analysis (Chapter 10) which is useful and easy to understand.

### The id concept

The id is a crude, primitive, instinctual drive in the unconscious mind, which seeks pleasure or gratification and avoids pain; therefore it is non-directional and lacks control. This core personality is aggressive and creates impulses that are destructive and domineering. Such pleasure seeking includes sexual drive and the demand for food, warmth and comfort. But as individuals develop and mature, most learn to control the id. Even then it remains a strong drive and is a basis of thinking and behaving.

### The ego concept

The ego is a conscious, logic-seeking drive which conforms to the external environment and interprets reality for the id, thus keeping it in check. The ego co-ordinates its perceptions and attempts to

cope with its surrounds. However, the two obviously conflict since the id seeks pleasure whereas the ego denies or postpones until a more convenient time. To resolve this conflict, the ego seeks support from the superego.

### The superego concept

The superego is developed in the unconscious mind by absorbing a society's morals and cultural values, and it becomes a conscience which provides the ego with norms that indicate right or wrong intentions. Development depends upon input from parents, teachers and other contacts; the individual is unaware of the superego; conflict between the ego and superego may occur; and the superego helps the ego to fight the id. According to Freud, the unconscious mind is a strong determining factor on behaviour that may defy rational explanation. Furthermore, even the individual concerned may be puzzled by it.

## JUNG

According to Carl Gustav Jung (1875–1961) everyone has many personality traits but they are used differently. A person who shows some strong traits is likely to possess certain others. This means there are trait clusters that form types of personality capable of being classified. These are grouped into four pairs (see below). Any person will show both aspects of each pair to a certain degree although one will dominate.

- *Introvert–extrovert*: This typology tends to be a continuum rather than discretely separate types. The introvert works alone, is diligent, independently minded and prefers to concentrate alone. The extrovert likes to work with others, is socially minded, freethinking and a good communicator.
- *Intuitor–sensor*: The intuitor is a creative problem solver, likes complexity and new concepts but they become bored if confronted with detail. The sensor is rather narrow in approach, avoids complexity, is practical, careful, patient and pays attention to detail.
- *Feeling–thinking*: The feeling individual empathises easily, prefers people rather than

objects and excels in persuading and compromising. But they appear to be disorganised, uncritical, illogical and overemotional. The thinking individual is objective, analytical and logical, so there is a tendency to be insensitive and to misunderstand values.

- *Perceiver–judger*: The perceiver is flexible, appreciates all sides of a problem or difficulty, seeks information but they may give up easily. The judger perseveres, is decisive and orderly but they may be impulsive and not admit errors.

## CATTELL

A further approach is the well-known trait theory proposed by R.B. Cattell in *The Scientific Analysis of Personality*. He distinguished between surface and source traits. Surface traits are on the surface of personality; examples are social–seclusive, wise–foolish, honest–dishonest and affectionate–cold. Source traits are deep-rooted; examples are good nature–suspicious attitudes, dominance–submissiveness, cheerfulness–depression and maturity–immaturity.

# Human characteristics

Many peculiarities in people fail to match and form a set pattern. Changes are noticed in some whereas others remain apparently unchanged. Some people act like sheep whereas others are intensely strong-willed and independent.

On the one hand, the human race seems to be very good at killing each other, standing by while others starve, behaving indifferently towards torture and discomfort of others, and lusting for power. On the other hand, it seems to be moving gradually forward towards higher ideals, a more responsible approach and more consideration for humankind.

Other noticeable features are many likes and dislikes, a wide range of hobbies and ideas, inability to think clearly, faith in the unknown, inability to recognise happiness until later when it is gone, and strong support for whatever they help to create.

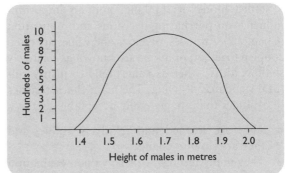

**Figure 9.1** Distribution of human differences: an example Distribution curves are normally bell-shaped, since most of the points fall around the average. This is particularly true of natural statistics; for example, there are more people who have approximately average intelligence, height, etc., than people who have values very far above average or very far below average.

## THE DISTRIBUTION OF HUMAN DIFFERENCES

If any one physical characteristic of people is measured and plotted on a graph, provided the sample is sufficient, a symmetrical bell-shaped curve will result (Fig. 9.1).

A similar distribution also exists in the hidden and more basic characteristics of people, such as desires, ability and disposition. These characteristics are exceptionally difficult to measure and considerable training and experience are needed before reasonable assessment is possible. For example, when meeting a stranger most people tend to form first impressions. These are invariably incorrect and adjusted later as they receive more information on the individual. Keeping an open mind and continually observing the person is necessary if a true evaluation is to be achieved. As opportunities occur for people to demonstrate their particular skills and natural abilities, their individual characteristics gradually appear. The supervisor should make sure these opportunities do occur.

# Attitudes

An attitude is an abstract concept that has no generally accepted definition. Certainly it is a form of settled behaviour, a means of indicating opinion, a settled mode of thinking, and an important influence on purchasing decisions and motivation (Chapter 9). Attitudes, opinions and values are often coupled together; opinions are known as relatively shallow ideas, whereas values tend to justify cultural standards of living. The main characteristics of attitudes that are generally acceptable are:

- They are learned and relatively stable, and they are slow to change.
- They imply feelings, beliefs, values, evaluation and a tendency to behave in a particular way.
- They affect habits, self-confidence, perception, and reaction to the internal and external environment.

## FOUR ELEMENTS OF AN ATTITUDE

- A behavioural tendency to act in a certain way towards an object or person. This intention to act (or conative element) means a particular action will probably happen (not will happen) if an opportunity occurs.
- Beliefs and disbeliefs involve trust or confidence in received information being true. This knowledge (or cognitive element) includes experience which provides some meaning to the (chaotic) state of the surrounding environment.
- Values are standards used to compare objects or people. Values are often classified as good or bad, appropriate or inappropriate, and desirable or undesirable. They may be held by the individual or by society.
- Feelings are the affective element which may be positive or negative, and they are essentially emotional.

## ATTITUDE AND BEHAVIOUR

Unfortunately, attitudes are not directly observable, therefore measurement of their strengths is difficult and tends to rely on asking individuals about their feelings towards a topic. But their behaviour is observable and from this emerged a concept (or assumption) that 'attitude tends to lead to behaviour'. In other words, behaviour follows naturally from holding a particular attitude. In reality many other pressures also affect behaviour, especially when group activity is

considered. Therefore, bearing in mind that attitudes vary in strength and may be modified, in 1970 D.J. Bem proposed the concept that 'behaviour tends to lead to attitude'. This idea has led to many motivation theories. However, considering group activity (Chapter 5), an interactive relationship exists between attitude and behaviour.

## BELIEFS AND VALUES

Managers tend to blame attitude when employees refuse to conform to their requirements, but attitude has many hidden components and there are many other pressures which need consideration. Indeed managers are often criticised for ignoring beliefs and values of individuals and groups.

The problem is that employees (at all levels in the organisation) have many different beliefs and values which cause exceptional difficulties when trying to design an environment that leads to high satisfaction and performance. Inevitably there is a gap between people's expectations and the real work situation. In recent years this divide has been aggravated by unemployment, demands for a higher quality of life, racial discrimination problems and green issues.

## PREJUDICE

Prejudice is an attitude which involves prejudgement and is held before direct experience. A prejudice may be negative, hostile, positive, unfair, inflexible, inaccurate, simplistic and not completely rational. Prejudices may be held about situations, machines, people or groups. They are a natural process of categorising, generalising and overgeneralising to form attitudes which may be discriminating and related to stereotyping, and which form an integral part of intergroup behaviour. A typical example is Sherif's survey of intergroup activity (Chapter 5).

Various techniques have been tried to reduce prejudices, but some aspects are impossible to remove such as unequal status, unemployment problems and complete fulfilment of psychological and social needs. Typical techniques which help are persuasion through advertising, legislation, attempts to improve mutual independence, and enforcing contact with the object or person involved.

## ATTITUDES OF NORMAL PEOPLE

A normal person's attitudes are formed by arriving at personal balanced opinions. Under suitable conditions, these opinions are open to adjustment through the acceptance of logical reasoning and provision of sufficient information to justify the change.

Although people may behave in different ways which tend to suit their own particular needs or best interests, they are all acting normally. Each person has his or her own method of dealing with problems depending upon emotions, reasoning and past environment. Moreover, an apparently abnormal or extreme reaction may be caused by further factors unknown to the supervisor.

## RESISTANCE TO CHANGE

Any new scheme or change will instinctively be examined from the selfish point of view and, if it pleases, acceptance usually follows. An element of doubt will create the tendency to reject the idea or to demand more information or assurance.

Security is very important to some people. If their security seems to be threatened in some way, a form of guarantee is necessary before the change visualised becomes acceptable. Any proposed alteration affecting pay, safety, working conditions or methods needs clarifying in the employee's mind to remove resistance. Perfectly healthy people will resist change from outside. However, individuals do change as it suits them. Living requires continual adjustment to social and industrial environments, although it is often a slow and laborious task. The fortunate ones adjust quickly, but to others the problem is insurmountable and they need special treatment before their minds can accept a change. An example is where a person suffers a bereavement and cannot face up to the drastic change in family life it entails.

The supervisor should accept that people do change their habits, outlook and attitudes, and have the capacity to improve. He or she should be able to recognise the ill-adjusted employee from a variety of indications, including nervousness, difficulty in concentrating, ailments, misunderstandings, unusual behaviour and poor general attitude towards work and people.

# Temperament

People think, believe, understand and perceive differently since they have mainly been moulded by their previous environment and inherited nature. Therefore, temperament (or nature) is complex and causes many misunderstandings; although with training, social aspects may be controlled and modified. An appreciation of this vast topic enables supervisors to be more discerning.

## BASIC TEMPERAMENTS

Research by Professor David Kiersey in 1984 concluded that there are four basic temperaments. Comprehensive information on each one is provided in his textbook *Please Understand Me*. Interesting applications of his findings are in selection procedures, self-assessment and assessing subordinates to utilise fully their capabilities. Only a brief reference is possible here, along with envisaged supervisory tendencies.

Patricia Hedges is currently operating a research project based on Kiersey's work. This project is designed to identify the temperaments of Mensa members to see whether they reflect the patterns of the general community. Her version of Kiersey's textbook is *Personality Matters*. The four basic temperaments are now listed.

### Sensing–judging

The characteristics of people with this temperament are:

- dependable
- painstaking
- hard and consistent work
- averse to change

Supervisory tendencies associated with this temperament are:

- sets rules, schedules and routines
- prefers orderly ways
- appreciates values, policies and purpose of an organisation
- chairs meetings effectively

### Sensing–perceiving

People with this temperament display the following characteristics:

- prefer variety
- routines bore
- thrive in crises
- are adaptable

Associated with this temperament are the following supervisory tendencies:

- good negotiator
- troubleshooter
- likes crisis situations and variety, but tends to ignore rules and regulations
- takes risks

### Intuitive–thinking

The characteristics of people with this temperament include:

- being creative and visionary
- having a flair for designing

Supervisory tendencies that could be expected are:

- instigator of change and improvements
- plans ahead
- enjoys public relations

### Intuitive–feeling

The characteristics of people with this temperament include being:

- people oriented
- optimistic
- humanitarian

Supervisory tendencies include the following:

- good motivator and communicator
- supports employees but tends to tire through overinvolvement

## Emotion

Emotion is much deeper and more pronounced than simple feelings associated with 'drives' since it involves environment, training and temperament, among other factors. Three responses occur with emotion: some physical or organic change, accompanied by an impulse to do something active about the situation, and a feeling which hastens the process of action. A person's temperament is recognisable from the way he or she controls emotions, moods and outbursts, and by his or her general emotional maturity.

## Basic mental processes

Basic mental processes help to explain why people sometimes behave in apparently illogical and unreasonable ways and how they are able to give meaning to their experiences and environment. Three important features are perception, mental levels and mental experience.

## Perception

Perception creates for each individual a unique picture of the world, a picture which differs from the real world. In other words, a person interprets a situation or the environment; they do not have an exact recording or registration of it. Perception uses all the sensory inputs: sight, hearing, taste, touch, smell, and feelings such as temperature change.

The ways people perceive themselves and the surrounding environment largely govern their behaviour. Consequently, it is essential to recognise the difference between a person's perceptual environment and the actual environment within the organisation. This difference or personal bias creates many emotional difficulties, personal problems and conflicts between supervisors and employees. Typical examples are communication breakdowns along with difficulties in judging, training, motivating and assessing the performance of employees.

People select, analyse and interpret sensory stimuli. The whole process is influenced by many factors, including their expectations, wants, background, experiences, values, beliefs, interests, attitudes, general views and the incentives they are offered. A compromise exists between what can be seen and what an individual is conditioned to see, will see, or will avoid seeing. Similarly, people hear what they want to hear, not the actual message, especially if it contains bad news or information that has a detrimental effect.

The following concepts should be related to this mental process and used to understand more clearly the conditions under which behaviour appears illogical or irrational.

## PERCEPTION AND SENSATION

All knowledge accumulated by a person depends upon the senses and their stimulation. These physical senses are hearing, seeing, touching, smelling, balance and tasting, plus so-called sixth senses such as extrasensory perception. Perception is more complex and broader than sensation. The process involves an interaction of selection, organisation and interpretation. Consequently, perception (a cognitive process) may filter, modify or completely change raw data received through the senses.

To avoid overcrowding at any time, the attention process selects information through deliberate or involuntary processes and discards the rest. This system works in the following ways:

- *Deliberate*: irrelevant, distracting or unimportant information is rejected to allow important information access to the brain.
- *Involuntary*: the subject matter or the form of presentation forces the brain to pay attention to it.

These factors may be subjective or objective depending on whether they are influenced by the receiver's personality. Objective factors include high intensity (loudness, brightness, etc.), sudden movement or change, repetitive but not monotonous stimuli, systematic patterning (logical arrangement), and novelty. Both processes are extensively used in advertising and communication (Chapter 14).

## PERCEPTUAL ORGANISATION: GROUPING

Stimuli are grouped together into a distinct pattern or framework by using the principles of similarity, proximity, continuity or closure.

- *Similarity*: If stimuli have something in common, they tend to link into a group. Typical examples are blue-collar workers (although each one is different); all shop stewards are categorised as a nuisance; and all sales representatives thought of as extroverts.
- *Proximity*: If members of a group are near to each other, they tend to be perceived as belonging together in terms of a characteristic. A group of sewing machinists in one room may be perceived as all being antagonistic if some of them constantly complain about working conditions; and a group of senior secretaries working together in one large office may all be considered as snooty although only two out of six actually are.
- *Closure*: This gestalt principle causes a person to perceive a whole when actually there are gaps fragmenting the whole. A supervisor may think he or she has complete agreement on a topic when in fact there is some opposition.

## THE CYCLES

Figure 9.2 shows the operation of two cycles associated with the perceptual process and external observable processes. The first cycle shows the internal data processing activity (perception). The second cycle includes perception and external observable processes; it begins with stimuli and cycles through the perceptual process, resultant behaviour and outcomes, before returning to stimuli. Note the way perception eventually changes stimuli when outcomes impinge on them, consequently presenting a new situation for the perceptual process. A complex series of cause–effect relationships exists.

## THE PERCEPTUAL PROCESS

The perceptual process may be divided into four components which form a cycle: attention and selectivity, recording, interpretation, and feedback to clarify and assist perception (these are within the dotted area in Fig. 9.2).

- *Attention and selectivity*: Initially the person is surrounded by stimuli, probably including people and many environmental conditions. Examples are (a) an argument develops between a supervisor and an employee outside

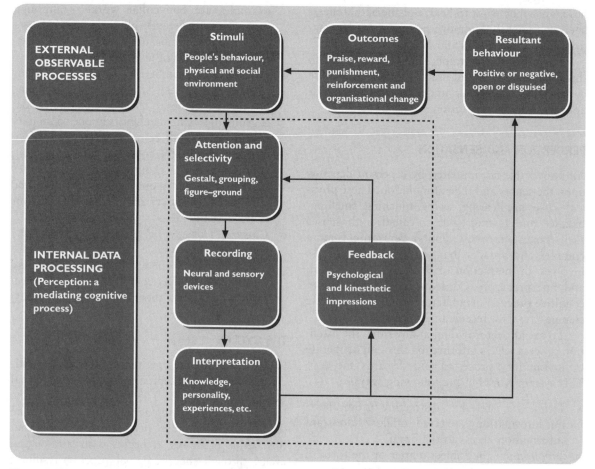

**Figure 9.2** The perceptual process and external effects
There are two cycles: (1) an internal mediating cognitive process (perception) and (2) an external process starting with stimuli, using perception, continuing with behaviour and outcomes, and returning to stimuli.

a manager's office, forcing the manager to intervene; (b) the internal phone rings during a discussion with an employee.

- *Recording*: Sensory and neural devices register the data in preparation for analysis and interpretation.
- *Interpretation*: Neural mechanisms interpret the situation. These are biased by many personal characteristics, e.g. personality, knowledge, intelligence, experience and motivation.
- *Feedback*: Links between this and the first component allow for corrections to first impressions and feed back stimuli which are of use to the perceptual process relating to reality. Kinesthetic mechanisms help to perceive dynamic situations that require rapid

adjustment; psychological mechanisms help to determine people's intentions. Examples are judging the speed of an oncoming car when deciding to overtake; assessing a manager's mood; or sensing when he or she is joking.

## EXTERNAL OBSERVABLE PROCESSES

Surrounding the perceptual process is external reality, which for this purpose consists of three processes (Fig. 9.2). The first is when stimuli enter the perceptual process and attract attention. The second is behaviour resulting from the perceptual process. The third is the outcome of the behaviour.

- *Stimuli*: These originate from people's actions, and physical and sociological situations.
- *Resultant behaviour*: Typical examples are when positive forms of behaviour generate helpful actions, and when negative forms cause unpleasant reactions. Changes in attitude may also occur, which could be identified or interpreted as favourable or unfavourable. Recognising this change is a controversial aspect and it depends upon a personal assessment of future behaviour if the related stimuli are identifiable and capable of assessment.
- *Outcomes*: These are the consequences of resultant behaviour such as praise and reward if behaviour suits the recipient, and punishment if behaviour displeases. Reinforcement may occur (Chapter 12) if the recipient encourages the behaviour pattern.

## PERCEPTUAL SELECTIVITY

An internal filtering process gives priority to vital stimuli. Selection depends upon its appeal to, and compatibility with, the individual's mental make-up, including values, needs and experience. External factors draw attention by means of size, intensity, contrast, movement, repetition and novelty of the stimuli. Thus, the whole process focuses attention on particular stimuli and allows for constant changes in attention as desired.

## SOCIAL PERCEPTION

Social perception plays a vital role in interviewing and in the employment situation since it attempts to explain how one person perceives another. Here are some of the major aspects.

### Profiles

Perception is strongly influenced by the characteristics of the perceiver and the person perceived. For example, if a manager feels pleased with life, possibly a more favourable impression will be created of someone who is averagely pleasant and attractive; whereas a manager who is displeased might be more than usually unimpressed by an arrogant and unattractive person.

- *The perceiver's profile*: The perceiver's characteristics affect those likely to be recognised in others. Therefore, endeavouring to form an unbiased picture of oneself makes it easier to see others more clearly.
- *The perceived person*: The person being perceived also has an effect on the perceiver. Examples are the person's status, stereotyping by status or role, and noticeable traits.

### Perceptual context

The overall environment in the concern that is created by management also biases particular meanings and values to the employee. Thus communications from managers and supervisors are distorted to some extent by the views employees have about them. Therefore, great care is needed when wording memos and notices, when speaking to employees, and when gesturing to make a point.

### Attribution

How people explain the cause of their, or another's, behaviour is called attribution. The tendency is to search for causes of behaviour and, when located to the satisfaction of the searcher, these causal attributions strongly affect perception. A typical example is to attribute a new sales representative's performance to the particular territory that was allocated, rather than to that person's ability and energy.

### Stereotyping

Perceiving another person as belonging to a single class or category is known as stereotyping. This means attributing favourable or unfavourable traits to the individual on that basis rather than on information about the person. Also, it implies general agreement on the attributed traits and existence of a discrepancy between these and the actual traits. Common stereotyped groups are managers, supervisors, trade union members, nationals and minorities. Here are some examples: managers are status conscious, the Germans are industrious, the French are great lovers, and the British are conventional.

### The halo effect

The halo effect is when a person's judgement of another is based upon one trait only, not a category as in stereotyping. Examples of these traits are ability, attractiveness, dependability and loyalty. An error will be compounded if a person allows the single trait to override all other traits in his or her perception of the individual. Typically, a supervisor may perceive a very good worker as being un-cooperative because he or she happens to be reserved; or a manager thinks the secretary is lazy because he or she will not type the manager's private letters.

### Perceptual barriers

A defence mechanism operates when a person is confronted with a situation that does not accord with a preconceived idea. This applies when a fact or an event is presented that is unacceptable or perhaps threatening in an obscure way. Typical cases would be agreement between a manager and trade union representative, or a confrontation between a supervisor and employee's spouse when the accusation of favouritism is put to the supervisor who is convinced that he or she treats everyone equally.

# Mental levels

There are assumed to be three mental levels. The supervisor should have some knowledge of how they work. He or she may then show a sympathetic understanding towards subordinates in certain situations, such as the examples given below.

## THE CONSCIOUS LEVEL

Consciousness may be described as knowing what is happening around us and being aware of our actions. Being able to concentrate on a particular task means a person can successfully block out all those distractions that are happening all the time. If concentration is disturbed by a passing van, a whistle blast, or any unusual noise, train of thought is lost and an error may occur. Some people find concentration more difficult than others; the slightest unidentifiable noise upsets them, or even a familiar sound may disrupt their train of thought. Their work capacity may be excellent, but unless there is low distraction in the immediate environment, productivity and quality will be poor.

## THE SUBCONSCIOUS LEVEL

All instructions and information flow into the subconscious mind, which retains the messages for recall at any time. Recent messages, which include information and experiences, are easily recalled within days, weeks or months, depending upon the individual. Some people have difficulty in remembering an event after a few weeks, whereas others find it easy. Failing to remember is not a crime; it is both thoughtless and inefficient to ignore the handicap when it is known, instead of making due allowances. The sensible supervisor will avoid placing people with poor memories in situations that call for a good memory as they are likely to fail.

## THE UNCONSCIOUS LEVEL

The subconscious connects with the unconscious mind and passes on all information and experiences for permanent storage. Although all experiences are stored, it seems that automatic recollection at any time is not possible. Recalling an event at will does not seem to work; often there is a time lag and suddenly, without any apparent effort, it springs into the conscious mind. Furthermore, a difficult problem may be put to one side and then, without warning, the answer presents itself. Similarly, all manner of information will appear without any conscious effort. An unfortunate effect occurs when a person takes an instant dislike to another for no obvious reason. Psychologists say this is due to an unconscious connection of the person with someone who caused unhappiness in the past. The danger of allowing first impressions to affect one's judgement is plain.

# Mental experience

The actual mental experience associated with awareness involves at any time the interaction of closely knit processes: feeling, willing and thinking. These are often called affective, conative and cognitive, respectively. Generally one overrides the other two, although they are also activated. For example, an employee notices a mistake in a colleague's work; the first person may feel the right course of action is to report it, but might will himself or herself to take no action, reasoning (or thinking) the mistake will be spotted by the usual procedures.

The subject of mental experience can only be glanced at, considering the complexity of other factors that are strongly connected such as the control feature known as sentiments, the influential feature known as disposition and the complexes associated with them. There is an extensive amount of material under this heading, but condensed it means people cannot be held responsible for their nature or temperament. With help, however, certain problems can be overcome if people learn to adjust and become more acceptable citizens and employees. The supervisor should advise employees to seek specialist help when the need is obvious.

# Sociology of work

Orientations to work may be classified according to the two extremes: the instrumentally oriented employee and the expressively oriented employee. One is more interested in financial reward while the other is more concerned with job satisfaction. Within this simple continuum framework (between the two extremes) various schools of thought have developed about human nature and work behaviour.

## THE SCIENTIFIC MANAGEMENT/HUMAN RELATIONS SCHOOL

The scientific management/human relations school is explained in detail in Chapter 10; briefly the ideas of economic reward as an incentive and the tendency for employees to slack if given the chance are fundamental. Also, if management relates to each employee and satisfies his or her self-interest, then full co-operation will be achieved. How individuals relate to each other is vital in this

psychologistic style, therefore the key features are participation, participative leadership and development of supervisory skills.

## THE ORGANIC/SYSTEMS SCHOOL

The organic/systems school emphasises the idea of society having an independent and determining effect on the individual. Thus the community, which is organic by nature and conforms to a social system, really decides how people behave.

## THE INTERACTIONIST SCHOOL

The interactionist school views the individual and society as mutually interdependent, not a one-sided deterministic relationship. Consequently, human behaviour is not caused by internal or external forces but by a process of interpretation of both forces, whereby a person constructs his or her own realities as a result of interaction with others.

## THE SOCIAL ACTION SCHOOL

The social action school considers the meaningful activity of the person and the grand questions of political, social and cultural change. People are considered to be rational and pursuing certain ends but there is not necessarily a direct relationship between their work and the outcome in terms of social order. People's actions often have unintentional consequences and lead to fundamental conflicts of value, interest and perspective.

## THE MARXIAN SCHOOL

The Marxian school proposes the idea that people achieve fullness of their humanity through their labour. The implication is that the conditions under which labour is performed are crucial. The argument that the worker is alienated is based upon three assumed points. But there are strong economic and social counter-arguments against this line of reasoning.

- The owner of a business has sufficient means of subsistence, whereas employees are dependent.
- Employees have to put in extra work over and above what is required for their own needs.

- Employees are restricted in their striving to achieve creative fulfilment.

# Class and status

A general belief is that achievement in the job decides promotion prospects. In modern organisations, however, apparently different skills are used in jobs as the hierarchy is ascended, which makes the belief suspect. Promotion prospects probably depend more on a willingness to fit into the power structure and on possessing appropriate cultural, class, status and background aspects that conform to the management pattern. Although there are examples of shop-floor employees making good, there is increasing evidence that class-related criteria are preferable to task-relevant criteria.

The class system may also be seen operating in trade unions where antiquated structures lead to competition among unions within companies and in industries. Furthermore, the tendency to emphasise class and status is openly displayed in companies (especially in factories) through the use of notices and rules: 'This door staff only', 'workers' canteen' and 'executive dining room'. Usually, workers clock on, staff book in, while managers simply arrive.

Employees also show concern for status. They may be sensitive to pay differences between jobs and, if they are transferred, the level of informal status of the new job. Commitment is more diffuse, there seems to be high trust, more discretion and more conception rather than execution of tasks.

Finally, sharp divisions are seen in the distribution of marketable wealth in the UK. According to Inland Revenue statistics for 1991, the most wealthy 1 per cent own 18 per cent, 10 per cent own 53 per cent, and 50 per cent own 94 per cent. Moreover, three significant ranges of the distribution are £0–5000 = 31.8 per cent, £50 000–100 000 = 8.9 per cent, and £100 001 and over = 7.3 per cent.

# Breakdowns in relationships

Relationships may collapse or break down for many reasons. The important ones are:

- *Unstable outlooks*: immaturity, varied social backgrounds, psychological problems
- *Poor social skills*: misinterpreting verbal and written messages, misunderstanding body language
- *Breaking rules*: standards are not taken seriously
- *Boredom*: lack of mutual interest, monotony in the group
- *Dissonant relationships*: different backgrounds involving religion, race and environment
- *Inequity*: negative feelings override positive ones, changes in pay and bonuses at higher levels which cause an increased organisational gap
- *Deception disclosures*: betrayal of trust
- *Conflict*: unacceptable levels of disagreement or disrespect
- *Cultural changes*: these include changes in interest, attitudes, education, training and job improvement
- *Relocation*: the distance between people or groups becomes too great for social activity

# Social influences in general

Social influences in general are viewed as a complex network of continuing interrelationships that affect behaviour. Collectively they include some topics already mentioned in this chapter and in Chapter 5, namely roles, status, class, culture, group formation, cohesiveness and norms. Also included is family influence, discussed in Chapter 11. An advanced society is highly structured, with a specialised economic nature. Consequently, an isolated individual has difficulty in surviving and learns to behave or satisfy needs in an acceptable fashion that avoids unpleasantness.

## SOCIALISATION

An individual learns to adjust to the social environment through socialisation. The process is a continuous one, beginning shortly after birth, and involving complex learning theory. The main components are the family, schools, peers and the media. Socialisation prepares the individual for the roles to be played; habits, beliefs, values and skills are learned; and knowledge is acquired. Many mechanisms come into play, such as imitation, identification, role playing, various mental processes and conditioning.

# The stress factor

Most people recognise stress in materials and machines because they see a physical effect – a rubber band will break if stretched too far; a fuse will blow if the load is too great. Indeed stress is occurring long before the result is witnessed, but the cause is accepted only when something drastic happens.

With people, stress also occurs internally and is not recognisable immediately. Some outward signs may indicate problems, but when a breaking point occurs the cause is often not recognised or investigated. This difficulty could be due to two situations. First, people may suffer with *underloading* or *overloading* of work; both are stress conditions. Second, there is the duration of stress; stress is usually classified as short-term or long-term. Short-term stress is suffered by many employees through unavoidable circumstances such as sudden sickness or termination of another employee, excessive urgent orders, and disputes or strikes. Long-term stress is more serious and may mean disastrous consequences. An overview of stress is given in Fig. 10.3.

## THE BACKGROUND

According to research, stress is viewed in many ways. Stress exists as a natural process when the body prepares itself for danger or attack; stress conforms to a natural cycle of body responses to fight or flight (termed distress) and when the fear or menace subsides it returns to normal; or the individual has feelings of stress which persist and cause comprehension and concentration difficulties. The latter view explains how ill-health develops and all activities appear to be threatening in some way.

Several reasons for this form of mental behaviour are usually accepted. First, it is the outcome of primitive ancestors (hominids) who were prey for the wild beasts. Second, the primitive ancestors who followed (*Homo sapiens*), gradually developed weapons to defend themselves, and finally became hunters to kill for meat. In brief, ancestors were subjected to flight and fight, which meant the body had to cope with excessive demands. These internal changes persist today and are called stress. They are recognised as internal sensations when people make a speech, fight or experience fear. Typical situations are criminal activities, feuds, wars, domestic life and business life.

## STRESS LEVELS

If a job is enriched, there may be difficulty in recognising the point at which an excessive mental load is reached. Conversely, it is equally difficult to assess when a person is underloaded. For instance, working on a conveyor belt might easily cause mental underload. Both situations, it is claimed by neuropsychologists, have detrimental effects on health and performance. Indeed stress can affect the state of mind of employees, making them more sensitive to feelings of social dissatisfaction. This complex subject is becoming increasingly important as more employers are realising it causes pathological, social and economic problems. Furthermore, stress levels depend upon the person; one type of stress may be good for one person but bad for another, and stress is often thought to be unquantifiable.

## DISPLAY SCREEN EQUIPMENT

In recent years the extensive use of display screen equipment (DSE) has caused many stressful conditions. Various acts and an EC directive are now in force; they are discussed in Chapter 21.

## DEFINITIONS OF STRESS

- An internal condition caused by a restraint of natural feeling, especially when compelled to behave against normal wishes.
- An excessive or inexcessive demand upon physical or mental energy.
- A constraining or impelling force that adversely affects a person's state of mind.

## SYMPTOMS

To create a feeling of well-being, the nervous system has to function between particular limits of intensity. If these limits are exceeded, the person soon experiences unpleasant feelings, which eventually may lead to a variety of pathological effects such as dyspepsia, headaches, insomnia and exhaustion. In some cases more serious illnesses may occur such as gastritis, ulcers and coronary disease.

The immediate outward signs of stress may be unusual behaviour, suddenly losing control, excessive tiredness, low performance, blaming others without cause, a sudden reddening of the face, trembling, sweating, hesitant speech or over-emphasis of a nervous habit. Inward effects are feeling irritated, a thumping heart, sweating uncomfortably, butterflies in the stomach, boredom, anxiety, unaccountable fatigue, loss of appetite, headaches, dizziness, breathing problems, grinding teeth, aches in the neck, shoulders and back, dryness of the mouth and throat, rashes, and nail and lip biting.

The psychological effects are inability to relax and concentrate; feeling keyed up, drained, irritable, tense, anxious, pressurised, pessimistic or inadequate; avoiding people and situations; overindulging in eating, drinking and smoking; insomnia; nervous laughing; and being accident-prone.

## OTHER ASPECTS

Reducing stress levels is discussed in the next chapter. Stress-related sickness is examined in Chapter 21, with particular reference to research findings; the effects on employees, supervisors and managers; and the role of senior management.

## QUESTIONS

1 How would you establish desirable superior–subordinate relationships?

2 Every individual is different. Discuss this statement and how it affects supervision.

3 Why have human relations been neglected in industry?

4 Human relations and higher productivity go together. Give your views on this statement.

5 How would you proceed to improve human relations in a department where poor relations existed between supervisors and employees?

6 Can the viewpoints of managers and employees be reconciled?

7 What is meant by 'divided loyalty' in connection with management–employee relationships?

8 Explain the importance of understanding human instincts as a means of improving the industrial climate.

9 What advantages can be gained by a supervisor who recognises that each subordinate is a separate individual?

10 Discuss fully the problem of trying to understand people.

11 How would you deal with a situation where employees complain about a colleague who sits next to them and suffers from body odour?

12 How would you react if a subordinate pulls your leg?

13 What action would you take if a subordinate complains that *your* superior ignores him or her?

14 If a subordinate offers you a gift of fifty cigarettes and says that they were a gift but that he or she does not smoke, what would you do? Explain your action.

15 How would you cope with a situation where a subordinate is continually critical of your actions but does not make constructive suggestions?

16 Discuss the implications of the distribution of human differences when dealing with employees.

17 What is the importance of the perceptual process when trying to understand an employee's behaviour?

18 Discuss why stress is considered to be an essential subject for supervisors to study.

19 How would you recognise that an employee is suffering with stress?

20 What action would you take if you were convinced that an employee was suffering with stress?

21 Discuss research methodology and its significance when considering human relations problems.

22 Explain the Johari window and its significance when first meeting a new employee.

23 Consider employees' expectations at work, related to their beliefs and values.

---

**CASE STUDY**

Paul Mason is a liberal-minded supervisor who tries hard to maintain good relations with his subordinates. On this occasion he is particularly bothered. Karen, one of his young employees, has approached him to see if he is interested in joining a video club that she has formed in the department. Paul is not interested but he can see no harm in allowing her to go ahead, so long as the club operates during breaks.

One of his older employees, with whom he is on friendly terms, casually mentions the club and tells him that the tapes are causing a 'bit of a stir'. Apparently they are a slight shade of purple, according to the rumours.

Paul calls Karen into his office and asks her to explain. She replies, 'Well, you didn't ask what they were like and you said it was all right'.

When she is told that the club has to close immediately, Karen becomes very obstinate. 'I've paid a lot of money for these tapes and I'm certainly not going to lose out on the deal. What are you going to do about it?'

*What action should the supervisor take? Comment on the original decision.*

---

**CASE STUDY**

Terry Browning has been leading a comfortable working life as a supervisor for some years. His group of nine maintenance engineers are co-operative and work well together. Two chargehands control the workloads, one of whom retired three months ago and was replaced by a good worker, Paul Cummings.

When Paul takes over, he declares that he will start studying supervision. Within two months his behaviour changes and he begins to air his recently acquired knowledge among his colleagues at tea breaks.

Terry, the supervisor, can see no harm in it until one day Paul raises the subject of conflict in industry. He outlines various frames of reference that might be used in analysing industrial relations issues. Finally he deals with the radical framework, stressing certain points such as capitalism and its reliance on rhetoric of social equality and rewards, whereas in reality, he claims, there is inequality in distributing rewards and in opportunities for advancement. He also raises the questions of unequal distribution of wealth, control of workpeople, issues associated with freedom, choice, independence and autonomy.

Terry can see that the group are impressed. Paul says, 'I couldn't understand what it was all about before, why I felt the way I did about going to work for someone else – but I do now'.

The group breaks up and Terry suddenly feels very concerned about Paul's successful manipulation of the group. Within weeks he is plagued with problems and it becomes obvious that the employees' behaviour has changed drastically towards him.

Paul simply smiles when he tackles him and says he cannot understand what has gone wrong. The other chargehand is also having difficulties and complains that Paul is indirectly causing discontent.

*What can Terry do in these circumstances?*

# 10

# Forecasting and influencing human relations

## Introduction

Influencing human relations in organisations depends mainly upon understanding people, developing appropriate management, anticipating changes and effects, using the main influential approaches, and applying overall control. Figure 10.1 illustrates the main aspects within these features.

To cope with these features, supervisors and managers must be able to apply interpersonal and conceptual skills, and thoroughly understand the human dimensions of the job. Supervisors are continually confronted by complex human problems.

Consequently, whenever possible, they should foresee them before they develop into crises and solve them in such a way that productivity and motivation improve.

Underlying this activity is an essential boardroom policy with long-term aims to support a behavioural approach, which operates alongside the other essential aspects of management. These include using human resource management; organisational psychology; organisational theory; and the fundamental managerial approaches, including collaboration, systems, qualitative and quantitative techniques, and technological factors. Understandably, the chief executive is a role model. If he is

**Figure 10.1** Influencing human relations: the main features

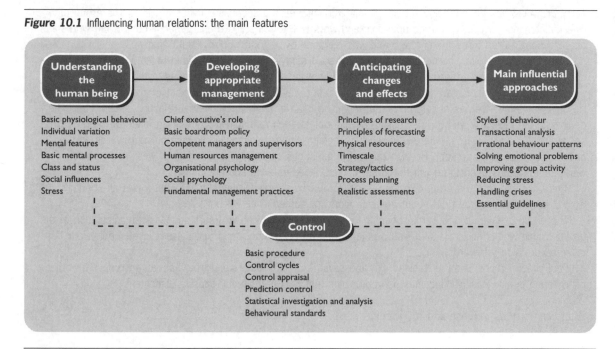

seen to be greedy, the employees will follow suit. If he is insensitive towards employees, they will react accordingly.

## MAIN APPROACHES

Some of the main influential approaches of forecasting and influencing behaviour are outlined in this chapter, but remember the subject is exceptionally complex. The following should at least help the supervisor to appreciate the breadth of information available and provide guidance on the approaches.

- research into improving human relations
- styles of behaviour
- transactional analysis theory
- irrational behaviour patterns
- emotional problems and how to solve them
- improving group activity
- empowerment
- reducing stress levels
- handling crises
- major causes of poor relations
- essential guidelines to improve human behaviour

# Research into human relations

## THE EARLY PIONEERS

Probably the first pioneer was H.V. Poor, editor of the *American Railroad Journal*. In the late nineteenth century he saw the need for recognition of the human factor to overcome the dangers of systemisation where people feel like cogs in a machine. Also he thought a kind of leadership was needed to overcome routine and dullness. Such leadership would create unity, an appreciation of the work and esprit de corps.

At the beginning of the twentieth century. F.W. Taylor and F.B. Gilbreth in the USA had concentrated on improving productivity by studying the operator, the job, tools and equipment, and working conditions. Outstanding improvements were achieved by the introduction of financial incentives, new methods, time and motion studies, rest pauses for workers, new types of tools, improved layout, and specialisation. However, these innovations did not always reach the visualised targets.

## THE HAWTHORNE STUDIES

In 1924 the Western Electric Company near Chicago decided to call in Elton Mayo, a professor at Harvard University, to study human behaviour. The company had already installed the systems of Taylor and Gilbreth, but the results were below expectations. Apparently productivity depended upon other factors that remained unknown.

The investigation was designed to test the effect of various factors on productivity by altering working conditions. Two equal-sized groups (A and B) of female operatives were formed and studied by Elton Mayo and his colleagues over a number of years. Lighting intensity was increased with group A and, as expected, output increased in sympathy. For no apparent reason, group B also increased its output, although the lighting was unchanged. The lighting was returned to its original intensity in group A and output increased further instead of falling back in sympathy.

In view of this unusual result, a whole series of experiments were conducted over a period of five years. Two voluntary female groups were formed and observed by the research workers who worked closely with the operators. All changes, which were made regularly every few weeks, were communicated to the operatives, who had the opportunity of commenting, asking for additional information, seeking advice, and airing any grievances.

This particular series of investigations was carried out in the relay assembly test room at the Hawthorne plant. Communication was ideal as information was allowed to flow freely in both directions. The supervisor had frequent conferences with the women, their views were requested and in some cases they were allowed to veto a proposal. The women had complete freedom to voice their thoughts and to decide their own working conditions.

A happy working group developed. The women worked freely and confidently with very little anxiety. A supervisory relationship was established which allowed them to feel a new sense of responsibility for their work. On the social side they seemed glad to be together in outside activities and enjoyed themselves through a sense of group solidarity which reflected itself in both the social and work environment.

The studies provided sufficient evidence to prove that factors other than pay and working conditions have a significant effect on output. However, there have been criticisms about the way the Hawthorne studies were conducted and in the interpretation of the results. Nevertheless, this first major study of people at work or in human relations raised important questions and many lessons were learned.

### Main conclusions

- When employees are in the limelight they feel important and begin to feel they are a vital part of the organisation.
- Seeking their opinions and ideas raises morale, encourages group spirit, and generally improves the industrial climate.
- Self-discipline emerges when a group is free to develop its potential and makes decisions affecting its members.
- Individuals should not be treated in isolation.
- Group belongingness and status are more important than cash incentives or good working conditions.
- The behaviour of workers is strongly influenced by informal groups.
- Managers and supervisors should accept there are social needs at work and attend to them to achieve collaboration.

## MODELS OF HUMAN BEHAVIOUR

Many models have been proposed over the years. Probably the most famous is E.H. Schein's contribution in 1965, which visualised the four classifications about the basic nature of people. The assumptions fit conveniently into the progressive nature of improving human relations since 1900. They are described below in chronological order.

### Rational–economic man

Self-interest dominates and is related to economic needs being satisfied by cash incentives. Two groups are identified: the passive, cash-motivated, calculative majority; and the minority who are the trustworthy, more broadly motivated, moral elite who organise and control the majority. This assumption is similar to Theory X, prescribed by McGregor and described in the next chapter.

### Social man

The second model sees people predominantly motivated by social needs and identifying themselves through relationships with others. This assumption is aligned with the Hawthorne studies and implies there should be more attention paid to people's needs and less to task needs. Also, it emphasises group activity and managerial roles of guide and supporter.

### Self-actualising man

Maslow has proposed that self-actualisation needs are of major importance to people. They are not social needs and they are described in the next chapter. People seek recognition, challenging work, increased responsibility, and achievement. In other words, increased autonomy satisfies self-motivation and maximises a person's potential.

### Complex man

The fourth model is more realistic and views people as being complex and variable. Their expectations vary and they demand individual treatment to satisfy the many motivational patterns. Consequently, managers must be adaptable, flexible, sensitive to the individual's personal requirements, and they must appreciate the subtle effects of teamwork.

# Styles of behaviour

Recognising mental features and basic mental processes were discussed in Chapter 9 as a method of developing recognition skill. However, the only immediately true recognition feature is the actual behaviour of the individual. This witnessed behaviour may be classified but often not explained immediately. So behaviour styles analysis is important because it provides the supervisor with the opportunity to deal more effectively with people when confronted with accusations, emotional problems and angry scenes (see below). The styles may be grouped in various complex ways; here is one convenient form:

- dictatorial style
- democratic style
- diffident style
- deliberative style
- defensive style
- belligerent style

Naturally they appear in the person sending information and in the person responding. To some extent, they determine the outcome of a communication or a confrontation, depending upon the style adopted by both parties. A person may adopt any of the styles illustrated below in certain situations, considering the hierarchy and its effects on people between levels, and in social and domestic situations. Consequently, it is not always advisable to label an individual with a particular behaviour style, although there are exceptions.

## PEOPLE'S RIGHTS

An important feature which may determine style is the question of people's rights. The operator has responsibility for producing acceptable work and has the right to receive criticisms if it is below standard. However, the criticisms should be made in a reasonable fashion and should not be so harsh as to cause excessive dismay. Similarly, the supervisor has responsibility for the work being done correctly; he or she has the right to receive the work at the standard laid down, and if below standard to indicate the errors and take appropriate democratic action.

# Dictatorial style

The aim is to win regardless of other people's feelings or rights to which they are entitled. Such extreme aggressiveness is not uncommon and sometimes disguised by benign approaches until the truth is revealed. Such manipulation is a dangerous practice because it creates a strong resentment and possibly violent reactions when the technique is discovered.

## APPROACHES

Dictatorial behaviour is recognised by:

- using insensitive techniques
- violating other people's rights and values
- dominating by only considering one's own rights, beliefs and opinions
- commanding in such a way that one's own contribution is considered paramount while other's ideas and work are thought to be unimportant

Here is an example: 'I do not expect you to hand in this rubbish after training. I don't want to hear any excuses; you have one week to improve or else!'

## EFFECTS ON THE SENDER

The possible effects in the short term are:

- low responses from the receiver
- tension released which reinforces this behaviour
- a sense of power and pleasant feelings

In the long term:

- feelings of guilt or shame
- possibly blaming others for one's behaviour
- feeling constantly under stress to guard against retaliation
- possibly a developing fear or hate of large groups who could overwhelm one's conduct
- feelings of isolation and not trusting friends
- developing a poor reputation and being despised by many employees

## EFFECTS ON THE RECEIVER

Possible effects on the receiver may be:

- feeling inadequate and knowing any ideas will be stifled
- feeling angry, hurt or humiliated
- harbouring thoughts of revenge or retaliation
- planning to avoid co-operation and avoid initiative
- planning to leave or transfer elsewhere
- becomes depressed and resigned to the treatment, if the person is weak

# Democratic style

The aim is to ensure both parties' rights and wants are considered in any situation. This means beliefs, values, needs and wants, loyalties, and all other internal human pressures, are allowed for when dealing with people. Therefore in any situation the following features are recognisable:

- standing up for one's own rights and beliefs
- accepting that all people have moral and legal rights
- using a direct and honest approach
- being sincere and just

The main approaches are now discussed, with comments, followed by the effects on the receiver. Finally a section on the assertiveness concept is included, because there is a tendency to use this term as meaning a democratic style. This is confusing since people interpret assertiveness in lots of different ways, many of which do not coincide with a democratic style. However, there are important rules of assertiveness often quoted. These are explained and are useful democratic guides.

## APPROACHES

### Informative approach

A plain statement is given to the receiver with no elaboration or explanations. The rights of both parties are recognised since the sender has the right to give the information and the receiver has the right to receive it.

> David, there are two orders for next week; the details are enclosed.

### Discerning approach

An augmented statement includes a mention of one's rights and the receiver's rights.

> David, there are no orders for next week so far. I shall tell you immediately if there is any change as I know it will cause you problems if there is a delay.

### Clarifying approach

An attempt is made to sort out differences between an agreement and an actual occurrence. It assumes there is a misunderstanding or a deliberate violation of rights.

> David, I did not realise the implications of failing to notify you early, which you outlined in your memo. I have instructed the chargehand to let you know immediately in future.

### Negative approach

The receiver confronts the sender with a negative reaction when he or she has received an insensitive communication that has caused problems, or has not received vital information on time. In this case the sender has ignored the receiver's rights either intentionally or unintentionally.

> John, you failed to give me the order from Jones Limited until late on Friday, when it was dated two days ago. This delay has caused considerable problems. I thought we had arranged for an immediate notification.

### Procedural approach

The procedural approach resorts to further action by applying a sanction laid down in existing procedures when the receiver does not respond to the sender's request, which is within his or her rights. In this case the receiver is deliberately violating the sender's rights.

> John, once again the order was received too late. I have no alternative now but to discuss this problem with the sales director.

### Questioning approach

The questioning approach is in common use to extract further information or where there is a communication problem.

> David, are you pressing the salesmen this week to pass orders in early in view of the transport problems?

## Comments

These approaches are simply snapshots which may form a sequence of activity. For instance, if there is an intentional violation of rights, a negative approach may produce a confirmation which would be followed by a procedural approach, notifying the other party that the case will be taken to a higher authority. All approaches conform to a democratic style where the rights of both parties are paramount.

## Effects on the receiver

Usually there should be:

- increased competence
- the tendency for people to work with rather than against the individual
- high quality performance from subordinates

## THE ASSERTIVENESS CONCEPT

The idea of being assertive is becoming more popular but is usually misunderstood because there are many meanings and misconceptions which are related to behaviourial styles. Assertiveness is mentioned here because a democratic style emphasises assertiveness when the term is used to mean insisting on one's rights.

Unfortunately, other meanings relate to different styles. Consider these meanings: justify by evidence or argument; being dogmatic, authoritative or arrogant; pushing; thrustful; forceful; emphatic; and outspoken. There are many more and they cause confusion when styles are discussed.

Some supervisors do not feel they are assertive but believe they use a democratic style, which is not surprising unless the particular meaning of assertiveness is stated first. For example, being assertive tends to be confused with belligerency and aggressiveness, which are much easier to use but very ineffective. Probably the term should be described as communicating directly, openly and objectively without causing offence or expressing undue emotion. This meaning implies the use of certain rules listed now which emphasise establishing correct relationships.

## SEVEN BASIC RULES

### Explain instructions

Disclose the full facts whenever possible for making or refusing a request. Usually people respond to this technique and co-operate when both parties are seen to be behaving sensibly and with due consideration.

### Use constructive criticism

A three-phase approach is ideal:

- Seek information on the reasons for the adverse behaviour.
- Ask for an opinion to ascertain whether the behaviour was thought to be incorrect.
- Advise on ways to improve in future.

There should be no doubt that the criticism is being applied, but offering help in any way is a fundamental requirement to show assertiveness.

### Consider compromising

Should the employee refuse to co-operate, seek reasons for the denial. If there are genuine reasons, attempt to compromise and try to gain agreement on a rearrangement that is helpful to both parties. If the reason is emotional with no foundation, there is obviously a behavioural problem which may be overcome by discussing alternative arrangements, without exercising authority.

### Remember people's rights

Always ensure that employees are not being overloaded with work. Appreciate that some people have great difficulty in saying no and standing up for their rights.

### Encourage mutual support

People expect praise when they have performed well. Showing such appreciation (even a thank you) helps to promote sound relationships, although the particular task is part of the employee's job.

## Encourage positive responses

The breadth of assertiveness is essentially a two-way process of developing a climate where personal feelings are expressed openly without fear of repercussions or adverse reactions. This implies that assertiveness must extend to using feedback, as in the case of showing appreciation and to improving credibility by admitting mistakes. Such errors should be automatically admitted to gain positive responses.

## Modify body language

Attempting to be assertive and not aggressive demands a strong body language discipline. Unfortunately, assertiveness may easily be destroyed by adopting non-verbal signals that do not coincide. For example, looking away when apologising may signify insincerity.

# Diffident style

The aim is to be dependent on others by avoiding conflict and pleasing them. To clarify this lack of self-confidence the faults are:

- being excessively modest
- failing to stand up for one's own rights and values
- always apologising for one's wants, opinions and beliefs
- failing to assert honestly one's feelings and beliefs

This state of mind assumes one has nothing to contribute, one's own rights are ignored, while other people's are considered more important and they have much to contribute.

> Errm, John, I'm sorry to say this batch of work is, well, it's below standard. The finishing department is complaining about it and I don't really know what to say.

## EFFECTS ON THE RECEIVER

Various feelings may include:

- being sorry for the individual because he or she is weak, unable to handle situations and problems, and cannot speak up
- feeling guilty if an advantage is taken of the individual
- being indifferent towards the supervisor
- being irritated by repeated indecision involving conflicts, problems and change
- eventually poor respect develops as integrity and honesty are often in doubt

# Deliberative style

The aim is to create a friendly, co-operative and helpful atmosphere. The deliberative style is ideal for coaching, training and debate, and coincides with collaborative management techniques. Naturally the right personality and temperament are important features which are recognised by:

- adopting a thoughtful and advisory approach
- offering advice and ideas
- carefully considering all factors for and against courses of action
- always being cautious, unhurried and calm
- achieving a reputation for being open and ready to discuss any situation in a rational manner

Sometimes this style is considered to be too laid-back, lacking drive and not showing sufficient initiative. Nevertheless, to adopt this style demands high expertise and a balanced personality, which many managers lack. Indeed in some unenlightened concerns it may mean the individual is overlooked for promotion.

> Hallo Ron, how are you feeling? We have a problem with this batch of work which is causing delays. I think we should go through the process now to find out the cause and then I can see what could be done.

## EFFECTS

- Ideal for developing autonomous teams.
- Encourages people to be self-disciplined.
- Helps to upgrade capabilities.
- Improves morale and productivity, when coupled with collaborative management.

# Defensive style

The aim of the defensive style is to be over-protective of one's own position, to be generally un-cooperative and disruptive. The defensive employee may be sullen, touchy, fitful, moody and melancholy. Indeed he or she may create a poor atmosphere by their mere presence and cause much ill-feeling and unhappiness. When approached for information they divulge as little as possible and glare if pressed for more detail. As well as being emotionally troubled, they may feel superior and feel their job is beneath them. Often they do not suffer fools gladly and may have bright ideas, which are not disclosed. They may feel insecure and resort to sulking if forced to undertake certain tasks.

## RECOGNISED APPROACHES

Here are some recognised approaches:

- *Resentful*: indignation is displayed subtly and bitter feelings may be expressed.
- *Withdrawn*: a general poor response, unsociable reactions, and a detached atmosphere.
- *Non-cooperative*: deliberately evasive and adopting a minimal response.

   I've had this batch slung back at me and it's not funny! I'm really mad at being on the receiving end and fed up with this situation. It's not my fault and I get the blame! How the blazes am I going to explain it to the works manager tomorrow?

## EFFECTS

- There may be a lowering of morale.
- There may be communication difficulties.
- The supervisor is seen as ineffective.

# Belligerent style

Similar to people with a defensive style, people with a belligerent style aim to erect mental barriers by displaying bad temper, being fitful and touchy, and generally being quarrelsome. At the slightest opportunity there are outbursts and, exceptionally, they will resort to violence. Very often they manage to hide this tendency at interviews and during trial periods. Also it seems that on occasions their attitude will change completely and they become very friendly when seeking love and attention. One view is they are always seeking love and attention, but they generate the opposite reaction.

## APPROACHES

The usual approaches are:

- *Aggressiveness*: offensive, disposed to attack, forceful and self-assertive.
- *Insolence*: offensively contemptuous, insulting, and uttering innuendos that cause fear.
- *Quarrelsome*: always ready to argue, pugnacious and generally objectionable.

   You idiot, haven't you got any brains? Get out of my sight before I really lose my temper!

## EFFECTS

The effects are similar to those for the defensive style. Firm action is needed but surprisingly these people often manage to escape reprimands for a long time for obscure reasons, such as being a boozing partner, nepotism, out-of-hours friendship, and weak management.

# Transactional analysis

Transactional analysis (TA) is a popular behavioural theory which helps people to understand themselves and their effect on others. Consequently, it is one means of understanding interpersonal behaviour (Chapter 14). The concept was developed by E. Berne in his book *Games People Play*, and popularised by T. Harris's book *I'm OK – You're OK*. Both are worth reading because, unlike many psychoanalytical theories, they are written in straightforward everyday language and are easily understandable. However, TA does not replace management theory and cannot solve all human problems. Certainly it is a useful tool for supervisors when dealing with people and for improving relations with customers. Three major areas are now briefly discussed: ego states associated with the individual, transactions between people, and life positions of the individual.

## EGO STATES

The ego concept was explained earlier, under the work of Freud. Remember, the ego represents reality, it attempts to restrain the impulsive id, and it uses the superego as a form of conscience. TA uses these concepts as a means of identifying three ego states: child (C), adult (A) and parent (P). They are patterns of feelings and behaviour which approximate to the id (child), the ego (adult) and the superego (parent). The child state is displayed by immature behaviour, being submissive or conforming or rebellious; also it includes happiness and creativity. The adult state displays maturity; it is rational; it uses problem solving and decision making; it is logical, fair and objective. The parent state tends to dominate; it is overprotective and critical.

All three states make up a balanced personality and indicate a mentally healthy individual. For example, the child state is useful when being creative, the adult state must judge which ego is suitable for a particular situation, and the parent state is essential in an emergency. Imbalance occurs when the adult state is unable to determine a suitable ego state for a particular situation.

## TRANSACTIONS

When two people communicate with each other, a transaction between their ego states occurs which may be complementary, crossed or ulterior. Any person may show all three ego states at various times but only one tends to dominate in a transaction.

A complementary transaction (Fig. 10.2) is where a message or behaviour from one person's ego state receives the expected response from another. Typically, P to C responded by C to P; A to A responded by A to A; and C to P responded by P to C. The A to A complementary transaction is most effective for interpersonal relations but the other forms also can achieve understanding and good communication. An example is when a supervisor says, 'The proposed output figures have been increased this week because of a rush order. Can you manage?' (A to A). The employee replies, 'I shall do my best, so long as the materials arrive on time. I'll keep you posted' (A to A).

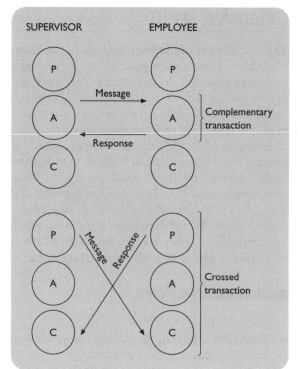

**Figure 10.2** Transactional analysis
A complementary transaction means the supervisor receives the desired or expected response. A crossed transaction means the supervisor receives an undesired or unexpected response, resulting in hurt feelings or frustration. A = adult, C = child, P = parent

A crossed transaction (Fig. 10.2) occurs when an undesired or unexpected ego state is received by the other person. Typically, P to C responded by P to C. This causes interpersonal conflict, resulting in possibly frustration and hurt feelings. An example is when a supervisor says, 'You must meet these targets or else you can expect trouble' (P to C). The employee replies, 'You gave me different figures last week. When are you telling the truth?' (P to C).

An ulterior transaction involves at least two ego states from one person, which confuses the receiver and upsets relationships. An example is when the supervisor says, 'I know I can rely on you', but means 'If you let me down you won't get a second chance'. This subtle form of transaction generally originates from insecure people who are unable to relate easily with others.

## LIFE POSITIONS

Transactional analysis claims that generally each person adopts one out of four life positions, which dominates the way he or she relates to others. The life position is generated from early childhood experiences, shows how a person feels about himself or herself, and therefore affects interpersonal relations. There are four life positions.

### I'm OK, you're OK

This healthy, positive attitude towards oneself and to others is clearly a distinct advantage when dealing with people.

### I'm OK, you're not OK

Feeling a high regard for oneself but not for others is immediately apparent when dealing with people and is obviously upsetting. Such authoritarian conduct is deplorable and common.

### I'm not OK, you're OK

Adopting a childlike position towards others naturally restricts the person's capabilities and is often noticeable in hierarchical organisations. Possibly this stance is through parental treatment or later unfortunate experiences. This may be corrected by applying modern collaborative techniques.

### I'm not OK, you're not OK

This unfortunate person has a low opinion of himself or herself and of others, which results in mental problems that need experienced counselling. This problem may be caused by poor health, unemployment, or failure at school or at work. Identifying such a person is not difficult as he or she tends to make this life position very clear when any transaction is involved. Typical remarks are:

> I've had it.
> If it weren't for you.
> There's no justice.
> Everyone's against me.

# Irrational behaviour patterns

Irrational or inconsistent behaviour may be traced to either one of two inherent situations, which have important differences. These situations are explained by theories of defensiveness and cognitive dissonance.

## DEFENSIVENESS

Defensiveness occurs when a person receives information that is threatening. Various defensive responses and reactions may appear. Typical responses are ignoring the threat and continuing to behave normally, denial by refusing to recognise the threat, recognising the threat but refusing to change behaviour or perception, modifying or distorting the threat by attempting to lessen its impact, or actually changing perception in some way, but this is unusual.

## COGNITIVE DISSONANCE

Cognitive dissonance applies when a person attempts to overcome an internal conflict, brought about when a person receives information that disagrees with his or her beliefs or attitudes, based upon knowledge already possessed. Cognitive dissonance relates to both perception and attitudes. It explains why people feel psychologically uncomfortable and seek to change their perceptions and possibly their behaviour in certain circumstances.

### Cognition

The basis of the theory is cognition, which is a way of acquiring knowledge. It involves imagination, reasoning, intuition and perception. Thus ideas or concepts are formed.

### Dissonance

Discord or tension (dissonance) occurs after a decision and involves two cognitions or perceptions: positive elements of the rejected alternative to the decision chosen, and negative elements of the chosen alternative. In other words, when two cognitions or perceptions are in conflict with each other after a decision, psychologically uncomfortable feelings appear.

To overcome this conflict, attempts are made to modify one of the incompatible perceptions to reduce tension and to create (hopefully) equilibrium. This may include revoking the decision, or changing an attitude or belief. As a result, people witness inconsistent or irrational behaviour.

### Research findings

Research findings suggest there are strong differences between reactions to information received which is consistent with a person's beliefs, and reactions to information received which is inconsistent with these beliefs or attitudes. This indicates why people do not change their opinions easily or do not necessarily accept new information as being correct. Furthermore, most dissonant information is presumed to be incorrect, therefore people distort or modify it, forget the information easily, or avoid exposure to it. The four examples given below help to clarify responses.

- If a heavy drinker cannot give up the habit, he tends to remain dubious about the harmful effects of alcohol. In other words, if information is given which is dissonant, the receiver rejects its validity. If the information agrees with existing beliefs, the receiver accepts the information as valid.
- An employee annoys his colleagues by saying he is sick but actually attends a football match when they are overloaded with work. Consequently they ignore him, so to compensate he claims the game was not worth seeing and volunteers to work over the forthcoming bank holiday weekend. In other words, when the information is dissonant, the receiver's memory distorts the information. If the information is consistent with existing beliefs, the receiver remembers it accurately.
- A clerk is un-cooperative with a lady in another section who has refused dates with him. Some of his colleagues agree with his conduct but others say he is mean and unfair. There is reaction from staff in the other section, and the clerk risks a reprimand from his supervisor. He decides to apologise and tells his colleagues he

did not really like her anyway. In other words, dissonance forces the receiver to avoid exposure to the message. If the communication was in accordance with existing beliefs, the receiver would seek further information.

- A supervisor has always used a manual system and believes in its accuracy and use as a means of evidence. When changing over to a computerised system, he has difficulty in operating the computer despite repeated attempts by the instructor to explain the procedures. In other words, the changeover is dissonant and the receiver easily forgets the new operating procedures. If the change is consistent with existing beliefs, the receiver remembers the instructions more easily.

## RESISTANCE TO CHANGE

Considering defensiveness and cognitive dissonance, there are clearly many reasons why an employee may resist any change in particular circumstances. These may be summarised as shown below.

### Irrational reasons

- Information which is apparently threatening.
- Information which disagrees with beliefs, attitudes and values.
- Rigid opinions causing suspicion of new information.
- If information is dissonant the employee's memory distorts it.
- Resentment through an incorrect assumption that the proposed change is a personal criticism.

### Alarm and insecurity

- Redundancy, termination, or increased workload, or changes in the job.
- The purpose of the change is unknown or ambiguous.
- No consultation or participation on the proposed change.
- Obvious faults in changes, such as incorrect timing, no training arrangements, and breaking up teams.

## Increased social and task pressures

- Relocation of workstation.
- Changes in working conditions.
- Revised training programme demanding more capability or new skills.
- Changes in responsibility and supervision.
- Revised work methods and new controls.
- Apparent downgrading of the job, authority and prestige.
- Insufficient information on new bonus scheme.

# Emotional problems

The supervisor will already be able to recognise the problem employee who is emotionally unstable because he or she will be spending more than a usual amount of time with that person. This unhappy employee has problems that cannot be solved in the usual ways because of his or her inability to adjust easily. The signs are antagonism towards management, the group and certain employees; ill health and absenteeism; a generally miserable mood; frequent and trivial complaints; and in extreme cases, complete breakdown, violence and excessive drinking.

## SOLVING EMOTIONAL PROBLEMS

This simple classification of individuals with emotional problems (and their responses under industrial conditions) defines three classes of people: normal, emotionally troubled and convalescent.

### Normal people

Normal people adjust readily to problems, provided the supervisor treats each person with proper understanding and sympathy when emotional stress is evident. The industrial climate must be right, with a friendly atmosphere throughout the organisation, a feeling of belonging, and support from superiors.

### Emotionally troubled people

They are many different types of people who feel unhappy and suffer generally. Their working efficiency is impaired and relationships with others are often unsatisfactory. They are misunderstood and their problems are aggravated if their complaint is not recognised. Trying to understand these people, who are fortunately in the minority, is wearing on the supervisor. They take up a lot of time. Often they cannot express themselves adequately, they do not make sense of situations, and they are generally looked upon as being a nuisance. Making the effort to understand them is worthwhile because it saves time in the long run and greatly assists them. Some of the types are given below.

### The insecure person

Insecurity is apparent when the need for praise is exaggerated. This reaches a point where any sign of apparent neglect, although unjustified, will cause the person either to react strongly against the supervisor or to resort to sulking for long periods. When approached he or she will possibly say there is nothing the matter or may pick on little faults and grossly exaggerate their importance. This individual is commonly known as difficult or touchy, and needs regular assurance of his or her usefulness and capabilities.

### Overdedication to the job

The person who places too much importance on the job at the expense of outside interests will find job satisfaction increasingly difficult to achieve unless he or she is able to advance in step with their aims. A person with this unbalanced outlook is unlikely to possess the right characteristics for promotion. This causes frustration if demands are thwarted. Possibly he or she may be persuaded to take up other interests in social activities or the company.

### The temperamental person

The temperamental person is continually pestering the supervisor with a whole range of problems such as registering dissatisfaction, making excuses, and generally being a nuisance. He or she appears to be suffering from a number of emotional problems openly expressed in continual upsets with colleagues and authority. The supervisor should try to avoid a direct approach and attempt to help the employee by seeking the cause of the trouble. This is hard to practise as the supervisor also has feelings and emotions that can stand so much provocation and no more. Within this group are the types who are often absent and are usually accident-prone (Chapter 21). Developing group spirit may help, so these individuals feel a stronger obligation towards their colleagues.

### The convalescent

Due allowance should be made for the person who has suffered a long illness or a breakdown and now wishes to lead a normal life again. The supervisor should treat the matter straightforwardly, informing employees of the person's return and insisting that the convalescent should be treated as an ordinary employee with no special concessions. This should provide the right atmosphere, which might otherwise cause embarrassment if too much fuss were made on the employee's return. Most people are naturally sympathetic and understand the person's feelings on these occasions.

# Group activity

Group activity was introduced in Chapter 5 and is an important feature in improving human relations. Further explanation here emphasises recognition of different types of social groups and research in human relations that have established the need for group spirit and autonomous workgroups.

## TYPES OF SOCIAL GROUP

There are many types of social group which all tend to merge into each other. Three main types may be distinguished:

- the gathering or crowd
- the club
- the community

First, the gathering of people at a football match, theatre or public meeting occurs when they have something in common. They are guided by events and are inclined to act impulsively and emotionally as a body, with no real objectives in mind.

Second, the club type of group is formed through active participation in sports and social activities, welfare or religious work. Club members have definite objectives and usually possess strong sentiments which create the desirable group spirit.

Third, the community type of group is a powerful, complex and stable organisation of individuals with strong common interests and high motivational potential. Force of circumstances governs its formation, and members play an important part in its organisation, daily operations and objectives. Each member has a particular responsibility and exercises self-discipline. Group loyalty provides a spirit, often known as esprit de corps, and this stabilises the group. The individual identifies directly with the group, which allow the member to assert himself or herself through the group structure and satisfy basic needs.

Although the community type of group is very desirable in industry, it is not frequently seen; the crowd type is more familiar. Some of the essential requirements for building up community groups in a concern are:

- forming the right organisation within each group of individuals and relating each correctly to other groups on soundly based principles
- creating stability by encouraging a low level of movement of group members – conditions should be arranged to minimise labour turnover
- reaching a stage of development in the industrial climate where each employee feels part of the company and has a pride in belonging to a particular group, which is recognised by management

## AUTONOMOUS GROUPS

Developments emerging from research following the human relations school have produced a strong emphasis on the creation of autonomous workgroups. Briefly, when changes are contemplated, a technology is not designed first and *then* the social organisation fitted to it. Essentially, *both* technology and organisation are used *alongside* each other jointly to optimise the two when designing workgroups.

## Research by Trist and Bamforth

One outstanding example illustrates the point. In 1963 Trist and Bamforth of the Tavistock Institute studied the effects of mechanisation at the coalface. Results showed that the technical innovations failed to provide social and psychological satisfactions expected by the miners in British mines, therefore productivity fell. The reasons were that new occupational roles and shift arrangements destroyed the closely knit groups, the relative autonomy they enjoyed and the variety of skills they used in small groups.

A different approach produced a better 'fit' by using the new machinery but allowing retention of the traditional social and cultural factors. Work tasks were grouped to form a logical whole task performed with minimal interference. Thus the criterion is to form the smallest group that can perform a whole task which, at the same time, will satisfy the social and psychological needs of its members.

Understandably, production orders cannot be replaced by autonomous teams. The hierarchy remains to determine policy, instruct lower levels on all the essential production aspects, and to achieve co-ordination through control. Although teams may appoint their own leaders (within each team), supervision remains to provide details of the job and the whole task, to assess and communicate feedback, and to recommend courses of action when deviations occur.

Certainly teams are encouraged to recommend changes, and these changes should be implemented as long as they fit the overall strategy. This technique is known as job redesign, the group technology approach, work restructuring, the cell system, flexible working teams, and group working schemes. It fits into the sociotechnical system and complies with new thinking that employees (and organisations) will not operate effectively if counterproductive management practices – considered by many to be necessary and unavoidable – are continued.

## Criticisms

The supervisor should note there are possible problems with autonomous groups:

- Instrumentalist employees, mentioned in Chapter 9, might not welcome job redesign.
- Employees may contend it is just another management tactic to extract more work for no extra pay.
- Some authorities claim engineers cannot work with social scientists to achieve the best 'fit'.
- The concept inhibits division of labour and specialisation of tasks.
- In some situations there could be expensive changes involved before installation, and possibly productivity would fall before improving later.

## Whole tasks

An example is a change from the conventional assembly line – say ten metres long, with short job cycles and operatives spread well apart – to a small working group with longer job cycles. The five employees in this group were given the job of building an automatic programme selector in a television receiver. The entire job (a whole task) included assembling, inspecting and correcting faults. Group members worked at their own pace, performed a larger job than before, and were trained to do any of the jobs. The group undertook new tasks, such as inspection, repair, drawing materials and accounting. It could choose the distribution of jobs according to individual preferences, and successive operations were taught to each other.

# Empowerment

The theory of empowerment is that employees have the ability and capability to contribute far more than is usually believed. Managers and supervisors are included because often they are frustrated when senior management style is traditional and outdated. Empowerment is developed to release the potential in everyone by removing traditional hierarchies and allocating appropriate authority to coincide with the development of capability which should ensure higher initiative and creativity.

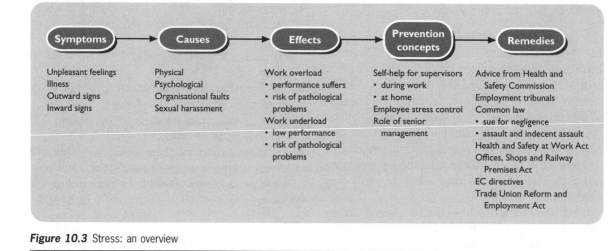

**Figure 10.3** Stress: an overview

## ESSENTIAL REQUIREMENTS

- The philosophy of empowerment should be accepted as the natural progression of research into improving behaviour where ultimately *self-actualising man* (or full creativeness) is achieved (Chapter 11).
- To satisfy empowerment theory management tends to coincide with the deliberative style (explained earlier).
- The organisational culture should avoid a bureaucratic or mechanistic style and concentrate on an organic style (Chapter 3). This means a loose structure, decision making lowered to appropriate levels, and flexible operations involving teams and appropriate grouping to solve problems.
- There needs to be a drastic change in outlook by all managers and supervisors to accommodate the philosophy of empowerment (Chapter 19).
- Human resource management is essential as attempts are made to overcome the strong influence of national culture, which may interfere with empowerment programmes (Chapter 4).
- Jobs should be redesigned to emphasise clear goals, initiative, challenging work, self-evaluation and adjustment, and appropriate authority and responsibility (Chapter 17).

# Reducing stress levels

Bearing in mind the remarks on stress in the previous chapter, influencing a person's behaviour may be severely disrupted if he or she is suffering with stress. The main features that help to recognise this problem and how to deal with it are the causes and effects, the problem areas, and how to control stress. An overview of stress is given in Fig. 10.3.

## THE CAUSES OF STRESS

One view is that the individual makes an event stressful, *not* the event itself. Considering that one form and level of stress may affect one person more than another, the two divisions are physical and psychological causes.

### Physical causes

Physical causes include excessive workload, causing musculoskeletal problems, repetitive strain injuries and visual fatigue; poor physical environment leads to problems with temperature, humidity, noise, vibration, etc.; low physical fitness and old age.

### Psychological causes

Psychological causes include mental workload problems and mental environment problems such as danger, confinement, mental atmosphere, and general reactions to a variety of factors like thwarted ambition, personality clashes and lack of job security. Typical problems are being promoted beyond capabilities, allowing work to become an obsession, depression, and excessive control. Other important causes are being subjected to poor management and poor control, such as suffering ambiguous objectives and conflicting priorities, excessive interruptions, low feedback, distorted feedback, and working in a poor organisational culture.

## THE EFFECTS OF STRESS

The results of stress when the optimum level is exceeded in either direction may be summarised as follows:

- *Overload*: performance suffers in some way and there is risk of pathological problems.
- *Underload*: low performance and pathological risks.

Although there is the argument that some people actually perform better under high stress conditions, they are in the minority (Fig. 9.1).

According to some theorists, more working days are lost through stress than through strikes. Absenteeism and sickness brought about by boredom and stress-related illness are said to be excessive.

## PROBLEM AREAS

In general terms the main problems are related to three features:

- poor management
- incorrect management style
- supervisory difficulties

There is often difficulty in persuading management that managing problems of stress *before* they occur is more cost-effective. The importance of management style is often neglected, or managers are insufficiently trained. This situation results in inconsistency, bullying and many other adverse features. Supervisors are not given sufficient training and development to cope with their own stress and employees' stress. Unfortunately, supervisors have to attempt stress management when the aforementioned problems exist.

In summary the main problems associated with stress are:

- Accurate measurement is difficult, so employees are incorrectly assessed for stress problems.
- The optimum level for each person is different and varies depending upon the form it takes and the degree.
- Each particular situation has different effects on different people.
- Physical and mental fitness affect the stress level experienced.
- Self-induced stress is possible: a person may deliberately cause someone to react against him or her.
- Some people manage to *cope* with stress but they do not necessarily know how to *manage* it effectively.
- More research is needed to achieve a better understanding of stress.
- Stress is a personal experience which is not necessarily related to success or failure at home or at work.
- Stress may prevent adaptive behaviour and may cause illogical behaviour.
- Many people do not recognise stress in themselves or in others.

## CONTROLLING STRESS

Stress control is still being researched, but many proposals are already available. This difficult topic should at least conform to three features:

- It should address the nature of control (Chapter 23).
- It should be related to particular problems associated with managers, supervisors and employees.
- It should explain the physical and psychological aspects of human beings (Chapter 9).

Conforming to these requirements means there is a strong emphasis on prevention rather than cure. Here is a typical programme:

- Apply prevention concepts.
- Adopt operational activities to reduce stress.
- Manage problems as they arise and use feedback to improve prevention concepts.

## PREVENTION CONCEPTS

### Self-help for supervisors

Taking the opportunity to read about stress is important because most stress-reduction suggestions become obvious as knowledge of the subject improves. Opportunities should be taken to attend courses on the general treatment of stress, including information and control by means of therapy techniques. Any uncertainty about an outcome usually leads to increased stress, therefore it should help to learn more. Using the proposals is far more demanding; it needs self-control and perseverance. There are many benefits in domestic and working life. The main features are listed below.

### During work

- To avoid angry scenes, always stand back from any situation and deliberately pause before speaking. Direct confrontations never seem to succeed.
- Do not be enticed into arguments that serve no purpose. In other words, do not allow others to induce stressful situations.
- Try not to worry too much or overanticipate; it may never happen.
- Try to solve a problem rather than remaining anxious about it.
- Sometimes a problem may be split into several small problems that are easier to solve.
- Try to improve time management techniques.
- Analyse obvious stressful events and attempt to rearrange, reduce or eliminate the causes.
- If possible, eat meals away from the workplace and take a break by walking and relaxing at the same time.
- Avoid taking drugs, smoking and consuming too much alcohol.
- Try to determine the inward signs of stress in oneself and respond accordingly.
- Avoid accepting tasks that are someone else's province.

- Delegation usually increases stress because routine jobs are handed down, which leaves more time to worry about intractable problems.
- By examining the favourable aspects of the decision, try to learn from the inevitable mistakes when dealing with more difficult tasks.
- Establish a more logical routine that avoids crises.
- Remember the priorities and so avoid crises.
- Accept the inevitable parts of the job that cannot be changed, but change those parts that are flexible and may be causing problems.
- Areas of uncertainty tend to increase stress, so concentrate on investigating these areas to avoid or reduce them.
- Try to be optimistic and confident; try to laugh at life. These attitudes lower stress and people appreciate them.

### At home

- Try to avoid thinking about work difficulties; if not, at least set aside a period to discuss them and stop when the time is up.
- Always set aside time to enjoy leisure activities which are not too hectic.
- Try to find time for some physical exercise; even walking is an excellent therapy.
- One view is that meditation techniques are essential.

### Employee stress control: supervisor's guide

- Remember that fitting the job to the employee is more effective than waiting for symptoms to appear.
- Attempt to assess employee stress levels by discussing workloads and listening carefully to any points that are causing difficulties in the job.
- Try to include some humour into the work during employee contact.
- Suspect stress when there is poor performance.
- Use work study but avoid setting standards that are too high or too low, and bear in mind environmental conditions.
- If an employee's job is obviously too demanding, make adjustments before it is too late.
- Remember the effects of underloading as well as overloading.

- Apply regulations on stress control outlined by various UK legislation and EC directives.
- At every opportunity discuss stress with employees, especially referring to workstyle, lifestyle, diet, domestic problems and the dangers of narcotics. Gain the employee's confidence and offer to help in any way.
- Remember that stress levels constantly change as circumstances alter. Therefore be on the alert for an individual's behavioural change.
- Constantly look for any outward signs of stress and respond accordingly.

### The role of senior management

The crucial role of senior management is obvious when the evidence from specialist research institutions is revealed on stress-related sickness (Chapter 21). Furthermore, the topic has received considerable publicity, some legislation now exists, and managing health risks is emphasised by many organisations. The main aspects of ignoring stress which should concern senior management are:

- Appropriate management of stress is more cost-effective than doing nothing to prevent it.
- Productivity suffers.
- There are increased costs on the National Health Service.
- Management may have an antisocial attitude towards individuals and family who suffer.
- There is an enormous effect on the economy of the UK.

Policy changes of a strategic and tactical nature are easily recognised when the psychological and physiological causes of stress are examined. To summarise, good management means identifying and controlling stress *before* it causes problems and leads to losses. The supervisor's role is limited unless senior management introduces a comprehensive programme.

# Handling crises

Invariably a crisis occurs because:

- An internal problem has been overlooked or ignored.

- An individual has allowed a grievance or situation to become out of hand.
- The supervisor has not developed a rapport with subordinates.
- An external problem suddenly appears with no warning or has been overlooked.
- Another department has not co-operated.
- A communication failure occurs which was not located earlier.
- There are clashes of personalities.
- Management has failed to notify the section of an important change.

A grievance or emotional situation usually starts well before the crisis point. Recognising the danger signals and solving these problems at an early stage highlights competence. These communication aspects are covered in Chapter 15, along with group discussions which help to identify situations.

Crises conveniently divide into an immediate emotional conflict between the supervisor and an employee, between employees, a problem with a customer, or a problem between the supervisor and a manager. The last one is discussed later in the chapter.

## EMOTIONAL CRISES WITH EMPLOYEES

Apart from the matters dealt with earlier, there remains the handling of direct conflicts with staff. Certain codes of conduct are essential:

- Always keep calm.
- Do not be pressurised.
- Try to defuse the crisis immediately by agreeing with the irate person, in an attempt to stop further outbursts.
- If the crisis is in a crowded workshop or office, find a private place, ask the person to sit down, and discuss the problem quietly.
- Try to summarise by writing down the main difficulties and giving the person the opportunity to raise the salient points.
- Use all the problem-solving techniques immediately or give the person a cooling-off period.
- Relieve some of the tension by assuring the person that everything will be done to solve the crisis as soon as possible.
- Be sure that all the facts are recorded and all the options are stated.

- Allow the person to give his or her views on possible solutions and ensure confidentiality.
- Close the discussion by ensuring there is agreement on all the factors involved and that there is a clear understanding of the next steps needed to solve the crisis.
- Remind the person that if anything has been forgotten, they should return immediately and clarify the situation.
- Do not delay implementing a decision when the cause of the crisis is known.

### Underlying factors

Some aspects are not immediately apparent; they generally include the following:

- There are always two points of view – one is known (the supervisor's), the other often remains hidden.
- Emotional difficulties may be difficult to trace through lack of background information.
- When people are angry they fail to provide a true account of the crisis.
- There may be collusion with other employees.
- The true cause of a crisis is often not revealed until after the problem is temporarily solved by coping with an apparent cause.
- There may be a tendency for the supervisor to blame others and so avoid embarrassment; but using scapegoats is inadvisable since eventually there are repercussions.
- People often seek a compromise, so be ready to give up something in return for co-operation or a settlement.

## EMOTIONAL CRISES BETWEEN EMPLOYEES

Direct conflict between employees should demand similar care as outlined above. Such interpersonal conflict is commonplace but its intensity varies. The usual reasons are:

- personality clashes
- unfair workloads
- favourable or unfair treatment
- different expectations of bonus, etc.
- different perceptions of situations
- reliance on another person's output

These reasons may be resolved by the supervisor's self-examination, discussions with personnel, changes in working practices, and possibly separating the two individuals.

## CRISES WITH CUSTOMERS

Besides the points mentioned above when dealing with irate employees, there are several features which are essential to secure and maintain a firm bond with a customer:

- Remember the customer is always right even when it is obvious that the company or an individual is not to blame.
- Taking the blame relieves the tension, it makes the customer feel partly satisfied immediately and it relieves indignation.
- Aim to solve the crisis quickly but do not make promises that are impossible to keep.
- If there are difficulties, typically when someone is not available or the essential information is missing, admit the problem and promise to telephone back or contact again soon. If there is a face-to-face confrontation in the circumstances, arrange for tea or coffee and make sure the customer is comfortable. Do not leave him or her standing at reception like an intruder.
- Take all the short cuts to find the answer and to satisfy the customer immediately.
- Remember to apologise and assure the customer that if anything else happens they should contact the company without hesitation. The aims are to please, to rectify the situation, and if possible to give a little token to bond the relationship, such as a sample.

# Major causes of poor relationships

Although outdated management (below) adequately explains the basic broad problem, the other sections may help to locate immediate causes of discontent.

## OUTDATED MANAGEMENT

Managers who have not moved with the times and fail to use modern approaches towards employees will cause general resentment, increasing friction and possibly strikes. Good intentions are insufficient if competence is lacking. Employees expect to hear the truth, to be trusted and be given credit when it is due. There is a strong need for ethical behaviour from managers, especially when the interests of others should be taken into consideration.

## EMPLOYEES' TRADITIONAL OUTLOOK

Inherited feelings towards management are tenacious and often correct. The view that management would quickly revert to its old ways if given the opportunity is difficult to counteract. This is reinforced due to increasing world competition forcing management to take unpopular decisions.

## INADEQUATE COLLECTIVE BARGAINING

Unless collective bargaining and the art of consultation are taken seriously, there will be a strong suspicion of management. True recognition of a trade union is non-existent until consultation becomes a regular, acceptable form of communication. Moreover, the conflict of loyalties tends to strengthen if the union, management and employees do not work together as a team. All three groups have a similar interest in survival.

## DIVIDED LOYALTIES

The industrial situation is confusing and irritating to many employees, especially those who are conscientious and strongly desire satisfaction from work. Loyalties seem to lie in many directions, considering colleagues, the group, the supervisor, management and the union. Other pressures complicate the problem, and it is understandable to see some people reach a confused state where they are prepared to submit to anyone's absurd schemes, which may mean abandoning their own principles to secure peace of mind. Others withdraw from industry and seek employment elsewhere to relieve the stress.

## POOR COMMUNICATION

Insufficient attention to the art of communication causes suspicion, distrust, antagonism, misunderstandings and a general feeling of neglect. The grapevine takes over if all the formal channels are not used, often with disastrous results. Employees feel management has no faith in them and that they are of little importance.

## MISUNDERSTANDINGS

Misunderstandings occur all the time; simple conversations are easily distorted and written communications are often a complete failure. The main reasons are the sender's difficulties, poor choice of communication channel, the receiver's difficulties, problems of expression and general situational problems.

## PERSONNEL POLICY MALPRACTICES

An excellent personnel policy is often treated in an absurd way by senior managers. Numerous examples of malpractice in all fields of personnel policy are obvious to employees. No one is fooled; often the personnel department is treated as a joke by managers, supervisors and employees; and personnel procedures become a facade. Typical areas of complaint are selection, appraisals, working conditions, unfairness, injustice and pay anomalies.

## CONFLICTING VIEWPOINTS

The views of management and employees are often opposed on questions of pay, output, working conditions and terms of employment. One group is thinking in terms of profitability, of cost and output, whereas the other group is thinking of sharing the profit by receiving more pay and benefiting from stability of employment.

## LOW INCENTIVES

The neglect of appropriate financial and non-financial incentives leads to severe frustration and low motivation (Chapter 11). Such a policy causes deep resentment, a poor external reputation, and effective prospective employees are difficult to recruit.

## INADEQUATE EDUCATION AND TRAINING

Employees expect to receive appropriate education and training for the job. Some also expect to be developed further for possible promotion. Certainly there is a strong feeling of the need for a mentor, a trusted and experience advisor, who will support them unselfishly.

## AN UNSOUND ORGANISATION

The incorrect use of specialists who appear to come between employees and supervisors upsets even a friendly atmosphere. Similarly, unsound application or disregard of the essential principles of organisation leads to confusion and agitation when conflicts occur. Working harmony is lost until a sound organisation is established and understood by everyone.

## CULTURAL VARIATION

A multiracial society encompasses differing cultures, which have varying effects on individual behaviour in the workplace (Chapter 2). Values, beliefs, customs, moral codes and ethical conduct vary and arouse strong, hostile feelings if managerial philosophy does not coincide with established standards.

Cultural conflicts at national and organisational levels are difficult to assess and resolve. They may include concepts of democracy, power interpretation, career stability and dominant value concepts associated with money, human relationships, concern for others and quality of life.

## SELECTING AND TRAINING SUPERVISORS

Management must appreciate the importance of providing each group with a carefully selected competent supervisor. A sound plan should include a continual search for supervisory ability and an effective education and training scheme. Such a plan demands expenditure and often a change in management's attitude towards supervision and its importance.

# Essential guidelines

Essential guidelines are divided into daily contacts with employees, individual recognition, opportunities to be taken during discussions and counselling,

some approaches on general conduct, and communication aspects.

## DAILY CONTACTS WITH EMPLOYEES

- Avoid making promises; although they may be sincere, changes often override situations and force revised thinking. An alternative is a balanced approach, illustrating the possible future situations which could upset plans.
- Admit an error or inadequacy and most people will feel sympathetic. Bluffing is a mistake and inevitably this will cause more trouble and expense later. Any admission of errors should be followed by prompt action to correct the fault.
- Avoid direct criticism wherever possible. A better way is to make a constructive comment and so evade an argument with someone who is probably already agitated by the situation. This does not give the impression of being too easy-going; the individual will appreciate the supervisor's sense of understanding and tact, and working harmony remains intact.
- Seek suggestions, especially when changes are necessary. Employees who participate are more likely to accept decisions and there is usually less friction.
- Welcome criticisms and complaints. Hopefully they will be more constructive if handled correctly by prompting and steering the conversation towards areas of improvement.
- Sometimes it may be difficult, but try to be pleasant. Resentment and misunderstandings are often caused by abruptness and a tough front. Always use common courtesies and avoid addressing employees by their surnames only.
- Give praise when it is due. Always show appreciation actively when an employee is putting in extra effort. Constantly impress on employees that their jobs are important.
- Always be particularly careful in dealings with the opposite sex. Avoid being familiar and bear in mind the emotional relationships which may exist in mixed groups. Words should be chosen carefully; the correct approach is essential. Someone nearby will always be ready to misinterpret a supervisor's intention and pass on

the incident and conversation to everybody, suitably distorted of course.

- Bear in mind the danger of being easy-going as this will retard efforts to treat everyone in the same way. Be continually on the lookout for incidents and do not trust to chance. Alertness to situations will ensure the slackers do not escape reprimands.
- Ensure the members of the group are not in conflict. Although people of different temperaments will work together happily, some will be antagonised because of conflicting beliefs. Where a clash occurs do not force people to work together. Other arrangements must be made to avoid more serious problems developing.

## INDIVIDUAL RECOGNITION

- Assess the feelings of employees regarding education, training and development. If a comprehensive training scheme exists, make appropriate suggestions. Remember that part of the supervisor's job is to act as mentor or coach.
- Undertake an academic study and a workplace study of people. Attempting to understand individuals is a continual and absorbing long-term process.
- Encourage employees to talk about themselves and their problems. Always give them undivided attention, be sympathetic, and offer advice where appropriate. Try to have a few words with each employee every day.
- Try to allocate the right jobs to the right people. Always ensure that the employee knows what is involved in a particular job before assigning it, otherwise an unnecessary burden may be placed on someone.
- Find time to have a good talk with each employee periodically. If the conversation moves towards private matters, avoid the temptation to be inquisitive. Leave the initiative to the employee. If advice is sought do not be too specific because the information received will be limited; the complete story generally remains unsaid.
- Question every action involving employees to ensure their self-respect is not affected in any way.

## DISCUSSIONS AND COUNSELLING

- Attempt to be a patient listener to grievances. Problems and complaints that are not completely explained, remain unsaid, or are repressed, all take more time to solve later on. Gain confidence by showing sincere interest and understanding, taking positive action where necessary.
- Always discuss problems with the employee's interests in mind.
- Arguing is futile – no one wins. Try to discuss subjects calmly, illustrate both sides of a case, seek more information if necessary, and always end on a friendly note to maintain a reasonable bond.
- Seek ideas and opinions to show recognition of capability. Use them in discussions with superiors, mentioning the source. Implement ideas on immediate situations without delay to avoid adverse comments.
- Try to foster teamwork between the union, management and employees to reduce the conflict of loyalties.

## GENERAL CONDUCT

- Behave ethically at all times to avoid suspicion.
- Demonstrate a genuine interest in people; do not use a facade to suit circumstances or personal gain.
- Treat collective bargaining seriously.
- Recognise and accept immediately there are two sides to any human problem.
- Fair treatment is essential at all times. Standard ways of dealing with employees in similar situations will show objectiveness or lack of personal bias. Having favourites is disastrous and will upset all efforts to improve relationships.
- Expect emotional reactions to changes. Inevitably the employee suffers in some way and will have difficulty in accepting economic pressures on the company which force unpopular actions.
- Do not hesitate to compromise if a mutual understanding of differences is demonstrated, and agree to discuss again later.
- Seek outside help and advice if there is a difficulty which demands more information or experience.

- Consider revising a rule if there is an obvious question of unfairness or injustice.

## COMMUNICATION ASPECTS

- Take every opportunity to provide feedback to top management on personnel policy malpractices. Depersonalise the information by explaining the effects on employees.
- Try to convince management that both financial and non-financial incentives are essential if there is a difficulty in this respect. Explain that employees must be given the opportunity to participate, set themselves objectives, and feel they are doing a worthwhile job.
- Unless good relationships are established, any attempt to place the company's interests first will fail.
- Carefully explain and discuss the reason for policy and rules of organisation. If employees are not satisfied with the explanations, endeavour to find more information or obtain explanations from management.
- If possible, stress the permanence and security offered by management to employees. Any feelings of insecurity, such as rumours of redundancy, may affect morale and output.
- Promotion should be open to everyone. Opportunities for advancement should be well publicised. When appointments are made the reasons should be stated clearly to those who are unsuccessful; thus resentment is minimised.
- Link the company's products or services and its aims with employees in such a way that they feel their jobs are worthwhile and that they feel proud of the company.
- Constant efforts should be made to ensure information reaches all employees. This information should at least include objectives, state of the business, competition, proposed changes to survive, and identifying newcomers.
- Counter any incorrect information circulating on the grapevine by injecting the actual information.
- Constantly check for any misunderstandings. Always ask if a communication is clear and seek confirmation of accuracy by asking the employee to repeat the information.

- Explain at every opportunity the reasons why conflicting viewpoints exist, especially in terms of coping with strong competition and the need to survive. Unfortunately, senior executives in some companies are labelled as 'fat cats' by the media when boardroom excesses are revealed. This irritates employees when they see attempts to cut costs at their level, and of course it destroys mutual trust.

## QUESTIONS

1 Discuss the various types of emotional problems that an employee may have to face at work.

2 How would you recognise the emotionally troubled employee and what would you do to help?

3 What is meant by the phrase 'a normal person'?

4 People don't change. Discuss this statement.

5 What is meant by resistance to change?

6 How would you deal with the insecure individual?

7 How would you explain the change in a person when he or she joins a working group?

8 Discuss the various types of social groups, illustrating your answer with suitable examples.

9 Write an essay on the Hawthorne experiments and include your personal opinion on the unusual effects that were discovered.

10 What is meant by group spirit?

11 Why are selection and training important factors in the problem of establishing good relationships with subordinates?

12 Traditional outlooks tend to thwart attempts to improve management–employee relationships. Explain this statement.

13 Discuss the various ways of improving human relationships.

14 On your first day as supervisor, an employee makes a rude remark as you go by. On the

second day a similar remark is passed by the same employee. What would you do?

15 If your best subordinate receives permission to attend a relative's funeral and, on your journey home, you see this person leaving the local football ground, what would you do?

16 How would you cope with a situation where an employee complains that colleagues refuse to speak to him or her?

17 An employee suddenly becomes very quiet and has nothing to do with colleagues. Outline the action you would take.

18 How would you deal with the following types of employee: sensitive, casual, aggressive, constantly grumbling?

19 Outline the main features of influencing human relations.

20 Discuss the main symptoms of stress and relate them to possible causes and the likely effects.

21 What are the major stress prevention concepts?

22 Outline the main styles of behaviour.

23 How can transactional analysis help you in forecasting behavioural problems?

24 Explain cognitive dissonance.

25 What are the essential requirements for the successful introduction of empowerment?

26 Explain the possible causes of emotional crises at the workplace.

27 Why is there emphasis on resolving crises with customers?

28 List the essential guidelines for influencing human relations.

---

**CASE STUDY**

The Truesome Tyre Company is an old-established firm with a good reputation for ethics and loyalty. Robert, the sales office supervisor, has studied hard and is conscientious at work. He knows that the present office manager will retire soon and, from chance remarks, he thinks he will certainly be a strong contender.

One weekend he attends a sailing course at Brighton. On Saturday evening the small group decides to pub-crawl in the town. At a crowded bar, Robert bumps into his sales manager, Sam Townsend. Looking very embarrassed, he acknowledges Robert and elbows his way from the bar. It was unlike Sam to be off-hand.

The following Monday, Sam calls Robert into his office and apologises for his abruptness. 'You know I would be obliged if you don't mention to anyone about seeing me with Pauline. I was supposed to be at a sales conference in Bradford. I'll do the same for you one day.'

Robert reddens uncomfortably and says, 'Of course, Mr Townsend, but, in fact, I didn't see your secretary there'.

The following month Sam is promoted to sales director. During a coffee break, someone mentions that Sam very nearly did not get the job because of some discrepancy over expenses.

Six months later, to Robert's dismay, he is passed over for the office manager's job. To everyone's surprise it is given to a supervisor with a poor reputation. Robert is convinced that his failure is due to Sam and his connection with the incident at Brighton.

In fact, Sam thought Robert *had* seen him with his secretary. The managing director had queried his expenses but knows nothing of the relationship with his secretary and Sam has not recommended Robert for the post.

Robert decides to see the managing director and complain. He explains everything and waits impatiently for a reply.

*Consider the question of loyalty and trust in this case. What would you expect the managing director to do?*

Harry Turnbull's superior was taken ill and so Harry was asked to stand in for him. Leaving supervision to Stan, one of his senior chargehands, he soon found his mind was fully occupied with his temporary position.

After a few days, he met one of the employees on her way to work.

'How is everything going, Josie?' he asked.

'Don't ask *me*!' Josie replied and walked off.

Feeling apprehensive, Harry decided to have a chat with Stan. When Stan arrived in the office he looked very worried. He said, 'I'm sorry, Harry, but I'll have to back out of this job. The others don't like me and they're giving me hell down there. I lost my temper with young Tim over some work he'd messed up on the first day. I'm sure he did it deliberately'.

*What courses of action are open to Harry in these circumstances?*

Jo Tavist, 26, joined Angle Superstore as a sales assistant four years ago. She is successful and likes her work. During a slack period, her supervisor loses her deputy in a redundancy programme and she is not replaced. Later business picks up and soon the supervisor is overloaded with work. She decides to ask Jo to help her as she thinks Jo is well-liked and she is pleased with her performance, which exceeds that of many of the 'old hands'. They are not informed, though, as she thinks it might upset them.

Jo is given the stock-level reports to complete and this means checking with other sales assistants. Next day she is absent and it is not until the third day that she reports back. To the supervisor's surprise, Jo hands her the reports and declares that she prefers not to be involved. After several attempts to seek an explanation the supervisor gives up.

By chance she overhears the end of a conversation between two of the older sales assistants, '. . . and that soon fixed Jo, lording it over us!'

*What were the likely causes of the problem? Could the situation be rectified at this late stage?*

# 11

# Motivation

## Introduction

The previous two chapters illustrated the complexities of the human being, how human relationships may be improved, and the many influences or factors that affect behaviour. They are associated with a psychological process called motivation.

Research in motivation has not found any exact laws to apply, but certain important theories, principles and tendencies have emerged. They are helpful in studying motivation and in providing some answers on how the mind functions, how to motivate, and why failures often occur. The overall situation is adequately expressed by Oscar Wilde: 'I sometimes think that God, in creating man, somewhat overestimated His ability'.

## Recognised features of motivation

There are certain features which help to clarify the meaning of motivation:

- Employees must be willing (possessing a motive) to undertake an activity and have the capacity to perform it.
- The degree of willingness of particular individuals in an organisation (or in a society) varies from high intensity to low intensity.
- In a modern society the tendency is for people in an organisation to have a low intensity level of willingness unless various forms of inducement (motivators) are applied.
- Motives (or drives) are complex and often conflicting within an individual.

- Satisfaction is only achieved when an effort (or drive) to reach a goal is successful; therefore motivation differs from satisfaction.
- Bullying (or excessive pressure) achieves a degree of productiveness in backward countries, but in modern civilised societies it is detested and replaced by motivating; therefore bullying differs from motivating.

The significance of these features is that improving relationships by influencing behaviour is reasonably straightforward, but improving behaviour that establishes motivation is a deeper, complex process. Although improved relationships helps initially, a comprehensive motivation plan must include the following four aspects.

- How to energise the inner driving force in a person.
- How to promote an acceptable level of motivation for the employee and the company.
- How to sustain this level during day-to-day activities.
- How to overcome difficulties that dampen the inner driving force to a point where motivation ceases.

## The background

For many centuries human motivation was explained as hedonistic, meaning an individual seeks pleasure and comfort, and avoids pain and discomfort. At the beginning of the twentieth century the idea of instinct-based behaviour emerged, as seen in animals. By the 1920s this concept was abandoned and replaced by a more complex theory of cognitive and environmental interactions governing behaviour. This theory raises the question of whether motivation is an unconscious process or if there is a conscious effort.

## UNCONSCIOUS MOTIVATION

A modern view is that some motives cannot be explained by a conscious process. These motives are based on learning but are not instinctive. They explain why certain behaviour is difficult to identify. Furthermore, they explain the effect of habits that are developed but not immediately recognised by that person. If unpleasant situations develop and confront an individual, the motive may be repressed. Unconscious motivation is still debatable and lacks research.

## DRIVE THEORIES

In 1918 Woodworth created a new concept – drive. He defined it as a unitary concept representing an overall activity level. In the 1930s the need for a more scientific perspective of motivation, as against instinctiveness, was partly satisfied by C. Hull. He proposed that motivation was a product of drive and habit. Drive was thought to be the energising internal influence that determines the intensity of behaviour. Habit was included to account for the learning influence on a person. This theory was extended later to include incentive as a factor to account for cognition in a person. In other words, people were influenced by their expectations. This theory generated considerable research, although some of Hull's ideas were suspect. Certainly it created a scientific research basis and its emphasis on drive, incentive (cognition) and habit (learning) was an important contribution.

## MODERN MOTIVATION

The outcome of research so far is the acceptance of a complex process involving many elements or factors which influence people in different ways and consequently defies a common definition. These elements include many terms: needs, wants, drives, motives, behaviour, goals, adaptability, incentives and expectations. There are many definitions from which to choose. Some of them are given below:

- An inner state that energises and directs behaviour towards a goal.
- An internal force that pressurises or moves an individual to take action towards achieving a goal.
- An internal process designed to satisfy a hierarchy of needs. This process is governed by many factors such as culture, perception, intellectual level, aptitudes and personality.
- An internal reasoning process involving strengths of desire, estimated probability of a successful outcome, and strengths of belief that a particular action will satisfy the need being considered at the time.

## PROBABLE ASSESSMENT ERRORS

The limited knowledge on motivation and its complexities must be related realistically to employees and the organisation. Because there are many known and unknown elements, clearly there is a very low probability of being able to assess accurately the cause of anyone's behaviour. Typical unknowns are:

- An employee may be suffering from exhaustion through sleepless nights with a newborn; he or she may not have disclosed the problem.
- A wrong word from the supervisor may unintentionally upset the employee and cause erratic output.
- A change in working position may cause the employee to feel unsettled and affect the quality of his or her work.
- A marital upset may cause loss of concentration.
- Gambling losses may cause depression.

# Factors affecting motivation

The main factors that affect motivation of people are the job itself, the company environment, external pressures on people, internal human pressures, individual capacity, and override features. There are many aspects within each main factor (Fig. 11.1). Furthermore, there is no way of accurately assessing each factor, or aspect within that factor; therefore the idea of calculating which mix is suitable for motivation is strongly suspect at present. In other words, it seems the priorities

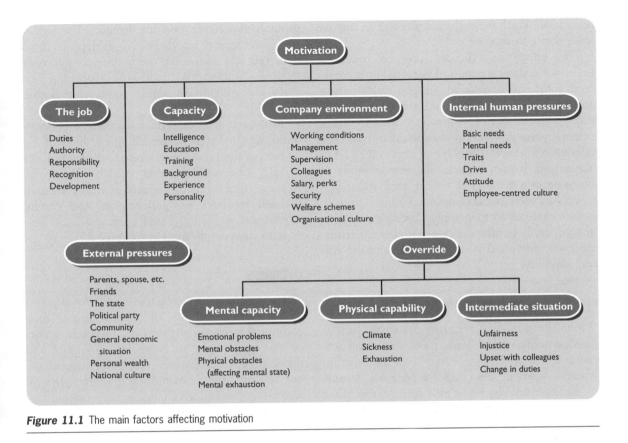

***Figure 11.1*** The main factors affecting motivation

and correct mixtures of factors vary with each individual.

There are many different ways of grouping all the aspects to form main factors. Figure 11.1 takes into account the various current theories about motivational factors, but it adds other factors which are often not mentioned when a certain concept is considered. Each factor is now discussed before the various concepts are outlined.

## THE JOB

The breadth of job content and the knowledge required are two features which have varied over the years. In the past, craftsmen possessed both in depth but they were naturally superseded by the factory and office type of employee who suffered narrow job content and knowledge requirements during the first seventy years of this century. Now the concept of job enrichment has reversed the process to satisfy the achievement motive.

## THE COMPANY ENVIRONMENT

The company environment covers all the internal features except the job itself. Examples are salary, bonuses, perks, organisational culture, the organisational structure, rules and regulations. Using these features alone to accomplish sustained motivation tends to fail. Their effect is often an initial rise followed by a fall to the previous level, although employees think the aspects are important.

## EXTERNAL PRESSURES

External pressures include national and local cultures, parents, spouse, relatives, friends, the state, political parties, the community, the economic situation, the media, and the individual capital possessed. Obviously they affect behaviour since people seek advice, listen to opinions and are generally being indoctrinated. An ambitious spouse, for example, can motivate by using subtle powers of persuasion which make the partner feel an intense inner desire to succeed.

The effect some people have on others is frightening: sheer strength of personality is sometimes sufficient to make an impressionable person go against logical reasoning and behave in very odd ways. The element of confusion caused by many external pressures should also be taken into consideration. If this factor plays an important part in motivation, it then becomes the responsibility of everyone in a country to ensure their influential powers are used to encourage motivation. The well-known chain effect then applies because someone, in turn, needs to take the responsibility for ensuring each individual is capable of exercising this responsibility.

## INTERNAL HUMAN PRESSURES

Within the individual are many pressures, such as physical needs, mental needs, traits, drives and attitudes, which affect motivation. Some are inherent whereas others develop during a person's lifetime.

Understandably, being able to recognise these in oneself is an advantage, but this is elusive since it depends upon having learned how to recognise them and make the necessary self-adjustments. Consequently, many people enter business without realising the importance of co-operation, co-ordination, self-discipline and self-control.

The outcome is suspicion and antagonism, often accelerated by poor management. Frustration develops since there is little opportunity to satisfy higher needs, and irresponsible behaviour develops due to healthy reactions to an unhealthy situation. Often highly absorbing hobbies are pursued to compensate for the inadequate work environment. These stress people who often arrive at work exhausted.

Adopting collaborative management (Chapter 2) avoids this predicament since a philosophy which absorbs all cultural aspects encourages employee commitment. An employee-centred culture overcomes frustration and develops mutual trust.

## CAPACITY

Capacity is closely linked with internal pressures. The main features are education, training, back-ground, experience and intelligence. The extent to which capacity affects behaviour depends upon matching the individual with the job not only from the 'square peg, round hole' aspect but also from the individual's ability to develop within that field.

Although it is healthy to stretch a person's mind, a job that is overreaching the limit of his or her capability will only cause frustration. Conversely, underutilisation is equally dangerous. In these circumstances the need is vital for rapid, detailed feedback on performance and careful adjustment of the job based upon results. (These aspects were emphasised in Chapter 9.)

## OVERRIDE

The so-called override factors upset the effect of all the previous factors, often regardless of their combined strength to motivate. Override occurs on the spot: it has an immediate, powerful and dominating effect on motivation by altering behaviour because of some mental incapability, physical incapability or sudden change in the situation surrounding the individual.

From the mental aspect, an emotional problem, a mental obstacle or a physical obstacle can suddenly appear which may completely throw the employee off balance and produce erratic behaviour. Similarly, from the physical aspect, feeling off-colour, sustaining an injury or suffering from a physical disability may produce unpredictable behaviour. A sudden change in a stable situation such as unfair treatment, an injustice or a change in the environment without due consultation, will again induce a similar effect.

All these features associated with override tend to destroy efforts to motivate in other factor areas. Indeed their effect frustrates many managers who abandon perfectly healthy schemes for the wrong reasons. In these cases, employees are often branded as being lazy, which really means either they are suffering from a mental or physical incapability or they are reacting strongly against some unfairness or injustice. The use of the word 'lazy' should be avoided because it immediately highlights the superior's complete inability to diagnose the individual's problem, as illustrated in the next section.

# The psychology of motivation

A scientific approach to motivation now includes certain recognised mental characteristics which produce a reasonable model. These characteristics include the concept, the process, the complexity of drives and their outlets, and the behaviour patterns which appear when barriers stop needs from being satisfied. Some ways of solving these problems when frustration occurs are included in the discussion.

# The motives concept

Motives that dominate behaviour may be sub-divided in various ways. A typical method is to divide them into three groups.

## BASIC AND MENTAL NEEDS

Basic needs are the desire to eat, to drink, to protect and to work; mental needs (or higher needs) include safety, esteem, self-fulfilment and creativeness.

## INTERNAL AND EXTERNAL MOTIVES

Satisfying internal motives is similar to satisfying basic needs and higher needs. External motives are dominated by outside factors such as temperature changes, other climatic conditions, dangerous elements like fire, water in connection with drowning, and so on. An external motive forces an individual to take action such as running to catch a bus or putting on extra clothing if the temperature drops.

## KNOWN AND UNKNOWN MOTIVES

Known and unknown motives are more complex and often difficult to analyse. Known motives are relatively easy to distinguish when actions occur such as ceasing to write through cramp, sitting down when the legs ache, and removing a coat if the temperature rises. Unknown motives are troublesome. Sudden inexplicable actions are confusing to all who are involved, including the one who may be acting in an illogical way. In extreme cases such actions are violent while other symptoms may be non-cooperation and sullenness. Often the real reason for this conduct is obscured by surface reasons.

There is also a favourable aspect to action resulting from unknown motives. A sudden upsurge of enthusiasm and willingness to co-operate are typical examples where a change has induced the person to act in a different way. In both favourable and adverse actions the driving force has emerged from within the person, and although an internal cause has motivated him or her to take a line of action, the reason itself may remain obscure.

Sometimes it is difficult to assess whether the motive is known or unknown. Certainly the reason will be connected with satisfying the needs already outlined, but the strength of these needs varies with each individual. Indeed some individuals easily satisfy their needs whereas others have great difficulty satisfying them.

# The process of motivation

The basic psychological process of motivation is often described as a need–drive–goal cycle. This concept is generally acceptable and the three factors are thought to be interdependent and interacting. Actual behaviour is more complicated because of many managerial and environmental issues. Nevertheless, this theoretical framework is a useful introduction (Fig. 11.2). Initially the three factors are examined. Analysis is easier if homeostasis and other processes are recalled from Chapter 9.

## NEEDS

A need, the first factor, is often described as an internal deficiency which is created because of the lack of homeostasis when a physiological or psychological imbalance occurs. Specialists, some of whom disagree, have drawn up a large range of needs. The existence of a hierarchy of needs was propounded by A. Maslow (see below).

## DRIVES

A drive, or motive, is established to satisfy a need. These drives are often defined as deficiencies with

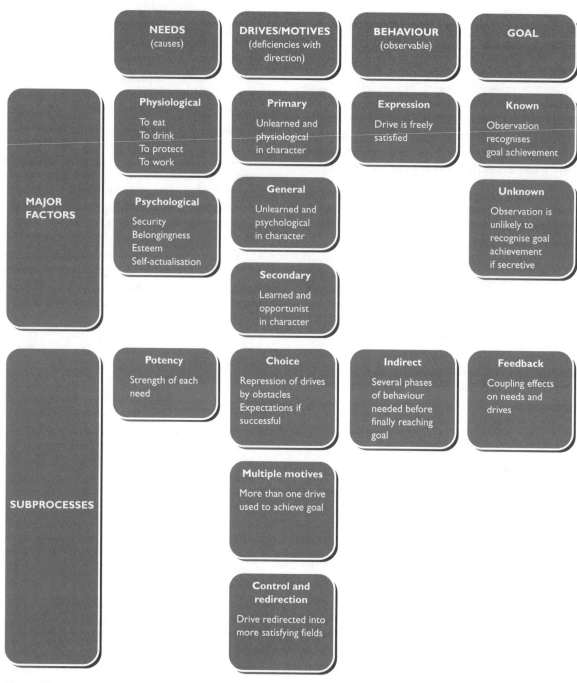

**Figure 11.2** A simplified motivation model
Major factors and subprocesses are indicated within the need–drive–goal cycle. The boxes should only be treated as building blocks.

direction because they are action-oriented and pressurise the individual into taking action to achieve a goal. They are often grouped into three categories.

### Basic or primary drives

Basic or primary drives are not learned; they possess a physiological character such as thirst, hunger, sex, sleep and pain avoidance.

### Unlearned drives

Like basis drives, unlearned drives do not develop through learning, but their character is more psychological than physiological. They often include achieving competence, inquisitiveness, persistence, experimenting and seeking affection. Unlearned drives are related in organisations to interactions with people and the breadth of a job. They maintain motivation provided the individual is given sufficient flexibility and opportunity.

### Secondary or learned drives

Secondary or learned drives are predominant in a modern society where basic needs are generally satisfied. There are strong associations with the use and misuse of power (Chapter 13), achievement, and status – in all its forms – which either create or destroy in various complex ways. Learned drives are an important feature of the behaviourist approach to motivation (Chapter 12) and in the learning process related to training (Chapter 19). Drives may appear in the conscious mind and force the individual into taking a certain line of action he or she might not have taken if given sufficient time to think. If one of the drives is suppressed, frustration may occur, causing loss of energy unless an adjustment is made.

### GOALS

The cycle ends with the achievement of a goal. Any attainment which reduces the drives and relieves a need is termed a goal. Considering homeostasis, the psychological and physiological balance is restored and the drive is cut off. Examples are eating food, drinking, being accepted by a member of a club, and passing an examination.

### MOTIVATED BEHAVIOUR

The theoretical model described above is only observable through behaviour. There are several reasons why it is doubtful whether motives may be accurately inferred from behaviour. Motives are often seen in various disguised ways, and more than one motive (or drive) may be expressed through one act. Individuals may also act in several different ways with the same motive in mind, or 'unlike' motives may be seen in similar behaviour.

Furthermore, behaviour may take on several forms in the expression of a motive. Instrumental behaviour is a form where an act only indirectly satisfies the need. For example, if an employee joins the company's sailing club, he or she may be a good yachtsman and is seeking recognition, so the act of joining is instrumental in nature. Another employee might join because he or she is seeking friendship, not being particularly interested in sailing. This form is called substitute behaviour. Finally, if an act directly satisfies the need, then consummatory behaviour is apparent, such as eating a meal.

# The complexity of drives

Drives or motives and their effects are illustrated here in four parts: (1) by giving five examples of secondary drives because of their importance; (2) by examining various outlets for drives; (3) by considering the barriers or obstacles that frustrate motives; (4) by outlining the behavioural patterns which emerge in reaction to obstacles and indicating how to solve such frustration problems.

### EXAMPLES OF SECONDARY DRIVES

### Aggressiveness

The drive to be powerful expresses itself in hostility, awkwardness, and being quarrelsome. In extreme cases, physical force is used such as shouting and banging the table violently. This drive is very close to the desire to escape when confronted with an intolerable situation. In proximity these two drives sometimes force a person into an unhappy state of mind. For example, he or she may want to attack a manager and leave the company because of a feeling of unfair treatment. If outside commitments restrict the person from taking this course, the resulting conflict causes severe stress. The results are often daydreaming, constant complaints and poor productivity. A popular individual may even gain support from colleagues, whose productivity will also drop.

Clearly all employees should have the opportunity to develop, which helps them to feel they are not just cogs in a large, impersonal machine. The chance to study and expand the job with equal opportunity to be selected for higher posts naturally needs stressing, as does the need for a policy of fairness and justice, and strict adherence to the policy by all managers.

## Acquisitiveness

The desire for protection and possession is directly associated with this drive. Sometimes it develops as a strong desire to control and possess power over others. Satisfying this drive means a manager should ensure company policy adequately protects employees by including secure employment, insurance, superannuation and other welfare benefits. Factors such as the national employment level, state benefit schemes, state retraining schemes, trade unions and staff associations, and the general feeling of job security, all contribute towards the employee's state of mind. Satisfying this drive, however, does not necessarily mean high productivity, since this factor is only one of many needing correct adjustment.

## Self-assertion

The drive to be important is closely linked with constructiveness. Receiving due credit for creating something is essential, but when a product or a system is divided into many jobs, the feeling of importance lessens because there is no direct association of the finished product with one individual. To compensate for this, an employee may turn to the group within which he or she is a member and enjoy group spirit if it is strong. Thus group dynamics must be considered (Chapter 5). This depends on the people in the group and the amount of attention given by management to this factor. Consistently fair and just treatment, careful counselling of each person's problems, development schemes for employees and a human approach all help to foster a keen group spirit.

The aim is to make each employee important. Trying to make a person *feel* important is insufficient because the feeling soon disperses as reality becomes obvious. Each employee must be placed in such a position that he or she *is* important and, knowing this importance, can actively demonstrate it to colleagues.

## Constructiveness

The strong drive to create probably causes more trouble in business than any other drive because, in so many jobs, the opportunity to create is omitted from job requirements. The effect is severe frustration, yet so often the whole concept of manufacturing processes and office work is usually based upon narrowing jobs down to relatively simple tasks.

People satisfy the urge to create by suggesting improvements, having job flexibility, preparing and discussing ideas, and knowing they actually participate in decisions affecting their jobs. Recognition of their contribution combines with self-assertion; they know they are important and they are actively contributing towards the success of the business. The disastrous effects of frustration if this drive is ignored are discussed later.

## Gregariousness

Another drive which is associated with group behaviour is the urge to belong to and be accepted by the group. Throughout life, the tendency to group together is seen everywhere and people will go to great lengths to be included in various social groups. The need to unite is probably close to mating and parental drives. Banning a person from a group is particularly harsh and inhuman. The victim may be driven to near-panic and many dangers result from such action.

# Outlets for drives

Driving forces, which compel a person to take action in a specific way, must be relieved or released through activity. If for any reason they are blocked, the effect is rather like an excess of steam which cannot escape inside a boiler. Sometimes the pressure builds until breaking point is reached and the boiler explodes. The three main outlets to satisfy drives are:

- expression
- repression
- control and redirection

The supervisor should be able to recognise symptoms indicating which outlet is operating and offer assistance, if necessary, by redirecting a person's energies.

### Expression

When the drive is freely satisfied by an activity directly connected with it, the term 'expression' is used to describe this normal outlet. An artist painting a picture and a strong-willed individual being appointed chairperson of a social club are typical of such outlets. A distinction may be drawn between two further examples: murdering an individual and publicly speaking for increasing the pensions of senior citizens. One could be called a barbaric or primitive approach to satisfying the drive and the other a civilised or cultured approach. When free expression is very difficult and the person feels restricted, he or she may unthinkingly repress the drive.

### Repression

To avoid nervous tension when an impulse is restrained, the drive may be repressed unconsciously and transferred out of the conscious mind. Unfortunately, this process of forgetting it or banning it from conscious thought is unhealthy or harmful. The painful experience continues to exist at another level, and usually the outcome is only a temporary repression. Suddenly the drive will break through, often at the most inopportune moment, which causes embarrassment and an even more painful situation. Partial repression of this nature causes various forms of perversion in certain circumstances.

Many difficulties experienced in business are the direct result of repression. The supervisor has a clear social responsibility to avoid placing employees in situations where repression may occur. Typical symptoms are poor co-operation, apathy, disinterest in the job and the company, maladjustment, antagonism and low concentration. Employees should not be forced into situations where there is no choice but repression. Inevitably retaliation occurs through verbal abuse or physical violence against a supervisor or, indirectly, the company. A much better approach is to control and redirect the outlet.

### Control and redirection

For those possessing a well-balanced personality there is ample opportunity to recognise the nature of the drive within them. With appropriate knowledge and experience they redirect their natural urges into more satisfying fields. Similarly, the manager should ensure supervisors can recognise drives and appropriate symptoms in their staff. Thus employees will be encouraged to adjust by redirecting them within the job and in other social pursuits within the company.

Redirection or sublimation usually occurs unconsciously. Consequently, someone with a strong constructive drive with no opportunity to exercise it at work may become involved in building complex model aircraft. Similarly, someone with a high aggressive impulse may be engaged in clerical duties at work, but in social life outside will be running a tennis club, organising help for senior citizens, or chairing a local residents' association. Such redirection is healthy and desirable. Unfortunately, in similar situations some individuals might develop unhealthy alternatives, such as pursuing criminal activities, bullying or perversions.

# Obstacles

When needs are not easily satisfied, the barriers or obstacles cause disappointment or frustration if they are not overcome. The effect is various patterns of behaviour (Fig. 11.3). To understand this reaction, the obstacles are examined by dividing them into two groups: internal and external.

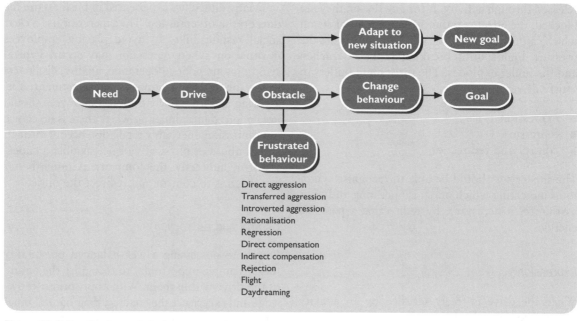

*Figure 11.3* Reacting to an obstacle

## INTERNAL OBSTACLES

An impressive array of internal barriers restricts a person from achieving the aims and needs he or she feels are desirable. A self-assessment of capabilities may mislead a person into believing his or her limitations are much higher than the true ones. Personal traits might cause inner conflicts when associated with both physical and mental restrictions. The person may lack the right degree of confidence, and inhibitions could restrict desires. Often the way people see themselves differs from the way other people see them. This situation is misleading and faults are not readily accepted, even when they are explained to people. Inability to self-analyse accurately causes internal conflicts which confuse, usually upset stability, and encourage mental exhaustion, apathy and a non-cooperative outlook.

## EXTERNAL OBSTACLES

The main groups of external obstacles are people, society and objective restrictions. The barriers people raise may be direct or indirect in intention. Where enmity or clashing interests are involved, there is often an obvious direct restriction, but occasionally this may not be known, as devious means of raising barriers are employed. Such devious treatment is bewildering as well as frustrating. Unfortunately, people like to use this technique.

When people satisfy their own desires and inadvertently stop or restrict someone else's efforts, an indirect effect occurs. The natural tendency to compete in an insensitive manner savours of jungle law, which is almost completely impersonal and often depends upon being in a certain situation at a certain time. Another factor is the effect of family and friends. In some circumstances they can apply restrictions which are difficult to overcome without causing an upheaval in domestic affairs.

Closely associated with this factor are the restrictions applied by the type of society within which the person has to live. Society pressurises to conform to certain codes of conduct which result in sanctions being applied if broken. The codes are learned through upbringing and education, but if they are unacceptable, the resulting conflict may cause change, the erection of insurmountable barriers or eventual adjustment.

Finally, the obstacles associated with objective factors include changes in the economic situation, international problems, governmental policies and even changes in the weather. All these aspects, plus many more not mentioned, cause people to react in various ways. These are now described.

## PATTERNS OF REACTION TO OBSTACLES

Reaction to obstacles takes on many different forms and combinations of forms. These frustration symptoms may be grouped into characteristics. When the characteristic is recognised, the type of obstacle is an important consideration in determining the course of action. The main characteristics are now discussed.

### Direct aggression

The usual symptoms that precede direct aggression are depression, sourness, sullenness and displeasure. A selection of symptoms may be expressed at every opportunity. Such tendencies are caused by a weakness which blocks needs and may suddenly express itself in physical violence and emotional outbursts. This primitive reaction is often seen in children and animals, but more refined versions are also displayed by adults who may shout, swear violently, use sarcasm and generally act in an overexcitable fashion.

Calmness, judgement and logical thought are affected. Whenever possible it is better to fight against the tendency and attempt to control it. When dealing with people suffering in this way the supervisor should give them time to cool off before reasoning with them. Furthermore, an essential requirement is to remain calm and not be provoked.

### Transferred aggression

When aggression is transferred to a false barrier, it is usually because the true barrier is unknown or it would be dangerous to use direct aggression against the barrier. In one sense, the irritation is controlled compared with direct aggression. It may be recognised when there are symptoms of peevishness, pedantry, constant complaints, criticisms, pessimism and a negative outlook.

The false barrier is generally of a weak nature, which gives the person the opportunity to bully or vent feelings freely, often with disregard for the harm this might cause. The supervisor should be aware of this possibility when dealing with complaints concerning the employee's colleagues. In these circumstances always provide ample opportunity for the person to explain the problem fully. Remember the art of listening and its effects, and demonstrate that the situation is understood and accepted. Solving the problem then becomes much easier.

### Introverted aggression

A sense of failure or a specific instance of failure may cause a poor energy level, depression, poor initiative and self-accusation. This failure results in self-punishment; the anger is directed inwards and causes introverted aggression. Examples are failing an examination, not being selected for promotion, or rejection by the opposite sex.

The person may be very quiet and unresponsive to questions regarding any problems. This situation demands careful handling and counselling may be helpful and essential if the behaviour continues. Begin with questioning techniques that encourage answers other than yes or no. Self-denial of this kind normally rights itself in time, but in some extreme cases it may even result in suicide.

### Rationalisation

When people have acted in a silly way or find themselves in a humiliating situation, they may unconsciously twist their motives. For example, an employee who fails to operate a machine properly after instruction may pretend not to care whether he or she can operate it or not. In another case the person may blame the mistake on someone else by insisting it is not his or her responsibility to check for errors.

When someone's self-respect is hurt, this emotional reaction may be expected: the person rationalises to justify his or her behaviour. Indeed solving problems logically becomes more difficult because the real causes are not acceptable at the time. Later the person may admit the fault when self-respect and esteem have recovered. Admission is not the aim; it is better to help the individual by not dwelling on the mistake but advising on how to avoid a similar recurrence.

## Regression

When behaviour becomes less practical than may be considered normal, probably the person is retiring into earlier primitive habits. Consequently, he or she neglects later acquired, more adaptive habits. This regression tendency is noticeable when a person insists on being incapable of performing a task but it is obvious this is untrue.

Initial symptoms are the inability to use knowledge, techniques or skills, along with signs of vague thinking, slovenly dress and the tendency to lose control easily. Usually it becomes more difficult to cope with the normal workload as interest wanes and there is poor concentration. Often it is difficult to locate the barrier before help is possible.

## Direct compensation

Direct compensation occurs when all the person's efforts are concentrated on trying to defeat the obstacle. The barrier is generally internal and caused by a weakness or lack of some requirement. Good adjustment is possible if these efforts succeed and are socially acceptable. However, over-compensation applies if the individual assumes an arrogant and excessively self-confident manner to cloak shyness and feelings of inferiority.

Sometimes a person may display co-operativeness at the time but fail to perform effectively later. Others may adopt a superior attitude with no justification. These people tend to avoid discussions and are poor listeners.

Exaggerating and stiffness in behaviour are general symptoms. Fixation is another form which means the person's energies are too strongly concentrated, resulting in a continual return to the same lines of thought or narrow thought patterns. Such patterns are illustrated by stubbornness, unresponsiveness to logical reasoning, and a tendency to argue with no firm foundation. Uncertainty underlies this form of behaviour, which is a desperate attempt to protect self-esteem. To overcome uncertainty the supervisor should be well prepared with appropriate responses and should display assertiveness.

## Indirect compensation

If a substitute goal replaces the original one, which is unachievable, an obsession to reach the substitute often occurs. All the person's efforts will be aimed in that direction. Although indirect compensation is a form of frustration, high performance often results if a domestic or outside social upset is traumatic and forces the individual into overemphasis on his or her employment. This imbalance is unhealthy. Other signs are wearing clothing unsuitable for the job and expressing absurd opinions.

## Rejection

Casting aside past unsuccessful efforts and trying to forget the problem as if it never existed are known as rejection or repression. To protect self-esteem and self-respect, unpleasant memories are forced into the back of the person's mind, thus making the conscience clear and uncluttered with humiliating thoughts.

In the subconscious mind these memories persist and affect behaviour and dreams. The symptoms are very little courage, poor energy, and projection (possessing a fault but refusing to admit it). Alternatively the person finds the fault with which he or she is suffering is very noticeable in others, and continually refers them to it. The reason for this strange behaviour is that the person's own desires and failures are projected onto other people's behaviour. Consequently, if the person sees this weakness in others then he or she will feel more secure.

## Flight

Flight is when an individual physically retreats from an obstacle. Examples are leaving a job if there is no prospect of promotion or transferring to another department to avoid a supervisor's criticism. Flight may be considered a good adjustment if the change is successful, but if the change worsens the individual's position, it will be a bad adjustment.

Internal obstacles may be subjected to a form of flight, such as resorting to alcohol or drugs, which only provide temporary relief. Persistent absenteeism and lateness are also symptoms. A more potent form is when a person gives up or shows resignation in the working situation, or adopts delaying tactics. Unfortunately, this condition is contagious to colleagues and may cause low morale.

The difficult task of attempting to discover why flight occurs and how to treat this reaction to an obstacle demands positive approaches by the supervisor. However, further counselling may be essential in some cases.

## Daydreaming

Near to flight is resorting to fantasy. Examples are being frustrated by petty irritations and apparently insurmountable problems. Daydreaming is a blessed release because immediate removal from the obstacle is made possible and time is available to regain control and drive.

Provided daydreaming is not continually preferred to reality, there is very little maladjustment; many people daydream. Maladjustment is noticeable when continual errors occur for no logical reason and there is no drive to develop further. When questioned, the individual tends to lapse into blank expressions, staring out of the window and, in extreme cases, seems unable to find words to express himself or herself.

### SOLVING FRUSTRATION PROBLEMS

The probable conclusions from this brief survey of frustration caused by motives being blocked either internally or externally are:

- Ensure employees are placed in suitable jobs appropriate to their capabilities.
- Monitor progress carefully to avoid frustration if the employee cannot cope with the job.
- Continuous assessment of employees is essential because people change due to various internal and external circumstances.
- The opportunity to develop further should be open to everyone.
- Employees need help in their jobs and with the social side of employment.

- Consider restructuring jobs to avoid frustration due to boredom.
- There are many needs to satisfy; concentrating on one group alone is insufficient.
- Employees are subjected to a wide range of pressures which easily upset performance: their way of life may not coincide with sustained high performance.
- External upsets and internal problems naturally affect employees' behaviour.
- Suitable organisational arrangements are necessary to cope with human problems; everyone has off-days and suffers from some form of frustration.
- The study of human problems is equally important as the technical problems if a supervisor is to be successful.

# Behavioural theories

The two main behavioural theories associated with an understanding of basic needs, motivation and job satisfaction are process theory and content theory. Research findings in these fields are inconclusive, so far.

### PROCESS THEORY

Various theories under the general heading of process theory attempt to postulate a formal explanation for the direction, amplitude and persistence of behaviour. Following the background to motivation, which generated research into drive theories, mid-twentieth-century ideas emerged emphasising that people make choices among behavioural alternatives on the basis of their knowledge. Thus people consciously calculate the relative pleasures and pains of various outcomes provided by alternative actions and they seek to maximise their total pleasure.

Within this concept there are three major determinants of action: reinforcement, drive (a need) and incentives. Either singly or in combination, they formed the major motivational models which were developed up to 1960.

Simplified, reinforcement means the effect on the individual of learning habit-forming activities.

Thus habit strength depends upon the situations which the individual has been subjected to in terms of magnitude and frequency. The energiser, or motivational component (drive), indicates the general level of pressure for activity. Incentive represents the pulling effects of rewards.

## CONTENT THEORY

Content theories attempt to suggest the specific identity of variables discussed in general terms by the process models. The history of content theory is located in the theories of instinct, which fell into disrepute at the beginning of the century as a result of the propensity to postulate a specific need for almost any human act. They achieved respectability again, however, when they were changed in concept to one of needs being acquired through the learning process.

Content theories are more concerned with specific rewards, the basic needs which may be identified and the strengths of incentives on offer. Consider job performance. One content theory may attempt to classify the strength of achievement possibilities, recognition, responsibility, promotion prospects and salary increases. Another theory may propose a different list.

# The behavioural scientists

So far, the motives that govern behaviour are seen to be extremely varied and capable of complex classification. The barriers that tend to destroy motivation force people into reacting in a variety of ways which are known as forms of frustration. A knowledge of the terms associated with frustration does not help unless the supervisor has the time to think and analyse employees. However, the supervisor can assist in promoting emotional stability with the aid of further information and with the idea of trying to help employees adjust to situations often outside their control.

An essential requirement to understanding fully the work of behavioural scientists is to read their books and papers. The main features of research findings and concepts of the well-known behavioural scientists now follow.

## ABRAHAM MASLOW

In 1943 Maslow wrote a paper entitled 'A Theory of Human Motivation', within which he put forward what has become the most widely accepted theory on the subject. He maintained the process of satisfying human needs is continuous: as soon as one need is satisfied another one takes its place. This implies that needs form a hierarchy of importance and when one need is satisfied it no longer acts as a sustained, effective motivator.

Maslow subdivided needs into the following groups which are in ascending order of importance, commencing at the lowest level:

- physiological needs such as hunger and thirst
- safety needs such as security and order
- belongingness and love needs such as affection and identification
- esteem needs such as desire and self-respect
- self-actualisation needs such as desire for self-fulfilment

The hierarchy breaks down when all the needs are developed. Although the needs remain, energy is spent differently on a continually changing basis as an attempt is made to satisfy all or any one of them. Furthermore, if a lower need is at risk, a higher need will be given up as the hierarchy reasserts itself. All the needs stay with a person regardless of whether he or she is at work, at home or at play.

### Exceptions

Maslow also pointed out that, in some circumstances, people would reverse the stages and ignore some completely within the hierarchy of needs. Typical examples would be the starving artist who would buy oils in preference to food, the struggling composer and the resting actor. These people will often willingly give up basic needs for self-fulfilment, although they are the exceptions. Many individuals are satisfied with lower levels of achievement and some, with low levels of ambition, are quite happy with the basic needs of life.

Higher standards of living and increasing social legislation affect the motivation level up to a point where social and egoistic needs become more important. If they are neglected, individuals will tend to be indolent, unwilling to accept responsibility and behave in an unreasonable manner.

## Conflict of needs

Furthermore, individual differences – such as cultural background, perception, physical and intellectual levels, aptitudes and personality – will affect the way people satisfy their needs. These aspects may induce a conflict of needs. For example, success at work may involve long hours which upset marital relationships.

Concentrating on one motivating factor alone has, at the most, only a temporary effect if it is already sufficiently satisfied. All factors connected with motivation closely interact with each other, and management's approach to motivation must cover all areas if the knowledge, intelligence and enthusiasm of employees are to be released into channels conducive to higher productivity.

Maslow's theory was first published in the *Psychological Review*, Volume 50, 1943. He also wrote many other papers, including 'A Preface to Motivation Theory' in *Psychosomatic Medicine*, Volume 5, 1943, and various books, one of them in conjunction with B. Mittleman, *Principles of Abnormal Psychology*, published in 1941.

## FREDERICK HERZBERG

Herzberg studied how the needs described by Maslow actually operate and has drawn certain conclusions which have received much publicity and achieved popularity in Britain. He analysed the main factors that result in either satisfying or dissatisfying experiences at work, concluding that satisfaction and dissatisfaction are not attached to the same factors.

Herzberg says that satisfaction comes through the job itself by the adjustment of motivators: achievement, recognition, the work, responsibility and professional growth. Dissatisfaction is induced through the environment by adjusting company policies and administration, supervision, working conditions, interpersonal relations, money, status

and security. Herzberg refers to this environmental aspect as *hygiene*; he considers that, although the hygiene factors are important and dissatisfaction should be kept to a minimum, only a fair day's work is possible if management concentrates on the environmental approach.

The approach through the job itself, however, seems to have a larger and more lasting effect. Concentrating on job design or job enrichment provides more satisfaction to the employee and in turn increases productivity. For a full appreciation of this motivation–hygiene theory, read two books written by Herzberg, *The Motivation to Work* and *Work and the Nature of Man*.

Many criticisms of this theory have also been published. The research undertaken by Herzberg was concerned mainly with accountants and engineers; therefore it is often suggested that his specific findings should be treated with discretion when dealing with shop-floor employees and clerical staff.

## ALDERFER'S ERG MODEL

Clayton Alderfer examined more recent evidence which caused him to reformulate Maslow's theory into three basic needs and refine Herzberg's two-factor or motivation–hygiene theory in the following way:

- *Existence needs*: desires for material substances that are in finite supply; typically food, shelter and money. The implications are that one person's gain is another person's loss; existence needs are not insatiable; and people reach a satisfaction level which is thought to be sufficient, therefore no one loses in times of plenty.
- *Relatedness needs*: the mutual sharing of thoughts and feeling with others. This assumes people desire to inform others and expect them to reciprocate. The communication should be open and accurate, regardless of any unpleasantness.
- *Growth needs*: the interaction of the person with the environment to develop ability and capacity along lines which are most important to that person. This assumes people seek to change their capacities according to their perceived requirements.

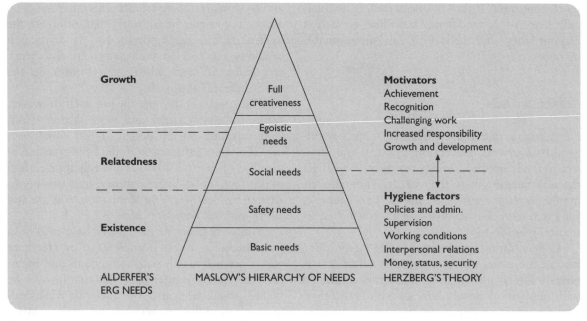

**Figure 11.4** Needs and motivation: three important theories

*Needs continuum*

Like Maslow and Herzberg, Alderfer felt there was value in categorising needs, but he viewed them more as a continuum. He disagreed with the ideas that a lower need must be satisfied before a higher need and that deprivation is the sole way to energise a need. A good example is growth needs, which may intensify the more they are satisfied. Figure 11.4 compares Alderfer's model with Maslow's model and Herzberg's model.

## DOUGLAS MCGREGOR

McGregor's work was based on his idea that effective leadership depended upon a manager's assumptions of the nature of management and about people. This idea was the keystone to his well-known contribution, Theory X and Theory Y. Although the reasoning behind these two theories is subtle, it does have the appearance of being simple. This misconception has resulted in a tendency to oversimplify McGregor's thoughts. To be sure of the correct concept it is essential to read his books *The Human Side of Enterprise* and *The Professional Manager* (1960).

*The assumptions*

McGregor stated there were two sets of assumptions about people; since then these assumptions have been interpreted in many different ways. Briefly Theory X and Theory Y – the terms given for these two assumptions – attempt to account for the way a manager can deliberately influence the behaviour of an employee. This influence is exerted through an underlying philosophy which is communicated by the use of all the techniques associated with contact between two people, such as speech, written notes, gestures, tone of voice, atmosphere and expressions.

Theory X is a philosophy which views employees as inherently disliking work; being unimprovable, needing to be coerced, controlled, directed and punished; avoiding responsibility whenever possible; and generally being unambitious. Theory Y is a philosophy which involves coaxing people through reward, praise, permissiveness and attention; it assumes people will work naturally, will exercise self-discipline and self-control in certain circumstances; and will have the potential for further development.

Both theories assume productive work is an unnatural form of behaviour and some form of pressure is essential to achieve it. The strategy behind Theory Y not only involves coaxing but also demands the structuring of work so that opportunities for further achievement and personal growth are possible.

## Misinterpretations

Some people incorrectly interpret Theory Y as completely abandoning the limits or boundaries associated with discipline and control. In other words, people should be allowed to do as they wish with no pressure to conform. This interpretation really amounts to anarchy. Unfortunately, employees tend to take full advantage of the situation when such an approach is tried. McGregor's work clearly anticipated the present vogue of job enrichment. He thought trust should be established by a collaborative effort where mutual support encouraged high motivation. He was Professor of Industrial Management at Massachusetts Institute of Technology.

## V.H. VROOM

Vroom's expectancy theory is complex and based upon three concepts: valence, instrumentality and expectancy. Valence means the strength of a person's preference for a particular outcome. Alternative terms are incentive, value or attitude. Instrumentality means the medium employed to achieve a goal. Expectancy means the probability that an action or effort will lead to a perceived goal.

The theory assumes the choices made among alternative courses of action are related to psychological events occurring with the behaviour. In other words, a person's behaviour is governed by (1) the strength of the desire; (2) an estimated probability of a successful outcome; and (3) the strength of belief that an action will satisfy the need. Although complex in total, expectancy theory strongly confirms that the supervisor should clearly explain incentive schemes, new work practices and the relationship between effort and rewards offered.

## L.W. PORTER AND E.E. LAWLER

Porter and Lawler refined Vroom's theory and assumed motivation (effort) does not equal satisfaction and/or performance. They treated motivation, satisfaction and performance as separate variables and implied that satisfaction is determined by the rewards which follow performance. Therefore, motivation does not lead directly to performance but is mediated by role perceptions, ability and traits. The outcome is that two main factors affect the degree of effort:

- psychological and monetary rewards that fulfil needs for security, esteem, independence and self-development
- expectation that increasing effort will result in receiving satisfying rewards

An important point is that effort and performance are different. Effort precedes performance and is the amount of energy exerted on a given task; performance is the result, which is objectively measurable.

## CHRIS ARGYRIS

According to Argyris, apathy and lack of effort are due to healthy reactions by normal employees to an unhealthy industrial situation, which has been created by management policies. He feels most people are naturally motivated to act responsibly, to be self-reliant and independent. Most jobs are structured, however, to create a childlike role, hence they lead to frustration which is demonstrated in defensive behaviour by employees to preserve self-respect.

Argyris feels people must have a sense of pride and accomplishment at work, but management still concentrates on financial rewards, job security and fringe benefits. Thus employees find little stimulation or dignity in work, and employment becomes a necessary evil. This is partially compensated by applying for pay increases as a penalty payment to offset lack of job satisfaction.

He also points out the difference between happiness and motivation. Making people happy does not necessarily motivate them. Conversely, a motivated employee is not necessarily happy.

## T-group training

A further aspect examined by Argyris was inter-personal relationships, which is the characteristic way of perceiving and dealing with each other. Apparently there is a tendency for managers and supervisors inadvertently to filter information and to have difficulty in giving their real views. This lack of personal competence can be improved, he says, by sensitivity training, or T-group training.

The method involves placing people in a unique situation which encourages openness and risk taking but discourages defensiveness and mistrust. Thus their behaviour should give them the opportunity to improve their communication effectiveness, to reduce the barriers affecting their relationships with other people, and to remove the filters that tend to distort information flow.

This unique atmosphere is created by operating informal sessions without a chairperson or an agenda. When the session commences, the participants soon realise a framework is needed where each individual plays a predetermined role if anything is to be achieved. Learning occurs as the group copes with this problem, each person seeing the effect of their tactics on the others, observing the personal bias effect and noting the distortion of information flow between them.

Argyris emphasises that T-group training does not solve management problems and he would not recommend its use in certain cases. Evidence shows this training helps to make a person a better listener, and he or she becomes more receptive to information from other people.

Argyris has written many articles and books. The well-known ones are *Organisation and Innovation, Interpersonal Competence and Organisational Effectiveness*, and *Integrating the Individual and the Organisation*. They should be read to appreciate his work, which includes his analysis of executive behaviour patterns.

## SAUL D. GELLERMAN

According to Gellerman, it is possible to make some generalisations about motivation from research findings: many motivational problems stem from the method of managing an organisation rather than the reluctance of employees to work hard; managers have a tendency to overmanage by narrowing employees' jobs and by making too many decisions at too high a level; and studying the employees' environment indicates reasons for their behaviour.

Gellerman's principle of psychological advantage stated that employees are motivated by their own desire to get by in the best possible way in the kind of world they think they live in. Thus employees are less susceptible to the influence of other people and more susceptible to their own drives, which presumably are partially governed by their standard of education, their degree of independence, and the demand for their particular services. Managers can play a part, therefore, by ensuring these desires can be satisfied by offering a change in the role an employee can play rather than concentrating on financial reward alone, although this is important. Gellerman recommends three approaches that have a positive motivational effect:

- to 'stretch' the employee by giving him or her more difficult duties above the level normally considered suitable
- to apply the principles of management by objectives
- to encourage participation by asking the employee for opinions before making decisions affecting his or her work

These and many other concepts are given in Gellerman's books *Management by Motivation, Management of Human Relations, Motivation and Productivity* and *People, Problems and Profits*.

## RENSIS LIKERT

The research undertaken by Likert is particularly interesting to supervisors. His findings indicate the importance of leadership quality and that certain basic patterns of supervision give the best results. According to the data, supervision and leadership style usually influence productivity far more than attitudes towards the company and job interest.

Likert states that supervision is always a relative process; a supervisor must adapt his or her behaviour to allow for the expectations, values and interpersonal skills of subordinates, colleagues and superiors. He maintains there are no specific rules of supervision which work well in all situations, but broad principles do apply to the supervisory processes and provide useful indicators of behaviour. These principles should always be used, bearing in mind the situation and the employees involved.

A fuller understanding of leadership styles, Likert's research work, and empirical tests are very useful. They can be studied in his book *New Patterns of Management*, published in 1961.

# Conclusion

Even a brief study of motivation theory as propounded by the above authors is sufficient to indicate the complexity of the science. There is a tendency for managers and supervisors to hear about a theory or a technique, try it, and abandon the idea for the wrong reasons. This is mainly due to misinterpretation of the theory, or pointing at apparent causes of failure instead of the real causes, or failing to appreciate other factors that override the behaviour of people in certain situations.

The social organisation in concerns is another important aspect affecting productivity. Society is rapidly changing and it is difficult to maintain a close touch with reality. People are reacting more strongly against undue pressure and general unfair treatment by management. The trend towards satisfying the more sophisticated needs is increasing along with more opportunities to develop a higher educational standard. The strong demand for management to adapt to these changes is obvious and cannot be ignored if attempts to motivate are to succeed and people are to be relieved of the multitude of senseless obstacles which frustrate them in many companies.

## QUESTIONS

1 How would you recognise high motivation and what are the essential factors that are needed to achieve it?

2 What part should management play in promoting high motivation?

3 Discuss the methods open to the supervisor for developing group spirit.

4 In your opinion how important is the human factor in connection with motivation?

5 If an employee accuses you of always giving him or her the difficult jobs and it is not true, what conclusions would you draw and what action would you take?

6 How would you explain that employees may receive pay increases, but that this does not lead to any difference in their attitude towards work?

7 What would you do about a situation where your group openly starts to 'carry' an employee for no apparent reason?

8 Behavioural science is based upon the assumption that behaviour tends to lead to attitude. Discuss this statement.

9 List the main factors that affect the motivation of people.

10 Outline the internal and external barriers that may stop an individual from satisfying his or her needs.

11 List the ways that people may react to obstacles which thwart their needs.

12 Write brief notes on the work of Abraham Maslow.

13 Discuss job enrichment.

14 Distinguish between a need and a drive. Explain their importance in analysing behaviour.

15 What is the difference between instrumental behaviour and substitute behaviour?

16 Give three examples of secondary drives and describe their significance in motivation.

17 Discuss the three main outlets for satisfying drives.

18 Describe Theory X and Theory Y. Give your opinion of their validity in modern industry.

19 Explain the complexity of drives with particular reference to aggression and assertion.

20 Describe the three groups of motives that dominate behaviour.

21 Learned motives are predominant in a modern society. Explain this statement.

22 What are the main features of motivation that help to clarify its meaning?

23 A modern view is that motives cannot be explained by a conscious process. Discuss this view.

24 Outline some of the definitions of motivation proposed through recent research.

25 There is a low probability that anyone's behaviour can be accurately assessed. What are the likely unknown elements that justify this statement?

---

**CASE STUDY**

Terry supervises a small section where keeping the staff motivated is considered to be his main role by his superior. There are three members who do not respond to his encouragement and it is obvious that new approaches are needed.

● *Daniel* is not easy to analyse. He is married with two children and enjoys home life. He is reluctant to work any overtime, but is conscientious and it seems he is happy to jog along without overexertion.
● *Fred* is reliable, loyal, but not assertive; this sometimes causes problems with other colleagues. He tends to keep to himself and people say he is shy.
● *Ken* is a lively individual, works well, expects more pay and will work overtime. His strong personality tends to work against him with colleagues, who say he is never satisfied with his lot.

*Explain the three members' behaviour considering the main motivational models. How would you attempt to improve their performance?*

---

**CASE STUDY**

Roden PLC is a medium-sized company producing a waterproofing product. Productivity must be improved to compete with overseas competition and to cope with the rising cost of chemicals. Personnel policy has included good pay for manual operatives, excellent working conditions and many fringe benefits.

Unfortunately, the workforce is not motivated beyond an average level for the industry. According to termination interviews, people are discontented because they are treated the same as colleagues who do a bare minimum and think that is sufficient.

The human resource manager is asked to comment by the managing director. 'I have already explained previously but we were not in difficulties then. It is not going to be easy now but there is still time if we are prepared to make some drastic changes.'

*Explain the probable motivational changes that should be introduced. Comment on the situation in terms of the content theory of motivation.*

---

Malcolm Candy has been supervisor of the hardware department in a well-known store for twenty-eight years and is due to retire within a year. In his department there are twelve employees, but no deputy supervisor. They muddle through when he is away. The store manager decides that a deputy should be appointed and asks Malcolm to put forward some proposals.

The situation as Malcolm sees it is that his department always seems to be the busiest in the store. New models, especially in electrical goods, are continually coming along, which is very demanding for him and his staff as the store's policy is that the staff must know how their sales products operate. However, everyone seems to get on well together and it is unusual to receive complaints. Pay is reasonable, even though there is no union recognition. From the employees' viewpoint there is no one like Malcolm and the current comment is 'We're going to miss him'.

In Malcolm's opinion there are three candidates:

- *Tom Janson*: the department's joker, well-liked, not serious-minded, work is exceptional, eight years with the company and age 35.
- *Susan Bagley*: quiet, a good worker, rather reserved, but with a talent for organisation, experienced background, three years with the company and age 42.
- *Gary Wittering*: the natural leader, wastes time, work just acceptable, respected, five years with the company and age 36.

*If you were Malcolm, what proposals would you put before the store manager?*

# 12

# Associated applications of motivation

## Managerial implications

Management's efforts to motivate employees should be based upon many fundamental influences and practices. The essential ones are:

- Employees should feel a strong reliance on managers who must ensure they live up to their expectations.
- Employees naturally expect managers to be up to date and competent.
- Managers must maintain an organisational community where employees feel they are an essential part and expect due respect and consideration as members.
- The needs and wants of employees must be recognised at all times.
- The practice of equitable treatment is essential.
- Managers should impress on employees that increased effort will lead to higher performance, which in turn will lead to desirable outcomes.
- Managers should ensure the organisation provides outcomes for employees which each individual values highly.

### ESSENTIAL FEATURES

Essential features are outlined to indicate their strong relationship with motivation theory and general management thought. The important features of leadership and power are covered separately in the next chapter.

- the behaviourist approach
- financial incentives

- appointments
- setting realistic goals
- designing the job
- coaching
- mentoring
- job satisfaction
- suggestion schemes
- employee participation

## The behaviourist approach

Behaviourist theory studies the behaviour of an employee and attempts to identify causes by varying the environment that precedes and follows behaviour. Although often considered under motivation theories, it differs fundamentally from them because thoughts, beliefs, attitudes and feelings are ignored. In other words, instead of focusing on inner aspects or inner motives, it concentrates on past and present features of reward and punishment, assuming that they determine behaviour. The idea is that behaviour is controlled by its immediate consequences.

The behaviourist school of thought in psychology has a high reputation for conducting extensive research in learning theories. Further reading on these and on memory factors is essential to appreciate the full background. The two main techniques, organisational behaviour modification and social learning theory, are outside the scope of this book. However, the main behaviourist principles are given below because of their importance and because many supervisors can relate them immediately to practical situations.

## BEHAVIOURISTIC LEARNING

Classical conditioning and operant conditioning are explained in Chapter 19. They form the basis for modifying behaviour through behaviourist techniques. The behaviourist approaches to them differ. As a reminder, note the difference in the concepts in the simple examples given below.

- Classical conditioning
    drive     = hunger
    stimulus = food displayed
    response = mouth waters
- Operant conditioning
    drive     = to satisfy a need (a cue)
    response = performing a task
    stimulus = receives pay

Therefore, classical conditioning is a process where involuntary responses occur through a stimulus; operant conditioning concentrates on the consequences of behaviour, not the causes. Operant conditioning has a greater impact on learning and partly explains organisational behaviour.

## Stimulus–response relationships

Stimulus–response relationships occur between superior and subordinate, between peers, and between employees and associations. Typically, a supervisor asks a subordinate to undertake a task (a stimulus or cue); if the performance (response) is acceptable and the supervisor congratulates him or her (a further stimulus and reinforcement), the response is strengthened. Consequently reinforcement not only strengthens the response that preceded it but also increases the possibility of the response occurring again.

Success is measured by noting whether future behaviour responds favourably to this particular stimulus. If it fails, another type must be tried. A classic example is the use of money as a reinforcer. If it produces improved performance more frequently, this type is successful, but until tested there is no guarantee. If it fails, another form of stimulus is tried and compared.

In other words, a reward (such as money) may not succeed as a reinforcer. This illustrates the true difference between rewards and reinforcers, although in practice they are generally treated as interchangeable terms.

## THE LAW OF EFFECT

The original theory of reinforcement which has stood the test of time is E.L. Thorndike's classic law of effect. Dating back to 1911 it still dominates and most behavioural scientists accept its validity.

Briefly the law states that given several responses to the same situation, those accompanied or closely followed by satisfaction in the form of reinforcement will be more likely to recur; those accompanied by or closely followed by discomfort in the form of punishment will be less likely to occur again.

Although there is controversy over some theoretical aspects and the nature of reinforcement is not fully understood, there is little doubt that behaviour can be changed by controlling reinforcement.

## Types of reinforcement

The forms of stimulus or types of reinforcement are usually classified under four headings:

- positive reinforcement
- negative reinforcement
- extinction
- punishment

Within each heading are a number of choices. They are contingently applied for positive reinforcement and punishment, and contingently withheld for extinction and negative reinforcement (Fig. 12.1).

The differences among the four types may be clarified initially by examining the aims, ways of achieving the aims and effects of each one. Positive reinforcement strengthens response and increases the probability of repetition, as does negative reinforcement. The positive reinforcement way is to use presentation of a desired consequence, while the negative reinforcement way is by terminating or withdrawing an undesired consequence.

Punishment differs from negative reinforcement. By applying a negative consequence to reduce the chances of repetition of that behaviour, it

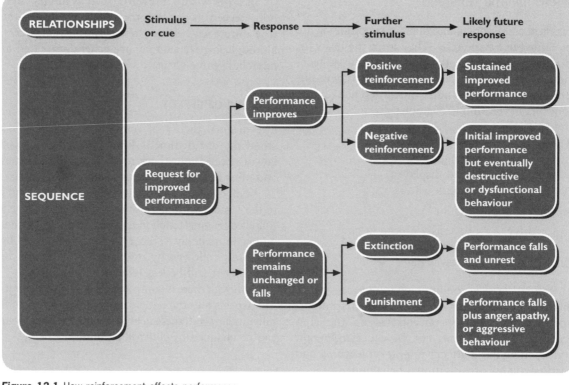

**Figure 12.1** How reinforcement affects performance

suppresses and implies that if an individual has a choice between punishment and no stimulus he or she would choose no stimulus.

Extinction differs from punishment. By stopping positive reinforcement when there is only a slight increase in performance, it tends to make the undesired response disappear, whereas punishment tends only to suppress.

## POSITIVE REINFORCEMENT

Positive reinforcement is a pleasant or desirable stimulus such as financial gain, praise, more attention, a visual sign of approval, or expressions of affection. A positive reinforcer is immediately applied when performance improves; the effect is to strengthen response and increase the possibility of the response recurring. Provided the appropriate positive reinforcer is chosen by the supervisor, success is assured.

The principle is to stimulate when there is any movement or response which indicates an improvement, not to wait until an acceptable performance level is reached. Consequently, the supervisor must be made aware of any favourable change immediately and time must be found to apply the stimulus.

Positive reinforcement should not be used when inappropriate behaviour is occurring. For example, an employee is not performing well and the supervisor adopts a patronising approach by attempting to boost morale. The employee usually knows the real reason for the interview and may feel he or she is receiving attention (positive reinforcement) when behaviour standards drop. A similar pattern is then adopted in future. In other words, to encourage undesirable behaviour, reinforce it positively.

## NEGATIVE REINFORCEMENT

An unpleasant or undesirable stimulus such as harassment or a reprimand is withheld or removed if performance is acceptable. Thus the employee avoids being constantly badgered or pestered, and behaviour improves. However, if productivity falls and harassment (punishment) begins, frustration and anger are created with inevitable results since the technique savours of social blackmail.

Negative reinforcement and punishment may be confused if both apply together. For example, if a person is not paying attention at a meeting and is embarrassed when asked a question, the effect is punishment through embarrassment and negative reinforcement by strengthening attention level.

## EXTINCTION

Extinction simply means that if a response is not reinforced it will eventually disappear. Often extinction means stopping positive reinforcement for only mediocre performance levels. This situation may occur due to a policy change or in a recession. Behaviour generally decreases and the risk of unrest is increased unless a revised positive reinforcement programme is introduced in an attempt to improve productivity.

A typical training example occurs during the learning period of a new technique. An employee will receive praise and a bonus for satisfactory progress, but the positive reinforcement stops when the employee is trained and placed in a job. No reward is offered for using the new technique and gradually performance declines.

If there is no external or internal reward such as financial gain, praise or job satisfaction, the tendency is to extinguish the particular behaviour. Consequently, an employee who suddenly suffers extinction by not receiving praise for his or her efforts, mediocre though they may be compared with others, will respond with lowering of effort. This emotional reaction, caused by cutting positive reinforcement, may also induce attitude changes towards colleagues, general dissatisfaction with the company and other forms of adverse emotional behaviour.

A common fault in managers is to adopt a stance where silence is intended to convey approval and praise to an employee when performing well. This high-handed approach is often accompanied by strong reaction from the manager if a mistake occurs or if behaviour of some description is unsuitable. An employee has to be very understanding and mature not to react adversely to such conduct. Usually the outcome in the long term is to seek attention through adverse behaviour, thus the manager is reinforcing lower performance tendencies.

## PUNISHMENT

The use of punishment is a complex practice which suffers with many major difficulties. One definition of punishment is any activity that weakens behaviour and its subsequent frequency. Opinions vary on its effectiveness; they range from warnings not to use it because of many undesirable side effects, up to its use as a drastic modifier of behaviour.

People dislike being punished, they strongly resent the punisher, and punished behaviour is only temporarily suppressed. In an attempt to overcome these difficulties, some ways of using punishment have been suggested:

- Before punishing ensure that an alternative form of behaviour is available which can then be reinforced.
- Recognise that punishment causes fear and anxiety which must be overcome before any permanent improvement in behaviour is possible.
- Punishment is always more effective at the time of the undesirable behaviour; a delay may cause misunderstandings.
- Punishment may become a reward for undesirable behaviour in certain circumstances, so always attempt to reinforce instead of punishing.
- Always be aware of possible physical reactions in some situations.
- After resorting to punishment, if the result is a favourable response always provide a reward or praise immediately.
- Try informative punishment by illustrating how adverse consequences may be avoided.
- Always ensure that punishment is associated with an unfavourable response and not confused with other responses.

Two important aspects should be remembered. First, severe punishment may stop poor behaviour but inevitable long-term side effects set in. Second, punishment tends to concentrate on the negative side by indicating something should not be done rather than on the positive side by indicating what should be done.

## CONCLUSIONS FROM RESEARCH

Positive reinforcement is most successful because it clearly indicates to the employee the rewards for desired behaviour. Extinction and punishment do not illustrate to the employee what is expected from him or her; they only show that poor behaviour is undesirable. However, this claim may seem unacceptable as most people are fully aware that a company seeks higher performance levels.

Negative reinforcement may increase performance but it also creates negative feelings because the employee knows that if the desired behaviour ceases, he or she will be subjected to harassment. Negative reinforcement and punishment are both negative control devices, although they may stop undesirable behaviour.

## APPLYING REINFORCEMENT

The two classes of reinforcement, primary and secondary, are considered before discussing their applications. Primary reinforcement satisfies a physiological drive such as hunger; examples are food, water and flight from pain. Secondary reinforcement is learned, acquired through prior association with a primary reinforcer, and cannot directly satisfy a physiological drive. Typical examples are financial reward, praise, encouragement and the opportunity to participate. Supervisors apply secondary reinforcement by offering money, approval, affection and attention.

### Application: financial rewards

Although the immediate application of financial rewards is desirable, scheduling may be continuous or partial in practice. Continuous application is costly and difficult to maintain over long periods as it needs supervisory and administrative time. The alternative is partial reinforcement, which is the application of rewards from time to time. This is more economic, more sensible and less cumbersome, but less effective as the desired behaviour takes longer to achieve.

Four ways of application are fixed intervals, variable intervals, fixed ratios and variable ratios. These terms are self-explanatory. A fixed time is arranged, say a week or a month, for payment of reward. Consequently, the tendency is towards uneven levels of performance. Variable intervals are random, thus the employee is unaware of the next payment date and the outcome is more consistent performance. Fixed ratios are simply based upon a number of output units, and often high performance levels are achieved if payment is immediate. Finally, variable ratios are similar, but the number of units is based upon a variance around a set average of productivity.

## APPLICATION: FURTHER CONSIDERATIONS

When using such reinforcers as praise, an essential practice is to determine carefully the behaviour to be reinforced. When using extinction and punishment a two-phase approach is possible by treating these devices to stop or reduce undesirable behaviour and, hopefully, as behaviour improves the opportunity is created to use positive reinforcement.

Choosing between extinction and punishment is difficult. Positive reinforcement has obviously failed as performance dropped. The reasons may be poor choice of reinforcement, a personal problem, or other factors. Counselling is needed and is more appropriate compared with resorting to extinction or punishment. However, using extinction immediately indicates to the employee that something is wrong and, provided the person is sufficiently sensitive towards low performance and the situation, he or she will connect the two changes. Such performance change must occur fairly recently and be noticed quickly, otherwise the employee may not connect the two. If the supervisor has neglected to act quickly or was unaware of low performance, which presumably has continued for a relatively long time, he or she may resort to punishment and rely upon positive reinforcement later.

# Financial incentives

The nature of Western society and the need to satisfy basic drives mean the desire to work is strongly linked to the desire for financial reward.

Money can certainly provide most comforts, but those who are wealthy always seem to claim it cannot buy happiness; at least they can be miserable in comfort.

## CHIEF EXECUTIVES' PAY

Bearing in mind the subject is motivation and its applications, especially related to employees, executive pay is controversial and often causes bitter feelings among the community when glaring cases of excessive greed are disclosed. The gap between take-home pay of chief executives and other employees has widened enormously since 1978. Over fifteen years the increase is about six times for chief executives and about four times for employees. Furthermore, these figures do not take into account bonuses at boardroom level and more benefits from tax cuts. Obviously some chief executives whose pay is thought to be exorbitant, think money is an important incentive, regardless of the effect on morale of other employees.

Arguably these executives are competent because they continue to hold their posts. They are in short supply and are a vital factor in the success of a company. Viewpoints of employees are interesting because their knowledge of chief executives comes through the grapevine. Unfortunately, chief executives have few secrets – actual performance levels, the effects on employees, and the quality of decisions are well known. Viewpoints of the community depend upon how it affects them. Typical factors are product or service prices, quality, profit levels, state and track record of the company, employee performance, strikes, pollution levels, dividends, reputation, moral codes and values.

### Debatable aspects

Debatable aspects include the following questions:

- Does competence include sensitivity towards the effect of conduct on employees?
- Is a chief executive's moral reputation important to the company?
- Should the pay level take into account greed, managerial philosophy and the organisational culture?

- Do exorbitant payments equal social blackmail?
- Who should equate exceptional performance with pay?

### Leadership side effects

As a leader, the chief executive has certain responsibilities. Leadership is a two-way process between the leader and followers (Chapter 13). A leader's behaviour influences followers' behaviour, and followers influence the leader's behaviour. In other words, followers tend to use the superior as an example. This mutual influence or interacting process explains to some extent industrial relations problems and employees' pay claims that seem excessive. Company culture tends to spread from the top.

## THE INFLUENCE OF FINANCIAL INCENTIVES

Financial incentives have a varying influence on output; the result depends upon many factors such as the wealth of the individual, the standard of pay already being received, the relative influence of social factors, the strength of the greed trait, general character and intelligence. If pay levels are high, the effect of a further increase may be negligible – perhaps a short burst of effort followed by a rapid fall to the original output level.

Two opposing views on financial incentives are often heard. One view is that a fair system is where people are paid for what they produce. In this way slackers are not supported by energetic workers. Another view is that this system upsets human dignity when people have to jump for the so-called jellybeans. The emerging questions are:

- Why do some people want to slack?
- How are scrupulously fair schemes arranged and operated?

Successful motivation in non-financial terms eventually eliminates the need for the first question. The second question is controversial since it is exceptionally difficult to design a comprehensive scheme that will satisfy all situations. However, all schemes must conform to a number of conditions and safeguards before non-financial forms of motivation may be applied successfully. These are now discussed.

## PERFORMANCE-RELATED PAY

Performance-related pay links financial reward with the individual, the group, company performance or any combination of these three. Generally it is restricted to cash reward, excludes various equity share schemes, but includes merit pay, various financial incentives and team performance improvements based on added-value or gainsharing schemes.

Although more popular now, doubts remain about its motivational effectiveness, the high costs of operating a suitable scheme, rewarding individual effort, and improving business efficiency. The organisation must be geared to competent and modern human resources management. Everyone should understand the system and be involved in operating and participating in it.

### Advantages

A properly conducted scheme may offer many advantages:

- Conscientious employees offering high performance are adequately rewarded.
- Successful teamwork is encouraged.
- Performance standards and targets become more sensitive.
- Corporate resources are used more economically, provided employees feel there are appropriate rewards for performance or contribution – not necessarily for their efforts alone.

### Critical issues

Critical issues include education and training, non-financial motivational factors, the capability to appraise and assess, the existence of a sound basic pay structure that allows for significant rewards and sufficient differential between performance levels, promptness of payment, just penalties for poor work, and immediate attention to queries. Success inevitably depends upon trusting top management, who must be fully committed.

### Essential requirements

Essential requirements vary from industry to industry. A sound scheme should be:

- fair, just, easily understood, and mutually acceptable to employees and management
- easy to operate considering evaluation of quantity, quality and wastage
- economic by avoiding high administration costs and high pay bills
- structurally sound by avoiding difficulties with grades, differentials and excessive pay
- designed to allow for beginners to earn reasonable pay and a guaranteed minimum pay for everyone

## PROFIT-RELATED PAY

Profit-related pay (PRP) was introduced by the government in 1987 as an incentive to employees to improve their employers' profits by taking a part of the profits free of tax. Many businesses are now operating PRP, which means a part of employees' pay rises and falls in line with the profits of the business. Employees should have a more direct personal interest in the fortunes of the firm, their jobs may be safer when market conditions are unfavourable and they benefit from the tax relief provided.

The Inland Revenue operates the voluntary scheme (which ceases in April 2000). Current regulations state that 80 per cent of eligible staff have to join it (those who abstain are excluded); 20 per cent of salary up to a maximum of £4000 (whichever is lower) is converted; this proportion of pay is tax-free; and a part of this proportion may be allocated an extra payment based upon the company's profit or withdrawn if profit is below the projected profit.

The employer usually operates the scheme for one year at a time and it does not form a term or condition of employment. The scheme is subject to alterations by the government, therefore the employer may withdraw at the end of any year; this should be made clear to employees.

## SCHEMES FOR MANUAL EMPLOYEES

The main types of pay schemes are annualised hours, day work, measured day work, graded day work, graded-level day work, piece work or premium bonus schemes, the points system and bonus schemes.

## Annualised hours

The annualised hours scheme is based on the number of working weeks in a year, multiplied by the number of weekly working hours, less holidays. Usually there are rostered and unrostered hours which are banked to give maximum flexibility. The trend in the UK is to extend the scheme to staff and service employees. The method is more common in France and Germany. Many claims of its advantages include more flexibility in matching hours of work to service needs such as seasonal demands, excessive premium payments for overtime are eliminated, there is more freedom to change daily working time patterns, and more opportunity to work fewer shifts.

## Day work

Day work is a simple, easily understood scheme where the employee is paid a standard rate, or flat hourly rate, or daily rate. Also called time work, it is suitable where standardisation of work is not possible and quality is important. The method may include a lieu bonus where employees are working near others who receive an incentive bonus. Day work is also used when it is uneconomic to introduce an incentive scheme or when output is not governed by the operator. Strong leadership is needed to compensate for the lack of incentive.

## Measured day work

In measured day work there is a flat rate as in day work, but performance is also measured and used to assess the payment of annual increments. Thus the method provides a form of competitive incentive.

## Graded day work

Graded day work bases payment upon a graded structure according to ability. The pay level is reviewed regularly and is partly subjective because merit rating is applied when degrees of skill are used as the yardstick. Alternatively, length of service may determine the increases, or output levels may be assessed over the period under review and used for appropriate increases.

## Graded-level day work

Graded-level day work uses work measurement. Payment is based upon a graded structure of proven performance levels. Advancement depends upon the employee demonstrating ability to perform at the next higher level for a probationary period. The scheme operates on mutual trust: the employee undertakes to work at a determined level and the management guarantees a wage level regardless of any change in circumstances.

## Piece work

Straight piece work is suitable for operators who need rewarding for exceptional ability. A fixed amount is paid for each unit of work produced of a set quality, payment being directly proportional to output. This sum is calculated by timing the unit of work at a reasonable speed of operation and relating it to the wage rate, plus an allowance to give the operator the opportunity to earn a bonus.

Setting rates may pose problems. The rate must be fair and should be fixed with great care because any change contemplated through an error in the original fix may disrupt good relationships. Some agreements are made not to pay less than the basic rate. Close inspection for quality is essential but close supervision is avoided as the scheme provides a strong incentive.

Regular checks for signs of overstrain are important, and the scheme must be run fairly. Clocking off the job may be necessary if delays occur. Certain rules are needed to clarify situations where additional tasks are involved that are outside the rate set. Allowances for fatigue and incidental tasks are normally built into the rate.

Other forms of piece work are simply variations such as differential piece work, which provides steps in the earnings to accommodate increased or decreased rates at certain levels. Many geared schemes may be used to make payment regressive or progressive at appropriate levels. For example, where quality falls off rapidly or if more enthusiasm is needed to reach a level where a higher bonus becomes operative.

### Premium bonus schemes
Premium bonus schemes provide a bonus when work is completed faster than the allocated

standard time. The savings are shared between the employees and the company. The three main schemes are the Halsey, Weir and Rowan systems, although there are many schemes in operation that are offshoots from these three.

A third of the saving is given to the employee under the Weir system, whereas half the saving is given under the Halsey system. The proportion of saving is variable under the Rowan system, which allows a bigger small-savings bonus than the other two. When half the time is saved, however, the Halsey and Rowan systems give the same bonus. The Rowan system also limits the increased earnings to nothing more than double.

A prerequisite of any system is the careful use of work study to determine the best way of doing the job, and to set a reasonable time for its performance (Chapters 24 and 25).

## Points system

The job is carefully evaluated on a points basis to provide a set number of minutes in which an operative working at a reasonable speed could complete the process. A point usually represents one minute, as in the Bedaux system, and an average operative is assumed to work normally at a speed of 60 points an hour. A basic rate is guaranteed and the bonus is calculated on about 75 per cent of the time saved.

## Group bonus schemes

Financial reward is based upon the combined output of the group. The effect is to bring each employee's work under the scrutiny of the rest of the group. Employees become dependent upon each other's work. Where they can help each other within the group, group spirit grows and output should improve.

Precautions are needed to ensure the group does not suffer unduly when a member is absent. Group size becomes critical and the bonus schemes should be so arranged that all groups have equal opportunities to earn more at the same differential of payment.

A degree of flexibility or allowance is essential to avoid restricting those employees who naturally work quickly. Group incentives also seem to induce a better overall standard of work compared

with individual bonus schemes. Close supervision is not essential as the group attends to slower members automatically. The system is essential where individual effort is difficult to measure, as in the case of track-laying teams.

## Profit-sharing schemes

Various profit-sharing schemes are extensions of the group bonus system. Generally they are offered to all employees who have about two years' service. The aim is to develop collective effort, although some individuals may not be able to correlate their work with the overall concern. Fair operation of the schemes, with full disclosure of figures, may improve confidence in management. However, other factors affect profits apart from employee effort.

Profit-sharing schemes are fairly common in large and small companies. The bonus is paid either entirely in tax-free shares or in taxed cash with an alternative of tax-free shares. However, the employee must leave the shares with the trustees of the scheme for three years before they can be received free of tax. The effect is a higher level of employee shareholding, which creates a dual role of investor and employee. These schemes should be distinguished from profit-related pay introduced legally in 1987, which includes loss sharing.

Justifying the profit-sharing scheme to investors involves convincing them that the percentage of profits paid to employees will raise further profits by more than this percentage as employees' productivity rises appreciably; hence higher dividends will be paid. This theory will work in practice provided management adopts a co-operative, participative approach and develops mutual trust. Profit sharing is not a remedy for incompetent management.

## Added-value schemes

Added-value schemes are based upon offering an incentive if a predetermined productivity level (based upon past efforts) is exceeded. Typical schemes are the Rucker plan and the Scanlon plan. Rucker conforms to the principle described above and the proportion of pay to added value in a set period becomes the norm against which future efforts are measured. A fund is established to hold productivity improvements, and it is paid out at set intervals. The Scanlon plan is often described as a social process where employees suggest productivity improvements and management propose a formula for sharing the gains.

## Comments

Payment by results (PBR) schemes may jeopardise the quality of work as employees focus on increasing output only. Therefore PBR could induce conflict between quality and productivity. A safer alternative is to use contingency management with emphasis on participation and quality circles (Chapter 27). In Japan, for example, emphasis on employee control has always been avoided and substituted by more modern approaches.

However, considering instrumentalism (Chapter 9), the importance of PBR should not be underestimated. Some people are prepared to accept monotony for high pay. Others with higher skills may become frustrated if their efforts are thwarted through hold-ups of materials, tools or assemblies, restrictive trade union practices and poor rate-fixing.

## SCHEMES FOR SALARIED STAFF

Salaried staff are usually paid an annual salary which is then subjected to either irregular or regular increases and fringe benefits. The amount is set by senior management generally in conjunction with the personnel department and the staff association or the union. The criteria include internal and external economic factors such as company policy on the going rates, demand and supply of specialist staff, and company profitability.

Staff who perform well naturally expect higher rewards. In some cases these rewards do not necessarily mean immediate financial gain but probably improved long-term promotion prospects. For the unambitious and the instrumentalists, the system may seem unfair. Even merit rating schemes suffer from inertia, although regular fair performance appraisals can partly overcome the difficulty. Unlike shop-floor work, if performance drops after the award, the enhanced salary is generally maintained. Hence the tendency for some individuals to work

hard, achieve permanent reward and then relax until the next opportunity. The main methods are now discussed.

### Fixed annual rate

A fixed annual rate is often set according to some form of legislative requirement. The rate is not subject to increments and is normally restricted to high-level posts.

### Annual rate

Most staff receive an annual rate, which may be subjected to regular or irregular increases such as those given below.

#### Incremental schemes
Job grades are established (Chapter 17) covering all the staffing levels. Within each grade a series of steps is listed and, provided the employee is competent, he or she may ascend the scales one step each year. Usually the scales overlap for promotion purposes. For exceptional performance, more than one step may be given.

#### Merit rating
Also described in Chapter 17, merit rating allows for extra reward based upon various levels of performance. Sometimes the concept may be applied more than once a year when appraisals are conducted.

#### Cost-of-living increases
Some companies adjust their salary scales once a year dependent upon the change in the inflation rate or in other similar economic assessments.

#### Bonus schemes
Typical bonus schemes are based upon annual profit share, commission on sales, success of special projects, or co-partnership shares in the company.

#### Overtime payments
Although arrangements vary, overtime is usually paid below a certain job grade. Sometimes a set number of hours is expected to have been worked before the person is eligible for overtime pay.

# Appointments

Supervisors should be allowed to develop employees' capabilities so that ambition and self-improvement are considered normal and a sense of opportunity is felt by everyone. Appointments should be conducted on sound scientific lines for the most efficient deployment of labour. Impartiality and fairness are essential to maintain good working relationships.

For some people promotion is clearly a strong motivator because, as a reward, it provides more power, more control, more pay, more status and the possibility of further promotion. Management saves the expense of advertising for the post, induction costs and possibly more training. Also it may be viewed favourably by employees if they consider the promotion is sound. However, a gap is created somewhere which generally must be filled. There is always the risk that the promotion is unsuccessful, and there are those who feel they should have been selected.

# Setting realistic goals

The importance of goals was stressed in the previous chapter, where the need–drive–goal cycle was explained. Setting such goals is a critical management practice. Studies by E. Locke seem to indicate that effective goal setting leads to improved performance. He emphasises that people strive to attain goals as a means of satisfying their emotions and desires. Indeed effective goals provide the directional nature of behaviour, resulting in action which may or may not achieve the goal. The consequences are feedback or reinforcement. Evidence indicates several interesting features. These features are subject to particular management styles which can override the effects.

- Employees should be encouraged to set specific, challenging but realistic goals, rather than vague unrealistic goals.
- Managers should not set unrealistic goals that are impossible to achieve. Unrealistic goals cause rejection by employees, so there is no impact on motivation; and if they are accepted, there is repeated failure resulting in severe frustration.

- Managers must ensure the proposed goals are accepted by employees.
- Employees who set themselves difficult goals seem to perform better compared with those who set easy goals.

## MANAGEMENT BY OBJECTIVES

A development of setting realistic goals was the launching in the 1970s of management by objectives (MBO). The title is misleading, since everyone normally works towards given targets and results are assessed. Management by acceptance of objectives is more accurate.

MBO is now largely disused because several major problems were encountered. The package offered by institutions was unsuitable for many companies whose culture did not coincide with the scheme. Often managers' ideas did not agree with the corporate whole; schemes were highly structured on an annual revision basis, demanding much administration; and the quantitative concept did not allow sufficiently for qualitative activities.

## PERFORMANCE MANAGEMENT SYSTEMS

Performance management systems (PMS) have similar characteristics to MBO. The aim is to organise work to produce the best possible results. Both schemes establish objectives for tasks within the job, recognise personal development and task-oriented goals, identify performance criteria, assess results periodically, and adjust accordingly. However, PMS recognises the importance of cultural features and includes:

- a statement of the organisation's aims, values and concepts
- identification of each organisational sector's objectives
- integrated schemes involving objectives and standards for managers and all staff
- quantitative and qualitative aspects of jobs
- systems designed on a tailor-made basis, not on the use of a standard package
- overall control by top management, not by a personnel specialist

Successful application depends on adherence to these principles, acceptance, flexible reviewing (not strictly annual), reducing administration to a minimum, and adapting to cultural change.

# Designing the job

The responsibilities and tasks in a job have a critical influence on an individual's motivation, satisfaction and productivity. Job design has been extensively studied, resulting in many different systems and approaches related to the problem of maximising productivity. A brief history of the main approaches is now discussed.

### SCIENTIFIC MANAGEMENT APPROACH

In 1911 F.W. Taylor published his ideas which included division of labour and task specialisation. He stressed standardisation, specialisation and work simplification. They had a strong influence on job design because efficiency can be improved in this way and their breakdown into various functions highlighted the importance of analysing tasks, matching the employee with the job, training, rewards and setting goals.

### JOB ENLARGEMENT

During the 1950s job enlargement was used to correct the adverse effects of Taylor's ideas which had been taken to the extreme, causing monotony and dissatisfaction. Enlarging the job meant increasing the variety of tasks, extending cycle times and introducing more skills.

### JOB ENRICHMENT

Herzberg introduced job enrichment in the early 1960s. Briefly it involved two categories: the motivators (factors intrinsic to the job) and hygiene factors (extrinsic to the job). The implication is that motivation will be achieved by enriching the job itself through the adjustment of achievement, recognition, the work, responsibility and professional growth.

### EMPOWERMENT

The concept of empowerment (Chapter 10) extends beyond job enrichment. The degree of authority is increased to embrace a philosophy which maintains that employees become dedicated to improving processes, eliminating waste, and fully contributing their ability and capability. This demanding change involves redesigning jobs (Chapter 17), introducing an appropriate organisational culture which coincides with empowerment (Chapters 2 and 3), and adopting a deliberative style of management (Chapter 10) that totally accepts empowerment and actively engages in fully supporting empowered employees.

### JOB ROTATION

Job rotation is self-explanatory and helps to reduce monotony and boredom. Its importance now relies on the impact of autonomous groups (Chapter 5).

### JOB ENGINEERING

Job engineering uses time and motion study combined with the person–machine interface factors. Particularly relevant is its development in autonomous groups.

### JOB CHARACTERISTICS MODEL

The job characteristics model supersedes previous theories and concentrates more on trying to achieve job satisfaction. R. Hackman and G. Oldham (1976) are mainly responsible for the model that summarises certain job characteristics which induce critical psychological states conducive to motivation. There are five job characteristics which divide into three psychological states.

#### Experienced meaningfulness

This consists of three job characteristics:

- variety of skills required to perform the job, including ability and flair
- identify with the task – being able to associate directly with the job which may be a number of operations that form a complete whole and are identifiable with the individual
- significance of the task – the degree to which the work has an impact on the next stage of work or on customer satisfaction

### Experienced responsibility

The job characteristic is associated with the degree of autonomy given to the individual. This would include authority, independence, discretion, determining procedures, checking for accuracy, and responsibilities.

### Knowledge of results

The job characteristic relies on the degree of feedback to the individual. This feedback should include detailed information on the effectiveness of performance.

### The process

The assumption is that an increase in the three psychological states causes higher performance and higher satisfaction. This is based upon the idea that internal rewards are felt when the person learns performance has demonstrated personal responsibility for achieving a task which he or she cares about. The outcome is a cyclical effect of self-generated rewards so long as the three psychological states that reinforce behaviour exist. When one disappears the process stops. In other words, the process continues until the internal rewards lose their attractiveness.

Unfortunately, an employee's perception of job content may not coincide with the actual job content, therefore changes are often needed to achieve the desired outcome. Also organisational design will affect outcomes. If mechanistic, employees may have low growth needs, indicating easy, routine jobs are desirable; organic designs indicate higher growth needs and job enrichment approaches.

The model is illustrated in Fig. 12.2. Certain individual differences are described below. The model is generally valid and serves as a useful guide for redesigning jobs and matching people with jobs.

### Individual differences

The process is influenced by the characteristics and qualities of individuals. These differences will determine the strength of the basic job characteristics leading to the three psychological states, and the extent to which these states will lead to high motivation. There are three characteristics of individuals which moderate the process:

- a person's strength of need for growth
- the level of knowledge and skills
- the personal effects of context factors

**Growth need strength**

Growth need strength relates to a person's needs such as self-fulfilment, self-respect and success. These growth needs were described in the previous chapter. If they are strong there should be a higher response to a job with high job characteristics and higher motivation. Similarly, the three critical psychological states are more likely to be experienced, compared with a person with lower growth needs.

**Knowledge and skills**

If a person possesses a high level of job-relevant knowledge and skills and is placed in a job with high characteristics, this combination should generate higher motivation. However, if a person lacks essential knowledge and skills, the outcome will be poor motivation and low satisfaction because of inability to generate the psychological states.

**Job context factors**

If important context factors such as pay, supervision, working conditions and fringe benefits do not meet expectations, motivation will be lessened in an enriched job. Therefore it is essential to offer a reasonable deal to generate high motivation and avoid dissatisfaction.

### Sociotechnical design

Sociotechnical design emphasises the need to change the overall climate of work in the organisation by establishing groups that successfully fit into the technological system and the social system. Such redesign should achieve a better quality of working life (QWL) and form more competent autonomous groups. This complex process includes joint decision making, strong collaboration, and mutual respect between groups and managers. Clearly the job characteristics model is absorbed into this approach, along with the concepts of autonomy (Chapter 5 and 10).

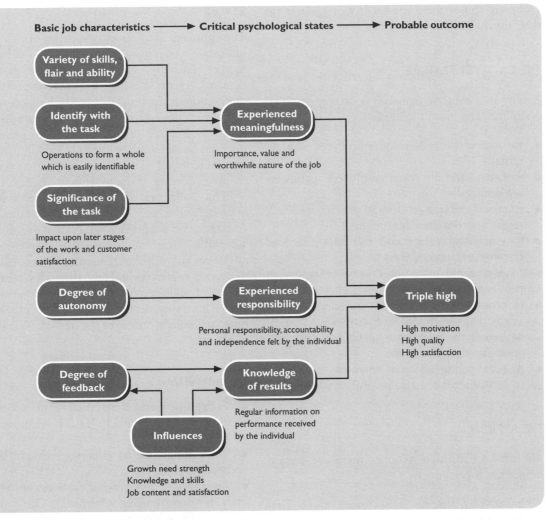

**Basic job characteristics** ⟶ **Critical psychological states** ⟶ **Probable outcome**

Variety of skills, flair and ability

Identify with the task

Operations to form a whole which is easily identifiable

Significance of the task

Impact upon later stages of the work and customer satisfaction

Experienced meaningfulness

Importance, value and worthwhile nature of the job

Degree of autonomy

Experienced responsibility

Personal responsibility, accountability and independence felt by the individual

Triple high

High motivation
High quality
High satisfaction

Degree of feedback

Knowledge of results

Regular information on performance received by the individual

Influences

Growth need strength
Knowledge and skills
Job content and satisfaction

**Figure 12.2** The effects of basic job characteristics
This diagram is based on the Hackman and Oldham (1976) model. Basic job characteristics affect three critical psychological states which determine probable outcomes; these three states are subject to three influences or moderators.

# Coaching

Coaching is an important feature for motivating and developing a group. Coaching is essential for autonomous teams (Chapter 19) who need a collaborative approach and a catalyst to help in improving competence. The significance of coaching is discussed by examining the tasks of the coach, which are usually the supervisor's new role; the catalyst feature, meaning an action that facilitates change; the approach; and the advantages. The development aspect is covered in Chapter 19.

## THE COACH

The coach is usually described as a facilitator who uses a specialised approach to develop and motivate a group. Often the supervisor will adopt this role after appropriate training. He or she should already be trained in the techniques and technologies applied by the group, possess interpersonal and conceptual skills and have appropriate leadership qualities. However, the vital point is that the traditional supervisor–subordinate relationship is dropped and replaced with a technique where the group recognises there is a facility or catalyst for their use, as and when they feel the need.

## THE CATALYST FEATURE

Acting as a catalyst demands a strong personal discipline. The usual functions are:

- to observe situations and employees' characteristics
- to listen carefully when employees' problems are outlined
- to review training results and provide feedback to the appropriate departments
- to emphasise values and the importance of training and experience
- to assess rapid and accurate ways of improving productivity
- to prompt and ask relevant questions in such a way that the employee discovers for himself or herself the answers to problems and situations needing decisions
- to avoid giving advice or answers
- to be open-minded and helpful at all times

## THE APPROACH

The use of a catalyst assumes there are certain fundamental principles:

- Improved dialogue releases more information to management.
- Comprehensive feedback on performance provides a measurement of training effectiveness and is an essential psychological feature for the employee.
- Focusing on employee interests, attributes and aspirations indicates probable responses to certain motivators.
- Encouraging personal responsibility and commitment is productive and emphasises important values.
- Fostering an employee-centred culture improves relationships and is a prelude to high productivity.
- An awareness of the importance and worthwhile nature of the job improves personal responsibilities.

## STYLES

The approach involves an emergence of two styles: indicative and consultative. The indicative style applies naturally where situations or problems demand urgent attention, but there is insufficient motivation, some resistance, or lack of knowledge and experience to cope. Parts of the approach are abandoned while others are used to emphasise urgency. Subtle ways of injecting vital information and overcoming resistance are needed to overcome the inadequacies of the individual or group.

The collaborative style uses the standard approach which applies where development, encouragement, confidence and mutual decisions are acceptable. Sometimes injections of information and advice on appropriate techniques become essential to develop employees and raise their self-esteem. The choice of style may depend upon circumstances where an assessment is based upon complexity, time available, a review of the outcomes, and time to adjust.

## THE ADVANTAGES

- Each group member may discover in time certain lessons and continue to learn from subsequent experience.
- Ways of building on employee strengths should become clearer.
- Appropriate discussions on weaknesses will help to encourage confidence.
- There is an improvement in recognition of attributes, aspirations and commitment.
- Existing skills and capabilities may be cultivated.
- An employee-centred culture is developed; this takes into account the national and organisational cultures, and it lowers frustration.

# Mentoring

Usually informal, mentoring is a way to offer help and guidance for personal growth and career development. A mentor is independent within the organisation, whereas a coach has a direct authority relationship with the individual. With mentoring it is possible to create a better rapport and a non-threatening atmosphere.

To fulfil this role is a demanding task where the ability to create the right approach is similar to counselling. There should be respect for the individual, job-related experience and skills, the ability to recognise and develop potential, human relations skills, and sufficient insight into the various problems confronting the employee.

Mentoring may be worthwhile providing the employee is co-operative and the organisational culture is suitable for such a programme. The scheme is likely to fail without sufficient sensitivity and sincerity within the organisation, and a mentor with expertise.

# Job satisfaction

The two main features of job satisfaction are job design and matching the individual with the job. The job includes all the intrinsic and extrinsic factors; matching includes all the characteristics of the individual. A general definition of job satisfaction is a perception of the job by the job holder, who determines a level of satisfaction based upon physiological and psychological needs. Put another way, it is a self-determined assessment of all the factors in the job that may please or displease, which are then aggregated to give a level of satisfaction. Clearly the subject is expansive and personal to each individual.

### MEASURING JOB SATISFACTION

An attitude survey is usually conducted where employees are asked to give opinions. This may be conducted in many different ways and include the use of specialists. Where displeasure in particular areas is felt by many employees, management may then take remedial action, concentrating on individual problems. A typical example is where a job does not match with the individual and attempts are made to redesign it so the person's characteristics are used more effectively. Other examples cover activities which may have been neglected and can be resurrected.

### SIGNS OF JOB DISSATISFACTION

There are many symptoms that could indicate job dissatisfaction. They include general discontentment,

low productivity, low morale, poor health, high labour turnover, absenteeism, extended breaks, poor timekeeping, and un-cooperativeness. Unfortunately, there are many other remote factors that may cause these symptoms. So unless personnel counselling clarifies the situation, there is no clear evidence upon which to base remedial action. Research on this subject has resulted in diverse reports.

### THE HUMAN FACTOR

The effects of experiencing different job satisfaction levels seem to vary from individual to individual. The main areas of thought are worth mentioning, but they lack clarity, and are sometimes conflicting and difficult to reconcile:

- Improved job satisfaction increases happiness and contentment but not necessarily productivity.
- Motivators will often improve productivity and job satisfaction.
- Elements such as the resources provided, financial rewards, relations with co-workers, and comfort may improve job satisfaction but not necessarily productivity.
- Improved productivity usually implies higher rewards, and together they should improve job satisfaction.
- Improved job satisfaction usually leads to higher morale, which should make the application of motivators easier and more likely to succeed.
- Improved job satisfaction may improve mental and physical health.

# Suggestion schemes

Many employees are already aware of better ways of doing their jobs. Others are capable of thinking about the problems and coming up with ideas that would save money for the company. A well-organised suggestion scheme, combined with good relationships, provides one way of encouraging employees to propose their ideas.

Everyone gains under a fair suggestion scheme. Relationships are improved, an excellent outlet for participation is provided, and employees are able to identify themselves more closely with the company. Even generally inactive employees are known to have submitted excellent ideas as the impetus to participate improves. The element of competition and the chance to be recognised incite people into action.

## LEGAL ASPECTS

To clarify the legal position, suggestion scheme rules should include a statement of how the employer and employees may use and disclose the suggestions. The suggestion scheme constitutes a contract, so the employer has legal obligations of confidentiality towards the ideas disclosed by its employees. This is an important feature of patent rights. Consider what happens when an employee's job does not include making inventions; what happens if a patent application is submitted by the company; and what happens when information is disclosed by the company to a third party if the idea has been rejected.

## LAUNCHING A SUGGESTION SCHEME

- *Publicity*: A full-scale campaign is essential if the information is to reach everybody. Posters should be prominently displayed and supported by letters to employees. Supervisors should be carefully briefed to give any additional information that may be required.
- *Boxes*: Suggestion boxes should be placed in well-chosen positions and accompanied by a supply of forms. The conditions of the scheme should be clearly stated on the form and indicate where the signature is required.
- *The supervisor's position*: The supervisor should thoroughly understand the philosophy, the importance of enthusiasm and the operation of the scheme. Fundamental requirements are encouraging the concept of generating employee contributions, recognising that ideas do not cast any doubts on the supervisor's capability, and ensuring the scheme is operated fairly to all employees' satisfaction.

## OPERATING THE SCHEME

A manager should be given the responsibility for operating the scheme. Finer details of the system will depend upon circumstances, but the essential points are that collections should be made regularly, they should be recorded, and acknowledgements should be sent out promptly. If privacy is requested, notification could be mailed to the employee's home address.

An efficient recording system is necessary to avoid errors. Each form should be numbered and a file raised to accommodate the correspondence and findings. A sorting scheme is essential to cover all the likely areas of suggestions. Each area should be represented by an executive who studies and investigates fully the proposals before recommending a course of action. Possibly a committee should finally approve or reject the suggestions and give appropriate rewards.

A rejection needs a carefully prepared and adequate explanation. On occasions a similar idea may already be in hand; in these circumstances proof is needed to show the employee that he or she was not the first to think of the proposal. Keeping careful records solves this problem.

The amount of an award varies from about 10 to 50 per cent of the savings for a year. Suitable publicity of awards should be given. Additional benefits such as a free holiday, attending special functions or theatre visits could be given periodically to all award winners.

A successful scheme demands time, expense and additional managerial effort. The gains are mainly twofold: financial economies and higher motivation of employees. There is a tendency for the scheme to lose impetus unless managers and supervisors continually show enthusiasm and full support. The main reasons why some schemes fail are:

- long delays in administering the system
- poor rewards
- inadequate reasons for rejecting proposals
- poor supervisory support
- suitable relationships were not established before commencement

## CONTROLLING THE SCHEME

Periodic comparisons of the number of submissions and acceptances give an indication of whether the scheme is proving successful. For this purpose, the following formulae may be used:

$$\frac{\text{Total suggestions submitted}}{\text{Average number of employees}} \times 100 = \begin{array}{l}\text{Submission} \\ \text{rate per 100} \\ \text{employees}\end{array}$$

$$\frac{\text{Total accepted suggestions}}{\text{Average number of employees}} \times 100 = \begin{array}{l}\text{Acceptance} \\ \text{rate per 100} \\ \text{employees}\end{array}$$

# Employee participation

In recent years there has been an upsurge of interest in various ways of involving employees in their work and work organisation. The participation concept admits employees are not just pairs of hands, they have a considerable amount to contribute, their needs have to be considered, and their wishes and expectations are important factors in determining the success of changes. This broad concept has been interpreted in many different ways, ranging from consultation, quality circles, autonomous groups, motivation theories, leadership style and consultative bodies through to employee control in industrial democracy.

## THE PHILOSOPHY

The achievement principle is widely accepted in society. It means people feel the distribution of rewards is fair because they believe these rewards are related to what is actually achieved at work or to the qualifications obtained to enable them to do the work. Thus the philosophy of participation is strongly imprinted in people's minds and may conform to any of the three basic approaches outlined in Chapter 2: unitary, pluralistic and radical. These approaches clarify industrial relations issues by stressing particular aspects of work conflict or organisational relationships. For details see the sections on constitutional management, democratic management and contingency management in Chapter 2.

## APPROACHES TO PARTICIPATION

Approaches to participation coincide with the three ideologies mentioned above, which are essentially rival frames of reference that attempt to explain work relations.

### Unitary

Work is reorganised within a unitary philosophy by consolidating consultation, job enrichment and quality circles. Thus the scope of work is increased to satisfy employee needs and to improve the company's efficiency in the national interest.

### Pluralistic

Pluralistic approaches establish structures and operating techniques in a situation where unions are sufficiently powerful to oppose management on equal terms. Thus management is willing to compromise in the interests of harmony and unity. Participative leadership, works councils and Whitley Councils (Chapter 20) are included in this philosophy.

### Radical

A joint approach is adopted through various models such as board representation for policy making, worker control, self-management and worker co-operatives. The radical philosophy applies where major inequalities and imbalances of power are accepted by management. The trend may be gradual or revolutionary. The Bullock Report (Chapter 20) explains the position in the UK regarding opinion and legislation.

## CONCLUSIONS

Considerable publicity has been given to successful schemes. In Japan the use of quality circles has proved to be worthwhile. Throughout the European Union, employee participation is a reality in terms of political, legal and social aspects. Sharing in the capital and profits is often a result of collective agreements, and in France it is a legal obligation. The scope of collective agreements is increasing and includes economic policies of companies and the organisation of their industrial and commercial affairs. Co-determination in Germany is well known.

There seems to be a danger that the characteristics of the situation, sociocultural and sociotechnical, may be incorrectly assessed when participation schemes are introduced, resulting in their failure. Such inaccurate assessment does not mean the concept itself is wrong. Similarly, problems are caused by lack of adequate preparation before introducing the scheme and by insufficient attention to education and training programmes.

## QUESTIONS

1 Explain the behaviourist approach and comment on its degree of realism compared with motivation theories.

2 Outline the types of reinforcement and their effects on performance.

3 Explain and give your opinion on the principle that forms the basis of positive reinforcement.

4 Discuss the difference between negative reinforcement and punishment.

5 Explain primary and secondary reinforcement.

6 Employees are just pairs of hands with little to contribute. If you were given this opinion by a supervisor colleague, how would you react?

7 My job's boring. If you must know, I come here for the money and because it's difficult to find work elsewhere.

If your best worker confronted you with this statement, what would you do?

8 Discuss financial incentives fully and give your personal opinion of their effectiveness.

9 How would you organise a suggestion scheme?

10 Do you think a suggestion scheme is worthwhile? Explain your viewpoint thoroughly.

11 Discuss the importance of setting realistic goals.

12 How would you include empowerment if you were asked to design a job?

13 What are the main job characteristics?

14 Explain the principle of coaching and its relationships with autonomous workgroups.

15 Outline an approach to coaching.

16 Explain the difference between mentoring and coaching.

17 Outline the effects of basic job characteristics.

18 Discuss the two styles of coaching.

19 What are the signs of job dissatisfaction?

20 Explain the philosophy of employee participation.

21 Discuss the approaches to employee participation.

Cynthia is relating to her friend the situation at her office. 'This girl Daphne actually sits there most of the day knitting and on senior secretary's pay. Her boss is nearing retirement *and* he says that so long as she gets his work done that's all he cares about. We're working flat out to keep up, but she never offers to help. In fact she said to Mandy, who was overloaded, "More fool you. Find a slack boss like mine and you're home and dry".'

Cynthia continues. 'My boss doesn't open her mouth. I take in the work, she signs it, hands me another tape and reaches for the phone. I started to complain about the office, but as soon as I mentioned Daphne she cut in, "Later, not now, I'm busy. You're already behind with that tape".'

Angela says that she gets the same treatment from her boss. She says she never gets a word of thanks. When she mentioned Daphne he scowled and told her it was none of her business and not to mix work with petty politics. She's heard on the grapevine that Daphne is related to the company secretary and she's been seen out with her boss.

Cynthia concludes, 'We feel we get punished for working hard while she's protected for doing nothing. It's unbelievable what goes on'.

*Analyse this case with specific reference to the behaviourist approach. What further evidence would you need before arriving at any conclusion? What could the secretaries do in this situation?*

Abraham Smithson, a managing director, spends Saturday afternoons on the golf course. During a round his golf partner, a company director, explains about the works council he has established recently. 'It keeps the employees quiet because they think they have a say but really it's the same old thing as the joint consultative committees we used to hold years ago.' He continues, 'We simply apply delaying tactics if we don't like the recommendations and, after a few meetings, they've forgotten what they proposed anyway. Gives them a chance to let off steam, you might say'.

'It sounds good', Abraham replies. 'Of course I've read all about participation and the Bullock Report but we don't need it. I rely on my production manager who holds meetings with the supervisors and they sort out all the difficulties. It's just another management gimmick that will be out of fashion in a couple of years.'

'It works well in Germany and Japan and, after all, they're our major competitors', a third partner cuts in.

'Maybe, but they're not British!' Abraham snarls. 'Their unions co-operate and they don't understand attitudes like "I'm all right Jack". You can't escape the fact that it's them and us over here and you've got to make the best of a bad job! Participation won't solve anything!'

*Comment on the attitudes displayed by the directors and relate your main points to the philosophy of participation.*

# 13

# Developing leadership, power and influence

## Introduction

Leadership, power and influence have a strong effect on the workforce and the organisation. They may be similar in some ways but not in others. An understanding of their differences and similarities is an important aspect of supervision. Indeed an accomplished supervisor uses all three techniques. However, they involve considerable knowledge and the use of many skills which are now outlined.

### LEADERSHIP

The controversial topics of leadership and power have been subjected to many specialists' opinions, considerable research and conflicting reports. Such intensive interest is obvious considering well-known leaders of countries and companies. Their reputations have ranged from patriots or moralists to tyrants or barbarians; and from strong to weak characters.

Few people have escaped the influence of leaders, and many employees have endured petty tyrants with low intellect and excessive greed. History is crammed with individuals who have been allegedly responsible for rapid economic growth, disaster, conquests, defeats, holocausts and revolutions. They often use 'devices' to stir up support such as religious creeds, religious cults and political creeds. Sometimes they manage to create mass hysteria, confused thinking, extreme aggressiveness and passiveness. They will even use disputed theories to gain power, typically evolution, to impress a nation that it has evolved into a master race.

New types of leader have appeared at senior and supervisory levels since about 1975. Certainly leadership remains one of the main factors determining group behaviour and there is a strong demand for leaders of quality. Unfortunately, exceptional leaders are rare and often unpredictable. At supervisory level the individual must be able to influence employees' actions and assess their needs. Indeed new leadership roles emerge when autonomous groups are introduced (Chapter 1). Figure 13.1 illustrates the main features that link leadership behaviour, leadership effectiveness, the objectives, power and influence.

To cope with these roles, the supervisor should possess sufficient knowledge of leadership, apply leadership skills and develop appropriate power. These features are divided into four parts for discussion before considering their positive influence in detail:

- leaders
- leadership
- developing leadership skills
- developing power

When leadership is correctly applied, employees actually enjoy feeling a strong commitment towards achieving organisational goals and perceive their own needs will be satisfied.

## Leaders

Certain characteristics distinguish leaders from followers and ineffective leaders from effective leaders. Unfortunately, these characteristics are often difficult to classify because leaders are

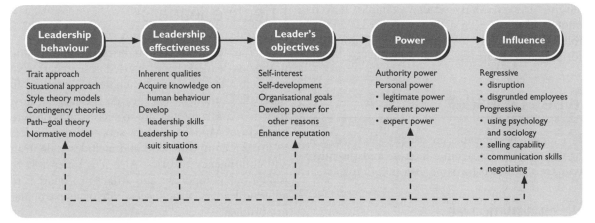

**Figure 13.1** Leadership, power and influence
Feedback (- - -) between all the features is a determining factor in the supervisor's effectiveness in adapting to changing situations.

affected by their followers, conditions and situations. One leader may be successful in one set of circumstances but not in others. Furthermore, some leaders are able to adjust easily to change and remain competent, whereas others fail to adapt and become ineffective. In these circumstances many definitions of a leader have been attempted and many theories propounded. The main features involved are definitions, views on leaders, types of leaders, and effective leaders – their influential capability and the influences exerted on them.

## DEFINITIONS OF A LEADER

Simple definitions are:

- capability to energise a group
- ability to mix correctly various skills which produce a driving force
- making people feel responsible
- inducing a dynamic common purpose to magnify the wills of employees, to inspire enthusiasm and to influence positively individual behaviour

Advanced definitions are:

- by engaging in a dynamic activity within a group, one person manages to influence all the other members voluntarily to contribute towards achieving established tasks and goals in a unique situation

- an outstanding member of a group who has the capability to create conditions within which all members feel a strong commitment towards achieving accepted objectives in a given environment

## VIEWS ON LEADERS

Specialists' views on leaders often depend upon their selection from a number of questions such as:

- Do leaders create followers? If so why?
- Do followers create leaders? If so why?
- Are leaders born or made?
- Why do leaders vary so much in character and still manage to be leaders?
- Why does the leader's power always seem to corrupt?
- Are there ideal characteristics in an effective leader?
- How do apparently weak leaders manage to survive?
- How does the situation affect leadership?

These questions receive diverse answers because appropriate leaders are selected to suit the proposed theory. Robert Maxwell managed to create followers and behave in a corrupt way regardless of staff empowered with high authority and responsibilities. Various leaders in British Airways were allowed to conduct dubious campaigns against

Virgin Airways. Many similar examples may be quoted. There is even a theory that a leader and followers is simply a natural phenomenon conforming to various laws of atomic physics.

# Types of leader

Five main types of leader are usually identified. The first three are of academic interest and the other two are significant for supervision.

### THE CHARISMATIC TYPE

Personality traits enable this well-known type to excel easily. Churchill, Kennedy and Hitler are in this category.

### THE TRADITIONAL TYPES

A traditional leader's position is conferred by birth, typically kings and queens. Obviously the class is severely restricted and many are doubtful leaders from the managerial viewpoint.

### THE SITUATIONAL TYPE

The situational leader is limited to circumstances where they can exert considerable influence due to their unique knowledge and experience. Obviously such leadership is only temporary since situations are subject to change.

### THE APPOINTED TYPE

Most managers and supervisors are appointed; this is because their influence is exerted from the position of authority they hold in the organisation. Some confusion will arise when they expect to exert power purely by virtue of their appointment and fail to see the differences between power, authority and leadership.

### THE FUNCTIONAL TYPE

Functional leaders practise modern contingency theory, which concentrates on what a leader *does* and discounts what he or she *is*.

# Effective leaders

Over the centuries the qualities of famous and notorious leaders have puzzled researchers. No acceptable list of traits, or whatever, seems to fit them all. Certainly what they do is clear, but how they do it and why they are so successful is open to conjecture. Modern thought sees effective leaders as using a composite skill and includes style, trait and contingency theories. Also it is unfeasible to isolate one component and attempt to relate it to all good leaders, their success rate or its particular importance.

### THE MAIN FACTORS

One approach is to agree the main factors, diagnose their implications, examine the leader's influential capability, and discover the influences exerted on the leader. The main factors are:

- A capability to inspire people. This means being able to infuse thought or feeling into people, to animate or create a feeling that influences positive responses to the leader's desires.
- To cope and adjust to the many influences exerted on the leader. This factor implies that the leader must behave towards individuals in accordance with these influences. In other words, many influences determine what a leader does and how he or she behaves.
- To take appropriate action to improve employees' behaviour dependent on circumstances.
- To be sufficiently sensitive towards individuals' differing motives and the situation in which they find themselves.

### THE IMPLICATIONS

The implications are often considered to be:

- Leaders are born with certain advantageous qualities.
- Leaders have the good sense to acquire knowledge on human behaviour and possess sufficient ability to develop appropriate leadership skills.

A leader's behaviour alone does not highly correlate with effectiveness; other factors play important parts. Consider two leaders placed in an identical situation. They may behave similarly, take the same steps, but achieve different results.

An effective leader finds the right balance between concern for people and concern for production. This means the supervisor is responsible for the work actually done by employees, who should receive sufficient attention to their development. Achieving this balance might persuade a supervisor to think less about himself or herself and more about employees.

# The leader's influential capability

The capability to influence followers is governed by the leader's characteristics, personal style, and status or position in the organisation. Together they determine the subordinate's responses to the leader's wishes. The major influences include the following aspects:

- *Personal characteristics*: charisma, assertiveness, self-confidence, and various favourable traits which cause subordinates to admire and identify with a leader.
- *Personal knowledge and experience*: competence through educational background, achievements and experience in industry and commerce.
- *Personal style*: the leader's behaviour towards followers, including a philosophical outlook acceptable to followers.
- *Rights*: rights to offer non-financial rewards, financial rewards, promotions and transfers.
- *Capability*: capability to punish or coerce subordinates.
- *Authority*: authority to change policies, rules and procedures.

# Influences exerted on the leader

Here are some of the many diverse influences exerted on a leader which may determine his or her behaviour and success. Invariably effectiveness depends upon some factors which are outside the control of the leader; therefore the element of luck is always present and must be accepted.

## SUBORDINATES' CHARACTERISTICS

Subordinates' characteristics are extremely varied as indicated in Chapter 9. They include traits, the distribution of human differences, temperament, class, status, educational level, conflicting viewpoints and general outlook. All influence the leader and affect his or her level of understanding. Furthermore, there is a noticeable tendency for the leader to behave differently towards people of differing backgrounds, males and females, young and old, and people with attractive and unattractive profiles.

## SUBORDINATES' PERFORMANCE LEVELS

Responses from subordinates obviously have an impact on the leader and determine his or her reactions to them. This action–reaction cycle includes the level of understanding, accuracy of feedback, and eventual termination of a cycle. Studies have shown that the performance of subordinates has more impact on the leader than the leader's behaviour has on subordinates' performance. Furthermore, as may be expected, competent subordinates tended to be related to less directive leaders, whereas incompetent subordinates tended to be closely supervised.

## PEERS

Inevitably there are pressures from peers who expect the leader to behave in a similar manner to themselves. Usually this established leadership pattern does not agree with the individual leader's ideas, but the strength of relationships with peers often overrides and creates conformity.

## SUPERIORS

The leader tends to treat subordinates based upon his or her superior's style. The superior usually acts as a role model which is accepted as an appropriate form of conduct to be adopted by the leader.

Therefore the leader may feel safer to conform and not offend the superior by deviating from the norm.

## THE ORGANISATION

The design of the organisation, corporate policy and human resources policy will naturally influence the leader's behaviour. Indeed the particular organisational approach (Chapter 3) will characterise the leader's style. Although this may not agree with the leader's own opinion, the behavioural pattern is dominated by factors such as the power of senior executives, promotion prospects and security.

## TASK SPECIALISATION

The functional aspects of subordinates' jobs influence the leader, who should conform to the overall requirements of the group. Typical examples are the relatively high flexibility allowed in a research laboratory where specialists work mainly on their own; and the relatively low flexibility in a production section composed of operators conforming to routine tasks.

# Leadership

According to P. Drucker, leadership is innate and cannot be taught or promoted. However, leadership is a subject for speculation. The art or practice of leadership has been extensively studied and has produced some conclusions but many different definitions. Undoubtedly there are diverse influences, considering the range of influential leadership capabilities and the extensive influences exerted on a leader. Contrary to the shallow thought that leadership is a one-way process, there is an interacting process or mutual influence which amounts to a complex two-way process between the leader and followers. This conclusion has been validated by many practical studies and it avoids any oversimplification of leadership as a subject.

The implication is that supervisors should recognise the ways their subordinates' behaviour is influencing them and be conscious of the situation where subordinates are influencing their leadership style. Similarly, the supervisor's superior should realise that the supervisor's behaviour is partly determined by his or her subordinates' characteristics.

A further implication is the importance of developing an employee-oriented style which should increase employee satisfaction and cause favourable responses towards this style, thus reinforcing a positive interaction.

## SOME DEFINITIONS OF LEADERSHIP

- A power relationship exists where subordinates accept or perceive that an individual has the right to prescribe their behaviour, but they have the right to respond.
- An interpersonal influence exercised by an individual and subordinates which is directed towards achieving specific objectives through a two-way communication process.
- The leader's behaviour towards subordinates and their subsequent responses in terms of performance and criticisms in a shared responsibility to achieve a desired objective.
- An interacting process where one person provides information in such a way that another person becomes convinced that the expectations will be beneficial if he or she behaves in the manner suggested and signifies acceptance through a change in performance.

## LEADERSHIP TRENDS

Many attempts to clarify modern leadership have caused conflicting viewpoints to emerge which create diverse styles and tend to justify a general opinion that very little is known about the subject. The emerging leadership problems are associated with the following modern organisational features:

- Rapidly changing technologies (Chapter 6) to achieve higher quality standards. These insist on leaders specialising more in reorganising, communicating changes, and coaching.
- Emphasis on highly trained employees (Chapters 17 and 19) to cope with new

technologies and advancing technologies. This workforce must be supported by updating training schemes, continuous training and effective coaching. This implies keeping in close touch with employees, listening and helping the thought processes.

- Empowering employees (Chapter 5) to take more responsibility and achieve a balanced outlook. This reduces tight control and involves the leader in supporting and encouraging employees.
- Delayering the organisation (Chapter 3) which dispenses with many middle managers and increases the importance of supervisors who are able to exert more influence on the remaining senior leaders as well as leading their own followers.
- The introduction of collaborative management (Chapter 2) has emphasised supervisory role changes involving the concepts of leadership. The emphasis on interpersonal and conceptual skills and the development of an employee-centred culture have concentrated on stimulating employee help and involvement. These factors have created a new type of leadership.

# Major theories of leadership

Six main theories of leadership have emerged over the past fifty years:

- *The trait approach* uses personal qualities to ensure success.
- *The situational approach* holds that a particular type of leader satisfies the immediate perceptions of people.
- *Style theories* concentrate on the behaviour and philosophical outlook of a leader towards employees.
- *Contingency theories* emphasise adaptive leadership behaviour, which varies depending on the situation.
- *Path–goal theory* incorporates expectancy motivation theory and use of power.
- A *normative model* attempts to illustrate how a leader should act in a number of given situations.

# The trait approach

Up to about 1950 most studies had tried to identify leadership traits, probably because in early times great leaders seemed to possess exceptional physical, mental and personality characteristics. These were perhaps essential to survive in battle and to dominate relatively simple communities. In these circumstances the assumption is that leaders are born not made, but research has indicated that heredity and early childhood experiences are very important.

Researchers' findings tend to disagree on which set of traits or qualities distinguish leaders from followers. Nevertheless, research has indicated a significant correlation between certain factors and effective leadership. Typical examples are:

- *Traits*: aggressiveness, assertiveness, dominance, integrity, independence, creativity, adaptability, confidence, emotional balance
- *Social qualities*: co-operative, tactful, popular, socio-economic status, interpersonal skills, participative
- *Abilities*: intelligence, conscientiousness, judgement, decisions, general and technical knowledge, fluency of speech

Other closely associated factors often mentioned are supervisory ability, initiative, self-assurance, broad social interests, maturity, respect for others, and an interest in people.

Although all leadership situations indicate certain common personal characteristics, it became clear that other aspects also influence leadership effectiveness. Nevertheless, personal traits and skills cannot be ignored.

# The situational approach

Notorious leaders like Hitler and Mussolini led researchers to conclude that such people came to power because there was a peculiar situation which demanded a particular type of leader. Thus, the belief arose that leaders are the product of a given situation. Castro and Roosevelt are good examples since they diagnosed the people's perceptions correctly and began programmes which appealed to them.

# Style theories

Style theories concentrate on the behaviour and philosophical outlook of leaders towards employees. To appreciate the thrust of these theories, four basic styles are now explained:

- The dictatorial leader uses the philosophy of fear.
- The autocratic leader directs and expects compliance; this type is forceful, positive and dogmatic, and exerts power by giving or stopping rewards and punishments.
- The democratic leader consults, encourages participation and uses power *with* rather than power *over* employees.
- The *laissez-faire* leader allows a high amount of independence; employees set their own objectives and decide how to achieve them.

The use of authority defines these styles, together with a philosophy variance ranging from fear, single authority and decentralised authority through to complete freedom from authority.

# Style theory models

Many models have been submitted by writers and institutes, based upon particular research findings; they fit into three groups. Their complexity demands considerable reading (see the bibliography), but a brief survey is now given.

## AUTHORITARIAN VERSUS DEMOCRATIC STYLES

McGregor's work on this concept is the foundation for many motivation theories. His Theory X and Theory Y (Chapter 11) clearly demonstrate the two opposing assumptions about behaviour and the supervisory stance adopted.

Likert's work in 1961 classified styles into four groups. They are based upon certain characteristics of the company: the degree of freedom employees feel about communicating with managers, and the amount of confidence and trust they feel the managers have in them. The groups (ratings) are:

- System 1 – exploitive authoritarian leadership
- System 2 – benevolent authoritarian leadership
- System 3 – consultative leadership
- System 4 – participative leadership, based upon teamwork or participation which demands confidence and trust

Research findings indicated a strong connection between System 4 and sustained high productivity. Likert stresses the application of three principles:

- Full use of the concepts and techniques of motivation.
- Development of a tightly knit organisation of workgroups committed to achieving organisational objectives. The groups should be interlinked by means of employees who possess overlapping membership in two groups.
- Establishment of high aims for managers and employees. The goals they are expected to achieve should be clarified with them.

Finally, Tannenbaum and Schmidt provided an example of a continuum of leadership behaviour (Fig. 13.2). Underlying these styles is the thrust to adopt a democratic style. The range of styles varies from authoritarian to autonomy.

## PERSONAL RELATIONSHIP VERSUS TASK ACCOMPLISHMENT

Concern for people as well as production is the theme of this model. Various grids and frameworks are constructed to indicate where a supervisor fits in relation to his or her bias towards group members and tasks. The four studies of interest are now discussed.

The Michigan Studies (1950) indicated that supervisors of highly productive sections were significantly more likely to be employee-oriented, whereas supervisors of less productive sections were production-oriented.

The Ohio Studies (1950s) indicated there were two distinct behaviour groups: consideration (relationship-oriented or consideration for people) and initiating structure (concerned with communication channels, allocating tasks and organising work processes). They were thought to be entirely separate dimensions.

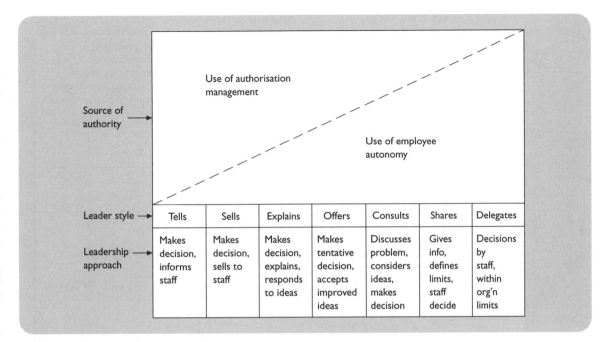

**Figure 13.2** Continuum of leadership behaviour
The range of styles is expanded by Tannenbaum and Schmidt into a continuum of behaviour. Underlying these styles is the thrust to adopt a democratic style and to emphasise the importance of a leader's behaviour.
(Adapted from Tannenbaum and Schmidt, 1957, *Harvard Business Review* Mar/Apr, p. 96)

The Michigan and Ohio Studies were used as a basis for the Managerial Grid and 3D Theory which are now explained.

### The managerial grid

This grid by Blake and Mouton (see the bibliography) is probably the most popular way of identifying leadership styles. The concept is that every manager has a deep-seated idea of how to manage, how to work with people, and how to integrate people and production. These thoughts may be clarified so that a better understanding of style is adopted by using the managerial grid. However, textbook learning is insufficient. Seminars are essential before the benefits are appreciated.

**Using the grid**

The grid is a framework on which styles of behaviour may be plotted (Fig. 13.3). A manager has to think about two factors: concern for the work (production) and concern for those who are doing the work (people). Usually there is more thought given to one factor compared with the other. These factors are plotted by using the horizontal axis – degree of concern for work – running from 1 (low) to 9 (high); and the vertical axis – concern for people – running from 1 (low) to 9 (high).

The resultant square indicates the degree of influence these factors exert. However, there may be two or more theories operating: one is dominant but when a manager is under pressure the style may shift to suit the circumstances. Appropriate training should improve teamwork. An indication of style is usually given as 1.1 inept; 9.9 team builder; 5.5 middle of the road; 1.9 country club; and 9.1 task.

### The 3D theory

The managerial grid only relates to two dimensions: concern for people and concern for production. W. Reddin introduced a third dimension – the situational impact on basic style. Consequently, more effective and less effective styles of leadership apply in practice. The original two dimensions

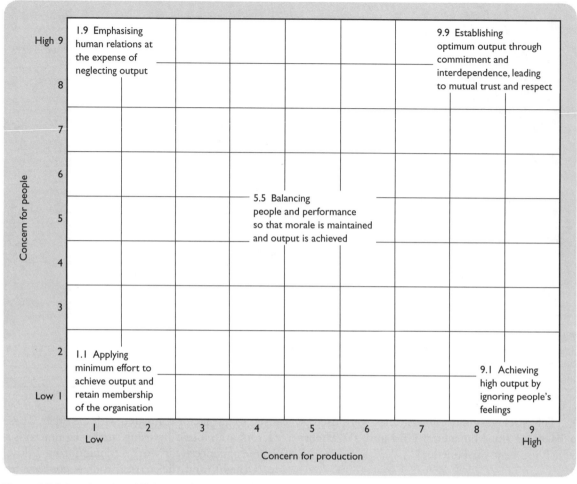

The grid area contains the following labels:

**High 9** — 1.9 Emphasising human relations at the expense of neglecting output

9.9 Establishing optimum output through commitment and interdependence, leading to mutual trust and respect

5.5 Balancing people and performance so that morale is maintained and output is achieved

**Low 1** — 1.1 Applying minimum effort to achieve output and retain membership of the organisation

9.1 Achieving high output by ignoring people's feelings

Y-axis: Concern for people (Low 1 to High 9)

X-axis: Concern for production (1 Low to 9 High)

**Figure 13.3** An adaptation of Blake and Mouton's managerial grid

are still incorporated (Fig. 13.4) where concern for people is portrayed as (CP) and concern for output as (CO).

Both theories (Blake and Reddin) are useful tools for management development and organisation development. Further reading is essential (see the bibliography) to appreciate fully the complexity of 3D theory. An indication of the styles is given below.

### Effective styles

- *Executive*: recognises individual differences, uses team management, and is a good motivator.

- *Developer*: maximises concern for relationships with people, minimises concern for output, and aims to develop people.
- *Bureaucrat*: minimises concern for both people and output, and is governed by rules.
- *Benevolent autocrat*: maximises concern for output, minimises concern for people, and causes resentment.

### Ineffective styles

- *Missionary*: maximises concern for people and minimises concern for output in inappropriate situations, and values harmony.

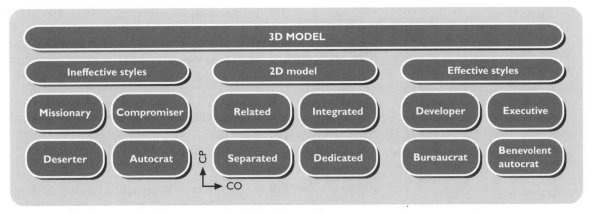

**Figure 13.4** An impression of Reddin's 3D model of leadership
The third dimension of effectiveness is added to the two-dimensional model, which is similar to the Ohio leadership studies and Blake and Mouton's managerial grid. The 3D model shows the situational impact on leadership, and the effective and ineffective styles that affect leadership. In the 2D model, CP represents concern for people and CO represents concern for output.

- *Compromiser*: concerned with both people and output in a situation where one is more important than the other, therefore is a poor decision maker.
- *Deserter*: minimises concern for both people and output, seeks to be passive in inappropriate situations, and avoids involvement.
- *Autocrat*: maximises concern for output and minimises concern for people in inappropriate situations, thus indicating lack of confidence in people and an obsession with work.

### SOCIO-EMOTIONAL LEADER VERSUS TASK LEADER

Harvard University identified two distinct groups of leaders in small-group behaviour. They were essentially mutually exclusive. This aspect is interesting since it agrees partly, but not wholly, with research findings on group dynamics (Chapter 5). Some leaders were task oriented, others were democratic, some were both task and relationship oriented, while others seemed unconcerned about either.

## Contingency theories

The following three approaches are based on the application of adaptive leadership behaviour,

which varies depending on the prevailing situation. They differ from trait and style theories since the multidimensional factors are taken into consideration.

### FUNCTIONAL LEADERSHIP

Functional leadership was developed by J. Adair and is often called action-centred leadership. The model is illustrated in Fig. 13.5 and consists of three components:

- individual needs
- team maintenance needs
- task needs

The components are related to the overall situation. The leader in these circumstances must be aware of the needs of the three components and should possess sufficient skill and training to meet them in accordance with the priorities of the particular situation.

Action-centred leadership is an apt description of the approach, which avoids emphasising personality, incorporates concepts in other theories, distinguishes between concern for individuals and concern for groups, and stresses the importance of acting in accordance with situational priorities. The examples in practice are the introduction of a computer in an office (individual needs), the

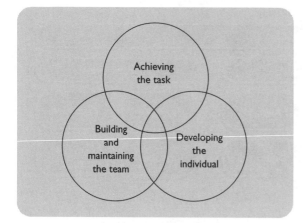

**Figure 13.5** Action-centred leadership
This model was propounded by Professor J. Adair. The three components are related to the overall situation. The leader must be aware of the needs within the components and must possess sufficient skill and training to meet them in accordance with the priorities of the situation.

introduction of a new engine involving changes in assembly and bonus schemes (group needs), and emergencies (task needs).

Individual needs or maintenance functions should include counselling to reveal the person's feelings, outlook and expectations; dealing with personal problems; assessing capability and training as required; and encouraging. Group needs or maintenance functions include counselling with the informal leader, building team spirit, aligning aims and goals, communicating effectively, setting fair standards, encouraging training, and liaising with other groups. Task needs or functions are directed towards planning, setting objectives, defining the tasks, allocating work and resources, and controlling.

## LEADERSHIP CONTINGENCY MODEL

F. Fiedler propounded that group performance was contingent upon the leader adopting the most effective style to suit the relative favourableness of the situation. According to Fiedler, the three major parameters which seem to determine the leader's effectiveness are:

- leader–member relations
- degree of task structure
- the leader's position power

The first two coincide with consideration for people and consideration for the task, both of which usually appear in style theories; the third is a combination of the leader's suitability for dealing with the situation, situation theory and task concepts.

## MATURITY LEVEL APPROACH

Hersey and Blanchard (see the bibliography) view leadership behaviour as depending upon the maturity level of subordinates, consequently they call it the situation approach. Maturity is interpreted as the individual's work experience, ability and willingness to accept responsibility.

Two forms of maturity are quoted: job maturity and psychological maturity. Job maturity measures skills and knowledge; psychological maturity measures the person's self-respect, self-image and self-confidence. Therefore high maturity demonstrates competence, assertiveness, self-confidence and high self-respect. Low maturity is the opposite and demands a more directive leadership style for a newcomer who needs role clarification and full support to avoid apprehension and confusion.

As the person improves, relationships change and more responsibility is sought. Supervision is gradually relaxed by changing style to include explaining reasons for decisions, clarifying contentious issues (selling style), and introducing more participation. Eventually a laissez-faire leadership style develops as the person reaches high maturity where independence, full responsibility, and quality workmanship are apparent.

Maturity is difficult to assess accurately and may be distorted by many influences such as the group and other individuals. These influences may affect self-confidence. Also the factors for high maturity may not all coincide; typically strong assertiveness does not necessarily mean high capability.

# Path–goal theory

Path–goal theory combines expectancy motivation theory and the use of power to smooth the employee's path towards achieving a goal. R. House and M. Evans developed the theory and both wrote papers on the subject. An adequate explanation includes a version of the four leadership styles, an identification of situational factors, and a description of the influencing technique.

## FOUR LEADERSHIP STYLES

- *Directive leadership*: Specific directions are given and people know exactly what is expected from them. The leader schedules the work, maintains standards of performance and encourages standard rules and regulations. No participation is allowed.
- *Supportive leadership*: A genuine concern for employees is shown; the leader is always approachable and friendly. Employees are treated as equals and a pleasant, enjoyable atmosphere is encouraged.
- *Participative leadership*: Suggestions are encouraged and used. However, after due consideration, the leader still makes the decision.
- *Achievement-oriented leadership*: Challenging goals are set for employees who see an open display of confidence in their abilities to perform well and achieve these goals. Trust is essential and personal responsibility is encouraged.

The inference is that different styles should be employed by the leader in different situations. Consequently, the approach differs from others. To provide guidance on the choice of style, two situational factors are employed.

## THE SITUATIONAL FACTORS

The situational factors have been identified as the employee's personal characteristics and the employee's working environment. After an appropriate assessment of these two factors, a suitable leadership style is chosen from the four listed above. The inference is that different styles should be used in different situations. Theoretically, the correct styles will be motivational because the employee's perceptions are positively influenced and they provide a smoother path through role and goal clarification and increased satisfaction.

### The employee's characteristics

The employee's characteristics are assumed to govern the degree of satisfaction and future satisfaction which is biased by the leadership style applied:

- *Ability*: If an employee perceives his or her ability as low, it is possible that directive leadership will be acceptable. But if the opposite perception prevails, he or she will probably find this unacceptable.
- *Needs*: The mental make-up of the individual, taking into account needs, drives and personality, may also influence the choice of style. For example, a strong drive for achievement would cause a favourable response to achievement-oriented leadership.
- *Locus of control*: If employees view what happens to them (or their future) as being under their control, this is an internal locus of control. Therefore a participative leadership style would be acceptable. But if the opposing view is held, the employees feel an external locus of control is operating, which means events are determined by influences outside their control. In this case directive leadership is more acceptable.

### The employee's work environment

The working environment is divided into three categories:

- employee's tasks
- the formal authority system
- the primary working group

These categories influence the amount of impact the leadership styles have on motivation and performance. They will decide the coaching, guidance, support and rewards the employee expects before effectiveness is likely.

## THE INFLUENCING TECHNIQUE

To accomplish successful leadership, House and Mitchell designed six steps for the leader to follow. The accomplishment of each step still depends on the appropriate choice of style.

1 Recognising and/or arousing subordinates' needs for outcomes over which the leader has some control.
2 Increasing personal pay-offs to subordinates for work-goal attainment.
3 Making the path to those pay-offs easier to travel by coaching and direction.

4  Helping subordinates clarify expectancies.
5  Reducing frustrating barriers.
6  Increasing the opportunities for a personal satisfaction contingent on effective performance.

This complex theory is very demanding but it is claimed that successful leadership behaviour is possible by following its principles.

# A normative model of leadership

Vroom and Yetton have attempted to establish a specific normative model illustrating how a leader should act and how decisions should be made in given situations. Other theories avoid these approaches, which have a limited use at present. The most recent complex model uses 5 leadership styles, 7 decision rules, 7 situational dimensions and 14 problem types. A separate in-depth study is essential to appreciate the use of the decision tree and all its components. Many managers find the model interesting and informative, but so far there are insufficient research findings to validate it and encourage its use.

# Leadership objectives

Leadership objectives are usually assumed to be aligned with supervisory and organisational objectives. Unfortunately, the assumption may sometimes be distorted when a supervisor pursues personal ends. Typical situations include practices associated with the rat race and empire building. Whether they contribute in any way towards achieving organisational objectives is debatable and depends upon the long-term outcomes, which will vary in each particular case. Presumably top management is aware of the practices and agrees with them; or disagrees but is powerless to interfere; or is unaware and out of touch with reality.

## INFLUENCING BEHAVIOUR

An effective leader is not necessarily an effective supervisor when he or she uses leadership to pursue personal goals. Leadership in this context is broader than management, which is considered to be a form of leadership, the aim being to achieve organisational objectives. Thus leadership is exercised at any time when a person is trying to influence behaviour.

The complexity of the scene increases when authority levels, group objectives, and formal and informal leaders are also considered. Group leaders may also visualise a number of different objectives. Choice becomes difficult and is partly influenced by the strength of top management, partly by power, how it is used, and how it contributes to ultimate ends.

# Developing supervisory power

Developing supervisory power is a way of improving co-ordination and it helps to achieve effective leadership. Such power does not mean bullying, malevolence or deceit. Benevolent power is implicit, which means influencing the employee by encouraging, heartening and demonstrating goodwill with some humanity. If power is successfully applied, the employee feels a strong desire to follow and work more willingly towards achieving goals. Probably he or she is influenced towards more responsible behaviour. Thus, more power is generated, which elates and encourages improved performance.

## POWER-SEEKING

Power struggles among people are inevitable and cause revulsion among those who have experienced misuse of power. The use of power should be learned with long-term effects in mind. The likely reaction from certain individuals should be expected. Power certainly satisfies some higher needs, therefore attempting to stifle drives to gain power frustrates a person and causes adverse reactions. When power-seeking, the supervisor's intentions could be self-interest, self-development or self-advancement, or to benefit the company, or combinations of these reasons. Inevitably managers and employees soon recognise the intentions, and possibly constructive conflict emerges which aids decision making.

## REPUTATION

The supervisor's reputation heavily depends on how power is used and developed. One belief is the authority inherent in the supervisor's position provides appropriate power, but considering a definition – the ability to get things done – this idea is suspect. Indeed relying on authority means depending on the superior, who may easily increase or decrease support. Such conferred power also implies that fear of the supervisor's disapproval gains employee support. In this situation, rewards and sanctions predominate, and possible reactions could be disastrous, especially with trade union support.

## AUTHORITY POWER

If a supervisor relies purely on authority power, or position power, he or she might be successful for a while, provided the situation is favourable. However, eventual change will be difficult to control and long-term effectiveness suffers as reactions to situations occur.

This effect could be dangerous if the 'successful supervisor' is promoted in the short term and a replacement finds reactions are setting in. Therein lies a selection principle: people should not be promoted because of quick results or the immediate favourable behaviour of their staff.

Whether employees accept a position of power depends upon many factors related to managerial prerogatives. Typical features are traditional contentions, employee attitudes and culture, trade union influence, and company climate.

## PERSONAL POWER

In a sense, personal power is the opposite to authority power because support comes from below the supervisor. Through charisma and the use of appropriate leadership styles, he or she relies upon building respect and appealing to employees' needs. This potentially volatile situation depends on how three types of power are used: legitimate power, referent power and expert power. The supervisor must have a legitimate right to influence behaviour (legitimate power), employees must perceive the supervisor as a potential leader (referent power), and he or she must possess sufficient expertise (expert power) to convince employees of this right.

Always there is the possibility the situation will change and employees will no longer support the supervisor for some reason. Consequently, effective leadership in the long term is possible only if the supervisor is successful in adjusting to inevitable changes in each individual's needs, the group needs and the organisation.

# Methods of developing power

- Attempting to dominate by using oral eloquence.
- Exerting mental pressure by using charisma.
- Developing friendships with powerful superiors and using these links to influence subordinates.
- Seeking alliances with peers to exert group pressure.
- Using an association by accepting a post and exercising influence through the automatic support of its members.
- Learning expertise in a new technology or discipline which is recognised as a critical feature for company survival or development.
- Finding weak points in the organisation and exploiting them in a variety of ways.
- Achieving effective performance by working hard, developing new roles and proposing new ideas.
- Establishing strong relationships with influential people outside the company who are able to exert pressure in some way.
- Creating a better impression through a variety of means, such as improving speech, education, technical and social skills, dress, manner and social work.

## THE EFFECTS

The use of a particular method has diverse effects on employees: fear, submission, obedience, capitulation, motivation, antagonism or retreat. Being able to forecast the response from superiors and subordinates is understandably difficult in practice. Choosing the appropriate methods improves the probability of advancement; since organisations are political arenas, healthy conflict reduces the risk of stagnation and the role system regenerates. Thus power seeking is essential, in one respect.

Exercising power can be equally destructive if used solely for self-development by ignoring the overall effect on the company. Examples are destroying someone's career by devious means, empire building, causing disruption between departments, and restricting information flow.

# The power game

The power game is often interpreted as a means by which the supervisor can impose his or her personal status or image and gain employee support and dependence. Winning power battles is essential for prestige since many of the supervisor's superiors and subordinates will also be engaged in power struggles and be watching closely for weak points. Those who are not actively involved will feel some frustration, but the process of winning also helps the supervisor's subordinates because this will elevate their power by association.

Careful planning of strategy and tactics in playing the power game allows the supervisor to establish certain objectives and make concentrated attempts to win essential battles. Losing those of minor importance may be tactically sound in circumstances where a subordinate's prestige is enhanced, but there is the danger of upsetting another subordinate.

## RULES

Whether people play according to rules or moral conduct depends on the reputation they hope to achieve or maintain. Some people change the rules to suit themselves as power develops and advancement follows, but everyone recognises this and opinions may alter. The practice is hazardous because it becomes lonelier as the hierarchy is ascended and enemies tend to increase in proportion to the degree of rule bending. Some specialists argue that an unhappy day arrives for the supervisor who looks for support, which is not forthcoming. This is all part of the power game and is healthy.

Many rules for playing coincide with those for developing good human relations. They come naturally to those who wish to develop a good reputation. Other rules have no boundaries and many underhanded techniques are employed by the ruthless individual looking for success at the expense of others. Debatable aspects are the effects on employee performance, the cut and thrust of business life, managerial ethics, moral codes of conduct, acceptable practices in other countries, and company survival.

# Power development concepts

A modern view places power within the realms of organisational politics. This term is interpreted by S.P. Robbins to mean any behaviour by an organisation member which is self-serving. Other notions are the structure and process of the use of authority and power to influence objectives not agreed by top management; ways to advance in the organisation; and a dynamic process that uses power to improve career prospects.

## TYPES OF POWER

Besides legitimate, referent and expert power, J. French and B. Rowan include reward power, which is possessing the capability and resources to reward employees, and coercive power, which is the capability to punish.

Combining these five types of power becomes a strong political power when applied by those with appropriate authority and capability. The outcome is an organisation that differs drastically from theoretical notions. The distribution of power among organisation members is usually biased in certain directions, often inducing callous treatment of some employees. Coalitions emerge, disappear and re-emerge in different forms, causing competition for resources and protection of certain individuals.

## POLITICAL STRATEGIES

Many political strategies for developing power have been proposed. A well-known example is by A. DuBrin, who drew up a list extracted from literature on the subject. Items included are strategies of divide and rule; avoiding decisive engagements; progressing slowly, one step at a time; forming and maintaining alliances with powerful individuals; and taking counsel with caution. Others are making a quick reputation by concentrating on one task immediately to gain attention; and collecting and using IOUs, which means doing favours but letting it be known that something in return is expected later. A long list of strategies was also compiled by R.H. Miles, while J. Pfeffer mentioned managing uncertainty, building alliances and controlling resources.

Probably political manoeuvring and power-seeking features have always been present in organisations. Possibly the mere presence of people and groups is sufficient to trigger such processes. Recognising, understanding and using politics and power seem to be essential requirements for the successful supervisor. Whether he or she is more effective as a result is debatable at present since research continues.

# Developing leadership skills

Armed with sufficient knowledge and theories of leadership, the potentially effective leader should be able to apply a straightforward approach to developing leadership skills. A logical and recognised programme for developing any social skill is:

- Attempt self-analysis.
- Spend more time on trying to understand group members.
- Develop a better understanding by concentrating on improving interpersonal relationships.

These three features are discussed shortly. There are many adverse influences which may upset a programme. Sometimes they are very powerful. They are mentioned and discussed elsewhere. However, the leader must accept the situation and concentrate on the overall philosophy.

## DEVELOPING SELF-ANALYSIS

Developing self-analysis relies partly upon acquiring the information given in Chapter 9 to convince supervisors that perception is important, followed by compiling a personal record, and diagnosing

strengths and weaknesses. Major considerations are how supervisors are perceived by others and how supervisors see themselves. The effects of interaction, reaction and acceptance should justify the need for self-analysis.

Self-opinion ranges from a low level of inferiority and opinion up to a high level of confidence and opinion. Most people crudely rate themselves somewhere along such a line but self-analysis to confirm their opinion or regrade themselves is unusual. The tendency is either to over- or under-rate, sometimes excessively. Indeed very few analyse themselves to reveal their strengths and weaknesses. Many tend to live in the past, picking on good or bad times, convincing themselves that if it were not for a particular circumstance they would be following a totally different career, generally one very much better than their present occupation.

Many also blame a relative, an individual or a company for the problems they face (or reject) because of previous experiences which have affected their career. To overcome such prejudices and excuses, a supervisor should find time for self-analysis or self-awareness, and attempt to be more self-objective. The exercise also helps to improve home and social life. Two techniques for this purpose are now outlined.

### Compile a personal record

Having acquired sufficient knowledge about human beings, the next step is to check with a friend, relative or colleague. This is achieved firstly by listing obvious features and those revealed through personal contact, and secondly by presenting them to the individual and asking for an opinion. The supervisor then builds up a personal dossier from this information. Included initially are features similar to those used when interviewing and selecting. More details are added as ideas occur. Areas demanding special attention will inevitably be highlighted as the leader diagnoses problems encountered with employees.

For those supervisors who are inexperienced in personnel selection techniques, there are two well-known examples to consult: the seven-point plan (published by the National Institute of Industrial Psychology) and the fivefold grading scheme by

J. Munro-Fraser (Chapter 16). Useful initial headings are:

- impact on other people
- abilities
- capabilities
- drive
- enthusiasm
- temperament
- prejudices
- confidence level
- introvert/extrovert tendencies
- physical make-up
- special aptitudes
- interests

A crude framework would be to start with behavioural, mental, physical and emotional headings.

### Diagnose strengths and weaknesses

Diagnosing strengths and weaknesses demands courage and honesty. The supervisor should approach others for information if the climate is right. Developing rapport with the right people who are willing to help takes time since they are often unwilling to be honest because of possible consequences. Usually someone's confidence will eventually provide new and often vital information. Suggesting a mutual exchange of information is often helpful.

### IMPROVING AN UNDERSTANDING OF EMPLOYEES

The second stage is an extension of self-analysis concepts, applying them to others within the group. They are no different from the leader in many ways, although each one will vary to some extent. Each person requires a particular approach, based upon previous experience. Taking the time to assess the individual's expectations is worthwhile because there is an increased chance of gaining a better understanding. Individual treatment to cater for expectations can only be based upon detailed knowledge and experience. Building up such information is time-consuming and costly, but there are many benefits. Span of control is another important feature since it becomes increasingly difficult to know each group member sufficiently well as numbers increase.

### DEVELOPING INTERPERSONAL RELATIONSHIPS

Developing interpersonal relationships depends upon the results of the previous stages and the leader's acceptance of other influences over which he or she has no control. Negative pressures must be expected from power groups such as militant shop stewards and belligerent informal leaders. These pressures should not be used as an excuse to avoid the exercise.

A fundamental belief in people is essential. This philosophy is demonstrated by the leader's behaviour, which must include remembering to praise and counsel when necessary. A part of the programme is to give adequate explanations of unpalatable actions which occur as company goals or survival take precedence. Whenever participation is feasible it should be used, but there are inherent dangers.

Inevitably the leader's actions will sometimes cause adverse reactions, followed possibly by a reaction from the leader which aggravates the situation. This hostility cycle must be broken immediately, consequently the leader's response must be favourable or acceptable.

It is exceptionally difficult for a leader to avoid his or her natural emotional retort when an employee behaves badly, but this is the only way to break the syndrome. For example, most people react to rudeness by reciprocating the rudeness. Avoiding this retaliation demands strong emotional control and self-discipline. An essential feature is understanding that pride and status are not lost by allowing an employee's reaction to pass unchallenged.

Of course there are limits, beyond which disciplinary procedures apply. Most reasonable people recognise and accept these borderlines. The risk of conflict is reduced if the supervisor attends to all the obvious requirements of employees. The effort and time spent reaps it own rewards.

# Influence

The management technique of influencing people means convincing them of the need to accept and use positive ideas or changes that will improve their performance and the dynamism of the organisation.

In general terms, influencing means persuading people to accept a point of view. Therefore, influence may mean moral power, dominant control, or an action which is perceptible by its effects. Unfortunately, influencing in general may also cause disruption in the organisation and disgruntled employees. This could be called regressive influence, whereas the management technique may be called progressive influence.

Leadership and power are influential factors but they may be used as a progressive influence or misused as a regressive influence. The distinction is important, because achieving a progressive influence is an art involving many skills.

## VIEWS ON INFLUENCE

- An effect when power is exerted on an individual.
- The result of using power successfully.
- The capacity to sell ideas.
- The capability to persuade individuals to take suggested courses of action.
- Convincing people that a viewpoint is correct and they should support the view.
- Persuading people to change their behaviour and commit themselves to proposed objectives.
- Setting a good example which causes an individual to aspire to similar behaviour.

## PROGRESSIVE INFLUENCE

Progressive influence implies identifying beneficial changes or creating ideas on where improvements lie in the organisation and being capable of bringing about the necessary changes through influential means. The technique involves a number of composite skills:

- using psychology and sociology
- selling capability
- communication skills
- negotiating

They are used in the following approach, which is essential to conform with competent supervision. Figure 13.6 illustrates the main features.

# A logical approach

Although the following framework may be partially short-circuited in practice, the main skills and techniques are now discussed. They are divided into six phases which are essential for the successful operation of progressive influence.

## PHASE 1: UNDERSTANDING ONESELF

The difficult task of self-analysis must be undertaken before an appropriate approach to various influencing skills is possible. The supervisor should have a clear picture of his or her impact and impression on people to avoid excessive frustration and misunderstandings of their reactions.

## PHASE 2: THINKING CREATIVELY

The outcome of self-analysis should indicate various features such as intelligence, drive, attitude, aptitudes, perception and temperament. These features have a direct bearing on the capability to think creatively and should be understood to avoid severe frustration. For example, supervisors with an intuitive–thinking temperament (Chapter 9) will have a distinct advantage over others with different characteristics. However, there are many techniques which everyone can use to improve thinking creatively. They include analytical thinking, lateral thinking, group discussions, brainstorming, synectics and morphological analysis, all of which are described in Chapter 8.

## PHASE 3: PLANNING VIABLE COURSES OF ACTION

Determining viable courses of action is not a straightforward exercise. It involves research and forecasting which are time-consuming but essential (Chapter 8). Within the planning phase lies a range of basic elements of supervision which are taken into consideration (Chapter 1) when a final course of action is chosen. In brief, the process involves the organisational structure and culture, psychological and sociological aspects, and control features.

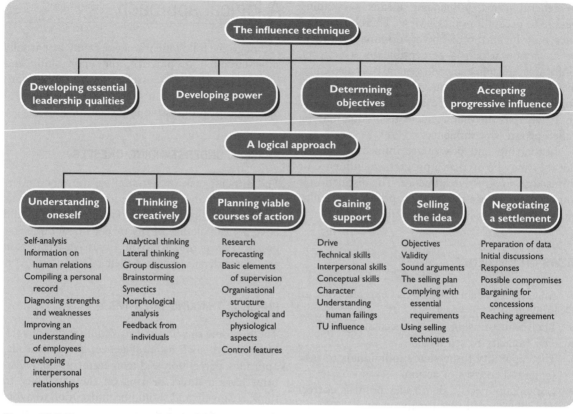

**Figure 13.6** The management technique of influencing people

## PHASE 4: GAINING SUPPORT FROM INDIVIDUALS

Gaining support from individuals demands competent supervision which should not be confused with selling the idea. All the features that determine an effective supervisor (Chapter 1) are essential before any degree of confidence and support from individuals is possible. There are two further aspects to consider in this phase, which have a critical effect on gaining support: human failings which the supervisor must recognise in him or herself, and trade union influence.

### Human failings

Employees recognise human failings immediately and they react strongly, often in subtle ways which a supervisor may not recognise. Examples that negate attempts to achieve progressive influence are greed; excessive ambition, leading to inhuman approaches; power lust, leading to unacceptable conduct; insensitivity to other people's feelings and reactions; deviousness and underhanded activities; jealousy and taking an unfair advantage to gain status; emphasising status, leading to mental barriers; rationalising adverse situations to suit personal gain; inadequate conscience level; unscrupulous conduct; and using money to gain personal ends which conflict with moral codes.

A confusing feature is that a supervisor or manager may introduce brilliant ideas but at the same time cause human problems. For instance, current cases often involve greedy senior executives with expertise who accept or arrange excessive pay and other increases for themselves. This insensitive action creates a disgruntled workforce whose pay is restricted to low percentage increases.

## Trade union influence

A close association with trade union representatives is needed to ensure their feeling towards possible changes is clearly understood. This feature helps to determine an approach for the next phase – selling the idea. Clearly there will be opposition if the idea may cause redundancies, changes in working conditions, or altered pay structures. Unfortunately, there are inevitable problems of this nature which have to be solved eventually.

## PHASE 5: SELLING THE IDEA

Many ideas are not exploited because of the person's inability to convince someone in authority of the need, or there is no opportunity to negotiate. Overcoming these difficulties is possible by selling. An indication of how to approach the sale is:

● Prepare the selling plan.
● Comply with the essential requirements.
● Use selling techniques.

### Prepare the selling plan

● Know the idea thoroughly, including the good and bad points, possible problems, costs, people, and the organisation.
● Clarify the objectives.
● Be convinced of the idea's validity.
● Identify sound arguments and a comprehensive framework.
● Outline a fallback scheme should the idea be unacceptable.

### Essential requirements for a successful sale

● Acquire a thorough knowledge of the subject.
● Obtain proof of validity.
● Have confidence in the idea.
● Develop the capability to sell.
● Be prepared to negotiate.

### Selling techniques

A successful salesperson feels he or she has a flair for selling, spends considerable time studying selling techniques, and practises constantly. However, expertise in all aspects of influencing people is obviously not possible for the supervisor. Here is an indication of the important factors:

● The idea must be sold; being too laid-back is fatal.
● Be confident, firm and friendly.
● Be completely open with information. Do not hold back if questioned. If the information given is wrong, admit it.
● Do not be critical if there is opposition. Accept the comments, let them pass, and be understanding.
● Always remain calm regardless of any provocation. Sarcasm and adverse comments are often emotional to demonstrate the person's importance. Comments may not stand up to argument, but allow for obvious mistakes and naive remarks.
● Try to find out the people's wants and play on them by showing how the idea can help them. This technique demonstrates an honest interest in other people's outlooks and objectives.
● When there is any form of favourable response, immediately pay a compliment and agree. The receiver's desire to show importance should release more enthusiasm and support. Listen very carefully for any hint of the reasons for support.
● Ask for points of view and attempt to answer queries from the other person's position and how it helps him or her.
● Avoid being drawn into an argument. Try every means possible to avoid them, as arguments are never won; they create ill-feeling and resentment. Always allow the person to save face.
● If possible, hint that part of the idea came from previous conversations with the individual.
● Emphasise the company's future and the need to improve the organisation to stay in business.

## PHASE 6: NEGOTIATING A SETTLEMENT

When the idea is sold there may be two courses of action. First, the manager will take over the scheme, submit it for approval at a higher level, and arrange for detailed investigations and changes. Second, the alternative is to arrange for the supervisor to negotiate the changes. These may include systems, procedures, administration, costs and organisational redesign. Each one may have to be negotiated as opposition is encountered. Invariably this involves personality changes, status changes and job changes. Negotiating in conflict situations was discussed in Chapter 5. Although some aspects are similar, the concept of negotiating a settlement to achieve a progressive influence should be carefully distinguished. An overall scheme that covers all eventualities, regardless of simplicity or complexity, usually includes four phases:

## Preparation

A comprehensive plan is essential which covers all the areas where changes are needed. These are listed and the proposed objectives outlined by submitting the requirements and any flexibility. All the data must be collated and available for acceptance of a proposed logical approach. With these features in mind, the bargaining tactics are decided by considering the probable concessions, the personalities, and the possible offers that may be submitted. In other words, be prepared to deal with any situation that may arise.

## Initial discussions

Opening discussions usually reveal the bargaining positions and can be compared with the ideal requirements. Diplomacy is now essential because there must be some give and take on both sides to make a settlement possible. The usual techniques are:

- Avoid making immediate concessions.
- Explore in more detail the proposals, objectives, attitudes, emotional factors and general behaviour.
- Try to assess the strengths and weaknesses, and probe without using too much pressure.
- Adopt a realistic approach by illustrating the minimum requirements and the advantages of concessions.

## Bargaining for concessions

From the information now available, bargaining can commence by highlighting the reassessments, attempting to take advantage of the weaknesses,

persuading individuals by indicating their gains if they abandon opposing ideas, and offering possible concessions to compensate for objections. The important features are to ensure give-and-take situations are suggested and kept open, to note reactions, and to offer a complete package as this will often look more attractive.

## Reaching an agreement

The three critical features to reaching an agreement are the obvious attitude changes, any silence when new proposals are submitted, and any favourable responses when further minor concessions are offered. Attempt to reach a settlement by summarising, indicating the fairness of the proposals to both sides, and the advantages for the organisation. Be prepared to compromise by giving up minor aspects if a firm settlement is suggested.

## QUESTIONS

1 Discuss whether it is possible to develop leadership skills.

2 An effective leader finds the right balance between concern for people and concern for production. Explain this statement.

3 Outline the main theories of leadership.

4 Explain functional leadership.

5 Write an essay on leadership styles.

6 Leadership objectives are assumed to be aligned with supervisory and organisational objectives. Discuss the significance of this statement.

7 Power struggles among people are inevitable. Is this statement a valid reason to develop supervisory power? Explain your viewpoint.

8 Define the term 'benevolent power'.

9 What are the dangers of relying on authority power?

10 Outline the methods of developing power.

11 Write an essay on the power game.

12 Explain reward power and coercive power.

13 How may leadership, power and influence be used in introducing changes?

14 How would you develop your leadership skills?

15 What are the main features of leadership, power and influence?

16 Outline the influence technique.

17 Consider the various views on influence and how a supervisor should use them.

18 What are the composite skills associated with progressive influence?

19 Understanding oneself and thinking creatively are important features when using a logical approach to influence. Explain the significance of these features.

20 How would you sell an idea to management?

21 There are many selling techniques which can be used to influence management to accept change. List the techniques that come immediately to mind.

22 If you are asked to negotiate a settlement, outline a logical scheme you would use.

## CASE STUDY

Tom is a new supervisor in a financial services department, which consists of four sections each containing twelve members of staff. The procedures critically affect other departments if there are delays. He seems to be dealing with crises most of the time and does not give sufficient thought when coping with problems.

Tom decides that he must delegate more work but has difficulty in locating suitable staff to undertake more authority. They all seem to be overloaded by providing urgent information to the representatives. Most of the telephone calls he receives are about queries on investment policies which he cannot answer and has to refer the caller to staff in the policy section.

The team of representatives is working well with the exception of one individual. He is obviously bright, with some experience of the work in the department but gives the impression of being bored.

Tom's budget is above his requirements for the year and there is sufficient for another member of staff. The sales targets are already being exceeded and there are two more months before the end of the year. Tom's superior is very pleased with his efforts but asks Tom how he is feeling and if he needs any advice. Tom is immediately conscious of the implied queries and says he will let him know.

*Outline the problems facing Tom. What should Tom do before seeking advice from his superior? If you were advising Tom, give an indication of the training needed to help him in this situation.*

## CASE STUDY

Over the past three months Mary, who works in a team of six operators, has been taking time off periodically. Her holiday leave is completed. About every three weeks she is absent for two days and her excuses range from migraine to backache. Her team covers for her and no compaints have been received. She is an excellent worker and respected.

*How would you conduct an interview with Mary in these circumstances?*

Two supervisors, Linda and Heather, are tipped for promotion to the vacant office manager's job. In terms of age, length of service, education and qualifications there is nothing to choose between them. Linda is smart but inclined to be short-tempered. Heather is more homely, with a good sense of humour and an excellent conversationalist.

Linda uses her assets well, develops appropriate relationships with managers and is known to get her own way. She can sense weak points in the organisation and several times has turned them to her personal advantage. Sometimes she is called a gold-digger.

Heather uses her strengths to develop good relations with the clerical union and with staff. Several of her ideas have been accepted by management and she has continued studying. Sometimes she is criticised for being too casual.

Both perform well in their jobs, they have a clean record and are hard workers.

*Consider the difficulties likely to be faced by the selection committee. What advice would you have given to Linda and Heather five years ago, considering the use of power?*

# 14

# Introduction to communication

## Important features

Successful communication of information between employees, peers and managers is an essential part of the supervisor's job. Achieving and maintaining effective communication is always a problem in any organisation, mainly because the topic is under-rated. Despite many well-known examples of disaster through poor communication, it continues to receive insufficient attention and training. Nevertheless, communication is frequently discussed at all organisation levels, most employees recognise its failings, misunderstandings occur frequently, and often it is one of the major difficulties facing management.

At global level, poor communication is often used as a reason for marital breakdowns, family feuds, ethical prejudices, the generation gap, and wars. Apparently the information in the mind of the sender is most unlikely to agree with the receiver's interpretation. The gap between the two causes the problem since people fill in the difference to suit their prejudices, personalities, values and culture.

### THE SUPERVISOR'S RESPONSIBILITIES

The supervisor's responsibilities include communicating operational information, ideas, industrial relations aspects and general information. The supervisor's four sectors of communication are subordinates, peers, management and clients. Employees expect to know everything at all times about their work and any subjects that interest or affect them. Peers expect to know any information about operations, relationships and matters affecting supervisors, so that harmony and good working relations remain established. Clients or customers expect to receive any significant information on the product or service, prompt service and courteous attention. Managers and top management expect full disclosure on all aspects, on time and in appropriate detail. Such information provides details for problem solving, decision making, reports, industrial relations activities, and determining policy on culture, trends, morale, motivation and human resources.

### TOP MANAGEMENT'S POLICY

For the supervisor to avoid severe frustration in attempts to improve communication, it is essential to stress the effects of top management's policy. The organisational culture depends upon the boardroom's policy towards effective communication, the obvious features being:

- disclosure and non-disclosure of information
- publicised and actual dedication to achieving effective communication
- fictional and non-fictional leaks
- releasing half-truths
- the degree of insularity and sincerity

### MANAGERIAL RECEPTIVENESS

Throughout the organisation employees usually accuse managers of low receptiveness to communication, although managers also have a responsibility for attempting improvements. Often excuses are made by managers who realise they are at fault. These excuses include lack of time and being easily

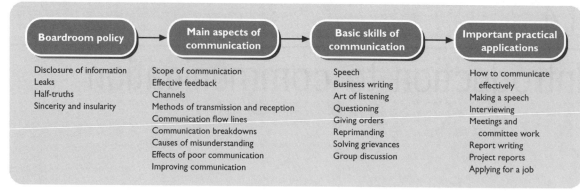

**Figure 14.1** Communication: an overall concept
The effects of boardroom policy on communication determine the success of communication practices. Attempts to improve communication will fail unless there is full support from the boardroom.

distracted. Some managers do not bother and may perform other tasks while the employee is speaking, such as reading a letter or memo, dialling a telephone number, speaking to a secretary, chatting with another manager, displaying boredom or disinterest, or adopting a blank expression.

These practices are guaranteed to increase the class gap, frustrate, irritate, and cause general distrust and suspicion. Indeed the busy manager will find that he or she is firmly establishing an even busier future.

### INFORMATION DISCLOSURE

Usually managers fail to understand that employees feel they should know situations at first hand, not through the grapevine. The same managers will expect to be directly informed immediately, expect to know their job descriptions and pay expectations; they will expect to have the right to a hearing whenever necessary, and to receive adequate explanations on any queries. Employees have similar expectations.

### COMMUNICATION: THE TWELVE MAIN ASPECTS

The overall concept is illustrated in Fig. 14.1, basic skills are discussed in Chapter 15 and important practical applications are covered in Chapter 16. The following aspects are covered here:

- observations on communication
- defining communication
- process models

- the scope of communication
- channels of communication
- networks
- methods of transmission
- methods of reception
- flow lines
- causes of misunderstandings
- effects of poor communication
- improving communication

## Observations on communication

The catastrophes caused by poor communication in this century aroused a strong interest in the subject. Throughout many diverse institutions and countries, research was conducted and gained impetus as the information explosion caused further problems. The outcome is an upsurge in knowledge but a failure to solve successfully many communication difficulties. The root cause of the problem is possibly the complexity of human beings and their unpredictable behaviour in various situations. Practical research has at least revealed certain observations:

- The only way people can influence each other is by an exchange of behaviour caused through a dynamic communication process.
- Communication depends upon the sender and the receiver. The message must be transmitted

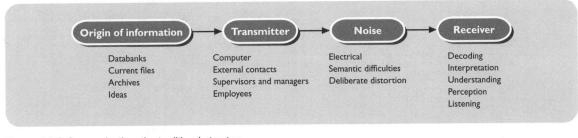

**Figure 14.2** Communication: the traditional structure
This concentrates on linear information flow, it is too noisy and it avoids the personal process.

to allow perception by the receiver who must provide effective feedback.

- The receiver's perception of the transmission is based upon experience, language and expectations.
- The strength of the transmission depends upon matching it with the receiver's desires, values and culture.
- Communication and information are often confused. Communication is personal and perceived; it is an interpretation. Information is impersonal and specific; it is a reasoned quantity.

Technically, communication includes the science and practice of transmitting and receiving information. In management terms, communication includes mechanical and electronic aspects, and organisational and interpersonal aspects. In psychological terms, perception governs communication by interpreting and determining the receiver's expectations. In this way, unexpected input is resisted by ignoring it or misunderstanding to suit expectations. Logically, to be successful the sender needs to know the receiver's expectations. This implies a close relationship where the receiver's ambitions, values and beliefs are disclosed.

# Defining communication

In everyday language, communication means the passing of information from one person to another. But in a different context it might be a means of getting in touch with another person. However, attempts to examine the communication process soon reveal many physical and psychological stages between sending and receiving.

## A TRADITIONAL MODEL OF COMMUNICATION

A traditional model of communication conforms to a comparatively straightforward linear information flow from sender to receiver, using physical and psychological stages which suffer with static and avoid the personal process. Many people do not even reach this level of understanding and have great difficulty in communicating. This traditional organisational structure of communication is illustrated in Fig. 14.2. The stages are self-explanatory.

## A DYNAMIC PROCESS MODEL OF COMMUNICATION

A close examination of communication indicates failure unless there is a dynamic process which incorporates an elaborate feedback system from receiver to sender. A broad model is shown in Fig. 14.3. It implies that information is ongoing, ever changing and continuous. All the stages interact and affect each other. This transaction concept means that everyone is engaged in sending and receiving information simultaneously. Each organisation member shares in the encoding and decoding functions, so everyone is affecting other members. The items to note are:

- *Encode*: Using language, etc., to convey the correct meaning and to draw attention, based upon knowledge of the receiver.
- *Screen*: A filtering process that accounts for language difficulties, emotional problems and general lack of understanding.
- *Channel*: Selection of the most appropriate channel increases the chances of the message arriving.

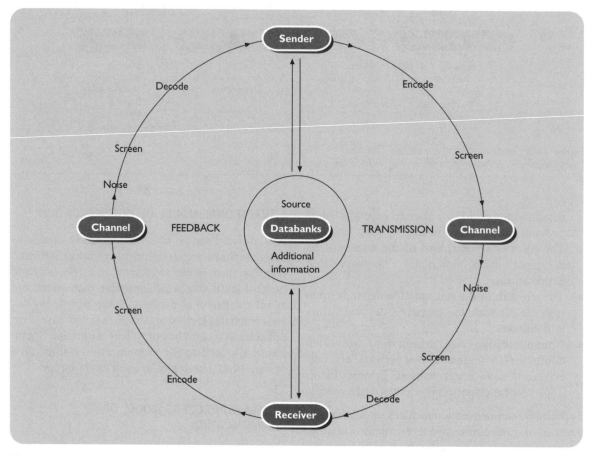

**Figure 14.3** Communication: a dynamic process model
This incorporates an elaborate feedback system; it is ongoing, ever changing and continuous; and it contributes to the central databanks. All the stages interact and affect each other.

- *Noise*: Any interference that occurs between transmission and reception. It may be a deliberate distortion of the message, a language problem, electrical static, or any problem that cannot be explained.
- *Decode*: Inability to receive correctly through poor concentration, inattention level, low interest, preoccupation with diversions, low level of understanding, and suspicion
- *Feedback*: The vital factor that signifies to the sender whether the desired effect is achieved. It provides the opportunity for adjustment by further communication processes to ensure comprehension and understanding.

This dynamic process relies heavily on the outcome through feedback to ensure the message is accepted as true, is remembered, and results in a modification of behaviour.

## Process models

Process models represent typical views which tend to overlap with general definitions. However, effective feedback is strongly emphasised by adopting certain recommended practices. These views are:

- a course of action starting with the sender and ending with the receiver
- a series of operations from an information source to a receiver
- a series of changes involving information passing through many stages, being utilised for action

or attitude change, and finally returning to the source to augment the original information
- a dynamic, continuing series of transactions leading to co-ordination

The process concept insists that the sender must allow the receiver to influence or persuade him or her to change the message in such a fashion that it becomes more acceptable to the receiver. Consequently, misunderstandings or rejections are avoided. Feedback loops are vital to operate this concept.

## EFFECTIVE FEEDBACK

Although feedback is treated as part of the process, it may also be envisaged as a communication process in its own right. Hence it will suffer from similar difficulties when the supervisor applies feedback to the employee. Typical features will be parallel with process stages, along with other critical aspects. These apply due to the sensitive nature of feedback in operating conditions such as checking performance and behaviour, constructive criticisms, correcting deviations and counteracting inaccurate instructions. Adopting certain practices may then avoid ill-feeling. Some examples are:

- *Objectivity*: This ensures the receiver appreciates the reason for feedback, such as avoiding a bottleneck in production or avoiding wastage.
- *Comprehension*: Sometimes the supervisor can easily misunderstand, especially when a subordinate is attempting to explain a complex situation.
- *Purpose*: The aim of feedback must be specific, not vague or general, otherwise further complications arise and frustration may develop.
- *Acceptability*: There should be no problem provided the information is useful and helps, trains, pleases or encourages the receiver.
- *Accuracy*: If feedback is inaccurate it will certainly antagonise, irritate or cause some emotional reaction. At the same time, some accurate information can be hurtful if it reprimands; due care and sensitivity are essential.
- *Timing*: The essential requirements are immediate comments, criticisms or reinforcement. Delay may cause insecurity, surprise, confusion and resentment (Chapter 12).

# The scope of communication

## INFORMATION THEORY AND SYSTEMS THEORY

The scientific study of communication is becoming increasingly important as research into operational faults and disasters mainly reveals errors caused by a low comprehension of information theory and systems theory.

Information theory is a scientific approach involving probability theory. The main thrust is a study of the transmission (encoding) and reception (decoding aspects). Also considered are functional roles and their contributions towards improving performance. Emphasis is placed on using statistical data to encode messages, employing electronic devices to transmit and receive, and selecting appropriate channels.

The application of systems theory (Chapter 3) in communication has developed into a system of operational management which accounts for the transformation of inputs through the various management functions of planning, organising, staffing, leading and controlling. The open systems approach allows for all interactions between the concern and its external environment, and transforms inputs into an effective means of producing outputs.

Information theory and cybernetics (Chapter 23) were both developed in the late 1940s, information theory by Claude Shannon and cybernetics by Norbert Wiener. Their ideas have now been refined and given impetus to computer technology and organisational systems analysis. Using these theories correctly ensures the integration of managerial functions, makes managing easier, and provides strong links with the outside world.

## INTERPERSONAL COMMUNICATION

Interpersonal communication is behaviourally oriented whereas information theory is mathematically oriented. The emphasis is on the transference of information from one person to another. The psychological processes involve perception, learning and motivating, as well as language, listening and non-verbal aspects of communication.

The interpersonal process is subjected to many influences within the individual, within the organisation (intra- and intergroup activities) and externally from the outside environment. This fundamental exchange of information between everyone in the organisation relies on the development and maintenance of sound human relations (Chapter 10). When operating effectively, the range of information extends to important features which are essential for top management to exercise competence. These include external information, marketing opinions, statistical data, and the changing attitudes and intentions of employees.

Effectiveness mainly relies on communication being easily understood, coping with queries immediately, avoiding personal objectives and obvious reactions, timeliness and comprehensiveness. Effective feedback is considered to be the vital element.

## ORGANISATIONAL COMMUNICATION

Organisational communication is a continuous transactional process since everyone is sending and receiving messages simultaneously. All organisation members are involved in encoding and decoding activities. Consequently, they are constantly influencing and affecting their behaviour.

Traditionally the structure of this communication type was visualised as a series of linear information flows, similar to a telephone network. Information was thought to consist of commands, directives, reports, enquiries and requests operating through the chain of command (Fig. 14.2).

Now the open systems approach incorporates all the external influences that disturb, make demands and cause operational difficulties. This is incorporated in the modern multi-stages process (Fig. 14.3) and conforms to sociotechnical systems and the contingency approach (Chapter 3).

# Communication channels

A wide range of formal and informal channels are available. More than one channel may be used to reinforce the message. The choice depends upon personal preference based upon the supervisor's knowledge of the individual (the receiver), experience and the environment. Communication channels form patterns or networks. In diagrammatic form they are grouped in various ways with one- or two-way communication facilities.

## FORMAL CHANNELS

Formal channels are easily recognisable, conform to military practice, and follow the direct authority lines shown in an organisational chart. Not so evident are the functional and staff channels explained later. These channels supplement the scalar process and ease overloads by operating a formal line of command from top to bottom of the organisation. Formal channels are connected with many official activities, such as joint consultative committees, discussion groups, personnel interviews and counselling, liaison with trade unions, company journals, posters and literature, policy publications, direct letters, noticeboards, conferences and suggestion schemes.

### Telecommunication channels

Within formal channels are telecommunication channels, including the telephone, cable, cellular, satellite communications, and the Internet (or Net). The Internet has revolutionised the market through the joining of computing with telephony to provide many computer networks all connected together. Thus, any computer may be connected to another and the users have access to enormous amounts of data.

The Internet provides many basic services such as electronic mail (e-mail), mailing lists, mail service robots, and gateways to other services. From the security aspect, it is possible to log on to any computer without the owner's knowledge. However, the access is restricted legally to those computers within the system.

Private networks based on Internet technology are called intranets. Intranets are used within a company to provide e-mail, internal directories, information manuals, and to link member companies together.

## INFORMAL CHANNELS

Informal channels operate unofficially through the grapevine, discussions with trade union officials, consultation, contacts with outside sources and services, and airing grievances and complaints. They work effectively because most organisation members want to contribute by passing on gossip, scandal and rumour as well as information. The three major informal channels are horizontal, ad hoc and line bypass. They are discussed in the section on communication flow since they are essentially spasmodic and operate as required. Nevertheless, they are critical and bind the structure together to form an effective working unit. The grapevine is a major informal channel.

## The grapevine

The grapevine operates through all members of the organisation. They pass on gossip, scandal and rumour to each other during their daily contacts at the workplace, in the dining room, and during social activities. When used properly the grapevine is a quick way of assisting the formal channels and it provides a guide to the effectiveness and accuracy of other channels.

## Dangers of the grapevine

Management is usually to blame if the grapevine plays a dangerous part in the communication system by betraying confidential information and spreading rumours based upon odd scraps of information and conjecture. Invariably the leaks may be traced back to managers' lack of circumspection – careless remarks over the telephone, leaving confidential papers lying around, imparting information to close associates without the appropriate authority, and so on. Few people are able to keep confidences completely to themselves.

Subordinates expect their supervisor to know the facts about rumours which are circulating. If supervisors do have confidential information they are then placed in the difficult position of deceiving employees, antagonising them by withholding the information, or betraying management's confidence. Management should prevent these situations occurring by issuing statements as decisions are made, or by ensuring no premature leakage is possible.

When any instructions are issued without acceptable reasons or when breakdowns in formal channels occur, the grapevine promptly takes over and creates the information, regardless of its accuracy. If the facts are not available from official or unofficial sources, someone always gives an opinion which is accepted as fact until proved false.

Employees want to know about the company, any current news which may affect them, proposed changes, and development of existing programmes. If information is withheld, the inevitable rumours will quickly destroy good relationships. Rumours cannot be stemmed unless management understands the situation and provides sufficient information for supervisors to pass on.

## Uses of the grapevine

- As a control check to ensure information reaches everyone in an undistorted form.
- As an informal means of supplementing formal channels of communication. Certain employees have a reputation for always being in the know. Many are informal leaders of groups and are usually good workers with a genuine interest in their job. The supervisor should make sure these people are supplied with the right information to pass on. If used properly, often this method of passing information is more effective because individuals pay more attention to those employees in the know.
- As a means of keeping up to date on events so that further information may be obtained from management and passed on quickly to subordinates before rumours develop.
- To counteract rumours. Management should supply the information and demonstrate, whenever possible, the truth by definite action.
- As a means of locating the malicious gossiper. There are generally one or two employees in a company who try to ruin personal reputations and lower morale by continually running down managers and supervisors. The slanderers can be discredited quickly if the truth is fed into the grapevine. An interview with the person responsible is essential to find out why he or she acts in this manner. Disciplinary action may be necessary to protect others against these spiteful activities.

## USING CHANNELS EFFECTIVELY

The effectiveness of formal channels is probably measurable by assessing how long information takes to travel from one place to another; how accurately it is transmitted; the responsiveness of employees;

and the cost per unit of manufacture. The correct balance must be achieved between speed of transmission, accuracy and effectiveness depending on the particular circumstances.

### Withholding information

Some supervisors have the mistaken idea that withholding information demonstrates power to subordinates. The reverse is the case as employees inevitably find out through other sources. If it is obvious the supervisor was aware of the information, he or she will be despised and distrusted. These other channels may also convey distorted versions of information, thereby causing further problems.

A similar situation will occur if a supervisor withholds any information from a superior. Regardless of whether the superior will be pleased or annoyed at receiving the information, it should come from the supervisor rather than from another source.

No manager or supervisor likes to be taken by surprise. He or she would much rather learn about problems and mistakes from a subordinate than first hear of them as complaints or reprimands from a superior. Early warning will give the supervisor the opportunity to investigate, correct the trouble, and prepare an adequate explanation.

# Communication networks

Choice of network depends on the degree of centralisation envisaged by management. Centralisation in this context means formal power to make decisions within the network. Thus 'centralised' means that one (or a few) has the power, whereas 'decentralised' means the power is dispersed among members. Perhaps concepts of participation, democracy, decision making, control and bureaucracy may appear to dominate choice, but the main thrusts are behaviour and communication factors. Other issues therefore emerge: specialisation, co-ordination and direction.

## CO-ORDINATING DECISIONS

Centralisation is undoubtedly the easiest way to co-ordinate decision making since all decisions are made by one person (or a few) and enforced by direct supervision. Difficulties may arise, however, if the person becomes overloaded due to an excessive number of decisions which need to be made. The only answer is to decentralise by appointing appropriate specialists, dividing the activities and supplying information as required. This action speeds up decision making, the structure becomes more sensitive to change, response is quicker, and more people are motivated because of increased responsibility and achievement.

When an organisation contains many networks, it is impracticable to describe it as centralised or decentralised because some parts may be centralised whereas others may not. To describe centralisation in these terms might mean comparing one organisation with another by commenting that one is more decentralised than the other.

## POWER DISTRIBUTION

Decentralisation is a dispersal of power among members in a network. However, a more specific description will consider the principle operating at organisation level. Therefore decentralisation will mean augmenting it with other organisational principles, such as the use of specialists and delegation. In most organisations, decentralisation through specialisation and delegation is usual. More unusual is decentralisation through power distribution to network members, which raises issues of industrial democracy.

## NETWORKS

Degrees of power distribution occur by altering the design of networks. A. Bevelas is well known for studying these 'communication nets'. Some examples and comments are given in Fig. 14.4. Certain features are indicated:

- Centralisation is high in fan and wheel nets.
- Communication restrictions are high in fan, chain, radial, wheel and Y nets
- Decentralisation is high in circle and all-channel nets where the power to communicate is shared equally and conforms to democratic structures: both tend to suffer from more noise, slower communication and an increase in errors.

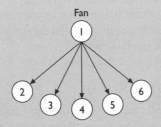

Fan

Power = 1
Centralisation tendency = high
Communication restrictions = high

Chain

Power = 3
Centralisation tendency = intermediate
Communication restrictions = high

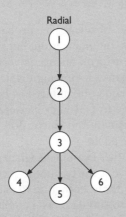

Radial

Power = 1
Centralisation tendency = intermediate
Communication restrictions = high

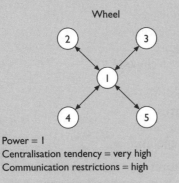

Wheel

Power = 1
Centralisation tendency = very high
Communication restrictions = high

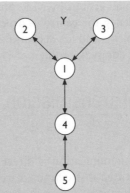

Y

Power = 1
Centralisation tendency = intermediate
Communication restrictions = high

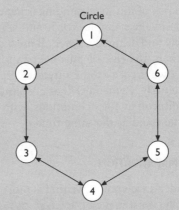

Circle

Power = equal
Centralisation tendency = nil
Communication restrictions = intermediate

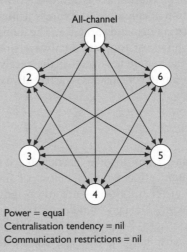

All-channel

Power = equal
Centralisation tendency = nil
Communication restrictions = nil

**Figure 14.4** Formal communication networks

Research with small groups by M.E. Shaw (1964) indicated a tendency for centralised nets to cope with simple problems and for decentralised nets to cope better with complex problems.

# Methods of transmission

## SPEECH

Although oral communication is direct and more personal than written instructions, care is needed in the choice of words and expressions. About 75 per cent of oral communication is misunderstood, ignored or quickly forgotten. The message should be given a little thought before being announced, otherwise the risk of misunderstanding is increased. Wherever possible use simple words and state the message slowly and distinctly. After all precautions have been taken, the risk of misunderstanding is still high, so always check to be sure the employee understands clearly. Remember that absolute concentration is difficult in noisy conditions, with other subjects on the mind at the same time.

## WRITTEN COMMUNICATION

From the sender's viewpoint, writing is more difficult as he or she must make up for lack of face-to-face contact which affects the tone of the message. Facial expressions and gestures are missing, which means much of the impact is removed from the communication. Being able to express a message clearly in writing demands practice. The danger of writing too much or too little is always present. Because of the remoteness factor, the receiver is inclined to jump to conclusions – nearly always the wrong ones.

## SIGNS

Indicators and signs form a particular class of visual communication where the loss of impact is a special problem. Notices are often ignored, e.g. No smoking, Danger, Handle with care, This way up, Press here, Keep within the white lines. The usual excuse is the person did not see them. Similarly, the use of flags, coloured lights and mechanical devices also has limitations because concentration is necessary. People should be constantly reminded, otherwise they tend to forget or overlook even the most glaring signs, especially after a little time has elapsed.

## ACTIONS

The best means of communication is positive demonstration by actually doing something. An action is immediately recognisable and the least likely to confuse. The reason is that the effectiveness of people's various senses is not the same. The sense of sight is about 87 per cent effective, hearing 7 per cent, and smell, touch and taste about 6 per cent. The well-worn saying 'Actions speak louder than words' makes good sense in communication.

## SILENCE

The use of silence is probably the most subtle form of communication, but when misused it is the stupidest form. Silence is very effective and harsh as a means of showing displeasure because a particular code of conduct has been ignored. Sending someone to Coventry causes the offender feelings of uneasiness and frustration, sometimes followed by near panic.

Another example is when a supervisor gives an employee a thirty-minute job five minutes before time, without bothering to enquire if the employee wishes to stay late. The employee's silence on the situation may be accompanied by a facial expression which is more than sufficient to indicate his or her feelings. Some of the effects of silence on people are:

- annoyance
- indifference
- disgust
- hurt feelings
- fear
- suspicion
- distrust
- amusement
- antagonism

They form an excellent list of feelings which must not be generated in employees. The danger of allowing false impressions to develop usually outweighs the effectiveness of silence, therefore this approach should be used with great caution.

## NON-VERBAL COMMUNICATION

Non-verbal communication (NC) may emphasise, clarify, or cause misinterpretation of a message. NC may be consciously or subconsciously recognised, depending on the people involved. In face-to-face communication body movement accounts for 55 per cent of the communication component, words about 7 per cent, and voice about 38 per cent. Also a knowledge of the particular person helps to assess NC. Each person tends to have certain body conduct which may not coincide with recognised NC signals and mislead a stranger. For example, wagging a finger may not mean aggression, covering the mouth may mean various problems, and touching may mean a gesture of friendliness without sexual undertones.

Significant features in interpreting NC are culture, class levels, age, sensitivity, sex, education, training and experience. However, people are influenced by all methods of transmission in the form of a total package. NC is an important feature and worthy of more study. M. Argyle (1975) outlined the practical applications. NC signals are classified in various ways; here are typical groupings.

## FACIAL GIVEAWAYS

Facial giveaways include many well-known features such as eye movements, expression, crying, grinning, blanching, blushing, dilating and contracting of pupils, changing gaze direction, blink rate, and narrowing and widening of eyes. They convey a wide variety of messages, typically to relate; to interact; show sexual interest or disinterest; and indicate deploring conduct, surprise or anger.

## CREATING AN ATMOSPHERE

Facial expressions are closely associated with atmosphere. The sour face depresses while the bright, cheery face enlightens. Changes in expression indicate changes in feelings, although some people manage to hide their feeling successfully whereas others use expressions to gain particular ends. Appropriate expressions are an essential part of conveying a message and help to give it impact and make it more easily understood. Everyone has the ability to create atmosphere, which should not be confused with silence. One person within a group can destroy a friendly atmosphere; this may result in either a tolerable or an intolerable situation. Atmosphere is highly catching, which probably accounts for the saying about the bad apple in the barrel.

## BODY MOVEMENTS

Body movements include gestures and other physical postures. Compared with continental countries, people in Britain have very few generally recognised gestures. These signs are helpful because everyone knows exactly what is meant when they are used. The V-sign is a typical example. Physical postures associated with eye movements are also effective. If the receiver slouches down in the chair, looks bored, and casts eyes to the floor, the sender should get the message that the topic discussed is boring. This pose may force a change of direction to a different topic. If favourable the immediate reaction could be sitting up, leaning forward, levelling of eyes with the speaker, showing a keen interest, and nodding agreement.

## PROXIMITY SIGNALS

People stake out their own 'territory' by setting both the spaces they occupy and their proximity to others. They tend to back away or retaliate if their territory is violated, and take offence. For a person to feel comfortable in certain situations there are rough distances to consider:

- *Intimate zone*: 6–18 in (152–457 mm) for those emotionally connected with the person.
- *Personal zone*: 18 in to 4 ft (457 mm to 1.219 m) for friendly talks and parties.
- *Social zone*: 4–12 ft (1.219–3.658 m) for newcomers.
- *Public zone*: 12 ft (3.658 m) for addressing an audience.

## BODY CONTACT

Touching (in many forms) is easily misunderstood, may invite violent reaction, and has strong sexual meanings. Touching is personal and should be avoided since a reputation of being a 'pawer' is easily gained.

## APPEARANCE

Clothes, cosmetics, perfume, wigs, jewellery and trinkets tend to convey a variety of meanings and are often misinterpreted. Probably people dress in certain ways to convey how they feel or to project an image.

## PHYSICAL CHARACTERISTICS

Physical characteristics convey particular meanings because of stereotyping and experiences with people in various categories.

## TIME FRAME

People are often grouped by means of their punctuality, hurried or leisurely approach, and application of rituals. Establishing rapport may depend on synchronised time frames, especially when cultural aspects apply.

## ENVIRONMENTAL FEATURES

Often people are assessed according to their general surrounds – typically a tidy, clean desk; appropriate furniture; and decor.

# Methods of reception

Methods of reception are divided into the various senses, the use of which may be improved with practice (Chapter 15). In communication, transmission and reception are equally important and should be examined with equal interest.

## VISION

The sense of sight is about 87 per cent effective. Visual perception relies on the way the brain organises the nervous impulses that come from the eyes. Thus the same object or framework could be seen differently by various people through the perceptual process (Chapter 9).

### Distortions

Vision is also affected by attitudes which the brain uses to interpret incoming signals. Attitudes may be thought of as points of view that alter reality or visual input (Chapter 9). Favourable or unfavourable attitudes govern thoughts on all features such as race, politics, social gatherings, religion, trade unions, groups of employees and sex. They also influence economic issues, trust or suspicion, and feelings of superiority or inferiority.

Attitudes also couple with opinions, which interpret visual accounts of events, behaviour, an object, or reading material. Thus a receiver of information through the use of sight has been influenced by factual occurrences and by attitude. Put another way, an opinion is an interpretation of facts which are influenced by attitude. However, an opinion is not a generalised conclusion, therefore opinions do not lead to attitudes but reflect attitudes.

Any individual tends to justify an opinion, the justification being a defence mechanism, not a cause of the opinion. If a justification is destroyed the opinion often remains, but if the opinion changes the defence changes. These details are important for the supervisor, who should always distinguish carefully the difference between facts and opinions. A supervisor who labels subordinates as lazy because of general suspicions towards employees may be expressing an opinion with little or no factual evidence. The other extreme is to give an opinion, such as 'improved air conditioning will reduce contamination', which is strongly supported by facts.

## HEARING

The sense of hearing is only about 7 per cent effective and needs high concentration and comprehension to receive a message correctly. There are many distractions at any time which cause hearing difficulties: environmental conditions such as noise; difficulty in concentrating; thinking about other matters; and being distracted by local movements of individuals. There are countless times in a day when people ask speakers to repeat what they have said. This wastes a considerable amount of time.

# Communication flow lines

Communication flow lines permeate the whole structure and must be fully utilised. Probably the two most important factors are speed of communication

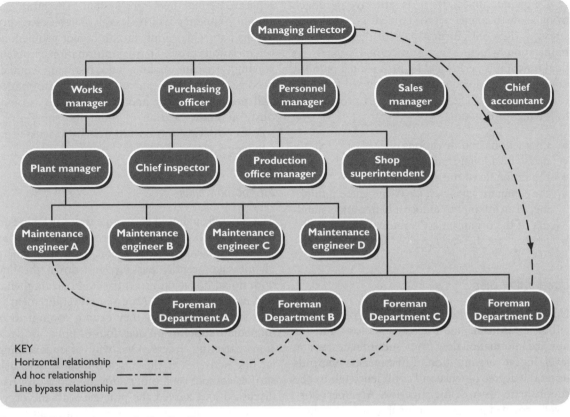

**Figure 14.5** Informal communication flow lines

flow and relevancy of the information in the flow lines. The supervisor always needs appropriate information, on time and without excessive overload. This depends upon:

- being able to state requirements
- the systems specialist's capability to provide them
- effective communication flow

Consequently, the supervisor should be able to solve problems, make decisions and accurately assess employee performance.

**THE SIX MAJOR FLOW LINES**

1 *Downward*: the traditional, authoritarian flow line conforming to lines of command.
2 *Upward*: the reverse of downward flow, conforming to formal lines and operating on a subordinate-to-superior basis.

3 *Horizontal*: the flow between peers who are accountable to the same superior.
4 *Ad hoc*: the flow between colleagues in different sections or departments.
5 *Line bypass*: the flow between a superior in one section and an employee in a different section at a lower level in the hierarchy.
6 *External*: the flow between any organisation member and outside people, including customers, suppliers and other companies' representatives.

*Informal flow lines*

Flow lines 3, 4 and 5 are informal and are illustrated in Fig. 14.5 to demonstrate their operational uses.

*Downward flow lines*

Downward flow lines suffer from delay, distortion and loss of information as they descend the line of command, unless there is effective feedback from below to counteract the tendencies. As already stressed, they only form a part of dynamic communication which is a transactional process. A dual function is performed by providing a path for downward transmissions and downward feedback to senders below. The downward part provides the following information:

- instructions and directions
- details on administration procedures and systems
- the rationale of the subordinate's job
- the company's policies, ideas and general thinking, in an attempt to induce a better understanding of the organisation's objectives and goals
- feedback for messages received from subordinates

## Upward flow lines

Upward flow lines also offer a dual function by providing a feedback line for transmissions and for upward information flow from 'subordinates' at any level in the organisation. Effectiveness depends upon the degree of trust and confidence felt by the subordinate towards the superior. At supervisory level, provided a sound relationship is established, subordinates should give full support, ideas for improvements, early warning of difficulties, participation, receptiveness to change and more acceptance of change.

A vital factor for co-ordination is the supervisor's desire to pass on information further up the line with a minimum of bias. Even adverse information that may damage the supervisor's image (in his or her eyes) must be transmitted. Supporting this flow line could be suggestion schemes, counselling, committees, the grapevine, complaints and grievances procedures, termination interviews, an open-door policy and the ombudsman.

## Horizontal flow lines

Horizontal flow lines are strongly connected with group activity (Chapter 5). Poor horizontal flow lines may divide a team. This danger applies equally to management and employee groups. The high risk of intergroup rivalry and cussedness in these circumstances causes group members to feel

separated from the larger system. Therefore the system boundary will be less permeable. Rigidity of this nature develops into an urgent problem as organisations grow. Sharing information, problem solving, decision making and resolving conflict become increasingly difficult. Group performance will probably be low and the supervisor is obviously at fault, bearing in mind the supervisory role of fostering intragroup activity discussed in Chapter 5.

## Ad hoc flow lines

The supervisor should encourage staff to expand ad hoc relationships with employees in other sections as this time-saving activity is vital. A situation where all messages rigidly pass up and down the line with no ad hoc arrangements should be anathema and must be avoided. An essential requirement is that staff should know they cannot commit their immediate superior on questions of policy or decisions affecting others. One way of encouraging ad hoc activities if there is a difficulty is to ask staff to contact each other after the supervisor has discussed and agreed the practice with the other employee's superior. Such sensible arrangements bring the organisation to life.

## Line bypass flow lines

Line bypass flow lines are very useful for avoiding trouble spots growing into major upheavals. Often managers further up the line are not made fully aware of difficulties because managers at lower levels either do not pass up any information that personally affects their image, or they distort the information. Usually the person nearest the adverse situation knows most about it. Probably he or she will provide a more accurate impression, so a logical approach is to bypass intermediaries and approach that individual.

A manager should not hesitate to use this approach if he or she feels dissatisfied with the way a situation is developing, doubts certain information, or if change does not occur as expected. Any sensible, trained manager or supervisor located between the two parties communicating in this way will appreciate the need to adopt such action.

## External flow lines

External flow lines harmonise with general systems theory which has already been stressed. Although some employees may not be directly contacting outsiders, they are invariably associated with the external environment through domestic situations, clubs and other gatherings. Often vital information is transmitted by these means, especially when managers meet their counterparts at golf clubs, social gatherings and various professional association meetings.

## COMMUNICATION BREAKDOWNS

Although all the channels, networks and flow lines are established, breakdowns still occur as well as misunderstandings. They are usually due to human problems that are created by poor management and organisation, poor selection, and ineffective systems and procedures. Typical breakdowns that tend to indicate their own solutions are:

- overloaded communication channels
- poor job descriptions causing overloads and delays
- incorrect instructions
- insufficient sifting of information to avoid an excessive number of messages and too much paperwork
- encoding and decoding difficulties
- lack of training to avoid excessive external and internal pressures
- unawareness of other employees' problems which leads to blocking vital information
- personality clashes and emotionally troubled people
- misuse of power and weak supervision
- corruptions of feedback

# Causes of misunderstanding

Causes may be grouped into five main categories:

- the sender's difficulties
- poor choice of transmission channel
- the receiver's difficulties
- problems of expression
- general situational problems

## THE SENDER'S DIFFICULTIES

Often the sender does not give sufficient attention to encoding the message in the most effective way for ease of understanding by the receiver. Such encoding may include the use of English language and translating into computer language. Also, using non-verbal expressions and gestures effectively should not be forgotten.

The sender must be able to assess the outlook, problems of understanding and the particular interests of the receiver. The right approach produces a more positive reaction and a better response to the message. Every person needs individual treatment, which means judgement plays an important part in successful communication. A friendly approach and giving information form only part of a far more complex programme (Chapters 10 and 11).

## CHOICE OF CHANNEL

The correct choice of channel is essential. There are many on offer such as oral or written forms: using the computer, telephone, fax, memo, letter, and so on. This linkage may be upgraded by using two or more channels to reduce the risk of failure or misinterpretation. Also there are many opportunities open for everyone to participate, such as chance meetings, group and departmental meetings, communication networks, e-mail, and general meetings.

## THE RECEIVER'S DIFFICULTIES

The most common problems are inattention when the message is decoded into thought; misinterpretation for a variety of reasons; and a psychological reluctance to understand the message correctly because of, say, prejudices or a fear of the consequences. They are some problems which are difficult to resolve without face-to-face contact. They include uncertainty of the message, incorrect assumptions, incompatible viewpoints, and inability to recognise any deceptions or deliberately omitted information.

## PROBLEMS OF EXPRESSION

### Educational level and experience

Allowance for an employee's level of education and amount of experience is essential otherwise a message can be so worded that it goes completely over the person's head. Embarrassment may prevent the individual from querying the message in these circumstances. The situation is not revealed until later when a problem arises because no action was taken by the employee. This problem requires careful treatment when it seems a subordinate has deliberately ignored an instruction. A wise action is always to ask first if the original message was clear.

A worthwhile exercise is to test the employee's capability to recognise the significance of messages. Individuals often tend to suffer with a shallow understanding of a message and fail to appreciate the deeper understanding. This difficulty extends to lack of knowledge associated with systems, procedures, priorities, client orientations, the supervisor's roles, and the job itself. Sometimes the problem employee will deliberately limit interpretation of the significance of a message and only use a narrow understanding.

### Interpretation of words

Words that have definite meanings, such as those describing buildings, furniture, tools, machines and workbenches are easy to understand. Confusion occurs, however, when the word describes more than one object. Additional words of description are essential in cases where misinterpretation is possible. Words that have vague meanings should be avoided whenever possible when describing the degree, condition or manner of things. Otherwise they must be explained or their meaning demonstrated. Some examples of vague words are given in the sentences below. A moment's thought will show how these instructions could be made more clear and precise.

- The job will be finished soon.
- Give the end of the tool a light tap.
- Hold the wire in the cutters gently.
- Slowly withdraw the assembly from the furnace.
- This job is urgent.
- Fix the bolt securely.
- Make sure the nut is tight.
- When the liquid is hot, dip the assembly in and out quickly.
- Press the valve in a little bit.
- Mix well before replacing the cap firmly.

### Abstract terms

Words that describe qualities or intangible things should not be used carelessly as their meaning will vary from person to person. Abstract words are often used when people wish to avoid being precise or have not thought about exactly what they mean. The tendency to be vague is because people feel more secure when they do not commit themselves and it requires less mental effort. The effect on subordinates, however, is one of frustration because they do not know where they stand. Some carelessly used abstractions are democracy, virtue, peace, morality, responsibility, conformity, truth, liberty, honour, religion, power, poverty, standard and progress.

### Technical jargon

Although technical terms have their place, they should be avoided in communications intended for those who are not acquainted with them. The full meaning is seldom conveyed and often completely misunderstood. Using jargon becomes a habit and some people even think its use makes them appear superior.

### Gobbledygook

Gobbledygook describes the style of speaking or writing which confuses because of its complexity. Often too many words are used where one would do, or long and uncommon words are used instead of short, simple ones. Here is an example of gobbledygook:

> The general arrangement in the drilling section has now been made untenable from the risk of fire point of view. The positions of the benches and drill stands have been altered considerably from the previous working layout that allowed the fitters, drillers and female assemblers free access from the gangways to the emergency exit which was installed three years ago in case of fire.

A suggested revision is:

> The rearrangement of benches in the drilling section has blocked the emergency fire exit.

Irritating shorter examples are:

- In the not too distant future = soon
- At this point in time = now
- Do you understand what I mean? = understand?

## GENERAL SITUATIONAL PROBLEMS

General situational problems must be considered when attempting to solve communication difficulties and to prevent future problems. Apart from the main issues discussed below, there may be legal, political and economic features as well as geographical, time and technological aspects.

The idea that communication is simply the passing of information from one person to another is quite common and some companies spend large sums of money with this thought alone in mind. Negligible results are achieved because the full process of communication must include motivating employees by appropriate leadership. This concept encourages self-discipline through persuasion, and aims at convincing employees that management and society want them to develop their capabilities fully.

### Inept managers

Often managers neglect the overall skill of communication. Typically, they avoid monitoring and controlling, they do not anticipate difficulties, and they neglect to ensure comprehensive coverage of information. Naturally this situation is created by top management and can only be rectified by action at this level.

### Company size

As a company grows, the problems of communication and misunderstanding increase in proportion. More specialists are introduced, each with their own problems of communication. Specialists are often misunderstood and misused when dealing with others who are unfamiliar with their particular functions. In the growing company, information passes through many more hands and remoteness becomes a danger as keeping in touch with everyone gradually becomes more burdensome. People are less familiar with the whole situation and so it is easier to misunderstand information.

### Poor organisation

In a poor organisation people are often unsure of their own authority, responsibilities and duties as well as those of their colleagues. Inevitably this causes considerable uncertainty about instructions, official backing and the importance of the message. Surveys show that poor organisation is common and many misunderstandings occur. The situation could be rapidly improved by clearly defining everyone's function.

### Previous environment

Memories of past treatment at home and in industry shape the attitudes of employees. If they have suffered injustices or harshness before, they will be on the defensive. They are often suspicious and prejudiced against their superior's intentions although the communication may appear to be clear. This inherent tendency to distort the message to suit the individual's attitude towards the sender should be recognised.

### Class consciousness

Some people seem to thrive on continually emphasising how much better they are in terms of bank balance, blood line, residence, previous schools, culture or accent. Such people are bores and some are unaware of the gulf they create between themselves, colleagues and subordinates by their immature attempts to assert themselves. This form of assertion is short-sighted since other people's reactions are more likely to be dislike, jealousy or contempt rather than admiration. Such feelings will distort the messages received and misunderstandings are inevitable.

### False reasoning

Reasoning must follow a set, logical pattern called syllogism. This is essential to avoid associating a statement of fact with some item of knowledge or another factual statement, and assuming a mistaken connection. Jumping to the wrong conclusion is easy. An example is given below of logical reasoning by deduction, followed by a statement of ridiculously obvious false reasoning:

| Sentence 1 | All dogs have four legs. |
| Sentence 2 | An alsation is a dog. |
| Conclusion | An alsation has four legs. |

| Sentence 1 | All dogs have four legs. |
| Sentence 2 | A cat has four legs. |
| Conclusion | A cat is a dog. |

Although the second example is obviously false, people are inclined to reason along similar lines, confusing facts with possibilities. A cat may be a dog on this basis, but without further information one cannot be sure. Always be particularly careful to check the sense of a statement when it is based on the relationship of two connected statements or facts in this way.

### Unsound arguments

- *Vague distinctions*: insinuating there are sharp divisions when there are indistinct differences. Examples are light or dark, black or white, sane or insane.
- *Inaccurate assumptions*: using supposition or intuitive reasoning. Such incorrect conclusions adopt premises which are only assumptions. These are often assumed to be true for the sake of argument or action. For example, a fuel gauge may give a false reading, consequently further checks are essential to verify.
- *Untested analogies*: suggesting a conclusion but not establishing it.
- *Invalid generalisations*: oversimplifying the evidence or by selecting instances favourable to a contention but ignoring those which conflict with it.
- *Unsound slogans or popular catch phrases*: used to confuse but often unacceptable unless justified.
- *Narrow arguments*: stressing one view when there are obviously many others.
- *Ambiguous words*: attempting to deceive or indicating favourable or unfavourable associations without any justification.
- *Diverting statements to confuse logic*: using complex techniques which may be very successful when subtly applied. They demand skilful manipulation of proposals; typically introducing irrelevant points or twisting words to suit the case.
- *Invalid syllogisms*: mentioned earlier.

### The wrong context

When conversations are overheard, a misunderstanding may occur because the opening remarks are missed, remarks which clarify the subject and throw light on the meaning. Here is an example of how the wrong impression can be caused.

He was inhaling oxygen, when suddenly the supply was cut off and he was dead a minute later.

The correct context was an incident in an operating theatre, but it could have been in an aircraft flying at high altitude, or in a space capsule on the moon.

### Thinking in terms of extremes

Some people develop a habit of judging or thinking in terms of extremes at each end of the scale. Consequently, they do not appreciate that problems and situations are many-sided affairs. Few events are so clear-cut and simple that they fit conveniently into a set pattern. There is a whole range of possible sides to a problem, each requiring separate consideration. For example, if a machine breaks down because a fuse has blown, the fuse could be replaced immediately. An engineer, however, might reason why the fuse burned out, make several checks and adjustments on the machine before replacing the fuse, and so save the company money and wasted time on future delays.

# Effects of poor communication

Poor communication will have a drastic adverse effect on production and individual relationships. Continual misunderstandings lead to confusion, mistakes, wastage and accidents. Employees become frustrated and morale drops, resulting in lack of motivation and low productivity.

**SYMPTOMS**

Unrest and possibly strikes follow when changes occur and reasons are not communicated. The usual sequence is that very little information flows upwards to managers, and the managers are unaware of the situation because complaints, grievances and trouble spots reach the lower levels of supervision and stop there. The general feeling of dissatisfaction spreads and poor co-operation is general throughout the company. Employees leave and labour turnover increases until the situation is recognised by management and attempts are made to improve communication. Many of these symptoms are measurable, so trends should be watched and appropriate steps taken.

# Improving communication

There are numerous ways of improving communication. They include understanding the basic aspects outlined in this chapter which highlight the trouble spots; developing the basic communication skills (Chapter 15); and using particular techniques (Chapter 16). Underlying any improvement plan should be an appreciation of the main aims:

- to improve the two-way process by ensuring everyone recognises the need for effective communication
- to recognise the need, and undertake responsibility for effective communication
- to reduce misunderstandings
- to satisfy any legal requirements
- to satisfy employees' misapprehensions
- to encourage everyone to participate and contribute towards achieving organisational goals
- to improve the industrial climate and culture by reducing suspicion, distrust and antagonism
- to convince each employee that individual responsibility for effective communication is an important part of the job

## AN IMPROVEMENT PROGRAMME

To satisfy the main aims, all supervisors and managers should recognise them, undertake appropriate training, and alter their operating methods accordingly. Top management should support the main aims and conduct an improvement programme. Apart from these aspects, there is ample scope for the supervisor to adopt a personal communication improvement plan. This may be achieved by using the information given here and in Chapters 15 and 16. To summarise, the following steps are essential:

1 Assess the effectiveness of present communication by conducting surveys based upon the main aspects discussed in this chapter.
2 Plan improvements to achieve the main aims by examining each aim, comparing it with the present situation, and noting the differences.
3 Relate each difference to the appropriate communication feature in terms of strategy, tactics and training.
4 Draw up detailed arrangements to achieve improvements.
5 Persevere with attempting improvements by appreciating that long-term aims are essential.
6 Follow up periodically to check on visualised changes.

## QUESTIONS

1 Explain the term *communication* and its importance in connection with production and human relations.

2 Discuss the main channels of communication and how the supervisor should use them.

3 Discuss the existence of the grapevine as an essential channel of communication.

4 Consider some of the common causes of misunderstandings and how they can be overcome by the supervisor.

5 How would you assess the effectiveness of communication in a company?

6 Why is communication so important in business?

7 Outline the means of communication and the possible dangers involved, if any, with each one.

8 How can a supervisor use the grapevine effectively?

9 State the advantages and disadvantages of one-way communication and two-way communication.

10 Why is it essential for formal channels of information to be supplemented by informal channels?

11 Withholding information unnecessarily can be dangerous. Explain this statement.

12 Discuss the effects of silence as a means of communication.

13 What advice would you give to a supervisor who cannot understand why employees ignore signs such as 'This way up' that are displayed at various points?

14 Why do subordinates and supervisors easily misunderstand information?

15 Outline the main communication networks and their uses.

16 What are the dangers of using non-verbal communication?

17 Why is feedback so important when communicating?

18 Outline the major communication flow lines.

19 Give some examples of non-verbal communication and their uses.

20 Discuss the process concept of communication.

21 Communication fails unless there is a dynamic process which incorporates feedback. Explain this statement.

22 List the range of communication process models.

23 What are the main classes of communication?

24 Explain the terms 'information theory' and 'systems theory'.

25 Interpersonal communication is behaviourally oriented whereas information theory is mathematically oriented. Explain the significance of these definitions related to supervision.

26 What are the supervisor's communication responsibilities related to subordinates, peers, management and clients?

---

**CASE STUDY**

Sid Prior is the sales manager of a large company that has ten showrooms at various towns in Surrey and Sussex. Each showroom has a manager and showroom supervisor. Randoph Amery joined the company eight years ago as a supervisor in Leatherhead. Sid was very happy with Randolph's performance appraisals and decided to groom him for promotion to a showroom manager. Accordingly he had transferred him to various showrooms over the past six years to gain experience.

Randolph began to feel uneasy about all the moves as he had thought Sid was pleased with him, although there was no word of promotion. Other supervisors he knew had been promoted. He kept thinking about his last appointment at Brighton where he felt there was considerable antagonism from John, the manager. Randolph had thought up some good ideas for improvements, but when he suggested them to him he was told to forget it. His wife was not happy with the situation, considering all their moves and no indication of promotion.

Sid began to doubt his plans for Rudolph after receiving a poor report from Brighton. At a company party it was obvious that Randolph's wife was unhappy. John, the showroom manager at Brighton, was retiring soon and Sid thought Randolph should at least try for the job.

*What would be the main points to raise with Randoph at the interview for the Brighton job? Discuss the questions of communication in the organisation, counselling, and performance appraisals, considering the events over the past eight years.*

---

The introduction of a typing pool at J.L. Conway, a medium-sized company manufacturing fishing equipment, has worked well. All managers use the scheme, although there is a tendency for the same typist to be allocated to the same manager each time as this approach provides some continuity. Strict devices are exercised to control output and balance workloads. The supervisor spends considerable time ensuring there are fair workloads.

Three incidents occur one Friday afternoon. First, Julie catches her finger in the cloakroom door and injures it sufficiently badly to slow down her typing speed. Second, Anna who works mainly for the personnel manager has helped her in the preparation of material for a weekend training course and is invited to assist her because her deputy has a domestic problem. Third, a rush job comes up unexpectedly, which means that even with a full complement of staff they will have to work on Saturday to complete it in time.

When the supervisor explains this to the typing pool, Julie complains that her finger is worse and Anna mentions her 'invite' to help with the training course. The supervisor becomes annoyed and says, 'Anna, your job is here. You can't go to the conference and that's that!'

*Comment on the conduct of the personnel manager, the supervisor and Anna.*

# 15

# Communication: basic skills

## Introduction

In the previous chapter the main aspects of communication were discussed and related to reception difficulties. Inherent in this communication process are basic skills which help to overcome many misunderstandings:

- effective speech
- business writing
- the art of listening
- questioning
- giving orders
- reprimanding
- counselling
- negotiating in conflicts
- resolving grievances
- conducting informal group discussions

## Effective speech

Effective oral communication overcomes many misunderstandings and creates an improved impression. Correct speech involves the rules of grammar; avoiding metaphors, slang and superfluous words; a distinct delivery and approach pitched to the listener; and the opportunity to demonstrate sincerity.

There are many views on the effects of speech. They account for varying reactions from the listener. For example, the range of outcomes if the impression is given of being upper-class or above the level of people employed as operatives or staff. Certainly some managers are irritated when they hear poor speech; equally subordinates may react if a supervisor does not relate to their speech level.

Moreover, a career-conscious supervisor with poor speech will often be at a disadvantage when considering job requirements at a higher level.

### SPEECH IMPROVEMENT

A personal assessment is possible by listening carefully to peers, managers and others, and noting the differences and effects. The use of a tape recorder helps to overcome personal assessment problems because often people are unaware of their speech difficulties until they hear a recording. Asking the advice of a trusted friend is also worthwhile. Some peers may insist that speech is unimportant, especially if they are seeking promotion. Try to avoid the following pitfalls:

- Careless speech – dropping aitches and slurring words.
- Incorrect grammar – which easily causes misunderstandings.
- Using clichés – hackneyed phrases which irritate: you know, I mean, sort of. People tend to concentrate more on waiting for the next cliché.
- Using American expressions that may not be fully understood: touch base, take on board, a new ball game.
- Using metaphors which some people may misinterpret:
  - Put your head on the block = take responsibility
  - Leave no stone unturned = be thorough
  - Food for thought = consider carefully
- Excessive mannerisms often send the wrong signals to the receiver: waving arms, banging the table, and hands on hips.

- Thinking out loud: openly displaying bad temper, causing a bad atmosphere, and interrupting other people's work.
- Forgetting to say please or thank you at appropriate times.

Speech improvement is always worthwhile but demanding on time and perseverance. Practical help is essential. Many speech therapists and courses are easily accessible for the ambitious supervisor.

# Business writing

Although most managers and supervisors may have extensively studied English grammar at school, many seem to have difficulty in writing a good memorandum or business letter. Numerous examples of bureaucratic verbiage are seen in letters from banks, the Civil Service, and large companies. There are exceptions, however, and these avoid any attempt to be vague. They concentrate on conciseness, sound construction, being informative, and frankness. This approach is ensured by using simple principles which identify the purpose of the communication, consider the reader, and conform to the relevance of each sentence.

The practical applications of report writing and project reports are detailed in Chapter 16. Improving writing skill is a straightforward process which follows a similar pattern to the previous section. Surprising progress is possible by attending lectures, reading appropriate literature (see the bibliography) and practising. The process is not mysterious or complex; it relies on simplicity and perseverance.

## MAIN ASPECTS

To improve business writing, the supervisor should concentrate on the purpose of the message, organise ideas into a logical structure, consider the style of writing which will be acceptable to the recipient, and attract his or her interest. Graphical presentation should also be considered. If a desktop computer is available, the use of a word processing package is invaluable for marshalling ideas, testing various layouts, and rearranging paragraphs to form a logical presentation. The main aspects are now discussed.

### Determine the purpose of the message

Deciding on the main purpose of the message is an important feature. Often messages are so garbled that much time is wasted trying to assess the real purpose. This may be because the purpose is often thought to include an opportunity to improve the company's image by impressing on the recipient involved strategies and vague objectives. They are usually of no interest and irritate the reader.

Sometimes there will be more than one purpose, in which case try to assemble the purposes in priority order. Samples of the purpose are to provide information on a subject, answer a question, give the results of a survey or activity, and recommend changes and certain courses of action.

### Arrange into a logical structure

A sound approach is to jot down all the ideas and points as they come to mind, rearrange into a logical pattern (Chapter 16), and divide into sections and subsections. Try to write an opening and closing sentence for each section, consider the main points in the sentences, and then write the main text. Remember to place the points in priority order and check that important issues have not been missed.

### Essential aspects

- Read the script through carefully and refer to problems of expression given in Chapter 14.
- A refinement is to use serial arguments which are often standard practice in reports. This means the argument is completed with a conclusion which then becomes the premise of the next, and so on. Here is an example:

  If more time is spent on ensuring that keyboard operators in the team are working in suitable conditions there should be less absenteeism. If there are fewer delays through absenteeism the team leader will have more time to concentrate on coaching. If coaching improves . . .

- Closely coupled with logical thought is the use of analytical thinking, including lateral thinking (Chapter 8).
- Use logical reasoning when outlining arguments using syllogisms (Chapter 14).

# Style of writing

Style is usually defined as a fundamental method of applying the principles of effective writing and interpreting grammar to gain a maximum impression on the reader. In other words, style is a way of presenting information or descriptive matter which achieves high impact.

Improving style is a demanding discipline involving practice and expanding knowledge of grammar and relevant principles. Apart from the pitfalls in the previous section, aim to keep the message simple, be realistic and always use correct language. Persuasion is not possible unless the reader understands.

## MAIN FEATURES

- Be positive by highlighting the favourable side of the subject. In other words, emphasise the pros and discount the cons.
- Be optimistic by praising the good points in such a way that feeling good is generated rather than degrading the subject.
- Avoid obvious prejudices by trying to maintain a balanced approach and disclosing all the views or issues under discussion. The writer's habits of thought or convictions are easily misconceived and often break down when tested.
- Avoid stressing self-motives or self-interest by adopting an objective theme.
- Clarify whether statements are factual, generalisations, opinions or ideas.
- Avoid using emotional words that tend to obscure the intended meaning, such as idiotic, silly, obstinate, common sense and obvious.
- Use generalisations carefully and try to clarify the intended meaning by adding such words as 'usually' and 'sometimes'.
- Using words is usually more effective than quoting numbers.
- A graph or picture is more impressive than many descriptive words.
- Use everyday language; avoid words the reader may not understand.
- Keep sentences and paragraphs short. Cut out any unnecessary words.

## AROUSING INTEREST

Most writers agonise over how to arouse the reader's interest. Famous authors have obviously perfected the art, and advertising agencies are forever experimenting with new ideas. The aims are to create a mental picture that appeals to the reader and to write in the reader's interests. Many volumes and courses are available on this aspect alone and there are hundreds of principles to use. Some important psychological points to observe are:

- Do not offend the reader's feelings. Never criticise an error or obvious false opinion.
- Respect the reader's points of view. Agree with any previous statements and make careful harmless suggestions to overcome a problem.
- Appreciate the reader's class or status. A safe approach is to avoid attempting to impress on the reader any superiority. Always assume humility by asking for advice, help or a favour.
- Recognise the reader's intelligence. Never flatter or attempt to be insincere. Appeal to higher motives, moral judgements and expectations.
- Stress the reader's importance and pride. This may be achieved by adding a compliment on any appropriate subject and asking for suggestions on any topic within the scope of the communication.
- Use motivational psychology by assessing needs, wants and interests. Indicate how to achieve them through action favourable to the requirements of the writer. Restrict the use of I and concentrate on You. In other words, limit what you want and expand on what they want.
- Avoid any form of pressure which might offend attitudes or perceptive interpretations. Use a friendly, co-operative style by praising, being objective, and using any social graces in written form.
- Invite the reader to take some definite action and explain how to achieve it, thus making the action easier.
- Whenever possible use irresistible words: save, free, latest, new. Avoid exaggerated words such as 'incredible'.
- Always write as though talking directly to the reader.

- Use concrete words: machine, factory, office. Avoid abstract words: democratic, ideology, love. Use dynamic words, not passive. Use active phrases: cut costs, save money. Avoid vague words.

## GRAPHICAL PRESENTATION

The use of visual techniques may improve the message and clarify complex details. There are many different approaches, some of which are only suitable for specialists to devise. The straightforward types of visual presentation are flow diagrams (Chapter 25), structure diagrams (Chapter 4), network diagrams (Chapter 23) and Gantt charts (Chapter 26). Bar charts, pie charts, pictograms, line graphs, trend charts, Z charts and frequency distributions are also very useful. They are illustrated in Chapter 23.

Graphical presentations may clarify data, they may arouse more interest if they emphasise an important point, and they may also strengthen the writer's approach. A brief outline of statistical methods is given in Chapter 23 to illustrate their use in control and in general presentation. Graphical presentations are equally useful in making a speech and in report writing (Chapter 16).

# The art of listening

The capability to listen attentively with genuine interest is an elusive quality for many reasons. It mainly involves being able to concentrate, adapting to high thought speed, and resisting the tendency to be bored. The art of listening is an essential requirement, not only in effective communication but also in many major aspects of management. These include employee morale and motivation (Chapters 11 and 12); marketing (Chapter 4); quality assurance (Chapter 27); leadership approach (Chapter 13); and work study (Chapter 25).

High concentration is difficult because thought is faster than speech. This allows the mind to wander ahead on to other subjects which may be more interesting. Much of what is said is then missed and the real message is not absorbed. If the speaker senses this inattention, the desire to

communicate is lost and communication breaks down in the early stages.

Avoiding the tendency to be bored easily is possible by carefully steering the conversation away from familiar areas and moving on to important subjects. However, avoiding any outward sign of boredom is essential when listening to well-worn complaints or subjects which are often repeated but very important to the speaker.

Genuine listening keeps the supervisor in close touch with employees. Regular contact provides a vital link for the free flow of new ideas, adaptations, and problems of a personal and technical nature. This philosophy establishes the co-operation of employees and it makes full use of them.

## RULES FOR BETTER LISTENING

### Maintain undivided attention

Use the spare time caused by higher thought speed to sift what is said into important and irrelevant points, examine them for validity, try to classify them and decide what is missing. Try to imagine what is coming next and link it with the change of mood or actions of the speaker. This flexible technique will fill the spare time and ensure the mind does not have the opportunity to wander.

### Find a suitable location

When practicable find a place with a minimum of distractions and interruptions. Noise and disturbances will ruin the continuity of a message for both parties and lead to mutual irritation.

### Show a positive interest

Some supervisors deliberately pretend *not* to be interested, but this should only be done when some diplomatic action is needed. For example, to discourage a request which will cause resentment if refused. Intelligent questions and comments in appropriate places help to convince the speaker that he or she is being heard with interest and understanding. The atmosphere should improve and the speaker is more likely to gain confidence and expand on his or her thoughts. In other words, listening should be dynamic and magnetic.

### Allow for distortion

Making due allowances for distortion applies to both supervisors and subordinates. Supervisors must recognise they are capable of distorting information as they receive it, and of discarding those parts that do not fit into their own outlook. Supervisors should try to treat the message objectively and ignore any personal feelings towards the speaker which might influence their reaction to the message. This does not mean discarding the personal approach of being friendly.

### Be co-operative and patient

Allow the speaker to hold the floor and say everything on his or her mind. Anything left unsaid grows and nags soon after. Check to ensure the full story is given.

### Record the conversation

Do not rely on memory; recalling a long conversation accurately is usually unrealistic. Recognise that memory is imperfect and details are often difficult to recall immediately, especially when many points have been raised which demand some action. Reassure the speaker by giving the reason for making notes.

### Practice constantly

Improve the art of listening by using the many opportunities to experiment away from the workplace: try to decipher a relative's conversation at home, use the radio and television, and listen to conversations on buses and trains. A sound procedure is to determine the main topic by sorting the major points from the side issues and by recognising padding. Look for particular techniques for emphasising the subject matter and note the words which arouse particular feelings and emotions. If there is time, write a summary and check on the facts for correctness and ambiguity. Look for ideas from facts and try to determine why there is an objection to certain words or phrases.

# Questioning

For success this skill relies heavily on effective oral communication, establishing a suitable rapport, and the art of listening. Questioning techniques are constantly used in a variety of situations and they save time when applied accurately. However, a supervisor may unintentionally block complete answers or receive wrong answers when he or she is in a hurry or frustrated by an incident. Employees are extremely sensitive towards questioning since they usually feel there is an ulterior motive which may adversely affect them. Therefore, always explain why the question is asked, consider the available techniques of questioning and choose carefully. Bear in mind people's likely reactions to questions (Chapter 9).

## SIX QUESTIONING TECHNIQUES

### Straight questions

Straight questions are simple requests, such as why, when, where, who, what and how. Generally they succeed in producing the information required, but this approach is crude and may offend if not courteously applied.

### Indirect questions

Indirect questions are ideal when dealing with capable, experienced employees who know immediately the reason for the communication. Typical examples: The floor is very oily around this machine. John doesn't seem very happy today. Output was down by 8 per cent yesterday.

### Searching questions

Searching questions usually apply automatically when an answer to a previous question is either evasive or too shallow. They demand care since it is obvious that pressure is being applied, so mental barriers must be reduced by adopting suitable disarming wording. Typical example: Yes John, I appreciate the supply position is causing a problem but could you tell me what has happened since we last discussed this one?

## Theoretical questions

Theoretical questions are useful at meetings and in dealing with capable individuals. The basis may be a speculative situation or problem which is based on mere theory. Generally the question does not deal with facts as presented by experience. It concentrates more on knowledge, but not with its practical application. In other words, suppositions are proposed. Two examples:

> John, you know Michael is thinking of moving to France. If you were to take over his job as chargehand what changes would you think about?
>
> Mike, supposing we switched the desks around so that Susan is nearer the terminal, how do you think she would react?

## Hypothetical questions

Hypothetical questions are closely allied with theoretical questions but the supposition is made as a basis for reasoning, without an assumption of its truth. They are useful as a starting point for further investigation from known facts.

## Loose questions

Loose questions are worded in such a way that people feel free to expand their answers and so provide more information. Questions that draw employees out must be carefully phrased. They demand practice to succeed. Typical approaches: How do you feel about taking over this job now that you've had time to think about it? I know it's early days but can you see some ways of improving the layout of these orders? Where do you think we went wrong?

## Follow-up questions

Finally there is the problem of failing to reach a satisfactory answer. This may be due to many reasons associated with relationships, poor communication or the environment. After an initial question it may be obvious from the reply that there could be a misunderstanding or an evasion. Pressing further may mean choosing a relevant point in the reply and seeking further information. Typical examples:

> Jane, you said that you would like to move away from Mary when we rearrange the office layout. Is there any particular reason for this?
>
> Roger, I thought you liked computer work but now you are saying its boring. Could you tell me what has changed your mind?

Unsatisfactory answers at this stage usually force the situation into more complicated discussions. These may involve considering effective communication, dealing with grievances, group discussions and interviewing (see below).

## TECHNIQUES TO AVOID

### Direct questions

Direct questions are authoritative and insist on an answer. Examples: Did you leave the machine unattended? Were you late this morning? Did you forget that letter?

### Rhetorical questions

Rhetorical questions are essentially provocative and really statements emphasising a malpractice that does not need a reply. In some ways the object is to forbid a reply and simply indicates exasperation. Example: How can we possibly be proactive and at the same time leave applications for the job way past the proposed starting date?

### Leading questions

Leading questions strongly suggest the answer should agree with the questioner's views. They are never really helpful and tend to test willingness to agree regardless of personal opinion. Examples: I think discipline needs tightening up, do you? He always seems to be away, don't you agree?

### Indiscreet questions

Care is needed not to fall into the trap of asking questions than can be interpreted as sexual, personal or of a private nature. Often they are purely inquisitive but may cause repercussions. Examples: Did you have a rough night, Sally? I don't think much of Bill as a man, Mary, do you? Mary replies: We are now engaged!

# Giving orders

## REASONS FOR GIVING ORDERS

Treat order-giving as a continuous process of passing information, checking and controlling. A true assessment of an individual's capabilities is then possible. Here are the main purposes:

- to achieve an objective by stirring people into action and giving them information on a situation that demands attention
- to indicate that a particular person is held responsible for performing a task by approaching the subordinate, discussing the situation and arousing in him or her a strong desire to deal personally with the particular situation
- to give the supervisor the opportunity to contact the subordinate and issue instructions in a way which will be acceptable
- to give the subordinate the maximum opportunity of consulting and participating in the situation so that he or she may develop capabilities fully and display potential qualities for promotion

## TYPES OF ORDERS

Although it is possible to classify orders into six main types according to method, there are many combinations based upon the words used, the tone of voice, facial expressions and gestures. There are four features which tend to influence the choice of method.

### The job in question

The order must be modified to suit the job to be carried out in particular circumstances. These circumstances may involve dirty work, difficult tasks perhaps with risks, disagreeable work, action which may have a detrimental effect on future relationships, or work of high importance.

### Other employees involved

The subordinate may have difficulties in approaching or dealing with others who are in close proximity to the job. Clashing personalities are not uncommon and a careful check is essential to avoid upsets and to make appropriate arrangements.

### The subordinate

To avoid adverse reactions the supervisor should recognise the effects of the order on the individual, considering personality, temperament, attitudes and other mental characteristics.

### Relationships

Relationships should include making allowances for relations between the supervisor and subordinates, the cultural factor and the industrial climate.

## SIX MAIN METHODS

### The command

A direct or autocratic order is essentially one-way and has an immediate effect provided there is an acceptable response. Simple or straightforward tasks carried out by normal people under favourable conditions are especially suited to this type of order where there is little to discuss. Here are some typical examples: Leave that and do this, Help them now, Do this, Get that. All should be accompanied with the usual courtesies, e.g. please and thank you.

The sensitive individual will often be antagonised by a direct order, whereas the lazy worker may be jolted into action. The order is emphatic and useful when diplomatic methods fail. The unreliable or troublesome employee may respond to this treatment, and in emergencies immediate response to direct orders is essential.

### The request

The request is more personal, tactful and arouses a friendly atmosphere of co-operation. The emotionally unstable employee is unlikely to take offence as the request softens, and displays understanding and sympathy. Here are some opening phrases: Could you look into this one? I wonder if you could arrange for . . . ? Would you mind having a look at . . . ? How about having a look at . . . ? How about having a go at . . . ? Do you think you could find out . . . ?

The request is particularly useful when employees have made mistakes. Usually they are aware of the error but even when they do not know, it is soon obvious after the request. Some ways of opening such a request: Would you mind correcting it? Perhaps you could have another look at this? Maybe you could go over this one again? Possibly you could improve on this?

## The suggestion

The suggestion is the mildest form of request. Mentioning the subject is sufficient to the reliable, experienced person who immediately sees the implication and acts accordingly. There is no demonstrated pressure behind the order, which is really thinking aloud. Examples: Lateness seems to be on the increase, The floor is rather dirty, There are more rejects this week, I have not seen the new assembly yet. The suggestion usually allows the receiver to develop his or her capabilities but the sender should remember the importance of follow-up, to allow for misunderstandings. Naturally the method should not be used to instruct a new, inexperienced employee.

## The open order

The open order allows the receiver the maximum opportunity to experiment and develop his or her capabilities. The supervisor gives information on requirements but leaves adequate room for the individual to decide how to perform the tasks. How much allowance depends upon the subordinate's experience and ability to perform the tasks within a time schedule, and the ability to deal effectively with any problem which may arise. The open order provides guiding principles together with additional essential information such as deadline dates. This method is particularly useful for developing potential leaders.

## Mutual effort

Mutual effort is only practicable when there is high morale and active participation in a company where everyone is working in the same direction towards the company's objectives. It means discussing the situation with employees and the union when they have a common objective in view. Reaching a solution takes longer but the results are more effective and permanent because everyone feels involved and committed.

This form of 'combined operations' uses everyone's knowledge and experience so the actual order is unnecessary. All concerned already know what has to be done and they go ahead without any persuasion. The basis of this technique is called the law of the situation, meaning the situation itself demands action which is determined by mutual discussion; thus reducing personality problems and depersonalising order-giving.

## Volunteers

Asking for volunteers is useful when it is obvious that choosing a subordinate will upset relationships and when the task to be done is particularly unsavoury. The call may arouse in someone the desire to be important, although this same person would probably refuse the task if approached directly. The danger of receiving no volunteers should not be overlooked when morale is low.

## CAUSES OF LOW RESPONSE TO ORDERS

## Poor approach

If the supervisor adopts the old approach of being the boss and completely ignoring more interactive methods of leadership, he or she will receive negative reactions. Today's employees are more independent, more aware of their rights, possess increased power, and will not tolerate harsh, illogical methods of supervision.

## Lack of information

If insufficient information is provided by management or passed on by the supervisor, the chances are the receiver will not fully understand the order.

Errors may occur and employees are less likely to respond well to a situation.

### Poor assessment of the individual

Unless the true attitude of the receiver is known and his or her experience is used through genuine consultation, the supervisor will not be able to communicate with that person or accurately gauge the response. Poor assessment stifles the individual and wastes his or her knowledge and capabilities to the detriment of the individual, other employees and the company.

### Low morale

Favourable responses to orders are unlikely when morale is low (Chapter 8). Although morale is difficult to define accurately, most people know what is meant by the term. State of mind, outlook, enthusiasm, collective attitude, sensitivity and co-operation all add up to morale. Building up morale takes a long time but knocking it down is easy and rapid. Many changes are needed to improve morale from a low level. They include improving sensitivity from boardroom members towards employees and fully understanding the effects of their decisions; more attention to human resources management and management competence; and ensuring effective communication.

# Reprimanding

Minor cases of a breach in standards of conduct or behaviour are dealt with by the supervisor. These cover minor misconduct, minor abuse of unwritten codes, and occasional poor performance. Reprimanding and counselling are sufficient unless the problem deteriorates into a major case involving a formal procedure for misconduct or gross misconduct. Misconduct and dismissal procedures are discussed in Chapter 18.

## REPRIMANDS FOR MINOR CASES

- A disapproving look.
- A few short words to remind the employee of the code of conduct expected from him or her.
- A quick joke to pass off the misconduct; this joke is suitably cloaked to make the point clear.
- A straightforward reprimand which is given in the right spirit dependent on the nature of the minor offence, forgotten officially, and appropriate counselling applied if necessary.
- Counselling the employee when circumstances indicate that advice should be given in such a way that plainly there is an offence but no direct reprimand is thought necessary.

## THE QUESTION OF DISCIPLINE

Negative or imposed discipline uses a system of punishments, which may be rebukes or penalties. The reprimand can easily destroy good relationships unless it is acceptable to the individual and the group as a whole.

Although acceptance depends on high morale, the way the supervisor handles the actual reprimand will be the deciding factor in individual cases (Chapter 12). The behaviourist approach explained in Chapter 12 demonstrates plainly the use of reinforcement in terms of negative reinforcement, extinction and punishment.

People tend to think of discipline as a system of rules and appropriate punishments when they are disobeyed. This system is quite common. The problem employee who is instinctively hostile towards authority calls for reprimands based upon a fair standard of rules and punishments; therefore, such a system is essential and cannot be removed entirely. Other forms of more sophisticated discipline demand both high morale and enlightened management.

A higher form of discipline emerges automatically if employees are well trained and allowed to participate more in their work, rather than being restricted to the simple performance of tasks. Ideally the supervisor should aim to develop employee self-discipline, although reprimanding and counselling remain inevitable in any organisational situation.

## DEVELOPING EMPLOYEE SELF-DISCIPLINE

When employees are given the opportunity to develop their capabilities, the group spirit and general working arrangements with supervisors foster a personal driving force within each individual. This drive is often called positive discipline, which urges employees to conform to rules and unwritten codes without restricting their enthusiasm.

The application of negative forms of discipline, such as penalties or fear of dismissal, fall into the background as people find new outlets for their energies through creativeness, a sense of belonging and greater freedom to develop their abilities. The supervisor must be sensitive to the degree of change as individuals begin to practise self-discipline and the organisational structure is rearranged to foster it.

The application of consultation and participation is a long process, which means both types of discipline have to be varied in proportion to suit the situation as it progresses. This process does not give the supervisor the opportunity to shirk responsibilities for the group he or she controls. Authority must continue to be used to make unpleasant decisions someone will disagree with at some time or another. A policy of fairness and justice includes imposing penalties, not only to correct the offender but also in fairness to those who are conforming to regulations.

## A REPRIMANDING PROCEDURE

Usually a company recommends a procedure and basic rules to protect the supervisor from violating any union agreements and legislation. A typical sequence is shown in Fig. 15.1, which includes a formal disciplinary procedure for major cases explained in Chapter 18.

### Alleged misconduct

The accusation may come from various sources such as another employee, a supervisor from another section, or another department. A careful approach is essential to clarify the problem; if there is no cause then the employee will be justifiably upset.

### Discuss with employee

The employee should be approached before investigating as invariably he or she will find out if investigations are started. This would cause a situation where underhandedness could be levelled against the supervisor. The individual will often have a different view and an explanation which may collapse the case immediately. The discussion should be recorded if the procedure is to continue.

### Identify the case

If the case does not resolve itself, the next step is to gather information and seek statements in an attempt to clarify the problem. This stage may determine whether an informal interview is worth pursuing. Often a few words of warning are sufficient if an emotional outburst in the heat of the moment was the cause.

### Confirm the breach

The supervisor should refer to the appropriate rules and procedures, and consult the personnel manager. When the problem is confirmed the employee should be informed.

### Conduct the informal interview

The art of interviewing is discussed in Chapter 16. The emotional condition of the interviewee is of paramount importance. Endeavouring to keep the discussions in low key is essential.

### Determine the outcome

If the case is straightforward and a decision is obvious, there should be no hesitation or delay. All the factors should be weighed up in the light of evidence, previous cases and the human aspect. Explain the rule, the reprimand for breaking it, and the penalties for further violation. Listen carefully to the offender's views and take into consideration any special circumstances. There are usually three choices. The proceedings at the interview and the outcome should be recorded.

- no action is required
- an informal warning accompanied by counselling
- counselling

### Follow-up

Follow-up must be conducted to ensure the offender is not harbouring any feelings of injustice and to ensure he or she is adjusting to the situation. Further

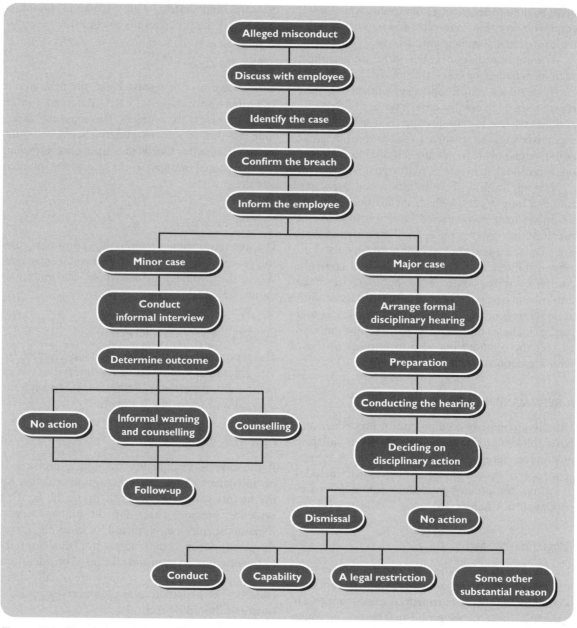

**Figure 15.1** Alleged misconduct: see Chapter 18 for major cases

counselling may be needed if there is any sign of reaction.

*Ensuring a fair hearing*

A number of questions must be answered before the offender will feel he or she has received a square deal. The person should understand fully the following points:

- the reason for the rebuke
- why such an offence demands a reprimand
- others committing a similar offence have not been excused
- the opportunity is given to discuss the offence

## BASIC RULES FOR REPRIMANDING

The essential requirements are to have a sound knowledge of subordinates, an understanding of human beings and human relations, the application of motivation, and a strong sense of fairness and justice. Supervisors should remember they too have good and bad points. These must be assessed when reprimanding. Their own good points should be developed when using a technique for dealing with awkward situations and they should take care to remember their bad points and attempt to reduce their effects on employees. Here are the basic rules.

1 Be impartial. Treat everyone alike.
2 Make sure the information on the case is correct and complete.
3 Be human. Remember that rules and regulations are guides for the supervisor, who should not interpret them too rigidly. Sympathetic understanding of other people's actions is essential.
4 Check the information with the individual. A good opening is to ask the offender for the facts, the offender's views on the case, and his or her opinion of the rules. This technique gives the employee's 'safety valve' a chance to blow a little and may avoid an emotional outburst later. The person's feelings are also made known to the supervisor early in the proceedings, which is an advantage.
5 Do not allow tempers to interfere in the discussions at any time. Although the employee may make outrageous remarks about the system and the company, remember he or she is under stress. Also the individual is entitled to give personal views, especially if asked.
6 Most people have a sense of fairness and are conscientious. If they commit an offence they expect repercussions. Prolonging a reprimand by lecturing on the subject only encourages feelings of antagonism and disgust to develop in the employee.
7 Be straightforward by explaining the occurrence, why it should not be overlooked, and the consequences if it is repeated.
8 Try to help the employee. Find out why the offence happened. Perhaps something is bothering the person. Attempt to win his or her confidence and find out the true cause. Avoid arguments and listen carefully to all comments.

9 When all the information is known, be constructive by taking some positive action whenever possible. Avoid any form of threat as this will immediately arouse aggressiveness and fear.
10 Another good opening is to praise the employee. Usually there is something noteworthy such as good timekeeping, consistently high output or low absenteeism.
11 Never be sarcastic. Some people do not realise they are being sarcastic until someone points out the fault. The habit easily develops because it inflates feelings of self-importance. Unfortunately, the receiver is sadly deflated and intense dislike, lack of confidence and insecurity soon follow.
12 Although timing is important, do not delay reprimands without good reason. Allowing reprimands to accumulate amounts to shirking responsibility. When a supervisor eventually loses patience, the offender will almost certainly be astounded and puzzled. He or she will have the excuse that nothing was said on previous occasions. A sense of proportion is essential, however, otherwise the supervisor may be continually rebuking staff, which is pointless.
13 Always think in terms of the offender's feelings. Avoid lowering his or her prestige in front of the group, thereby forcing the person to retaliate to save face. In brief, make sure any unpleasantness or difficulties are discussed privately, out of sight and hearing.
14 Do not be offhand after the reprimand. Continue to be firm and friendly because only immature supervisors hold grudges after they have reprimanded. Subordinates quickly recognise this fault.

# Counselling

The counselling process usually implies that the counsellor (the supervisor) possesses expertise in a particular subject. This expertise may be used to help a person by providing the opportunity to discuss, examine and understand more clearly the problem. In addition, to consider appropriate courses of action, and to help in arriving at a decision.

## TYPES OF COUNSELLING

Counselling is considered to be an important feature in reprimanding. It maintains good relations and heals any feeling of injustice if the alleged misconduct was untrue. Other types of counselling are:

- work-related difficulties, such as poor performance due to insufficient training, poor selection, or changes in the job
- preparing for another job which may involve adjustment and removing any apprehensiveness
- dealing with minor misconduct
- a personal work-related problem involving a physical aspect, or relationships with peers
- a domestic problem related to a marital situation or to other crises
- a personal problem involving mental health, alcohol or drug abuse

The employee may approach the supervisor for advice if sound relationships exist. Naturally there may be difficulties if the personal problem is complex, in which case the supervisor suggests the employee should see a personnel specialist. Similarly, the supervisor should not become involved in difficult psychological or marital problems.

## HINTS ON COUNSELLING

- Allow the employee to lead the discussion if possible. If not suggest possible help in any situation where the employee seems embarrassed.
- Listen attentively without interruption, until the employee has exhausted the subject.
- Any queries should be raised as open-ended questions with no hint of intimidation.
- Try to direct the conversation as diplomatically as possible. In other words, try to steer the discussion in a subtle way by avoiding conflicting approaches.
- When opportunities occur attempt to summarise by seeking agreement on subjects before continuing.
- Look for hesitations, and illogical or invalid statements. Try to probe further without causing offence.

## SUMMARIES

At the end of the session there may be the opportunity to summarise, or possibly to leave the situation open-ended without a summary if the case is complex. Some causes of the problem may be obvious after the discussion. Possibly the time could be right to suggest them to the employee. Typical examples are:

- ill-health for various reasons
- domestic problems
- emotional difficulties
- feelings of insecurity caused by bullying, harassment and losing prestige
- resistance to proposed changes
- communication problems
- capabilities failing
- education and training problems

If the interview is obviously deteriorating, the supervisor should stop the discussion, consult the personnel manager, and arrange for a formal disciplinary hearing. A simplified counselling process is illustrated in Fig. 15.2.

# Negotiating in conflicts

Negotiating in conflicts is the ability to discuss a conflict situation with those concerned and so reach a compromise or agreement or bring about a desired result which is acceptable to the parties. Fortunate people have a flair for negotiating which involves being diplomatic, assertive and using essential principles. However, applying negotiating skill varies when there is conflict between groups (Chapter 5) and in solving grievances covered in the next section. Negotiating situations arise when there is a need for the supervisor to increase his or her power position in discussions, or to gain some benefit, or when there is conflict between two employees or between the supervisor and an employee.

## CONFLICT

In the employment situation conflict is probably occurring everywhere as people struggle to dominate, fight for safer positions, and clash over

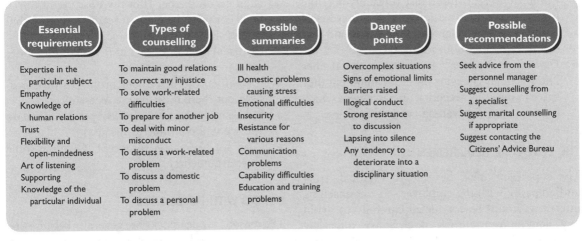

**Figure 15.2** A simplified counselling process

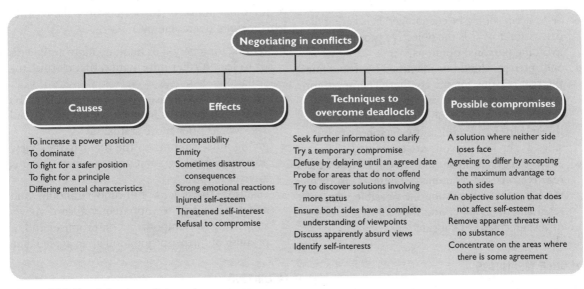

**Figure 15.3** Negotiating in conflicts: main processes

principles and many other factors. These cause incompatibility, enmity and sometimes disastrous results. The basic causes of conflict are the differing characteristics of people. Principles, attitudes, temperament, perception, experiences and wants all combine in an individual who is often confronted with others who have differing mental characteristics. Unless the individual is mature, considerate, experienced and appreciates other people's feelings, there is a strong emotional reaction.

## MAIN ASPECTS OF NEGOTIATING

There should be consideration for the emotional situation, relationships, and the 'atmosphere', before deciding to summarise. Inevitably the employee should understand the reason if an acceptable conclusion is reached and the expectations of the supervisor should be made clear. The main process of negotiating in conflicts is shown in Fig. 15.3.

- *Compromise*: A compromise is usually possible by discussing the situation until the interests of both parties emerge and a solution is found that satisfies them without losing face.
- *Diplomacy*: Diplomacy is essential so that neither side is actually changing his or her mind but they agree to differ by accepting an agreement which is of maximum advantage to both parties.

## THE ESSENTIAL REQUIREMENTS

The supervisor must be able to establish trust and empathy with the employee. The counselling interview should be conducted carefully to avoid any deterioration into a disciplinary interview (Chapter 18). Disciplinary rules and procedures must abide by a set pattern according to legislation and a code of practice (Chapter 18):

- Self-esteem should be encouraged by steering the discussion towards the objective problem, thus avoiding personal opinions.
- Self-interests should be identified by discussing the real reasons for the conflict. The apparent reasons proposed are usually emotional reactions against the person who is perceived as a threat. More acceptable answers appear to both sides as the real reasons are examined.
- Areas of agreement should be sought when the real reasons are examined. These areas form the basis for determining the possible ways of resolving the conflict and they allow the areas of disagreement to subside.

## DOUBLE MEANINGS

Often negotiators do not always mean what they say. There are various accepted phrases with hidden meanings and they are used to establish defensive or aggressive positions that invite further discussion. If there is any doubt it is advisable to probe further by guessing at the meaning and inviting comment. Some examples are:

- My best offer is . . . (My boss may increase it)
- I don't think it is possible (I am prepared to bargain)
- This is out of the question (Let's talk about it)
- I can't see any point in continuing (Why don't you make a suggestion?)

- I can go no further (But my boss might do)
- I will consider the offer (It seems acceptable but I must show some reluctance)
- My usual limit is 3 per cent (I would offer more for some concession)
- It is difficult to meet your proposals (It is possible but there must be a concession)
- It does not seem a fair deal (Explain your views and we will continue to discuss)
- I can see no reason to accept (Give me some more arguments)

## COPING WITH DEADLOCKS

The reasons for deadlocks are generally because one side cannot produce more arguments, there is an emotional obstacle, both sides refuse to budge on a particular point, a sudden refusal to compromise, or for some political reason. Possibly these problems may be overcome by:

- retiring for a period to think up more arguments or to seek further information that clarifies the situation
- attempting to defuse emotional problems by trying new approaches that would not offend and would offer more status
- giving more support to the other party's view and reassuring by some means where there is any suspicion
- ensuring there is a full understanding and adequate respect for apparently absurd views
- suggesting a temporary compromise and a promise of further negotiation at an agreed date

## MEDIATING

Sometimes the supervisor may be asked to act as a mediator. Mediating should be distinguished from negotiating: it is a voluntary, advisory, private function where a neutral person attempts to reach a negotiated acceptable arrangement between two parties. This difficult role has essential characteristics. The person should be unconnected with both parties, be objective or impartial, offers suggestions (not decisions), and be able to conduct informal proceeding successfully. He or she is essentially a facilitator or a problem solver. Both parties must agree to accept the mediator, but they are free to withdraw if they wish.

*Basic principles of mediating*

- Remain neutral by treating both sides alike, therefore do not argue.
- Avoid discussions on people and minimise emotional tendencies by accepting statements without question at first.
- Attempt to clarify obvious emotional statements by rephrasing, quoting evidence, careful questioning, and summarising to seek agreement.
- Always accept that conflict exists but try to steer the discussions towards objective solutions.
- The mediating role means discussing issues with both parties, allowing them to reach their own conclusions, and steering them towards decisions which resolve the conflict.

# Resolving grievances

Resolving grievances demands the use of many skills involving day-to-day operational skills and negotiating process skills. Essential tasks are to know the basic causes of grievances which enable the supervisor to recognise grievances in their early stages of development. Often a grievance procedure is established in the company and used when informal resolving of grievances fails. The supervisor's role is essentially active because the actual negotiations with the employee should start early before the mental irritation or grievance develops. This involves continually assessing the individual, watching for changes in behaviour, and recognising likely problems occurring through changes in organisational or operational conditions.

If these changes in behaviour are missed, negotiating process skills commence when the grievance is aired by the employee. Such skills include careful listening, correcting communication difficulties, reaching a complete understanding, and attempting to resolve the grievance. The aim is to solve the grievance quickly in the most effective way. Knowingly allowing an employee to seethe for weeks is inviting disaster. All these features are now discussed.

## DEFINITION OF A GRIEVANCE

A grievance is any situation or act that is unfair in the eyes of the complainer. The cause may be the act of a manager, a supervisor or an employee, or a situation which is allowed to continue and develop. The grievance may be held by an individual, a group, a section or even a department. The complainer may be personally involved or may act as a representative for others. At this stage it is unimportant whether the grievance is actually right or wrong. If the employee thinks there is a legitimate complaint, other factors are by the way.

## BASIC CAUSES OF GRIEVANCES

Some knowledge of the reasons why employees complain and the causes of their complaints will help in minimising grievances. Early action ensures the grounds for complaint are prevented from appearing. To avoid a complaint in a few days' time, sufficient information should be passed to satisfy any suspicion concerning a particular action. Employees complain for two main reasons:

- because they are emotionally unstable
- because they feel there is some unfairness or injustice

*The problem employee*

The problem employee is easily recognised by the experienced supervisor. There are continual waves of complaints from the employee, which are mostly settled by carefully explaining the truth which has become distorted in his or her mind. Unfortunately, some of these employees are beyond the stage where the supervisor can help. When readjustment is not possible, replacements may be necessary and every effort should be made to persuade the individual to seek medical advice.

The inexperienced supervisor may easily confuse the problem employee with one who has a legitimate problem which is hidden by a steady stream of petty complaints. These minor grievances are a symptom of a more basic grievance. This does not emerge until the employee has full confidence in the supervisor who should listen carefully with sympathy and understanding.

*Lack of understanding*

The second basic cause of grievances covers all those activities of management and supervision which, for many reasons, are unacceptable to employees. This situation could be summed up as lack of training and the insensitive understanding of people by managers.

In more detail, the situation includes poor communication when breakdowns occur in both directions; poor organisation, which is aggravated by violation of principles; unsound policies and rules; general lack of fairness and justice; poor working conditions; overloaded supervisors who do not have sufficient time to assess subordinates and ensure smooth running of the section; inability of supervisors to assess subordinates; favouritism, which may be intentional or unintentional; poor training schemes for managers, supervisors and employees; jealousy between individuals and sections; and rumours and gossip. There are many more causes but this cross-section indicates the depth of the problem which faces the supervisor.

## RECOGNISING GRIEVANCES

A grievance is recognisable in two phases:

- Phase 1: when the event occurs which caused the grievance to materialise in the person's mind.
- Phase 2: when the person voices the grievance to someone in authority.

### Phase 1

The real difficulty in recognition occurs in phase 1. Such recognition is very demanding on the supervisor, who must be continually on the alert by watching for danger signs to appear. He or she should be looking for:

- changes in attitude in seasoned employees
- antagonism
- suspicion
- indifference
- carelessness
- daydreaming
- rudeness
- slacking
- absenteeism
- frequent cloakroom visits
- gossiping
- general carelessness

Successful discovery of a grievance in its early stages is time-consuming; the supervisor must be continually in close contact with subordinates to assess the situation. He or she must know each individual sufficiently well to notice changes and be able to identify the likely causes. When the supervisor has gained the employee's confidence, he or she will feel able to ask the supervisor immediately for more information, for reasons, or for fairer action. The natural tendency to hold back complaints and suffer unnecessarily is reduced.

### Phase 2

Recognition in phase 2 is obvious as the grievance is aired by the employee. However, the apparent grievance often differs from the real grievance, which is more deep-seated and usually hidden until careful listening reveals flaws.

## THE RANGE OF SKILLS

Grievances may be recognised during two phases of development. The first phase is an initial mental irritation or feeling of unfairness and injustice when a change occurs. The breadth of this change covers all the organisational changes which may happen daily or occasionally, and changes within the individual. The second phase is, in a sense, a supervisory failure when the ill-feeling is missed and its progress leads to a grievance which is brought to the attention of the supervisor.

Considering the application of skills, day-to-day operational skills in phase 1 include continually assessing the employee; anticipating, forecasting and planning changes; identifying changes or assessing the effects when changes are introduced; and helping the employee to adjust to changes. In the second phase, negotiating process skills include careful listening to the employee, communicating effectively, taking action, and follow-up. These supplement negotiating skills in conflict situations discussed previously.

There is no doubt that in the long term the time spent in the operational phase by observing and settling difficulties in their early stages is economical. In the negotiating process phase, the adverse effects and long sessions needed to disentangle the grievance which has reached a complex stage of

| PHASE | CONDITION | BASIC CAUSES | RESOLVING TECHNIQUES | SKILLS |
|-------|-----------|--------------|----------------------|--------|
| Phase 1 | Recognising mental irritation | The problem employee<br>• low readjustment level<br>• mental difficulties<br>• poor job selection<br><br>Lack of understanding<br>• poor communication<br>• unsound policies<br>• unfairness and injustice<br>• poor working conditions<br>• incorrect assessments<br>• favouritism<br>• poor training schemes<br>• jealousy<br>• rumours and gossip | Offering sympathy and understanding<br>Explaining in detail<br>Persuading to seek medical advice<br><br>Correcting personal problems<br>Correcting communication breakdowns<br>Correcting organisational breakdowns | Day-to-day operations<br>• continually assessing the individual<br>• anticipating, forecasting and planning<br>• identifying changes<br>• helping the individual to adjust |
| Phase 2 | Grievance reported by employee | Failure by supervisor to recognise mental irritations<br><br>Failure by supervisor to realise the overall effects of change | Identifying real causes<br>Correcting misunderstandings<br>Correcting incomplete impressions<br>Arranging transfers or job changes<br>Recommending rehabilitation<br>Offering guidance | Negotiating process<br>• careful listening to the grievance<br>• communicating effectively<br>• taking action<br>• follow up |

**Figure 15.4** Resolving grievances
Phase 1 avoids a mental irritation developing into a grievance. Phase 2 indicates a failure by the supervisor to assess difficulties in the early stages.

development are frustrating and damaging to morale. Furthermore, the risk of resorting to a formal grievance procedure is increased. The two phases are illustrated in Fig. 15.4.

## DAY-TO-DAY OPERATIONAL SKILLS

Day-to-day operational skills are essential to avoid resentment, stored-up anger, and arguing when the supervisor is missing. Poorly handled changes cause bickering, divert concentration on the job, lower productivity and upset teamwork. The following skills involve the supervisor in gradually developing a personal technique for resolving difficulties as he or she becomes more experienced in understanding people. How to assess their feelings and their reaction to suggestions and advice must be considered.

### Continually assessing the individual

The supervisor should attempt to know as much as possible about the individual. The essential requirements include studying the employee at work and in social activities, and assessing sentiments, background, attitudes and general outlook. Accurate assessment is a long, painstaking process. However, to avoid spending an increasing amount of time handing grievances later on, a proportion of the supervisor's time must be allocated to these assessments.

### Anticipating, forecasting and planning

Anticipating, forecasting and planning were discussed in Chapter 8. They form an important part of the supervisor's day-to-day activities and are essential to support operational skills.

## Identifying changes in individuals

Changes in individuals may be caused by many personal problems such as overestimating or underestimating capability, and a lowering or a raising of self-image. All these may affect relations and attitudes to changes. There may be concern for organisational changes, keeping the job, poor relations with peers or the supervisor, some injustice, or inability to develop on the job. The supervisor should consider exploring various fields of anxiety such as an uncertain future, over- or underwork, relationships in general, and technical incompetence. The employee may rationalise any of these causes into resentment and ill-feeling.

## Helping the individual

Do not delay approaching the individual. Take the initiative and try to persuade the person by various indirect means to talk about the suspected difficulty. This may be achieved by asking appropriate questions that lead on to those topics which may be the cause of the resentment. Always listen with sympathy and openly show understanding. If there is any doubt ask more questions until all the queries are clarified. In these early stages there are various methods to employ such as:

- informing the employee if the difficulty involves a technical change or uncertainty on following instructions
- advising, by illustrating or suggesting different approaches which will give the employee the opportunity to adjust more easily rather than harbour ill-feeling
- discussing the change, noting any reactions and guiding accordingly
- counselling

Counselling is the preferable approach because it involves a rapport with the person so that intelligent discussions are possible. These discussions lead to the person gradually establishing a more realistic approach to the difficulty, thus arriving at a self-induced solution which is far more satisfying and permanent. Counselling is ideal for personal difficulties. The person is persuaded to think and arrive at new conclusions which relieve the tension. The inevitable follow-up is made easier because the approach is more positive by asking the person how his or her ideas are working out.

## NEGOTIATING PROCESS SKILLS

When the individual approaches the supervisor with a grievance, remember that he or she is already emotionally aroused and feeling frustrated. This confrontation is demanding on the supervisor, who must remain calm and often be prepared for outbursts and possibly some abuse, which is to be accepted until the initial reactions have died down.

## Listening to the grievance

The art of listening has been discussed earlier in the chapter. Listening to an employee airing a grievance tends to be frustrating because there is a strong temptation to think about the causes, the blame and how to prepare a defence. These are the supervisor's emotional responses which will hinder unless the employee is persuaded to provide the full story first.

## Communicating

Invariably the employee's perceptions and prejudices will distort the situation and these will need to be corrected carefully to avoid further ill-feeling. Time must be allowed for questions to clarify any misunderstandings and incomplete impressions.

People often have difficulty in explaining their thoughts clearly and they may be embarrassed or nervous because of this problem. They may be unsure of the real cause of the grievance themselves until the whole question is talked over carefully and calmly.

There is the possibility that a combination of events at work and at home may eventually arouse the individual into thinking he or she has a grievance. Unfortunately, people are easily upset. They need help and friendly advice. These are often sought from the supervisor who can create the right atmosphere. A small irritation may become a large grievance in the employee's mind and must be treated as it appears to that person.

Eventually there will be some frustration and communication problems on both sides as misunderstandings persist. Interpersonal communication and the causes of misunderstanding were explained in Chapter 14. They should be thoroughly understood and used to ease the situation until the climate allows for a thorough understanding.

## Taking action

Some grievances can be resolved by patient listening and showing a complete understanding of the complainer's feelings. If the employee's position is sincerely appreciated and consolation is given, it relieves the tension and emotional disturbance, although no action is possible. The employee may then feel the position is understood and the grievance has been solved. Similarly, the complaint may be relieved by genuine praise for good work and an assurance that all the conditions under which the employee works are known and understood.

Other situations demand some positive action – not reassurances or promises that cannot be kept. Shallow promises are fatal and highlight the weak supervisor. If a supervisor cannot deal with the situation because it is outside his or her authority, the facts must be reported objectively to the superior. The risk of distorting the story to cover any error on the supervisor's part is not worthwhile. If the superior interviews the employee and the story does not agree with the supervisor's report, the supervisor's position is not an enviable one.

Often a possible grievance is solved simply by providing the employee with information. If the supervisor had not withheld this information, he or she should investigate the communication breakdown. Regardless of the way the grievance is resolved, follow-up is essential to ensure the employee is feeling settled and adjusting.

## A GRIEVANCE PROCEDURE

A competent supervisor usually settles most grievances easily, because they often arise through misunderstandings. An informal settlement is far more satisfactory but unfortunately there are exceptions when the grievance is beyond the solving point by the supervisor. These may occur through a poor interviewing procedure for the job, a drastic change in the individual's outlook through a domestic situation, a serious deterioration in relationships, or a serious career problem. In these circumstances there is usually an established formal grievance procedure. The main steps are:

1 The supervisor should keep a record of informal discussions for his or her personal reference. Although informal, the supervisor may be questioned on previous difficulties and they should be accurately presented. Sometimes both parties sign the informal records as being accurate.
2 Discuss the employee's difficulties with the superior before resorting to the grievance procedure. Possibly a solution may be found at this level.
3 Seek advice from the trade union or staff representative. Ensure all the information is available, including the names of persons who may help, dates and relevant documents.
4 If all these avenues fail, write a formal request for an interview.
5 Give the name of the person who is selected by the employee to be present.
6 Ideally members of the panel should include the personnel manager and a senior manager, but the arrangement varies. The supervisor and employee provide evidence along with any other parties the employee cares to name.
7 The actual interview should be conducted in a friendly manner. However, the procedure should follow a strict code, comply with any legal requirements, and ensure the employee feels there has been a fair hearing.

## Possible solutions

Apart from negotiating activities, there may be indications leading to many factors which involve a disciplinary procedure and dismissal problems; these are discussed in Chapter 18. Nevertheless, the grievances may often be resolved at this level by proposing a transfer, change of job within the terms and conditions of the employment contract, solving a personality clash, further training, rehabilitation, or guidance on a domestic problem if the employee so wishes.

# Conducting discussions

The basic skill of conducting group discussions with subordinates is separated here from group activity (Chapter 5) and formal meetings and committee work discussed in the next chapter. Often the supervisor may decide to hold an informal group discussion on many different topics to discuss the difficulties and try to clarify the situation. Such get-togethers are an important part of effective communication. They encourage participation and improve morale.

Usually the supervisor acts as discussion leader, may prepare a few notes if there is time available or simply discuss the topic after stating the object. Ideally the group comprises those directly affected by the topic and members who may contribute through their knowledge, experience and ideas. About five or six members are sufficient to allow everyone to participate.

## RELEVANT FEATURES

Properly conducted discussions can improve the quality of decisions provided the following features are remembered. But in practice the discussions are often hasty, short and consist of anyone who is available.

- To avoid wasting time arguing about opinions, essential information should be given for discussing factual aspects.
- Participation by group members usually increases the chances of the decision being accepted.
- Groups tend to be cautious where employees are in some way at risk, and less cautious when organisational risks are discussed.
- A well-balanced group may increase the accuracy of decisions.
- Groups may inhibit creativity if allowed to follow a set pattern, but they may offer more effective evaluations of ideas.

## HANDLING DISCUSSIONS

Some typical ways of leading discussions are general comments on the problem or topic; proposing solutions or decisions; evaluating the proposals; and choosing the most appropriate decisions.

## GENERAL COMMENTS

- Align comments on fact-finding by avoiding any premature solutions.
- Clarify any facts by discussing other possibilities.
- Avoid accepting opinions as facts.
- Avoid any bias or prejudices being emphasised too strongly.
- Do not expect members to hold figures or complex information in their heads.

### Proposing decisions

- Analyse carefully any proposed solutions that may lead to a decision without sufficient evidence.
- Try to emphasise new ideas rather than old ways of overcoming a problem.
- Press for different solutions until a good cross-section of the group is committed.
- Seek out the advantages and disadvantages of each proposal.

### Choosing the decision

- Careful weighing-up without emotion is essential.
- Try to avoid the influence of stronger group members who may silence others.
- Minority proposals are not necessarily the weakest.
- Remember the supervisor takes the final responsibility and must decide, using his or her own knowledge and experience if there is deadlock.

In circumstances where time is limited, the supervisor should develop an appropriate communication skill. This consists of acquiring knowledge on conducting group discussions, and developing a technique from this knowledge which successfully restricts discussions within the timescale and arrives at a sensible answer.

## QUESTIONS

1 State how the supervisor can improve his or her performance in the art of listening.

2 What are the main purposes of giving orders?

3 What factors should be borne in mind when giving orders?

4 Discuss the main ways of giving orders and suggest suitable situations for their use in each case.

5 In what circumstances would a supervisor resort to a direct command and when should its use be avoided?

6 Many supervisors blame their subordinates when they receive a low response to their orders. Comment on this statement.

7 How would you encourage self-discipline among your subordinates?

8 When should a supervisor use negative forms of discipline?

9 What precautions should be taken before reprimanding a subordinate?

10 What advice on reprimanding would you give to a newly promoted supervisor?

11 Suggest a logical procedure for dealing with a reprimand.

12 What action would you take as a supervisor if you saw an employee from another department deliberately damaging a machine?

13 How can a supervisor use subordinates' complaints constructively?

14 Discuss the basic causes of employees' complaints and the role of the supervisor when dealing with these problems.

15 How would a supervisor recognise the symptoms of a complaint before it is aired by the employee?

16 Outline the basic steps in solving a grievance.

17 How would you conduct a group discussion?

18 List typical outline procedures to determine alleged misconduct.

19 Discuss a counselling process emphasising the danger points.

20 Outline the main process of negotiating in conflicts.

21 Discuss the importance of effective speech.

22 How would you improve your business writing?

23 List the six main techniques of effective listening.

24 Why is it important to attempt resolving a grievance in phase 1?

25 Discuss how to resolve grievances in phases 1 and 2.

26 Discuss the day-to-day operational skills that are essential to avoid resentment.

27 What are the main steps of a grievance procedure?

---

**CASE STUDY**

Andrew was due to retire in five years. He was the most experienced fitter, always performed well, and had refused promotion two years ago. His supervisor decided to make some changes in view of some likely heavy orders arriving soon, but this situation was not discussed with the employees.

Andrew tackled the supervisor saying the changes were not common sense and he refused to co-operate. Andrew's action caused others to refuse the instructions and general unrest developed quickly.

The supervisor suspended Andrew. A delegation insisted that the supervisor should reinstate Andrew. The supervisor told them it was not their concern and unless they conformed with the changes he would take further action. The works manager was notified and the supervisor reported that Andrew was the problem and always caused trouble.

*What is likely to happen now in these circumstances? Comment on the supervisor's actions. Visualise the organisational culture in this company.*

Sarah Pringle has been employed as an office supervisor for twelve years in the typing pool. Her office manager, without warning, tells her that two XYZ word processing machines are being delivered the next day.

Sarah meets her training advisor who arrives with the machines. She explains that part of the deal is a free three-day training scheme for three typists. Sarah picks the best workers and tells them that they are going on a course.

When they return all three insist that they cannot work the new machines because they are too complicated and make their backs ache. One threatens to leave if forced to use the machine. The other two are equally hostile and say they are going to see the staff representative.

*Consider why these reactions could have been foreseen by Sarah. Comment on the manager's approach to installing new machines of this nature.*

# 16

# Communication: practical applications

## Introduction

This chapter looks at some of the important practical applications of communication for the supervisor:

- how to communicate effectively
- making a speech
- interviewing
- meetings and committee work
- report writing
- project reports
- applying for a job

## How to communicate effectively

Any plan for communicating effectively should conform to a scientific or logical method. A general approach is suggested below and is illustrated in Fig. 16.1. The plan may be applied to most types of communication. Here are the main steps a supervisor should take; any omission of a step may reduce effectiveness.

- Clarify the purpose of the communication.
- Consider the type of communication.
- Obtain the relevant information.
- Assess the receiver.
- Determine the best means of communicating.
- Decide on the channel or channels to use.
- Assess oneself.
- Arrange the communication.
- Transmit the message.
- Check for understanding.
- Follow up.

### CLARIFY THE PURPOSE

The question to be asked is, What should be the result of the communication? Care is needed to avoid stopping short of the real objective because of shallow thinking. For example, if conflict exists with another department, the true purpose is to resolve the problem, not simply to blame an individual. Similarly, if another department complains of poor service the purpose is not to make excuses but to ensure the fault is located, removed, and the department notified accordingly.

### CONSIDER THE TYPE

The type of communication to effect change may take many forms, such as an order, a warning, submitting a report or memorandum, a discussion or an interview. Often more than one type may be used. Choosing the appropriate type (or types) is an important step and this determines the significance of the communication.

### OBTAIN THE RELEVANT INFORMATION

Although time is nearly always against the supervisor, he or she must attempt to gather as much information as possible on the topic. Information is often most easily obtained informally by talking to the people who are close to the problem or situation. Often their information will contain less distorted material.

After the information is located, it should be examined and classified. Surplus information should be discarded and the remainder translated into simple, straightforward language for easy transmission.

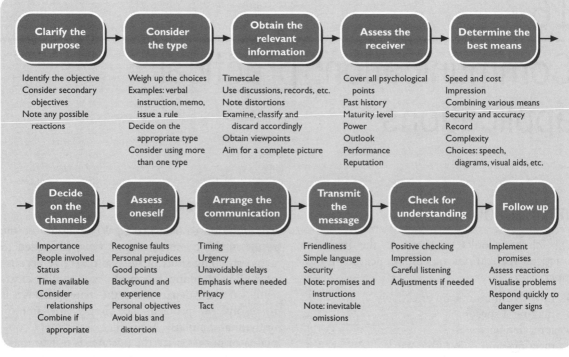

**Figure 16.1** Effective communication: the sequence of principal steps

The recipient's viewpoint must be borne in mind; if any vital information is missing, the grapevine will fill the gap. The supervisor should check that the message is complete, otherwise he or she is deliberately or unintentionally creating a distorted picture in the receiver's mind.

### ASSESS THE RECEIVER

Make sure all aspects have been considered when assessing the person who is to receive the message. The individual's job, background, education, experience and present social and domestic life, all mould outlook and account for present mood. History should be noted, bearing mind any possible previous injustices and problems.

Unfortunately, some individuals persist in adopting an immature approach to a communication. For various reasons a shallow understanding of a message may override its significance. This may be intentional if the receiver feels threatened or is vindictive. The opportunity may be taken to misinterpret deliberately if there is any ambiguity.

In these circumstances a thorough knowledge of the person is essential. This will determine the appropriate methods of communicating, and ensure the message is absolutely clear with careful checking.

### DETERMINE THE BEST MEANS

Choosing the best means of communicating in the circumstances depends upon cost, urgency, security, accuracy, impression on the recipient, the need for a permanent record, and the complexity of the message. Combining different means may be essential when the information is complex. This would include considering speech, diagrams, notes and visual aids, as well as the obvious formal means.

### DECIDE ON THE CHANNEL

The choice of channel depends upon a variety of factors such as the number of people involved, the importance of the information, status of the individual or individuals concerned, and the time available. If one person is involved and the message is important, a face-to-face discussion through the formal line of command may be needed. Unimportant information can be passed on verbally through a third party, or a note may suffice. A number of channels could be used simultaneously if many people are involved and they should all receive the information at about the same time. This may be essential to maintain good relationships when union officials and fellow supervisors are concerned with the information. When in doubt use many channels to avoid both repercussions if someone is overlooked and the dangerous effects when individuals resort to the grapevine.

## ASSESS ONESELF

Being honest with oneself is difficult. Self-analysis includes recognising faults and personal prejudices, as well as the good points. Supervisors too are influenced by their background and experience. Personal objectives must be considered, along with the gains and losses incurred through intended actions. These will determine the need to understate or overstate the case. There is always a tendency to distort information received and transmitted to suit personal bias. Also to bias information that complies with a particular specialisation which may cause difficulty in understanding other specialists' viewpoints.

## ARRANGE THE COMMUNICATION

The main factors to consider are timing, contacting other people who may be involved, the importance of the message, the recipient's timetable, the need for privacy, avoiding interruptions if continuity is essential, and tact. In some cases all these factors would not apply.

Correct timing depends mainly on the type of communication to be used and the urgency of the message. Promptness is essential for reprimanding and discussing grievances. However, there is often more latitude with other types of communication. There may be unavoidable delays if arrangements have to be made for another person to be present such as a union official or a superior, in which case the delay must be explained to the individual as soon as possible.

An urgent message obviously demands prompt action and consideration for the receiver's timetable. An important message which is delayed until, say, two minutes before the recipient's lunch break will obviously cause a half-hearted reception if it means rearranging to deal with the message.

Further aspects are the question of privacy and avoiding interruptions and distractions. Although these are important and essential with some types of communication, they are unavoidable in some establishments, owing to pressure of work and poor working conditions. Tact is vital in these situations.

## TRANSMIT THE MESSAGE

To minimise distortion, create a friendly atmosphere, use clear, simple language and foster a genuine sense of security. In this way the receiver should respond without fear or suspicion. Carefully noting instructions and any promises made is essential. This ensures future communications on the subject agree with the original arrangements. Although a mistake or omission made later may be unintentional, the supervisor will have difficulty in convincing subordinates.

## CHECK FOR UNDERSTANDING

Do not assume the message is clearly understood. There must be a positive check. This means not relying on a nod of the head or silence. Some people are afraid to admit they do not clearly understand a message. Others cannot be bothered to query a message and make excuses later if there is any ambiguity. Checking is an integral part of the effective communication process. Failing to check is like setting the hands of a clock correctly, but forgetting to wind the spring. Checking also impresses the message more deeply. Listening carefully to the response or reaction is essential. This ensures respect from the recipient and often more information emerges as a result.

## FOLLOW UP

If any promises are made by the supervisor during the closing discussions, they should be put into effect quickly. The follow-up process should include assessing any reactions, checking to see whether the desired result is achieved, and carefully noting any trouble spots which are developing. Appropriate follow-up means visualising any possible problems that could arise and being prepared to respond quickly if any danger signs are spotted. Follow-up is often the most neglected step because many supervisors expect the message to be sufficient.

# Making a speech

## INTRODUCTION

A supervisor will eventually have to make a speech either at work or on a social occasion. This may take various forms such as a presentation, introducing a speaker, an impromptu speech, a speech at a conference, or a formal platform speech. A presentation may be an informal or formal speech to a small group, or to an individual. The aim of the speech may be to provide information in various formats to suit the audience, or to motivate by using various audio techniques.

The three essential factors are thorough preparation, practice and developing confidence. The points mentioned on speech as a basic communication skill (Chapter 15) and the previous section on how to communicate effectively are also important.

### Thorough preparation

This expansive subject includes a number of features:

- the audience
- the aims of the speech
- the subject
- planning the speech
- conducting the speech

### Practice

Standing up and speaking to someone, or even speaking alone, helps to overcome hesitations. Also the use of a tape recorder indicates obvious faults, and repetition helps to correct them. Attempt various introductions and decide which one seems most appropriate. Practise as many times as possible as there is no doubt this method improves performance. Press for advice from the listener, if there is one who is willing to help, and do not forget to thank him or her.

### Developing confidence

Expect to be nervous at the event – practically everyone suffers including the professionals. This anxiety is natural, produces adrenaline which helps in communicating, and usually this feeling disappears quickly. Using antidotes is a contentious subject involving strong positive and negative views. The particular individual and state of mind are critical features. Thorough preparation and practice help to ease tension and promote a friendly approach. If there is time for a complete rehearsal, this tends to overcome hesitation, improves timing and portrays outward confidence.

## PRELIMINARY PREPARATION

Although there never seems to be sufficient time, preliminary preparation enables the speaker to present a coherent talk which will appeal more to the audience. To achieve this the aims of the talk must be decided, the audience should be carefully assessed, the communication features considered, and the subject for discussion must be thoroughly researched.

### Decide on the aims

The purpose of the speech determines the subject material, the way it is presented, and the appropriate title. Typical aims are:

- to explain a method
- to give a point of view
- to provide background or detailed information
- to outline a skill
- to propose or persuade a course of action
- to lead a discussion
- to summarise certain conclusions

### Assess the audience

The three considerations are to note their knowledge and experience on the subject, their attitude, and their capability to absorb the content and amount of information in the speech.

### Existing knowledge and experience

Naturally the audience is going to be bored unless the subject material is new to them. Therefore it is essential to assess their knowledge and experience. Do not rely on the arrangers who have chosen the subject. Check on the material that other speakers have used.

### Attitude

Assess the attitude of the audience by noting their appearance, if the opportunity occurs. Their impressions are easy to see; they may be friendly, hostile, indifferent, sceptical, interested or puzzled. Consider carefully what is on offer which causes the audience to attend. Typical answers are helping to solve problems, make decisions, improve their knowledge, and being able to seize any opportunities.

### Capability

Determine whether the audience is used to absorbing information at talks and whether the subject is likely to cause excessive strain. These aspects will depend upon intelligence level, likely expectations, characteristics, background, and self-interests.

### Communication features

Audience input will be achieved through sight, hearing, and possible touching. The speaker must please these sensory inputs by considering many principles which determine receptivity or perception (Chapter 9). Some of the important rules are now discussed.

### Sight

- Avoid distracting mannerisms and excessive movements which may distract the audience. Typically, pacing up and down, shuffling notes, slouching, smoking, and gesticulations with hands or other objects.
- Remember to smile and be natural.
- Use a pointer and stand to one side when illustrating items on a chart or blackboard. If the detail is complex, produce copies and distribute them.

- Use various approaches to liven up the talk so that the eyes of the audience do not become fixed. Examples are visual aids and blackboard work.
- Look at the audience all the time, apart from indicating points on visual aids and referring to notes.
- Try to focus on every member periodically.
- Do not pretend to see the audience; members seem to be very sensitive to offhand approaches.
- Use gestures sparingly to emphasise important points.

### Hearing

- Monotonous delivery lulls the audience into poor concentration. Keep the speech alive, distinct and active by varying the pitch, volume and speed.
- Maintain attention by using 'we' and inviting comments rather than adopting a straight lecturing approach.
- Ensure that everyone can hear.
- Give individuals the opportunity to digest information by pausing in appropriate places, otherwise important points may be missed. Appropriate pauses are an art, as any comedian will confirm. Try to avoid nervous pauses.

### Touching

A distinct advantage with some subjects is to give the audience the opportunity of handling the object under discussion. For example, the soft feel of a particular material, or the exceptional lightness of a component, is demonstrated far more effectively with hands-on experience. It is quite acceptable to save time by having the audience pass the object from one member to another during the talk.

### Investigate the subject

Considering the audience, the aims and the degree of depth for the talk, it is now possible to conduct appropriate research. A suggested approach is to:

- Check the accuracy of existing information.
- Decide on the information needed.
- Determine where to locate the information.
- Consider theories, ideas and current research.
- Seek advice from peers and friends.
- Be thorough.

## PLANNING THE SPEECH

### The content

Write each idea or item on a separate card and assemble the cards in a rough order of delivery, bearing in mind the structure (see below). Try to develop the story from a logical beginning through to acceptable conclusions. Consider revising the order or obtaining more information if obvious gaps emerge as the sequence is examined. Usually about six main topics are sufficient for an audience to assimilate, considering possible questions. Often there is too much information to deliver. This means drastic pruning to provide a concise presentation without too much detail which the audience will probably not remember.

### Prompt cards

The final stage is to adapt the initial cards into prompt cards for delivering the speech. Each prompt card should contain abbreviated information, highlighting the major features. The cards provide a useful means of memorising, reminding as the speech develops, avoiding any omissions, and completing the speech on time.

### The structure

#### Introduction

Try to think of a point which will alert the audience immediately and arouse their interest. Their self-interest is always worth considering as this will appeal and demand their attention. Provide an outline or framework of the talk and disclose any important sources of information.

#### Main aspects

The major topics are now outlined. Arguments must be presented clearly, bearing in mind the themes which are essential to assimilate, background information of interest, and examples.

#### Conclusions

Restate the main topics that must be remembered. Give reasons for their importance and how they can be used.

#### Questions

Be ready for obscure queries and searching questions on the information given, such as where located, accuracy and possible conflicting research disclosed. Be honest if the answer is not known and check up later.

### Audio and visual aids

Audio and visual aids are useful to liven up the talk and usually communicate a message with higher clarity and persuasiveness, if properly applied. A variety of aids is available such as samples, diagrams, models, charts, graphs, photographs, projection machines, and films. Care should be taken with size for everyone to see properly, minimum detail to avoid excessive intake, clear presentation, and using a balanced number of aids.

### General points

- Sometimes there is little or no time to prepare, in this case bear in mind the audience will always have difficulty in following long, complex sentences.
- Emphasise key points first and do not expect people to recall many facts and figures.
- Always be sincere because most listeners easily detect hesitation or overemphasis when attempts are made to mislead.
- Whenever possible use personal experience to illustrate a point.
- Use a logical sequence of arguments.
- Distinguish between facts, inferences and value judgements.
- Avoid too much detail; too much detail may bore an audience and people who desire details can put questions at the end.
- Try to keep the speech as short as possible.
- Use jokes with great care; jokes often fail unless relevant, new and really amusing.
- Allow for a rehearsal if possible; there is always a tendency to overrun the talk, so check with a tape recorder, note obvious weak points and revise.

## CONDUCTING THE SPEECH

1 Start on time, first impressions are important.
2 Check the timetable periodically with the plan.
3 Remember the audio and visual aids.
4 Remember to use the prompt cards.

5 Try not to hesitate if the place is lost, but continue regardless. Probably the audience will not even notice so long as the discontinuity is not too obvious.

6 Do not be afraid to pause and repeat information if necessary.

# Interviewing

Whenever the supervisor is speaking with another person and information is being exchanged, he or she is interviewing or being interviewed. This broad interpretation of 'interview' goes beyond the general impression that interviews are solely connected with employment.

A wide range of interviews take place every day on topics such as induction, training, grievances, suggestions, pay, merit rating, discipline, policy, regulations, operating problems and personnel counselling. The term 'interviewing' in this sense is an active two-way process of exchanging information, ideas and opinions between people, whereas the term 'communication' is the dynamic linkage between people throughout the company. The exception that illustrates the difference is a direct order which is one-way and not an interview; nevertheless it is a communication.

## DEFINITIONS

A general definition is when two people are exchanging information on a particular topic by using various interviewing techniques, making judgements and expressing opinions. An interpersonal approach is to define interviewing as a conversation (language) with a purpose (the objective), supplemented by observations (nonverbal behaviour and the use of senses) to explore a situation. An approach in psychological terms is a meeting between two people who use their interpersonal and conceptual skills, knowledge and experience, to analyse and make assessments which are influenced by motivational and perceptual factors. Considering the aspects of communication discussed in Chapter 14, similar features apply which are equally important and help in determining the success of interviews.

## INHERENT PROBLEMS

Interviewees tend to create impressions of what they think they are or would like to be, which of course is natural but misleading to the interviewer. Similarly, when individuals pass on information the tendency is to give favourable impressions of themselves. In this way the information received is distorted to conform to this pattern of behaviour.

Being able to establish an interviewee's previous record on any topic is difficult because of all the situations and variables over which the individual has no control. Furthermore, interviewers are inclined to allow personal prejudices to dominate opinions. This fault should be remembered, but being completely objective is obviously not possible.

## TYPES OF INTERVIEW

### Closed interviews

Closed interviews usually follow a set pattern of asking questions that are planned to cover all the requirements of the interview. They may be direct, in the form of a diagnostic checklist of questions, or patterned to provide a comprehensive questionnaire which may be used by a number of interviewers for comparison purposes. High skill is required to overcome a stereotyped approach. Learning the questions and varying their order help to remove a rigid or formal effect.

The advantages of closed interviews are that all the essential information is gathered quickly and the interviewee is given sufficient information to make a decision on fairness, justice and the topic under discussion. Careful planning is needed to cover all the aspects of the topic. However, the closed interview tends to be impersonal unless the right atmosphere is established by the interviewer, who should be skilled in creating an informal approach, which is difficult considering the direct pattern. Consequently, it is unlikely to stimulate opinions and disclose feelings.

### Open interviews

Open interviews offer more scope for the skilled interviewer to make a better assessment of the individual. The object is to put the interviewee at ease, draw him or her out on the subjects under discussion and steer carefully on to new topics. The open interview is unstructured but closely linked to the closed interview as both have the same object in mind – to obtain and give particular information. However, only one opinion is revealed in the open interview.

### Self-controlled interviews

When suggestions, complaints or grievances are presented, the self-controlled interview allows the interviewee to express himself or herself fully without worrying about time limits. The interviewer plays a 'near passive' role by listening sympathetically and agreeing periodically with the interviewee. If the interview starts to close prematurely, the interviewer must be sufficiently skilled to encourage the interviewee to gain confidence and air thoughts openly.

### Group discussions

A well-conducted group discussion is an excellent way of exchanging information and fostering new ideas. However, its effectiveness depends upon the right atmosphere of co-operation and enthusiasm being induced. The discussion may be controlled with a specific topic in mind or as an open discussion. The group approach was discussed fully in the previous chapter.

### Board or committee

The individual may be subjected to a number of interviewers who are known as a board or committee. The interviewee will probably feel nervous when confronted by say six people who in turn ask questions based upon their own particular experiences of the topic. Assessing how the person copes with such an ordeal is part of the technique, but there are variations. For example, the individual may be interviewed privately by each board member. Their opinions are then examined and analysed by the board. Decisions may be made in various ways, such as majority voting. Provided members use a structured approach, this method is more successful.

## THE ART OF INTERVIEWING

Effective interviewing involves many skills, an extensive knowledge and experience of human beings, and the development of sensitivity to improve assessing, analysing and making judgements. This demanding and sometimes thankless task is naturally influenced by the interviewer's characteristics, especially perception and attitudes, and the capability to be objective, within reason. Consequently, the art may be summarised as:

- forecasting and compiling a comprehensive plan (Chapter 8)
- persuading the person to feel at ease and relaxed by adopting behavioural techniques, ensuring seclusion and privacy, and establishing a favourable rapport
- asking the right questions and follow-up questions (Chapter 15)
- recognising misleading answers and elaborations by careful listening (Chapter 15)
- sizing up accurately as the interview develops
- avoiding the interference of personal prejudices

Interviewing skills within the art are usually difficult to learn and develop. Certainly improvements are possible by studying interviewing knowledge available in many books on the subject, and by practising with the aid of a competent tutor.

### The basic skill sequence

The main features of interviewing include the art of interviewing, the inherent problems and the basic skills; they are illustrated in Fig. 16.2.

1 Conversing in a casual manner – aiming to lull the interviewee into a feeling of security and confidence.
2 Phrasing questions in such a way that the answers provide comprehensive coverage of the objective.
3 Interpreting the answers, considering honesty, full coverage, attempts to mislead, hesitancy, omissions and inconsistencies.
4 Cross-examining to clarify the answers by probing and using the what, where, why, how, who, techniques, etc.
5 Recognising eventually the deliberate omissions, half-truths and weaknesses.

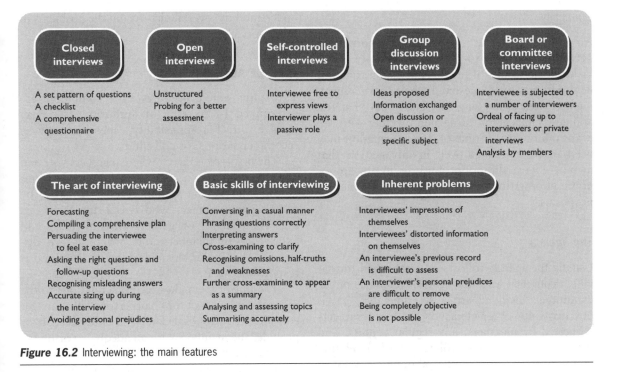

| Closed interviews | Open interviews | Self-controlled interviews | Group discussion interviews | Board or committee interviews |
|---|---|---|---|---|
| A set pattern of questions<br>A checklist<br>A comprehensive questionnaire | Unstructured<br>Probing for a better assessment | Interviewee free to express views<br>Interviewer plays a passive role | Ideas proposed<br>Information exchanged<br>Open discussion or discussion on a specific subject | Interviewee is subjected to a number of interviewers<br>Ordeal of facing up to interviewers or private interviews<br>Analysis by members |

| The art of interviewing | Basic skills of interviewing | Inherent problems |
|---|---|---|
| Forecasting<br>Compiling a comprehensive plan<br>Persuading the interviewee to feel at ease<br>Asking the right questions and follow-up questions<br>Recognising misleading answers<br>Accurate sizing up during the interview<br>Avoiding personal prejudices | Conversing in a casual manner<br>Phrasing questions correctly<br>Interpreting answers<br>Cross-examining to clarify<br>Recognising omissions, half-truths and weaknesses<br>Further cross-examining to appear as a summary<br>Analysing and assessing topics<br>Summarising accurately | Interviewees' impressions of themselves<br>Interviewees' distorted information on themselves<br>An interviewee's previous record is difficult to assess<br>An interviewer's personal prejudices are difficult to remove<br>Being completely objective is not possible |

**Figure 16.2** Interviewing: the main features

6   Further cross-examining or rephrasing in such a way that it appears as summarising or a clarification, if the answers are vital requirements. Here are two examples: How would you deal with this situation from what you have indicated so far? Could you describe again how you would cope with this problem?

7   Analysing and assessing each topic discussed.

8   Summarising and concluding with a mutual understanding of agreements or decisions.

# Meetings and committees

Committee work provides an opportunity for people representing the functions or sectors that come under the committee's sphere of activity to meet and act as a group. Under the guidance of a chairperson, information and ideas from each sector are pooled and discussed to reach accurate, balanced decisions. Provided the meeting is conducted properly, closer co-ordination between sectors should automatically follow.

Ideally, committee work is an excellent means of supplementing the organisation framework because it provides a meeting ground for individuals from different parts of the company who would not normally be in direct contact with each other. Purposeful control and suppression of self-interests are difficult to achieve; consequently, some committees have a poor reputation and are known as time-wasters. However, invaluable work can be done at meetings to co-ordinate activities and improve the effectiveness of the organisation. The success of committees depends upon preliminary arrangements, chairing the meeting, membership, type of authority and attending meetings.

## PRELIMINARY ARRANGEMENTS

Often the committee secretary, or sometimes the chairperson, attends to preparations. They include the objectives; choosing and advising committee members; dates, times and locations; preparing and distributing the agenda; arranging any visual aids; place names, name tags and refreshments.

## Continuity

An important feature is gathering information between meetings to ensure continuity. This includes the results of previous decisions, queries, new information requested at the previous meeting, progress of ongoing subjects, policy changes, and new subjects for the agenda together with relevant information. Some of this information may need to be circulated well in advance so that members have the opportunity to locate appropriate information, and perhaps write a paper on proposals.

## The agenda

Usually the agenda follows an established format which complies with the terms of reference of the committee. Included are a set timetable, previous items not completed, new business, subjects requested by members, any regular reports, and statutory items arising. All information relating to the agenda is distributed about one week in advance.

## THE CHAIRPERSON

A competent chairperson is essential. He or she must conduct the meeting firmly, use the correct procedure and plan carefully throughout the life of the committee. Effectiveness depends upon identifying the important issues and reaching agreement, controlling strong members and protecting the weak, noting reactions from listeners and acting accordingly, and summarising progress regularly.

## COMMITTEE MEMBERS

Competent members subordinate their own interests and the group's interests to the common interest: the objective set for the committee. The chairperson can control this factor when it is obvious, but unfortunately self-interest may prevail when specialists are drawn together. Besides solving problems, the meetings help people to appreciate other points of view and so broaden their outlook. As the body of knowledge grows, people have to specialise on narrowing fronts, which increases the difficulties involved in trying to understand the overall picture and the problems of other specialists.

## TYPE OF AUTHORITY

The status and procedures of a committee are determined by its type of authority. This may involve direct responsibility, specialist advice, recommendations, or consultative views.

The first type is direct, where members vote and are responsible as a committee for the decisions it implements. The second type is advisory, by assisting the manager who is chairing the meeting. The chairperson gathers the knowledge and experience of members and proposals are discussed. Then he or she makes the decision and is responsible for it.

The third type makes recommendations to the manager, who is not the chairperson. The manager considers the proposals later and either accepts or provides the members with an adequate reason for their rejection.

The fourth type is consultative, where representatives from management and employees are brought together to give their views. Theoretically, communication by these means ensures that information is received by all interested parties.

## ATTENDING MEETINGS

1 Study the constitution of the meeting, which gives the rules for conducting proceedings.
2 Ask the secretary's advice on suitable dress for the meeting.
3 Study the previous minutes of the meeting, the agenda and any information forwarded in advance.
4 Prepare any facts or figures which are needed to support proposed views.
5 Send a written apology or telephone the secretary immediately if attendance is not possible.
6 Plan to arrive at least five minutes before the meeting commences.
7 During the meeting, always address the chairperson unless directed otherwise.
8 Think carefully before speaking, as people judge others by their words and ideas.
9 Make speeches clearly, slowly and with brevity.

10 Do not take offence at criticisms of proposed views. They are probably made with as much sincerity. Remember the object of group discussion is to consider the best solutions to problems through team effort, which means constructive criticism, putting forward ideas and arriving at several conclusions.

11 Listen attentively and use the spare time to think over proposals.

12 Criticise constructively and tactfully.

13 Ask questions if there is uncertainty about any point, or if the decisions reached are unclear.

14 Avoid making any comments and suggestions after the meeting. The time to speak is at the meeting. Failure to comment until later indicates insecurity.

### Informal meetings

Small informal meetings are often held for various purposes. Within reason and circumstances they should be conducted along similar lines to a formal meeting; this avoids slovenly behaviour and helps to achieve objectives.

### THE MEETING AS A MEANS OF PERSUASION

On some occasions the supervisor may have difficulty in persuading management to take an obvious and essential course of action. When these circumstances are known to everyone and management remains indifferent, it is possible to ask for a meeting to discuss the question.

In many cases this will be agreed. Often it is worth writing a paper for the meeting outlining the main points and recommendations so that the managers are fully aware of the situation. Usually management has already acted to avoid embarrassment by the time the meeting is held. The time is then used to clarify the arrangements.

# Report writing

An efficient communication system has to rely, to some extent, upon the conscientious provision of written reports. Neglecting to render worthwhile reports may result in disastrous blunders, poor decisions and wasted time.

A report is defined as a written account of an event or situation, together with relevant facts, figures and recommendations, where required. The purpose is to provide information to those who are concerned with or responsible for taking some action on a situation.

Every supervisor who is responsible for a number of subordinate supervisors soon realises the importance of the reports received from them. However this person, in turn, must attach similar importance to the reports he or she sends to superiors. The supervisor will expect the reports received to be clear, accurate, concise, logically arranged and on time, so he or she must conform to similar standards in making his or her own reports.

The main features of report writing are as follows. Summaries of the main features of report writing are given in Fig. 16.3.

- types of report and how they are used
- readability, to reduce the risk of being ignored
- a recommended procedure which provides a logical framework
- the essential requirements of a report

### TYPES OF REPORT

#### Personal accounts

Personal accounts include presenting information as witnessed at the time, on events such as accidents, social disturbances and disciplinary action.

#### Routine reports

Routine reports include all information passed to control points on topics such as production, progress, machine breakdowns and idle time, which are everyday occurrences.

#### Special reports

Special reports are for unusual, involved events. A report includes investigations and analysis of information, illustrating the significance of findings and often recommending courses of action. Careful planning and a logical approach are needed, otherwise the reader will spend considerable time

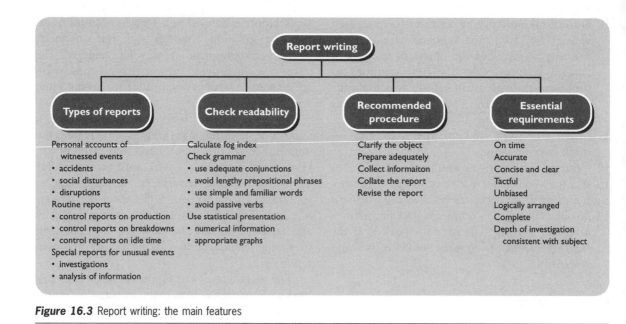

**Figure 16.3** Report writing: the main features

reading through the material in an attempt to sort out the sequence of events and the points to be noted.

## READABILITY

Reports must be easy to read and easily understood, otherwise the reader will be distracted by the wording and rapidly lose interest. Two helpful techniques are the fog index and the statistical method.

### The fog index

The fog index increases in value as the writing becomes foggier. It is calculated in the following way:

1   Work out the average number of words in each sentence in a passage of about one hundred words by dividing the total number of words by the number of sentences. The final sentence in the passage should be included or excluded depending upon which word count is nearest to the hundred-word total.
2   Count the words containing three or more syllables in the passage, but exclude proper nouns and easy compound words. This means

excluding words beginning with a capital letter, and words such as 'extend' or 'repress' when they appear as 'extended' or 'represses'.
3   The results of the first and second steps are added and together multiplied by 0.4 to give the fog index.

A passage with an index of 6 is very easy to read, while an index of 17 is extremely difficult to read. The fog index may be improved by restricting a sentence to about two ideas and 18 to 22 words.

### Grammar

Grammar has been discussed under speech and business writing (Chapter 15) and in making a speech, in this chapter. To improve the fog index there are other grammatical points worth noting.

● Keep sentences short but vary their length and structure.
● Link and relate sentences to each other.
● Use adequate conjunctions (and, but, with, that, etc.).
● Avoid lengthy prepositional phrases (for the reason that = because).
● Wherever possible use familiar words with few syllables.
● Avoid passive verbs.

## Statistical method

Statistical presentation is an important requirement. Appropriate graphs and figures often impress far more than wordy notes. Brief descriptions of statistical methods and various graphical presentations are given in Chapter 23. The use of a computer with an appropriate package is also helpful, along with an appropriate textbook on statistics.

## RECOMMENDED PROCEDURE

- Clarify the object of the report.
- Prepare adequately – method of investigation, area to cover, etc.
- Collect information.
- Collate the report.
- Revise the report.

## The object

Make sure the aim of the report is clear. Any ambiguity or uncertainty in the terms of reference should be clarified before proceeding further. The terms of reference must give sufficient detail to establish accurately:

- the topic of investigation
- the limitations, if any, of the enquiry
- the purpose of the report

## Preparation

Prepare a framework of investigation first before making enquiries and collecting information. Work can then proceed to a flexible plan which may be revised as necessary when new information becomes available.

The plan should take into account an assessment of the likely difficulties, the time factor, amount of co-operation from employees, degree of secrecy, amount of detail required, known availability of facts, possible repercussions from certain individuals, and any special requirements for the report.

The reader must also be considered when drawing up the plan. An assessment based on personal knowledge, previous experience or discreet enquiries will enable the writer to decide how much detail is needed. This will depend on information already known to the reader, whether technical jargon or plain language should be used, and the reader's likely reaction to the significance of the findings.

## Collecting information

Collection of information and ideas should proceed according to the plan. The sources of information are found by personal knowledge or by using the 'chain method' – asking one person who suggests another, and so on. Careful observation, reading and experimenting form part of the technique.

Make notes immediately whenever possible and in sufficient detail, as very brief notes are often difficult to decipher later. The use of rough sketches is a good memory aid. An important precaution is always to identify the source of information.

## Collating the report

The first draft of the report should be written within a suitable framework, usually with the following headings. The report must also be dated and signed.

**The subject**
Terms of reference should be stated in full. In some instances the source and date of a directive should be given, especially if copies are to be sent to various departments.

**Introduction**
The method of conducting the investigation should be given, together with any major difficulties which were encountered. Any major gaps in the report must be mentioned along with an assessment of their importance. If background information is considered to be of use, it may be mentioned at this stage. Any relevant information which does not fit conveniently into the rest of the framework of the report may be included in this section. Examples are the general attitude of employees towards the subject, degrees of secrecy, explanations of courses of action, or necessary technical jargon.

### Findings

The findings form the main body of the report, which includes all the facts presented in a logical sequence and in an unbiased manner. Whenever possible, a good plan is to tabulate the facts. This has the advantages of improving clarity for the reader and easier preparation for the writer.

### Conclusions

An analysis of the facts and all the inferences and value judgements should be included in the conclusions. Adequate explanations of conclusions drawn from the facts are essential, otherwise the reader will be unable to assess their value. Logical conclusions based upon a number of facts are generally straightforward and immediately acceptable, but if experience and judgement are included in the basis, this should be stated.

### Recommendations

Recommendations are based upon the findings and conclusions. If there are a number of choices they should be weighted with arguments for and against each one. Some important factors could be the cost, time, disruption of production, human problems, availability of supplies, and space.

### References

References to any documents or books should be listed in this section. Sufficient information is essential for easy location. Naturally this section may be omitted if no references are mentioned.

### Summary

A brief outline of the report is needed for some people who have insufficient time to read the full text. The correct meaning of each section must be conveyed. Figure 16.4 gives an example of the layout of a summary page.

TITLE Page 1

Terms of reference ....................................

Introduction .............................................. Date .................

Summary of findings

1 ..............................................................................

2 ..............................................................................

3 ..............................................................................

4 ..............................................................................

5 ..............................................................................

Conclusions ..............................................................

Recommendations ......................................................

(Signature)

***Figure 16.4*** Summary page of a report
A single-page summary helps everyone, especially those who are short of time. Its layout should be clear and logical.

## Revision

Whenever possible, wait at least a few hours before attempting to revise the first draft. A break provides sufficient new insight which helps considerably in rendering a more balanced report. The document should be read critically and objectively. Try to be ruthless and remove all unnecessary words. If a person can be found who will give an honest, helpful view of the report, the second draft should be submitted to him or her for comment.

## ESSENTIAL REQUIREMENTS OF A REPORT

A report should meet these requirements:

- on time
- accurate, concise and clear
- tactful and unbiased
- short and simple sentences
- a clear objective
- state a case and then support it in clear language
- easily understood terms
- logically arranged and complete
- the depth of investigation is consistent with the importance of the subject
- the conclusions and recommendations are aligned with the information
- illustrations should be used where words are inadequate to promote attention and for clarity
- stimulates interest, otherwise no one will read it

# Project reports

Some examination boards require course members to investigate a problem or situation by collecting appropriate information, analysing it, arriving at logical conclusions and making suitable recommendations. Apart from using information preceding this section, further notes are now given on the choice of subject, the investigation and the report.

## CHOICE OF SUBJECT: FOUR PHASES

### Write down immediate ideas

Rather than agonise over whether a situation or problem is suitable, write down the immediate difficulties being experienced or the obvious faults surrounding the job. Take into account procedures, systems, control, etc. Note there are inevitably hundreds of suitable subjects in the immediate vicinity.

Choose subjects which appear to be straightforward and of sufficient depth to warrant investigation. They should demonstrate obvious improvements immediately and are considered worthwhile in terms of savings, improving efficiency or increasing effectiveness.

### Consider the work involved

Add to each idea a rough plan of the possible work involved. Bear in mind interviews, studying the immediate situation, guessing at possible avenues to be traced away from the workplace, assessing the people to be contacted, and forming a general impression of the project's breadth. Even seemingly simple situations and problems become complex when investigated in depth. Often this is why they exist.

### Decide on the category

Sort ideas into categories: problem solving, procedural rearranging, cost saving by simplifying, and so on. Use work study techniques to categorise them. When complete, consider which one suits the available knowledge and personal experience.

### Select two or three

Write a framework of ideas for each one. Discuss with the manager for an opinion. Discuss with the tutor for an opinion and approval. Choose the most suitable subject.

## INVESTIGATION

- Always be diplomatic towards the people who are involved. They may feel apprehensive, even hostile, if there are obvious improvements they have ignored.
- If hostility is met and there is no improvement, consider an alternative project rather than create an incident.
- Avoid any personal prejudice. Try to present facts not opinions, unless there is no alternative.
- Information may be obtained by asking someone and by observation and research. Use all three to confirm if there is any doubt.
- Always seek permission before overstepping any sectional boundaries.
- Revise the plan if new evidence reveals a difficult problem.
- Try to identify effective lines of enquiry to save time, especially if generalisations are appearing.
- Consult the manager if advice is needed. This serves two purposes: he or she may be flattered and will not be taken by surprise at the end if made aware of progress and problems.
- Revise the desired objectives if there are difficulties.
- Use work study techniques.

## THE REPORT

- Make several attempts before choosing an appropriate arrangement.
- Avoid very brief headings. Convey their meaning plainly. For example, avoid 'stock', use 'finished goods stock'.
- Avoid including information which is not strictly relevant. Questions to ask are: Does this particular information lead to the conclusions and recommendations proposed? Is it of use to justify the recommendations proposed?

- Emphasise significant information to avoid doubt as to the validity of conclusions and recommendations.
- Try to provide balance by minimising space on minor subjects and maximising space on major factors.
- If recommendations are controversial, indicate how the proposals will harmonise with other sections.
- Include details of alternative proposals which were abandoned. Give reasons so that questions are anticipated.
- Remember to include acknowledgements, especially help and advice received from the manager.

# Applying for a job

The uncertainty of employment, rapid change, redundancies, and strong competition for jobs have caused an increased interest in this subject and an increased demand for specialist advice. Many self-help textbooks are available, an increasing number of consultancies and agencies give guidance to those who register with them, and specialist organisations will design and produce a CV for a fee. For those supervisors who prefer a personal approach, there are three main areas on which to concentrate:

- the introductory letter
- the CV
- the interview

## THE INTRODUCTORY LETTER

Apart from conforming with good business letter writing discussed in the previous chapter, the first consideration is to choose advertisements which are worth a reply. Avoid wasting time applying for unsuitable jobs, because the sifting process when letters are received immediately rejects obvious mismatching. Carefully read the advertisement and note the immediate requirements. These may include a CV or a letter of application briefly outlining the career pattern. Do not deviate from the instructions as this will irritate and cause more administration.

## PREPARING A CV

### Aims of a CV

- To provide sufficient information which is relevant to the prospective post.
- To appeal strongly to the reader by assessing the main features that will attract attention and provide a favourable impact.
- To demonstrate thoroughness, preciseness and conciseness.

### A suitable framework

The aims of a CV can only be fulfilled by careful planning, rearranging and meticulous thinking. The main approaches are to determine a suitable framework, gather and sort all the data, pay close attention to the obvious pitfalls, and use logical progression. A typical acceptable plan is to provide all personal details, including the obvious particulars, date of birth, marital status, and main interests; education, including schools and colleges, qualifications and dates; and career, including job titles, companies, authority, responsibilities, special assignments, achievements, and reasons for leaving. Avoid gaps by giving explanations. Propose references should they be required.

### Fundamental requirements

There are many hints on writing which help to ensure CVs are actually read and not discarded. Here are the important ones:

- Remember the essential details – name, address, telephone number, age, present occupation, education, skills and experience. Often some are omitted through carelessness.
- Honesty is rated highly. Attempting to lie is always dangerous. If believed at the time, there is a risk of the falsehood being discovered later, which could mean instant dismissal and further problems when applying for future jobs.
- Many claims of minor interest are taken at face value, such as being an animal rights campaigner. But there is always the danger of meeting an employee with similar interests which become embarrassing and may destroy promotion prospects.

- Do not take the risk of making false claims. There is the possibility of asking for documents later for some reason, or the interviewer may know someone outside who can verify.
- Check carefully for correct grammar and spelling mistakes; avoid jargon and overlong words.
- Be concise, be precise on dates and be positive.
- Emphasise strengths, particular skills, etc., for the prospective job; emphasise ambitions and other relevant aspects.
- Ensure the layout is logical, neat and highlights important features.
- Try to demonstrate a logical career progression and emphasise aspirations.
- Two or three pages are generally sufficient, but one page is not enough.
- Do not overemphasise education or other interests.
- Give evidence of achievements, but avoid excessive detail on historical aspects of say fifteen years ago.
- Use reverse chronological order for previous jobs, mentioning quantifiable results such as leadership successes, budgetary control, cutting costs, improving productivity, and modern techniques.
- Avoid emphasising subjects which may be difficult to discuss intelligently at an interview.
- Be businesslike and try to imagine the interviewer's requirements.
- Ask a friend to read the CV and encourage criticisms.

## THE INTERVIEW

Following a CV, the interview will naturally be used to assess the suitability of the individual and verify the information received. Some of the hints on writing CVs apply here. Also there are various codes of conduct which help to create the right atmosphere.

### The first impression

The initial impression and the first few minutes are still considered to be important, although they may easily mislead the interviewer. Five essential features are:

- Look well groomed – avoid an unusual hairstyle, earrings (for men), ostentatious clothes, and general untidiness. In other words, a non-controversial appearance is worthwhile and avoids irritation.
- Avoid alcohol on breath, impoliteness and disinterest.
- Do not slouch in the chair.
- Try to smile.
- Remember to say good morning, etc.; if the interviewer greets first, remember to reply.

### Acceptable conventions

During the main part of the interview there are certain conventions which will, at least, please the interviewer:

- Always be honest: a skilled interviewer instinctively recognises the truth, a half-truth, a lie or exaggeration; they will probe to verify.
- If attempting to mislead be ready for cross-questioning.
- Recognise the skilled interviewer; he or she will be listening most of the time and guiding the discussion. Only amateurs talk a lot, learn little and guess.
- If any questions are unclear or ambiguous, do not hesitate to seek clarification.
- Try to give concise, logical answers. Although this is not easy, persevere by practising. Bear in mind there may be assumptions behind questions.
- Do not volunteer further information unless there are clear signs that it will help to secure the job. However, there are some aspects that might cause difficulties later, in which case it may be wise to volunteer information. Typical examples are marital problems and financial difficulties.
- Try to maintain an open, frank approach with emphasis on the job (not on pay), and on a willing attitude.
- Avoid giving false impressions; there are many testing devices that soon reveal the truth.
- At the end, thank the interviewer for the opportunity to attend.

## QUESTIONS

1 Discuss the importance of developing a good interviewing technique in connection with supervision.

2 Describe how you would conduct an employment interview.

3 The importance of reports is often overlooked. Discuss this statement.

4 Outline a logical approach in preparing a written report.

5 Discuss the essential requirements of a report.

6 What advice would you give to a colleague who is going to attend his or her first meeting as a member of a committee?

7 Put yourself in the place of a new employee and describe your feelings and what information you would hope to receive from your supervisor.

8 Outline a logical method of communicating effectively.

9 Discuss the importance of external aspects of communication in connection with the supervisor's role as a leader.

10 Outline the various types of interview.

11 Discuss the fivefold framework, illustrating the main features of the plan.

12 Thorough preparation is essential before making a speech. Discuss this statement indicating the main features to consider.

13 How would you plan an effective speech?

14 List the main types of interview and their uses.

15 Competent interviewing is an art. Discuss this statement.

16 How would you prepare a CV?

17 Outline the essential requirements when applying for a job.

18 Name the four essential features to remember when you are subjected to an interview.

19 Outline a procedure you would follow when writing a project report.

20 Consider how you would decide on an appropriate project.

---

**CASE STUDY**

Arthur explained to his supervisor that his wife was very ill and that his two children aged 5 and 7 years were unable to cope when they arrived home from school. He suggested leaving at 3.30 pm for a few weeks until her health improved. The supervisor agreed but two weeks later he overheard in the dining room that Arthur's wife had changed her job and was working as a postwoman. There was nothing wrong with her and she had been seen several times delivering mail recently.

*What steps would you take in this situation?*

---

Sally Newton, young and single, is warned about the men in her department of a well-known travel company by her superior before she takes over the supervisor's job. The caution is expected as the eight men, most of them young, have a reputation for being teasers and not being tolerant of favouritism.

On the first day, Sally soon finds herself attracted to Bob, a popular man in the group. She cannot keep her eyes off him and inevitably it takes only a few days for the other men to notice. She deliberately spends the minimum amount of time necessary with him, knowing the risks. Bob soon becomes aware of Sally's interest and makes it obvious, it seems, that he is equally attracted to her.

Sally, being no fool, is sure that the other men are wise to the situation. She is uncertain as to whether Bob is setting her up or is genuinely interested in her. Several weeks pass and everything goes smoothly in the department. Package holiday bookings boom beyond their previous high levels and there are very few hitches.

Her superior is delighted, praises her and adds, 'Incidentally, Sally, what are you going to do about Bob?'

*How would you answer if you were Sally, after you had recovered your composure? How would you account for the successful running of the department from the information given?*

# 17

# Employment: recruitment and associated practices

## Introduction

Usually a supervisor will be involved in many of the tasks which make up an effective recruitment procedure and associated practices. An extensive knowledge is required to contribute successfully and considerable practical training is essential.

The complete process is expensive, complex and demanding. Mistakes are costly and severely restrict activities in the workplace and administration. Many employees have been distressed, overstressed, and suffered many problems through misplaced individuals. Also, if the newcomer is installed in the wrong job, he or she will suffer stress and encounter human problems with associates. In this event probably further education and training are needed to rectify the situation, which is an additional expense. Naturally productivity suffers through mistakes.

There are many different recruitment processes seen operating in practice. No ideal procedure exists, but a comprehensive plan and conscientious operation with appropriate skills will reduce the risk of error.

### THE RECRUITMENT PROCESS

A typical recruitment procedure is outlined in Fig. 17.1, which provides appropriate columns for decisions. Decisions may be agreed, rejected or revised, and finally authorised. Thus the procedure is designed to incorporate flexibility, based upon opinions and fact-finding to determine any revisions. The main phases of a recruitment procedure are discussed shortly.

### ASSOCIATED PRACTICES

There are many associated practices of recruitment which determine the effectiveness and accuracy of any programme. The important ones are equal opportunities, appropriate practices of civil law, remuneration and manpower planning (see later).

## A recruitment procedure

Although there are many variations in practice, a typical process would conform to a number of main phases in sequential order. These should be examined in Fig. 17.1 and referred to as each phase is outlined. A supervisor will often take part in conducting many of these phases. The degree of involvement depends upon the personnel department, if one exists. The specialist activities outside the supervisor's expertise would either be covered by personnel or by an appropriate consultant within or outside the company. The procedure for induction is often considered to be an operational feature of employment and is dealt with in Chapter 18.

## Phase 1: Propose the vacancy

The vacancy may emerge for various reasons:

- termination of an employee
- transfer of an employee
- increased workload
- restructuring the section for various reasons

Discussions with personnel at this phase may overcome the problem if there are other vacancies, transfers or proposed changes being considered.

| PHASE | DECISIONS | AGREED | REJECTED | REVISED | AUTHORISATION |
|-------|-----------|--------|----------|---------|---------------|
| 1 Propose the vacancy | | | | | |
| 2 Investigate the situation | | | | | |
| 3 Justify the vacancy | | | | | |
| 4 Prepare a job description | | | | | |
| 5 Prepare a personal specification | | | | | |
| 6 Determine suitable sources | | | | | |
| 7 Initial screening of applications | | | | | |
| 8 Selection inverviewing | | | | | |
| 9 Engagement | | | | | |
| 10 Preparation for arrival | | | | | |
| 11 Induction | | | | | |

Procedure completed

Signature .............................     Date ...............................

Personnel manager

*Figure 17.1* Recruitment procedure

## Phase 2: Investigate the situation

Before a programme is developed there may be immediate questions which will clarify the situation when the answers are examined. Typical examples are:

- Is the work involved in the proposed vacancy essential?

- Is it possible to reorganise and split the work among existing employees, possibly with some overtime?
- Are all employees in the section fully utilised?
- Could the work or a sector of the work be sub-contracted?
- Does the workload warrant a full-timer, a part-timer or a temporary worker?
- Have work study, automation and mechanisation been considered recently?

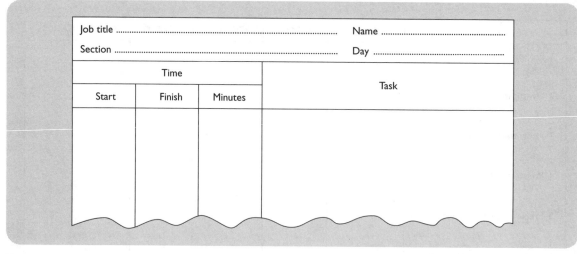

| Job title ........................................................... | | | Name ........................................... |
|---|---|---|---|
| Section ........................................................... | | | Day ........................................... |
| Time | | | Task |
| Start | Finish | Minutes | |
| | | | |

**Figure 17.2** Daily task sheet

## ESSENTIAL REQUIREMENTS

When the above questions have been answered and adjustments considered, some practices remain which will justify whether a newcomer is needed, determine the newcomer's duties, and show why the job is necessary. There are five main practices which may be used when adjustments have been discussed:

- job tasks
- activity analysis
- job analysis
- job evaluation
- functional analysis

# Job tasks

A surprising number of tasks and the time element involved in completing them are often forgotten and neglected. Therefore an attempt should be made to record all the details on a daily basis, which is worthwhile although time-consuming. A simple example of recording for an office is given in Fig. 17.2. In conjunction with activity analysis and job evaluation, it provides a sound framework for employment purposes, control and work study.

# Activity analysis

To achieve a comprehensive picture, the activities of a section should be analysed by tabulating all the tasks. The survey should include an appropriate title for each activity, the time spent on each one, the employee's name and any other useful data. An appropriate form may be easily drawn up. The layout will depend on the circumstances, but a typical example is given in Fig. 17.3 as a guide.

# Job analysis

Job analysis is conducted to determine the essential characteristics of the job. It is a fundamental activity and is used in many different ways by personnel. There are two main approaches:

- traditional narratives on tasks, procedures, responsibilities and personal attributes
- describing the job in behavioural terms

The first approach is often viewed as job-oriented, emphasising the technological aspects; the second approach is often viewed as worker-oriented, emphasising the human behavioural aspects. An investigation should use both approaches. In summary, job analysis is the systematic investigation of work in two stages.

Section ..........

Week commencing ..........

| Activity | Supervisor | Hrs | Clerk A | Hrs | Clerk B | Hrs | Clerk C | Hrs |
|---|---|---|---|---|---|---|---|---|
| | | | | | | | | |

***Figure 17.3*** Weekly activity form

### Identifying task-oriented aspects

- title
- nature of work
- methods employed
- purpose
- place of work
- tasks
- value of tasks
- supervisory aspects
- standards established
- any special working conditions

### Identifying worker-oriented aspects

- mental demands
- skills involved
- competencies
- knowledge requirements
- experience requirements
- personality requirements
- any special education and training

### BASIC METHODS OF INVESTIGATION

Methods may be used singly or combined, depending upon their relevance to the job. They are called observation, interviews and questionnaires. Direct observation reveals most information on the job, and judgements are possible on the personal aspects of the work, so long as there is high manual content and low mental processes, including discretion. Interviewing demands careful preparation and a structured systematic approach to determine all the aspects of the job. Questionnaires should be planned to cover all the aspects.

In the large organisation a job analyst may be used to investigate and complete a job description. In the small company, the personnel officer or an outside consultant may be used.

## Job evaluation

Job evaluation is a systematic approach to the problem of determining the value of a job in relation to others so that a fair pay scale may be applied. It is essential to have a scientific basis for assessing all factors involved in a job. Although personal bias or opinion cannot be eliminated completely, new techniques are being developed which will eventually make job evaluation more scientific.

Judging the relative values of jobs is difficult within one department and becomes exceptionally difficult when applied to different industries. With sufficient experience, the superior should be able to make a reasonable assessment. Opinions vary among supervisors, however, and there should be a determined attempt to be as objective as possible.

Successful introduction of job evaluation depends, to some extent, on the ability of supervisors to make sound assessments and on the careful compilation of the pay structure. A good scheme should result in a reduction in labour turnover and an increase in morale and output. Correct placement of employees in suitable jobs is made easier after job evaluation. The publication of job classifications clearly indicates the duties, authority and responsibilities of each employee, which means everyone knows what is expected both of themselves and others.

## THE PROCEDURE

A scheme is usually based upon particular standards that provide a fair comparison between various jobs. The main factors under consideration are:

- physical and mental effort
- education and training
- experience
- degree of authority and responsibility
- particular skills and aptitudes
- appropriate competencies
- working conditions

A detailed examination of the job is essential. For this purpose a suitably designed form should be completed and the findings then carefully assessed on a comparative basis.

When all the jobs have been assessed, they are arranged in sequence of value and related to the pay structure, using the most logical method possible. The important aspects which help to determine job evaluation are:

- the methods of evaluation
- a job grading scheme
- merit rating
- working hours
- flexible working hours
- flexiwork

## METHODS OF EVALUATION

### Points rating

Points rating attempts to rate each factor of the job by allocating an appropriate weighting of points. Each factor may be assessed within a range of 0 to 10 points, or 0 to 20 points if a wider choice is desired. An example of a form using the points rating system is given in Fig. 17.4. The total number of points is calculated and matched against a pay table, which is designed on a points pay-rate basis.

### Factor comparison

Factor comparison is a variation of the points rating system. The main difference between the two schemes is that only five factors are used for factor comparison:

- mental
- physical
- skill
- responsibility
- working conditions

Key jobs are chosen to represent various pay levels. The pay for each job is proportioned according to ratings for the five factors. From this information a value can be placed on each point and appropriate rates may be calculated for those jobs that fall between the key posts.

### Ranking

Ranking is the other main method besides points rating. Ranking involves judging each job as a whole and attempting to assess its relative value by ranking a whole job against another whole job. Part of the system is preparing a job description and grading levels for allocation of pay. It does not show the degree of difference between jobs, which is a disadvantage for the large company where a wide variety of jobs usually exists. In the small business the method is likely to be more suitable due to its simplicity and the reduced range of jobs is probably easier to define.

### Classification

This method may also be used. Before the jobs are ranked, the scheme determines the grades and salaries within which prepared job specifications are fitted. Personal judgement is used to group and rank the jobs.

## A JOB GRADING SCHEME

Although the four methods of evaluating jobs obviously need considerable personal judgement, they are often called scientific methods. An example of a job grading scheme that clarifies the levels in office work is offered by the Institute of Administrative Management:

**Figure 17.4** Job evaluation form with points rating

- *grade A*: simple or closely directed tasks requiring no previous experience to perform them.
- *grade B*: simple tasks requiring only a few weeks' training, closely directed, carried out within a small number of well-defined rules, checked and following a daily routine.
- *grade C*: routine tasks following well-defined rules, requiring a reasonable degree of experience (or a special aptitude), amounting to a daily routine and subject to short period control.
- *grade D*: tasks requiring considerable experience, some initiative, predetermined procedure and a slightly varying daily routine.
- *grade E*: tasks requiring a considerable amount of discretion and initiative (or a specialised knowledge) and responsibility for the work undertaken.
- *grade F*: tasks demanding an extensive amount of responsibility and judgement or the use of professional technique, such as legal work, accounting or engineering.

## MERIT RATING

A number of steps is normally incorporated within each of the grades mentioned above. Staff are placed on a particular step depending upon their expected performance. Adjustments are made in a number of ways, such as annual increments, further qualifications and merit. A typical merit rating scheme submitted by the Institute of Administrative Management is outlined below.

| Merit grade | Classification |
|---|---|
| 1 | beginner |
| 2 | qualified |
| 3 | experienced |
| 4 | superior |
| 5 | superlative (ready for promotion) |

The aim is to encourage higher performance standards by means of financial reward. Opinions vary on its success since the scheme depends upon subjective judgements, including views on co-operativeness, creativeness, competence and initiative.

## WORKING HOURS

According to data from the European Commission's statistical office (Eurostat), the average British working week is 43.4 hours (including overtime). This figure is three hours longer than the EU average of 40.3 hours and is the highest in EU countries. British men work about 45 hours a week and British women are the only ones who work for more than 40 hours a week. According to the TUC, in the UK there is a 'culture of commitment' for white-collar staff to work 'voluntary' overtime; while employers are requiring blue-collar workers to work longer hours rather than engaging extra staff. The EC Directive on Working Hours is discussed later.

## FLEXIBLE WORKING HOURS

The urgent need for increased flexibility to cope with fluctuating customer needs, cost control and productivity has forced many companies to use flexible working hours (FWH), along with employing temporary workers, teleworkers and home workers. A standard scheme sets a core time, maybe 10.00 am to 4.00 pm, when everyone should be present; and a flexible time outside these hours which is negotiated individually. This arrangement differs from staggered working hours where employees choose the starting time which determines the finishing time.

The main reasons for introducing FWH are to improve timekeeping by relieving rush hour travel, to solve domestic problems, to cope with work surges and slack times, to reduce absenteeism, to improve working conditions, and to treat employees as responsible people.

Careful planning overcomes many workload problems created by FWH. To cope with work surges, there are schemes where the employee builds up additional hours of work and takes appropriate time off later. An example is to set core hours and a clocking system to build up additional time above the weekly hours. Such time may only be taken off during the current month, and any time over eight hours in the month is forfeited. The requested time off needs the supervisor's permission to avoid busy periods.

## FLEXIWORK

Flexiwork abandons overtime pay and replaces it with appropriate time off. Theoretically the approach is simple and sensible considering factors of competitiveness, wanting to reduce costs and to maintain stable employment. Often flexiwork is mentioned during discussions on productivity bargaining. In practice, many obstacles have to be overcome before a firm arrangement is possible.

Usually workloads vary, causing very busy times and slack times, which create economic control difficulties. If employees and trade unions agree, it is feasible to work long hours during busy periods to satisfy orders on time and take time off to compensate when work is slacker. Naturally a one-week period would be replaced by a month or a quarter. This system is often called a working time account. Typical problems are equating time off with overtime, recessions and seasonal or cyclical variations. Both sides could gain because costs would be lower, redundancies could be avoided and extra bonus schemes could be awarded during successful periods.

Two other forms of flexiwork involve training employees to perform other tasks. These tasks are to maintain machines during slack periods and to reduce the workforce to core groups that are augmented by part-time or temporary staff as required.

# Functional analysis

In connection with job evaluation, the supervisor may feel a complete or partial revision of the activities within each job is needed. This situation often arises when a company is growing rapidly or has developed on a stop-gap basis. The purpose of functional analysis is to improve performance by adopting a more logical approach to the activities within each job and revising job descriptions where necessary. This differs from activity analysis (see earlier), which aims to provide an overall picture of all the activities within a section. The analysis may be conducted in two stages. It forms part of a procedure for assessing and improving the organisation described in Chapter 3.

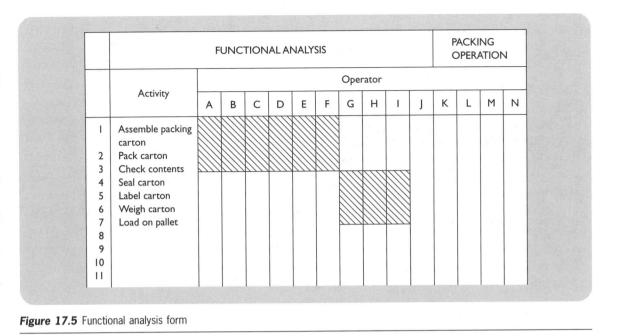

**Figure 17.5** Functional analysis form

## Stage 1: Functional analysis

A complete survey of all the activities conducted within a department is recorded. The two main details noted are the particular activity and the employee who is responsible for it. In many situations a number of employees will be performing similar activities. A typical example of a form which may be used for analysis is given in Fig. 17.5.

## Stage 2: Job analysis

The activities are now rearranged to form a more logical pattern among the employees. The knowledge and experience of operators are taken into consideration, along with any other relevant factors which will affect the allocation. Fig. 17.6 illustrates the type of form which can be used for this purpose and provides a simple example. The information offers valuable data for the preparation of job evaluation forms.

# Phase 3: Justify the vacancy

From the results of phase 2 a comprehensive justification should emerge. These results are

substantiated by detailing the findings of a job design programme which is now described.

# Job design

Job design was discussed in Chapter 12, where the main approaches were summarised and their importance was established as a strong motivating influence. The two main aims of job design are:

- To satisfy technological and technical aspects. Coping with this aim is straightforward because technological data is usually available and continually revised by companies.
- To satisfy personal and social aspects. Many difficulties arise when attempting to cope with humanising the job; consequently, this aim is often abandoned or neglected. A useful analogy for this situation is to imagine the absurdity of building a space probe for a ten-year trip and then considering accommodation for the astronauts.

The way jobs are designed has a critical effect on behaviour and satisfaction. Good design may make employees feel happy, comfortable and motivated;

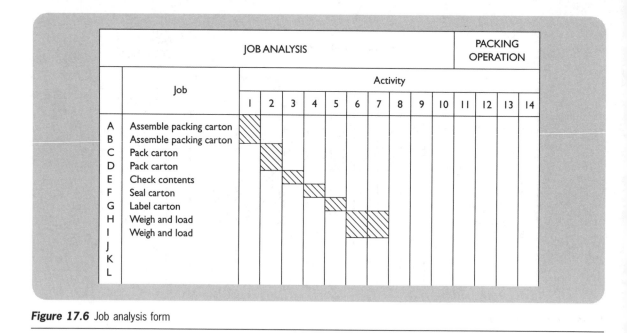

**Figure 17.6** Job analysis form

poor design can induce the opposite. The reasons for these effects are now examined and recommendations offered to counter poor design.

## HUMAN PROBLEMS

Many managers and supervisors are fully aware of the human problems associated with job design:

- the effects of differing values
- forced uniform pacing
- repetitiveness
- very short cycle times
- poor working arrangements
- unreal or distant objectives
- difficulty in communicating with colleagues

The problems have a critical effect on productivity and job satisfaction. Surprisingly managers are often aware of them and their effects, but the reasons for not pursuing job redesign programmes remain undisclosed.

## THE ORGANISATIONAL CULTURE

A variety of features make up the organisational culture in a company. They include boardroom policies (mostly unwritten), personnel policies, acceptable managerial and supervisory practices, job grading and evaluation schemes, class and status boundaries, shop steward practices, and many worker group practices. Combined they influence a manager or supervisor to adopt certain stances rather than others, which may well affect his or her view of job redesign.

In essence the social tools in companies are there but the appropriate organisational culture may be missing. Consequently, there is a deadlock, perhaps with a few successful attempts to overcome the difficulty. Latest theories on job design seem to be focusing more on these problem areas. They may be related to the complete role of the individual in a productive type of organisation.

## MODERN JOB DESIGN

The new approach is a twofold scheme. First, using the existing idea of incorporating the personal needs of the individual and the sociological aspects surrounding the job with the organisational structure that correlates these two aspects. Second, adjusting the technology by treating it as a variable factor rather than a fixed configuration around which other aspects are manipulated. Consequently, this approach coincides with sociotechnical systems discussed in Chapter 3. The aim is to develop a more responsible, autonomous job by adopting the following concepts:

- working at a pace that suits the individual
- enlarging or enriching the job, either by adding more operational tasks or by including such activities as ordering materials, setting up machines, servicing machines and plant, inspecting the work, some accounting operations, and rotating jobs
- making the individual (or the group) responsible for a cycle of activities needed to complete a particular assembly, a sector of work or the whole product, depending on circumstances and technological feasibility
- placing responsibility at its lowest level (not supervisory level) for rate of working, output, quality and material wastage
- encouraging the interdependence of the employee (or the group) on other groups for effectively progressing a cycle of activities
- encouraging autonomous behaviour by every means possible; typically developing self-regulation, self-evaluation, self-adjustment, self-establishing individual or group objectives, self-discipline, and participation in all discussions that may affect the working group

## CURRENT CHANGES

The six concepts given above indicate the complexity of change and the urgent need to continue with research. Eventually hypotheses and prescriptions to validate redesigning jobs may become more acceptable and workable within the framework of the technology, the individual, group activity and other influences.

### The empowerment feature

Part of the empowerment process is to redesign the job so that the individual feels free to develop and fully use ability and capability. The aim of modern job design is aligned with this process, which emphasises clear goals, initiative, challenging work, self-evaluation and adjustment, and appropriate authority and responsibility. Successful

empowerment (Chapters 5 and 10) also depends on the deliberative style of behaviour and the organisational culture.

### Quality of working life

Attempts to improve the quality of working life of employees involve not only job design but other features described elsewhere in this book. Quality of working life (QWL) embraces all aspects that affect human satisfaction in the working situation. Consequently, participation, career development, the employment contract, health, safety and welfare are some of the important considerations.

# Phase 4: Prepare a job description

The usual way to prepare a job description is by referring to the job analysis to produce a written statement of important information on authority, responsibilities and duties, and their interactions with operational and organisational activities. The description should be accurate and complete, giving a good overall picture of the most important aspects. The details are outlined in Fig. 17.7 and should always include a detailed analysis or breakdown of the actual job. However, the kind of individual required to perform the job is shown in the *personal specification*.

# Phase 5: Prepare a personal specification

Preparing a personal specification may be separated from a job description or sometimes combined in a complete job description. A separate treatment avoids confusion and emphasises the behavioural or work-oriented aspects of a job. Included are physical and mental specifications, skills, competencies, education and training, occupational experience, various aspects of personality, and attitudes. These are indications of the main requirements for successful performance in a job.

```
                          JOB DESCRIPTION

1  Job title      Name ............................................  Section ........................................

                  Location ....................................  Department ................................

                                                               No. employed .............................

2  Job summary    Authority ..................................................................................

                  Responsibilities ..........................................................................

                  Duties ........................................................................................

                  Relationships .............................................................................

                  Operations .................................................................................

                  Procedures ................................................................................

3  Purpose of the job ...............................................................................................

4  Physical working conditions ................................................................................

5  Social nature  Individual ...................................................................................

                  Group ........................................................................................

                  Supervisor .................................................................................

6  Education and training requirements ...................................................................

7  Conditions of employment   Remuneration ............................................................

                              Hours of work .............................................................

                              Holidays .....................................................................

                              Pension .....................................................................

                              Welfare schemes .........................................................

                              Benefits .....................................................................

8  Career prospects ...................................................................................................




                                        Signed ..........................................................

                                        Title ..............................................................

                                        Date ..............................................................
```

*Figure 17.7* Job description

For senior vacancies there is a tendency to use a composite job description because it may be argued the work reflects more strongly on personal qualities. A separate specification is a useful aid in interviews, where consideration for both specifications allows for essential features and those that may be desirable. Nevertheless, judgements cannot be avoided. Figure 17.8 illustrates a typical personal specification.

| JOB TITLE | DEPARTMENT |
|---|---|
| 1 Appearance<br>(essential requirements) | |
| 2 Preferable age<br>(any limitations considering the internal & external environment) | |
| 3 Educational qualifications<br>(desirable and essential, considering status and contacts) | |
| 4 Manual skills<br>(inherent, special aptitudes, and helpful competences) | |
| 5 Particular competences<br>(aids to productivity) | |
| 6 Mental skills<br>(inherent and essential) | |
| 7 Experience<br>(degree of varied experience required) | |
| 8 Standard of intelligence<br>(range limits of IQ, matching with satisfaction) | |
| 9 Physical health<br>(demands, stressful situations, any disabilities) | |
| 10 Interests<br>(level of activities, connections with the roles) | |
| 11 Motivational factors<br>(assertiveness, initiative, thought processes, energy or drive) | |
| 12 Personality<br>(characteristics for the job, introvert or extrovert, tendencies, friendly approach) | |

Agreed
Signed
Title

**Figure 17.8** Personal specification

# Phase 6: Determine suitable sources

Phase 6 has three stages: attracting suitable candidates, locating suitable sources, and designing an application form. The first stage involves designing an advertisement which will encourage replies. The message must convey the right information to the right people. The second depends upon choosing the appropriate media. The third is a specialist's job to design an attractive application form.

## INTERNAL APPOINTMENTS

The advantages and disadvantages of internal appointments are often stressed and debated. Such appointments may stimulate morale and motivate other employees, reduce induction time, and indicate more easily the potential and personnel record of candidates. However, there is a risk of ill-feeling among those rejected and the risk of missing new ideas from newcomers. Also there might be rumours of 'jobs for the boys', nepotism or favourites; and a lowering of morale if the newly appointed member fails to perform well and causes upheavals.

## THE DRAFT ADVERTISEMENT

The draft should clearly describe the vacancy. Typical items to include are job title, department, group, pay structure, location, key competencies, physical and mental skills, roles, authority and responsibilities. In addition, some priorities within company policy may be outlined, such as strong client orientation, working smarter, behavioural orientation, concern for quality, and an innovating outlook.

## LOCATING SUITABLE SOURCES

Locating suitable sources is a straightforward task and demands choices that depend on cost, urgency and appropriateness, considering the labour market and its prevailing state. Deciding sources may be influenced by personnel policy restrictions, the use of consultants or employment bureaux, the advertising budget, degree of secrecy, and whether the prospective candidate is already in employment. With these influences in mind the choices may be selected from external or internal sources. External sources include advertisements in national and local newspapers, trade and professional journals, jobcentres, employment bureaux and specialist consultants. Internal sources include noticeboards, the company magazine and the distribution of letters to selected employees.

## DESIGN OF THE APPLICATION FORM

This is an important promotional feature which should use specialists. After reading the advertisement and applying, the candidate's first impression is created when the form is received. The application form should provide further information, be arranged to supply all the relevant information to the company, and become part of personnel records.

# Phase 7: Initial screening

Assuming all the relevant information is received from prospective candidates, the procedure should be to run through the following list and choose about six candidates for selection interviews:

- to sort into categories those who are obviously unsuitable, borderline cases, and those worth interviewing
- to establish a plan for checking on critical features which affect the choice
- to update information in personnel records for future reference
- to check the favourable applications with existing records

# Phase 8: Selection interviewing

Depending upon company size, the existence of a personnel department and the system in operation, the supervisor may be involved in three different ways:

- to assess a candidate's suitability from the technical aspect only
- to make a general assessment for comparison with the personnel manager's opinion
- to make a comprehensive assessment and select the most suitable candidate

A strong view is the prospective superior should make the final decision. Consequently, he or she may then be held accountable for the selected applicant's performance. Also, it helps to have opinions from those who will have working relationships with the candidate. To avoid any criticisms of nepotism the appointer's superior should approve, but not make the decision.

The main features now discussed are:

- effective selection
- exchange of information
- definitions of a selection interview
- approaches for planning the interview
- the selection interview, with particular reference to the introduction, exchange of information, the conclusion, the interviewer's notes, and general aspects
- selection tests
- references

## EFFECTIVE SELECTION

The essential requirements are a clear understanding of the job to be filled, comprehensive information on the applicants, a realistic image of the company, and the selection and attraction of the most suitable applicant.

## EXCHANGE OF INFORMATION

Successful selection in the long term depends upon a comprehensive exchange of information between the interviewer and the applicant. An accurate assessment of each applicant's capabilities and background provides sufficient information for a sound decision. Equally important is an accurate portrayal of the company which indicates all the features that will affect the prospective employee's proposed job, development and career. If these do not match the applicant's desires, eventually there will be discord.

## DEFINITIONS OF A SELECTION INTERVIEW

Three examples help to clarify the supervisor's role when interviewing:

- An exchange of information between an employer's representative and an applicant, the aims being to present an image of the company to the applicant and to assess the applicant's suitability for the vacancy.
- An opportunity for an applicant to demonstrate his or her suitability for a particular job, and to learn about the company.
- A conversation (using language) and observation (using non-verbal techniques of the senses), in an attempt to discover an applicant's ability, capability, experience, personality and suitability for a particular job.

# Approaches

Various plans may be used to assist the interviewer. These may be observed as obvious faulty approaches or workable approaches by considering the use of the following factors:

- relatives and friends, because they will be grateful and support the interviewer
- personal preferences, including instant dislikes and hunches
- the candidate's background and experience in the hope that previous good performance will continue
- appropriate attitudes that coincide with requirements
- behavioural patterns as effective predictors of future performance levels
- objectives of the job related to the candidate's past performance objectives and successful achievements
- assessments on the basis of comprehensive plans that include a full range of requirements in a job

### The seven-point plan

The seven-point plan was devised by Professor A. Rodger of the National Institute of Industrial Psychology. Here are its main features:

1 *Physical make-up*: Has the candidate any defects of health or physique that may be of occupational importance? How agreeable and appropriate are appearance, bearing and speech?
2 *Attainments*: What type of education has the person had? How well has he or she done educationally? What occupational training and experience have he or she had already? How well has the candidate done occupationally?
3 *General intelligence*: How much general intelligence can the person display? How much general intelligence does he or she ordinarily display?
4 *Special aptitudes*: Has he or she any marked mechanical aptitude, manual dexterity, facility in the use of words or figures, talent for drawing or music?
5 *Interests*: To what extents are the candidate's interests intellectual, practical–constructional, physically active, social, artistic?
6 *Disposition*: How acceptable does the person make himself or herself to other people? Does he or she influence others? Is the candidate steady and dependable, self-reliant?

**Table 17.1** The fivefold framework

| Headings | | Grade E (bottom 10%) | Grade D (lower 20%) | Grade C (middle 40%) | Grade B (upper 20%) | Grade A (top 10%) |
|---|---|---|---|---|---|---|
| Impact on others | | Dirty clothes and sullen expression Difficult to understand with manner causing avoidance by others whenever possible | Rather scruffy in appearance with local accent and limited vocabulary Manner rather off-putting due to lack of self-confidence | Undistinguished in appearance while speech and manner attract little attention Difficult to call to mind after interview | Well turned out Expresses self with enough confidence to meet most situations | Very pleasant to talk to; shows interest in what one says Has considerable attraction in other ways |
| Qualifications and experience | General education | Incapable of normal education; school for educationally subnormal | No recognised qualifications in examination passes Low achiever at school | GCSE Grades D–G | GCSE Grades A–C to A level | University degree from pass to honours level |
| | Vocational training | Left to pick up the work alone | Unsystematic on-the-job training, limited to work to be done | Systematic training at work with part-time classes, but no publicly recognised qualifications | BTEC National or Higher National or similar standard at local college | Equivalent to a university degree at higher education institutes |
| | Work experience | Unskilled work on simple tasks that call for the minimum understanding | Semi-skilled on jobs that have been pre-planned and are carried out to set standards | Work calling for varying levels of skills and knowledge Mainly routine involving little planning or decision making | Middle or supervisory management posts, responsible for day-to-day operations | Higher management, mainly concerned with long-term planning |
| Innate abilities | | Mentally subnormal | Slow in understanding and tending to make oversimplified interpretations | Capable of taking in everyday affairs but has difficulty in understanding new or complicated ideas | Above average intelligence, but lacks the extra spark that would push the pendulum into grade A | Quick and active mind capable of taking in all sorts of information, interpreting it effectively and thinking up new ideas |
| Motivation | | Incapable of supporting self and completely dependent on other people | Lacks initiative to find means of applying effort satisfactorily Tends to rely on others to organise work and spare time | Motivation adequate for routine work, provided someone is available to deal with unexpected problems | Hard-working, with enough initiative to overcome day-to-day difficulties | Very high level of drive and enthusiasm; always succeeds in finding outlets that provide self-realisation |

*Table 17.1* cont'd

| Headings | Grade E (bottom 10%) | Grade D (lower 20%) | Grade C (middle 40%) | Grade B (upper 20%) | Grade A (top 10%) |
|---|---|---|---|---|---|
| Emotional adjustment | Incapable of adapting to normal social roles and frequently requires special treatment | Has difficulty in meeting the demands of normal roles and tends to be found 'awkward' by colleagues | Fits into normal roles acceptably but may become emotional when anything unforeseen crops up | Tends to be accepted in central roles as others find they can depend on candidate in difficulties | Capable of social roles that involve continuous stress; remains calm and rational in the most difficult situations |

7  *Circumstances*: What are the person's domestic circumstances? What do the other members of the family do for a living? Are there any special openings available for this person?

### The fivefold framework

The fivefold framework was introduced in 1950 by J. Munro Fraser. The headings are:

1  Impact on others
2  Qualifications and experience
3  Innate abilities
4  Motivation
5  Emotional adjustment

An assessment of each of the five grades is based upon the distribution of human characteristics mentioned in Chapter 9. The main features are illustrated in Table 17.1.

## THE SELECTION INTERVIEW

This section should be read in conjunction with the art of interviewing (Chapter 16). Particular attention to impression and procedures is needed because there may be external candidates who will be judging the company, as well as internal candidates. The aim of the interview is attempting to find the person most suited for the particular job. This demanding task is difficult even for professional interviewers. The three phases of interview are the introduction, exchange of information and the conclusion. These are discussed, followed by some interviewer's notes and general aspects.

### The introduction

Reception arrangements and appropriate accommodation are important factors in establishing the confidence of the applicant. Every attempt should be made to put the individual at ease. Naturally he or she is nervous and time should be allowed for the candidate to settle down. Any quick assessment should be avoided and the interviewer must be extremely careful not to give the wrong impression, because the applicant will be judging the interviewer as well during these critical early stages. A courteous technique is to notify the candidate of the interview programme. All questions should be clear, and sufficient time allowed to complete the interview thoroughly. At the beginning, a short chat on any topic that is familiar to both parties helps to relieve the tension and establish a friendly relationship.

### Exchange of information

As the interview develops, the information conveniently flows in both directions. The interviewer should be seeking attitudes as well as facts, which can only be found by listening carefully to assess pauses, evasiveness, embarrassment, overelaboration or sketchiness. The interviewer is not there to impress, nor to show personal feelings. Making a true assessment demands concentration and, if there is a doubt, the topic should be clarified by asking further questions until the position is clear. A sound technique is to ask practical questions on how the candidate would respond in particular situations. Ensure all aspects have been covered and that the interview runs smoothly.

## The conclusion

The interview will gradually draw to a close naturally and sufficient time should be allowed for this to happen. Both sides will run out of questions, but the interviewer should allow the applicant a little time to think of any further points, which are often forgotten under the stress of the interview. The applicant should be thanked courteously for attending and be allowed to bring the interview to a conclusion if possible. No doubt should be in the applicant's mind about the job or the company. He or she will then feel the interview has been fair with the fullest opportunity to state a case for being appointed to the position.

## The interviewer's notes

- Use all possible checks: application forms, CVs, tests, the interview, and references.
- Develop interpersonal and conceptual skills to a high standard for effective interviewing.
- Improve interviewing performance by further training and development.
- A well-practised interviewee may easily mislead, lie successfully, give half-truths, and present a false image by demonstrating a totally different character.
- Arrange for a specialist to check on the interviewee's asserted skills.
- Try to avoid discrimination, personal prejudices and personal bias.
- Avoid hasty decisions. Wait until all aspects have been covered and then attempt an overall assessment.
- Do not believe in paranormal powers to size up a candidate at a glance or after five minutes.
- Avoid any questions related to sex discrimination. They could include references to spouse, care of dependants, children, plans to expand the family, engagement, divorce, marriage, domestic problems, personal circumstances, and personal problems. The risk is an allegation of sex discrimination at an employment tribunal, unless there are exceptional circumstances warranting such information for a particular job.

## General aspects

- The failure rate of selection interviews is often claimed to be high. Everyone in the organisation tends to be hypercritical of appointments, consequently newcomers are always under close scrutiny. No one knows how the other applicants would have performed if they had been appointed, but mistakes are often obvious.
- Some employees always suspect nepotism. Unfortunately, they can often quote a classic case: the executive's secretary who has a pretty face, pretty legs and is pretty hopeless.
- Selection is always a compromise. There is seldom a perfect match between the successful applicant and the requirements of the vacancy.
- An interview assessment is a poor predictor of performance. The best prediction of performance, according to some specialists, is to discover accurate information on previous records of success. However, one never knows the degree of reliance placed on the applicant's subordinates in previous jobs.
- In most job descriptions there are paradoxes in the abilities required, because of restrictions in the organisation. The degree of intelligence and knowledge may not relate to routine work. Initiative and drive are often stifled because of restricting procedures.

## SELECTION TESTS

Selection tests are standardised psychological tests designed to make objective measurements of particular characteristics such as intelligence, personality, attainment and aptitude. Specialists conduct the tests to ensure their validity and reliability. Selection tests provide useful additional information or confirm existing information, but they only supplement the interview.

Internal assessment centres have been developed by some large companies as a further aid. They conduct a variety of selection methods, including participating in group situations, interviewing, testing and practical exercises. Studies have shown significant improvements in selection standards. The centres offer a two- or three-day programme but are expensive to operate, so independent centres offer a service to smaller concerns.

## Personality tests

Personality tests are so-called objective tests that produce a personality profile. Unfortunately, the questions are easy to remember if they have been taken before. The applicant may guess the personality requirements for the job, so manipulation is probable. The validity of such tests is often questioned since opinions on the job requirements vary and often the findings are vague or irrelevant.

Recently there is more interest in psychometric tests that assess personality by using 'the occult power of divining profiles of people by contact'. The tests claim to assess dominance, social and analytical skills, determination, influence, interaction with people, and stress levels. However, there is some scepticism about the validity of the tests when related to actual job achievement and the way they are conducted.

## Intelligence tests

The validity of intelligence tests is often disputed, especially when people score a high IQ (intelligence quotient), which does not seem to agree with their general performance levels. Certainly extremes of intelligence levels are verifiable with appropriate tests, but there is strong disagreement on their usefulness as many definitions of intelligence are vague.

## REFERENCES

Applicants will either provide only copies of favourable references or suggest referees who will support them. However, seeking references is essential because the applicant may be bluffing. Although applying for written references should be undertaken, there is a risk that the information given may not be true or complete. People are often reticent to commit themselves fully in writing when their disclosures may be detrimental. A safer way is to telephone or meet the referee. In face-to-face situations people are often more prepared to give broad hints and suggestions, and to indicate their true feelings by using body language techniques.

# Phase 9: Engagement

Offers of employment are usually conditional upon receiving appropriate references and a satisfactory medical examination. Terms and conditions may be sent by letter, a printed document, or by a letter of appointment and an employee handbook. Other terms for clarification are any probationary period; pension schemes, private health insurance; arrival procedure which may include issuing a security pass; announcements to employees; and issuing any protective clothing or uniform. A modern personnel department will certainly use an engagement checklist (Fig. 17.9). Each item should be completed with no omissions that may cause problems later.

## PROBATION

In some companies a probationary period is required for about six months. This assessment might be conducted by the newcomer's supervisor every month. Progress is discussed and a note is placed in the individual's personal file.

There could be a three-month review and any problems should be mentioned, along with how they should be solved. At the end there could be a satisfactory performance level or remaining problems, in which case there could be an extension. If there is no improvement at the end of the extension, discussions follow with the personnel manager.

## LAW OF CONTRACT

Agreements between two parties are commonplace. They include contract of employment, contract of work, and contracts of sale. The law of contract attempts to provide rules and conditions on such agreements. The essentials of a valid contract are:

- *Offer and acceptance*: one party must make an offer to perform a function or to pay a certain price, whereas the other party must unconditionally accept the offer.
- *Intention*: both parties must intend to create a legal relationship, not simply a social relationship.
- *Consideration*: both parties must show consideration by performing an activity in return for benefits received.

| ENGAGEMENT CHECKLIST | | | |
|---|---|---|---|
| Surname<br>Forenames<br>Address<br>Telephone | | Department<br>Job title<br>Supervisor | |
| Item | | Date | Authority |
| 1 Interviewer<br>2 Offer letter sent<br>3 Acceptance received<br>4 Referee<br>   telephoned/meeting/letter<br>   accepted/rejected<br>5 Referee<br>   telephoned/meeting/letter<br>   accepted/rejected<br>6 Referee<br>   telephoned/meeting/letter<br>   accepted/rejected<br>7 Birth certificate seen<br>8 Health insurance form completed<br>9 P45, bank, pay department<br>10 Driving licence checked<br>11 Entry on database<br>12 Supervisor/manager notified<br>13 Induction programme<br>14 Probation completed | | | |
| Completion date | Personnel manager | | |

**Figure 17.9** Engagement checklist

- *Capacity*: parties must be fit to enter into a legal agreement, thus minors (under 18), mentally disabled and drunken people are generally excluded.
- *Genuine consent*: if there is any duress or mistake, the contract is invalid; typical examples are mistaken identity or the use of any undue force.
- *Validity*: any illegal act, such as misrepresentation, failure to disclose essential information or unlawful intent, renders a contract invalid.

## THE EMPLOYMENT CONTRACT

The employment contract may be verbal or written, provided there is:

- an offer
- an acceptance
- a consideration

The consideration consists of the pay and terms offered, provided the individual is ready, capable and willing to work.

A verbal contract in these circumstances means that although the person may not have actually started work, the employer can only break the contract by giving notice. Usually the employer will pay in lieu of notice.

### Written evidence

Under the Trade Union Reform and Employment Relations Act 1993, written details of employment must be given to all employees who work eight hours a week or more, and have been employed for one month. Details should be received within two months, and if the employee leaves after one month there is still a right to receive details. The written statement should include:

- the names of the parties to the contract of employment
- the date of commencement (if the contract is for a fixed term, the date of expiration should be stated)
- the date from which continuous service began
- the job title or a description of the work
- the place of work; if various places of work apply they should be specified
- the scale or rate of pay or the method of calculating remuneration
- the intervals of payment (weekly, monthly, etc.)
- hours of work, including any terms or conditions associated with this aspect
- the terms and conditions relating to holiday periods and holiday pay, which should include calculations for accrued holiday pay and rights to pay during periods of sickness and convalescence due to injury
- length of notice the employee should give and is entitled to receive
- the name of an individual whom the employee may consult and to whom the employee may apply for redressing grievances, the procedure to follow and any other relevant details
- a statement of any works rules
- details of pension rights if any
- whether a contracting-out certificate in respect of the state pension is in force
- details of any relevant collective agreements that directly affect the terms and conditions of employment and the persons by whom they were made.

## Working abroad

If the employee is required to work abroad for a period of more than one month, the statement must include:

- the period for which the employment abroad is to last
- the currency in which the employee is to be paid
- any additional pay or benefits
- terms relating to the employee's return to the UK

## Changes in terms and conditions

Any changes made after commencement of employment must be given in writing within a month. These changes are subject to mutual agreement and are binding on both parties. If any change without mutual agreement is detrimental to the employee, there could be a claim of constructive dismissal or for breach of contract.

Under common law the contract may be terminated by giving due notice and re-engaging the employee on new terms and conditions, but this would not stop the employee from claiming unfair dismissal. After proper consultation, the conditions may be varied in certain circumstances such as business need. However, the employer must prove he or she had acted reasonably if the employee claims constructive dismissal.

## Employee bargaining

An employee may negotiate for changes which, if accepted, become part of the employment contract. If the outcome is a verbal agreement at the time, the changes should be written into the contract, as mentioned above.

## Custom and practice

Negotiations for changes are often conducted by a group of employees or by trade union representatives. They may be accepted and introduced but not necessarily written into the contract, although legally essential. Probably some changes are considered to be obvious such as No smoking signs in certain areas, and additional health and safety precautions. These aspects are usually covered in particular legislation.

## COMMON LAW ASPECTS

If an employment contract does not mention certain duties, common law provides implied duties which are binding on the employer and the employee. Common law, or judge-made law, is based upon cases heard by judges who apply certain principles. The outcomes are written down in the form of case law or law reports, and they form binding precedents.

There should be a balance between powers of employers and protection of employees. The balance is determined by binding precedents created by the courts and by government legislation. There are many implied duties for the employer and the employee. Case law is extensive and forms the basis for many legal battles, especially in films. A specialist should be consulted if there is any question of common law rights.

## MOONLIGHTING

Moonlighting means undertaking a second paid job undisclosed to the first employer. Certain risks are likely: fatigue during first employment, impingement of business interests if working for a competitor or establishing and running a similar business, and disclosing confidential information.

The supervisor should report any suspicions for further investigation since there are courses of action open to the employer. For example, it may be written in the employment contract that moonlighting is expressly forbidden. There is also the common law principle of an employee being loyal and showing fidelity. If this implied term is questionable, under the law of contract there could be a case. Similarly there are questions of trust and confidence as implied terms.

# Phase 10: Preparation for arrival

Preparation for arrival is often neglected and there is too much reliance on making last-minute arrangements at the time of arrival. Unfortunately, the newcomer is strongly influenced by induction impressions and these should always be made as favourable as possible. The planning process should cover all the induction techniques of an operational nature (Chapter 18).

# Phase 11: Induction

Induction completes the recruitment process by ensuring the newcomer is integrated into the organisation quickly, with a minimum of problems arising. To achieve high performance the newcomer must be made to feel at home and welcome within the group. Feelings of anxiety and uncertainty are normal, but a competent supervisor using a comprehensive induction programme should soon overcome these difficulties.

Considerable information should be given on an informal basis during the first few days. In a large company, a formal induction programme is probably more economic on a company-wide basis, held periodically as sufficient newcomers become available. The topics may include a tour of the offices and factory, the aims of the company, the roles of various departments, and a history of the company. Many companies also provide a handbook which covers all the details of the concern and information of interest.

There is a case for stressing the need for information and all the details of the job to coincide with the offer of employment. There is a legal and moral obligation to conform, but unfortunately this sometimes does not happen. Consequently, relationships are upset from the beginning and often they never recover.

The main details of induction are covered in the next chapter, which deals with the operational aspects of employment. These details include the personnel department's part, further assistance, the supervisor's part and the procedure.

# Associated practices

Associated practices help in determining the effectiveness and accuracy of any programme. The important practices now discussed are:

- equal opportunities
- appropriate aspects of civil law
- remuneration
- manpower planning

# Equal opportunities

Progressive companies are promoting equal opportunities and operating programmes which stress the business benefits. These schemes include the need for co-operation from employees, customers' needs, the measurement of progress through feedback from employees and customers, and guiding principles. Campaigns are conducted on various appropriate subjects. The main areas covered include career breaks, access to support services, disability, flexible working, harassment, parental and paternity leave, compassionate and emergency leave, and customer service.

# Civil law and employment

Attempts to clarify the rights and duties of individuals and businesses towards each other are written in many acts. The Department for Education and Employment (DfEE) provides a service regarding legislative aspects of employment. Local jobcentres issue a full range of detailed publications for employers and employees. These free booklets are concise and provide up-to-date and comprehensive information. The main aspects of particular relevance to employment recruitment and associated practices are now outlined.

## LAW OF TORTS

The law of torts concerns civil wrongs; it clarifies the situation when an injury is suffered or there is an infringement of rights. Typical torts are when a person or a business has been negligent, has trespassed, caused a nuisance or defamed an individual's character. Rules are provided that decide whether any damages may be claimed for an injury. Simplified, they insist there is a loss through an injury caused by negligence or intent or failure to do something that should have been expected or having done something that should not have been done.

## DATA PROTECTION ACT 1998

Data protection control covers certain manual data and computerised personal data. Conditions are stipulated on processing of data and individual rights which include the right to be informed about processing, about obtaining copies of data, and how to secure legal remedies. There are eight principles for using personal data which must be used:

1 Fair and lawful processing.
2 Used for lawful purposes only.
3 Adequate, relevant and not excessive.
4 Kept up to date and accurate.
5 Kept no longer than is necessary for the purpose.
6 Processed according to the rights of the data subject.
7 Proper security to prevent unauthorised or unlawful processing, or accidental loss, destruction or damage.
8 Not transferable outside the European Economic Area unless the receiving country ensures adequate protection levels and there are appropriate safeguards.

### Complying with the act

All employees should be aware of the implications concerning data for customers and internal contacts. Specialist advice should be sought on any condition. The main aspects are:

- Customers have a right to see all data held on them.
- Customers must be given more information upfront on the data held and its uses.
- Customers may obtain a court order insisting that erroneous data is removed.
- Any erroneous data passed to a third party must be corrected if inaccurate.
- Employees have a right to obtain a copy of their personal file.
- Manual customer and employee files must be appropriately controlled.
- Any automated decisions should have an appeals procedure.
- Sensitive data must be adequately safeguarded.

Careful reading of the act is essential to clarify the meanings of personal data, conditions for processing, sensitive data, manual files, accuracy, retention, access rights, security control, and many other aspects.

## THE COMPUTER MISUSE ACT 1990

The Computer Misuse Act 1990 states that it is a criminal offence for anyone to access or modify computer programs or data, or to attempt to do so, without the owner's authority. The police have the power to prosecute people who misuse computers, and the act complements security procedures. These procedures should identify those authorised to use the computer system and apply access controls. There are three offences under the act:

- unauthorised access
- ulterior intent
- unauthorised modification

These offences are detailed under Sections 1, 2 and 3, and should be carefully read. Proving the offence is also covered.

## DISABILITY DISCRIMINATION (EMPLOYMENT) REGULATIONS 1996

The Disability Discrimination (Employment) Regulations 1996 exclude small employers with fewer than twenty people. There are numerous provisions affecting recruitment and selection, terms and conditions of service, promotion and transfer, training, occupational pension schemes and insurance, retention of disabled employees, and harassment.

Disability is defined as those who would generally be considered to be disabled through physical or mental impairment that has a substantial and long-term effect on ability to carry out normal day-to-day activities. There is further protection even if a person has recovered. Guidance on definitions of reasonable adjustment and arrangements, and the Code of Practice is essential. Employers are expected to adopt a 'reasonable adjustment' approach to accommodate disability.

## EMPLOYER'S LIABILITY (COMPULSORY INSURANCE) ACT 1969

Section 1 states that all employers shall insure, and maintain insurance, under one or more approved policies with an authorised insurer or insurers against bodily injury or disease sustained by their employees arising from and in the course of their employment in the UK. A copy of the certificate of insurance should be displayed at all places of business and in a prominent position where it can easily be seen and read.

## EMPLOYMENT LIABILITY (DEFECTIVE EQUIPMENT) ACT 1969

An employer is considered (deemed) to be negligent if an employee dies or is physically injured due to a defect in plant or equipment supplied at work. Should employers pass responsibility back to a manufacturer or supplier of the defective product, that is a matter for them. This strict liability for death or physical injury is extended to the community in the Consumer Protection Act 1987.

## THE EMPLOYMENT ACTS 1980, 1982, 1988, 1989 AND 1990

Throughout the 1980s a series of Employment Acts were designed to restore balance in employment legislation. They are complicated and need careful study. The many facets of employment covered include trade union ballots, codes of practice, exclusion from trade union membership, unfair dismissal, maternity rights, protection for non-unionists, picketing and industrial action, and union members' rights.

## EQUAL PAY ACT 1970

The Equal Pay Act 1970 states that a woman doing the same, or broadly similar, work to a man in the same employment qualifies for equal pay and conditions of employment. A similar provision applies if she is in a job that may differ from those of men but is considered to be of equal value through the findings of job evaluation. Any disagreements on this aspect may be referred to an employment tribunal for a decision.

The Equal Opportunities Commission (EOC) was established to promote the objectives of the act. The commission may conduct formal investigations into discriminatory practices and issue 'non-discrimination notices'. Breach of such a notice may be enforced by injunctions in civil courts. The commission carries out research, advises the government on ways to improve the legislation, and may assist and represent individual complaints.

## LAW REFORM (PERSONAL INJURIES) ACT 1948

An employer is liable for any personal injuries of an employee caused by a fellow employee.

Moreover, the Law Reform (Personal Injuries) Act 1948 makes void any provision in a contract of service or apprenticeship that excludes or limits an employer's liability in respect of personal injuries caused by another employee. In certain circumstances an injured person may claim damages from the employer and from the Industrial Injuries Scheme. To prevent this form of double compensation, the act states that one-half of any industrial injury benefits received for five years from date of injury must be taken into account against any earnings loss or profits arising from the injuries if actions for damages for personal injuries are undertaken.

## NATIONAL INSURANCE (INDUSTRIAL INJURIES) ACT 1965

An employee who is injured at work may claim damages from the employer if the employer is negligent. Negligence is interpreted according to the tort of negligence. Negligence must be the *cause* of the accident. Often the employer is not to blame for the accident, therefore the employee cannot make a claim and possible hardship may result through loss of pay. These cases were covered under the Workmens' Compensation Acts 1890. However, they were inadequate and eventually replaced by the Industrial Injuries Scheme in 1946, which operated from 1948 and was consolidated in 1965.

## PUBLIC INTEREST DISCLOSURES ACT 1998

The Public Interest Disclosures Act 1998 protects whistleblowers who want to report various matters such as fraud, health, safety, welfare, and anticompetitiveness practices. It amends the Employment Rights Act 1996 by adding protective provisions. In brief it means an employee has the right not to be subjected to any detriment by any act, or any deliberate failure to act by an employer, done on the grounds that the employee has made a protected disclosure. Theoretically, the act should improve employees' rights. However, the apparently 'difficult' employee may still have career prospects affected, so disclosures need to be made with care.

## RACE RELATIONS ACT 1976

The Race Relations Act 1976 replaces the 1965 and 1968 acts and makes unlawful any discrimination on the grounds of colour, race or ethnic or national origin. It applies to employment and the provision of goods, facilities and services. Individuals who feel they have been discriminated against in employment may complain to an employment tribunal. The act established the Commission for Racial Equality, which has similar powers to the Equal Opportunities Commission (EOC).

## SEX DISCRIMINATION ACT 1986

Discrimination in employment on the grounds of sex or marriage is prohibited under the Sex Discrimination Act 1986. Such discrimination applies to interviews and other selection procedures, benefits such as opportunities for training and promotion, and any action that may be detrimental to employees, such as short-time working or dismissal.

The act goes further by stating that discrimination is unlawful in relation to membership of, and benefits and facilities provided by, trade unions and any other organisations (such as professional bodies) that substantially influence the possibility of an individual carrying on an occupation. Any pressure exerted on another individual to discriminate unlawfully and the publishing of discriminatory advertisements are also prohibited. The act applies to all employees, even if only one person is employed, and conforms with the ruling of the European Court of Justice. Detailed information is available in a free booklet, *A Guide to the Sex Discrimination Act.*

An individual feeling discriminated against in employment on the grounds of sex can make a complaint to an employment tribunal. A conciliation officer of the arbitration service ACAS will attempt to settle the problem. If this fails, the complaint will be considered by the tribunal, which has the power to declare the complainant's rights and/or award compensation against the employer and to recommend action that, if not complied with, could lead to increased compensation. The tribunal may also declare a case of general discrimination that can be made the subject of a formal investigation by the Equal Opportunities Commission.

## Exceptions

The Sex Discrimination Act 1986 provides for exceptions in certain posts where a person's sex is a genuine occupational qualification. The criteria are:

- for reasons of physiology or authenticity
- in social and personnel work where teams of both sexes are essential
- in a predominantly single-sex institution where members of one sex are legitimately important to the character of the institution
- on grounds of propriety and privacy, which would be affected if the opposite sex were employed

## SOCIAL SECURITY ACT 1990

The pensions provisions of the Social Security Act 1990 assist members of personal and occupational pension schemes to establish their rights. A Pensions Ombudsman is created with the power to investigate a complaint even if it occurred before the ombudsman's appointment. Various obligations are placed on the employer. These include giving the government power to restrict the investment of assets for approved schemes in anything connected with the employer, limited protection against the effects of inflation for deferred pension benefits and pensions in payment, and extra protection for the employee if the scheme is wound up.

### The Barber ruling

In 1980 Douglas Barber was made redundant at the age of 52 by Guardian Royal Exchange. He was offered a deferred pension because the severance arrangement only offered an immediate pension to anyone within ten years of state pension age (65 for men and 60 for women).

He sued since there was a breach of Article 119 of the Treaty of Rome, which forbids sex discrimination in matters of pay. The European Court of Justice ruled occupational pensions and redundancy payments to be paid; therefore Barber won his case on the grounds of sex discrimination, which is illegal.

## TRUCK ACTS 1831, 1837, 1896 AND 1940

The Truck Acts protect employees from bad practices connected with pay, such as paying in kind instead of in cash or by cheque, and forcing employees to spend their money in a particular shop owned by the employer. The Payment of Wages Act 1960 was introduced to bring the Truck Acts into line with modern practice. Employers are permitted to pay employees in the following ways, provided written agreement is obtained from them:

- payment into a bank account
- payment by postal order or money order
- payment by cheque

## WAGES ACT 1986

Deductions from pay are clarified in the Wages Act 1986, which applies to employers and self-employed contractors engaged by an employer. The fundamental rules are:

- Money must not be deducted from pay due to an employee.
- The employee cannot be forced to pay back any money from his or her pay.

The exceptions to these rules are:

- Statutory deductions, such as income tax and National Insurance.
- Payments to third parties, e.g. a court order to pay a fine.
- Employee requests, such as union subscriptions, sports club fees, or an external pension fund (the request must be in writing).
- Agreed deductions for say spoilt work, absenteeism or lateness; the agreement must be in writing before deductions are made or stated in the contract of employment; a written note must be handed to the employee who should sign a receipt.
- Accidental overpayment of wages or expenses may be deducted from later pay.

Additional rules protect employees in retailing. Included are a variety of occupations, such as bank tellers, petrol station attendants, cashiers, milkmen and bus conductors.

## TRADE UNION REFORM AND EMPLOYMENT RIGHTS ACT 1993

### Time off work

An employer must normally allow time off work for employees to carry out public duties as a Justice of the Peace, or as a member of a number of listed authorities, or to carry out industrial relations duties, or to take part in activities of an independent, recognised trade union of which they are a member, or to look for another job if being made redundant, or to attend antenatal care appointments, or to carry out duties or undergo training as a safety representative, or to carry out duties as a trustee of an occupational pension scheme. The amount of time off is 'as much as is reasonable'. There are set rules. Time off with pay is given unless carrying out public duties.

### Maternity rights

All pregnant employees, regardless of their length of service or hours of work will have a right to:

1 Take a 14-week period of maternity leave.
2 Benefit during that leave from all their normal terms and conditions of employment, except for wages and salary.
3 Be offered a suitable alternative vacancy, where available, if they would otherwise have to be made redundant at any point during that period.
4 Return to work following a longer period of maternity absence, lasting from the end of the maternity leave period until 29 weeks after the week of childbirth; provided items 1, 2 and 3 above are met.

These maternity rights implemented the employment protection requirements of the EC Pregnant Workers Directive. There are also regulations which protect all women against dismissal on maternity-related grounds and which give new rights in relation to suspension from work on maternity grounds. Additional maternity rights are covered in the Employment Protection (Consolidation) Act 1978 and the Social Security Acts 1986 and 1992.

## WORKING TIME REGULATIONS: EC DIRECTIVE 1998 (STATUTORY INSTRUMENT 1833)

The Working Time Regulations protect the health, safety and welfare of employees at work. The new rights and obligations relating to work and rest include:

- A limit to an average 48-hour week: opting out must be in writing and there is a right to cancel by giving 7 days notice.
- A limit on night shifts of 8 hours average in each 24-hour period.
- Health assessments for night workers: if there are health problems connected with working nights there is an automatic right to transfer to day work.
- Minimum daily and weekly rest periods: 11 hours of consecutive rest in each 24-hour period; an uninterrupted rest period of not less than 24 hours in each 7-day period.
- Rest breaks: an automatic right to a minimum uninterrupted rest break of 20 minutes wherever work is over 6 hours.
- Adequate rest breaks for monotonous or repetitive work.
- A guarantee to 15 days of paid annual leave, rising to 20 days after 23 November 1999.

## NATIONAL MINIMUM WAGE ACT 1998 (AMENDMENT) REGULATIONS 1999

Detailed rules are set out on the rate of the minimum wage, exemptions, how to calculate the hours, the elements of pay that count, and details of record keeping.

# Remuneration

The question of financial incentives has been covered in Chapter 12, but the other major aspects of remuneration are achieving a fair system, a right to an itemised pay statement, and deductions for union subscriptions. Responsibility for recommending a pay policy and negotiating pay rates comes under the personnel department, which operates a pay scheme as fairly as possible. Within such a scheme the maintenance of correct differentials – through the operation of a merit rating scheme – is of particular importance to the supervisor. His or her recommendations provide the personnel department with appropriate information for establishing new rates, potential upgradings and promotions.

## RIGHT TO ITEMISED PAY STATEMENT

Employees working between 8 and 16 hours a week have the same right as those working longer hours to receive an itemised pay statement (except in firms with fewer than 20 employees, where they will have to complete a five-year qualifying period of continuous service). The statement should include gross pay, net pay, variable deductions and fixed deductions.

## DEDUCTION OF UNION SUBSCRIPTIONS FROM PAY

An employer may make deductions from a worker's pay for union subscriptions. This is known as a check-off deduction and is a voluntary arrangement by the employer, but there must be prior written consent from the worker and a renewed consent every three years. If there is an increase in the amount, the worker must be given at least one month's notice and a reminder that consent may be withdrawn at any time.

# Manpower planning

Manpower resources must be utilised as effectively as possible because being able to compete successfully in present-day markets depends on the accurate prediction and control of future labour costs. Furthermore, corporate or strategic planning must include manpower implications in setting objectives. Often companies have been confronted with labour supply problems which could easily have been avoided by careful manpower planning.

## DEFINITION

Manpower planning is generally recognised as a strategy for acquiring, utilising, improving and retaining a company's labour force. Four phases are distinguishable:

- Evaluate the present manpower resource by collating personnel records.
- Set a forecast period and calculate the manpower losses by estimating (1) the effects of wastage (terminations, retirements, etc.); (2) changes in labour productivity (alterations to hours and conditions); and (3) labour market demands.
- Assess the manpower requirements for the end of the forecast period; this will involve looking at output per employee and utilisation of manpower required to achieve objectives.
- Draw up a manpower plan to cope with the difference between existing resources and forecast resources for the end of the period, taking into consideration the estimated losses.

## OBJECTIVES

- To avoid any shortage or surplus of labour over a significant period.
- To discover at an early stage any critical aspects of labour which may demand attention.
- To control accurately the costs of labour and any associated ancillary costs.
- To anticipate redundancies and early retirements.
- To determine the optimum cost balance between plant and manpower utilisation.
- To forecast the cost and types of training schemes for managers and employees.

## ESSENTIAL REQUIREMENTS

The consultation and participation of employees and unions should be conducted by manpower planners, who must be supported by senior management. Adequate communication with employees helps to explain the importance of manpower planning and its part in achieving company objectives. The personnel department has a critical role in ensuring records are immediately available, up to date and accurate. Other aspects which may affect the supervisor are associated with the operation of manpower planning. They include the centralisation of manpower planning responsibilities, the length of the forecast period, the forecasting technique to be used, and the degree of accuracy recommended.

## THE SUPERVISOR'S PART

The degree of involvement depends partly upon the size of the organisation and personnel policy. Usually the supervisor will be associated with the co-ordinating mechanism of informing, consulting and fostering support from employees. This aspect has deeper implications than first suspected.

A good supervisor will possess useful information on each employee's personal circumstances and opinions, which might affect the employee's stay with the company, his or her possible transfer, or promotion. Thus an efficient manpower planner will endeavour to utilise the supervisor and always include him or her in relevant discussions with management. The supervisor in turn will be seeking such information and, with management's help, achieve genuine exchanges of views.

In the small firm, the supervisor may be confronted with more complex manpower planning tasks, although the problem is often easier to solve and less demanding on the use of advanced statistical techniques outside the scope of this book.

## QUESTIONS

1 Outline a typical recruitment procedure which incorporates sufficient flexibility.

2 Consider the importance of a daily task sheet and activity analysis.

3 Outline a procedure for job evaluation.

4 What are the methods of job evaluation available to a supervisor?

5 Discuss the advantages and disadvantages of flexible working hours.

6 How would you conduct a functional analysis?

7 Outline the main features of modern job design.

8 Discuss the ways a supervisor may become involved in selection interviewing.

9 A comprehensive exchange of information is essential for a successful selection interview. How may this be achieved?

10 Outline a typical engagement checklist.

11 Discuss the objectives of manpower planning and the part the supervisor should play.

12 What are the essentials of a valid contract?

13 What should be included in a written statement for the employment contract?

14 What advice would you give to a new supervisor regarding civil law and employment?

15 Outline a method of conducting a job grading scheme and illustrate your answer with suitable diagrams.

16 How would you assess a candidate's suitability from the technical aspect?

17 What advantages are likely to accrue from the establishment of an efficient selection procedure in a company?

18 List the records you would expect to find in a personnel department and explain their uses.

Genco is located in a small isolated town. The company produces small general items, packaged for supermakets; it works on a low profit margin. Three supervisors control 140 operatives, of which 90 are part-time unskilled women who are engaged in finishing, packaging and labelling. Personnel policy is to pay low wages, allow flexitime, provide good working conditions and pay an annual bonus provided output and quality targets are reached each month.

Carstyles, a well-known company, decided to open a subsidiary in the town. The jobs made available are mainly for part-timers to mind modern machines. Pay is better than Genco and the hours of work are three hours less a week.

Within a few weeks the part-timers are leaving Genco at the rate of about eight a week. The supervisors and workforce are having to work overtime to maintain output. At an emergency meeting the works manager reported that the workforce is already complaining about excessive overtime. The managing director commented that there did not seem to be any loyalty towards the company and assumed if they increased the pay, Carstyles would follow suit. The personnel manager was asked for an opinion. He mentioned that some time back he had suggested various changes but these were not taken up.

*Suggest possible reasons why the part-timers were leaving, apart from higher pay. What are the probable changes suggested by the personnel manager in these circumstances? What action could the managing director take now to salvage the company?*

The large production shop in Reefolds Ltd is divided into 18 sections which are spread over a wide area. The workforce consists of mainly skilled fitters and there is a reliance on their capabilities to maintain quality. The 18 supervisors rarely meet each other, each being concerned with maintaining output and relying on personnel to solve most problems.

Liz is a bright, highly skilled fitter whose consistently high performance is admired by her friends and her supervisor. She comes up with good ideas which are quickly adopted. According to her personnel record she is an excellent worker. Some employees wonder why she has not been promoted after 12 years' service.

After a short interview, Richard, the supervisor of section F, has agreed to accept Liz as a replacement for a retirement. His section is in a remote part of the factory. Next day he is contacted by Nigell, Liz's present supervisor, 'I've heard you're taking over Liz from me. I'm glad in one way and sorry in another. I'll guarantee she will be your best worker'. Richard replied, 'What's the bad news?' Nigell confided in Richard and warned him, 'She's a shocker! A whistleblower with plenty of barrack-room lawyer experience. What she doesn't see she makes up from gossip'. 'Charming', said Richard, 'No wonder it wasn't mentioned at the interview; now I'm stuck with her. I suppose they think she can do less harm as we're out of the way'.

Within a month, the situation had changed dramatically in Section F. Richard could not help noticing the atmosphere and several employees had complained about the working arrangements. The team seemed to be upset and production was falling. Richard decided to check with his chargehand and asked what was going on. 'As if you didn't know! It's Liz; she's on to everything and never seems to stop stirring it up. Trouble is they think she's marvellous and anything they don't like, they let her know. She keeps talking about this new act and insisting they have their rights.'

*What would be your recommendations to Richard now? Examine the possible reasons for this situation in view of the new legislation to protect whistleblowers.*

When Jack joined Herralad a year ago he had misled personnel by stating he was a supervisor at Strickens for five years and he provided a false reference. In a short time his success as a supervisor became well known and his team had exceeded targets for the past three months. Appraisals were favourable and his superior had recommended him for a management development course.

By coincidence, a newcomer, Roger, had worked for Strickens and remembered Jack as a payroll clerk who was always very helpful with queries. Roger was surprised to learn that Jack was a supervisor and decided to introduce himself and congratulate him on his new post. When they met, Jack felt embarrassed and could not believe his misfortune. Roger noticed Jack's reaction when they met and was puzzled.

*What should Jack do in these circumstances? How much of the blame for the situation was due to personnel?*

# 18

# Employment: operational aspects

## Introduction

Survival depends upon the effective performance of the total workforce in a concern. Such performance implies measurement of the work, setting objectives, assessing the employees' efforts, and adopting various operational tactics in attempts to improve performance and develop the workforce.

Initially, the supervisor will be expected to take over a newcomer on arrival at the section and conduct a thorough induction programme. Following this procedure there are many other operational aspects, which include performance appraisal, day-to-day performance, transfers and promotion, resignations, discipline, redundancy, suspension, lateness and absenteeism. From the motivational aspect, the operational aspects will be carefully adjusted to suit the approaches which were detailed in Chapter 12. Clearly enlarging jobs, enriching the job or empowering employees demand an appropriate emphasis which was explained in Chapter 10.

## Induction

First impressions form a permanent mark in the newcomer's mind. If they are unfavourable, changing the individual's outlook towards the company takes a long time. A personnel department has the opportunity to create a good impression from the beginning at the interview stage, if given a free hand. In view of the high cost of labour turnover and the importance of first impressions, it is surprising to see some personnel departments tucked away in the most unattractive part of the company or at the end of long, bleak corridors.

### THE PERSONNEL DEPARTMENT'S PART

A list of information the personnel department normally provides for a new employee is given below:

- organisation charts and an explanation of where the new employee's job fits into the overall plan
- a booklet on terms and conditions of employment – the personnel officer should explain any items that are not clear and mention any which are likely to be altered in the near future
- a clear statement of the authority, responsibility and duties of the job and the job title
- an outline of possible channels of promotion
- details of the company's education and training schemes and the name of the training officer
- a plan of the workshop or office showing all the usual facilities, which should include cloakrooms, washrooms, medical services and the dining rooms
- the names of the immediate superior and the superior in charge of the department where the new employee will be working
- commencing salary or pay, the scale of pay increases and any financial incentives which are in operation, making sure the new employee fully understands the pay scheme
- an outline of the social activities and the name of the welfare officer or the individual who arranges such activities

- hours of work, tea and coffee break times, lunch times, starting and finishing times, and any allowances for clocking and times for washing
- general amenities, such as bicycle sheds and car parking arrangements
- information on the trade unions and where to locate the union representatives
- advice on safety and a copy of the company's written safety policy
- background information on the company, its achievements, products and objectives

## FURTHER ASSISTANCE

The personnel officer should carefully explain that the new job will mean some adjustment to new surroundings, new colleagues and work methods. He or she must emphasise the personnel department is there to assist and offer advice whenever anything is bothering the new employee. A good impression is created if the employee's legal rights are made known. For example, legislation on health and safety (Chapter 21) and employee relations (Chapter 20). After a formal introduction to the supervisor concerned, the personnel department officially hands over the newcomer.

## THE SUPERVISOR'S PART

The next step of induction begins at this point. Thorough preparation by the supervisor is equally important as planning for induction in the personnel department. This should include a knowledge of the individual and details of the section and workplace.

### The individual

Know all the essential information about the person, such as the employee's name, clock number, job, background, education, experience and assessment.

### The section

Pass on the necessary information about the newcomer to colleagues and other individuals who may have contact with him or her.

### The workplace

Ensure the place where the newcomer will be working is tidy, clean, and that all tools and equipment he or she will need are obtained beforehand and in good condition.

## PROCEDURE

Make all the arrangements beforehand which may be needed for special passes, forms for social activities, beverage and meal tickets, and any handouts which are not passed to the employee by the personnel department.

### Arrival

Give the newcomer a warm welcome. Introduce him or her to all colleagues in the group and mention in passing any special interests. This will give the newcomer an opening for future conversation with colleagues.

Try to put the person at ease by chatting on general topics but without giving the impression of being too interested or overinquisitive about personal affairs. If the newcomer reacts against this approach, take the initiative and discuss other topics such as social and sports events.

Provide the new employee with as much information that can be assimilated at first. Do not expect him or her to remember everything. Be prepared to repeat information several times on different occasions. This may seem tedious, but remember strangeness is caused by lack of information on people, the job and surroundings.

Make sure his or her authority, duties and responsibilities in the job are clear. Also ensure the newcomer knows the person to whom he or she is responsible. Explain the job in more detail and question the person to see if everything has been clearly understood. The learning and teaching period is covered in the next chapter.

Supplement earlier stages of induction by discussing the terms of employment and regulations in more detail. This procedure is essential as there may be small but important variances due to local conditions which the personnel department could have easily overlooked. The employee should also be given a further opportunity to ask any questions which may have arisen since the interview with the personnel officer. Transport problems, holidays, insurance schemes, social activities, pay problems and working arrangements often need more advice.

### Checklist

Naturally there are many small points to be covered under the general topic of working arrangements and inevitably a few are overlooked. Keeping a complete checklist of all the points to tell the new employee overcomes this problem and saves embarrassment later. The list would include the following points where appropriate:

- danger areas
- special regulations concerning smoking
- departmental and sectional boundaries
- allowances for washing
- locker and cloakroom facilities
- maintenance rules
- fire hazards and procedure
- special routines concerning tools, oils, equipment
- use and issuing of safety devices
- first aid
- emergency arrangements

### Work assignment

Check that the employee clearly understands the assignment. If the job involves working a particular machine or being at a control point, make sure the employee realises the importance of being on the spot and knows the procedure to follow if he or she leaves the workplace for any reason. The procedure for tool and materials requisitions should be outlined. The chargehand, leading hand or a responsible employee should act as a guide during the initial period, helping as much as possible to develop the right practices and attitudes in the newcomer. The importance of the work and its place in the general pattern of production should be stressed.

### Follow up

The object of induction is to make newcomers feel part of the organisation, which enables them to contribute fully their capabilities. This sense of belonging is not achieved in a few days; it takes weeks and often months before a new employee really settles in, therefore induction must be treated as a lengthy learning process. The supervisor should check periodically to note progress, see if he or she can assist and help with any problems. There will be at least one difficulty bothering a newcomer and the supervisor should try to gain the individual's confidence by careful questioning and noting reactions.

### The probationary period

Usually the newcomer is on probation, during which time the superior's responsibilities are to monitor performance and progress to ensure job requirements are met. Also training may be needed to correct any deficiencies. At the end of probation there should be at least an informal assessment. In some cases a formal interview is conducted to explain assessments of performance, to invite comments and to determine whether the post should be made permanent.

# Performance appraisal

Appraisal usually means a periodic review of a person's performance by conducting a formal documented interview, by referring to informal records, or operating an established system. Other terms in use are a staff development review, development needs assessment, and a performance review. The difference between monitoring and appraisal is important. Monitoring implies continually checking and reviewing performance, providing feedback, ensuring deadlines are met, correcting problems immediately, and maintaining informal records in preparation for the eventual appraisal. Appraisal is conducted periodically, formally recorded, uses appropriate feedback, and recommends education, training and development needs.

## BENEFITS OF APPRAISAL

An effective system is expensive in investment, time and effort. Provided appraisal is taken seriously and conducted competently there are many compensating benefits for the company, the appraiser and the appraisee.

### The company

A successful organisation may be created by identifying the data for manpower planning and succession; using the data for education, training and development; demonstrating commitment to employees; and improving communication between managers, supervisors and employees. Continuous improvement in competencies is possible by ensuring everyone is aware of their core roles and responsibilities, their objectives, and their performance contract.

### The appraiser

Appraisal provides the means of improving employee performance, receiving effective feedback, assessing management style, clarifying objectives, resolving difficulties, and discussing poor performance with a structured approach.

### The appraisee

The appraisee has the opportunity to discuss their opinions on performance, to give feedback on many topics, to hear and learn from constructive criticism, to suggest training needs, to consider career prospects, to clarify objectives, and to learn about the appraiser's expectations for the next period.

## BASIC PROBLEMS

- Unenthusiastic managers and supervisors who find appraisal and record keeping are time-consuming, and who have difficulty in conducting interviews.
- The system seems to suffer with inertia over training programmes, pay arguments and agreeing performance.
- The art of interviewing is not sufficiently developed.
- Through previous adverse experiences of appraisals employees have no faith in the system, become disgruntled and cannot agree with criticisms, especially when promotions seem to be based on favouritism or nepotism.
- The system may fall into disrepute and is treated as a joke when appraisers are frustrated by

higher management's attitude; everyone goes through the motions of complying with the regulations, but there is no faith in the scheme.
- Expertise is needed to identify a system that is best suited to the organisation, considering culture and managerial techniques in use.

## METHODS OF APPRAISAL

Assessments should apply at all levels in the organisation to achieve maximum effectiveness. On the administrative side of the organisation an annual assessment might be conducted by the supervisor, the supervisor's superior, the personnel department, or colleagues, and supplemented by self-assessment.

Assessments by the supervisor may be simply a summary from continuous feedback, supplemented by intensive questioning and self-assessment. The superior's assessment may be more objective. However, using employee's peers should be treated with caution because there might be some vindictiveness or jealousy. Nevertheless, their opinions may be more accurate, being based upon close contact.

On the production side, performance is usually more obvious, but the accuracy of the pay scheme should be considered, remembering the well-known saying: Those who get the credit are not always the producers.

There are four identifiable methods of appraisal which may vary in complexity. Downward appraisal or downward feedback is the usual technique. Upward appraisal or upward feedback is now thought to be an essential part of a total programme. Self-appraisal is useful when an employee undertakes a more active and responsible role. Finally a multi-sided method is a complex technique involving everyone surrounding the appraisee.

### Downward appraisal

Downward appraisal may include not only assessing current performance but also assessing latent talent, personality traits and manpower requirements. Naturally there is a heavy reliance on the appraiser to portray an accurate evaluation.

## Upward appraisal

The current view is to augment downward appraisal by persuading the subordinate to criticise formally his or her manager. Upward appraisal (or upward feedback) allows for adequate impact on disclosure of vital information for development plans and for the effect on hierarchical levels, considering empowerment and collaboration. The aims are to appraise honestly, assess the results and discuss with the superior ways of improving performance.

Negative views are that the technique is too radical; too unsettling; too daunting; and it provides an outlet for spite, grudges and jealousy. Positive views far outweigh the snags, as may be expected, because the tool provides information on the superior's or manager's performance, weaknesses and strengths, and style. Furthermore, the technique gives employees more empowerment, the opportunity to participate in an appraisal process which before was only one-way, and provides a feeling that subordinates' views are valued.

## The process

1 Discuss the proposals with managers and supervisors to gain support.
2 Notify employees of the proposals emphasising honesty and no danger of repercussions.
3 Either ask for opinions in writing or hold a meeting with the manager present. The superior listens and notes the comments. Obviously there must be no personal animosity on either side.
4 The manager discusses the results with a counsellor who analyses and summarises. This part is crucial and demands considerable expertise from the counsellor.
5 An improvement plan is proposed by the counsellor, who seeks approval from the manager. Usually the plan is designed to correct weaknesses, build on strengths and possibly change management style.

## Observations

- Upward appraisal is not more accurate than downward appraisal and suffers with the same difficulties; this view is often thought to be biased, lacks sufficient contact to provide sound opinions, and suffers with inexperience to judge accurately.
- Some schemes are used to reward a manager if the results are favourable; this practice may be suspect unless great care is exercised.
- Accurate feedback and sound counselling provide an excellent means for developing a manager by using various techniques such as coaching from more successful colleagues.
- Generally a manager is surprised at the comments but after discussion he or she admits the problems and welcomes the opportunity to break down the barriers and improve performance.
- Subordinates are usually enthusiastic about the scheme provided the manager is determined to improve, since the results should lead to more empowerment, letting employees deal with their own problems, increased coaching, and general development.
- The technique is viewed as a tool for change by generating ideas and more rapid positive response from the hierarchy.
- A few managers cannot accept the programme, in this case it seems they do not fit into the company's human resources policy and may be asked to consider their position in the firm.

## Self-appraisal

A more active and responsible role by the employee is achieved with this technique. The form to be used varies considerably, depending upon the approach. A more personal style might be to divide the form into sections with headings such as How I have progressed, My breadth of knowledge, What I hope to accomplish in the next period, How I plan to go about it, How management can help. The supervisor may go through the same process, using a more formal form before arranging for a discussion with the employee to agree on the various factors. Generally the question of remuneration is omitted from these talks. Self-analysis of this nature is demanding on perceptory powers. A useful guide was outlined in Chapter 13 in the section on developing leadership skills.

## Multi-sided appraisal

Multi-sided appraisal involves evaluation by those above, below and to the sides of the appraisee. Often the method is referred to as 360° feedback. The ideas are that more accurate assessments of good teamwork are possible from peers, and judging management and leadership skills is more accurate from subordinates. Confidentiality is essential, so a facilitator is employed for debriefing. The process involves detailed analysis and the expertise of a psychologist, who assesses strengths and weaknesses, identifies more skills training, and indicates further general training and development. The total exercise is time-consuming for everyone, but appraisals are now thought to be very important and worth the extra effort and expense.

## APPRAISAL: THE ESSENTIAL PHASES

### Planning revisions

The appraiser should refer to the previous appraisal, any directives from personnel or the superior, and the training programme for the current period. Armed with this data the following items should be established:

- agree performance standards and objectives
- revise if necessary any competencies related to the appraisee's roles
- check the training and development schemes and note any discrepancies

### Monitoring performance

Monitoring performance is a continual process of collecting and recording data, noting any relevant conversations, recording any situations or incidents, and summarising coaching. The essential points are:

- Record all details on achievements and the way they were achieved.
- Record all details on misunderstandings and mistakes or upsets that caused incidents.
- Relate achievements and problems to the performance contract, and forecast responses and reactions.

- Ensure the employee knows that records are kept, along with their purpose, their confidentiality and safeguarding.
- Persuade the appraisee to keep similar records and ensure data collection is known at the time, along with appropriate feedback from the appraisee.
- Avoid pre-empting assessments and ratings until the period is complete, so ensuring an accurate overall performance level.
- Plan provisionally for education, training and development needs as monitoring indicates.
- Plan the actual appraisal meeting to cover all incidents.
- Record any coaching and the outcome.

### Preparing for the appraisal interview

Preparation should follow the situational approach discussed in Chapter 16. The essential requirements are:

- Establish a suitable time and pick a quiet location.
- Write a loose agenda to provide sufficient flexibility for the appraisee to digress if he or she wishes.
- Notify the appraisee (face-to-face) well in advance; provide a clear, comprehensive brief; and advise the appraisee on how to prepare for the meeting.
- Allow about an hour for the meeting and reconvene if more time is needed.
- Talk with other people who have close contact with the appraisee.

### Preparation by the appraisee

The appraisee should be thoroughly prepared otherwise he or she will agonise later on many points that should have been raised and were forgotten. A sound programme for the appraisee is:

- Read the agenda and note anything to be added.
- Read the performance contract and relate to actual performance.

- Note strengths, weaknesses, enjoyable parts, particular difficulties, help or lack of it from superior, and ways other people can help.
- Be ready to exploit successes and provide adequate reasons for difficulties.
- Consider the forthcoming period and note any possible problems, further training requirements, opportunities and likely achievements.
- Listen carefully at the interview; remember that the appraiser is attempting to help in every way possible and is seeking advice.
- Accept criticism as a means of finding ways to improve performance, not as a personal slur.
- Be ready to discuss openly any ambitions and changes.

## Conducting the appraisal interview

The art of interviewing, basic skills and feedback were discussed in Chapter 16. These are fundamental requirements for appraisal interviews. These additional features ensure the success of the meeting:

- Start by making sure the appraisee fully understand the objects of the meeting. Impress on him or her to listen carefully, ask questions if there are any queries, take notes, and make suggestions on any topic.
- Complete the assessment form at appropriate intervals (Fig. 18.1).

**Figure 18.1** Appraisal interview assessment form

| Category | Performance | | | | Development recommendations |
| | Standard | Actual | | | |
| | | Below | Adequate | Above | |
|---|---|---|---|---|---|
| Core responsibilities | | | | | |
| Roles | | | | | |
| Interpersonal skills | | | | | |
| Conceptual skills | | | | | |
| Technical/technological knowledge | | | | | |
| Outlook | | | | | |
| Appraiser | Date | | | | |

COMPETENCIES ASSESSMENTS

| THE PERFORMANCE CONTRACT | | | | |
|---|---|---|---|---|
| Category | Standard | | | Comments and recommendations |
| | Below | Adequate | Above | |
| 1 Main objectives | | | | |
| 2 Subsidiary objectives | | | | |
| 3 Roles | | | | |
| 4 Competencies summary | | | | |
| 5 Overall contribution | | | | |
| Initial overall assessment | | | | |
| Appraiser | | | Date | |

*Figure 18.2* Preliminary appraisal evaluation form

- Explain that the appraisal should signify areas where performance can be improved by coaching, training and development in knowledge, skills and effectiveness.
- Discuss tactfully the importance of trying to improve current behaviour by various means, including relations with peers.
- Seek advice on how to improve communication in the section or department, stressing the need to receive adequate feedback.
- Emphasise all the positive achievements.
- Discuss openly any misunderstandings and incidents by seeking agreement and correcting any misapprehensions.
- Give ample opportunity to discuss any other topics.
- Avoid any remarks that are aggressive, racist, sexist, religious or disciplinary matters.
- Always use praise where appropriate and offer constructive criticism or advice where it is obviously helpful.
- Ask the appraisee to read the assessment and check it is a correct record of the discussions. Ask them to seek advice if there is any change in the job that should be noted on the performance contract and to pursue the agreed development arrangements.

- Close the interview by discussing the next period, asking for any positive proposals, and thanking the appraisee for attending.

### Evaluating the appraisal

There are many evaluation techniques, some of which have already been criticised. They range from an overall assessment of quantity and quality of work, through to involved evaluations that demand high appraisal skills which only a few people possess. The difficulties are accurately weighting the various items, being objective, applying fairness and judgement, and reaching complete agreement with the appraisee.

The aim should be to consider broadly all the items, avoid any mathematical calculations, and use a feeling or judgement to arrive at the overall assessment. One view is that two assessments are needed: one for training and development purposes, the other for financial reward. Another view favours a two-stage evaluation that overcomes the difficulty. This involves a preliminary assessment for comments and recommendations (Fig. 18.2), followed by an overall assessment for financial reward discussed below.

### The overall assessment

The assessment for financial reward may be based on the workforce being divided into sectors of a normal distribution curve, a straightforward merit system or a simplified evaluation which is easier to assess. These three methods are now discussed.

### Performance contract levels

The workforce is considered as a whole and the way people's performance fits into a normal distribution curve is illustrated in Chapter 9. This bell-shaped curve could be divided arbitrarily into categories. An example is to evaluate on a basis of five performance levels:

1 *Well below performance contract*: They fail to achieve objectives considering quantity and quality of work (say 2 per cent of workforce).
2 *Below performance contract*: They reach some objectives, but lack in commitment or are below some appropriate achievement standards of competence (say 13 per cent of workforce).
3 *Achievement of performance contract*: They attain all objectives, are conscientious, and contribute towards improving the quality of work in the section (say 70 per cent of workforce).
4 *Above an adequate performance contract*: They are seen to be better performers compared with others, tend to exceed the set objectives, highly valued, and an asset to the section (say 13 per cent of workforce).
5 *Well above an adequate performance contract*: They are rare, high performers, creative, highly effective, admired, and their advice is sought by peers and superiors (say 2 per cent).

### A merit system

This rating uses five grades as a means of evaluation:

1 Excellent
2 Very good
3 Average
4 Below average
5 Poor

### A simplified evaluation

A simplified evaluation restricts assessment to five main groups which are then used to make an overall assessment. Applying a merit system to each group indicates a rating for overall evaluation.

- relating overall performance to the performance contract
- performance of related skills
- special contributions, including behavioural competencies
- attempts to raise standards
- relations with peers and superiors

# Day-to-day performance

The competent supervisor will be constantly aware of changes in behaviour through daily observation of employees. Some of these changes will pass off quickly and performance will return to the expected standard, whereas other changes will cause lasting poor performance. People have off-days for many reasons but the severity of the change and the impression created are the important aspects. Also the duration and any pattern which develops over a few days. In other words, poor performance may be acute or chronic.

### ACUTE POOR PERFORMANCE

Naturally everyone suffers with acute poor performance occasionally, perhaps through a hangover, a heavy cold, other sickness, or an emotional upset at home or at work. During normal everyday contact the supervisor may ask how the person is feeling if there is an obvious incident which has been noticed. Depending on the response, help may be offered; or if there is a particular problem, further investigation is needed to find the cause.

Another situation may arise when a pattern emerges of reduced performance every Friday. Keeping appropriate records is important to provide evidence when the individual is confronted with the case. Apart from a domestic difficulty there may be a particular task undertaken on that day which causes an upset. The three important features to remember are judgement, sympathetic understanding and an offer to help.

### CHRONIC POOR PERFORMANCE

Should performance suffer beyond an acceptable time, say a few days, then further discussions are essential. These discussions must be conducted with care and due diplomacy because there is obviously a severe change of behaviour. Three main phases are apparent: preliminary investigations, informal discussions, and formal discussions if informality fails.

## Preliminary investigations

There are certain areas which may indicate the reason for poor performance. They should be checked first and all the information noted. Typical investigations would include:

- Is there a change in workload which has significantly altered the job description?
- Are there any personality clashes or changes in relationships within the group?
- Are there any organisational changes which may have caused an emotional problem?
- Is there a change in physical or mental health?
- Is there a change in attitude that is noticeable to colleagues?
- Are there any domestic circumstances which are causing a problem?
- Is there a communication breakdown?

Naturally some of these questions are unanswerable without further discussion with the individual, colleagues and personnel. However, there may have been significant indications during previous discussions which were overlooked at the time.

## Informal discussions

Informal discussions should be on friendly terms with a view to helping the person to adjust. Two situations are possible: the individual recognises there is a problem or the individual is unaware of the change.

### Acceptance of the problem

If the person recognises the change in performance, appropriate counselling (Chapter 15) should clarify the case and provide various solutions. Discussion usually leads to a mutually acceptable way of rectifying the difficulty. The supervisor must take all the essential steps to correct any situation associated directly with the work. However,

if other circumstances apply, the person should agree to seek appropriate advice from personnel.

### Rejection

If the person does not accept the situation there may be various reasons:

- an emotional problem causing considerable stress
- a communication difficulty which causes ambiguity
- inappropriate feedback which does not allow the employee to comment
- lack of training to perform any additional tasks to set standards
- the job description is not fully understood

Clearly the supervisor could be at fault in some of these cases. Also there may be difficulties with the supervisor's superior. Any emotional problems demand the immediate help of personnel through counselling and professional advice.

## Formal discussions

Should there be no improvement after several attempts to correct poor performance, formal proceedings are unfortunately essential. They are discussed in Chapter 15 under reprimanding, counselling, and resolving grievances; and in this chapter under discipline and dismissals.

## THE CONTROL FACTOR

Supervising day-to-day performance demands high skill and the art of dealing with employees. Sufficient flexibility and sensitivity are essential but effective control is equally important in achieving high productivity. The importance of the control factor is discussed in Chapter 23, which explains the logic and basics of control and control cycles. These features align supervising day-to-day performance with the tactical approach of directing activities to achieve an objective, according to predetermined plans and standards.

## Controlling flexitime

In situations where the employee builds up additional working hours and takes appropriate time off later, the supervisor should be aware that abusing the procedure is possible unless sufficient control is applied. The employee may easily accumulate unnecessary time by spreading out the workload. To counteract this tendency there should be appropriate scheduling of work and regular checks, without causing any feelings of excessive pressure.

# Transfers and promotion

A transfer may have to be arranged if an employee has a health problem, a personality clash, boredom or monotony for various reasons, or a physical incapability. Also if an organisation problem arises through reorganisation, redundancies or resignations.

## PROMOTIONS

Potential promotions are key issues because of the benefits incurred: improved pay and status, more power, and often increased perks. Promotion possibilities arise as employees reach higher levels of competence through training and development schemes. An internal promotion always receives considerable attention from employees because of the advantages and disadvantages associated with the scheme.

### Advantages

- Morale might be improved, except for those who fail to be promoted.
- Management is keen to take an interest.
- Encouragement for development and effort.
- No extra external costs, or internal training and induction expenses.

### Disadvantages

- Finding a suitable replacement to fill the vacated job.
- Competence in one job does not mean similar competence in another job.
- The tendency for everyone in a hierarchy to rise to a level of incompetence.

## PROBLEMS WITH PROMOTIONS

- Insufficient terminations to create appropriate vacancies.
- Matching employees with vacated jobs.
- Contraction periods and varying workloads that thwart proposals.
- Avoiding the halo effect (Chapter 9).
- Interpreting experience is an essential requirement: often experience means being in the same job too long, and running out of ideas and drive after a few years.
- Interpreting loyal service as competence.
- Ensuring that managers and supervisors conform to personnel procedure.

## POLICY VERSUS POWER

An effective system improves the quality of the workforce, relies upon central control from personnel, and depends upon operating a fair and just approach by managers and supervisors. Personnel policy usually emphasises equal opportunity for everyone to progress and apply for vacancies. This policy becomes a sensitive issue when a transfer or potential promotion arises.

If the procedure is continually flouted and the scheme becomes a joke, morale suffers, and managers and supervisors are labelled accordingly. The misuse of power is always obvious: poaching employees, telling employees not to apply for a vacancy, favouritism and nepotism, and disastrous appointments.

A responsible senior management ensures the procedure is effective by authorising personnel to ensure co-ordination and to report any diversions from personnel policy. Managers and supervisors are made accountable for providing accurate information to personnel and for ensuring fair practices. Any misuse of power should be dealt with severely as the truth is known through the grapevine.

# Resignations

Often employees avoid divulging the true reason for resigning, although this is important because it may indicate a problem such as a flaw in personnel policy, poor supervision and management, low morale, the ineffectiveness of selection interviewing, poor performance appraisal, or an unsolved grievance. Usually an external reason for leaving is revealed without any probing, such as being offered a better job or suffering a domestic problem.

Some companies offer a termination interview conducted by the personnel department, as well as an interview by the supervisor or the manager. This form of personnel counselling may reveal information that forms the basis for negotiating a mutual settlement to avoid the resignation.

## LABOUR TURNOVER

Compiling trends in labour turnover may indicate vital data for revising policies. Such trends will include reasons for leaving and comparisons using the following formulae.

### Crude rate

Crude rate expresses labour turnover as a percentage of the number of people employed:

$$\frac{\text{Number of terminations in one year}}{\text{Average number of employees (in same year)}} \times 100 = \frac{\text{Labour turnover}}{(\%)}$$

This is the standard form of measurement. However, there is no indication of the length of service of those leaving, or the stability of the labour force. The aim is to reduce the percentage labour turnover.

### Labour stability

Labour stability provides a fairer presentation for the year and may be extended to longer periods if the information is available:

$$\frac{\text{Number of employees with a year's service or more}}{\text{Number of employees at start of the year}} \times 100 = \frac{\text{Stability}}{(\%)}$$

A high percentage stability indicates a stable workforce, but if it is considered to be too high the manpower establishment may be top heavy.

### Fringe turnover rate

Fringe turnover rate provides a percentage turnover of short-term employees:

$$\frac{\text{Number of employees who joined and left within one year}}{\text{Average number of employees during the year}} \times 100 = \frac{\text{Fringe turnover}}{(\%)}$$

If the percentage is high this indicates problems with such aspects as selection, induction and working conditions.

### Influencing labour turnover

Influencing labour turnover has depended upon research and covers the whole area of management, the organisation and individuals. Researchers have investigated labour turnover for many years and arrived at a multitude of reasons. Most explanations suggest three broad areas:

- *General economic factors*: alternative opportunities, prevailing employment levels, comparative pay, level of economic activity.
- *Organisational factors*: job dissatisfaction, size of work unit, promotion prospects, pay levels, supervisory relations, peer group interaction, job content, autonomy and responsibility.
- *Personal factors*: age, length of service, marital status, number of dependants, education and skills levels, and personality traits.

These factors depend on the particular situation and may be conflicting. Major reviews have varied. For example, Pettman in 1979 identified two main features: perceived desirability of movement by employees, and the perceived ease of movement. Angela Bowey in 1974 identified processes which are either 'push' or 'pull'. Push processes help to propel employees away, whereas pull processes attract employees from the organisation.

Being able to influence labour turnover is bewildering in these circumstances. However, the major features of competent management and supervision, applications and techniques in total, have a profound effect.

## TERMINATION METHODS

- *Fair dismissal*: the reasons include low capability, lack of qualifications, poor performance, violation of rules, or poor code of conduct.
- *Redundancy*: market depression, seasonal business or organisational change.
- *Resignation by employee*: promotional gain, better company located, domestic problem, dissatisfied or personal circumstances.
- *By notice from employer*: in accordance with the contract of service or under the provisions of the Employment Protection (Consolidation) Act 1978; however, the employer may still face a claim for redundancy pay or unfair dismissal.
- *By agreement*: when both parties agree to terminate the contract; if both agree to new terms and conditions, a new contract replaces the old one.
- *Retirement*: reaching retirement age, physical ill health, mental ill health or company succession plans.
- *Frustration*: which includes incapacity such as illness, death of employee, and imprisonment.

# Discipline

Although everyone understands the need for discipline it remains an emotional subject. Job security is at risk, so there must always be consistency and fairness when applying discipline. This implies that managers' and supervisors' level of toleration should be similar and that the personnel manager should apply a detached judgement.

Discipline may be viewed as a two-stage process. The first stage is for minor cases involving misconduct, occasional poor performance, abuse of unwritten codes, or a breach of a specific rule. These aspects are handled on an informal day-to-day basis by applying warnings, counselling and training. If a minor case fails to correct the problem and behaviour deteriorates, or a serious case occurs, the second stage involves a formal disciplinary procedure. This must conform to the Trade Union Reform and Employment Rights Act 1993 and the ACAS Code of Practice. All organisations employing twenty or more employees must provide

certain details of disciplinary procedures, provided the employees work eight hours or more a week. A note should be given to the employee specifying disciplinary rules and the person to whom he or she may apply if there is any dissatisfaction with the disciplinary decision. The ACAS booklet *Discipline at Work* should be used to comply with a disciplinary procedure outlined under the ACAS Code of Practice on Disciplinary Practice and Procedures in Employment.

## MEETING THE ACAS CODE

- It must be in writing and state to whom the code applies.
- Provision for quick administration and an outline of the various disciplinary actions.
- Provision for informing the employee of the complaint and providing the employee with the opportunity to state his or her case before any decision.
- State the management levels that can take the various forms of disciplinary action and emphasise that immediate superiors do not normally have the authority to dismiss without referring to senior management.
- The right of an employee to choose a trade union representative or peer to accompany him or her at the disciplinary hearing.
- State that an employee cannot be dismissed for a first breach of discipline (except for gross misconduct).
- Conduct a careful investigation and give the employee an explanation for any penalty applied.
- Include a procedure for the employee to appeal.

### Formal disciplinary hearings

Formal disciplinary hearings are a sensitive issue for the employee if for some reasons the manager raising the complaint has incorrect information and the supervisor disagrees with the hearing. The hearing is sufficient to sour relationships permanently when there is no case to answer. All disciplinary action must be preceded by a disciplinary hearing. The main features are:

- Inform the employee of the complaint and give all the details.
- Ask the employee to state his or her case, give an explanation, and call witnesses if necessary.
- Adjourn the hearing to consider the complaint, decide whether it is proved, and decide the penalty if proved.
- Reconvene the hearing and inform the employee of the decision.
- Advise the employee of the right of appeal, record the disciplinary action, and follow up in writing if there is a written warning.
- Monitor and follow up by noting the date for revising the standard, arranging a review meeting and noting conduct in the long term.

In the case of the hearing having no foundation, although the ACAS code does not mention it, the manager should be morally bound to apologise and attempt to rectify the situation by explaining how the error occurred and the action taken to ensure a similar hearing is avoided.

### The appeals procedure

The appeals procedure must be plainly defined, the employee informed at the hearing, and confirmed in a follow-up letter. Prudent action is to appeal in writing within the stipulated time. The appeal should be heard by the next highest level of management or a senior manager. The reason for the appeal should be examined along with any new evidence. The outcome should be in writing and if the proper procedure has been shown to be neglected, a new hearing should be convened.

In the event of the disciplinary action being proven unfounded, management has a moral obligation to apologise and try to rectify the error to the employee's satisfaction. Obviously management is seen to be incompetent and insensitive in not checking the information first before proceeding to a disciplinary hearing.

### FORMAL WARNINGS

Disciplinary sanctions are usually formal warnings, suspensions and dismissals. Formal warnings should also follow the ACAS code, and in the case of written warnings they should state the reasons, the standard expected, the time limit to achieve the

standard, the penalty if the time limit is exceeded, and the right to appeal.

The routine should state the number of warnings in the procedure, the authority to give a warning at each level of offence, and the duration of the recorded warning before it is removed. A typical routine is:

- first offence – verbal warning
- second offence – first written warning
- third offence – final written warning

Usually the line manager gives the warnings, senior managers hear appeals, and the personnel department maintains records to ensure there is evidence available for any employment tribunal hearing. Subsequent warnings after the first warning do not necessarily have to be for the same reason. Also a further penalty may apply for any poor performance or misconduct.

### Counselling

As already discussed under reprimanding and counselling in Chapter 15, and under counselling in Chapter 7, any cases should be subjected to counselling by the supervisor first before resorting to the formal disciplinary procedure. Often appropriate counselling provides sufficient help or advice to the employee, who immediately improves.

# Dismissals

The authority to dismiss an employee is a serious and responsible duty which demands the application of absolute fairness. Where a personnel manager is not employed, the right to dismiss may rest with the supervisor at department level, but higher management would normally sanction such an action first. The supervisor should know the relevant employment legislation and strictly follow the procedures. The Department for Education and Employment (DfEE) booklet PL714, *Fair and Unfair Dismissal*, should be obtained and any queries settled.

The introduction of a personnel manager normally changes the system; they take final responsibility for dismissal. The supervisor recommends the action to the personnel manager who considers the case objectively. In the eyes of the employee an appeal to an individual outside the immediate jurisdiction of his or her superior is much fairer.

Supervisors in these circumstances often feel their status is lowered, some power is lost or their authority is reduced. However, if supervisors are relying upon such forms of authority and power, they obviously do not appreciate the value and effect of supervision that allows appeal to an outside authority.

## THE BACKGROUND

### Incompetent management

The real blame for dismissal may lie with management when employees are placed in unsuitable jobs, or when no help is given to the employee confronted with new surroundings or changes in duties. The dismissal should be avoided if possible, especially where the fault is two-sided. Much can be done to help employees to adjust. The effort is worthwhile on grounds of economy and morale alone.

### Personality clashes

Apart from problem employees, inevitably there are some personality clashes. Clashes may occur between the supervisor and employee, and between employees. They are often difficult to resolve and cause many emotional problems which flare up into scenes that cause dismissal. The supervisor should be constantly looking for such problems. The sensible, human approach is to separate the parties involved.

### Supervisory problems

Poor co-operation, absenteeism, lateness, laziness, rudeness, dishonesty and carelessness all seem to indicate a supervisory problem. If help is given at the time when the employee becomes disgruntled, it may prevent an untenable situation developing.

### Incompetent employees

The individual may suffer with low ability or lack of correct training. This means that selection procedures are faulty or the training scheme is inadequate. The employee is blameless in either case.

### Loss of capability

The reason for loss of capability may be a mental problem or physical incapacity. Some large companies provide rehabilitation centres to assist the employee with a physical or mental handicap. New jobs are located, which often means a demotion. However, provided the approach is made in such a way that the employee feels it is worthwhile and they are not downgraded in front of colleagues, the demotion is usually acceptable.

## DEFINITIONS OF DISMISSAL

- The termination of employment by the employer with or without notice.
- Employee's resignation with or without notice where the employer implies that he or she is not to be bound by the contract of employment.
- The expiry of a fixed-term contract without renewal.
- The employer's refusal to allow a female employee to exercise her legal right to return to employment after the birth of her baby.

Dismissal may be construed to be fair or unfair. This subject is featured in various acts, codes of practice, guides on rules and principles, conciliation through ACAS, and considerations by employment tribunals. The sensitive nature of dismissal, along with employers' and employees' legal rights, demand careful study. To avoid heavy costs in disputes there should be strict adherence to procedures, and often advice sought from specialists.

## RELEVANT DOCUMENTS

- Trade Union Reform and Employment Rights Act 1993
- ACAS Code of Practice on Disciplinary Practice and Procedures in Employment
- ACAS booklet *Discipline at Work*
- Employment Protection (Consolidation) Act 1978
- Employment Acts 1980, 1982, 1988, 1989, 1990

- DfEE guide *Dismissal – Employees' Rights*
- DfEE booklet *Industrial Relations Procedure*
- The Employment Rights (Dispute Resolution) Act 1998

# Fair dismissal: five reasons

## CAPABILITY

Capability covers three situations: work below the standard required, an extremely serious error, and incapability through ill health.

### Below standard work

A procedure for substandard work is outlined in *Discipline at Work*. Briefly the main terms are:

- Employees should know the standards of performance required.
- If standards drop they should be interviewed and the reasons recorded.
- If further training is required to reach the standards, this should be offered; alternatively other work should be offered.
- If standards remain below requirements, the employee should be warned of the consequences and the warning recorded.
- If there is no change, the employee should be dismissed with due notice or payment in lieu.

### An extremely serious error

The ACAS handbook indicates that if an employee commits an extremely serious error for the company, an appropriate warning is not needed. Fair dismissal is acceptable provided the company's disciplinary procedure clarifies that in these circumstances there will be dismissal.

### Ill health

#### Frequent short-term absences
If the employee has not consulted a doctor, he or she should be advised, asked to submit the cause of the problem, and provide the doctor's proposal to improve the condition. The employee should undertake treatment and be warned of possible action if absences continue. If there is no improvement there should be further warnings. Provided the absences are causing operational difficulties, dismissal may be necessary to overcome the adverse effect on the business, not because there is doubt about the genuineness of the illness.

#### Long-term absence
Arrangements can be made to overcome operational problems in this case. However, if the absence continues for a long period and there is no sign of improvement in the condition, dismissal may become necessary on the grounds of capability. Clearly there is a moral code to consider. Before deciding, it is essential to consider the employee's length of service and previous record. A procedure would be:

- Remain in close touch with the employee and help in any way.
- Keep informed on possible changes in health.
- Seek medical advice from the doctor.
- Consult the employee to explain possible termination, or suggest an alternative job involving less strenuous work or part-time work.
- Perhaps suggest early retirement, or pay in lieu of notice if there is termination.

When approaching the employee's doctor it is essential to use the procedure outlined in the Access to Medical Reports Act 1988. The act should be consulted for various requirements and strictly followed.

## CONDUCT

The company's disciplinary procedure should be carefully followed, paying particular attention to written evidence. Failure to conform in any way will usually lead to confirming unfair dismissal, regardless of the employer's valid justification.

The appropriate statutes and codes of practice should be strictly followed because the employer will need to demonstrate that managers have acted reasonably by taking into account equity and the substantial merits of the case. Demonstrating reasonableness, conducting a proper, full investigation, and appropriate warnings are complex and demand the advice of a specialist. There are many key points to consider, such as remembering that disciplinary action is viewed as a means of encouraging improvements, not to dismiss.

Gross misconduct means a serious offence that warrants the penalty of summary dismissal – dismissal without notice or payment in lieu. An essential element is suspension on full pay while a full investigation is conducted, followed by a disciplinary hearing with the employee present. Suspension without pay is possible if mentioned in the contract of employment.

Typical causes of gross misconduct are malicious damage to company property, theft from employees or the company, assault, falsifying expense claims or company records, gross negligence, abuse, insubordination, and flagrant disregard of health and safety regulations.

## REDUNDANCY

The vexed question of redundancy involves social responsibilities of management, competitiveness, many legal requirements, careful planning, and complying with a complex number of trade union, employer and employee rights. These features are discussed later. Redundancy is a fair reason for dismissal but great care is needed in establishing objective criteria when selecting jobs for redundancy and in controlling the redundancy programme.

### A LEGAL RESTRICTION

Dismissal is fair if the company would be breaking the law by continuing to employ an individual. An example is where public safety is at risk, such as employing a lorry driver whose driving licence has been revoked. The company should act reasonably by offering alternative employment, if possible, before dismissal.

### SOME OTHER SUBSTANTIAL REASON

All other cases for fair dismissal require some other substantial reason. Similar restrictions apply such as proving there is no alternative employment, impartial procedures carefully followed and recorded, and no indication of unreasonable conduct by the company. An example is a proven imperative to reorganise which implicates the employee who refuses to comply with essential changes.

# Unfair dismissal

All employees, irrespective of their length of service, hours of work or age, may apply to an employment tribunal if they feel they are unfairly dismissed. In these circumstances the employer must establish and justify the reason for the dismissal. The tribunal decides whether the employer acted reasonably or unreasonably in deciding the reason as sufficient for dismissal. Many aspects are included in the decision such as the guidelines issued by ACAS on disciplinary practice and procedures, the administration resources of the company, and its size.

The employer may have to pay for legal representation, collecting the facts, choosing witnesses, and the time needed to attend the tribunal. Avoiding the risk of unfair dismissal procedures is partly possible by ensuring line managers and supervisors are fully trained on dismissals, by establishing comprehensive disciplinary procedures, and carefully complying with them. Adequate consultation with the personnel department at all times is essential.

## MATERNITY-RELATED GROUNDS

Provisions in the Trade Union Reform and Employment Relations Act 1993 state that the dismissal of a woman will be automatically unfair, regardless of her length of service or hours of work if:

- it is on maternity-related grounds and takes place during her pregnancy or statutory maternity leave period, or during the four weeks following the end of that period if she has since then been incapable of work due to a medically certified illness; or
- it occurs after the end of her statutory maternity leave period and is on the grounds that she has taken or availed herself of the benefits of that leave; or
- it is on grounds of a health and safety provision which could give rise to maternity suspension; or
- it is on grounds of redundancy and the employer has not first complied with the

requirements to offer her any suitable alternative vacancy which is available; or
- she is unfairly selected for redundancy for one of the above reasons.

An employee who is dismissed at any time and for any reason while she is pregnant or during her statutory maternity leave period will be entitled to receive a written statement of the reasons for her dismissal without having to request it and regardless of her length of service or hours of work.

## TRADE UNION ACTIVITIES

Dismissal is automatically unfair in the following circumstances:

- membership or proposed membership of an independent trade union
- taking part or proposing to take part at any appropriate time in an independent trade union's activities
- refusal, or proposed refusal to become or remain a member of a trade union that was not an independent trade union

## REDUNDANCY EXCEPTIONS

Dismissal on grounds of redundancy will be unfair if:

- The employee was selected for dismissal on account of trade union membership or activities.
- The employer unreasonably disregarded the customary arrangements or the agreed procedure relating to selection of employees for redundancy.
- The selection was unfair for some other reason; for example, the employer failed to give adequate warning of redundancy or failed to consider alternative employment for the employee.

## CONSTRUCTIVE DISMISSAL

A tribunal may rule that an employee who resigns because of the employer's conduct has been 'constructively dismissed'. This means the employee was unfairly dismissed because the employer's action was a substantial breach of the employment contract. Examples are:

- arbitrarily demoting the employee to a lower position or a poorer paid position
- accusing an employee of theft
- swearing at him or her

## DISCRIMINATORY DISMISSAL

If dismissal relates to sex, marital status or race, the nature and scope of these provisions are covered under the Sex Discrimination Act 1975 and the Race Relations Act 1976. Originally there was a cap of £11 000 on awards, but this was removed by the Sex Discrimination and Equal (Remedies) Regulations 1993 and the Race Relations (Remedies) Act 1994.

## CLAIMING UNFAIR DISMISSAL

An application form IT1 is obtained from any jobcentre and sent to the Office of Employment Tribunals. The office forwards it to the employer, along with form IT3. Form IT1 should be completed carefully as the information becomes the basis for the case.

When ACAS receives form IT3 both parties are invited to consider conciliation or a compromise agreement, which are settlements out of court. If there is no conciliation, each side presents its case at an employment tribunal and may call witnesses. Each side may cross-examine the other and sum up. The tribunal then retires, decides and communicates its decision to the parties, usually on the same day.

## APPEALS

An appeal is only possible on a point of law. The procedure is to apply within 42 days of receiving the official written decision to the Employment Appeals Tribunal. Further appeals are possible to the Court of Appeal and the House of Lords.

## THREE REMEDIES

- *Reinstatement*: the employee is treated in all respects as though the dismissal has not occurred.

- *Re-engagement*: the employee is re-employed but not necessarily in the same job or on the same terms and conditions of employment.
- *Compensation*: most employees seek compensation that consists of a basic award and a compensatory award; in some instances there is an additional award and a special award.

# Redundancy

Often companies are forced into declaring some of their jobs redundant because of market depression, a seasonal variation in business or essential organisational changes. To remain competitive at home and abroad a company may need to increase mechanisation or automation programmes, which may also result in redundancies.

The social responsibilities of management in these situations are complex. For example, a decision not to automate may throw the whole labour force into unemployment if the company becomes insolvent.

The legal requirements are equally complex. They include regulations on lump sum repayments, periods of notice, rights of trade unions and employees, and complaints procedures. The appropriate acts, EC directives and special orders should be studied before taking any action.

The Department of Trade and Industry (DTI) may be consulted when planning redundancies and calculating payments; its free helpline is 0500 848 489.

## DEFINITION OF REDUNDANCY

Redundancy is defined in the Employment Protection (Consolidation) Act 1978: when an employer has ceased, or intends to cease, to conduct business at which the employee was employed; or has ceased, or intends to cease, to conduct business at the place where the employee was employed. Redundancy will also occur when the requirements of a business for employees to do work of a particular kind, or for employees to do work of a particular kind in that place have stopped or diminished, or are expected to stop or diminish.

In the Trade Union Reform and Employment Rights Act 1993, redundancy handling procedures are extended to implement the EC Collective Redundancies Directive 1992. Thus the definition of redundancy is widened to include any dismissals for reasons not related to the individual. This accommodates other circumstances where an employer may be considering dismissing an employee, such as reorganisation or reallocation of duties that did not result in there being a diminution in the needs of the business for workers to carry out work of a particular kind.

Note that the job is redundant, not the employee.

## THE RIGHTS OF TRADE UNIONS

An employer has a duty to consult with appropriate trade unions about proposed redundancies to see whether there are ways of reducing the numbers involved or of mitigating the effects of redundancy. If the employee is not a member, the employer must still consult the trade union.

Under the Trade Union and Labour Relations (Consolidation) Act 1992, an employer who proposes to dismiss as redundant any employee should consult the representative of the union. This applies where there is an independent trade union recognised by the employer regarding the class of employee concerned.

The act also states that when 100 or more workers are to be dismissed within 90 days or less, the employer must consult at least 90 days before the dismissal. If 10 or more workers are to be dismissed within 30 days, consultation must be at least 30 days before the dismissal. In addition, an employer must provide reasonably full information in writing and include:

- the reasons
- the numbers and descriptions of employees involved
- the total number of employees of any such description
- the proposed method of selecting the employees
- the proposed method of conducting the dismissals, taking into account any agreed procedure, including the period over which the dismissals will occur

Under the Collective Redundancies and Transfer of Undertakings (Protection of Employment

Amendment) Regulations 1995, employers must consult with elected representatives of all employees if redundancies involve 20 or more employees. Employers will be able to choose whom they wish to consult, such as trade union officials or other elected employees. Also the elected representatives must be given time off with pay to do such duties and will be protected against sanction.

If the trade union replies, the employer must consider the points raised and reply to them, giving reasons if he or she rejects any of them.

## Complaints

The trade union may complain to an employment tribunal if an employer has not met the consultative requirements. Before the hearing an ACAS conciliation officer must have the opportunity to consider whether he or she is able to help the parties settle the dispute. The officer may be asked for help by either party or may proceed independently.

## Protective awards

If the tribunal upholds the claim, it may make a 'protective award'. This amounts to one week's pay for each week of the protected period, up to a maximum of 90 days' pay for 100 or more redundancies within a 90-day period; 30 days' pay for 10–99 redundancies within a 30-day period; and a maximum of 28 days' pay if fewer than 10 redundancies. The amount may vary depending upon the seriousness of the employer's default.

## THE RIGHTS OF EMPLOYERS

In certain circumstances it may not be reasonably practicable for an employer to meet fully the requirements for minimum consultation periods, disclosure of information or the manner of dealing with the union's representations. In these special circumstances the employer must do all that he or she can reasonably be expected to do to meet the requirements. In defence an employer must show he or she did fully comply, or state the special circumstances, or show that all possible steps were taken to comply.

## THE RIGHTS OF EMPLOYEES

Employees who are declared redundant should be notified as soon as possible, be given as much notice as possible and have reasonable time off to seek new employment. The employer should ensure a fair and agreed selection method is applied for redundancy. Obvious steps should be taken such as stopping recruitment and overtime, commencing short-time working, insisting that those over retirement age retire, seeking volunteers and trying to cut back through natural wastage. Consultation with remaining employees to maintain morale is fundamental.

If an employee is covered by a protective award, he or she has a right to be paid a normal week's pay for the protected period, whether that person is still working for the employer or not. However, there are certain conditions which need to apply before these rights may be claimed.

An employee who is still employed will be paid under a protective award only when entitled to payment under the contract of employment or under statutory rights during a period of notice. For this purpose the whole remaining part of the employment is treated as if it were a statutory period of notice. Thus an employee who goes on strike, or is absent from work without leave and without good reason, or is granted leave at his or her own request, or has time off from work under certain other provisions of the Employment Protection (Consolidation) Act 1978, will not be entitled to payment.

An employee who is absent under contractual holiday arrangements, or who is ill, or during any period where the employer has no work available for that person, will be paid. An employee who is fairly dismissed for a reason other than redundancy, or who gives up the job during the protected period without good reason, will lose the right to payment for the rest of the protected period.

## Offer of renewed or new employment

An employer may offer to re-engage an employee in his or her old job or in a different but apparently suitable job before the end of the protected period. If the employee refuses the offer without good reason, he or she loses the right to payment for the rest of the protected period. However, the employer must be able to show that the alternative job was suitable. Each case is judged on its merits.

### Right to a trial period

An employee who accepts an offer of a different type of job is allowed a trial period to see if the job is suitable. For calculating continuity of employment, this trial will be regarded as starting from when the employee's old job ends, even where there is a gap between the two jobs. The trial period will normally continue for four weeks after the employee starts work in the new job.

An employee who leaves the job for any adequate reason or who is dismissed for a reason connected with the new job during the trial period, keeps the right to payment under the protective award. However, he or she will lose the right to payment for the rest of the protected period if the job or the training is given up without adequate reason or the employer dismisses that person fairly for reasons not connected with the changed terms of employment.

### Extension of trial period

The trial period may be extended to retrain the employee for the new job by agreement between the employer and employee. The agreement must be made before the employee starts work in the new job, it must be in writing and must specify the date the trial period ends. The terms and conditions of employment will apply after the trial period ends.

The period allowed for trying out the new job is the same length as under the redundancy payments provisions. However, the employee has a right to a trial period if he or she starts a different job with the same employer at any time during the protected period. The employer may offer the new job before or after the end of the old job.

## COMPLAINTS

If an employer does not pay the money under a protective award, the employee has a right to complain to an employment tribunal. Where a number of

employees are concerned in a single protective award, a test case could be arranged by agreement between the parties, including the union concerned.

A complaint can be made within three months from the last day for which there has been failure to pay. If tribunals consider it was not reasonably practicable for the employee to make the complaint in time, they can allow longer. Application forms are available from local DfEE offices and the Employment Service Division. A copy of the completed form will be sent to a conciliation officer of ACAS who will, at the request of the parties or on the officer's own initiative in appropriate cases, consider whether he or she can help settle the complaint without the need for a tribunal hearing.

The employee or employer can seek help from the conciliation officer through the nearest ACAS regional office. Where conciliation is not possible or fails, the tribunal will hear the complaint. If justified, it will order the employer to pay the employee or employees concerned the money due to them under the award.

## SELECTING EMPLOYEES FOR REDUNDANCY

Where it is necessary to reduce the number of employees in a similar job category, the criteria for selection should be agreed with the trade union. Plainly an objective method is essential and should be published. In the long term there is the critical problem of retaining those employees who are vital to the company's future.

There are many ways to select such redundancies: last in, first out (LIFO); early retirement; level of skill and qualifications; volunteers; performance level; attendance record; and disciplinary record. Each one has its problems and appropriate counselling is essential.

## REDUNDANCY PAYMENTS

Under the Redundancy Payments Acts 1965–69 a lump sum payment is established which applies to most employees. Usually, all people engaged under a contract of service as employees are entitled to redundancy pay. Indeed even a volunteer for redundancy may claim, but there are exceptions for certain people who are excluded by circumstances or statute. The scheme takes into account age, length of service, a minimum qualifying period and compensation varying according to pay level.

The employer must provide a detailed statement of the lump sum payment in writing. This should include the following three important factors:

- *Length of service*: service over 20 years may be ignored and only completed years are included; for example, 5 years and 11 months would be counted as 5 years of service.
- *Actual current weekly pay*: amounts over a certain pay level may be ignored; a maximum figure is subject to annual review by DfEE.
- *Payment scales*: each year of service fits into one of three pay bands:

  | | | |
  |---|---|---|
  | ages 18–21 | $\frac{1}{2}$ week | |
  | ages 22–40 | 1 week | |
  | ages 41–63 | $1\frac{1}{2}$ weeks | |

  At age 64–65 the amount is reduced by 1/12 for each complete month the employee exceeds 64 years.

*Length of notice*

Apart from redundancy pay, the employee is entitled to the contractual period of notice or statutory period of notice, depending on which is longer, or payment in lieu.

**NOTIFICATION TO THE SECRETARY OF STATE**

An employer must notify the Secretary of State for Education and Employment if there is a proposal to make ten or more employees redundant at one establishment within a relatively short period. This action allows the Training Enterprise and Education Directorate (TEED) to take any necessary measures to redeploy or retrain redundant employees, and government departments and agencies to consider any further steps to avoid or minimise the redundancies. Similar enforcements apply in terms of disclosure of information. Moreover, the employer's defence of 'reasonable practicality' also applies. There are penalties for non-compliance.

# Suspension: main causes

## MEDICAL SUSPENSION

Sometimes employees are suspended if they have been continually exposed to hazardous substances at work, which might damage their health.

## MATERNITY SUSPENSION

An employer must offer alternative work if a new or expectant mother may be affected by any health or safety risk and the risk cannot be removed. In circumstances where there is no alternative work the employee is suspended.

## LAY-OFFS

An employee is 'laid-off' if the employer cannot provide work on a day when he or she would normally do so because the business is not working at its usual level. This action depends upon the contract of employment between employer and employee as to whether the employer is entitled to lay off the employee.

*Guarantee payments*

There are various regulations and rules that apply concerning entitlement to a statutory guarantee payment. Most employees have an entitlement, and there is a procedure for complaints through the employment tribunal.

# Lateness and absenteeism

High levels of lateness and absenteeism adversely affect output, productivity, profits and morale. ACAS estimates that in the UK over one million employees are absent every day. The CBI estimates that absenteeism costs industry over £5 billion a year, which is four times higher than those for major overseas competitors. The Industrial Society calculated that 11 days off a year were taken by the average shop-floor worker. The journal *Director* estimated that 200 million days were lost each year. Clearly it is worthwhile for any company to assess these factors and establish suitable control procedures.

Apparently some companies do not even recognise the problem for various reasons, such as lack of systematic records, not distinguishing between genuine reasons and excuses, being unaware of the effects, and poor supervision. Modern companies, however, take absenteeism seriously and their personnel policy usually incorporates the principles of being understanding, sympathetic and applying a flexible approach. Also, managers and supervisors are advised to be fair and friendly, and to take prompt and consistent action.

The importance of the problem is demonstrable when the effects are shown to permeate the whole company. The burden of covering for latecomers and absentees often falls on the rest of the employees, who must apply extra effort and suffer the additional strain of trying to do more than one operation at once. Such unnecessary stress on supervision and employees is unfair. Continually trying to rearrange operations and machine loading inevitably causes some hold-ups and idle time, which is reflected in lower output and possibly poor quality work.

## REAL AND APPARENT CAUSES

Some causes of lateness and absenteeism cannot be avoided. Inevitably employees suffer with domestic difficulties, sickness, mishaps and other unfortunate situations such as transport hold-ups, fatigue and oversleeping. These real causes are acceptable in a modern society, but there are other apparent causes which may indicate organisational and motivational problems. Distinguishing between the two causes demands a policy that establishes and maintains comprehensive records, counselling to find out the real reasons, appropriate disciplinary procedures, careful control and remedial programmes.

One general view of British people is that provided they have sufficient for a home with acceptable comforts, a car, a holiday, and facilities for the children, there is little incentive to work conscientiously, or to improve the pay packet for the sake of the country. Two causes of lateness that are particularly difficult to control are the misuse of alcohol and the effects of narcotics.

## MISUSE OF ALCOHOL

Misuse of alcohol is a main cause of absenteeism; it also causes poor performance and safety problems in the aftermath. The problem raises two issues: the use of counselling and treatment, and disciplinary procedures.

### Counselling and treatment

Some companies have introduced an alcohol policy which offers advice and treatment but does not necessarily avoid the disciplinary process. An employee may seek help or the company will refer the case to an independent section. A referral usually applies if the employee is agreeable. Such treatment does not eliminate any disciplinary procedure but may cancel such action if the treatment is successful. Indeed an employment tribunal would expect to see assistance, similar to that in any ill-health situation but support dismissal if the employee fails to co-operate or relapses into the old drinking habit.

### Capability and conduct

Although most disciplinary procedures would include drunkenness as gross misconduct, the circumstances must be considered carefully. The two features are capability and conduct; both demand a thorough investigation to decide whether ill health through an alcohol problem affects capability, or the degree and extent of conduct warrants disciplinary action. Employment tribunals clearly insist that the medical aspects should be fully investigated and pursued first before resorting to disciplinary procedures. Dismissal may be accepted if an employee is drunk at work, causing a safety hazard, behaving offensively or refusing to leave work. Such gross misconduct would usually be interpreted as fair but there may be problems if there are particular circumstances.

## NARCOTICS

A narcotic is a substance which induces, among other effects, drowsiness, sleep, stupor or insensibility. Within this category are drugs and tobacco. Drugs policies in companies tend to be unusual except for the practice of dismissal through gross misconduct. Policies on anti-smoking are now common, although the subject remains controversial because smokers claim to have rights too, despite the effects of passive smoking. Nevertheless, smoking is recognised as a major hazard. Smoking and non-smoking areas are widespread at work and in public areas. Under the Health and Safety at Work Act 1974 the dangers of passive smoking are recognised and employees have a right to a smoke-free environment. If employees consider there is a risk to health, they may call in either a health and safety inspector or an environmental health officer.

## Warning signs of drug addiction

Addiction to illegal street drugs or pharmaceutical drugs is not easily recognised and demands experience and knowledge to detect. Furthermore, it is more likely that a member of a group will not be on drugs. However, the supervisor should be aware of the problem and be alert to possible indications that seem to arise more often.

Unfortunately, there are many warning signs that could be confused with other reasons. These may be emotional changes, absenteeism, lateness, absences from the job position, drowsiness, accident-proneness, suspicion of theft, and sudden aggressiveness or irritability. Other indicators are loss of interest in general topics, sniffing frequently, jerky movements or dilation of the eyes, furtive behaviour, unusual smells, stains or marks on the body, loss of appetite, balance difficulties, and unexplained damage to belongings.

Clearly accusations must be avoided. If there is any suspicion of drug abuse, the supervisor should report the problem to personnel or a senior manager.

## RECORDS

Establishing a suitable system of records involves an assessment of the main features. They include individual records of timekeeping and absences, statistical information, isolating sections where conditions seem to be at fault, and personal opinions through counselling in an attempt to review the causes. Underlying such record keeping is the conscientious support of managers and supervisors;

they must distinguish between genuine causes and excuses, and attempt to match other factors with the problem.

## Checklist

1 A means of recording attendance.
2 Any deviation from recording attendance should be confirmed by agreement with the supervisor.
3 The supervisor is responsible for checking attendance, ascertaining the reason for absence, and arranging counselling as required.
4 Confirmation of absence by notifying the supervisor, by a written note, or by a sickness self-certification form.
5 Absence returns sent to the personnel department for compilation of statistics, including sickness records.
6 Recording by the personnel department of excessive absenteeism against set allowances, and any action established by agreement with the union.

## DISCIPLINARY PROCEDURES

Disciplinary procedures must be absolutely fair, agreed with the union, recognised as acceptable by the employees, and operated in a strictly democratic way. The difficulties are choosing a suitable warning procedure, defining the meaning of a poor history, and determining the sanctions to apply. Some companies apply pressures by cutting pay, stopping bonuses, suspension, discharge after a number of warnings, loss of seniority, and loss of holiday rights.

## Checklist

1 A signed agreement from each employee who should be made aware of the rules, sanctions, allowances and how to claim them, control procedures, and appeals procedure.
2 A regular update of justifiable absences which should be carefully worded, recorded and notified to everyone.
3 A regular update of unjustifiable absences, which should be agreed with the union, recorded and notified to everyone.

4 A review procedure to discuss any problems, liaise with unions, and consider absence statistics.

## THE SUPERVISOR'S ROLE

Provided supervisors are trained to undertake responsibility for control and are given the necessary discretion and authority, they are in the best position to monitor absenteeism. No doubt the line managers should be involved in the sanctioning of disciplinary procedures unless there is an arrangement for automatic action within the framework.

### Control mechanisms

1 A personal record for each employee detailing appropriate information on absences.
2 A control chart recording lateness and absenteeism for each day of the month (Fig. 18.3).
3 An absence return form submitted to the personnel department on a weekly or monthly basis (Fig. 18.4).

4 Statistical returns to management. Typical comparisons may be completed for each period, such as a month or a year, by using the following formulae. The second formula may be applied on a basis of hours, shifts or days.

$$\frac{\text{Total number of days}}{\text{Average number of}} = \frac{\text{Average number}}{\text{of days lost}}$$
$$\frac{\text{lost through absence}}{\text{Average number of}} = \frac{\text{of days lost}}{\text{per employee}}$$
$$\text{employees for period} \quad \text{for period}$$

$$\frac{\text{Total number}}{\text{of days lost}} \times 100 = \frac{\text{Days lost expressed}}{\text{as a percentage}}$$
$$\frac{\text{Total planned}}{\text{days}} \times 100 = \frac{\text{of planned}}{\text{working time}}$$

### Employees' responsibilities

Supervisors should ensure that all employees understand their responsibilities when they are late or absent. These include:

Figure 18.3 Monthly lateness and absence chart for one department

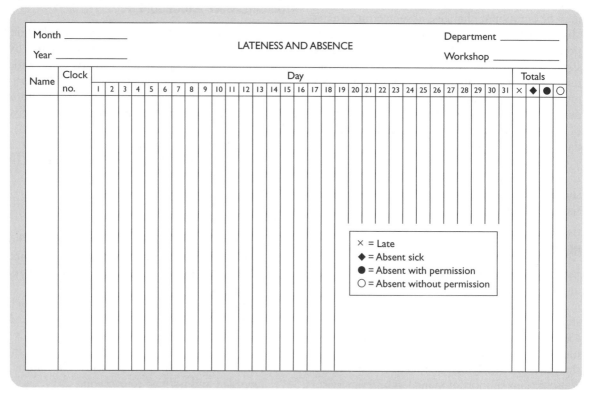

| | | Absences | | | Week commencing | | |
| Name | Clock no. | Date | | Total hours absent | Reason | Medical certificate (after 7 days) | Remarks |
| | | started | ended | | | | |
| | | | | | | | |
| | | | | | | | |
| | | | | | | | |
| | | | | | | | |
| Supervisor | | | | | Department | | |

**Figure 18.4** Absence returns may be weekly or monthly

- Inform the supervisor as soon as possible directly or indirectly through a relative or friend.
- Provide details of the reason.
- If the sickness is beyond seven calendar days, write confirming the reason and provide a doctor's certificate.

## THE SUPERVISOR'S RESPONSIBILITIES

### During absences

- Maintain a record of lateness and absences, and complete appropriate control charts and statistics for management.
- Contact the employee at regular intervals and keep a personal record.
- If there is no contact on the eighth day and no medical certificate is received, inform the personnel department immediately.
- The supervisor should arrange for a visit if the absence is prolonged. Good practice is to telephone for an appointment well in advance, take a friend, and check with personnel.
- Seek advice from personnel if there is any doubt about any aspect.

### After absences

- Welcome back the employee.
- Ensure the individual feels sufficiently better to start work.

- Discuss the reason for the absence, but be careful to avoid confrontations if there are doubts about the genuineness of the absence. Avoid sensitive areas of a personal nature.
- If the reason is work-related, discuss the possibilities of improving the situation to avoid a recurrence.
- Consider referring to personnel if there are problems such as the need for medical or other specialised advice, a desire from the individual to discuss the case with a third party, or a trend in their absence record that demands further discussion and counselling.

## MANAGERIAL CONTROL

Excuses for absenteeism are usually related to faulty organisational aspects or a poor personnel policy, both of which are management's responsibility to correct. There are many areas to consider which easily lead to absenteeism unless they are assessed accurately and adjusted. Typical examples are:

- disgruntled feelings over pay and increases, especially when they do not match with boardroom increases
- poor financial incentives to encourage good attendance
- poor working conditions
- ineffective working arrangements that cause major disruptions if someone is absent and

do not encourage more responsibility among employees
- poor productivity packages that do not penalise those who place a heavier workload on others if they are absent
- an inadequate occupational health programme and no promotion of health education
- no overall control at board level to review the statistics and the system, and to implement any changes to improve the situation

## QUESTIONS

1 Discuss the question of induction.

2 Draw up a list of information which you think a new employee should receive before he or she starts work.

3 What arrangements should be made to receive the new employee on the first morning at work?

4 Discuss the problem of transfers and promotion in connection with fairness and justice.

5 How would you conduct a termination interview?

6 What action would you take if labour turnover began to increase in your department?

7 Employees are often discharged through no fault of their own. Explain the implication of this statement.

8 How would you deal with an employee who is continually late? Include in your answer the reasons for the actions you would take.

9 As a new supervisor, outline a plan to improve lateness and absenteeism which are particularly bad problems in your section.

10 State how you would conduct a fair programme of assessment for each employee under your control.

11 Discuss the problem of labour turnover and the importance of keeping appropriate records on this topic.

12 If your company were forced to contract, discuss the various ways of deciding which employees should leave. Give your personal choice of the method to be used and explain the reasons for your choice.

13 What are the benefits of effective employee appraisal?

14 Outline the methods of employee appraisal.

15 What are the essential phases of an appraisal programme?

16 Draw up an appraisal interview assessment form.

17 Daily observation of changes in behaviour of employees is an important feature of supervision. Discuss this observation.

18 Examine the difference between acute poor performance and chronic poor performance.

19 Describe informal discussions and formal discussions when dealing with chronic poor performance.

20 What are the basic reasons usually leading to dismissal problems?

21 What is considered to be fair dismissal?

22 Outline an employee's rights relating to dismissal.

23 What are the warning signs of alcohol and narcotics problems in an employee?

24 Discuss the question of coaching and counselling associated with day-to-day performance.

## CASE STUDY

Jane took a fortnight's holiday but did not return on the following Monday. She telephoned to say she was suffering with backache after the long flight. On her return on Tuesday, her supervisor told her the one-day absence would be treated as holiday. Jane replies she would prefer it as a day off sick. The supervisor agreed but when the personnel weekly record reached the manager he refused and told Jane it would be treated as a day's holiday. The supervisor confronted the manager as he had already agreed the arrangement with Jane and thought it was common sense. The manager replied that it was a question of principle; last year Jane did the same thing before the supervisor had taken over the section.

*Outline the causes of this situation. Consider ways of improving organisational relationships to avoid future occurrences of this nature.*

## CASE STUDY

Joan was very annoyed with Susan. Apparently, Joan had mentioned casually to her that she had thought up a much better way of assembling a component which took half the time. Some weeks later Susan told the supervisor, was rewarded £200 and had been promoted. Joan complained to the supervisor but Susan denied that Joan had mentioned the new way.

*What could be done now in these circumstances?*

## CASE STUDY

Rose had been working five evenings a week in a local bar to make more money for her childrens' clothes. One evening Mary and her boyfriend visited the bar and waved to Rose. Next day Rose, who worked full-time, was called to the personnel manager's office to account for moonlighting in the evenings. According to her supervisor she was making more clerical errors recently and was very quiet.

Rose immediately suspected Mary because she received work from Rose and was having to waste considerable time rectifying Rose's mistakes. An angry scene developed and Rose was told to have the day off to cool down. Mary was not guilty as Rose had supposed. Rose's situation at home was well known and another clerk had reported her.

*Comment on the supervisor's conduct in this situation. Consider the role of the personnel manager when Rose's domestic situation is known and moonlighting is reported.*

# 19
# Training the workforce

## The importance of training

Any country with a highly trained workforce has a distinct advantage over those which have neglected this vital factor. Future prosperity is probable if such a country has a sound economic environment, which includes appropriate pay rates and high productivity. In the UK there has been a shortage of skilled labour since World War II and many companies have shirked their responsibilities for training and developing employees. This situation has contributed to the slow rate of economic growth. Some top managers even contest the installation of a training programme on the grounds that it is costly and time-consuming. They claim that many other pressing jobs should receive priority and that training is uneconomic because the trained employees leave and other firms receive the benefit. Training is an essential part of the supervisor's job. If this activity is neglected, the time spent on other aspects of supervision increases sharply, resulting in false economy. Other matters demand far more time, cost and effort than training, without showing effective results.

In 1884 the Royal Commission on Training Instruction considered the key reason for Britain's poor competitiveness to be a neglect of training. Successive governments have not solved this problem (Chapter 6). In 1964 the Industrial Training Act was passed. Training boards for each industry were established to plan, supervise and advise on training schemes, and to control standards. For various reasons many boards were abandoned. Now only seven boards remain. In 1985 evidence of a very low level of investment in training in the private and public sectors of organisations in the UK was published by Coopers and Lybrand in *A Challenge to Complacency*. The reasons were thought to be complacency, scepticism, ill-informed companies, and inept personnel practitioners. Now the business environment is changing so rapidly that any country which is unable to develop its human resources at the same rate will inevitably decline.

### LONG-TERM DEVELOPMENT: THREE PHASES

#### Education

Education is the main contributor. An effective system produces knowledge and capabilities, along with the provision of character building, the formation of cultural background, and ideas for careers and achievement.

#### Training

In the short term, training provides a source for the individual to achieve competence in technical and technological aspects, in performing tasks, and in improving skills. To be effective these learning activities must be integrated and applied at all organisational levels in a continuous development programme.

#### Continuous development

Continuous development should be an extensive programme which concentrates on improving the breadth of knowledge and skills related to modern approaches. Examples are:

- empowering everyone to use initiative and creativity
- participating in business process re-engineering by contributing ideas on structural changes, more efficient activities and increasing effectiveness
- ensuring that the whole organisation is customer-oriented
- aiming for higher quality and reducing waste
- applying the advantages of teamwork and autonomous activities

These examples illustrate the complexity and extent of holistic management. Continuous development is essential for the survival of any business in an increasingly competitive world.

## COMPETENCIES

As explained in Chapter 1, the Management Charter Initiative (MCI) introduced units of competence in 1992 under the title of Management Standards. This scheme has emphasised a national standard for an individual to reach in a particular job.

Jobs at all levels should have an appropriate mix of knowledge and skills requirements. Under this scheme an individual who wishes to qualify as competent to perform a particular job may submit to an assessment of competence by a range of methods. National Vocational Qualifications (NVQs) are offered at various levels; levels 3 and 4 apply for supervisors or first-line managers.

## PERFORMANCE IMPROVEMENT: THREE TYPES OF TRAINING

- Manual skills to develop reflexes and the capability to use machines, devices and tools in the workplace or in the office.
- Basic clerical skills to develop all the skills in memorising, learning procedures and systems, using communication devices and other office skills.
- Higher clerical skills to improve long-term effectiveness by developing mental and creative skills, problem solving and decision making.

### Social behaviour training

A fundamental training problem is how to change attitudes and social behaviour at work. The main thrust takes into account the characteristics described in Chapter 9. As a reminder, attitudes are related to the immediate environment; perceiving and reacting to the environment; and the learning process. They are relatively enduring; slow to change; and imply feeling and evaluation. This type of training is complex and demanding on top management strategies involving organisational culture. To avoid frustration, the supervisor should appreciate the major difficulties involved, considering the nature of attitudes and their association with beliefs, values and behaviour.

# The supervisor's role

If the supervisor is restricted by a company's inadequate human resources development policy, he or she may help to improve the situation by learning about appropriate skills and using them on the training and development of employees. In these circumstances the supervisor's role extends to finding and using employees' hidden strengths, giving employees the opportunity to improve, and helping them in every way possible to reach their maximum potential. Often there is little time available as the emphasis on short-term objectives overrides sustained sensible training programmes, so courage and perseverance are essential.

Essential features which enable the supervisor to fulfil the training role include:

- *A planned training programme*: appreciating the various training programmes, the breadth of training, which includes improving performance levels, delegating, managing safety, and examining a typical training programme.
- *The learning process*: understanding how people learn and the way they cope with certain management skills. Also how to use learning styles that influence learning capability and effectiveness in problem solving and decision making.
- *Behaviouristic learning*: understanding people's behaviour by examining the causes (known as classical conditioning) and the consequences (known as operant conditioning). These indicate, respectively, the operation of emotional responses and need responses.

- *Training methods*: knowing the methods available and their use dependent upon improving knowledge, improving manual and other skills, and developing supervision for promotional purposes.
- *The training environment*: appreciating the advantages and disadvantages of various locations, coaching in certain situations, and using guides to learning.
- *Training manual skills*: using a logical sequence of instruction for all schemes involving skill development.
- *Problems of training existing employees*: being able to persuade and stimulate employees to accept change and learn new tasks. Using techniques, including coaching of autonomous teams, to achieve effectiveness.

# Planned training programmes

As explained in Chapter 3, under organisational development (OD) a planned programme is an essential requirement. However, various schemes are seen in companies. These may be divided into three sectors:

- *Organisational development*: These are comprehensive programmes established by a competent senior management. Everyone expects to have the opportunity to be educated, trained and developed within the company's organisational culture.
- *Sectional or group programmes*: These are arranged often on an ad hoc basis to satisfy changes, such as the installation of new machines or devices, introducing new procedures, or launching a new product.
- *Individual programmes*: These are usually based upon the selection interview and feedback from performance appraisals.

Within these schemes are four important aspects: the scope of training, newcomers, delegating authority, managing safety, and a typical training programme.

## THE SCOPE OF TRAINING

A natural sequence for the new employee is selection, induction, training and development. For existing employees there should be a continuous programme of training and development. This avoids under-utilisation of the workforce. A realistic programme to achieve full utilisation includes formal education and training schemes run or arranged by the personnel department, and localised training applied by the immediate superiors.

The scope of training permeates all activities in the organisation. Competence levels of employees rely on effective training schemes. Each employee should learn to recognise the vital part he or she plays in all features of an organisation, which embraces collaboration, structural soundness, overall effectiveness and control.

## NEWCOMERS

Newly trained employees and newcomers naturally need special attention until they are proficient and capable of working entirely on their own. Even those who are already skilled expect and should receive training in their particular job, which invariably differs in some respects from similar jobs they may have done previously.

An essential part of issuing instructions on work, rules, regulations and procedures is to provide training in any aspects that are new or unusual. Whenever new methods are introduced on the recommendations of work study engineers or as a result of the supervisor's study of existing methods, such changes demand additional training.

## DELEGATING AUTHORITY

Successful delegation depends upon recognising employees' potential and their effective training for the tasks to be delegated. Further training of employees to expand their capabilities and prepare them for promotion is essential for their morale and improved effectiveness.

Often the supervisor relies on deputy supervisors to assist and take over part of the supervisory planning and organising of activities, as well as straightforward tasks. Here the supervisor's responsibility is to ensure employees are adequately trained to cope with these tasks. The supervisor has frequent opportunities during the daily routine to demonstrate methods and give reasons for his or her actions to the deputies, thus giving them an invaluable insight into the job.

## MANAGING SAFETY

Comprehensive training as well as sufficient close supervision is needed to reduce the accident rate. Although safety is discussed in Chapter 21, the importance of training is stressed here because of the distress and anxiety that unnecessary accidents cause to employees and their families.

Inadequate training is often the cause of accidents; it embraces such features as ignoring safety regulations and speeding up task time. An assessment of accidents over a period will indicate particular areas where more training is required to reduce dangerous practices. Extra instruction helps to convince employees of the full danger of various bad working habits.

The legal requirements for safety that affect both employer and employee are discussed fully in Chapter 21. However, the supervisor should remind staff of their duties under Sections 7 and 8 of the Health and Safety at Work etc. Act 1974, and of the powers of inspectors under Section 20.

## A TYPICAL TRAINING PROGRAMME

Most training programmes follow a logical and straightforward approach which conforms to any comprehensive procedure, but usually they will be augmented and structured to suit a situation:

1  Investigate the job description, the job in practice, and job analysis. These findings should indicate the knowledge, experience and skills required for each job.
2  Examine the job holders to discover their levels of knowledge, experience and skills. This information should be available already but updating is not always conducted regularly.
3  Analyse steps 1 and 2 to identify education, training and development needs for each person.
4  Compare with the organisational development programme, or the manpower plan, or the managers and supervisors.
5  Prepare a schedule to coincide with the planned changes and priorities.
6  Conduct the programme with appropriate control and staffing.
7  Evaluate periodically by conducting appraisals, feedback arrangements and personnel records on transfers and terminations.

# The learning process

Learning leads to a relatively permanent behavioural change due to practice and experience. Consequently, successful learning is demonstrated by a difference in behaviour – voicing knowledge unknown previously, performing new skills or adapting to a new situation.

Learning is naturally a dynamic process, whereas training provides the opportunities to learn. Professor C. Hardy states, 'Learning means both keeping on top of your subject and developing your personal capacity'. Furthermore, he emphasises the importance of learning from experience or learning from hindsight. There are two features of the learning process that give an insight into how the process works and how learning styles affect learning capability.

## UNDERSTANDING THE PROCESS

In everyday experiences the learning process is simple: if a child puts his hand on a hotplate and burns himself, he has learned rapidly and painfully to avoid touching hot objects. In complex situations the learning process is more involved. An experience may occur through seeing an event, or reading about a theory, or performing an act. To learn from this experience it is essential to think about the event or reflect on the observation, and then to draw conclusions, generalise or decide to investigate. Investigation may involve experimenting, being creative and applying ideas, or simply making decisions.

Briefly this learning process involves four steps: experience, review, conclude and plan. Various basic skills are applied: observing, analysing, creating or visualising, problem solving, decision making and evaluating.

In motivational terms the learning process may also be viewed as a stimulus–response relationship (Chapter 12). The four steps are drive, stimulus, response and reinforcement.

Clearly, these two theories stress certain factors inherent in the learning process. They are:

- the needs and wants of individuals
- the importance of appraisals, planning and objectives
- the application of many basic skills
- encouragement, advice and adaptation

The importance of the learning process is stressed when learning styles are examined, as they influence how people learn in various situations and the way they cope with certain management skills.

## LEARNING STYLES

Individuals possess particular learning styles that influence their learning capability and their effectiveness in problem solving and decision making. According to D.A. Kolb's ideas (1974) there are four major learning styles: activist, reflector, theorist and pragmatist. An individual learns more easily from a particular style, but some fortunate people adapt easily to any learning situation. Nevertheless, when the four styles are examined, learning supervision and management involves the use of all four styles, considering the need for reading, listening to lectures, tackling difficult tasks, observing and analysing, using logic, and being well organised and practical.

### Activist style

Activists are enthusiastic, action-minded, optimistic, open-minded, and enjoy crisis firefighting. They learn more easily when given difficult, challenging tasks; when offered new experiences; and where the learning situation offers drama, excitement and crisis. They tend to be bored with passive or solitary roles such as reading, listening to lectures, watching, and not participating.

### Reflector style

Reflectors are thinkers, observers, cautious and easy-going. They like collecting and analysing data, and tend to take a back seat at meetings. They learn more easily by watching, thinking over all the factors, deciding in their own time, and analysing carefully. They dislike the limelight and being forced to choose with insufficient information.

### Theorist style

Theorists are detached, inquisitive, analytical and logical. They tend to be recognised as being thorough, serious-minded and boffins. They learn more easily when listening, or reading about concepts based on

logic or rationality; when confronted with facts, figures and models; and when they are intellectually stretched. They dislike ambiguity, lateral thinking and flippant approaches; so they are overcautious, resist being forced, and avoid vague situations.

### Pragmatic style

Pragmatists are practical, well organised, set goals, and plan for action. They are essentially matter of fact; enthusiastic when confronted with ideas, theories and techniques; and are down to earth. They learn best when dealing with practical issues, and learning techniques that easily display practical applications. They dislike vagueness, open-ended discussion and theoretical ideas.

# Behaviouristic learning

The principles of learning emerge only from behaviouristic theory, therefore its bases are important. There are two concepts: classical conditioning and operant conditioning. Both are well known and sometimes called connectionist theories.

## CLASSICAL CONDITIONING: PAVLOV'S DOGS

- *Before conditioning*: A dog is hungry (drive); after being shown food (stimulus) its mouth waters (response) and eventually it is fed (reinforcement).
- *During conditioning*: Similar to the first experiment, but a bell is rung (conditioned stimulus) when the food is shown (unconditioned stimulus) and salivation occurs (unconditioned response).
- *After conditioning*: The bell is rung (conditioned stimulus) and the dog's mouth waters (conditioned response) although no food is present.
- *Conclusion*: The dog is now conditioned to respond to a new stimulus (the bell); the response is a reflex action (conditioned reflex).

### Applications

People respond in a similar way; many fears and other emotions are learned by classical conditioning, therefore certain emotional responses can be traced back to this process. Examples are:

- conditioning children to respond to a raised finger, a frown or a raised eyebrow
- conditioning staff to respond to a stare, a tone of voice or a gesture

Elementary examples are shock from a loud noise (stimulus) resulting in jumping (response); buzz of a wasp resulting in fear; and sight of blood resulting in revulsion.

## OPERANT CONDITIONING

Operant conditioning has far more impact on learning. Behaviour is explained by concentrating on the consequences of behaviour not the causes. This means the learner is active or takes the initiative by responding without an unconditioned stimulus; the response is due to a need.

In other words, during classical conditioning the unconditioned stimulus is a reward and presented every time; but in operant conditioning the reward is given only if the response is performed. To satisfy a need – a need means wanting something – is called positive reinforcement; the need to escape from a situation is called negative reinforcement.

B.F. Skinner, an American psychologist, conducted famous experiments in operant conditioning using the so-called Skinner box. The sequence of operant conditioning should be clear:

- The learner is motivated to satisfy a need.
- A response is evoked to reach a goal (stimulus).
- If successful, a response achieves the goal and the stimulus acts as a reinforcer; thus the response strengthens. If unsuccessful, there is no reinforcement and the response weakens.
- After repeated reinforcement the behaviour becomes conditioned.

### Applications

Elementary principles are:

- Performing a task (response) leads to payment (stimulus).
- Working hard leads to receiving praise.
- Crying leads to receiving attention.

Incentive schemes, praise at appropriate times, many motivation theories, and the study of behaviour rely partly on operant conditioning.

# Training methods

The main sectors of employee training that determine the methods employed are:

- developing knowledge that serves a dual purpose of providing information for the job itself and, if correctly applied, providing information which should improve attitudes
- developing manual and other skills
- developing supervision for promotional purposes

The four major training methods are trial and error, the traditional method, the analytical method and an integrated approach.

## TRIAL AND ERROR

In a company adopting trial and error, employees are either placed on their own and learn the job by performing operations, making mistakes and correcting them; or they watch another employee, ask questions and copy the operations. Such unsound methods are still common.

In this way the trainee picks up bad habits, which are difficult to break, so he or she is unlikely to become proficient. If an employee is asked to help a trainee, there is no incentive to assist. Invariably time is wasted, which affects the employee's pay in the case of piece work and bonus schemes. These forms of training are slow, disrupt organisation, are relatively expensive and generally ineffective.

## TRADITIONAL METHOD

The traditional method follows a rigid pattern which suffers with two interconnecting major faults: the learning plateau and possibly severe frustration when progress is prematurely halted. The scheme follows a set routine:

1  Explain the whole job.
2  Demonstrate the operations.
3  Practise the operations slowly and carefully.

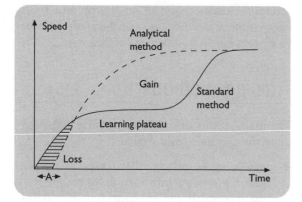

**Figure 19.1** Overcoming the learning plateau
The analytical method of training overcomes the learning plateau normally encountered using the standard method. It starts with exercises that involve no productive work, so there is a time lag (A) before production begins.

4 Increase speed until the learning plateau is reached.
5 Place a trainee on the job under some form of supervision.
6 Eventually increase the speed to that of a proficient employee.

### The learning plateau

When the whole job is explained and the speed of *all* the operations is gradually increased as proficiency improves, a point is reached where improvement stops. In other words, a learning plateau is reached and no further development occurs until improvement recommences.

The plateau is illustrated in Fig. 19.1, where the traditional method (or standard method) is contrasted with the analytical method (see below). Many reasons have been suggested to explain the cause of the learning plateau. One reason is that the skills which are acquired in the early stages of training are not capable of being developed to the advanced stages of full-speed operation without being modified.

### THE ANALYTICAL METHOD

The analytical method is efficient, time-saving and dispenses with the learning plateau. The scheme follows a pattern:

1 Conduct basic exercises.
2 Break down the job into its individual skills.
3 Demonstrate each skill separately.
4 Practise each skill until full speed is reached.
5 Gradually combine the skills and parts of the job, maintaining full speed until the whole job is performed.
6 Place the trainee on the job and allocate periods of practice at full speed under supervision.
7 Gradually increase the practice periods until the whole day is spent at full speed.

Considering the problems with the traditional method, there is a strong case for learning each small part of the job separately, using the advanced skills from the beginning, until full speed is attained. The trainee can then concentrate on increasing speed by intensive repetition without being concerned about the overall job until he or she is proficient at all the required skills.

On assembly line jobs where the operator controls the speed of work, the feasibility of the analytical method should be carefully examined. There may be snags such as increased training time, breaking down the job into skills, and the problem of slowing down advanced skills to speeds that can be readily assimilated. However, these snags should be weighed against the savings which can be made by avoiding the learning plateau.

### AN INTEGRATED APPROACH

An integrated approach is based upon scientific principles of learning and psychology. The principles of learning, guides, type of job, the learner's ability and experience, and the environment are all integrated. A set procedure is followed on a step-by-step basis which allows the trainee to develop rapidly.

Usually there are three stages which are divided into considerable detail. Stage 1 conducts an investigation into available facilities to provide sufficient information for preparing the plan. This stage includes accommodation, visual aids and learning materials which are useful when choosing the methods for stage 2. Stage 2 covers lecturing, handouts, discussion, practical demonstrations, examples, practice and improvisation. Stage 3 outlines the important aspects of the plan, such as objectives, the budget, organisation, the programme, allocation of trainees, methods of instruction, training environment, progress reports and follow-up.

## Stage 1: Investigating available facilities

### Accommodation

The supervisor has to cope with the accommodation that management is prepared to offer. Often this is inadequate and amounts to a rearrangement of facilities at the workplace. In some establishments a separate training centre is available to supplement training at the workplace. Also allowances are made to accommodate trainees on the shop floor, so they can practise, listen to lectures and watch demonstrations.

### Visual aids

Visual aids are intended to assist the instructor by supplementing verbal explanations. Many useful aids are cheap and require a small amount of preparation. Blackboards and flipcharts allow the instructor to develop ideas visually, step by step. Diagrams and models can be produced cheaply, and they effectively demonstrate practical work. There are many expensive aids such as overhead projectors, slide and cine projectors and television, but remember they are aids not ends in themselves.

Only one aid should be used at a time and without any fuss, otherwise the trainees give more attention to the aid than to the subject matter. To avoid any delays, the aid should be checked beforehand to ensure the equipment runs smoothly. Learning occurs when the trainee becomes mentally involved in the process by seeking out knowledge, asking questions and visualising the operation. Actual practice is the natural complementary process from which the trainee learns by relating physical experience and visualisation of the operation.

### Lecturing material: the job breakdown

Adequate preparation of lecturing material is essential. This ensures a smooth presentation of the procedure in correct sequence and provides an opportunity to check the current method. The critical points should be emphasised by providing comprehensive explanations and appropriate practice.

A job breakdown should contain the current step-by-step account of the operation. The usual method is to watch the operation, build up the steps by asking questions and ensure the steps are in the correct sequence. Probably records may be obtained from the work study department if one exists.

Make sure the most effective method or standard method is being used by the operator. If there is time, another opinion helps to assess the job breakdown. Adequate preparation also ensures that any questions will be answered with confidence and understanding of the difficulties trainees are likely to experience.

## Stage 2: Choosing the available methods

### Lecturing

In its narrowest sense, the lecturing method is used to give information to trainees, who are more or less limited to playing a passive role of listening. As their knowledge of the topic increases, the one-way process of lecturing is gradually replaced by the two-way process of teaching, which includes participation using the questioning technique. The instructor continually checks by asking questions to see whether the knowledge has been absorbed accurately, and trainees are encouraged to ask questions to supplement the lecture. Lecturing is a fundamental method of imparting information, concepts and explanations. Although the theory and a guide to the practice of a skill can be imparted, there is no guarantee that performance will improve.

### Coaching

Coaching is more advanced and demanding (Chapter 12). The coach should possess effective interpersonal and conceptual skills (Chapter 1), should care about equipment and should be obsessive with details. A correct rapport is essential and the trainee must feel free to discuss strengths and weaknesses, problems and values. The employee should be already trained to a certain level, or be performing the job, so that full advantage of the technique can be taken. The coach provides the means for further development through the use of various skills that prompt, explain, help the employee to think and reason, and feel more confident. The coach does *not* advise, or give answers to problems or decisions. The technique is an essential part of development in autonomous teams.

### Handouts
Lecturing may be supplemented by distributing duplicated copies of notes on the subject matter and any additional information. Dictation is avoided, saving considerable time and energy. Suitable reading matter such as textbooks and periodicals may be recommended for further study.

### Prearranged discussion topics
Prearranged discussion topics are outlined in the training programme so that trainees can read in advance of the lecture, make notes and consider appropriate questions for discussion. This encourages participation by arousing an interest in the problem areas of the topics; it should raise lively discussions and increase the absorption rate.

### Discussion
Successful discussion depends upon establishing a group who possess similar basic knowledge of the topic, who come from varying backgrounds, and with sufficient experience and size to give a balance of opinions. Discussion is a popular technique for airing problems because it stimulates individuals into thinking up new ideas and encourages more participation. Discussion groups are usual in supervisory and management courses. There are various more elaborate schemes:

- *Seminars*: These are conducted either by asking a member to give a lecture on a given topic or by holding a discussion on a topic to stimulate an exchange of ideas under a chairperson from the group.
- *Case studies*: Information on a problem is given and the group attempts to find a satisfactory answer by discussing and analysing the case.
- *Role playing*: This involves members actually taking part in controlled situations by assuming the identity of a supervisor, for example, and dealing with a complaint.
- *Business games*: These are similar to role playing, but more involved. A number of members may participate on similar lines and, when properly conducted, they soon tend to live the part.

Gathering a group of employees from the workplace often causes a certain amount of disruption, and management may object to this. However, the gains may be considerable, not only from the training viewpoint, but also because of the excellent suggestions which can emerge.

### Using examples
Some topics are difficult to explain by speech alone. This predicament can often be solved using suitable examples to illustrate the situation or point. Some of these aids are sketches, diagrams, models, pictures, analogies and anecdotes.

### Practical demonstrations
Skills are mainly acquired by imitation and practice. Naturally the only way a trainee can imitate an operation is to watch a practical demonstration and be provided with the facilities to copy and practise it. The demonstration must be clear, have a strict, logical sequence and adhere to the standards given in any handouts. The complete operation should be demonstrated. Any particular problems are pointed out and accompanied by illustrations of special techniques and critical points.

### Practice
The vital stage in acquiring a skill is reached when practice begins. Continual practice is essential, together with assistance from the instructor, who should regularly check and correct when necessary. The trainee must be encouraged if progress is poor, as it is easy to become disheartened. This must be accompanied by positive criticisms, showing the correct method and techniques. Quick learners must be watched to see that speed is not leading them into bad habits. Slow learners need moral support, appropriate sympathy and extra help.

### Improvisation
All trainees should practise the art of improvisation. Improvisation invariably starts as lecturing ceases. Questions are asked which usually demand a degree of improvisation. If a topic is difficult to understand, the instructor will have to think up examples and illustrations on the spur of the moment that are in tune with the atmosphere at the time and meaningful to that particular group. Successful improvisation demands a broad and deep

knowledge of the subject matter, plus the ability to expand a point and to construct suitable teaching material at a moment's notice.

## Programmed learning
Programmed learning was developed by B.F. Skinner, famous for operant conditioning. The subject matter is presented in a sequence of simple stages; it is learned at the trainee's own pace and checked by self-testing. Presentation is by means of a teaching machine, a teaching book or display screen equipment controlled by a computer. Each frame or page contains some information and a question to check comprehension. The method is rapid, creates interest, is useful for teaching facts and procedures, and the effects are long-lasting. The programmes are expensive and difficult to update, therefore many trainees are needed to justify the cost.

## Software training packages
Software training packages present self-check exercises which enforce continual interaction between the trainee and the programme. Mistakes are rectified by replay, and the depth of learning can be varied. The learner's interest is aroused by the technique and self-pacing is assured.

## Stage 3: Establishing the plan

## Objectives
A good plan is based upon clear objectives which should be stated and understood by everyone who is concerned with the training scheme. Some of the aims of training are to improve the quality of work, increase output, increase productivity by reducing errors, reduce the accident rate, and create positive attitudes.

## The budget
Management must agree a budget to cover all possible expenditure for equipment, teaching materials, a training centre and instructors.

## Organisation
It is essential to appoint individuals who are responsible for training generally and for particular training schemes. They must have sufficient authority to act within the overall framework of training programmes so that arrangements may be put into practice and controlled effectively.

## The programme
An assessment should be made of all the training schemes that can be accommodated. Each scheme will be titled and timetabled with sufficient detail and suitable progress points to form a logical sequence of training at different levels. An overall schedule may then be drawn up to accommodate the schemes, perhaps on a half-yearly basis. The programme should be as simple and flexible as possible to cope with probable alterations later on.

## Allocation of trainees
Allocation should be made on a fair and logical basis in accordance with personnel policy. Selection of suitable trainees and choice of training are additional factors that depend on circumstances. To avoid any misapprehension, publicise the method and results of allocations.

## Methods of instruction
Deciding upon the methods of instruction will depend upon a number of factors, including training environment, the budget, the standard of trainees and existing facilities. The initial decision about methods depends upon whether the aim is to acquire knowledge on a particular subject or to acquire a skill.

## Training environment
Where a choice of facilities is available, full use should be made of the advantages of each training environment. As a general guide, the quiet atmosphere of a classroom is ideal for lecturing and discussions; a training centre may accommodate lectures, demonstrations and practice; the workplace provides the atmosphere of reality and is therefore useful for advanced practice.

## Progress reports
Adequate control depends upon the conscientious recording of progress and results. Measuring performance and improvements at appropriate stages in training will ensure corrective measures can be taken, such as additional tuition or, in extreme cases, removal of a trainee from the course. The reports are normally stored in personnel records,

and the records are used to prepare statistics for management appraisal. The trainees should also see the reports as part of the normal practice of informing the individual of his or her progress.

### Follow up

A good training scheme is essentially a continuous process. Genuine interest in the progress of trainees *after* the course is essential for successful follow up. Sometimes further training or retraining may be necessary; sometimes rapid progress may result in promotion. Recording such information is vital for statistical purposes when linked with progress reports. Assessment of long-term results may indicate changes which need to be made in the training programme. Individuals might develop bad working habits after certain periods on machines or practice in the job. These may be corrected in subsequent training schemes by additional emphasis at the appropriate stage of the operation. Long-term effective control of training relies upon conscientious follow up.

# The training environment

Training may be conducted at the workplace or at a separate training centre. The correct attitude and approach to learning is also a factor to be considered as this has a substantial effect on the success of the training.

### LEARNING AT THE WORKPLACE

The supervisor is usually responsible for training at the workplace and is the instructor. This is an additional burden, but an important aspect of the job. Allocation of time becomes more difficult as less time will be spent on supervising. The success of the scheme depends upon his or her ability to instruct and to spend sufficient time with the trainee.

### Coaching

Coaching is effective provided there is a thorough understanding of the principles. It has already been fully described in current trends of supervision (Chapter 1), in collaborative management (Chapter 2) and in the application of motivation (Chapter 12). Coaching is an essential part of a development programme for autonomous teams.

### LEARNING AT A TRAINING CENTRE

There are fewer distractions in a training centre; this provides the trainee with suitable conditions for concentrating and learning, although the element of reality is probably missing. The use of a specialist instructor is an obvious advantage, provided suitable discipline makes up for the loss of workshop atmosphere. The trainee receives more attention and guidance on his or her weaknesses, assuring more rapid progress.

# Useful guides to learning

Useful guides to learning have evolved through research into the learning process and are mainly derived from classical and operant conditioning theories. A typical example is reinforcement, probably the most important principle of learning as it predicts *and* controls behaviour (Chapter 12). But remember that each person is unique and may not fit conveniently into a set pattern.

### PLANNING

Although it is essential to draw up a careful plan of training, such aspects as current alterations, difficulty with a particular topic and coping with slow learners must be allowed for in the schedule. This flexibility avoids adherence to a rigid programme which itself becomes the objective; the true objective must be to produce trained employees.

### TRAINEE ABILITY

The instructor should assume the effective selection of trainees has provided him or her with individuals who are capable of learning and have sufficient ability to perform the tasks involved. Lack of confidence in the trainees is immediately apparent to them and has an adverse effect on the learning process. Displaying confidence builds up enthusiasm and spurs individuals on to greater efforts.

## MOTIVATION

Creating the desire to learn or being able to motivate trainees is part of the instructor's job. The reasons for and advantages of learning a job should be stated to make the trainee feel the exercise is worthwhile, considering definite objectives in mind, such as financial gain, regrading or increased status.

## LEARNING RATE

Although people learn at different rates, there is some uniformity in the progress of learning. Many factors determine the rate and pattern: intelligence, flair, degree of interest, physical strengths and weaknesses, resistance to change, established working habits, lack of incentive, and sometimes deep psychological resistance. Age itself is unimportant, provided the person's mental and physical powers are not failing, although strength and experience are considerations. Also the job content is a major factor, considering the types of task, knowledge and skills requirements, and monotony.

## LEARNING CURVES

An important feature for the supervisor is an ability to explain the rate of learning. The rate of learning mainly varies according to the task being learned. There are four learning curves which help to understand the patterns to be expected.

### Decreasing returns curve

The decreasing returns curve (Fig. 19.2) is negatively accelerating; it starts rapidly then gradually slows down until learning practically stops. This represents the most usual way of learning. Most mental and motor tasks of a specialised routine nature tend to conform to this pattern. Motor functions are those requiring dexterity or manipulative activity; this muscular control is unrelated to mental functions. Hence a very intelligent person may be awkward when assembling a simple piece of machinery.

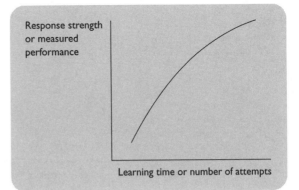

**Figure 19.2** Decreasing returns curve
Applies to most mental and motor tasks of a specialised routine nature.

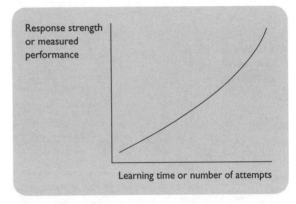

**Figure 19.3** Increasing returns curve
Applies when a completely unfamiliar mental or motor task is learned, such as highly skilled lower-level tasks.

### Increasing returns curve

The increasing returns curve (Fig. 19.3) charts a positively accelerating learning process that produces increasing returns (the opposite to decreasing returns). Learning begins very slowly but gradually it becomes very rapid. The process is more unusual and occurs when a completely unfamiliar mental or motor task is being learned, such as highly skilled lower-level tasks.

### S learning curve

The S learning curve (Fig. 19.4) conforms initially to the increasing returns curve and followed by the decreasing returns curve. Therefore it is often

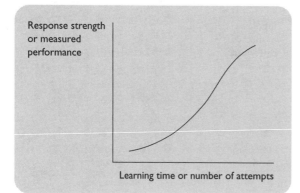

**Figure 19.4** S learning curve
Applies when some experience already exists, so that a complex process evolves when the unfamiliar task is tackled and insight occurs.

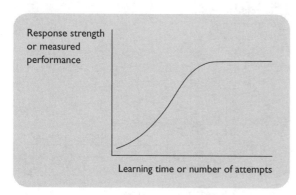

**Figure 19.5** Learning plateau
Applies to low-level or monotonous tasks. Motivation triggers improvement when the plateau is reached.

known as a combination of the first two curves. Theoretically all learning occurs in this way when an individual starts with no relevant experience. In reality some experience already exists and a complex process evolves when the unfamiliar task is tackled and insight occurs. It typically represents an experienced technician learning a new and highly skilled task.

## Learning plateau

The cause of the learning plateau was explained earlier (Fig. 19.1). The usual pattern (Fig. 19.5) for low-level or monotonous tasks is a slow start, sudden improvements and finally a levelling off to a plateau. Behavioural techniques are essential at this point to motivate the individual to improve further.

## THE CORRECT SEQUENCE OF LEARNING

Effective learning of skills occurs when movements are performed in the correct sequence. Therefore, although this may be an uneconomic procedure because of excessive waste, the process is essential. Skill is largely developed through muscle sense that registers for example the movement of a lever, then using the degree of sensation, it automatically decides the next movement to be carried out. Familiar examples of this effect are handling the steering wheel in a car and changing gear.

## DEPTH OF UNDERSTANDING

Creating a deeper understanding of the job and the process is better than imparting a superficial knowledge of the job. The success of this more sophisticated training method largely depends on the intelligence of the trainees and their keenness to possess a deeper understanding of the principles and their wider application. Those with considerable insight into their work as well as ability are more versatile and become valuable assets to the company.

## INSTRUCTION

The process of passing on information may be carried out in a variety of ways: explanation by direct speech, written notes, practical demonstration, and examples illustrated by a range of visual aids. Passing on knowledge must, however, be distinguished from the process of learning. Learning is an active process in which the trainee must be physically and mentally involved.

## SIMPLIFICATION

Some instructors deliberately complicate the job to stress their own importance because they know the answers. It is psychologically bad to influence the trainees with continual propaganda on the difficulties and complexities of the job. The instructor must make the operations look easy, show they can be performed easily and not allow trainees to form the impression that even the expert finds the job difficult. Encouragement and confidence are important to the trainee. Therefore it helps to arrange the programme so that teaching the easy tasks comes first, followed by the more difficult ones later.

## THE TRANSFER OF LEARNING

In a retraining programme there may be some parts of the new job that were a part of the old one. This so-called *identical elements principle* explains why the trainee may find learning a new task is easier if the principle applies. However, the parts must be identical for *positive transfer* of learning. For example, a clerk may excel at interviewing staff, but being placed in a *client* interview situation involves some different approaches.

If previous experience creates difficulties in learning a new task, a *negative transfer* applies. Examples are being presented with a strange computer program, a telephone operator facing a different model of switchboard, or an operator confronted with a new electronic console on a machine.

Transfer through principles is a simple theory which shows that experience theoretically helps in retraining. For example, a clerk who understands filing in strict alphabetical order would have no difficulty in transferring to new document filing procedures.

## THE ABILITY TO DISCRIMINATE EFFECTIVELY

Many jobs involve processes or operations that demand a particular type of response to certain situations. The response may be to push a button, pull a lever, stop a machine, or process a piece of material in many different ways, depending upon requirements. The situation that demands attention may be made evident by lights, sound, touch, visual appearance and measurement.

The training process should develop the correct response to situations. Associations should be built up so the trainee learns to use the most suitable sense organs to provide an adequate response to the situation as it arises. A simple example would be to check the smoothness of a surface by touch rather than by sight.

Another example would be the operation of a transfer machine where the operator is expected to press a button when twenty-four red lights are all glowing. The response to a number of lights may be much slower to learn than reaction to more familiar signs, like a bell or a buzzer sounding. The operator must learn to judge when the critical moment is coming.

## PRACTICE

Continual practice or participation forms an essential part of the learning process. The trainee must be given the opportunity to ask questions; examine the machine, the tools or the work in hand; try out the process; show the results of his or her efforts; discuss the queries or problems; and so become absorbed in the process of learning. A genuine interest in the job should develop as the trainee notices improvements and is appropriately encouraged when he or she performs the operations correctly. The instructor should indicate any errors or bad practices and demonstrate the differences to show the advantages of performing a process correctly.

## USE OF ANALOGIES

When trainees are confronted with strange or complex assemblies or operations, it is helpful to explain the assembly. For example, by showing a similar device that is more familiar to them and indicating its likenesses to the unfamiliar assembly.

## THE IMPORTANCE OF REPETITION

The instructor should remember that learning is easier and lasting impressions are achieved by repeating the information or demonstrating the technique many times. Most individuals' powers of absorption are limited, so repetition is essential. If difficulty is experienced, repetition should also be supplemented by varying the approach and giving different examples.

## SPACED REPETITION FOR LEARNING SKILLS

Skills are acquired more easily when there is a carefully planned number of regular learning periods over a length of time, rather than in the same number of lessons grouped closely together over a short period. Although this scheme is often difficult to arrange in many industrial conditions, it should be used wherever possible.

## CONTINUITY

Because of the nature of change in processes, design and machines, training is essentially a continuous activity. Newcomers, transferees and existing employees all require training as changes occur. Follow up becomes very important to ensure employees use the correct methods for performing operations.

## PROGRESS REPORTS

All trainees should have immediate and regular reports on their progress so they can correct and practise to a scientific programme.

Unless criticism or praise is given quickly, valuable time is wasted by all concerned. Emphasis during the early stages of training should be placed on the correct method. Incorrect ways will continually appear, but they should not be highlighted by drawing attention to them unduly. Repetition of the *correct* method at these times is more positive and directs the efforts of the trainee in the right direction.

Asking questions regularly helps to keep trainees alert and fosters their feelings of actively taking part in the learning process. The question should be phrased so that an explanation is required. This will immediately show whether there is a true understanding of the subject rather than a simple yes or no, which is uninformative. If any particular difficulty appears, the instructor should deal with it immediately. Regular reviews of progress also provide an opportunity to summarise the important aspect.

# Training manual skills

Training manual skills is intended for the workplace and the office where there are manual skills involving the use of machines and devices. The main steps in an instruction plan are:

- Prepare the trainee.
- Explain the job.
- Demonstrate the operations.
- Practise the operations.
- Check performance.
- Follow up the training.

This plan follows a logical sequence of training which is fundamental to all schemes for acquiring a skill. The analytical method of training is ideal for developing skills and should be remembered when examining the logical sequence below, considered by many instructors as the basis of most schemes.

## PREPARE THE TRAINEE

Reduce nervousness and concern by attempting to establish a friendly relationship with the trainee. Take the person's mind off the subject of training for a while. Useful information can be gained by asking the trainee to talk about previous jobs. This provides a lead to giving general information on the product, the processes involved, where this particular job fits in, and its importance. The trainee's interest may be further aroused by giving more details of the objectives of the company and his or her part in achieving them.

## EXPLAIN THE JOB

The job should be outlined first but with sufficient detail for the trainee to appreciate its significance. At this stage explanations should be given on special tools or equipment, standard layouts, measuring devices, specifications, drawings, job language and materials. To encourage conscientiousness the trainee should also be told the value of the equipment, tools, materials and assemblies, and be instructed on safety precautions, cost of waste and the importance of high standards.

## DEMONSTRATE THE OPERATIONS

Each important step should be adequately explained, shown and illustrated. Key points must be stressed. The trainee should be as near as possible to the operation position. The instructor should ensure all stages are clearly understood, which means he or she must be painstaking and check the effectiveness of the teaching by constantly asking questions. A run-through at normal operating speed is followed by a slowed-down version, to the point where each movement may be clearly seen and connected with preceding and subsequent movements.

## PRACTISE THE OPERATIONS

When the trainee feels sufficiently confident to attempt the operation, he or she should do a trial run under close supervision. A complete run of the whole operation at normal speed is recommended, but it is not always possible owing to economic considerations such as the high cost of materials.

### Mistakes and memory lapses

Errors must be expected considering mental levels discussed in Chapter 9. The errors should be corrected immediately and more detailed explanations should be given to avoid repetition. Asking the trainee to explain the tasks as they are performed helps to memorise the key points and hastens the learning process.

Often the cause of a mistake is a lapse of memory or forgetfulness. The degree of forgetfulness varies depending upon the situation and previous events. Determining the cause is difficult, but memory may be improved by eliminating the obvious reasons. These reasons are usually loss of concentration, nervousness, ingrained poor practices, insufficient repetition of the main features, conflicting new practices with old ways or values, and slow adjustment due to strange or distasteful aspects. Practice continues until the instructor is satisfied with the performance.

## CHECK PERFORMANCE

Performance checks are made when the trainee is working alone. A nearby colleague or supervisor should take over to offer immediate assistance when needed, and the instructor should check frequently for any deviation from the correct method. Continued personal contact is needed to boost the trainee's spirits at this time. Questions should be asked on any work problems. Extra coaching should be gradually diminished as performance improves.

## FOLLOW UP THE TRAINING

Follow-up ought to be considered as a process that continues indefinitely. If good relationships have been established, the instructor will be able to encourage and make employees feel more important by taking an interest in their progress on a long-term basis. Any bad working habits which may appear later must be checked and any advice that is desirable should be given freely.

This broad interpretation of follow up should be encouraged as it provides a close-knit system of communication for promotion and other purposes. Sufficient information should flow between the personnel department, the supervisor, the instructor and post-trainees to provide more reliable indications of the true working situation.

# Training higher clerical skills

A long-term programme is essential to develop mental and creative skills at this level. These skills include using creativeness and ideas, taking the initiative, feeding back information, communicating effectively, being resourceful, accepting change and being confident. Such development may lead to supervisory promotion. Many techniques are used:

- *Seminars*: structured discussions on various appropriate topics.
- *Role playing*: playing various parts in simulated situations.
- *Case studies*: dealing with a situation alone or in a group, which demands problem-solving and decision-making techniques.
- *Coaching and mentoring*: help and advice when performing various tasks.
- *Self-help*: guidance on self-development from textbooks, situational experiences from reading material, and live problem-solving and decision-making opportunities.

# Problems with existing employees

## INCAPACITY

Employees' physical and mental health may deteriorate, preventing them from doing the job successfully. They may have suffered an illness or an accident, or be under emotional stress. Dealing with this condition may be difficult. Sometimes employees persuade themselves that the blame for their shortcomings lies with the supervisor who continually gives them the 'hard jobs' to perform. The supervisor must be equally persuasive and convince them of the need to be retrained for a different job.

## PRODUCTION METHOD CHANGES

Most employees will appreciate the economic necessity of keeping up to date with production processes in the face of competition. Obsolescent machines must be replaced; new and more suitable materials must replace the old; and the introduction of better methods is essential. Unfortunately, these changes often cause human upheavals which include the retraining and regrouping of employees. Adequate explanations are essential, otherwise there is less chance of achieving co-operation.

## FLUCTUATIONS IN OUTPUT

Seasonal products and demand changes cause output fluctuations, which often result in temporary redundancy. The introduction of patterned seasonal products (such as ice-cream in summer and hot dogs in winter) solves the problem of output, but demands a more versatile workforce where many employees are capable of performing more than one job.

Existing employees need persuading and encouraging to learn new jobs. Important factors such as losing face in front of colleagues, breaking up working groups, separation from particular colleagues, and resistance to changing a long-established routine should all be considered. Reasonable solutions to such problems must be established before interviewing the employee.

Adequate information on the background to these changes will help adjustment. If the employee can see and accept the reasons for any changes, the possibility of agreement and co-operation is greater.

## COACHING AUTONOMOUS TEAMS

A fundamental feature of autonomous teams (or empowerment) is the redistribution of organisational power to improve the achievement of corporate objectives. This form of organisational development relies upon appropriate employee development, which means comprehensive training schemes and competent coaching.

If team members are not highly trained, they will not be able to use their increased responsibility competently to achieve objectives and satisfy customers. Furthermore, effective coaching and full support from top management are essential to cope with changing technologies. These changes should cause alterations to processes, provide continual development and maintain motivational influences. The motivating aspect of coaching was discussed in Chapter 12.

### Coaching: the main aspects

- Systematically plan the sessions, bearing in mind changes, weaknesses in members, the informal leader's role, and scheduled production.
- Progressively develop members to maintain correct team relationships, motivate, and encourage receptiveness.
- Use a collaborative approach to maintain the correct rapport (a communication relationship). Members should see the coach as a facilitator or catalyst when they feel the need to discuss their strengths and weaknesses, and want appropriate training.
- Avoid any tendency to control closely. But regular appraisals are essential to assess the success of coaching and to provide feedback for the adaptation of performance goals for the teams and individual members.
- Adopt counselling techniques in a democratic fashion to encourage autonomy and to provide information on techniques and technologies.
- Influence members whenever possible to believe in their capabilities, to be self-disciplined, and to encourage initiative. Remember that employees generally prefer to win respect through their

achievements, which should be strongly coupled with their area of responsibilities. Thus a higher degree of fulfilment is derived from their work along with an enhanced contribution towards organisational objectives.

- Remind members of their strengths and the need to attend to their weaknesses. In this way they develop and fully exercise their capabilities.

- Provide the team with feedback on customers' views so that members appreciate why processes need to be changed and they understand the use of coaching to ensure their efforts are pointed in the right direction.

## Coaching problems

Coaching tasks are very demanding on patience; they need considerable psychology and collaborative techniques. Problems are easily caused by creating the wrong impression, being too directive, overstressing weaknesses, not depersonalising changes, being subjective, forgetting to avoid criticism and arguments, and trying to exert power.

Clearly the concept must be understood by everyone. This should be seen as *sharing power* in such a way that teams feel fully committed to reaching goals and so achieving a higher degree of self-fulfilment. An inherent danger is the feeling by the coach and other managers that power is being lost as team members develop higher standards of capability.

Solving these problems when they occur is a difficult role. This requires ingenuity and perseverance to restore the philosophy of autonomy, and to achieve more confidence and higher morale. Much depends upon the personality of the coach, the leniency of team members, and the capability of the informal leader within the team.

## QUESTIONS

1 Why is training considered to be so important?

2 Discuss the supervisor's fundamental task of training.

3 Discuss the question of training schemes, mentioning their effectiveness and any limitations.

4 What is meant by the 'learning plateau' and how can it be overcome?

5 Discuss the analytical method of training, mentioning the advantages.

6 Suggest some useful guides to training that would assist the supervisor in improving his or her capability as an instructor.

7 Discuss the problem of acquiring a skill.

8 Outline a planned programme of training.

9 Draw up an instruction plan for acquiring a skill.

10 What difficulties should a supervisor be prepared to overcome when retraining existing employees?

11 What are the aims and advantages of an organised training programme in a company?

12 Discuss the problem of skill shortages in the UK.

13 Explain classical conditioning and its possible use to the supervisor.

14 Discuss the importance of operant conditioning in training schemes and in the study of behaviour.

15 Describe the programmed learning technique and coaching.

16 Explain the development process and the concept of continuous development.

17 Learning is naturally a dynamic process, while training provides the opportunities to learn. Discuss the significance of this statement.

18 What are learning styles?

19 Discuss the essential features of effective coaching.

20 Consider the likely coaching problems when applied to autonomous teams.

**CASE STUDY**

John's performance appraisal had not been satisfactory. His superior had suggested more supervisory training in view of his group's low ratings compared with the others in the department. John was aged 50 and had been promoted from the group to supervisor five years ago. The group members liked him but he was not supportive, relied heavily on them to sort out problems, and seemed to give the impression that he could sit back now and relax.

John had attended previous supervisory courses and his superior had received excellent reports on his performance. No weak points had been mentioned and his strengths were noted as being a good leader, reasonable capability at problem solving and decision making, and able to mix easily with course members.

*Which topics or competences on a course would be suitable for John in these circumstances? Is this situation attributed in any way to John's superior or to the selection system in the company?*

**CASE STUDY**

Chris Tanger is being groomed for promotion. She has been a supervisor on the clerical side of the business for five years and her superior is pleased with her performance. The personnel manager arranges for her to work closely with one of the middle managers on the maintenance service side of the business.

As Chris has expected from her studies, the approach of this manager to staff does not coincide with her own ideas. Although she thinks the treatment is insensitive, it seems to work very well. Everyone seems to respect Mr Winston and the department works smoothly.

When Chris is being interviewed by the personnel manager six weeks later, one of the questions that comes up catches her unprepared: Did you know that Mr Winston is disliked by most of his staff *and* he knows it?

Chris replies, 'I must admit I didn't realise that. I think he is a bit hard on them but they don't react openly towards him.'

*For what reasons would the personnel manager have chosen Mr Winston for Chris?*

# 20
# Employee relations

## Introduction

The term 'employee relations' (or industrial relations) covers relationships and all the complex bargaining and discussion between management and trade unions, and management and employees. These activities may be formal or informal, involve certain legal machinery, and use accepted negotiation procedures.

Employee relations (ER) is an important feature of any economy. Sound ER has a beneficial influence on a country, but poor ER can cause economic damage. Unfortunately, attitudes tend to dominate negotiations, rather than adherence to facts. Managers seem to rely on generalised assertions and personal judgements. Trade unions face many accusations such as being out of date, too militant, too powerful, too political, and sometimes of holding a country to ransom to win a dispute. Figure 20.1 illustrates the main features of employee relations.

## THE UK INDUSTRIAL STRUCTURE

There are distinct sides in the UK which directly oppose each other, namely trade associations and trade unions. They blame each other for the country's economic problems and for the exclusion of co-operative dialogue. Furthermore, the situation is aggravated by a polarised society where extremes of opinion are expressed on the Establishment, the distribution of wealth, status-conscious attitudes emphasising cash reward and benefits, and short-termism. All these aspects naturally have an effect on economic growth.

### Short-termism

The concept of short-termism means that all parties (including owners, investors, institutions, managers and employees) concentrate on extracting as much cash as possible from the system in the shortest possible time. Thus long-term

**Figure 20.1** Employee relations: the main features

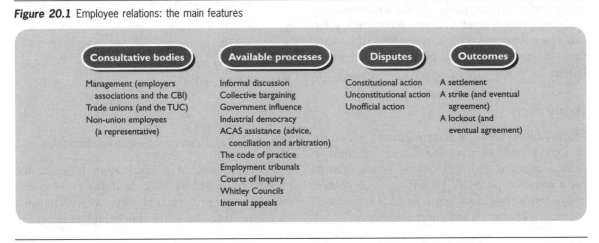

programmes of wealth generation from industry are neglected, which is a disastrous national policy.

However, there is an increasing realisation that economic survival depends upon long-term development and close co-operation between the two sides of industry. Certain changes are now noticeable as foreign companies invest in the UK. Japanese and American philosophies are becoming more influential.

The question of responsibility for short-termism and who should change their ideas is often debated. The parties involved tend to blame each other for not accepting their particular responsibilities. Co-operation and commitment are the key issues.

## VIEWS ON EMPLOYEE RELATIONS

People perceive ER in many different ways that depend mainly upon their views on society, politics, personal experiences, legislation and the purposes of ER. The characters and institutions involved take up various stances based upon additional aspects such as psychological opinions, sociological opinions and economic opinions. The result is a complex, practical system prone to breakdowns. Such entrenchment is attributed to various theories: Marxist, unitary, pluralist, social action, and systems.

### Marxist theory

Marxist theory is often interpreted as accepting that social change is inevitable and causes class conflicts. These conflicts arise between social groups with varying power levels within society. Such competition involves opposed economic interests where one group owns the means of production for profit, and the other group provides labour for pay.

### Unitary theory

Unitary theory relies on everyone acting within the national interest by accepting that an organisation is an integrated and harmonious whole existing for a common purpose. Thus there is no conflict of interest, strong team spirit, and ER is based on mutual co-operation and common interest.

### Pluralist theory

Pluralist theory relies on compromises, logical argument, the development of good personal relationships, and a free exchange of information. These are achieved when the workforce surrenders some autonomy and recognises some rights of owners, whereas the owners or management recognise employees' rights to organise, legally oppose, and bargain over procedures and financial rewards.

### Social action theory

Social action sees the behaviour of individuals relying on many influences that determine their subjective approaches at the expense of structural features in the organisation. Thus individual choice and social action emerge from social situations where the parties interpret their roles and behave accordingly. In practice the structural influences such as political and economic situations cannot be ignored. However, the many personal influences such as goals, experiences, interaction, expectations, norms and values, have a powerful effect on negotiators.

### Systems theory

Systems theory assumes the two parties develop rules and procedures to operate ER and produce agreements. Here the industrial or business environment is paramount when rules are formed and reformed. Clearly this environment must include all the appropriate aspects, some of which are:

- corporation wealth
- market share
- budgets to remain competitive
- economic factors
- size
- location
- the workforce
- internal and external power relationships

A system model of a breakdown is when the parties' views do not coincide at any point in discussions. Compromise is possible only when some views coincide and some understanding exists.

## THE LABOUR MARKET

In democratic countries the labour market is usually a complex and diverse institution. This consists of many sub-markets where people offer their abilities, capabilities, knowledge and skills to concerns who try to cope with manpower needs. Besides the sub-markets, a variety of representative groups collectively form a structure or network. The labour market has a strong influence on ER and company practices, including pay levels, collective bargaining, terms and conditions of employment, recruitment, selection and human resource management.

### Slack and tight states

All consultative bodies are affected by the situation in the labour market. Also employers, employees and prospective employees are directly influenced by its state. If slack this usually means employment is relatively high, employers have more scope to pick and choose, and they have more control over pay in some circumstances. However, there is still difficulty in locating people to suit requirements. If there is a tight state, this usually means low unemployment, employers have an increased difficulty in locating suitable people, and they have to raise pay levels and standards of terms and conditions to entice prospective employees.

### Influences on the labour market

- The level of investment in industry
- General economic activity
- The rise and fall of industries
- Technological changes
- Birth and death rates
- A willingness by the community to seek employment
- The education and training system
- Wars and political practices

### Characteristics

The structure of the labour market is mainly determined by prices for labour. These prices are affected by trade union bargaining power, government policies, taxation, income thresholds provided by social security, and social changes.

### The knowledge factor

Unfortunately, there is an inadequate knowledge of the labour market for many reasons. Consequently, people have difficulty in taking advantage of the situation. This causes the following difficulties:

- Employers are unable to determine accurately the pay and conditions they should offer.
- Employees are unable to assess their true worth.
- Government policy making is hazardous.

### Trade union policy

Trade union membership is related to labour market changes; therefore union policies must be adjusted to structural alterations. Trade unions may attempt to reduce this impact in the short term by applying apprenticeship controls, insisting on job demarcation, refusing to accept new technologies that affect labour requirements, seeking closed-shop agreements, and pressing for higher pay and improved conditions.

According to research, trade unions have managed to increase pay rates beyond the level that market forces suggest should be the case. However, in the long term it seems market forces prevail and are moderated by traditional thoughts on social aspects and acceptable differentials between occupations.

In authoritarian countries, oppressive regimes dominate the labour market to suit their requirements. For example, Nazi Germany disbanded all trade unions in 1933, but they were re-formed in 1945 when democracy was restored.

## THE SUPERVISOR'S ROLES

A knowledge of ER is essential to enable the supervisor to speak intelligently with employees and to avoid obvious bias towards any particular party when the subject is discussed. Furthermore, he or she may be involved in negotiations or disputes, and be participating in daily contacts with shop stewards or union representatives.

To fulfil these roles the following main features of ER are now discussed: collective bargaining, the changing scene of ER, negotiations, legislation, industrial democracy, the consultative bodies, disputes and procedures, the rights of employees and trade union members, and relationships between the supervisor and the shop steward. These topics provide sufficient knowledge, and when linked with other chapters in Part Two they form a basis to develop appropriate skills.

# Collective bargaining

Collective bargaining is a process where trade unions representing their members negotiate with employers. Successive governments have strongly supported sensible collective bargaining by making recommendations and passing appropriate laws. Bargaining for manual employees may be conducted at an industry level, especially in manufacturing industries, and at local levels. At national levels, minimum wage rates are often agreed for skilled and unskilled groups. At local levels, negotiations are conducted for each job classification. Similarly, hours of work are set but shift numbers and lengths are decided locally.

### BARGAINING UNITS

To gain strength, trade unions tend to group together to form bargaining units. These units may cover an established group of employee such as all operators. Salaried staff and perhaps skilled employees would form separate units. These units might cover an industry, a company, a department in a company, all the employees below first-line management in a company, or just some of them.

This scheme sometimes suits employers because fewer negotiating bodies may emerge, which often means leap-frogging claims are avoided and negotiating time is probably reduced. However, some employers resist this move by refusing to recognise the union's case to negotiate for a group or by trying to exclude certain groups.

### PRODUCTIVITY BARGAINING

Productivity bargaining attempts to reform the traditional process where each party gives and receives concessions that amount to zero gain for both sides. It should produce an agreement where employees agree to changes that aim to create more effective and economic production. Consequently, employees gain an increased income and the company gains increased profits.

Typical changes include a more flexible workforce; eliminating demarcation; reorganising working hours to restrict overtime; and reducing overmanning by redeployment, retraining or voluntary redundancy. Productivity bargaining does not guarantee a fixed increase in pay since it depends on future results and relies on both parties having a vested interest in identical proposals.

# The changing scene

Up to about 1960, bargaining units concentrated on traditional approaches relating to pay, working hours and holidays. During the 1960s it extended to include fringe benefits. This change occurred through a continuation of full employment and nationalisation programmes, governmental incomes policies, and weak sterling. About thirty-five years of full employment caused both negotiating parties to concentrate on other features such as pensions, lay-off pay, pay structure changes, and productivity bargaining.

### THE 1980S

In the 1980s there was a drastic downturn in the economy and a rise in unemployment. This caused an increased awareness of fundamental faults in the British economy and an increased resolve to take more positive action to rectify them. Typically, the media focused on poor industrial performance, inflation, standards of living and overseas competitors. The Conservative government elected in 1979 adopted policies to reduce inflation, reduce trade union power, and encourage free enterprise. Six main features emerged:

- Trade unions could no longer strongly influence government ministers; they were not treated by the government as partners in a so-called social contract; they were practically ignored by the government; and they were powerless to resist legislation to regulate their activities.

- Many managers established new channels of communication. This meant they could bypass trade union representatives and communicate directly with employees.
- More harmony developed between managers and trade union representatives. Trade unions responded more favourably towards problems presented by managers, and they suggested ways of solving them.
- The industrial climate appeared to improve as legislation reduced the monopoly power of trade unions. For example, the number of recorded disputes in 1985 was the lowest for fifty years and the number of days lost through strikes dropped from 29.5 million in 1979 to 0.75 million in 1991.
- Trade unions adopted new tactics to tempt employees to join them.
- More comprehensive consultation developed on many economic and non-economic issues between various parties at many different levels.

## THE 1990S

The slow recovery rate and increased overseas competition forced companies to search for new ways of reducing unit labour costs. The industrial and business climates altered drastically as complexity and uncertainty increased, and unpredictable change became commonplace. Good ER was once viewed as providing fair pay, stable employment and a good working environment. Now it is dominated by the customer, external competition and technological innovation. Organisations face critical problems of performance, design and motivation. Consequently, employees are threatened with transfer or termination, which involves insecurity, low protection, and changed ideas on performance and reward.

The problem is not new but now people recognise it, and that is vital for survival. Employees have to accept new techniques such as business process re-engineering, empowerment, downsizing and flexibility. These essential techniques have changed traditional ideas of sound ER. Modern views of good ER seem to lean more towards the following policies:

- giving employees full information on the state of the company and the industry, to show clearly the need for changes
- consulting with employees to seek the most acceptable ways of dealing with competition, to search constantly for improvements, and to work closely with customers
- providing the best possible arrangements for those employees who suffer due to essential changes
- involving employees at all stages of programmes to improve productivity and to encourage creativeness and flexibility
- ensuring that all boardroom decisions regarding pay, bonuses, share options and other benefits are seen to be fair and just for everyone

# Negotiations

Negotiations tend to rely upon the aims of the parties involved, government influence and the process adopted by the participants. The supervisor should be able to appreciate these aspects when discussing a current situation with employees and superiors.

## AIMS OF THE PARTIES

Although the aims of the two parties obviously differ, there could be some common ground. For example, to prevent high calibre employees leaving and taking up jobs abroad, to make the company more productive and so repel competitive pressures, and to avoid disputes that adversely affect the community. Ideally both parties should recognise the importance of profit, productivity, investment and the community.

### The union's aims

The union's aims should be based on consideration for all employees as well as its members, because bargaining units may also include non-members. Their commitment and aspirations may differ from the union's ideas. Consequently, a balance has to be found that minimises conflicting views. Usually the aims in priority order are:

- To press for pay increases.
- To improve working conditions.
- To reduce working hours.
- To encourage non-economic features, such as representation on boards.
- To be included in decision-making activities.

## Employers' aims

- To reduce or maintain labour costs, or to allow for reasonable increases to keep high calibre employees.
- To avoid damaging disputes and poor publicity.
- To keep in line with general conditions of employment in other companies or industries.

## GOVERNMENT INFLUENCE

Various governments have attempted to influence pay settlements, either through a planned economy or non-interventionist policies. Evidence from econometric studies and economic models supports the claim made by many business people that a slower growth in pay would mean more jobs. One Treasury review suggested that if real pay were to rise to a level 1 per cent lower than otherwise, that would eventually lead to between 0.5 per cent and 1 per cent more jobs, that is 110 000 to 222 000 more people would be employed.

As the UK's largest employer, the government can strongly influence pay settlements and the type of settlement, by setting norms related to productivity. Nevertheless, the shortage of labour from 1945 to about 1979 obviously had some influence on pay levels as market forces operated. Also, it is arguable whether trade unions exercised monopoly power that prevented market forces deciding. Companies are certainly concerned with labour costs, which are determined not only by pay but also by fringe benefits, administration costs for each employee and the productivity levels for the workforce.

## THE NEGOTIATING PROCESS

The supervisor should discover how negotiations successfully escape from entrenched positions, how different behaviour patterns are used to cope with situations, and how communication plays a part. Here is an indication of the negotiating process, which is usually in five stages.

### Planning

Planning considers the situation and the environment. The employer will assess the financial state of the business, sales orders and competition. Also, the claim is subjected to a detailed analysis, an examination of the policy and strength of the union, and an assessment of employees' feelings. The cost of various increases is calculated and plans are completed to offset them, perhaps through a productivity deal.

### Presentation

A claim is presented by the union. Assessments by both sides determine priorities and possible outcomes. Parties will be seeking opinions on possible objectives, the degree of co-operation which can be expected, and general responses to negotiations.

### Integrative bargaining

To avoid deadlocks, the negotiators must show a willingness to abandon their entrenched positions to some degree. They must use various cross-cultural skills to demonstrate some flexibility. By taking various stands and altering stances, a more personal approach gradually develops and person-to-person skills become demanding. Thus proposals and counterproposals ensue until common ground is reached.

### The decision

Persuasive skills gradually erode the unacceptable features of the claim until a satisfactory compromise is reached. Each party must judge what is acceptable, followed by one party adopting a closing technique such as attempting to summarise and stating a decision. After clarifying minor points, the issue is resolved.

### Commitment

Enforcement of the deal depends on feelings of moral obligation; negotiated agreements are seldom legally binding. The union's representative must sell the deal to the members and receive majority support for it. Communication is important since misunderstandings later become embarrassing for both sides.

When the deal is ratified, the union's representative reports to the employer to record the agreement and arrange for its implementation. The employer should ensure the agreement is understood by managers and supervisors, and clarify the reasons for the agreement. This essential communication link provides a firm basis for discussion with employees so that criticisms may be countered with arguments based on direct knowledge, not hearsay.

# Legislation

Sensible collective bargaining has always been stressed in committees established by various governments. In 1891 the Royal Commission on Labour supported the use of negotiations through representative machinery. Similar support was given by the Royal Commission on Trade Unions and Employers Associations in 1968 (the Donovan Report).

The Whitley Committee of 1917 even established two hundred Joint Industrial Councils to fill the need for negotiating machinery at national level. These councils are non-standardised structures, but the majority of national agreements on pay and conditions of employment have been negotiated through them.

When the Donovan Report was published, about five hundred negotiating arrangements for manual employees were known to exist between employers (or employers' associations) and trade unions. About two-thirds of the working population had their terms and conditions of employment regulated by collective bargaining. Legislation on ER (usually termed industrial relations) is often seen in three chronological phases.

## RESTRICTED LEGISLATION UP TO 1970

During the first half of the twentieth century middle-class opinion thought the standard of living and working conditions should be improved.

However, such change should be introduced on a voluntary basis by moderate trade unionism, collective bargaining, and a restricted application of common law and government legislation.

## LABOUR POLICY FROM 1971

The Labour government's policy was to pass laws that shifted the balance of power in bargaining to favour the trade unions. In 1971 the Industrial Relations Act was passed. This attempted to create a legislative framework acceptable to all parties. The enactment caused controversy, mainly on the grounds that legislation cannot cover all the facets of a relationship between employer and employee. Further laws were passed in 1974 and 1976 that successfully achieved a shift in power to the trade unions. Two notable acts are the Employment Protection Act 1975 and the Employment Protection (Consolidation) Act 1978.

### Employment Protection Act 1975

The Employment Protection Act 1975 promotes the improvement of industrial relations by means of the Advisory, Conciliation and Arbitration Service (ACAS) and encourages the extension of collective bargaining. New rights and greater job security which were given to employees are now contained in the Employment Protection (Consolidation) Act 1978.

### Employment Protection (Consolidation) Act 1978

The Employment Protection (Consolidation) Act 1978 brings together under one enactment the provisions on individual employment rights previously covered in other acts: the Trade Union and Labour Relations Act 1974, the Contracts of Employment Act 1972, the Redundancy Payments Act 1965 and the Employment Protection Act 1975. The rights conferred in those acts are in no way altered, nor are the corresponding obligations on employers. The vast majority of sections and schedules which have been consolidated from the earlier acts are repealed with some exceptions.

By 1979 many views thought trade union power was excessive and continuing to grow dangerously. Shop stewards were seen to be exerting pressure that reduced the effectiveness of the economy. The Conservative Party argued strongly that trade union power should be reduced by legislation that restricted industrial action and the closed shop, and democratised union activities. Thus the balance of power between employers and unions would be readjusted to favour employers.

## CONSERVATIVE POLICY FROM 1979

In 1979 the Conservative Party won the general election, followed by four consecutive elections. Their proposals covered a lengthy programme usually referred to as a threefold labour legislative plan:

1 to repeal the Industrial Relations Act 1971
2 to legislate afresh on collective and individual employment rights
3 to launch 'industrial democracy' (research for this part of the plan was conducted by the Bullock Committee)

Many of the issues were studied in depth in the UK and in overseas countries. By the early 1990s industrial relations were regulated mainly by law that included relations between employers and employees, and between employers and trade unions. Claims were made that trade union power had been successfully curbed to a satisfactory level. The plan is now discussed. A main section is included on industrial democracy because of its importance in the European Union.

## REPEAL OF THE INDUSTRIAL RELATIONS ACT 1971

The first part of the plan was the statutory replacement of the Industrial Relations Act with the Trade Union and Labour Relations Act 1974. TULRA, as it is often called, repealed the 1971 act but re-enacted, with some changes, the provisions of the older act regarding unfair dismissal, along with certain supplementary provisions.

TULRA provided a new, fuller portrait of the trade union, its immunities and the legal position of the collective agreement. Schedule I of the act received much publicity since this covered the basic rules of unfair dismissal as well as the jurisdiction and procedure of industrial tribunals. In 1976 over 31 000 applications were received by the industrial tribunals for unfair dismissals alone, which illustrated the importance of this single region of employment law. These provisions are now contained in the Employment Protection (Consolidation) Act 1978.

## STATUTES PASSED SINCE 1979

The second part of the plan contained legislation on many industrial relations topics. The statutes passed during the long term of the Conservative government restricted trade union power in many areas, including taking industrial action, enforcing closed shops, and picketing disputes. The acts need careful study and specialists should be used to interpret the provisions. Those most often quoted are mentioned below.

### The Employment Acts 1980, 1982, 1988, 1989 and 1990

The Conservative Employment Acts are covered in Chapter 17. They deal with many topics including trade union ballots, codes of practice, exclusion from union membership, unfair dismissal, maternity rights, protection for non-union members, picketing and industrial action, and union members' rights.

### Trade Union and Labour Relations (Consolidation) Act 1992

All employees may decide whether or not to belong to an independent trade union of their choice and to participate in its activities. There are remedies if an employer dismisses an employee on the grounds of trade union membership or non-membership, or if any action is taken to prevent or force an employee becoming or not becoming a member of an independent trade union. The same applies if an employer attempts to discriminate against an employee. Some of the main provisions are:

● Collective agreements between employers and trade unions are not intended to be legally enforceable unless they are written and expressly affirm they are to be binding.
● Time off with pay for carrying out union duties. This includes negotiations with an employer,

representing members on disciplinary matters, and paid time off for union officials to take training in appropriate matters.

- Employers have a duty not to take action against employees when, at an appropriate time, they take part in trade union activities.
- All closed-shop dismissals are automatically unfair.
- Specific areas for consultation are covered for consultation in the event of redundancy proposals.

### Trade Union Reform and Employment Rights Act 1993

The Trade Union Reforms and Employment Rights Act 1993 implements, in varying degrees, the requirements of social directives issued by the European Union. These include Equal Pay Directive 1975, Collective Redundancies Directive 1975, Equal Treatment Directive 1976, Acquired (Employee) Rights 1977, Social Security Directives 1979 and 1986, Insolvency (of Employer) Directive 1980, Written Statement of Contract of Employment Directive 1991, and Protection of Pregnant Women at Work Directive 1992.

It also provides for the scrutineers of union elections to inspect, if necessary, the union's register of members' names and addresses for accuracy; to ensure all candidates are treated equally; and to appoint an independent person to store and distribute voting papers and count the votes. It abolished the Wages Council system but the Wages Council Orders still exist unless negotiated to the satisfaction of both parties.

### EMPLOYMENT RELATIONS BILL 1999

The government has published this bill to implement the provisions of its Fairness at Work White Paper 1998. Many details are not yet available. There are changes in the following aspects: unfair dismissal awards, family-friendly provisions, maternity provisions, parental leave, time off for domestic incidents, union representation at disciplinary and grievances procedures, protective rights to all individuals except those 'genuinely' self-employed, fixed-term contracts, part-timers' rights and code of practice, and amendments to

Employment Agencies Act 1973. The timetable for legislation is unclear. Within the bill the Secretary of State is given power to introduce regulations for some provisions that are not included in the bill itself.

### APPROACHES TO STATE INTERVENTION

Although all political parties admit pay is a significant factor in economic control, their approaches differ. The Conservative Party aims to reduce trade union power and its influence on pay and productivity. The Labour Party has to gain trade union co-operation by legislating and adopting policies that please the unions. Unlike some European countries where industrial relations law is based on positive rights for unions, UK laws are based upon immunities. Thus trade union power is used to gain improvements or to defend its position.

# Industrial democracy

The third part of the Conservative government's plan was to encourage industrial democracy (ID). ID has a number of alternative terms and meanings. Each one tends to indicate an emphasis on a particular aspect. Typical terms are employee participation, employee control, participation and co-determination. Typical meanings are:

- industrial harmony between all parties involved
- joint decision making between management and employees
- shared control of policy making
- an accepted system of employee representation on the board of directors
- joint participation in designing jobs
- established works councils where employees have an equal voice with management on various activities

In the UK the role of ID has been debated for many years, as might be expected. The controversial aspects have been viewed with suspicion by some parties, nevertheless practices in the rest of the European Union forced the Labour government to establish a committee of inquiry in 1975, headed by Lord Bullock.

## THE BULLOCK REPORT 1977

Lord Bullock's brief was to consider the effective methods of extending ID, accepting the situation for its radical extension to representation on boards of directors. The recommendations were controversial within the committee. A minority report of employers' representatives was published by three of the members, who broadly alleged that industry in the UK was not yet ready for such fundamental changes as were envisaged in the majority report. In the body of the report, the committee envisaged its creed as follows:

> We believe that there must be a joint approach to decision-making in companies, based upon equal representation of employees and shareholders on the board. In our view it is no longer acceptable for companies to be run on the basis that in the last resort the shareholders' view must, by right, always prevail.

The committee envisaged a basic legal framework 'of necessity, complex' but allowing great freedom for each individual company to create its own board of directors. This device clearly indicates that the success or failure of ID depends on co-operation between management, trade unions and non-union employees. An independent Industrial Democracy Commission was advocated to provide 'advice, conciliation and ultimate decision for those within a company whose task it is to devise an agreed system of employee representation on boards'.

The German model of a two-tier board was considered unsuitable, although the minority group favoured it. The unitary board was favoured, with an 'ultimate responsibility for decisions'. These systems are discussed soon.

### Opposition to the report

Hostile reaction from the UK's business interests caused controversy which might be summarised as implying that the Bullock proposals, regardless of whether they are right or wrong, were too radical for employers. The Labour government issued a White Paper in 1978 that embodied many modifications. However, in 1979 the Labour government was defeated and the new government did not pursue the findings.

## THE PHILOSOPHY OF INDUSTRIAL DEMOCRACY

The disastrous consequences of poor relationships between employers and employees in the UK are well known. Equally obvious is the need for Britain's managers and trade unionists to revise their ideas on ID, individually and collectively. Many reasons are often given for lack of industrial harmony. Some of the glaring examples are:

- failure by employers to recognise the strength of trade unions
- the continual use of outdated methods of treating employees
- reliance on obsolescent managers who are out of touch with reality
- failure in appreciating the educational level of employees who understand far more about industrial and commercial operations than is generally imagined
- completely underestimating the ingenuity and capability of employees

Employees must also take some of the responsibility. Often there is a tendency to take advantage of management and the company if the opportunity arises. Examples are improving on their share of perks, slacking whenever possible, bargaining for excessive pay claims if they think they can hold the company or an industry to ransom, and not co-operating. This selfish approach, often at the expense of fellow employees in other industries, is indicative of one of the basic problems that prevails in industry and commerce.

Finally, the trade unions must also take their share of the responsibility for lack of industrial harmony. Some trade union leaders openly declare their political beliefs and even go so far as to admit their aim is to overthrow the government in office at the time. Others develop a minority interest in improving earnings and conditions for a particular group of trade union members, despite the discontent this creates in other groups. Certain unions have held the public to ransom at times and issued grave warnings, such as anticipating industrial chaos under particular conditions. Cases of excessive militancy by some shop stewards, outdated policies and general misuses of trade union power have also been levelled against trade unions in recent years.

## PROBLEM AREAS

- Does a particular formal approach to ID seen operating well in a foreign country mean that a similar approach would be successful in the UK?
- How can a trade union equate nominating some of its members to a board of directors with its freedom of action?
- How would collective bargaining be affected considering this second point?
- Would employee nominees to a board of directors have sufficient expertise to contribute at this level in the organisation?
- How can enthusiasm be generated among employees to participate effectively in management decision making?
- If one of the declared objectives of a trade union is to develop a minority interest by improving earnings and conditions for its members despite the discontent of other groups, how does it reconcile this aim with the national interest?

## INDUSTRIAL DEMOCRACY IN THE EUROPEAN UNION

European practices may be divided into three sectors: the unitary board, the two-tier system, and works councils. The European Union (EU) has been pressurised for some years to introduce compulsory measures to improve industrial democracy. However, the measures and suggestions have not been successful, according to many views, but the Works Council Directive has been popular, except in the UK.

### The unitary board

The unitary board means there is one main board of directors who supervise the managing director and company, and decide overall policy and planning. Examples are seen in the UK, France, Italy and Sweden.

### The two-tier board

A two-tier board means there is a supervisory board and a management board. The supervisory board usually appoints the management board and makes major policy decisions. The management board controls day-to-day problems, agrees official contracts and generally runs the business. Examples are seen in Germany, the Netherlands and Denmark. In Germany the supervisory board may veto business decisions. About 50 per cent of its members are employees who can influence the company's strategy. Some views are that a consensual style of decision making is encouraged and that often the board only acts as a rubber stamp. The management board undertakes a proactive decision-making role in practice and one worker representative is elected on the board.

### Works councils

Works councils are established in most EU countries under the EC Works Council Directive 1994. The directive did not apply in the UK since the government opted out from the Social Chapter in 1991. The Social Chapter is now accepted and by the end of 1999 new regulations will be introduced to include the EC Works Council Directive. Some UK large companies have similar schemes already in operation. Works councils are at workplace level; members are elected by the workforce and are often dominated by trade union representatives. A typical works council may have three rights:

- to be given information on financial performance and future prospects
- to be consulted on strategic aspects
- to participate (co-determination) in deciding issues on the management of personnel

These issues may include working conditions, holidays, shift working, promotion, dismissal, welfare and social facilities. Works councils have a limited capability when strategic policy making is involved.

# Consultative bodies

The main consultative bodies are the employers' associations and the trade unions. At this level, pay negotiations are usually handled directly without referring to the two central federations (the Confederation of British Industry and the Trades Union Congress) for active assistance. The federations advise, provide information and statistics to their members and give their views to the government, the national press and international organisations. Their officials sit on a number of councils and committees that advise the government and statutory bodies.

## EMPLOYERS' ASSOCIATIONS

Employers have generally grouped themselves together within a particular industry but not to any set pattern. Their associations may be small, local groups, sections of an industry or a whole industry at national level. Some of these associations were formed to cope with industrial relations problems. In addition, they were organised to deal with trading and commercial problems. Sometimes an association deals only with trading questions.

### Origins

Early employers' associations were established in some trades in response to union pressure at the beginning of the eighteenth century. Among them were master printers, shipwrights and cotton garment production. By 1889 the increased impact of trade unions caused national associations to form in shipbuilding, boots and shoes, cotton spinning and engineering. Their objectives were to keep a common line and help one another in resisting union pressure, particularly to help any member who was singled out for union attack.

By 1915 national associations were well established. By 1935 they were about 270 strong with about 1500 local and regional branches. In 1968 the Donovan Commission listed 1350 employers' associations who were negotiating pay and conditions of employment. These are federated now to about 85 national organisations, most of them members of the Confederation of British Industry. They negotiate with trade unions to reach national collective agreements.

### Roles

The roles played by employers' associations vary depending upon overall policy. Some have an enlightened policy and actively promote good relations between employers and employees. They offer practical advice and information on pay standards and conditions of employment, training programmes and specialised services. Others are rather negative in their approach by examining proposals and advising revisions based upon the protection of members' interests. They seldom initiate action themselves.

### Activities

The associations adopt a low profile approach and make decisions by consensus. They usually offer guidelines for members in contrast to rigid decisions applied by trade unions.

### Organisation

A typical organisation has a small number of full-time staff, controlled by a director who is responsible for the daily activities of the association. Also there are representatives from member firms and officials who form a central committee. This committee meets about four times a year to formulate policy and to elect such committees as are considered necessary. The chairpersons of these committees usually meet regularly with association officials to co-ordinate activities.

## THE CONFEDERATION OF BRITISH INDUSTRY

The Confederation of British Industry (CBI) represents the employers' associations at national level and internationally. The nationalised industries and many individual companies are affiliated to the CBI, which puts forward the views of all these groups to the government. CBI representatives are members of a number of government advisory committees and voluntary bodies who deal with labour problems. The CBI annual conference discusses policy issues but no votes are taken. The council has twenty-six standing committees that decide policies.

### Royal charter objectives

1  To provide for British industry the means for formulating, making known and influencing general policy in regard to industrial, economic, fiscal, commercial, labour, social, legal and technical questions, and to act as a

national point of reference for those seeking industry's views.

2 To develop the contribution of British industry to the national economy.

3 To encourage the efficiency and competitive power of British industry, and to provide advice, information and services to British industry to that end.

## TRADE UNIONS

Employees have organised themselves into trade unions in most industries today. The process has been long, involved and often haphazard in growth, consequently there is a complex structure of many different types of union. Gradually the movement is becoming more organised and uniform as amalgamations and mergers of the smaller unions into larger ones continue.

There are about 320 unions of which 80 are affiliated to the Trades Union Congress (TUC). Total membership peaked in 1979 at over 12 million but has been declining to about 7 million in 1998. Compared with some countries the UK membership is strong at about 29.5 per cent. In the Netherlands membership is 25.5%, Japan 24%, Germany 23.9%, Italy 22.6%, and USA 14%. The proportions of membership vary in different business sectors and represent about 40 per cent of all employees. About 26 million people are in employment, including 3 million self-employed. Some are barred from union membership, typically the armed forces and the police. Others, such as senior managers, are unlikely to be members. Collective bargaining applies to around 17 million.

### Trade union decline

An important feature is to appreciate the growth of trade unions before 1979. Various reasons given include war, social unrest, government influence to keep industrial peace by legislating in favour of trade unions, business economic cycles, and more large-scale business structures. There are many influences that operate; they vary in intensity depending upon economic, political and social situations. However, the drastic decline of trade unions since 1979 is usually attributed to the rise in unemployment (the business cycle) and the Conservative government's aims to reduce trade union power while in office.

### Revised strategies

Trade unions obviously hope to stop the decline by pursuing certain strategies. These strategies may include improving services to members, changing unpopular aims, recruiting members in new industries, and merging with each other to form powerful blocs.

Clearly the main objectives of protecting and helping their members remain. They are achieved by negotiating for higher pay and improved conditions of employment. However, an urgent need is recognised for more *joint consultation*, which should be distinguished from *joint negotiation* for pay and conditions of employment.

The modern approach is *participation* according to the TUC. Such collaboration may mean focusing relationships in an international direction and framing partnership agreements which emphasise working together to increase profit and provide a fair share for both parties.

### Four forms of organisation

- the professional workers' union for clerical, administrative or executive workers (rapidly growing membership)
- the craft-type union for skilled trade (static membership)
- the industrial union for all workers in an industry, such as mining (static membership)
- the general labour union for workers below the skilled level (static membership)

### The four-level structure

- A *shop steward (delegate or collector)* collects dues, handles complaints and grievances, and operates from the workplace.
- A *branch secretary* is elected, deals with matters within the branch area and is an important liaison link.
- A *district controller (or regional controller)*, salaried and full-time, heads powerful committees and links with the central organisation by mean of intermediate committees.

- *A general secretary* heads the central organisation, is responsible to a national executive committee, is salaried and full-time, and may be elected in various ways.

### Registration

Any organisation of workers (such as staff associations) or employers may apply for registration to the Certification Officer who is appointed by the Secretary of State after consultation with ACAS. Certain provisions are necessary, including having the power to alter its own rules, being independent and controlling the application of its own property and funds.

There are many advantages of being registered and obtaining a certificate of independence. They include the right to demand information from an employer for collective bargaining purposes; the right of employees who are members of an independent trade union to have paid time off work to engage in union duties; the right to refer a recognition issue to ACAS; and the right to tax exemptions in respect of investment income and in capital gains devoted to the payment of provident benefits.

### THE TRADES UNION CONGRESS

The trade union movement is represented as a whole by the Trades Union Congress (TUC), to which most large unions belong. An annual conference attended by delegates from affiliated unions discusses TUC and union affairs, political aspects and economic issues. The main functions of the TUC are:

- to agree and issue the trade union movement's policy
- to be consulted by the government
- to be consulted on interunion disputes
- to propose legislation which benefits and protects its members

The TUC expanded the aims of unions when it gave evidence to the Donovan Commission in 1965. Included were:

- to achieve full employment and national prosperity

- to improve public and social services
- to achieve a voice in government

However, a strong comment often voiced by critics is that when trade union leaders had enormous power and were keen to tell the public what needed to be done, the results were devastating: many strikes, low productivity and 25 per cent inflation.

# Disputes

Failure to settle a dispute by collective bargaining generally leads to a stoppage of work through either a strike or a lockout. Such stoppages not only affect the interests of the parties concerned but also have serious repercussions on the national economy. Strikes usually occur to support pay claims. Three types of dispute may be seen:

- *Constitutional action* when all the procedural steps have been completed with no agreement.
- *Unconstitutional action* when a breach of dispute procedure occurs before the problem is discussed at all stages. Unfortunately, views on this differ. Employers see breaches as a failure by unions to conform to an agreement. Unions see breaches as a moral means to avoid coercion by employers because a procedure is too slow or unfair.
- *Unofficial action* when the union does not support the strike. Such action may be constitutional or unconstitutional.

### PROMOTING SETTLEMENTS

For many years, successive governments have attempted to introduce effective machinery for promoting settlements. This machinery has taken the form of advice, conciliation and arbitration. Conciliation means introducing a third party who attempts to help the parties in dispute by suggesting possible solutions that may be acceptable to both. There is no question of compulsion.

Similarly, arbitration is a voluntary process where both parties agree to submit the dispute to a person (or persons) who will give a valued opinion. The parties also agree to accept this opinion or award beforehand. Figure 20.2 shows a simplified

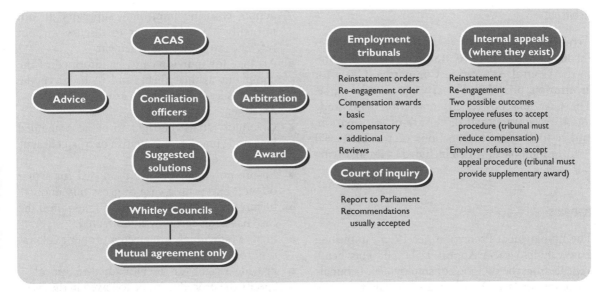

**Figure 20.2** Negotiating machinery for employee disputes

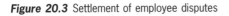

| Disputes | Settlements |
|---|---|
| Contract of employment | Recorded |
| | Corrected |
| Redundancy | Declaration – postponement |
| | Protective award |
| Unfair dismissal | Reinstatement |
| | Re-engagement |
| | Compensation |
| | Reduction of compensation |
| | Supplementary award |
| Equal pay | Arrears payable up to two years |
| | Equal treatment |
| Equal opportunities | Declaration of rights |
| | Compensation |
| | Corrective action |
| | Non-discrimination notices |

**Figure 20.3** Settlement of employee disputes

indication of the negotiating machinery which is available, and Fig. 20.3 lists the disputes and possible settlements.

## THE ADVISORY, CONCILIATION AND ARBITRATION SERVICE (ACAS)

The aim of ACAS is to promote the improvement of industrial relations by strengthening collective bargaining and by assisting in various ways when a dispute arises. ACAS is independent, meaning it is not under government control.

### Advice

Employers are offered advice on a wide range of industrial relations and employment matters. They may seek assistance from ACAS officers in helping to settle disputes. ACAS may conduct inquiries into industrial matters and publish its findings. A code of practice has been produced called *Disciplinary Practice and Procedures in Employment*. This provides guidance on how to draw up disciplinary rules and procedures, and how to operate them effectively.

### Conciliation

Under the Employment Rights (Dispute Resolution) Act 1996 ACAS may conciliate in disputes over redundancy payments. Employers may, in most cases, seek the assistance of an ACAS conciliation officer when a trade union or employee complains to an employment tribunal. The officer will try to settle the dispute by agreement between the parties rather than resorting to a tribunal hearing. As a matter of course, a copy of the complaint submitted to an employment tribunal is sent to a conciliation officer.

### Arbitration

Arrangements may be made to settle disputes through arbitration. ACAS may refer disputes to the Central Arbitration Committee (CAC) for arbitration, provided the parties concerned agree. The CAC has powers in connection with trade union recognition and disclosure of information, and it took over the functions of the Industrial Arbitration Board, which included cases involving fair wages.

### Appeals

The Employment Protection Act 1975 established a new Employment Appeal Tribunal. This hears appeals from the decisions of employment tribunals on points of law. Also it hears appeals from the decisions of the Certification Officer on points of law and fact when the dispute concerns either an entry on the list of trade unions or applications for certificates of independence. *The Industrial Relations Handbook* is an appropriate guide.

## THE CODE OF PRACTICE ON DISCIPLINARY PROCEDURES

The aim of the code is to help employers, trade unions and individual employees by providing practical guidance for promoting good industrial relations. The code encourages improvements in individual conduct. Failure to observe any code provision does not render a person liable to proceedings. However, in the event of a dispute being taken to arbitration, or being put before the Central Arbitration Committee, the code shall be admissible in evidence. If any provision in the code appears to be relevant to the case, it will be taken into account.

The essential features of disciplinary procedures are they should:

- Be in writing.
- State to whom they apply.
- Provide for matters to be dealt with quickly.
- Indicate the disciplinary action which may be taken.
- State the levels of management which have the authority to take various forms of disciplinary

action, ensuring immediate superiors do not normally have the power to discuss without reference to senior management.
- Arrange for individuals to be informed of the complaint against them, and to be given the opportunity to state their case before decisions are taken.
- Give individuals the right to be accompanied by a trade union representative or by a colleague of their choice.
- Ensure no employees are dismissed for a first offence, except in a case of gross misconduct.
- Ensure no disciplinary action is taken until the case has been carefully investigated.
- Ensure individuals are given a proper explanation for any penalty imposed.
- Provide a right for the individual to appeal.
- Specify the procedure to be followed in the event of an appeal.

### The supervisor and the code

The initiative lies with management for establishing adequate disciplinary rules and procedures. However, for them to be fully effective, they need to be accepted as reasonable by both supervisors and employees. Therefore, all levels within the organisation should be involved when new or revised rules and procedures are being formulated.

Some degree of interpretation of rules is inevitable and the supervisor should ensure employees know and understand them. Verbal explanations are essential as well as the distribution of written copies. They should form part of an induction programme for new employees. To avoid misunderstandings, the supervisor should explain the likely consequences of breaking rules and indicate clearly the type of conduct which could lead to summary dismissal.

### An acceptable disciplinary procedure

- Establish the facts immediately, including statements from witnesses.
- Consider a brief period of suspension with pay while the case is investigated.
- Interview the individual before any decision or penalty is imposed and give him or her ample opportunity to state the case.

- Advise the individual of his or her rights under the procedure, including the right to be accompanied.
- Decide whether to give a formal oral warning in the case of a minor offence or a written warning if it is more serious.
  - Set out the nature of the offence and the possible consequences of further offences.
  - Tell the individual that the warning, oral or written, constitutes the first formal stage of the procedure.
  - If the supervisor decides to give only an informal warning for the purpose of improving conduct, then the previous item does not apply.
  - Remember to satisfy the test of reasonableness of action in all circumstances, not forgetting to take into account the employee's record and any other relevant factors.
- A further breach of discipline could warrant a final written warning. This should include a statement that any recurrence will lead to suspension or dismissal or some other penalty.
- The final stage could be disciplinary transfer or disciplinary suspension without pay. This depends upon an express or implied condition of the contract of employment, or dismissal, according to the nature of the misconduct.
- Disciplinary suspension without pay should not normally be for a prolonged period and such a course of action demands special consideration before it is taken.
- Details of the disciplinary action should be given in writing to the employee or employee's representative. This does not apply to an oral warning.
- Notify the employee of any right of appeal and how to conduct such an appeal in terms of procedure and the people involved.

### Advice for all staff

- Do not assume the trouble will disappear.
- Seek immediate advice from the union or staff representative.
- Seek clarification if there is any confusion on the question of criticism.
- Keep signed and detailed notes of any informal discussions where performance is criticised.

- If asked to attend an informal or formal interview, seek advice immediately and be accompanied by a representative.
- Ensure there are full details available, including names and relevant dates of people involved.
- Do not withhold information from the representative.
- Do not make a statement without advice.

### Exceptional cases

Occasionally special consideration must be given in circumstances where using the standard disciplinary procedure may be too rigid or complying with it is too difficult. Three typical examples are:

- If the full disciplinary procedure is not immediately available for some reason, then special provisions are essential. Nightshift employees may not be able to consult a trade union representative; there may be no one in authority to take appropriate action; or there could be problems associated with remote working sites.
- There may be an apparent attack on a union's functions if a union official has committed an offence. This could lead to a serious dispute. Consequently, it may be more diplomatic to give an oral warning until the circumstances of the case have been discussed with a senior union official.
- A criminal offence outside employment may not be sufficient to dismiss an employee. Consideration should be given as to whether the offence makes the employee unsuitable for his or her type of employment, or whether he or she would become unacceptable to colleagues.

### EMPLOYMENT TRIBUNALS

Employment tribunals have already been explained in Chapter 17, and they were formerly known as industrial tribunals. They also feature generally in disputes. The Employment Rights (Dispute Resolution) Act 1998 introduced an arbitration scheme which serves as an alternative to the previous industrial tribunals. New provisions provide power to determine a case on written evidence alone, when both parties agree, or without a full hearing when it is undefended.

The Industrial Tribunals Act 1996 is superseded in some respects. Now tribunal chairmen may sit alone in some cases. This is a further encroachment on the three-person tribunal concept and reduces the importance of lay members. Professional advice on the system is essential for individual employees who wish to complain to the tribunals under employment laws passed since 1964.

## COURTS OF INQUIRY

Under Part II of the Industrial Courts Act 1919 the minister may appoint a court of inquiry to investigate the causes and circumstances of a trade dispute and submit a report. Such a dispute would naturally be of high importance where an impartial opinion is thought necessary in the public interest and when other methods of negotiation have broken down.

The court has the power to call witnesses who give evidence under oath, to ask for any relevant documents, and to sit in private or public as it so desires. Its findings or recommendations carry no legal weight. However, because of its impartiality, the decision is invariably either accepted outright or provides a firm foundation for further negotiation between the parties, which usually leads to an agreement. Any report (and any minority report) must be laid before both Houses of Parliament.

## INTERNAL APPEALS

Where an internal appeals procedure exists in a company, the Employment Rights (Dispute Resolution) Act 1998 has two provisions. They encourage employers to settle disputes in this way and to penalise whichever party fails to implement the procedure. The penalty or reduction must not exceed two weeks' pay. Two situations may occur:

### Employee refusal

An employee may choose not to accept an employer's appeal procedure against dismissal when given written notice and appropriate details of the procedure. In this case the employment tribunal must reduce the compensation award by a suitable amount.

### Employer refusal

An employer may have an appeals procedure but prevents an employee from using it. In this case the tribunal must provide a supplementary award.

# Individual rights of employees

- To take a complaint to an employment tribunal on a wide range of jurisdictions under the various employment laws passed since 1964.
- To receive a written statement of the terms and conditions of employment, provided they work at least 8 hours a week and within 2 months. Any changes should be in writing within 1 month.
- To receive a certain minimum period of notice after 4 weeks' continuous employment; the duration depends on length of service. The employee will usually be entitled to pay during notice. After 4 weeks' continuous employment, the employee is required to give a minimum of 1 week notice.
- To qualify as a person entitled to a full range of legal protection, provided continuity of employment of 16 hours a week or more can be shown, or if he or she has worked for the same employer for 8 or more hours a week (but less than 16) for 5 years or more.
- To receive itemised pay statements showing gross pay, net pay and the amounts and reasons for all variable and fixed deductions. As an alternative, fixed deductions may be shown as a total with the amounts and reasons supplied in a separate annual statement, which must be amended during the year if the occasion arises.
- To receive guarantee payments for a limited period during short-time working or lay-offs. The employer must make this payment only if a full day's work is lost, the limit being £9.50 a day and it is guaranteed for 5 days in any calendar quarter. Payment is excluded if there is no work due to action involving other employees of the same or an associated employer.
- To receive normal pay (up to a maximum of 26 weeks) during medical suspension covered by special health and safety regulations,

following examination by an employment medical adviser or an appointed doctor.

- To be a member of, or take part at an appropriate time in the activities of, an independent trade union. Dismissal for these reasons is automatically unfair.
- To refuse to join a non-independent trade union or to object to joining on religious grounds any trade union whatsoever. Dismissal for these reasons is automatically unfair.
- To choose a union of their choice and not be refused membership by the union unless there is no commonality of interest with the union's membership and on the grounds of conduct.
- To be allowed reasonable time off with pay during working hours to carry out trade union duties if the employee is an official of an independent trade union. Furthermore, this applies to receiving training in trade union duties provided it is concerned with industrial relations.
- To take reasonable time off without pay for the performance of certain public duties such as Justice of the Peace, member of a local authority, member of a statutory tribunal and member of certain health, education, water and river authorities.
- To take reasonable time off with pay while under notice of redundancy to seek new employment or to make arrangements for retraining. The entitlement is also based upon the employee having been continuously employed for the minimum qualifying period by his or her present employer.
- If a woman is expecting a baby, she has a right not to be dismissed because of her pregnancy or for a reason connected with her pregnancy. If her condition does not allow her to do her job adequately or her continued employment while pregnant is against the law, she must be offered a suitable alternative job if one is available.
- A woman is entitled to maternity leave, time off for antenatal care and statutory maternity pay. Dismissal during maternity leave is automatically unfair, regardless of length of service or hours of work and other benefits.
- To complain to the Certification Officer or industrial tribunal against unfair or unreasonable disciplinary action. This aspect is discussed

in detail in Chapter 17, together with rights regarding redundancy payments.

- To claim from the Department for Education and Employment any outstanding pay as a result of an employer becoming insolvent.
- To reject any attempt to deduct money from pay unless there is an agreement in writing.
- To refuse paying back any money from the pay packet to the employer; exceptions are statutory deductions and lawful payments to third parties.
- To be informed by all data users if they hold relevant records on the employee. To have right of access to them and to demand corrections or deletions if appropriate.
- To consent in writing for a check-off deduction of union subscriptions. Renewed consent is necessary every 3 years.

# Rights of trade union members

Various acts, particularly the Employment Acts 1988 and 1989, provide rights to members. The aim is to balance or check union power. The main rights are:

- to terminate union membership
- unrestricted participation in union activities
- unrestricted right to join a union
- not to be unjustifiably disciplined by a union in such cases as not supporting or taking part in a strike, or alleging that a union representative has behaved unlawfully
- to be balloted before industrial action
- to apply to the commissioner for the rights of trade union members for assistance to take legal action against a union
- to see the union's electoral roll and check its accuracy
- to inspect the union's accounts and be accompanied by an accountant
- not to be unreasonably expelled in a closed-shop situation
- for trade union officials to seek time off for union activities
- to take legal action against the union's trustees if suspected of using funds for unlawful purposes

# The supervisor and the union representative

Although the supervisor needs a sound knowledge of the procedures and regulations controlling industrial relations, the day-to-day contact with these problems will be through the shop steward or union representative. A sound and friendly relationship is essential to keep employee friction to a minimum. The problem of establishing and maintaining such a relationship is complex and demanding. The supervisor and shop steward or union representative not only have to consider the other's viewpoints but also to withstand pressure from employees and management in various ways. When a situation is aggravated by temperamental employees and outdated management, disputes are difficult to avoid, so the problem is now examined from a variety of viewpoints.

## THE EMPLOYEE

The employee is continually reminded through daily occurrences at work and a steady stream of publicised cases, of injustice and victimisation of various descriptions and intensity. Resisting the influence of this constant external pressure is difficult. Consequently, he or she feels insecure and sensitive to any suggestion of injustice and harshness.

Employees obviously feel the need to belong to an association that supports them and fights for their rights. Even those who are not members of any employees' association are mindful of the role it plays and would probably join very quickly if their continued non-membership meant disbanding the association.

Whether employees are misguided, have incorrect attitudes or wrong impressions is beside the point. They distrust management, strongly feel the need for protection and are prepared to stand by the association that supports them.

## THE SHOP STEWARD OR UNION REPRESENTATIVE

Most representatives are very conscious of their responsibilities to the union and its members. They are voluntary appointments and recognised as officials in negotiating procedures. Many are untrained in a role which is difficult to fulfil adequately without a true understanding of employee relations and all the associated activities. Both trade unions and educationists are aware of this situation and are actively engaged in improving training.

The representative's job is time-consuming; essential qualities are leadership, patience and the ability to sift fact from opinion. He or she has the power either to improve the atmosphere within an establishment with due co-operation from supervisors and management, or to destroy relationships, often with disastrous consequences for all concerned, including employees. Although representatives are appointed to represent the will of their colleagues and demonstrate union policy, they also have a social responsibility to act in an impartial and fair manner. In circumstances where they sincerely feel colleagues are unreasonably biased, they must have sufficient courage to disagree with demands and stand by their word.

## THE SUPERVISOR

Whether real or only apparent, any attempt by a representative to undermine the supervisor's authority will naturally provoke hostile reaction. Unfortunately, shop stewards often create this impression in performing their duties. Consequently, the supervisor feels he or she is losing prestige in the face of criticism and interference.

The soundness of the supervisor's position depends mainly on management's policy towards supervision and the degree of active participation in negotiations which is allowed at supervisory levels. If queries, complaints and grievances are to be settled quickly, the closest point to the trouble is on the shop floor or the office, which gives the supervisor a distinct advantage. The supervisor is more familiar with the situation than is management, therefore he or she should be able to tackle the problem with a minimum of disruption. This is provided all the adequate information and agreements are known.

## MANAGEMENT

General board policy determines management's attitude and relationships with representatives. This is largely governed by procedural agreements and awareness of the need to work together. Individual managers may find themselves working strictly to set terms which tend to cause unnecessary rigidity and narrowness of outlook. Obviously this is not conducive to friendly working relationships. Competent managers recognise the importance of supporting the supervisor and developing friendly relationships among the parties concerned. Active steps to encourage participation and achieving co-operation must come from senior management. Without this philosophy the efforts of supervisors and representatives will be wasted.

## WORKING TOGETHER

Good relationships between supervisor and representative depend on each party appreciating and recognising the other's position and the role each plays. The foundation of understanding and the good sense of both parties will provide the opportunity to improve employee relations.

The supervisor should appreciate the need to keep the representative fully informed of any problems, plans, grievances, complaints and possible changes. The representative should not be surprised by any action which would cause loss of prestige in front of colleagues. Similarly, the supervisor should look for an adequate return of information from the representative. This exchange of information is vital to improve communication and confidence. The information should include adequate explanations of changes and all the known facts whenever possible. Any reasonable person will respond to this straightforward approach and try to co-operate.

There is always the possibility of being faced with an antagonistic representative who is suffering from an emotional problem. Standing firm in these circumstances and being scrupulously fair is essential. Employees must see evidence of fairness and justice, which should be demonstrated at every opportunity.

The supervisor reserves the right to discuss any problems which employees put forward, but the representative should be present if a union agreement is the cause. Similarly, the supervisor should try to settle all problems at this level with the co-operation of the representative, who should ensure colleagues abide by the set procedure. Each case should be judged on its merits. All the facts and essential opinions must be considered to reach a solution that satisfies both parties.

Working together in this way produces mutual respect and a marked improvement in the workplace atmosphere.

## QUESTIONS

1 Discuss the function of the employee relations officer.

2 Why should the supervisor need a reasonable knowledge of employee relations?

3 What is meant by collective bargaining?

4 Explain the role played by employers' associations and the Confederation of British Industry.

5 Describe the growth and organisation of trade unions. Comment on the organisation and effectiveness of their activities.

6 Discuss the part played by the Trades Union Congress in employee relations.

7 What is meant by the terms 'conciliation' and 'arbitration'?

8 Explain the purpose and effectiveness of arbitration.

9 What is a court of inquiry?

10 Give your personal advice to a new supervisor in dealing with the shop steward.

11 Discuss the functions of shop stewards.

12 What are the main difficulties that the supervisor and shop steward have to face when trying to work together?

13 Outline the use of joint consultation in industry.

14 Discuss the changing role of the shop steward.

15 State the main tasks of the Certification Officer.

16 What is meant by industrial democracy?

17 Outline the general aims of the Employment Protection Act 1975.

18 Outline the rights of trade union members.

19 Discuss the systems view of a breakdown in employee relations.

20 Outline the main features of employee relations.

21 Outline the negotiating machinery available for employee disputes.

22 List the individual rights of employees.

23 Discuss the rights of trade union members.

---

**CASE STUDY**

Raymond had conducted a performance appraisal for John, who had joined him three months ago. When John first arrived his lateness record was good, but after six weeks he began to be late at least three times each week. Complaints were received from the staff and John had been warned three times but there was no change. His excuse was always the same, 'I overslept'.

Earlier Raymond had learned from another supervisor that John had a very bad lateness record in his previous job. Apparently the staff became antagonistic and this probably caused John to apply for a transfer.

Raymond was annoyed because the personnel department had not mentioned it at the time. At the appraisal interview John mentioned he was keen to progress and demanded time off to attend part-time day classes. Raymond flatly refused and said his lateness would have to stop before he would consider part-time studies.

Two weeks later the staff union representative spoke with Raymond. 'John thinks he is being victimised because you refuse to sanction time off for part-time study. I know about his lateness but he insists on making a case for it.'

*What action could Raymond have taken before the appraisal? Consider the conduct of the personnel department. How would you continue the conversation with the staff union representative?*

---

**CASE STUDY**

Andy, the supervisor of the sheet metal department, had been called by Robert, the personnel manager, to discuss the dispute over the bonus scheme. Robert outlined the problem, 'It seems Eric, the shop steward, is insisting that the system is unfair compared with the assembly department. Trouble is that when we introduced it last year it was made deliberately complex to cover the more lucrative scheme and make it more attractive for newcomers to join the assembly department when we were short of operators'.

George, the works manager, arrived and said, 'My budget is tight this year as you know and I haven't got spare cash available for an increased bonus. In any case what's it going to cost?'

'It's going to be at least £3000 a month.' George become agitated and replied, 'Can't afford it and that's that! This is a fine mess. You know we've been negotiating with Alenco Metals to take over some of Andy's metalwork at a cheaper rate. That's going to mean redundancies too'.

Robert turned to Andy, 'Well, what do you think? You know Eric well enough to guess what will happen now'.

*Consider the main features of this case and the likely attitude of Eric, the shop steward. Discuss the possible choices of negotiation tactics in this situation.*

---

Tom Johnson's promotion to supervisor is greeted calmly by Charlie, the shop steward who has worked with him on the shop floor for three years. They have got on well together. Charlie always gives Tom the latest information before the previous supervisor receives it from management. It is a standing joke and Tom always takes full advantage of his advance knowledge.

Now the tables are turned, he soon learns how irritating it is being the last to find out what is going on. Eventually he complains to his superior. To his amazement he is told that his promotion is mainly due to his strong relationship with Charlie. He is expected to keep up the good work and not to 'rock the boat'.

Unfortunately, Charlie has other ideas and does not confide in Tom any longer.

*What should Tom do now? Outline the communication and industrial relations problems that are likely to exist in this organisation.*

# 21
# Health and safety

## The background

Over five hundred people die and several hundred thousand suffer injury and illness each year through risks taken at work. The control of risks should be a high priority in companies, considering the distress and anxiety unnecessary accidents cause to employees and their families. There are also questions of the financial burden on the state, lost production, compensation and repair costs.

Lack of moral fibre, a casual approach and ineffective control are three of many accusations levelled at management. The essentials for improvement are:

- more research into occupational health and safety
- more enforcement and stronger legislation
- developing social responsibility in managers and owners
- creating a safety-conscious workforce

Boardroom policy on health, safety and welfare is an important feature. The moral and legal obligations are illustrated in Fig. 21.1. This emphasises expectations and outcomes when this feature is taken seriously by senior management.

## Work-related illness

Health-at-work research shows that 30–40 per cent of all sickness is caused by a mental or emotional disturbance. The remaining percentage accounts for a wide range of health risks which are capable of causing a variety of illnesses.

Some examples given by the Health and Safety Executive are handling heavy or awkward loads, poor work postures, repetitive or forceful movements; breathing in and handling hazardous substances; high noise levels; vibration from hand-held tools; exposure to radiation and biological agents; and various stressors, including excessive workload or work pace, and conflicting priorities. Stress-related sickness is now considered to be an important factor in work-related illness.

## Reducing health risks

Preventing health risks leading to illnesses is possible by identifying and controlling risks *before* they cause problems and situations. Anticipating health difficulties when organisational changes occur is essential. A typical procedure to manage work-related illness follows the usual pattern of problem solving and decision making (Chapter 8) oriented to health risks:

1 Establish the health standards according to legislation.
2 Examine the workplace and equipment to find the hazards. Pay careful attention to employees at work and to the use of their tools. Discuss the work with employees to seek opinions.
3 Compare findings with sickness absence records and seek advice or data sheets from suppliers. Often health hazards are not immediately obvious.
4 Make decisions based upon four main aspects: the risk assessments, the precautions needed to

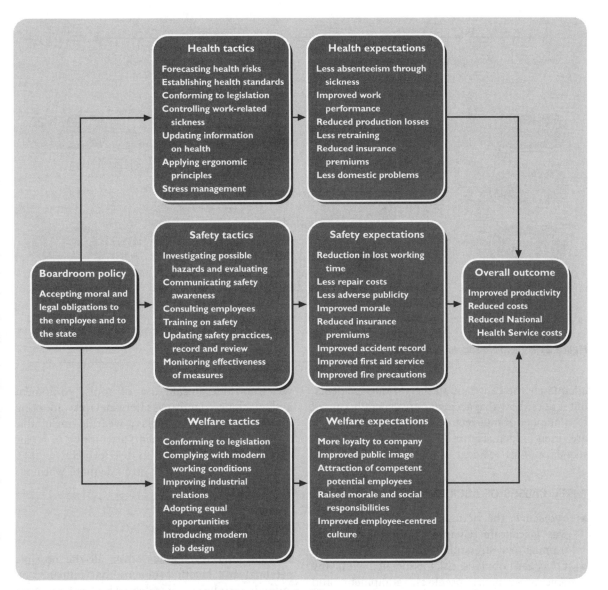

**Figure 21.1** Moral and legal paths to achieving improved productivity

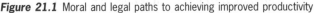

conform with standards, the steps identified to correct the causes, and the priorities by using sickness records.

5 Take action to remove the causes, bearing in mind that often problems are known but taking action is delayed for various reasons.

6 Monitor the results by checking records and following up to ensure control measures are maintained.

## Safety at work

Although research into safety at work has been extensive, the resulting evidence is conflicting and incomplete. Certainly studies suggest that personality, emotional problems, age and poor group relations contribute to high accident rates. Furthermore, research indicates that theories do not explain

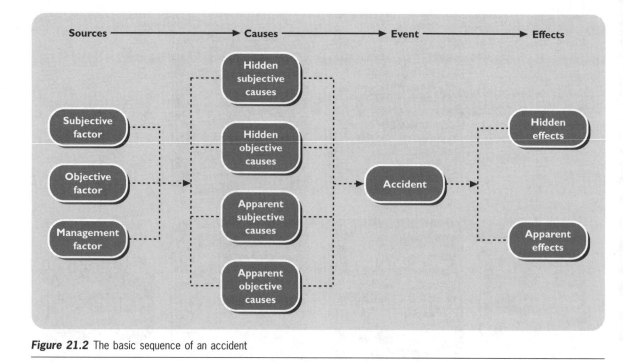

**Figure 21.2** The basic sequence of an accident

adequately the causes of all the various accidents, but it does show that accidents are generally caused by a number of interrelated factors, some of which are often hidden. Figure 21.2 illustrates the basic sequence of an accident.

## THREE CAUSES OF ACCIDENTS

- *Subjective*: the victim's perception of the risk was inaccurate (Chapter 9) through lack of training or a stressful condition.
- *Objective*: obvious risks associated with any objects such as premises, equipment and machines, etc.
- *Management*: failure to communicate the risks of accidents to employees, failure to take adequate precautions, and failure to control stress.

## FOUR TYPES OF CAUSE

### Apparent subjective causes

Apparent subjective causes may be any unsafe action or an omission by an employee to take reasonable care. There are many occurrences

which include unsafe use of tools, equipment and machines; ignoring safety devices; adopting unsafe positions; horseplay; wearing unsuitable clothing; abusing equipment; attempting to repair equipment; and failing to use protective gear, secure loads properly, or give adequate warnings of danger.

### Hidden subjective causes

Hidden subjective causes cover all the possible personal and health problems that influence an individual to behave unsafely. They include stress of various types, domestic difficulties, misunderstandings, taking short cuts, physical and mental disorders, avoiding discomfort, and failing to follow regulations.

### Apparent objective causes

Apparent objective causes are usually due to poor quality plant and machinery, or poor working conditions such as insufficient maintenance of machines, inadequate warning systems, hazards of many kinds, and dangerous equipment.

### Hidden objective causes

Hidden objective causes are usually due to inept management, poor local control, poor design of safety devices, unusual wear not covered by maintenance of plant, and poor preventive maintenance. Managers and supervisors may fail to communicate safety precautions, conduct inadequate training programmes, and fail to adopt or maintain adequate safety regulations.

# The effects of accidents

## APPARENT EFFECTS

Apparent effects are the obvious direct results of an accident. They include minor and major injuries, damage to equipment and machines, and *claim payments* made through insurers.

### Hidden effects

The indirect consequences may be considerable for the victim, such as reduced earnings, domestic upsets, disrupted personal life, and prolonged suffering from the injury. The company may suffer in many ways since the overall irrecoverable costs are generally overlooked. An outline of the costs that may be incurred illustrates the severity of any accident:

- lost time of injured employee
- lost time by managers and supervisors who help the injured person, arrange for the job to be covered, investigate the cause, prepare accident reports, and so on
- lost time by other employees whose work may be delayed through assistance, curiosity, sympathy, interruption of supplies, or damaged machinery or equipment
- labour and materials to repair any damage, including making the arrangements
- immediate first aid and travel expenses to hospital
- adverse publicity in local and national newspapers
- effect on morale
- welfare and benefit schemes
- loss of productivity

- increased insurance premiums if there is a poor accident record

## ACCIDENT THEORIES

Attempts to classify so-called *accident activators* have produced many theories. Positive correlations with accident rates exist in three main features:

- *Age*: young workers through inexperience and irresponsibility, and older workers through a reduction in physical and mental capabilities.
- *Health and physical characteristics*: related to a particular job.
- *Inexperience*: during the first five months in a job.

Complex theories include accident-proneness, maladjustment to stress, lack of job involvement, trying to avoid work, industrial conflict, anxiety, pure chance, biased liability, and an unconscious self-destructive tendency.

# Safety management

According to the British Safety Council, accidents are caused and/or allowed to happen. Indeed most accidents need not be inevitable; with efficient safety management they could be avoided. Their survey showed that all other accidents can be controlled by measuring and controlling *near hits*. Management at all levels should record accidents of a serious and minor nature, damage and *near misses*, and act upon the resulting information.

It seems accidents are the predictable result of minor incidents that lead to minor injuries and fatal accidents. This situation is often known, but many accept accidents as inevitable and treat the accident rate as almost unavoidable.

The Health and Safety Commission states that people working in manufacturing companies employing less than a hundred people run a higher risk of a serious accident. Apparently the reasons are that small firms tend to lack experience, expertise or access to health and safety information and networks. In an attempt to overcome this difficulty, the commission has produced the booklet *Essentials of Health and Safety at Work*.

- Stress-related sickness
- Safety legislation which attempts to protect the employee
- Calculations of injury rates for control purposes
- The supervisor's role
- Ergonomics
- The implications of environmental protection

# Stress-related sickness

The urgent need to reduce stress-related sickness is still slowly being recognised as various specialist institutions have revealed serious statistics. An estimated 180 000 cases are reported annually of stress or depression caused by work pressures. About 80 million working days are lost annually through stress, and about 3 per cent of employees are admitted as psychiatric outpatients through high stress levels. According to the Confederation of British Industry, the annual cost of mental health problems at work is about £3.7 billion.

Chapter 9 discussed the definitions, levels and symptoms of stress; Chapter 10 examined how to reduce stress. An overview of stress was shown in Fig. 10.3. In this chapter stress-related sickness is summarised from information provided by the medical profession and health and safety organisations. These organisations have concentrated on four levels: the employee, the supervisors, managers and senior management. Each sector is now discussed.

## EMPLOYEES

Research has shown a surprising number of major stress ailments, such as coronary disease, peptic ulcers and hypertension, are more common at the *base* of the organisation. The general impression is the opposite. Even minor discomfort and pain mar performance. The basic problem is often associated with bad habits: sitting or standing for long periods, too little or too much exercise, and taking an excess of mild drugs or stimulants (cigarettes, coffee, aspirins).

The need to keep physically fit and healthy is often neglected. Usually employers overlook the need to emphasise this point to employees and do not take positive action to help solve the problem. Rapid cures are possible for many of the minor ailments, but many people suffer from inertia and need a strong mental push before they will take remedial steps.

## SUPERVISORS

Supervisory performance is also impaired through minor discomfort and pain caused by stress. The basic problems apply and supervisors should recognise the need to take remedial action. Stressful situations are occurring all the time for supervisors. Some examples are meeting employees, peers and managers face to face; attending meetings; telephone calls; dealing with crises; and coping with situational problems concerning people.

### Coping with mental stress

There are many viewpoints on stress which should be of personal interest to the supervisor. A study of the subject is worthwhile and sometimes essential for those who aspire to managerial positions and who feel they are suffering unduly. The main contributors who could be of help are J. Deese, W.T. Singleton, H.W. Magoun, N.H. Mackworth, J. Parrot, A. Fassina, M. Carruthers and J.V. Brady.

## MANAGERS

A classic research project still influences management thinking today. Friedman and Rosenman studied managers in 1959 and found that they tended to fall into one of two personality types: type A and type B. Type A managers suffered over six times more heart attacks than type B managers.

- *Type A* showed a high degree of competitiveness, quick thought and action, and were conscious of time and deadlines. Typical descriptions would be thrusters, extremely competitive, aggressive, hasty, restless, impatient, hyperalert, tense, and feels under pressure.
- *Type B* is the reverse of type A. Typical descriptions would be free of habits, no type A characteristics, no time urgency, no free-floating hostility, does not flaunt accomplishments, plays it for fun, and relaxes without guilt.

## Recognising type A managers

- Explosively accentuates various key words in speech.
- Brings discussions around to topics he or she likes.
- Is always urging people and asking if they have finished a task.
- Does everything in a hurry.
- Tries to do several things at once.
- Thinks about other subjects when people are talking.
- Feels guilty when relaxing and doing nothing for a while.
- Suffers from a chronic sense of time urgency.
- Tries to do things faster than other people.
- Suffers from obsessions.

## Recognising type B managers

- Listens to others patiently without interrupting them.
- Concentrates on one task at a time.
- Creates a placid atmosphere.
- Possesses an unhurried approach.
- Has the knack of taking the heat out of situations.
- Relaxes when the opportunity occurs.
- Reads books that require concentration.
- Enjoys food and takes time over meals.
- Has absorbing hobbies.
- Lives by the calendar, not for the day.

## General recommendations

There seems to be a tendency for managers and supervisors to take on type A characteristics. For those who wish to avoid this trend, a variety of sources offer advice. Some suggestions are simply good sense and come naturally to most people if they *stop and think*. The descriptions and ways of recognising the two types should provide ample reference for seeing these characteristics developing in oneself or others.

There are broad headings of advice for overcoming the negative aspects of type A behaviour. They include techniques to still the mind; adjusting attitude and behaviour; avoiding excessive smoking, alcohol and food consumption; exercising; avoiding stressful personal relationships; learning how to relax; solving domestic and marital problems.

## SENIOR MANAGEMENT

Many stressful situations causing stress-related sickness are created by inept senior management. Insufficient management training, poor personnel policy, insensitiveness and poor organisational design are probably the bases for many stressful conditions. All these aspects may be remedied by senior management.

Extensive reviews are required for situational problems; selection; appraisals and rewards; training and development at all levels; organisational development; rehabilitation; and the application of relaxation techniques. These reviews are costly but must be weighed against the total expense of stress-related sickness, which in itself demands the expense of keeping appropriate records and possible legal fees.

## The legal aspect

An employee may claim for negligence in certain circumstances where stress has caused illness. However, the employee cannot simply claim the job is too much for him or her and seek redress. The employee (the plaintiff) must prove the employer could reasonably have foreseen that the system of work would lead to a material risk of damage to the employee's health; and they must prove a direct connection between stress at work and the illness suffered.

The employer is under a duty of care and should provide a safe system of work that will not cause psychiatric damage through volume or character of the employee's workload. Therefore there is a danger that a stress-related illness might cost more than direct absence expenses if the plaintiff proves negligence and damages are awarded.

## Managerial strategy

Recent research has indicated four major stress areas that can damage people's health:

- excessive workloads
- consistent long working hours

- a bullying boss
- sexual harassment

To overcome the general trend, senior management should adopt a firm strategy by establishing stress audits, a stress control programme, and a stress counselling service.

# Safety legislation

In addition to the social obligations of health and safety, there are three main sources of law which protect the employee:

- *Common law* is unwritten, established by custom and supported by precedents (created by judges); it is known as case law.
- *Statute law* consists of parliamentary acts; it overrides common law in the event of conflict.
- *EC directives* are issued by the European Commission (EC) within the European Union, under Article 118A of the Treaty of Rome; the articles and regulations are binding and directly enforceable in UK tribunals and courts; they take precedence over UK domestic law.

## WORK SAFETY HOTLINE

The work safety hotline eliminates long, technical research to find appropriate information on a subject from an expanding mass of regulations. Offered to British Safety Council members, the computerised system provides an answer to an enquiry within the hour.

## COMMON LAW

Under common law there is a liability for safety of employees. Employers may be sued for damages if they do not provide safe and reasonable systems of work. If employers ignore this obligation to take reasonable care and avoid unnecessary risks, a civil wrong or tort of negligence is committed. The injured person may sue for damages, and in serious cases the state may consider the offence a crime and prosecute.

Another legal aspect of safety arises when an employee commits a civil wrong or tort during the course of his or her employment, such as injuring another person. This means that if an employee carries out an improper action while working which causes injury to a colleague, although he or she may have been expressly forbidden to do so, the employer is liable for the civil wrong and damages provided the employee was told *what* to do and *how* to do it. This is known as *vicarious liability*. If a person is told what to do but has complete freedom as to how the work is done, the relationship changes to one of employer and independent contractor, in which case the employer is not liable.

## STATUTE LAW

Health and safety law is complicated and drafted in complex legal language. Professional advice is essential. Courts are considered competent to interpret and apply the acts, within which certain words and phrases raise difficulties as to their exact meaning and implication.

Some acts often mentioned are Alkali Works Regulations Act 1906, Agriculture (Poisonous Substances) Act 1952, Agriculture (Safety, Health and Welfare Provisions) Act 1956, Explosive Acts 1875 and 1923, Petroleum (Consolidation) Act 1928, Radioactive Substances Act 1960, Mineral Workings (Offshore Installations) Act 1971, Mines and Quarries Act 1954, Nuclear Installations Acts 1965 and 1969, Railway Employment (Prevention of Accidents) Act 1900, Road Traffic Acts and Transport Act 1968, Shops Act 1950, and the Health and Safety (Young Persons) Act 1997.

## ACTS REQUIRING SPECIAL ATTENTION ARE

### Factories Act 1961

The Factories Act 1961 contains a number of provisions which include precautions concerning machines, fire risks, lifts, cranes, boilers, floors, tanks, masks and goggles, removal of offensive fumes and dust, some health and welfare requirements, and regulations in dangerous trades. Accidents which result in death or affect pay for more than three days, and specify fires or explosions as the cause, must be notified to the factory inspector. A general register is required to record accidents and other aspects of safety. Figure 21.3 shows a

## ACCIDENT REPORT

Name .....................................................     Date .........................................................................

Staff/works ...........................................     Time .........................................................................

Clock number .......................................     Place ........................................................................

Department ...........................................     Supervisor ...............................................................

Section .................................................

Description of injury ...........................................................................................................

Cause of accident ...............................................................................................................

Treatment ............................................................................................................................

Hospital ................................................     Rehabilitation course ...........................................

Doctor ...................................................     Date ........................................................................

Date ......................................................     Results.....................................................................

Action to avoid recurrence ................................................................................................

Directive issued ..................................................................................................................

Date ....................................................................................................................................

Circulation ..........................................................................................................................

Authority .............................................................................................................................

Remuneration ......................................................................................................................

Absence: From ........................................   Time ..........................................   Date ...............................

To ............................................   Time ..........................................   Date ...............................

Reductions ...........................................................................................................................

Compensation ......................................................................................................................

Records ...............................................................................................................................

Entry general register .........................................................................................................

Factory inspector notified ..................................................................................................

Employee's record card ......................................................................................................

Circulation: Pay supervisor ................................................................................................

Safety officer ...............................................................................................

Works manager ..........................................................................................

Personnel manager .....................................................................................

Date .......................................................   Signature of supervisor ..........................................

**Figure 21.3** Accident reports: this form should satisfy regulations

typical accident report for internal use which would provide sufficient detail for the register and for control purposes. Factories, construction and demolition sites, civil engineering sites, docks, shipyards and electrical stations are covered by the act.

## Offices, Shops and Railway Premises Act 1963

The Offices, Shops and Railway Premises Act 1963 applies to rooms in which people work and to other parts of the premises, such as stairs, passages, landings, storerooms, entrances, exits and yards. Although the coverage is extensive, there are some kinds of premises which are excluded. All employees, whatever their occupation, are protected. Usually the occupier is responsible for complying with the act. Inspectors have powers to enforce the act and there are penalties for non-compliance.

### General requirements
Detailed provisions cover cleanliness, overcrowding, temperature, ventilation, lighting, sanitary conveniences, washing facilities, drinking water, accommodation for clothing, seating arrangements, seats for sedentary workers, eating facilities, floors, passages and stairs, fencing off exposed parts of machinery, cleaning of machinery, training and supervision of people working at dangerous machines, prohibition of heavy work, first aid and general fire precautions.

### Duties of employers and occupiers
The enforcing authority must be notified immediately of any accident that causes the death of a person employed to work in the premises or disables any such person for more than three days from doing his or her usual work. Premises must be registered by completing the prescribed form.

### Duties of employees
It is an offence to do wilfully and without reasonable cause anything likely to endanger the health or safety of people employed on the premises. It is also an offence to misuse wilfully or interfere with or, without reasonable excuse, remove any equipment, appliance, facilities or other things that have been provided to meet the requirements of the act or regulations.

## Health and Safety at Work, etc., Act 1974

The Health and Safety at Work, etc., Act 1974 is an enabling act because it is broad and generalised in nature rather than giving considerable detail. Powers are given to the Secretary of State for Education and Employment to introduce EC regulations and codes of practice on specific health and safety matters. The Secretary of State, in turn, acts through the Health and Safety Commission.

In other words, the act is a broad framework from which future legislation will be introduced to make up a comprehensive body of legislation (including existing acts) on health and safety. The main approaches are:

- to overhaul completely and modernise the existing laws covering health, safety and welfare at work
- to create a Health and Safety Commission
- to provide a range of new general duties for employers
- to reorganise and unify the various government inspectorates
- to impose new powers and penalties for the enforcement of safety laws
- to establish new methods of accident prevention and new ways of operating future safety regulations
- to adopt and implement EC directives on health and safety
- to establish codes of practice instead of regulations whenever possible

### Codes of practice
Codes of practice may be formulated by people in industry with practical knowledge, they may be written in non-legal language which should be more easily understood, and they are easily revised to keep up with changing technology. The codes are not statutory requirements but they may be used as evidence in courts of law. Anyone charged with a contravention of a statutory provision will have to prove the practices used were better than or at least as good as the relevant approved code. Contrary to traditional legal practice, the person will be guilty until proved innocent.

### General duties of the act

Within the provisions of the act there are a number of general duties mentioned which apply to employers, employees and people other than employees. These duties are extensive; all of them should be read carefully. They include duties relating to premises, harmful emissions into the atmosphere, and articles and substances used at work.

### Enforcement of the act

Two bodies were established: the Health and Safety Commission and the Health and Safety Executive. The commission is responsible to the Secretary of State. It makes agreements with government departments, or others, to perform functions on their behalf, and maintains the Employment Medical Advisory Service. Also it has some responsibility for the control of *process* risks associated with fire precautions.

The commission's operations are applied through the Health and Safety Executive, which appoints inspectors who have certain powers. These powers include the right to enter premises at reasonable times, to investigate as they think fit, and to issue improvement notices, prohibition notices and apply penalties.

### Control of Substances Hazardous to Health (COSHH) Regulations

The COSHH Regulations are wide-ranging and include regulations and approved codes of practice (ACOPs). They explain to all employees their responsibilities and guide employers on how to implement a training strategy. The regulations apply to substances brought in and anything hazardous to health which is processed, manufactured or produced at work. In brief, a company should comply with the following guidelines:

- Appoint and train a COSHH nominee who will be responsible for complying with all the requirements.
- Publish a written policy, giving objectives, responsibilities, and systems to identify and control health risks.
- Identify and assess hazardous substances.
- Establish and maintain a register of all hazardous substances.

- Notify the COSHH nominee of any new purchases likely to be hazardous.
- Adequately control the storage and use of hazardous substances.
- Issue appropriate protective clothing.
- Inform personnel of all the health risks.
- Implement any recommended medical surveillance and closely monitor the results.

### The Environmental Protection Act 1990

The Environmental Protection Act 1990 refers to any activities which are either prejudicial to health or a nuisance, such as smoke, dust and smells. In this case the environmental health officer has similar powers to those under the Noise and Statutory Nuisance Act 1993. The COSHH Regulations and the Environmental Protection Act are of particular relevance to respiratory problems and sick building syndrome.

#### Respiratory problems

Work-related asthma is caused by exposure to respiratory sensitisers, substances which may trigger irreversible reaction in the respiratory system. According to the TUC and the National Asthma Campaign, about 400 000 suffer asthma as a direct result of their work. They claim this is the fastest-growing occupational disease and it causes over one million working days lost in a year.

#### Sick building syndrome

The World Health Organisation (WHO) defines sick building syndrome (SBS) as non-specific symptoms of malaise – particularly irritation of the eyes, nose and throat, lethargy, headaches, nausea and dizziness – which people experience in a building but which improve or cease on leaving that building. The Health and Safety Executive published a research review stating that the causes of SBS are not clearly established despite extensive research. Even the best modern buildings are not immune.

The main risk factors are possibly problems associated with ventilation, airborne chemical pollution, micro-organisms found in airborne dust, high temperatures when combined with low humidity or other factors, poor lighting, and many personal and organisational circumstances such as routine tasks. Apparently any source of stress or general dissatisfaction, while unlikely to be a primary cause, could lead to the reporting of SBS. The research review emphasises that evidence for the risk factors being causal agents is limited and points to the importance of looking at what may be behind them.

### Noise and Statutory Nuisance Act 1993

The Noise and Statutory Nuisance Act 1993 provides the local authority environmental health officer with the power to serve abatement notices. The person responsible for a statutory nuisance can be required to abate, prohibit or restrict its occurrence or recurrence. Failure to comply is a criminal offence.

**Noise levels**

Excessive noise is a major health hazard. Regular exposure for eight hours to noise of over 85 decibels accelerates normal age-related hearing loss and may cause tinnitus, a continuous ringing in the ear. The degree of risk depends on noise levels and length of time of exposure. Employers have a statutory duty to reduce noise levels as far as is practicable. The factory inspectorate's code of practice states a limit of 90 decibels. Where machines exceed this level they should be masked, prominent warning notices should be displayed, entrance to such areas controlled, and ear defenders must be worn.

**Ways to reduce noise**

- Use inexpensive instruments to measure noise and take appropriate action.
- Use noise defenders such as earplugs, ear valves and earmuffs.
- Mask machines, saws, generators, compressors, etc.
- Seek advice from employees by asking if the work is affecting their hearing, typically by having to shout to be understood by someone two metres away.
- Examine data supplied with machinery as manufacturers must provide information if there is high noise emission.
- Trade union representatives can seek guidance from the TUC.

**Ways to reduce exposure time**

- Rearrange part of the work to a quiet place.
- Use job rotation.
- Use quiet restrooms.

### Health and Safety (First Aid) Regulations 1981

The Health and Safety (First Aid) Regulations 1981 state that employers must determine the requirements for first aid. A first aid box should be provided in an appropriate place. If there is an appointed first aider, he or she must have passed an approved course and be retested every three years. If no first aider is appointed, a person should be given the function and their responsibilities should include taking control in the event of an accident, calling an ambulance if required, and monitoring a first aid box.

### Fire Precautions Act 1971

The Fire Precautions Act 1971 includes specific and detailed requirements. Various regulations under the Fire Precautions (Places of Work) Regulations 1994 and EC directives also apply. The initial act demands an inspection and issue of a fire certificate in most workplaces. These are arranged through the local fire authority.

### Trade Union Reform and Employment Rights Act 1993

The Trade Union Reform and Employment Rights Act 1993 includes provisions which protect employees against victimisation by their employer for taking specified types of action on health and safety grounds. It implements the EC Health and Safety Framework Directive. All employees, regardless of length of service, hours of work or age, may claim to an employment tribunal if they are dismissed, selected for redundancy or subjected to any other detriment because they:

- carry out or propose to carry out any activities which they are designated by their employer to carry out in connection with preventing or reducing risks to health and safety at work

- perform or propose to perform any functions they have as official or employer-acknowledged health and safety representatives or committee members
- bring to their employer's attention, by reasonable means and in the absence of a representative or committee with whom it would be reasonably practicable for them to raise the matter, a concern about circumstances at work which they reasonably believe are harmful to health and safety
- in the event of danger which they reasonably believe to be serious and imminent and which they could not reasonably be expected to avert, leave or propose to leave the workplace or any dangerous part of it, or (while the danger persists) refuse to return
- in circumstances of danger which they reasonably believe to be serious and imminent, take or propose to take appropriate steps to protect themselves or other persons from the danger

## EC DIRECTIVES

The European Commission (EC) adopts directives on minimum health and safety requirements. Each directive is implemented by separate regulations under Section 15 of the Health and Safety at Work Act. Information is available from the Health and Safety Executive. Member states are given deadlines to integrate requirements into their domestic laws. Failure to integrate is no excuse since an employee is able to rely directly upon a directive.

### The EC Framework Directive on Health and Safety

The EC Framework Directive on Health and Safety extends existing health and safety arrangements in the UK by applying management principles to workplace health and safety, which include managing risks and reducing risks to acceptable levels.

### The new regulations

- They are not qualified; this means they must be strictly complied with; *not* considering cost and other factors which may be reasonable or practicable to apply.

- They may give rise to a civil action for breach of statutory duty if the provisions are not complied with and someone is harmed as a result of the negligence.
- A risk assessment must be conducted of all work hazards.
- Risks must be reduced by applying adequate control.
- Risks must be assessed bearing in mind anyone else affected by work activities.
- Hazards and risk information must be shared with other employers, which includes those in adjoining premises, other site occupiers, and sub-contractors entering the premises.

### Further EC directives on health and safety

There are five other directives coupled with the framework directive. They cover health and safety requirements for the workplace, the use of work equipment, personal protective equipment, manual handling of loads, and display screen equipment. Each one is now outlined.

### Workplace (Health, Safety and Welfare) Regulations

The Workplace (Health, Safety and Welfare) Regulations cover many existing statutory requirements in the UK, including the Factories Act and the Offices, Shops and Railway Premises Act. Various UK acts will be eventually repealed or revoked. The range of workplaces has been increased, the regulations are clearer, and the aim is to promote good housekeeping in the workplace.

**The requirements**
Some of the specific duties are not mentioned in current UK legislation, although they are implied in the general duties of the Health and Safety at Work Act. The requirements include the following topics:

- *Housekeeping*: maintenance of the workplace, equipment and facilities, cleanliness and drainage.
- *Working environment*: ventilation, temperature, lighting, room dimensions and space, workstations and outdoor workstations, and restrooms.

- *Facilities*: seating, rest areas, clothing storage, rest facilities for pregnant women and nursing mothers, toilets, washing, eating and changing facilities.
- *Safety*: falling objects, floors, glazed doors, gates, escalators, falls from heights, passages, windows and skylights.

## Provision and Use of Work Equipment Regulations

The Provision and Use of Work Equipment Regulations place general duties on employers and state the minimum requirements to deal with selected hazards for industry. Work equipment includes everything from hand tools through to machines of all types, and up to a complete plant. The term 'use' covers everything, such as starting, stopping, installing, dismantling, programming, setting, transporting, maintaining, servicing and cleaning.

### General duties

- Consider the working conditions and hazards in the workplace when selecting equipment.
- Ensure equipment is properly maintained and suitable for the intended use.
- Provide employees with adequate information, instruction and training on the equipment.

### Specific requirements to protect workers

- Control systems and control devices
- Danger caused by equipment failure
- Guarding of dangerous parts of machinery
- Isolation of equipment from power supplies
- Lighting
- Maintenance operations
- High and very low temperatures of parts and materials
- Stability of equipment
- Warnings and markings

## Manual Handling Operations Regulations

The Manual Handling Operations Regulations include any manual handling operations that may cause injury. The main regulations are:

- a risk assessment of all manual handling operations
- if possible avoiding hazardous manual handling operations

- if there is a risk, this must be reduced to the lowest possible level
- employees must be trained to make full and proper use of equipment and inform the employer of any injury or condition which may affect performance of their duties

## Personal Protective Equipment at Work (PPE) Regulations

Suitable personal protective equipment must be provided for all employees who may be exposed to risk. Risk includes radiation, hazardous substances, falling objects, and foul weather. PPE includes most types of protective clothing and equipment, but should only be relied upon as a last resort.

### Main regulations

- An assessment of risks involved in a task.
- Provide and maintain or replace PPE free of charge.
- Provide information, instruction and training in the use of PPE.

## Health and Safety (Display Screen Equipment) Regulations

The Health and Safety (Display Screen Equipment) Regulations set out minimum health and safety requirements for using the majority of display screen equipment. They do not replace old legislation but cover a new area of work activity for the first time. Display screen equipment (DSE) includes conventional screens and other display processes such as LCD or microfiche, process control screens, CAD screens, and computer-generated graphics. A 'user' is an employee who habitually uses DSE as a significant part of normal work, but there are no set rules since duration and pace of continuous use should be considered.

### Main risks

- *Physical musculoskeletal problems*: they include upper limb disorders (ULDs) and repetitive strain injury (RSI).
- *Visual fatigue*: possibly sore eyes, headache and impaired vision, and in some cases permanent eye damage.

- *Stress*: generally caused by the working environment or poorly designed tasks.

## Workstations

Employers must analyse DSE workstations to assess risks and reduce them to a reasonable level. Assessments should be systematic, appropriate to the possible degree of risk, and comprehensive. Records should be kept and checklists used during assessments. When problems are identified all reasonable practical measures should be applied to minimise the risks, such as:

- adjusting or relocating equipment
- providing footrests, anti-glare screens, etc.
- replacing equipment
- training
- redesigning tasks
- screen cleaning

## Minimum specific requirements

- display screens with a stable image, adjustable brightness and contrast, swivelling and tiltable screen free of reflective glare
- tiltable keyboards (separated from screen) with a matt surface, clear key symbols, and adequate space to facilitate use
- work desks with a low reflective surface, adequate space for comfort and working conditions
- document holders, adjustable or rigid, that minimise awkward head and eye movements
- work chairs, comfortable and stable, that allow for ease of movement, can be adjusted for height and tilt, and include a footrest if needed
- working environment with satisfactory conditions for surrounding space, lighting, noise reduction, humidity, ventilation, low reflective surfaces from surrounds, and a negligible level of radiation

## Task design and software

To reduce the risk of stress, task design should give users the opportunity to exercise discretion, provide feedback, and participate in task planning and design. Software should be appropriate to the task, be adaptable and simple to use, provide assistance to the user and feedback, allow for variable input rates, and avoid in-built quantitative monitoring.

## Daily routine

Short, frequent work breaks are recommended and rest periods should be taken away from screens if possible.

## Visual aspects

Users have the right to an eye and eyesight test, before and during work at regular intervals. Employers should provide free basic spectacle or contact lenses to correct vision, and free tests.

## Provision of information

Employers should provide the following information to employees and others working under their control. All the regulations are supported by detailed guidance from the Health and Safety Executive.

- entitlement to eye and eyesight tests
- provision of basic spectacles
- measures used to protect users or reduce risks
- provisions for work breaks and any changes in activity
- entitlement to health and safety training
- entitlement to training if there is a substantial change in the workstation, or if the user has been absent or engaged in other work for a long period

# Injury rates

Statistical analysis of the immediate cause of injury in a company can indicate the avenues to follow for accident prevention. For example, one industry analysis may show that only one injury in every hundred arises from accidents involving hand- or power-driven machinery, but forty out of every hundred injuries arise from handling materials, and so on. For control purposes, the following four formulae are often used to indicate trends in accidents and to form a standard basis for comparison in industry.

## FREQUENCY RATE

The frequency rate is given by:

$$\frac{\text{Number of lost time accidents} \times 100\,000}{\text{Total man hours lost}}$$
$$= \text{Frequency rate}$$

The term 'lost time accident' refers to one that stops the employee from working at his or her normal job beyond the day or shift during which the accident occurred. A reduction in the frequency rate indicates less frequency of accidents. A satisfactory figure should be lower than 1.

The calculation uses the number 100 000 as this is thought to be about the number of hours worked by an employee during their working life.

## DURATION RATE

The duration rate is given by:

$$\frac{\text{Total man hours lost}}{\text{Total number of lost time accidents}} = \text{Duration rate}$$

The term 'duration rate' is the average number of hours spent away from the job by an injured person. To avoid distortion, fatalities are not included in the calculation.

## INCIDENCE RATE

The incidence rate is given by:

$$\frac{\text{Number of reportable accidents} \times 100\,000}{\text{Number of persons at risk}}$$

$$= \text{Incidence rate}$$

## SEVERITY RATE

The severity rate is given by:

$$\frac{\text{Number of man hours lost} \times 100\,000}{\text{Number of man hours worked}}$$

$$= \text{Severity rate}$$

## ACCIDENT REPORTS

Accidents must be notified to the relevant enforcement authority. Under the Notification of Accidents and Dangerous Occurrences Regulations 1980 (NADO) any fatality, major injury or any prescribed dangerous occurrence should be reported immediately on the telephone and confirmed in writing within seven working days. Furthermore, all accidents resulting in incapacity for more than three days should be recorded and forms completed for industrial disablement or sickness payment if the Department of Social Security so desires. Also, the absence should be reported to the Factory Inspector. The injury is then termed 'reportable'.

## RIDDOR

In 1995 updated regulations were introduced. The Reporting of Injuries, Diseases and Dangerous Occurrences Regulations (RIDDOR) unified all previous reporting procedures for injuries. Employees are obliged to report *all* injuries due to acts of violence and any other incidence of certain diseases which are listed in RIDDOR. The regulations should be consulted since the revised list of accidents is extensive.

# The supervisor's role

Although management may ensure that all possible electrical and mechanical precautions are taken, the personal aspect of safety precautions rests with the supervisor. Employees should be convinced that safety is mainly a question of attitude and that safety awareness must be constantly kept in mind during working hours. Occasionally a serious accident occurs that could have been avoided. For peace of mind alone, supervisors cannot afford to ignore their role in these circumstances. The main aspects of the supervisor's role in promoting safety are now outlined.

## ASSESSING RISKS

A careful examination of all likely hazards and the existing precautions is essential to reduce the risk of accidents and injury to health. The categories to consider are physical, psychological, chemical, biological, ergonomics and housekeeping. Note that a hazard is anything with a potential to cause harm and includes a machine, a substance and method of work. The main hazards are:

- *Physical*: noise, light, heat, radiation, vibration, pressure, mechanical, electrical, fire, explosive and transport.
- *Psychological*: fatigue, general stress, volume or rate of work, individual responsibility, job situation, and level of intelligence.

- *Chemical*: single or repeated exposure.
- *Biological*: HIV, hepatitis B, leptospirosis, Legionnaires' disease and bacterial infections from cooling and cutting fluids.
- *Ergonomic*: worker characteristics, man–machine interface, and environmental effects.
- *Housekeeping*: physical, psychological, chemical, biological and ergonomic.

## A logical assessment procedure

1. Systematically seek out all possible hazards.
2. Consider the dangers and who is at risk.
3. Evaluate the risks, check whether there are any existing precautions and decide whether more precautions are needed.
4. Record findings and report to management.
5. Review periodically and revise as necessary.

## AVOIDABLE HAZARDS

Stumbles, slips and trips account for over one-third of major injuries each year. Problem areas should be identified and action taken to avoid these hazards. The Health and Safety Executive recommends a five-step approach:

1. Identify slip and trip hazards. Check on uneven floors, trailing cables, spillage areas, and any probable hazards that could cause injury.
2. Decide who might be harmed and how. Who comes into the workplace? Are they at risk?
3. Consider the risks. Are the precautions already taken sufficient to deal with the risks?
4. Record the findings if there are five or more employees.
5. Regularly review the assessment. If there are any significant changes, make sure that precautions are still adequate to deal with the risks.

## Examples of immediate improvements

- *Cleaning and maintenance*: train employees in the correct use of any safety and cleaning equipment.
- *Lighting*: replace, repair or clean all lights so that obstructive and slippery surfaces are easily seen.
- *Floors*: ensure the surfaces are sound by attending to any loose finishes, holes, cracks, worn rugs and mats, etc.
- *Passages or corridors*: clear any obstacle and do not block.
- *Obstructions*: keep all areas tidy by removing any trailing cables, objects or obstructions likely to cause stumbles.
- *Footwear*: provide suitable footwear which will reduce the risk of slips and trips.
- *Spillages*: clean up immediately and erect appropriate signs.
- *Stairs and slopes*: provide handrails, improve lighting and ensure the treads are sound.
- *Steam and smoke*: relocate or control by redirecting away from risk areas, improve ventilation and post warnings.

## ACCIDENT-PRONENESS

The problem employee is invariably accident-prone, probably because he or she has great difficulty in concentrating for any length of time. Those unfortunate people who are suffering from some nervous disorder are often unsuitable for operating machines. This manifests itself in periods of moodiness, temperamental outbursts, un-cooperativeness and general antisocial conduct. They are a menace to nearby colleagues, who may be injured by their sudden lapse of concentration.

Some individuals who suffer from hypochondria are frequent visitors to the sick bay and, through their lost vitality and general concern over their health, they become accident-prone. Whether their complaint is real or imagined is beyond the scope of the supervisor to determine, but he or she must take action to place such employees where the hazards are low.

The importance of maintaining a regular, careful watch on employees is highlighted when considering safety. The emotionally unstable employee is recognisable in chronic cases because of personal contact over a period, but normal people will suddenly change under the stress of a domestic or social problem. A sudden development of emotional instability makes the person very susceptible to accident-proneness and should be removed from a hazardous job until he or she recovers.

## AIDS

The free booklet *AIDS and the Workplace: A Guide for Employers* is available from the Department for Education and Employment (DfEE) and has already been sent to many companies. The supervisor should obtain a copy since it includes a number of useful points, such as dealing with potential problems, standard precautions, unfair dismissal, and threats from employees. The main theme is that anyone infected with HIV or suffering with AIDS should not be treated any differently.

## DISPLAY SCREEN EQUIPMENT

The supervisor should know the EC Directive on Health and Safety (DSE) Regulations which were outlined earlier in the chapter. These regulations must be strictly complied with and may result in a civil action if someone is harmed as a result of negligence. The main aspects to remember are detailed regulations on workstations, minimum specific requirements, task design and software, daily routine, visual requirements, and provision of information to employees.

Often managers do not take the regulations seriously and fail to appreciate the stressful conditions created when standards are neglected. Managers in other European countries have welcomed the information as a means of achieving higher productivity and competitiveness. The supervisor should bring the regulations to management's attention if they are neglected and the obligations are not being fulfilled. Remember that under the Trade Union Reform and Employment Rights Act 1993 there is ample protection for employees.

## APPROPRIATE WARNINGS TO EMPLOYEES

The supervisor should note that warnings of a general nature are insufficient. Employees must be warned if a certain job carries a risk of injury. They should have the risks explained to them along with the reasons why they are being warned. They should also be told what action to take if any symptoms appear.

## CLINICAL CONDITIONS

The supervisor should be aware of the rapid increase in upper limb disorders (ULDs) and repetitive strain injury (RSI) during recent years. Both conditions are due to repetitive work using hands, arms and legs, and they cause a reduction in productivity and costly insurance claims. Employees who have suffered include keyboard operators, rapid assembly production workers, and workers in service industries.

Typical clinical conditions to be aware of are pain, tenderness, and swellings irritated by movement or pressure. The common types of RSI are synovitis (inflammation of tissue that lines the inside of joints), tenosynovitis (inflammation of the sheath surrounding a tendon), tennis elbow (pain over the lateral aspect of the elbow), tendinitis (inflammation of a tendon), carpal tunnel syndrome (compression of the median nerve between bones and ligaments of the wrist), and bursitis (inflammation of a small sac of tissues between tendons and ligaments, often called housemaid's knee and dustman's shoulder).

## CONTROL OF SMOKING

Careless smoking habits cost lives, fire damage and serious health risks for the smoker and the passive smoker. Many companies now have a smoking policy which attempts to minimise the risks. The policy usually includes prohibited smoking areas, such as where any flammable liquids or gases are stored; where combustible materials are present, including woodworking workshops; any area infrequently visited; and communal areas, including food preparation and consumption. This policy should be explained and issued both verbally and in writing. Various precautions are often enforced which conform to stipulations in insurance policies:

- A fire point with fire extinguishers should be available near to all smoking areas.
- Smokers should be segregated from non-smokers if they so wish; also under the Health and Safety at Work Act employees must be protected from the dangers of passive smoking.
- Smoking areas should have receptacles for discarded matches and cigarettes, and ashtrays emptied daily into metal containers.

- Notices should be displayed to identify smoking and no-smoking areas.
- Furniture and furnishings in smoking areas should be made with non-inflammable materials.

## ELECTRONIC SAFETY PRECAUTIONS

The supervisor should liaise with the safety representative and the representative responsible for new technology installations. The devices should be checked in operation – preferably before their introduction – to assess any health or safety hazards. The workplace should be examined to ensure all ergonomic aspects have been properly considered.

Employees should be informed of any particular dangers associated with high voltage equipment. They should be instructed not to tamper with devices. The British Standards Institution has published a useful guide entitled *Electrical systems in office furniture and office screens*. New hazards are emerging as information technology develops. Defective plugs, sockets and leads cause more electrical accidents than do appliances. Considering the consequences, employees should be made aware of the dangers and should be encouraged to report immediately any defects, to switch off equipment before unplugging or cleaning, and to be safety conscious. The supervisor should be vigilant, regardless of electricians' inspections. Visual inspections of electrical connections are essential as faults may develop at any time.

## PROTECTIVE CLOTHING

The effectiveness of protective clothing such as goggles, gloves and boots depends upon the employee's good sense and the supervisor's watchfulness. The tendency to discard the protection often occurs if it hampers the work or if the employee considers its use an additional burden rather than a safety precaution. Besides that, there is always the individual who has a false idea of courage and discards the device to show off prowess. In some instances people simply forget and, inevitably, the lapse coincides with the accident.

The supervisor must try to discipline employees into always observing safety routines as a personal protection. Periodic campaigns are unsuccessful as the accidents nearly always occur between the periods of enforcement. Continuous checks and appropriate reprimands are essential, although they are demanding on the supervisor who is inclined to allow safety to be overshadowed by production problems through pressure of work.

## SAFETY ATTITUDE

Most accidents are caused by various forms of neglect, such as careless use of tools or machines, failure to wear protective clothing, taking risks (including horseplay), inconsideration for nearby colleagues, lack of concentration and failure to use safety devices. All these faults amount to a poor attitude towards safety.

Improving safety attitude hinges upon human relations and the supervisor's ability to create a team spirit that encourages employees to work safely. The supervisor must set the tone of safety consciousness by insisting on thorough checks for possible hazards on new and existing machinery, and by insisting on correct methods of working all the time. This attitude towards accident prevention must be clearly demonstrated to employees whom the supervisor must train and discipline to observe all precautions.

Working safely is habit-forming and rapidly develops into group pride in maintaining accident-free workplaces where employees appreciate the dangers and stupidity of taking risks. Surveys indicate that most accidents could have been avoided by taking more personal care, so fostering the correct attitudes in employees can reduce the accident rate to a low figure.

## TRAINING

Lack of experience and poor training also cause many accidents. Therefore an essential part of any training scheme is to emphasise safety and the correct method of performing a task. Bad habits must be corrected as they appear, and the supervisor should constantly check new and existing employees. Allowing a newcomer to work alone before a suitable level of competence is reached, is inviting disaster.

## WORK RATE AND FATIGUE

As the rate of working increases, the risk of an accident rises in proportion. Similarly, fatigue also contributes towards higher accident probability. The problem is to find a safe working rate, using the best method and the optimum working period to keep fatigue and the accident rate to a minimum. To maintain and improve productivity in these circumstances, the setting of standards is essential through the use of work study techniques (Chapters 24 and 25).

# Supervisor's safety summary

1 Ensure all health and safety measures are implemented within the area of the supervisor's responsibility.
2 Ensure safe working methods are always used.
3 Always use the main methods of risk control: elimination, isolation, substitution, extraction and guarding.
4 Insist on the maintenance of good housekeeping.
5 Conduct a daily inspection of the area, machines, tools, ancillary equipment, and so on.
6 Issue safety equipment and protective clothing as laid down by management and legislation; ensure they are used at all times.
7 Report all accidents, near misses and hazards.
8 Train employees and induct newcomers to ensure the job is thoroughly understood and they are proficient.
9 Liaise with the superior on all aspects of safety, health and welfare.
10 Remind employees that they have a duty to take reasonable care to ensure they do not endanger themselves or anyone else; to co-operate with management and others in meeting statutory requirements; and to avoid misusing anything provided in the interests of health or safety at work.
11 Communicate developments and changes in procedures.
12 Provide any information requested by the safety representative on such things as substances, processes or pieces of equipment. If there is any doubt as to the accuracy of the information, make this point clear.

13 Ensure every employee is aware of all possible fire hazards, the fire procedure and any related procedures.

# Ergonomics

Ergonomics is the study of human capabilities and performance in relation to the demands of the job. The knowledge accumulated by biological scientists in their study of operators and their working environment is now being applied more in industry.

For many years designers in industry concentrated on *machine* design because it was the limiting factor, but recently the situation has changed. The *operator* is now the limiting factor. The result is the study of the anatomical, physiological and psychological aspects of the operator, who must be viewed as an integral part of the machine.

Operators are subjected to many stresses and strains of a mental and physical nature as they become machine minders. This situation is recognised now and many health and safety requirements are in force. In particular, the six EC directives described earlier apply to many ergonomic features. The various aspects of ergonomics dealt with below help to reduce mental and physical fatigue.

## ANTHROPOMETRY

The measurement of the physical dimensions of the human body is known as anthropometry. The findings of anthropometric study are essential for the correct design of seats, benches, machines and other equipment used by people. The British Standards Institution Advisory Committee on Anthropometrics has recommended dimensions which are published in booklet BS 3404, *Anthropometric Recommendations for Dimensions of Office Machines, Operators' Chairs and Desks*.

Conventional seating is a typical example of incorrect practice which results in unnecessary fatigue and therefore affects operator performance. The so-called conventional height for seats is 457 mm; and according to specialists, this is too high for about 50 per cent of the working population. The mean lower leg length is 432 mm for males and 381 mm for females, so the maximum suitable height should be no more than 432 mm.

Many items of furniture already fit the regulations but there are some suppliers who pay particular attention to design flexibility and colour aesthetics. The emphasis is on offering safe units that provide comfort and relaxation, non-reflective surfaces and the avoidance of sharp corners.

## APPLIED HUMAN PHYSIOLOGY

The study of applied human biology reveals that improvements are possible in the general working environment. It considers the function of the body in relation to applied forces and the tolerances it can stand in various surrounding environments. Such factors as noise, heat, light, vibration and heavy physical effort are measured and the effects recorded.

Numerous booklets are available that give adequate information on maximum and minimum levels for each factor. In addition, the use of kinetics in handling and lifting activities is essential to avoid strain and injury. The Royal Society for the Prevention of Accidents (RoSPA) conducts courses and issues leaflets and posters illustrating the essential points for smooth and easy handling of all kinds. The Health and Safety Executive offers a wide range of free booklets covering appropriate legislation, general guidance, risk assessment, physiological aspects, dangerous substances, and many aspects in various industries. To contact HSE books telephone 01787 881165 or fax 01787 313995. Many HSE books are also available for purchase.

## APPLIED PSYCHOLOGY

Applied psychology studies the operator's ability to receive information in various forms through the different senses, to process the information and to take appropriate action. Its importance and its application are illustrated by an experiment conducted during World War II on the ability of a radar operator to concentrate on the display screen for long periods. Tests proved concentration was lost after thirty minutes: clear signals were not seen after that time lapse because of monotony and mental fatigue. Similar dangers exist today where critical processes and procedures demand long periods of concentration.

The design of dials provides a further example. Visual displays of information can confuse and they can easily be misinterpreted unless careful attention is given to their design. Control movements connected with visual displays can cause a serious error if they do not conform to expected standards. Examples are turning a wheel in a clockwise direction, resulting in the movement of a pointer to the right; or pushing a lever forward, resulting in a pointer moving forward or upward. A right-handed person finds a clockwise turn is anatomically more natural.

Confusion may occur when movements are learned or made through experience. For example, in the UK a downward movement switches on the light whereas in the USA a downward movement switches off the light.

## APPLIED BIOLOGY

Applied biology informs the scientific design of visual displays, the established optimum rate at which an operator can receive information, and the planning of suitable surrounding conditions. The study in human beings of physical structure and capacity includes the following topics: an understanding of the bone structure; the physical effects when work is performed, the production of energy and the disposal of resultant waste; the receptors (nerves) which feed information to a central control mechanism that processes and takes decisions which are transmitted through the motor system (nerves and muscles) to appropriate points of action; and the self-governing system that automatically controls the heart, glands and other parts of the body which function without conscious effort.

## ASSISTANCE ON ERGONOMICS

There are many software packages which may assist companies that are unable to find an appropriate ergonomist. They include information on DSE-based ergonomics, stress relief, an assessment of the workstation, possible risks, and non-conformity with the regulations. Some suppliers act as consultants, perform workplace audits, make recommendations and train staff.

# Environmental protection

There is increasing recognition that environmental pollution can affect employees and the local population, especially if the clean-up is inadequate. Many environmental implications involving clean air, smoking, hazardous substances, road traffic, town and country planning, and water have resulted in considerable legislation. Global warming is being taken more seriously. A green analysis includes all processes from raw materials to products; ozone-depleting emissions; waste management; and green labelling of products.

## LEGISLATION

The supervisor should be aware of current legislation if he or she is involved in any environmental activities in the company. The main acts are Clean Air Act 1968, Consumer Protection Act 1987, Control of Industrial Air Pollution Regulations 1989, Control of Industrial Major Accident Hazard (CIMAH) Regulations 1985, Control of Substances Hazardous to Health (COSHH) Regulations 1988, Control of Pollution Act 1974, Environmental Protection Act 1990, Health and Safety at Work Act 1974, Road Traffic Act 1986, Town and Country Planning Act 1990, Water Act 1989. Also there is BS7750: 1992 *Specification for environmental management systems*.

## EFFECTS OF COMPETITION

The benefits for a company to create a green corporate image are gradually being realised. Cases are now given considerable adverse publicity as Greenpeace and other organisations actively pursue any opportunities to show companies are ignoring pollution. Environmental pressures are being exerted on companies by various market forces such as competitors, the community, suppliers, consumers, shareholders and employees.

## MANAGERIAL RESPONSIBILITY

Effective environmental management is essential to demonstrate responsibility for the natural and physical environment, and to recognise the effects on the community. Many companies have introduced an environmental policy that obviously has social and economic benefits. They have also distributed a code of practice for managers to apply.

## ENVIRONMENTAL POLICY: TYPICAL ITEMS

- A strategy to improve the environment within the company's control, with appropriate responsibility to a senior manager.
- A plan for managers and employees to become environmentally conscious through appropriate training programmes.
- Monitor all possible pollution risks and take immediate action when weaknesses are located.
- Use natural resources whenever possible.
- Provide products and services that are safe and which minimise environmental damage; provide full information to the consumer.

## QUESTIONS

1 Give a brief account of the supervisor's responsibility in connection with the safety of subordinates.

2 How can the supervisor establish a safety-conscious group under his or her control?

3 You are asked to attend the first meeting of a newly formed safety committee. What topics would you expect to be raised and what suggestions would you put forward?

4 Discuss safety in connection with maintenance of machinery and equipment.

5 What precautions could a supervisor take to minimise the risk of accidents?

6 How would you deal with an employee who refuses to wear goggles when operating a machine that has a high eyesight hazard?

7 An employee suddenly has two accidents within a few days. What action would you take?

8 Describe the formulae used for control purposes to provide information on the frequency rate and duration rate of accidents.

9 Draw up a suitable framework for an accident report form.

10 What is the Health and Safety Commission?

11 What are the powers of health and safety inspectors?

12 Explain the significance of European directives.

13 Outline the range of activities that may cause serious problems in the office environment.

14 List the installation and design features that are essential to reduce fatigue when operating display screen equipment.

15 Discuss the importance of ergonomics in the working environment.

16 Write an essay on environmental protection.

17 Outline the basic sequence of an accident.

18 Discuss the importance of stress-related sickness.

19 Outline type A and type B personalities and their effect on health.

20 What are the four major stress areas which can damage people's health?

21 Discuss the main risk factors related to sick building syndrome.

22 What are the ways of reducing health risks at work?

23 What are the main causes of accidents?

24 Discuss the supervisor's role in preventing accidents.

25 Outline a logical procedure to assess risks.

26 List a five-step approach to deal with avoidable hazards.

27 Discuss the problem of environmental protection.

---

**CASE STUDY**

The safety officer was very concerned recently about the poor use of machine guards in the factory. The supervisors had been urged to increase output, consequently they tended to ignore the guards because the operators claimed they slowed down their work and affected their bonus. The safety officer complained to the works manager; but the works manager was not sympathetic and it seemed obvious he was also being pressurised. However, it was agreed to take the matter further.

After three weeks there was no change. The safety officer decided to write to the managing director pointing out the duties of employers under the Health and Safety at Work Act. The inevitable serious accident occurred the following week and it was attributed to misuse of the machine guard. An inspector from the Health and Safety Commission conducted an investigation.

*Consider the situation of the safety officer in these circumstances. Are there other implications that contributed to the accident?*

---

**CASE STUDY**

A gas explosion had severely injured five operators and caused considerable damage. At the investigation by an inspector, the safety officer said he was informed that the smell of gas had been reported by several operatives about five minutes before the explosion.

The safety officer had immediately seen the works manager and urged him to clear the area. This advice was ignored and the maintenance department was told to find the leak. The safety officer became very angry and threatened to call the fire brigade because there were electric motors in the vicinity. He ran into the workshop shouting to everyone to leave the premises at once. The explosion occurred before the evacuation even started.

*Did the safety officer do everything possible to avoid the catastrophe? How much blame could be attributed to the works manager and the supervisors in the workshop?*

For the second year running, Mike Robins receives a certificate for his department's safety record. He puts a congratulatory memo on the noticeboard, along with the award.

Later on he is chatting with one of the chargehands, who criticises the memo: 'It seems to me that people are getting pretty fed up with all this pressure on safety. They know their stuff and they resent all these safety checks you keep giving them'.

Another chargehand joins them: 'I've had similar moans. Why don't we give it up for a while and see how it goes? They think you're after promotion and driving them too hard'.

*How should the supervisor respond to this question? Consider the chargehands' role in this case.*

# 22

# Welfare

## Introduction

The welfare of employees in the UK has undergone a transformation in the twentieth century. Today enlightened companies and prospective employees view welfare as an important factor. Existing employees see welfare as one consideration when deciding whether to stay with a company. Many companies include welfare as a factor in their personnel policy and in achieving higher productivity.

The broad meaning of welfare includes health and safety at work because of their obvious connections. Also included are avoiding physical and psychological harassment, protection from personality clashes, avoiding jealousy practices, and banning any coercion from managers and supervisors.

A limited meaning of welfare is the employee's social well-being, a satisfactory state of immediate surroundings and the workplace, avoiding physical and psychological interference, and assistance in many ways including unofficial benefits (perks) and official fringe benefits.

To accommodate these definitions the following aspects are included: an outline of legal requirements, many of which are detailed in other chapters; the social responsibilities of managers and supervisors, considering working conditions, employee relations, equal opportunity, modern job design, physical and psychological harassment, and workplace counselling; and details of many fringe benefits usually available in many companies. These aspects are outlined in Fig. 22.1.

## Legal requirements

Major changes in the law are now in force. They directly affect health, safety and welfare as the new European Union regulations are implemented and absorbed into the UK legislation. As a result

**Figure 22.1** Welfare: the main features

the two main sources of law that protect the employee are:

- *European Union legislation*: regulations (or directives) issued by the Council of Ministers under Article 118A of the Treaty of Rome.
- *English legislation*: includes common law and statute law.

## EU LEGISLATION

The regulations or directives are legislated and issued by the Council of Ministers. This institution is also known as the European Council, consequently they are called EC regulations or EC directives. Many are already in force under the Health and Safety at Work Act. However, these regulations provide clarification, they are more explicit, and they use new approaches. The directives are explained in Chapter 21. They cover:

- The framework
- The workplace
- Work equipment
- Personal protective equipment
- Manual handling
- Display screen equipment

## ENGLISH LEGISLATION

English law may be grouped under two headings: civil law and criminal law. A civil offence does not concern the community; it deals with the relationships between private individuals when redress for grievances is sought legally. The remedies are damages (payment of money) or an injunction (either forbidding or commanding some course of action). A criminal offence is against the community. The police may take action even if the victim involved declines. The offender is punished by either imprisonment or a fine.

Some offences are both criminal *and* civil wrongs. For example, an industrial injury may involve a breach of the Health and Safety at Work Act *and* provide grounds for damages at common law. Under common law the employer has an obligation to provide safe working conditions, which include the place of work, machinery and equipment. This obligation is reinforced by the Health and Safety at Work Act.

# Legislation

Considerable legislation has been introduced in recent years to safeguard employees' interests and to improve their general position. The existence of relevant legislation is likely when most problems of welfare are raised. Legislation extends to four main areas: employment and associated practices, operational aspects of employment, industrial relations, and health and safety.

Chapter 17 discusses the main acts concerning contracts of employment and associated acts protecting employees; protection of employees' personal records; insurance against bodily injury or disease sustained during employment; employers' liability for defective equipment; redundancy, dismissal and disputes; employees' rights and job security; equal pay for men and women; supervision, advice and planning of training schemes; personal injuries; racial discrimination; damages for industrial injury through employers' negligence; social security; sex discrimination; pensions protection; bad practices connected with pay; restrictions on pay deductions; maternity rights; and minimum pay levels.

Chapter 18 looks at passive smoking, terminations, disciplinary procedures, dismissals, redundancy, and misuse of alcohol. Chapter 20 covers industrial relations matters, including trade union members' rights and restrictions, employees' rights, collective bargaining, and disputes. Chapter 21 examines health and safety, including vicarious liability, control of substances hazardous to health, general working conditions, employees' duties to take care, and accidents.

# Responsibilities

The social responsibilities of management are now far more extensive. There are many reasons for this; here are some of the important ones:

- the high cost of the National Health Service which is partially due to stress-related sickness and poor working conditions
- the high premiums of insurance schemes partially related to accidents, working conditions, and workplace change

- the effects of productivity when social responsibilities are ignored or neglected
- the effects on morale when the welfare expectations of employees are considered to be unimportant

Although provisions are quoted in various acts and directives, there is also some interpretation because they sometimes use the following terms: suitable, adequate, sufficient, minimising, a high standard.

## ACCEPTABLE STANDARDS

A particular workforce may have certain expectations which will be of a higher standard, compared with the requirements of an act or directive. A conscientious management will recognise this situation. Discreet enquiries and assessments are essential to ensure these expectations are met. Bearing in mind these aspects, the following topics may assist in choosing suitable standards.

## WORKING CONDITIONS

Working conditions have received much attention and detailed regulations are issued in various acts and directives outlined in Chapter 21. The main items are the workplace, cleanliness, overcrowding and ventilation, workplace design, temperature and humidity, lighting, seating requirements, lavatories and washrooms, cloakrooms, noise, respiratory problems, and sick building syndrome.

## WORKPLACE DESIGN

Most musculoskeletal problems are caused by poor workplace design. They create aches and pains, resulting in about 5.5 million working days lost each year. Musculoskeletal disorders involve a variety of sprains and strains affecting muscles and joints. Particularly at risk are the neck, shoulders, back and upper limbs. The results may be slipped discs, hernia, backache, tenosynovitis, tennis elbow, carpal tunnel syndrome, and repetitive strain injury.

Most problems are easily preventable, without heavy expense. The main risks that can be properly managed are:

- poor working positions such as incorrect seating, and standing for long periods
- infrequent position changes such as sitting, standing, or stooping for long periods
- poor working environment
- excessive application of force or grip
- difficult manual handling tasks
- highly repetitive tasks
- too demanding deadlines
- a combination of any of the above items

The conscientious manager and supervisor will easily reduce the risks by using good sense, seeking the help of an ergonomist, and referring to many textbooks on the subject.

## EMPLOYEE RELATIONS

The importance of sound employee relations is generally acceptable. However, many debatable issues remain. Opinions vary, but often employees feel their welfare depends on the strength of the trade unions who support them. Employees sometimes feel that management's attitude towards their welfare is to reduce or maintain it at a set level. The outcome of new schemes affecting welfare often seems to be a subtle way to lower welfare standards. Trade unions have no bother in condemning these schemes as having an adverse effect.

Some companies strive to improve welfare by strengthening relationships with trade unions representing employees and emphasising the importance of working together. Arguable features are whether this is due to recognising social responsibilities and their effect on productivity, or due to the effects of trade union power.

## EQUAL OPPORTUNITIES

Convincing all employees that the company practises an equal opportunities policy remains a difficult managerial task. Inevitably some employees think they are more equal than others, while others are bigoted. Certainly the strict application of legislative requirements helps, but often justifying decisions on selection, transfer and redundancies to everyone's satisfaction is not possible. The undercurrent of discontent and feelings of injustice easily affect the general well-being of employees when any case involving equal opportunities is discussed. This adverse aspect of welfare is likely to remain.

## MODERN JOB DESIGN

Modern job design was discussed in Chapter 17. From the viewpoint of welfare the approach has a critical effect if it is ignored. Essential features are personal needs, the sociological organisation structure, and treating the technology as a variable and not a fixed configuration. They coincide with sociotechnical systems outlined in Chapter 3, absorb current changes, and embrace the quality of working life (QWL).

## SEXUAL HARASSMENT

Preventing sexual harassment is a serious managerial responsibility, which should include an appropriate policy. This could be a written statement issued to all employees that emphasises sexual harassment will not be permitted or condoned, and that anyone should complain immediately if it occurs. A procedure may be installed which guarantees prompt, corrective action, including a disciplinary guide for managers and supervisors.

Usually a policy allows for those who do not wish to proceed formally and it provides for informal ways of settling the difficulty. Everyone should know the meaning and extent of sexual harassment, and the possible consequences. An effective scheme includes adequate training for managers and supervisors to ensure full implementation, counselling by qualified individuals, confidentiality, and a comprehensive complaints procedure.

Sexual harassment is broadly interpreted and includes any verbal abuse or suggestive remarks, meaningful physical contact, leering, innuendos implying sexual favours, compromising invitations, and physical assault. The test for sexual harassment appears to be whether the complainant finds the remarks or actions offensive. A clear distinction must be made between friendly attention reciprocated by the other employee and unwanted or unpleasant behaviour that creates fear, indignation or distress. In other words, an exchange of pleasantries or obviously attentive harmless remarks are acceptable. One industrial tribunal defined sexual harassment as 'unwelcome acts which involve physical contact of a sexual nature which, if proved, would also amount to offences under common law such as assault or indecent assault, and also conduct falling short of such physical acts which can fairly be described as sexual harassment'.

Such criminal offences come under the Sex discrimination Act 1975. Note that anything done by one employee to another in the course of employment shall be treated as if carried out by the employer. An employee may also claim constructive dismissal (Chapter 18).

One problem with sexual harassment is that everyone does not fit into the same mould. Some people actually welcome attention in the form of suggestive remarks and they encourage it. Others find similar remarks offensive. The person making the remarks takes a risk because sometimes individuals change rapidly and may suddenly take offence.

## BULLYING

Bullying is common but often not recognised. Bullying causes many problems, typically stress, low morale, absenteeism, increased employee turnover, demotivation, fear, desperation and humiliation. Such detestable treatment of employees is often disguised when inept managers adopt this mode of behaviour in vain attempts to control. Peers may use it in personality clashes and jealousy situations. Psychopaths may also adopt this behaviour. Unfortunately, the practice extends to most activities outside companies.

### Definitions

Bullying may be defined as abuse of power, persecution, and physical or psychological oppression. The Health and Safety Executive uses the term 'work-related violence' and defines it as 'any incident in which a person is abused, threatened or assaulted in circumstances relating to the work'. Verbal abuse and threats are most common, while physical attacks are comparatively rare. However, employees who deal with the public may risk aggressive or violent behaviour.

## Subtle bullying

- An employee is accused of poor performance and disciplinary proceedings are started. Although performance is low it is not the employee's fault, but the manager's, who installed a scheme which failed. The humiliation of a disciplinary interview and lengthy explanations are unnerving for the employee who is blameless. However, the side effects are worse when other employees discover the truth.
- A manager misuses power by exerting excessive pressure on an employee to complete a task involving considerable time outside working hours. Bullying takes the form of veiled threats of being passed over for promotion and threatening to write poor appraisal reports.
- Picking on a particular sensitive feature of an individual and continually mentioning it to embarrass and downgrade. This may be a facial disfigurement, height, clothing, or speech habit. The practice may be mentioned privately or within other employees' presence.
- Embarrassing a person at a meeting by voicing derogatory remarks, making fun of an explanation, or ignoring a comment.

## Confronting bullying

The strong need to confront bullying must be accepted by management, considering the implications which involve not only financial and personal difficulties but also legal reasons similar to those expressed under sexual harassment. A typical programme will include the following steps.

### Identify bullying

A competent manager or supervisor will identify bullying by various means such as considering the symptoms, changes in behaviour patterns, changes in the atmosphere at the workplace, and a lowering of performance levels. Many excuses appear for low motivation such as poor morale, people talking of leaving, high employee turnover, and incapability.

Employees should be given the opportunity, and encouraged in private, to complain if they feel threatened. The supervisor should make it known that if they are aware of any form of bullying it should be reported in confidence. Sometimes employees feel reluctant to divulge incidents for various reasons. Here the supervisor should gain people's support by explaining the problem, guaranteeing confidentiality, emphasising the dangers, and stressing that any form of abuse is deplored and not a part of the job.

### Determine immediate action

Make a note of any particular problem areas and potential hazards. Consider all the steps that are essential to conform with legal requirements. Under the Management of Health and Safety at Work Regulations 1992, the risks should be assessed to protect employees from exposure to reasonably foreseeable violence. Assessment should include planning, organising, controlling and reviewing.

If the case involves non-consensual physical violence, the enforcing authority should be notified under the Reporting of Injuries, Diseases and Dangerous Occurrences Regulations 1995 (RIDDOR). Employees should be informed and consulted under the Safety Representatives and Safety Committees Regulations 1977 and the Health and Safety (Consultation with Employees) Regulations 1996. Determining action to conform with these acts should include:

- establishing a programme to identify those employees at risk
- ensuring that job redesign is considered to reduce violence, such as planning procedures so that cash is not held in situations where robbery is made attractive, avoiding vulnerable situations where an employee is alone, and adopting precautions to reduce the risk of robbery
- adopting training schemes where risks are outlined and identified in particular occupations
- ensuring the surrounding environment copes with security, such as using video cameras, appropriate locks and safety devices

### Take action

Ensure all precautions and cases follow recognised procedures. Revise a policy statement on violence if the circumstances indicate any failings. Maintain appropriate records that should provide ample evidence if any legal action occurs later on.

### Follow up regularly

Situations may change rapidly and often the risk of violence is overlooked when procedures are altered. Continual checks and updating are essential. The use of safety committees and a review of incidence records should identify progress and the possibility of using further measures.

### Rehabilitate victims

To avoid stress the victims should receive appropriate treatment. This may include counselling, transfer to another job, further training, leave to recover from the experience, legal assistance, a sympathetic understanding from management, and the use of various victim support organisations.

### A caution

The supervisor and the victim need to check carefully on the *real* attitude of the human resources department and the company towards subtle forms of bullying. There may be a political reason why the department ignores such cases even when there is ample evidence. Typically, the bully has a good cost-cutting record, therefore the board's policy dictates 'performance at any price'. Such short-sightedness is deplorable.

### WORKPLACE COUNSELLING

A workplace counselling service is now an essential feature of employee welfare. This concept originated in the USA and is often called an employee assistance programme. The aims are:

- to help employees cope with high stress levels
- to provide assistance in adapting to changes involving downsizing and restructuring
- to give advice on family problems and financial problems
- to inform and advise on narcotics

Many problems affecting work performance and welfare are not work-related. Many employees are now working under greater pressure, consequently counselling services help to support them by trying to avoid severe depression, personality disorders and narcotics abuse.

Although in-house counselling is useful, an outside service may reassure employees of confidentiality and possibly provide a wider range of available information. Naturally the supervisor will be generally counselling employees on a daily basis as described in Chapter 18. Such features as lateness, absenteeism, personality clashes and work problems are constantly being processed through counselling techniques.

# Benefits

Most companies have a wide range of benefits. Some benefits are official or formal and add to company status. Others are unofficial or *perks*, which employees tend to take for granted with or without management's knowledge. Traffic in these perks is sometimes unbelievably high, resulting in heavy losses to the company. Some examples are the use of the company's petrol pump; taking items such as raw materials, components, products, tools and stationery; and using machines and equipment for private purposes.

### OFFICIAL FRINGE BENEFITS

- *Assurance schemes*: There are many schemes, including death-in-service benefits which provide some security for the family if the employee dies while working for the employer before normal retirement date.
- *Financial assistance*: Help with further education, loans with subsidised interest rates for house purchase, season ticket loans, discounts on purchases of certain products, and reduced prices for company products.
- *General benefits*: Gifts for long service, bonuses, free luncheon vouchers, anniversary payments not directly connected with employee output, examination success awards, staff introduction awards, privileged banking facilities, holiday travel discounts, marriage gifts, nurseries for young children of employees, and Christmas gifts.
- *Insurance schemes*: Various insurance schemes to cover retirements, sickness and injury, private medical treatment, and voluntary personal

accident and sickness schemes. Special terms are given by insurance companies for such groups.

- *Job or status-related benefits*: These include company cars, executive share option schemes, mobile and house telephones, expense accounts, and provision of accommodation.
- *Medical schemes*: Annual contributions for private medical treatment through independent health care associations or through group discount schemes. Large organisations may employ a nurse and medical facilities, including a medical room, a restroom, and a company doctor on a part-time basis.
- *Payment for non-working time*: Within this category are various national agreements and legislation that cover holiday pay, including bank holidays. Some companies aim to help employees balance more easily their workload and domestic commitments. They may offer allowances for career breaks, part-time further and higher education during the day, compassionate and emergency situations, parental difficulties, paternity leave, visits for house purchase, and other legal reasons.
- *Pension schemes*: These vary from a defined personal pension scheme to a *money-purchase* personal pension scheme. The defined scheme will provide a pension on retirement directly related to final salary and length of service. The money-purchase scheme will provide a fund to purchase the most appropriate type of pension to suit the employee's circumstances. Schemes are subject to Inland Revenue approval and are established under trusts. Furthermore, schemes may be funded totally by the employer or partly by the employer and employee, respectively known as non-contributory schemes and contributory schemes.
- *Personal advice*: Professional assistance if an employee has a personal problem related to work or other activities.
- *Share schemes*: These include share option schemes and profit-sharing schemes (Chapters 6 and 7).
- *Social facilities*: A wide range of social and recreational facilities in the form of dining rooms, sports clubs, social clubs, outings and entertainments.

## QUESTIONS

1 Discuss the question of perks or unofficial benefits.

2 Outline some of the benefits offered to employees under various welfare schemes.

3 Explain how the law protects the employee.

4 Give a general outline of the Factories Act 1961.

5 What statutory regulations exist concerning pay and conditions of service?

6 Explain the legislation on National Insurance.

7 To what extent would you consider that working conditions affect the attitude of employees towards management?

8 Do you think there is any connection between the quality of working conditions and the quality of work in a factory?

9 Is it possible for the supervisor to promote the health of subordinates?

10 If the social and recreational facilities are poorly supported in a company, what do you think are the likely causes?

11 Outline the legislation that provides for compensation of operators in the event of industrial injury.

12 What are the main features of welfare?

13 Discuss the social responsibilities of management related to welfare in a progressive company.

14 What are the likely benefits for a company if welfare is taken seriously?

15 Besides the obvious ones, what are the symptoms of subtle bullying?

16 What immediate action should the supervisor take to deal with bullying?

17 What are the aims of workplace counselling associated with welfare?

18 Discuss the formal and informal ways of settling sexual harassment.

19 What is meant by constructive dismissal, related to sexual harassment?

A chemical company was located by the side of a river. Jones took his lunch break by the river bank and one day noticed the water was murky. On checking, he could see a pipe under the surface was pouring out a dark liquid. Jones reported the pollution to Eddie, his supervisor. Eddie promptly told him to ignore it as all companies dumped waste into rivers these days because of the high cost of dumping elsewhere and profits were already low. When Jones told his wife, she agreed it was not worth the risk of taking the case further for fear of redundancies if the company were forced to spend more money removing the waste.

Next month Eddie confronted Jones, saying that the company was in trouble over polluting the river and accused him of shopping the firm. Jones denied it but Eddie obviously did not believe him. Eddie started to make life difficult for Jones by giving him the unpopular jobs and generally being objectionable. Finally Jones lost his temper and swore at Eddie, who promptly suspended him. Jones appealed to the personnel manager for support, but the manager sided with Eddie who started the dismissal procedure.

*What could Jones do now? Comment on the supervisor's behaviour and the personnel manager's behaviour.*

Amy Thomas, in the accounts office, is very agitated when she approaches her supervisor, Andrew Ralton. 'I have just seen Michael, the new computer operator, going through my coat pockets. When he saw me he left hurriedly. What are you going to do about it?'

Andrew calms her down and suggests that they should check to see if anything is missing. They walk over to the coat rack at the end of the office. Amy examines her pockets and pulls out a lighter. 'This isn't mine!' she declares. 'That's Ron's, I'd recognise it anywhere!'

They check and Ron remembers that it was in his raincoat pocket. Going through his raincoat pockets he pulls out a bunch of keys and says, 'These aren't mine, but my cigarette case is missing.'

It takes about fifteen minutes to sort out the contents of the coat pockets, as others are also involved. Andrew tackles Michael who strongly denies going through Amy's pockets. 'Amy's got it in for me because I'm a faster worker than she is. She doesn't like it because I won't take breaks. She won't talk to me in the office now, not even to say good morning. She probably did it herself to get me the sack', Michael declares.

*How should the supervisor proceed now?*

It is one month before the Christmas party and Terry remembers clearly last year's fiasco when he had agreed to a disco. The older employees had complained that they could not hear themselves talk because of the noise. The volume was turned up and down repeatedly.

At the meeting the older members say they will not support another disco party, but the younger members insist on a disco. There are insufficient numbers for two parties, which would defeat the object anyway.

*How could this problem be resolved to satisfy both groups?*

# Suggested projects for Part Two

**Project 1**
Attempt an assessment of morale in your company:
- List all the possible factors which affect morale and investigate each one.
- Draw up a summary of your findings and suggest constructive methods for improving the situation.

**Project 2**
Write an account of five human problems on the shop floor from your own experience. Each account should include your personal observations, the opinions of other colleagues wherever possible, the causes of the problem, the actual situation as it arises, the way it is solved and any after-effects. Attempt to summarise your work and furnish suitable conclusions.

**Project 3**
Investigate the operation of the grapevine in your company. Classify the rumours, sources and accuracy and estimate the effects. Do *not* attempt to trace the *human chain* back to the original source of information. After an adequate number of cases has been established, attempt to draw conclusions from your work.

**Project 4**
Carry out a continuous survey for about four months to ascertain the number of occasions when problems or trouble spots arise through a breakdown in communication. Classify the causes (such as lack of information, misunderstandings) and summarise the findings, making suitable recommendations.

**Project 5**
If the company's personnel policy is publicised, investigate the effectiveness of its operation in practice. Choose a group and study each individual's reactions and problems within the province of personnel policy. Tabulate and explain your findings with a view to criticising constructively the policy, its interpretation by management and the reactions of employees.

**Project 6**
Prepare and maintain a record of negotiations between management and the trade union in your company. Include such aspects as date, subject, negotiations, results and follow-up. Attempt to assess the effectiveness of the talks and the possible causes of disagreements when they arise.

**Project 7**
Maintain a record of negotiations between yourself and the shop steward. The report should include all relevant details of the talks and each disagreement or problem should be amplified to show the possible causes and the opinions of both sides. Prepare a summary of your conclusions, indicating some of the basic problems or difficulties encountered and how you would overcome them if given the opportunity.

**Project 8**
Attempt to assess the importance of welfare in your company. Make notes on individuals' reactions to welfare facilities, their complaints concerning welfare, whether schemes are supported and the general attitude towards welfare. Write a comprehensive report on the welfare situation and include your recommendations.

**Project 9**
Examine the jobs of five employees who have the reputation of being lazy. Consider whether they would benefit if the jobs were enriched.

**Project 10**
Study the job structures in your section and attempt to enrich them.

# PART THREE

# Controlling the work

# 23

# The nature of control

## The importance of control

The term 'control' has many meanings: power of directing, ability to restrain, means of restraint, standard of comparison for checking inferences deduced from experiment, or as a verb meaning to dominate or to regulate. Any term which has a variety of meanings leads to confusion in practice unless the meaning intended is carefully explained.

### THE FOUNDATIONS OF CONTROL

Control breakdowns will occur if any of the foundations are ignored. Furthermore, all employees with accountability will be wasting time attempting to control effectively without adequate back-up and essential information. The following foundations need to be understood and accepted before considering the next section:

- There are clear levels of responsibility for all activities within the organisational structure.
- Each person knows exactly the terms and conditions of control allocated to him or her.
- Each person has the capability to take appropriate action within the limits of the job, or to understand the importance of resorting to a higher authority if in doubt.
- Each employee above and below the person with control knows these terms and conditions.
- Comprehensive plans are communicated so that everyone knows their personal and organisational expectations to achieve objectives.
- A clear and integrated organisational structure.
- An established communication system for channelling deviations to everyone who is concerned and responsible for the activities.

### ESSENTIAL FEATURES FOR THE SUPERVISOR

After a brief look at business control, the chapter goes on to consider these important aspects:

- basic theory of control
- control appraisal
- problems of control
- types of control
- the complete control process
- the supervisor's role
- quantitative techniques
- statistical method
- establishing standards

## Business control

Control as applied to business may be defined as the direction of activities to achieve an objective according to predetermined plans and standards. Various aspects of control are needed to implement this broad definition. They should be carefully explained to all employees. The opportunities to discuss the implications of control should be given to avoid misinterpretation and to outline the apparently conflicting viewpoints in practice.

## Basic theory of control

A sound understanding of certain logical steps which form a basic procedure ensures that all activities have occurred in accordance with the plan. The basic procedure is:

- Set standards.
- Check performance.
- Correct deviations.

This procedure is the basis for control cycles which apply to production, operations and administrative processes. The concept seems obvious and any normal person with good sense would automatically conform to this simple practice.

Some senior managers believe the idea is too elementary or they choose to ignore it. The result is a series of famous cases where top management has failed to comply and it has cost companies enormous sums and embarrassment.

Unfortunately, a supervisor may not have complete freedom to control effectively. Consequently, he or she should insist on a clear brief which outlines limitations and restrictions.

# Basic control procedures

The basic theory of control is clearly oversimplified. Control procedures are complex and involve various loops and cycles to ensure effectiveness. The two main control groups are (1) production and (2) operations and administrative processes. They are now described to illustrate the importance of feedback, the continuous process of adjustment, and the expectations and levels of performance envisaged.

## CONTROL CYCLES FOR PRODUCTION

The basic control procedure does not indicate the logical sequence involved in a control cycle since *checking performance* covers the whole process of feedback of information and comparison of the actual with the standard. The procedure for starting a machine illustrates a simple example and is called a *closed-loop system*. Omitting the feedback in any system produces an *open-loop system*.

| Cycle | Observation |
| --- | --- |
| Instruction and action | Press starter button |
| Feedback of effect | Machine refuses to start |
| Information | Electric power is off |
| Adjustment | Switch on power |
| Instruction | Press starter button |

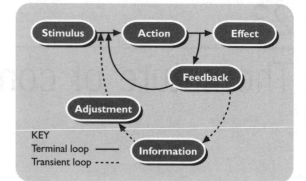

**Figure 23.1** Terminal and transient loops in control
There are three reasons why an effective control cycle must contain a transient loop: (1) to give feedback on any failure to achieve the desired result, (2) to give information on the cause of failure, and (3) to provide adjustment that rectifies the problem. The cycle is repeated until the terminal loop is successful, providing (a) appropriate action and (b) feedback on the success.

## A CLOSED-LOOP SYSTEM

Closed-loop control is illustrated in Fig. 23.1, which should be studied carefully. Cycles of action are represented as loops. A fault is corrected by means of the *transient loop*. The *terminal loop* is only completed when the action taken to start the machine is successful; that is only one terminal loop can be made for each event. This means that after one loop is completed to start the machine, the next terminal loop may be to feed the machine, and the next to switch it off. But the transient loop must be repeated in the same sequence until the action is successful, i.e. until the machine is finally started.

### The sequence

Under normal conditions a transient loop must be followed by a terminal loop before a stimulus (instruction) is satisfied. If an action fails to achieve its purpose, a sequence of five (three plus two) steps is necessary. The transient loop operates in three steps:

- *Feedback* notifies the controller of the failure.
- *Information* provides a reason for the failure.
- *Adjustment* should rectify the fault.

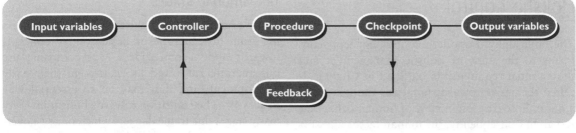

**Figure 23.2** Basic control procedure
Control is a continuous process of adjusting input variables to produce the desired output effects. These variables are also called parameters.

Then the terminal loop must follow in two steps:

- The original instruction is repeated.
- Feedback notifies the controller that the desired effect is achieved.

If the transient loop is unsuccessful, the five steps are repeated until the terminal loop is completed. The waste of time and frustration may be considerable when transient loops continually occur through poor control, such as faulty feedback of information and ill-considered adjustments.

### Constant deviations

Control is essentially a *continuous process of adjustment* to situations, such as steering a vehicle which is constantly deviating from a straight course. This aspect of control is illustrated in Fig. 23.2. The input factors are those variables which may be altered by the controller when corrections are necessary. When properly manipulated, these factors can alter the output variables according to need in the particular circumstances. A simple example is riding a bicycle. The input variables, such as steering, rate of pedalling and use of brakes, are manipulated by the rider to adjust the output variables, direction and speed, according to desire and conditions.

#### CONTROL CYCLES FOR OPERATIONS AND ADMINISTRATIVE PROCESSES

A procedure for operations and administration activities usually involves a more complex approach. Due to the questions of choosing expectations and the envisaged performance, a more subjective assessment should include some flexibility and

initiative. Difficult situations may arise such as customer contact and unusual queries. The control cycle theory for machines still applies, but is related to a more sophisticated approach.

The employee should clearly understand performance expectations and the standards required so that the work is balanced to meet the aims of the team involved and the marketing concept. Thus the person's behaviour within the team is an important factor. This affects consistent delivery of effective results, which is associated with the individual, the team and organisational performance.

# Legislative control

An important aspect for managers and especially directors is to conform with the requirements of UK company law and EU directives. Company directors are particularly at risk (Chapter 7) if legislation is ignored. This form of business control should be rigidly applied regardless of the behavioural aspects (see below).

The breadth of legislative control extends to promotion of the product or service; conforming with various codes related to selling, warranties, after-sales service, and health and safety regulations: Inland Revenue requirements; financial aspects of company law; and many other laws relating to conducting business operations.

Appropriate control systems and procedures must be seen to conform and be liable to scrutiny by external authorities. The rigidity of legislative control naturally tends to be in conflict with both empowerment and flexible working arrangements unless the reason is carefully explained.

# Holistic control

The philosophy of modern control concepts conforms to the aims of holistic management and the essential requirements outlined in Chapter 2. Often this move towards holism is thought to be a natural progression in view of human behaviour research. Consequently, the human factor and survival are recognised and the dangers of bureaucratic control avoided. The important points are now briefly repeated.

## THE HUMAN FACTOR

Apart from the underlying assumptions of holism, the vital points are:

- maintaining a suitable balance between essential controls through rigid, strict rules and adopting principles that remain within legal limits
- flexible operating conditions which allow empowerment to operate successfully
- applying motivational techniques and developing an employee culture
- continually revising controls to achieve maximum effectiveness

## SURVIVAL THROUGH HOLISM

To achieve the correct balance a twofold approach involves:

- encouraging creativeness and innovation
- ensuring control processes provide correct, current information on the financial and legal situations

## THE PHILOSOPHY

Modern control implies the following main concepts:

- a holistic shift by *all* managers to an appropriate management strategy
- an employee culture which involves everyone in continuously improving controls and operational effectiveness
- customer-oriented controls that ensure the customer comes first

## TRANSITIONAL STAGES

Many arguments highlight the problems of moving from bureaucratic or basic control concepts towards modern control ideas. Most companies use bureaucratic rules and procedures in their early development, and they may be an essential way to survive. The transition towards holism involves many stages due to the dangers which must be overcome. Some of these difficulties demand long-term projects and drastic, sincere policy changes.

The idea that introducing modern control is easy and straightforward is an illusion. There are many examples of failed attempts by top management. No one is fooled by distributing policy statements or literature which do not coincide with reality. Alert trade unions soon investigate and smash shallow changes which give wrong impressions. Considerable harm is done to relationships by attempting to fool employees.

# Control appraisal

An appraisal should take into consideration all the input activities associated with production, operations and administrative processes. From the three steps of control (set standards, check performance, correct deviations) it is possible to develop a more elaborate appraisal of how processes are organised. This is essential before any effective system of control can be applied. The appraisal may involve a number of control questions. They are listed below together with the various functions or sources which provide a means of answering them.

## CONTROL QUESTIONS

1  Who is responsible for each section of the work and for doing the work?
   *Refer to organisation plan – division of responsibility and delegation (Chapter 3).*
2  What is the work content?
   *Refer to job description (Chapter 17).*
3  How is the work to be performed?
   *Refer to method study (Chapter 25).*
4  How long should the work take to perform?
   *Refer to work measurement (Chapter 25).*
5  Where should the work be performed
   *Refer to method study and layout (Chapter 25).*

6 When should the work be performed?
*Refer to planning and scheduling (Chapter 26).*

7 What is the cost of performing the work?
*Refer to accounts and costing (Chapters 28 and 29).*

8 How is work performance regulated?
*Refer to human relations, motivation, cost reduction and progress (Chapters 11, 12 and 30).*

9 How is the quality of work checked?
*Refer to quality control (Chapter 27).*

## THE ESSENTIALS OF EFFECTIVE CONTROL

All organisational sectors must conform to many control principles and maintain a continuous control process. Control information should be as complete as possible, quantifiable, easily understood, concise, and acted upon immediately where necessary.

Underlying these important aspects should be adequate training at all levels, clear objectives for everyone, effective organisation where authority and responsibility are comprehensively covered, and an employee culture that recognises the dangers of ineffective control.

### Typical principles

- *Standards* are set to agree with performance expectations and to conform with the nature of the work and the organisational situation.
- *Predictions* on possible deviations are forecasted, repeated, updated and compared.
- *Deviations* based upon the exception principle (Chapter 28) are immediately transmitted to appropriate sources or centres for action.
- *Corrections* are undertaken on a timescale appropriate to the urgency of the deviation related to the work and the organisation.
- *Communication flow* to all relevant sections affected by the corrections should be comprehensive, easily understood, and economic in operation.

## ADVANTAGES OF EFFECTIVE CONTROL

Provided the control process is clearly explained to employees they should receive:

- exact information on performance expectations and standards required
- coaching and support from the supervisor
- comprehensive reviews and feedback at regular intervals
- more effective supervision of day-to-day performance (Chapter 18)

The organisation will benefit in many ways:

- increased productivity
- balanced workloads for all employees through identification of low performance and rapid adjustments
- a recognised fair control procedure which should improve morale and motivation
- an effective coaching scheme with established objectives
- improved communication
- identified training and development needs
- more accurate assessment of performance for future advancement and reward

# Problems of control

Many problems arise in the final stage of correcting deviations. The capability to correct effectively depends upon knowledge, experience, imagination and judgement. All these are overshadowed by an unexpected occurrence such as a power cut, a machine breakdown, or an accident.

The problem of size may easily defeat control with such obstacles as feedback delay, the excessive growth of information flow, the general haze over operations which increases with size and complexity, human problems, and lack of time to think through difficulties. These problems are multiplied at higher levels of management, where additional external factors and uncontrollable variables impede decision making, often when speed is essential.

Criticism of any person who is controlling is exceptionally easy. Immediately some form of action is taken, the situation is changed and further adjustments may be needed. This may appear illogical or contradictory to someone who is unaware of all the facts. Constructive criticism is far more difficult.

## COMPUTERISED CONTROL

In situations where imagination and judgement are not needed, control may be programmed in a *computer system*. Properly adjusted, this automatic control process is more efficient than human operations. However, there is the risk of breakdown which causes delay, possibly irritation for staff and clients, sometimes loss of information if not programmed correctly, and may be disastrous if the system is performing a critical function. An example is a machine that administers drugs to patients automatically. This computerised infusion pump controls blood pressure by monitoring and administering a drug through a drip into the blood stream. Results show it consistently controls blood pressure better than a nurse operating a drip manually.

## REAL-TIME INFORMATION

One advantage of computerised control is the use of real-time information, i.e. data made available on the outcome of events as they occur. Many operations may be captured for real-time control. Examples are booking seats in an aircraft, transmitting sales data in supermarkets to a central storage point to update stocks, and reserving holidays. The benefits depend upon whether real-time information is of direct and crucial use. In some situations the correction procedure is long, therefore the expense is not worthwhile. In most business situations, day-to-day controls are helped by real-time information.

## SECURITY

Security measures are essential to safeguard the company's information, and to satisfy legislation on data protection. Management should ensure the types of control are adequate, and that rules and procedures are followed. The supervisor should check the systems in practice and consider any preventive or remedial steps to improve control. Internal audits should also examine approaches, check on realistic standards, and consider any possibility of security breaches.

### Disasters

Unfortunately, systems and procedures may fail, so contingency plans are a key feature of control. Security must be maintained during systems failures and the supervisor should be ready to take corrective action to minimise their effects.

# Types of control

## FEEDBACK CONTROL

The basic control procedure is based upon feedback. Feedback has many practical failings and its capability is limited. It indicates what *has* happened and provides a correction. Being reactive in this way is essentially responsive to an external stimulus or a reciprocal act.

## PREDICTION CONTROL

A more effective control is achieved by a feedforward system which explains what *will* happen if action is not taken. But accurate forecasting is difficult. The accuracy can be improved by conducting forecasts repeatedly, updating each time, and comparing results. A feedforward system of control is much easier using a computer. PERT networks (see below) also use this concept.

### Applications

Extreme cases, such as weather forecasting for farmers and alerting safety measures, highlight the hazardous nature of some events. However, more predictable situations occur daily, and these fall mainly into two groups: effective action and ineffective action. Suppose a car ascends a hill, the driver may consciously press the accelerator further to maintain a set speed. But a heavy lorry will be forced to change gear to climb the hill and so lose speed. If the aim is to climb the hill with no imposed time limit, *both* actions will be successful (effective action). If the aim is to keep to a set speed, the lorry driver's action will be unsuccessful (ineffective action).

## The concept

The idea is to analyse *input* (feedforward) not *output* (feedback), noting the interaction and adjusting input before output occurs. Prediction control is essential in some manufacturing processes when any surges or changes occur within the process and are noticeable at the input stage. Thus adjustments to compensate can be made.

Although arguably feedback is involved in prediction systems, there is a distinct difference. Information feedback occurs on the input side to make possible adjustments to input before output occurs. Feedback from output is still essential to verify results since there is no guarantee of complete success. Briefly, to operate prediction control the supervisor should:

- Identify the important input variables.
- Construct a model to illustrate their interrelationships.
- Collect data regularly on input and inject this into the system.
- Note the differences between planned and changed inputs.
- Assess results and conduct further alterations to achieve maximum success.

## The main difficulties

Apart from incompetent supervision, the main difficulties may be:

- the effectiveness of forecasting (Chapter 8)
- managing business information (Chapter 30)
- throughput instability factors

## Throughput instability

Throughput instability may be spasmodic and increasing or decreasing in intensity. All processes are affected. Besides affecting material flow, instability occurs in maintenance, services, cash flow, systems and procedures. Consequently, it involves management control at strategic levels and supervisory control at tactical levels. Both aspects concentrate on reducing the degree of instability and the rate of movement from a determined stable condition, in accordance with plans. The main causes of instability are external influences, internal influences and workforce problems.

### External influences

External influences depend on the type of business. Marketing changes in fashion, urgent orders, new competitors, and new legislation are typical examples, along with fluctuations in deliveries of materials, price changes and seasonal effects. Collectively, they cause prediction difficulties for management.

### Internal influences

Many managerial decisions directly and indirectly affect throughput. These effects may be intentional such as introducing a new line, reorganising, revising plans, and changing education and training programmes. Unintentional effects include incompetent decisions associated with motivation, marketing and projects. Using prediction control reduces unstable workflow in these circumstances. However, supervisory control resorts to a basic control pattern when the influences cannot be predicted at this level.

### Workforce problems

There is a fundamental need to apply prediction control as a means of assessing the effects of policy decisions and tactical decisions on the workforce. Most decisions have some effect on motivation and employee productivity. Unforeseen problems such as resistance, increased employee turnover and other disruptions may be avoided.

## PROACTIVE CONTROL

Proactive control avoids analysis of prediction control. Being proactive means adopting a culture that includes:

- being constantly aware of the likely significance of information as it is received
- alerting any sources immediately of the likely effects

These two features obviously require capability and experience.

There is always the risk that the proposed event may not happen, but this is safer than not communicating the forecast and allowing someone later to be surprised at the outcome. A simple everyday example is to hear rain is forecasted and alerting someone to take an umbrella. If it rains the action is successful. If it remains dry the umbrella is useless and the action is unsuccessful, but the probability of rain occurring makes the exercise worthwhile.

Proactive control is an essential part of effective supervision and should always be practised. The important aspects associated with it are the development of conceptual skills (Chapter 1) and using the principle of forecasting (Chapter 8).

## The complete control process

Here are twelve major features which provide an example of the complete control process. They include the processes outlined in Chapters 17 and 18 on employment, and the emphasis on setting standards of performance based on method and time study detailed in Chapter 25.

1 Establish a job description from an agreed plan.
2 Agree performance levels, expectations and standards with the employee and record information.
3 Review performance regularly and record all relevant information.
4 Provide detailed feedback to the employee and agree the information with him or her.
5 Predict events which will occur from the information received and take action.
6 Adopt proactive approaches by alerting appropriate individuals of possible changes, although there is no proof.
7 Provide appropriate coaching from the supervisor or a specialist, as required from feedback.
8 Repeat items 4 and 7 to ensure adequate support and improved performance within the brief, through informal reviews.
9 Bear in mind the three possible situations for standards of performance:
   (a) below standard – agree an action plan to reach the appropriate standard with the employee
   (b) standard maintained – praise, recommendations, etc.
   (c) above standard – praise, rewards, etc.
10 Continue with reviews.
11 Take action if the standard below expectations (9a) persists:
   (a) informal warnings within an agreed procedure
   (b) formal disciplinary procedure
   (c) downgrading the employee.
12 Ensure all appropriate records are maintained.

## The supervisor's role

The supervisor's role may be divided into three main groups that follow the sequence of a basic control procedure:

- collecting and distributing data
- identifying performance problems
- rectifying problems and making recovery plans

### COLLECTING AND DISTRIBUTING DATA

Collecting and distributing data is relevant to performance appraisal and day-to-day performance discussed in Chapter 18, and to the employee performance control cycle. Closely related are the concepts of setting standards and being proactive. The main aspects are:

- Agree clear performance *expectations* with the employee so that his or her aims are in line with the team's efforts and that efforts are focused on important areas of the job.
- Monitor performance by noting behaviour and the impact on the team. Record any positive or negative examples for future reference, but avoid focusing on personality.
- Provide feedback on a regular basis and endeavour to give constructive remarks, noting reactions.
- Persuade the employee to keep a record of performance problems and to consult when there are difficulties.

### IDENTIFYING PERFORMANCE PROBLEMS

Although there may be an obvious performance problem, there is always the difficulty of identifying the cause or causes:

- skill deficiencies (Chapter 19)
- aptitude difficulties (Chapter 9)
- motivational problems (Chapters 11 and 12)
- personal circumstances (Chapter 22)
- conflict within the group (Chapter 5)

- inappropriate methods, time allocation and quality standards (Chapters 24, 25 and 27)

Performance problems are sometimes exasperating because the causes may be either real or apparent. If the apparent cause is recognised, this may lead to examining a long chain of bewildering events before locating the real cause.

## RECTIFYING POOR PERFORMANCE

Rectifying poor performance involves using appropriate techniques and adopting a recovery plan. Many techniques are available, each one appropriate for a particular situation. They have already been discussed and they include:

- individual training by the supervisor
- coaching and support by the supervisor or a specialist
- attending internal or external training courses
- advising on personal difficulties from the personnel manager and various specialists

### Adopting a recovery plan

An agreed recovery plan between the supervisor and the employee is essential to achieve substantial benefit from the process. The main features are:

- Outline the specific objectives.
- Allocate dates for review.
- Agree the recovery programme with all the people involved.
- Resolve any particular issues that arise during the process by immediately discussing the difficulties with the employee and any specialist who is involved.
- Clarify with the employee at the start of the recovery programme the procedure to follow if performance does not improve.

# Quantitative control techniques

The term 'management science' also includes quantitative control techniques. Their purpose is to aid planning, controlling and decision making by using complex formulae which provide data and models quickly in a suitable form. Four of the many choices are considered here.

## CYBERNETICS

Cybernetics is the study of communication and control mechanisms in machines and living creatures. It has enormous potential for improving the effectiveness of industry and influencing its future. The science of cybernetics is complex and extensive. Briefly, the cybernetic attitude accepts industry as *actually* living or working as if it *were* living.

Considerable progress has been made since a group headed by Norbert Weiner, the American mathematician, called this science 'cybernetics' in 1947. His group of scientists had been working together for about five years on the problems of control. They realised common ground existed between control systems in a number of different sciences. Consequently, a number of eminent statisticians, mathematicians, biologists, sociologists, logicians, psychiatrists, engineers and other specialists commenced research with a common aim.

The engineers were particularly interested in applying this new science to automation and computer sciences. Considerable progress has been made in this direction. The basic notions of cybernetics are outside the scope of this work; for more information see the bibliography.

The basic cybernetic model is similar to the open system described earlier. The interrelationships in an organisation operate by means of communication networks which are self-regulating and cope with environmental changes. Thus homeostasis (or a stable condition) is achieved by having reliable information feedback to control points that adjust automatically to changes.

If the system is *deterministic* – changes in behaviour are completely predictable – there is no problem. Temperature changes and sales order movements would be in this category. If behaviour is *probabilistic* – involving estimates or possible changes – only trial and error will determine the correct input/output in the system. Examples are advertising a product and attempting to assess sales orders or throwing a dice once and attempting to determine the result.

Sometimes bionics is thought to be synonymous with cybernetics; together they have been compared to two sides of a coin. Bionics attempts to develop machines through biological design principles whereas cybernetics attempts to understand organisations through making analogies to machines.

## OPERATIONAL RESEARCH

Operational research (OR) is difficult to define accurately. Briefly it is the application of scientific analysis and careful reasoning to provide a quantitative basis for measuring possible courses of action. Consequently, it is a general aid to decision making and there is no limit to the breadth of its application in industry.

The term OR was coined in World War II when various specialists were grouped together to study wartime operations, such as setting up radar systems and fuse-setting for depth charges. Since then many large companies have introduced OR to study such problems as the optimum loading of machines, efficient use of staff, economic methods of transportation, stores congestion, effective maintenance schemes, and optimum stock levels.

Today OR is applied throughout industry and other fields in many countries. OR societies are established and international conferences are held regularly. The approach is to use a basic planning procedure and apply sophisticated mathematical concepts and models to determine optimum courses of action. Such techniques as linear programming, queuing theory, critical path scheduling, replacement theory, and stock control theory demand specialists who are usually advisors. Also existing staff are often trained to operate certain OR techniques.

The main difficulties are finding suitable staff with mathematical backgrounds and managerial experience to approach problems, and coping with the large amount of computer time required. An inevitable problem is the X factor. This applies when some activities defy measurement because of intangible or probabilistic situations. In these circumstances guesswork takes over.

### Applications

Operational research may be applied in any complex situation, such as involved sequential activities, bottlenecks, probability difficulties, choice of action, location queries, scheduling, optimum level requirements, economic quantities, determining priorities, and improving systems and procedures. Many books are available which describe techniques and applications (see the bibliography).

## NETWORK ANALYSIS

Network analysis covers a number of techniques for planning and controlling complex projects. Two typical forms are the *critical path method* (CPM) and the *programme evaluation and review technique* (PERT). In many ways they are similar and represent sequential relationships between activities by a network of lines and circles. The activities are coupled to show how the total time may be reduced to a minimum. Such optimum coupling is called the *critical path*. CPM assumes an *accurate* time for an activity whereas PERT *estimates* the time. CPM is used typically for large construction jobs, PERT for highly complex projects such as a space shuttle.

### A basic network

Figure 23.3 is a simple illustration. Circles represent an event, which is a significant point of time and marks the start and finish of an activity. Lines indicate activities that take time to complete. In the diagram the minimum project time follows the thick line; this is the critical path:

$$30 + 6 + 5 = 41 \text{ minutes (events 1, 4, 5 and 6)}$$

All these events are critical. To avoid delay they must be completed on time. Spare time is called *float*. For example, operator B uses 22 minutes (10 + 10 + 2) with 8 minutes to spare before event 4. Float values indicate where improvements lie.

Even drawing up this simple arrangement immediately raises queries that may not have been obvious before:

- Is the team a good idea?
- How critical is the time to complete the whole service?
- How many other ancillary activities are involved?
- How many engines are being serviced?

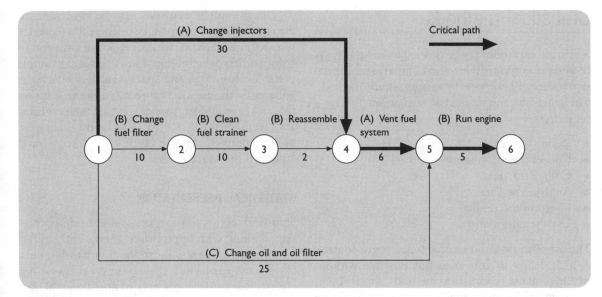

**Figure 23.3** A simple network
This part of a diesel engine service illustrates the critical path. B has 8 minutes of spare time (float) which could be used to clean the air intake, plus 6 minutes of extra time between events 4 and 5. The team (A, B, C) could therefore cope with extra ancillary tasks.

## Computerised networks

In practice many thousands of events and enormous amounts of data become difficult to handle. Computer graphics and appropriate programs help to solve the problems, which may include rearranging sequences successfully in parallel and utilising float times. In this way all the advantages of network analysis are covered. They include rapid presentation of data and graphics for immediate control and co-ordination; assisting in planning; identifying critical data immediately; and presenting data for calculating cost, times and resources required, further summarised as appropriate.

## SIMULATION

Simulation has been used for many years. A model of a process or system is developed to predict reactions to input changes. The model is an attempt to resemble reality by using a quantitative or mechanical approach to illustrate how the situation will be affected when inputs vary. The predictions use probability theory to supply answers to the variables; this means the models are not

precise, they are incomplete, and they tend to be oversimplified.

A typical problem for simulation would be to predict the effects on sales volume of certain variables, such as competition from China in the next two years, changes in world trade and effects of new technologies. This complex model would be computerised because many runs are essential under different economic conditions. Here is the basic procedure:

- Define the problem carefully.
- Assemble the data.
- Develop a model.
- Test in various ways.
- Gather more appropriate data for experiments.
- Run the simulations.
- Analyse the output.
- Rerun the simulations with appropriate changes.
- Repeat the testing and simulations as necessary.

Other applications include computer games and various training simulations for driving cars, piloting aircraft and operating machines.

# Statistical methods

Statistical methods may be defined as various ways of abstracting, classifying and comparing information for control purposes by using scientific methods. The stages in a statistical investigation follow a set pattern:

- Define the reasons for the investigation.
- Collect the information required.
- Collate the data.
- Analyse the data.
- Interpret the results.
- Use the information.

The use of statistics is essential for effective control. A high degree of control is not possible without making full use of statistical methods; this includes drawing valid conclusions and making reasonable decisions on the basis of scientific analysis.

The use of a computer has eased the problem of processing numerical data. But sometimes there remains the tendency to use oral, written or visual means of information rather than resorting to numerical information.

## ADVANTAGES OF USING STATISTICS

- Statistics reduce the breadth of disagreement which might occur in a discussion when attempting to determine a decision.
- Subjective ideas, theories and opinions may be challenged or supported by presenting numerical information.
- Gossip, rumours and uncertainty may be dispelled.
- Arguments based upon particular circumstances or isolated cases may be removed.
- Systematic collection and analysis of data are more likely to be accurate.

## THE PROBLEM OF INTERPRETATION

An important feature which is often forgotten is that two sets of figures can only be accurately compared when they are measured in the same units, e.g. all data in pounds sterling or all data in kilograms. Also they should be expressed in the same way, e.g. all fractions, all decimals, all percentages.

Unfortunately, statistics may be easily abused through incorrect interpretation. There is a tendency to use those statistics which support a case and to ignore others which oppose it. A classical example is the explosion of the space shuttle *Challenger*: apparently the engineers forecasted the O-rings on the rocket would rupture at freezing temperatures and recommended not to launch; the managers used incomplete data to contest the forecast and launched the space shuttle.

## STATISTICAL PRESENTATION

Statistical reports to superiors should be simply presented along with appropriate graphs and figures. Graphs often impress far more than wordy notes. Should the supervisor wish to impress his or her efforts, it is surprisingly easy to portray numerical information in a better light. For example, graphs can have their scales manipulated to produce large variations in presentation, e.g. not starting the $y$-axis from zero and using a logarithmic axis. Naturally this tactic should be considered when receiving statistical information. Statistical information should apply not only to control reports but also to business writing (Chapter 15) and report writing (Chapter 16).

## ANALYSIS OF INFORMATION

The main aspects which may be used in control reports are graphical representations. These include bar charts and pie charts, pictograms, graphs, trend charts, frequency distributions, histograms and frequency polygons. Other forms of analysis include methods of stating accuracy, tabulation and numerical methods. These are extensive and may be obtained from any book on statistics.

# Graphical representation

## BAR CHARTS

The three main types are illustrated in Fig. 23.4:

- *Simple*: the height or length of each bar indicates the value represented.
- *Multiple*: separate components of the total are shown as separate adjoining bars.

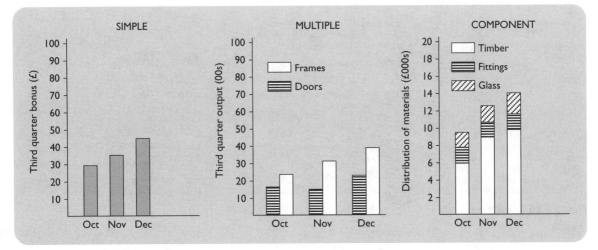

**Figure 23.4** Three kinds of bar chart

- *Component*: the bars are subdivided into the different components of the total, represented either as actual figures or as percentages.

## PIE CHARTS

Pie charts create a quick impression of the structure of the total information by presenting the parts as sectors of a circle. Often the percentages or values are entered in each sector. The angle of the sector is calculated by multiplying the percentage by 3.6, e.g. 20 per cent is represented by $20 \times 3.6 = 72°$). Accurate comparison of segments is difficult where there is little variation, but their use is ideal where obvious comparisons can be illustrated (Fig. 23.5).

## PICTOGRAMS

Pictograms are easy to understand provided the symbols representing a particular quantity are simple and the quantity is clearly stated. Smaller quantities are represented by fractions of the symbol and larger quantities by a number of the symbols. If the symbols are arranged in line, the effect is similar to a bar chart. Figure 23.6 illustrates a typical arrangement.

## GRAPHS

The graph or line chart conveys the relationship between two variables by plotting a curve or a

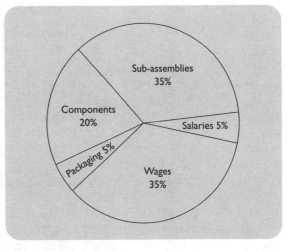

**Figure 23.5** A pie chart

straight line. A graph is constructed by drawing two lines at right angles to represent the variables. The dependent variable is plotted on the vertical axis ($y$-axis); the independent variable is plotted on the horizontal axis ($x$-axis). Figure 23.7 illustrates the layout of a graph.

When data items are classified chronologically, the time series is plotted as an independent variable on the $x$-axis. For example, output per month would be portrayed by drawing the months on the $x$-axis and the range scale of output on the $y$-axis (Fig. 23.7). To avoid distortion the scale should

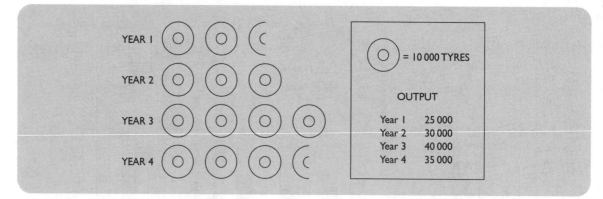

**Figure 23.6** A pictogram

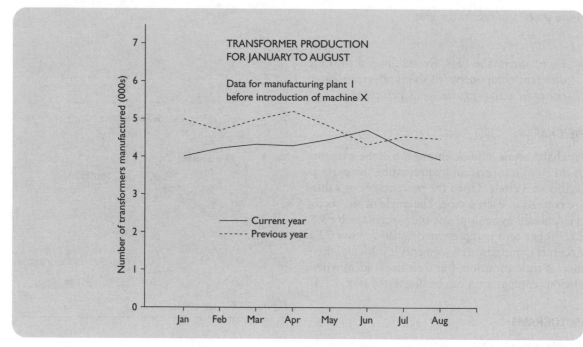

**Figure 23.7** A graph
Plot the dependent variable on the vertical axis (*y*-axis); plot the independent variable on the horizontal axis (*x*-axis). To prevent distortion, the scale on the *y*-axis normally begins at zero. Label the axes clearly and provide a key to any symbols.

start at zero for the dependent variable. Attention to detail is important when preparing a graph otherwise it will not convey the correct impression. Details must be remembered such as inserting a title, the source of data, the key to co-ordinate lines if more than one is used, and naming the variables clearly with sufficient information.

## TREND CHARTS

A fundamental problem of control is the fluctuations in demand for production caused by seasonal market conditions. The use of line graphs which give current output figures of set periods (such as weeks or months) can be misleading and difficult

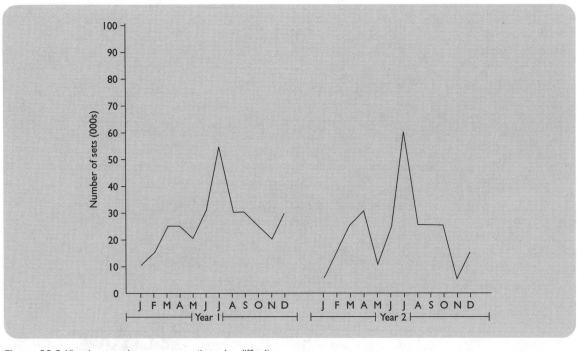

*Figure 23.8* Visual comparisons can sometimes be difficult

to interpret by comparing one year with another. Figure 23.8 illustrates this problem: at any time during year 1 an estimate of the trend compared with year 2 is likely to be inaccurate.

This problem may be overcome by using annual figures for comparison and plotting the moving annual total (MAT) or trend. The trend line dispenses with seasonal fluctuations and gives a clear indication of the true position compared to the previous year. The MAT or trend is calculated by deducting the monthly figure for the previous year from the annual total and adding the current monthly figure. The result is plotted and it becomes the new annual total; a similar process is used to calculate the next month's MAT, and so on. This is illustrated in Fig. 23.9; to allow comparison, similar statistics are used in Figs 23.8 and 23.9.

## Z CHARTS

The Z chart is useful for illustrating the overall picture of monthly figures (or similar statistics), the moving annual total, and the cumulative total. The effect of plotting these three lines resembles the letter Z, as shown in Fig. 23.10. The data is prepared in the same way as figures for trend charts, and the cumulative total is calculated by adding each monthly figure to the total for the previous months.

## FREQUENCY DISTRIBUTIONS

Frequency distributions present a mass of data in a simple and meaningful way. They give all the data and the number of times each piece of data occurs. To reveal the pattern, the data is usually grouped into classes. The total number of frequencies must always equal the total number of occurrences.

The variables are the factors being measured. They may be discrete or continuous. Discrete variables are measured in whole numbers only, e.g. 11 operators or 17 machines. Continuous variables are measured in quantity or extent, e.g. operator height = 1.2 m, a cement load = 7.23 tonnes, and

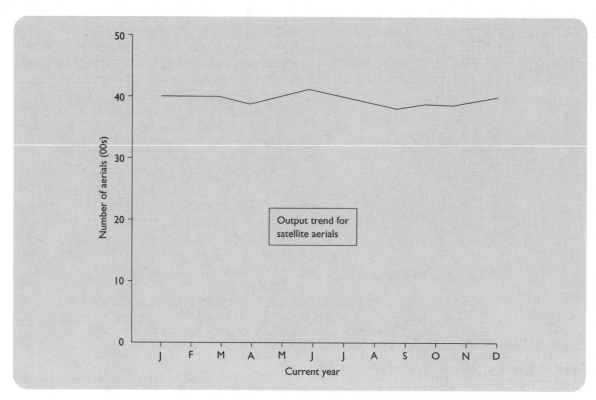

**Figure 23.9** Moving annual total
The moving annual total or trend is calculated by deducting the relevant monthly figure from the previous year's total and adding the figure for the current month. To obtain the moving annual total for May 1999, take the year May 1998 to April 1999, subtract the figure for May 1998 and add the figure for May 1999. To obtain the moving annual total for June 1999, take the moving annual total for May 1999, just calculated, subtract the figure for June 1998 and add the figure for June 1999. Continue like this for each consecutive month.

can be expressed in fractions of a number. This is an important feature when deciding on the class limits. Working groups may be classed according to numbers, 1–4, 5–9 employees, etc., but if lengths of steel rod were classed in this way, no provision would be made for lengths which were more than say 1.25 m and less than 1.5 m. Figure 23.11 shows a discrete frequency chart.

## HISTOGRAMS

A diagram illustrating the frequency distribution of a continuous variable is known as a histogram (Fig. 23.12). Class intervals are plotted along the *x*-axis and distribution is shown as rectangles measured against the frequency scale on the *y*-axis.

The area of the rectangle representing each class is also proportional to the frequency in that particular class. The histogram should not be confused with bar charts which show magnitude.

## FREQUENCY POLYGONS

Frequency distributions may also be plotted as *frequency polygons*. Take the topmost side of each rectangle and mark its midpoint, then join the midpoints together (Fig. 23.12). The line can only be plotted when the class intervals are equal. Where the class intervals are very small this will produce a *frequency curve*. The area enclosed by the frequency curve or polygon should be equal to the area of the histogram.

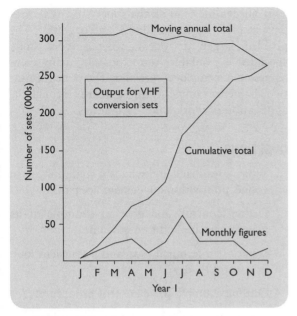

**Figure 23.10** A Z chart
A Z chart is obtained by plotting the monthly figures, the
moving annual totals and the cumulative totals on one graph.
The cumulative total for February is the sum of the figures for
January and February; the cumulative total for March is the
sum of the March figure and the cumulative total for February;
the cumulative total for April is the sum of the April figure and
the cumulative total for March.

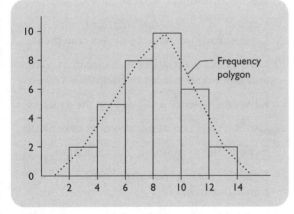

**Figure 23.12** Histogram illustrating a frequency polygon
A histogram is a graph of a frequency distribution. It is not a
bar chart; the area of each rectangle should be proportional
to the number of observations in its class interval. The class
interval is represented by the width of the rectangle. To
construct a frequency polygon, take the topmost side of each
rectangle and mark its midpoint, then join the midpoints
together; the polygon may be smoothed into a curve. The
curve should extend to the axis, half a class interval beyond
the classes at the two extremes.

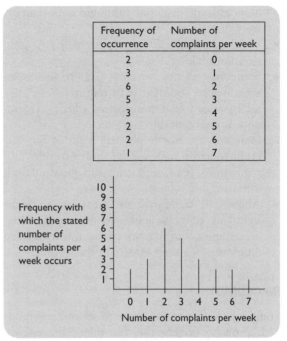

**Figure 23.11** Discrete frequency chart
This frequency distribution gives all data and the number
of times each piece of data occurs. It is only suitable for
variables which are discrete, i.e. measured in whole numbers.
Continuous variables are measured in quantity or extent and
are plotted on close intervals; see Figure 23.12.

# Establishing control standards

Scientific control is not possible unless most of the
variable factors involved in a process are measured
and standards are established. However, there is
no point in setting a standard for control unless it is
economic. In other words, the cost of establishing
a standard must be justified and it must not be more
than the value of return from the activity.

Standards may be set for factors such as
methods, times to complete tasks, performance,
quality, forms, equipment, working conditions,
grading individuals, work batches, layout, materials and tools.

### ESSENTIAL FEATURES

- Standards are measures for the application of
  vital controls.

- Standards are essential minimum requirements for planning and forecasting.
- Standards are flexible measurements to help decision making.
- Standards are not for employees to use as set measures to conform with requirements; they are bases or foundations below which performance is unacceptable.
- Standards do not imply any form of bureaucratic function such as conforming to rules and regulations, and restricting imagination and initiative.
- Above all, standards are measures to highlight and recognise achievements, imagination, creativeness and inventiveness; and to reward employees for their efforts in these roles.

## INACCURACY

Some supervisors are reluctant to set control standards, probably because they fear their estimates will be inaccurate. This possible error is of no importance. The vital point is to provide some basis against which the actual figures may be measured, consequently the reasons for the deviation may be ascertained and corrective action taken if necessary. If the actual figure is justified after investigation, the standard is revised and no harm is done. The process of scientific control has then commenced.

## THE DANGER OF EXCESSIVE ACCURACY

Measuring to a high degree of accuracy is time-consuming and may be self-defeating. Good sense is needed to ensure that decisions are not delayed unnecessarily through excessive accuracy. If an approximate figure will provide sufficient data for control, there is no purpose in being absolutely accurate. Naturally where financial matters are concerned there are other risks to consider, such as not conforming to legal requirements and providing misleading data for cash flow purposes.

## THE USE OF SPECIALISTS

Usually performance is related to pay schemes and various assessments. Clearly an essential requirement in these circumstances is to set standards that are acceptable to employees and trade unions.

This burden may fall on the supervisor, who may have to measure, set standards, and negotiate. The problem largely disappears when a work study specialist is available. Unfortunately, many companies do not employ a specialist. Therefore the next two chapters examine setting standards through the application of work study techniques.

## QUESTIONS

1 What is feedback and why is it so important in connection with management control?

2 Define 'control' and give an example of its meaning as applied to a machine.

3 What are a terminal loop and a transient loop in control theory?

4 Outline a simple basic control procedure.

5 Discuss the basic steps that are necessary to set up control of a plan.

6 What is meant by control appraisal?

7 State the main aspects of control in a business and give a brief account of each one.

8 Control may be said to be a continuous process of adjustment. Discuss this statement.

9 Control is an essential part of supervision. Give a reasoned account of this statement.

10 Give a brief description of operational research and mention the main techniques it covers.

11 How can network analysis help the supervisor?

12 Outline the main applications of cybernetics.

13 Explain the term 'model' in simulation.

14 Describe some typical applications of operational research.

15 Using the philosophy of modern control is an essential part of supervision. Explain this philosophy and how the supervisor can apply it.

16 What are the dangers of control that a supervisor is often confronted with in day-to-day situations?

17 Standards should be carefully explained to employees. List the main aspects of this statement.

18 List the foundations of control.

19 Outline the essential features of control that the supervisor should fully understand.

20 Describe the basic theory of control.

21 Explain holistic control.

22 Detail the main types of control.

23 Effective supervision relies upon proactive control. Justify this statement.

24 List the twelve main features of a computer control process.

25 Outline the quantitative control techniques available to the supervisor and in what circumstances they could be used.

26 List the stages of a statistical investigation.

27 Using statistics is essential for effective control. Discuss this statement.

28 How would you ensure that your reports to superiors are likely to be read?

29 What are the essential features to remember when establishing standards?

---

## CASE STUDY

Alfred is 55 years old, has worked in the company for 30 years, and is employed as a clerk. He is a slow worker now, careless, and interrupts others by chatting and asking questions. Andrew is a new supervisor and has decided to tolerate Alfred, considering his length of service. One day Helen, a conscientious clerk with a good record approaches Andrew. She insists that Alfred is becoming a nuisance, hindering her work and making innuendos. Andrew decides to interview Alfred, outlines the problem of interrupting people's work, but does not mention Helen's name. Alfred strongly denies the complaint and says he can't stand the sight of Helen.

*How would you continue the interview?*

---

## CASE STUDY

Stephen Braddock is employed in a large department store as the store detective. While in the cosmetics section he overhears two women talking about a lipstick one has just bought. 'And what do you think? She gave me change for a ten pound note instead of a fiver!' He contacts the supervisor, Jill, and explains. At the end of the day Jill checks the till. The takings agree with the tally roll.

*What would you do about this situation? Consider Jill's action related to the possible explanations.*

# 24

# Setting control standards

## The importance of work study

The reliance on standards in all control processes was stressed in the previous chapter. Consequently, the supervisor has a responsibility to ensure method and time standards are used effectively to achieve scientific control. Setting such standards is a skilful activity. In the absence of a practitioner, the supervisor has to undertake this activity and it requires considerable practice to become proficient. Furthermore, within the expanding field of work study, there are many other means which may help in establishing appropriate standards.

The burden of improving productivity through the application of new operations still falls on the supervisor, even when a practitioner is employed. Sufficient faith in the effectiveness of new methods is essential and may depend upon the supervisor's knowledge of work study. There is always the danger that the supervisor may be so engrossed in procedures, methods, timing, recording, controlling workflow, etc., that he or she neglects the employees who put the methods into practice.

### THE HUMAN ELEMENT

Employees should have a thorough understanding of the reasons for using standards. This factor has already been stressed previously. The standards that are set may interfere with drive and effort unless the supervisor pays sufficient attention to the human element and stresses they are foundations only. Such foundations or bases are minimum levels below which performance is unacceptable. A balance is possible to satisfy both aspects of using the benefits of standards *and* attending to the human problems of operations control. This is achieved by providing guidance and encouragement to maintain motivation and morale, and ensuring the production tasks do not override the human element.

Finally, employees usually recognise the fairness of requirements for output and quality. If they are given the opportunity they will work at their own pace to suit their personality and to achieve the desired results. Consequently, they enjoy more freedom and the supervisor can relax close control; but this partly depends on competent supervision in other areas.

### A COMPREHENSIVE PLAN

Considering the nature of control and the human factor, clearly there are crucial features inherent in embarking on any scheme for setting control standards. They include a concise presentation of all the aspects associated with standards, appropriate counselling to remove resistance and overcome personal problems, involving everyone at the beginning, and stressing the need for suggestions and ideas. Studying the work follows set patterns outlined in the next chapter, and the vital use of all the human aspects.

Finally, the implementation of improvements and findings is equally important if resistance is to be avoided. This involves concern for people in all respects, including apprehensiveness, fear of redundancy, training problems, and adequate counselling. Consultation with other sections or departments is essential to avoid repercussions

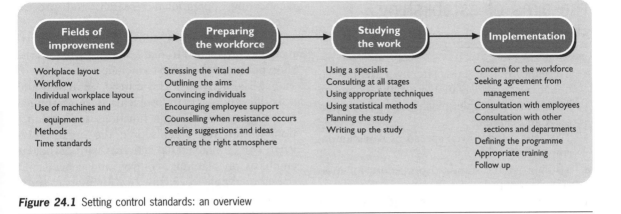

**Figure 24.1** Setting control standards: an overview

later on. This factor should be viewed as a continuing process of follow up to ensure any snags are dealt with quickly. An overview of the whole process is shown in Fig. 24.1.

## ESSENTIAL ASPECTS

To satisfy the above requirements, the supervisor should have a working knowledge of certain aspects which provide a firm basis for discussion with employees and for using work study effectively. These are discussed now and summarised below.

- definition of work study
- aims of establishing control standards
- the scope of work study
- the application of work study
- organisation and methods (O&M)

# Definition of work study

Work study may be broadly described as a scientific study of any form of work. It includes such factors as people, machines, equipment, tools, materials and layout, with a view to increasing productivity by improving the effectiveness of each factor involved.

Cruder forms of work study naturally commenced at a time when human beings first used their brains to reason out a better way of performing a task, such as trapping an animal for food. Nowadays work study is highly sophisticated and continually expanding. Many techniques use complex scientific calculations and computers. All these modern techniques are not concerned with increasing the speed of the processes. They are aimed at locating the optimum utilisation of individuals, machines, processes, materials, equipment, space, and any other factors which are involved in the particular work under investigation.

## OPTIMUM UTILISATION

The usual interpretation of the phrase 'optimum utilisation of individuals' is that people must work harder to increase productivity. This should be expected because people confuse the *optimum* 'the best' with *maximum* 'the greatest'. Employees may see some people being idle – often through no fault of their own – while others are working well beyond a normal rate. Forcing people to work beyond a normal rate or natural rate does not, on the whole, achieve increased output. Many problems arise, including low morale and stress.

The aim of optimum utilisation is to create a favourable utilisation of individuals, which means minimising fatigue and ensuring *all* concerned perform a normal day's work.

Far greater savings are possible by improving methods, more detailed planning and control of work, and effective utilisation of machines and other facilities, than by driving employees at too high a rate.

# The aims of establishing standards

- To indicate the most effective use of economic resources available to the company. This includes people, machines, space, equipment and capital.
- To create a more even spread of work among employees.
- To improve the standard procedure for more effective control.
- To aid planning by providing standard times and procedures.
- To establish fairer pay schemes by carefully assessing job values and performance.
- To assist in creating a more contented workforce. The streamlining of production should eliminate many sources of frustration and tension, providing management does not neglect the human element when introducing changes.
- To increase productivity. This should help to bring economic benefits both to the company and to the community.

# The scope of work study

For the purpose of explanation only, work study is divided into *method study* and *work measurement*. Method study attempts to find better ways of performing jobs with available facilities; and work measurement determines the time a proficient employee takes to perform a specified job, based upon a given level of performance.

In practice these two sectors are closely integrated. Usually method study comes first, followed by work measurement, which is based upon the revised method. Measuring the work will often reveal more improvements which are then incorporated.

The field of work study is expanding continually. Consequently, there is some degree of overlap in new terms and techniques which are emerging from the study of various aspects. For example, there are many terms which mean more or less the same as work study, such as production engineering, organisation and methods, methods engineering, operational research, and process re-engineering.

The scope of work study as a service department has broadened from the study of work on the shop floor and the office to include a vast range of managerial activities. This critical, analytical and scientific approach to problems is now applied to new projects; all main functions and subfunctions within the organisation; the organisation itself; and all managerial activities with particular emphasis on planning, control, and general and operational policies. Figure 24.2 attempts to show the modern extent of work study and to indicate its complex developments with the overlapping of techniques and terms.

## THE WORK STUDY PRACTITIONER

The supervisor should possess some knowledge of the qualities and aims of a work study practitioner. The object is not to be critical of the practitioner's shortcomings, but to assist in achieving the purpose of helping the supervisor and the employees. The practitioner's reputation rests entirely with the supervisor and employees. They can make the proposals work well or ruin them. Most practitioners are aware of this situation. Inevitably the practitioner needs the supervisor's help and the assistance and suggestions of employees. Any supervisor who deliberately forestalls and attempts to create the wrong atmosphere between the practitioner and employees is hindering both parties and openly displaying ignorance and conceit.

## THE INDIVIDUAL AND WORK STUDY

Unfortunately, there is an inherent belief that any suggested change in the way a person performs work is a direct reflection on his or her ability. This belief applies to everyone. Furthermore, a superior has the same feeling when proposals are made to change a subordinate's way of working. This natural resistance may be overcome by sound explanations of the need and scope for improvements. People should then realise that work study is only an extension of the specialist function, it is very time-consuming, and it is not a personal criticism of their methods.

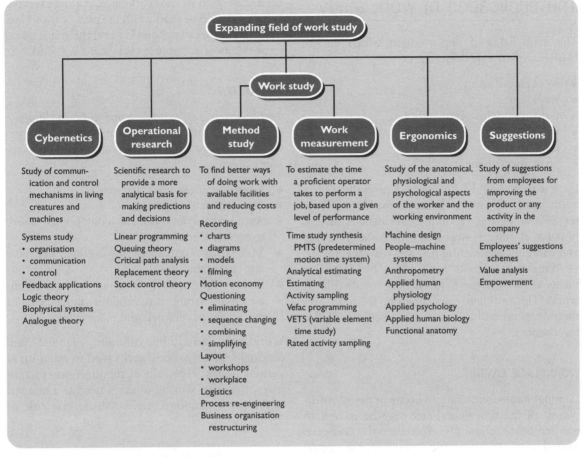

**Figure 24.2** The expanding field of work study

## Typical attitudes

Employees are usually inclined to wait for the *supervisor* to propose better ways of doing the work. They probably think it is the responsibility of the supervisor. Perhaps suggestions have been ignored in the past, consequently apathy has developed. Of course, some take the initiative and develop their own short cuts. There is also the attitude that new methods mean more work, and job changes may mean redundancy. People are not inclined to take the risk of bringing about changes, especially if they are already happy and secure in their jobs. This natural resistance to change is understandable. The supervisor must accept the problem as a challenge to convince employees of the necessity for progressive thinking and the dangers of lagging behind in productivity.

## Encouraging employee support

The case for work study is strengthened if the supervisor remembers that often individuals are disinclined to ask for more work. Most people take the work they are allocated and spread it very accurately over the time available. Management should provide appropriate briefings, including (if feasible) guarantees on such difficulties as redundancy, pay and incentives. Supervisors should attempt to create a desirable atmosphere to achieve co-operation.

# The application of work study

The main fields of improvement which do not involve capital expenditure are:

- workplace layout
- workflow
- individual workplace layout
- use of machines and equipment
- method study
- work measurement

Each aspect should be examined carefully and in accordance with method study procedure (Chapter 25). Some degree of improvement is always possible if time is spent studying the situation and carefully considering possible rearrangements.

Employees always have ideas for improvements as they are most closely concerned with the work. The problem is persuading them to give their opinions and to co-operate during and after the changes.

## WORKPLACE LAYOUT

Gradual and subtle changes occur in many workplaces all the time: a cabinet may be moved to accommodate a supply of materials, a bench moved nearer to an electrical point, and so on. As processes and output change, some rearrangement occurs. Unless the supervisor maintains a constant check and plans, even the best layout gradually deteriorates into a muddle, especially if individuals are allowed to move equipment without permission.

### Surveys

Periodic surveys of workplace layout are worthwhile. The usual problems are storage; keeping gangways clear; maximising the use of overhead space; locker location; and the siting of benches, desks, machines and equipment. The problems should be listed and possible solutions noted. Important aspects to consider are safety; existing location of supply lines such as air, electricity, water and gas; and workflow.

One useful method for trying out ideas is to make scale models of all the workplace furniture by making cardboard cut-outs and locating them on a scale plan of the workplace. All the essential supplies should be marked on the plan. Various layouts may be arranged quickly and the snags noted until the most suitable arrangement is found.

## WORKFLOW

Transporting is an expensive operation so eliminate each unnecessary movement of materials, paperwork and assemblies. The main principles to apply are:

- Rearrange flow lines that cross.
- Avoid backtracking.
- Avoid any congestion at vital points where materials feed the line.
- Make due allowances for testing, verifying and inspection points.
- Ensure the correct sequence of operations which are arranged to minimise movements of materials, paperwork and assemblies.

Workflow should be carefully planned and checked regularly. Bottlenecks tend to build up at various points, especially at the junction of gangways. Effective workflow saves time and temper, is far more economic, and reduces the risk of accidents.

## INDIVIDUAL WORKPLACE LAYOUT

A number of advantages may be gained by attending to poor individual workplace layout. These include reducing employee fatigue and frustration, avoiding the risks of accidents, and improving output and quality of work. The usual reasons for this problem are:

- lack of forethought
- overcrowding
- changes in job content
- untrained employees
- disregard for new work study techniques

The principles of general workplace layout equally apply to individual workplace layout. Workflow is an important feature and should be related to:

- arrival and departure points of materials and assemblies

- positioning of jigs and fixtures
- the siting and use of the most appropriate tools.

## USE OF MACHINES AND EQUIPMENT

Existing machinery and equipment may be obsolescent, obsolete or partly unsuitable. This factor causes frustration and affects output and quality. Nevertheless, the supervisor's responsibility is to make the best possible use of these facilities. Blaming management or predecessors for buying unwisely is not an excuse to ignore the responsibility. Precious capital has been spent on these items and they should be fully utilised by careful planning to avoid the company suffering a loss.

The supervisor may make recommendations for replacements and additional mechanisation, but they must be justified through savings in time and labour plus improved quality. The supervisor should appreciate that capital expenditure is a complex and risky part of management's job. One major error of expenditure in a small concern may result in the eventual liquidation of the company. A certain amount of sympathy and understanding is essential where the need for expenditure seems obvious, but management is inclined to be cautious for no apparent reason.

## METHOD STUDY

A critical study of the operations performed in a job is an essential part of the technique of method study (Chapter 25). The supervisor should adopt a questioning attitude towards each activity in the work, with a view to eliminating, combining, changing the sequence of, or simplifying various activities. Most jobs can be streamlined in this way. Productivity should improve when adopting the principles of motion economy as well, due to the application of quicker and less fatiguing methods.

## WORK MEASUREMENT

An assessment of the time jobs take to perform is obviously essential for planning and control. The supervisor does not have to be a specialist to time a job within reasonable limits, provided the application and techniques of work measurement are followed (Chapter 25). Helpful aspects are experience of the work and a working knowledge of employees who are performing the operations. Neglecting time standards is inviting disaster when pay schemes, costings and estimates are arranged. The set times should be acceptable to employees before they can be used for financial incentives.

# Organisation and methods

The application of work study applies equally in the office, where it is known as organisation and methods (O&M). All office or administrative activities need to be carefully questioned and justified. For full co-operation from clerical staff, the changes recommended and implemented demand similar diplomacy, human skills and understanding.

The gains may be considerable when bureaucratic procedures and systems are examined and changes made to suit modern control techniques and a customer-oriented culture. The benefits are:

- fewer repetitive tasks
- fewer interruptions
- reduced frustration
- more flexibility
- an improved service to employees and customers
- a range of economic advantages.

Provided staff are consulted and involved in the studies, there should be increased enthusiasm, general acceptance of change, reduced staff turnover, and the opportunity to broaden the range of tasks in a job.

Problems of supervision are similar to those encountered on the shop floor. Often managers and supervisors are forced to spend most of their time running the departments, and seeking improvements tends to fall into the background. Provided the company is sufficiently large, it is worthwhile to employ an O&M officer. This specialist should inform management on new techniques and information technology, advise on changes, and assist in introducing more effective systems.

## QUESTIONS

1 Discuss the importance of work study in connection with higher productivity.

2 How would you convince an employee of the necessity for work study?

3 Explain the terms 'method study' and 'work measurement' and show their interrelationship.

4 What are the main problems that confront the work study practitioner during the normal course of duties?

5 How can the supervisor assist the work study practitioner?

6 What part must management play if the suggestions for improving work are to be successfully employed?

7 What should the supervisor do if an employee strongly objects to the presence of a work study practitioner at the workplace?

8 What are the main fields of improvement to consider when setting control standards?

9 How would you prepare the employees before starting a scheme to set control standards?

10 Implementing control standards is an art. Discuss this statement.

11 How would you convince an employee that optimum utilisation of the workforce is essential?

12 Outline a comprehensive plan to embark on a scheme to set control standards.

---

### CASE STUDY

At a supervisors' monthly meeting, the main subject was a rumour that the company intended to introduce business process re-engineering. Michael said, 'We all know what that means; cost-cutting and headcount reduction. I've heard it's drastic and dangerous considering customers and losing good people'. Douglas said, 'Why don't they discuss it with us first? We've been agitating to use work study for ages now and no one had taken any notice. Now some idiot has come up with this one!'

Robert was getting cross, 'It's jobs for the boys! A golf course decision you can guarantee. I propose we try again and make a presentation to the managing director this time instead of talking about it to the works manager'.

Michael retorted, 'You're wasting your time. I'll bet its already arranged and we'll be the first to suffer!'

*Outline the possible problems in this situation. Write up a suitable presentation for the managing director.*

---

### CASE STUDY

'Roger keeps giving me the rotten jobs and I'm fed up with it!' declares Ron Evans, an old hand who is quite capable and could easily tackle more difficult tasks successfully. 'Why not give these youngsters a go? I want some straightforward work for a change.'

'I know, Ron, but the trouble is they can't cope, as you well know', sympathised the supervisor.

*What work study techniques could be used in these circumstances? Comment on the supervisor's role in this case.*

# 25

# Establishing methods and time standards

## Introduction

The importance of setting methods and time standards has already been stressed under the nature of control (Chapter 23). Without the aid of a specialist, the supervisor has to undertake this task. Adopting work study techniques with confidence may be achieved by reading and remembering the information in this chapter and practising continually.

Even if work study specialists are employed, the supervisor still needs to understand what they are doing. He or she should be able to discuss the techniques intelligently with the specialists. Active participation by the supervisor is needed during investigations and meetings, because the supervisor's knowledge and experience help to broaden opinions and provide ideas for improvements.

Whenever possible, the terms used in describing the various techniques conform to the definitions in the *Glossary of Terms in Work Study*. This is issued by the British Standards Institution (BSI) and reproduced with their kind permission.

## Setting methods

### BSI DEFINITION OF METHOD STUDY

The systematic recording and critical examination of existing and proposed ways of doing work as a means of developing and applying easier and more effective methods and reducing costs.

### Method study procedure

A logical sequence is usually divided into five stages (Fig. 25.1):

**Figure 25.1** Setting methods: a simplified procedure

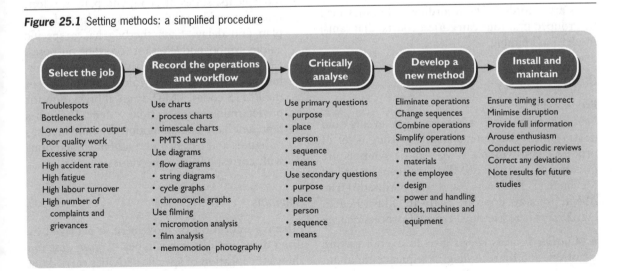

| Select the job | Record the operations and workflow | Critically analyse | Develop a new method | Install and maintain |
|---|---|---|---|---|
| Troublespots | Use charts | Use primary questions | Eliminate operations | Ensure timing is correct |
| Bottlenecks | • process charts | • purpose | Change sequences | Minimise disruption |
| Low and erratic output | • timescale charts | • place | Combine operations | Provide full information |
| Poor quality work | • PMTS charts | • person | Simplify operations | Arouse enthusiasm |
| Excessive scrap | Use diagrams | • sequence | • motion economy | Conduct periodic reviews |
| High accident rate | • flow diagrams | • means | • materials | Correct any deviations |
| High fatigue | • string diagrams | Use secondary questions | • the employee | Note results for future |
| High labour turnover | • cycle graphs | • purpose | • design | studies |
| High number of | • chronocycle graphs | • place | • power and handling | |
| complaints and | Use filming | • person | • tools, machines and | |
| grievances | • micromotion analysis | • sequence | equipment | |
| | • film analysis | • means | | |
| | • memomotion photography | | | |

- Select the job to be studied.
- Record all the appropriate facts.
- Critically examine the facts.
- Develop a new method.
- Install and maintain the new method.

## SELECT THE JOB TO BE STUDIED

Usually selection is based upon economic considerations. Where costs are abnormally high there is a good opportunity to make considerable savings. The signs which reveal likely areas for investigation are:

- trouble spots
- bottlenecks
- low and erratic output
- poor quality work
- excessive scrap
- high accident rate
- excessive overtime
- high fatigue
- high labour turnover
- high number of complaints and grievances

## RECORD THE FACTS

A clear picture of all existing operations and flow of work should be drawn, to provide a sound basis for examining the system followed. This stimulates ideas for improvements, ideas which are seldom apparent until the overall scene is portrayed. Faults become more obvious when operations are recorded. The recording techniques may be grouped into four categories: charts, diagrams, models and filming.

### Charts

#### Process charts

Process charts take a sequence of events and portray them diagrammatically by using a set of process chart symbols. Two sets of symbols are in common use: the ASME (American Society of Mechanical Engineers) and the Gilbreth. The ASME is more popular. Both are illustrated in Fig. 25.2. There are three types of process charts:

- *Outline process charts* give an overall picture of one job by recording in sequence the main operations and inspections. An example is given in Fig. 25.2.
- *Flow process charts* set out the sequential flow of a product or a procedure by recording all the events under review. The flow process chart activities may record the operator (operator types), or the use of materials (material type), or how the equipment is used (equipment type). An example is given in Fig. 25.3.
- *Two-handed process charts* record the activities of an operator's hands or limbs in relationship to each other.

### Timescale charts

Timescale charts are used for recording the activities of more than one subject at once and for recording all the movements taking place in an operation. There are three types:

- *Multiple activity charts* record the activities of two or more subjects using a common timescale to show their interrelationship. The subjects may be operators, machines or equipment.
- *Simo charts* use film analysis; 'simo' is an acronym for *simultaneous motion cycle chart*. The chart records simultaneously on a common timescale the *therbligs* or groups of therbligs performed by various parts of the body on one or more operators. The term 'therblig' was given by Frank Gilbreth to each of the specific divisions of movement, according to the purpose for which it is made. The divisions cover movements, states of being and pauses: select, grasp, assemble, inspect, transport loaded, rest, plan and delay. Each therblig has a specific colour symbol and letter for recording purposes.
- *PMTS charts* record all the movements taking place in any operation by using one of the PMTS codes. PMTS is an abbreviation for predetermined motion time system. The codes represent basic human motions by combinations of figures and letters and qualifying conditions with corresponding time values.

### Diagrams

Effective indication of movement is achieved by using diagrams of various types. A *flow diagram* shows the location of specific activities carried out

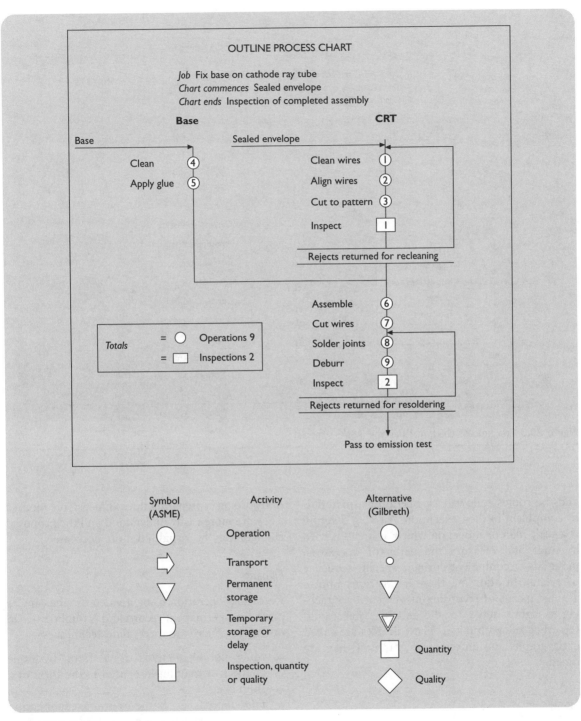

**Figure 25.2** Outline process chart

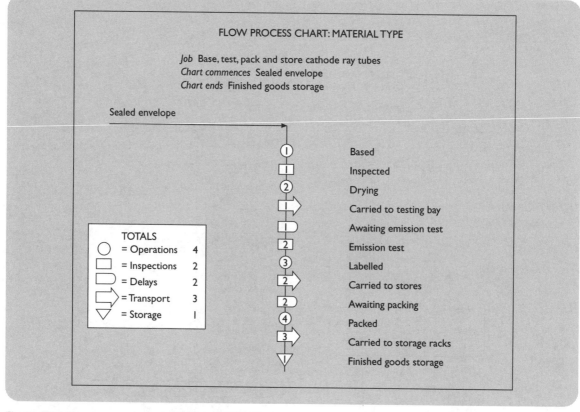

**Figure 25.3** Flow process chart: material type (ASME symbols)

and the routes followed by operations, materials or equipment in their execution. A *string diagram* is a scale plan or model on which a thread is used to trace and measure the paths of operators, materials or equipment during a specific sequence of events. In addition, there are various photographic means of recording movement by attaching a light source to the moving object and recording the path taken. These devices are called cycle graphs and chronocycle graphs if they are timed.

## Models

A popular method is to draw a scale model in two dimensions. Cut-outs or loose templates are used to indicate the positions of machines, benches and equipment on the model. A more expensive method

of recording is preparing three-dimensional models. They are more easily understood and the proposed changes may be visualised more accurately.

## Filming

Recording operation using a video or cine camera provides a permanent record and is unobtrusive in operation. There are three main techniques:

- *Micromotion analysis* is a frame-by-frame analysis of the film, prepared in the form of a simo chart.
- *Film analysis* is a frame-by-frame examination on film of an operation to determine the state of activity of the subject during each exposure.
- *Memomotion photography* is a form of time-lapse photography which records activity by a camera adapted to take pictures at longer

intervals than normal; this makes it possible to record activities continuously over a long period.

## CRITICALLY EXAMINE THE FACTS

An objective attitude is essential for the examination of any work if a new method is to be satisfactorily evolved. Any personal bias towards people or the work must be ignored in favour of a broad outlook free of narrow viewpoints. Vital features are a painstaking attention to detail and an analytical, logical approach.

### The questioning technique

A critical examination of the recorded operations is conducted by means of the questioning technique. Each activity in turn is subjected to a systematic and progressive series of questions. There are two stages in this technique: primary and secondary questions.

### Primary questions

The primary stage queries the fundamental need of the performance, place, person, sequence and means of every activity recorded. The main headings for the primary questions would be:

- *Purpose*: Is the work needed? What is achieved? Why is it needed?
- *Place*: Where is the work done? Why is it done there?
- *Person*: Who does the work? Why use that particular individual?
- *Sequence*: When is the work done? Why is it done at that time?
- *Means*: How is the work done? Why is it done it that way?

A thorough understanding of the existing method should emerge, if all these questions are answered correctly. Clear indications of improvements in various sectors should be seen at this stage.

### Secondary questions

The next stage subjects the primary answers to secondary questions. The secondary questions determine whether possible alternatives of purpose, place, people, sequence and means are practicable and preferable. Some typical questions would be:

- *Purpose*: Could the work be altered or eliminated in any part? Is the whole operation needed?
- *Place*: Are there other places available? Is there a more convenient place?
- *Person*: Who else could do the work? Could a less skilled person do the work with some alterations?
- *Sequence*: When else could it be performed? Would it be cheaper if performed earlier or later?
- *Means*: How else could the work be done? Are the principles of motion economy used? Are the most suitable machines and tools used? Could the working environment be improved?

## DEVELOPING A NEW METHOD: FOUR FACTORS

### Elimination

The first consideration should be whether the operation can be abandoned entirely. The operation may *appear* necessary until a more searching enquiry reveals it no longer serves any purpose in the end product.

### Change of sequence

The merits of the existing sequence should be considered. When satisfactory proof of the need for the operation has been found, a change of sequence may be justified by improving workflow and removing unnecessary or duplicated work. For example, an assembly may be carefully cleaned at one stage, receive dirty treatment at the next, and then be cleaned again. A more glaring type of sequence fault occurs when an assembly must be partly dismantled to fit a component and then reassembled.

### Combination

Combining operations is always a possibility. The gains may be considerable so it is worthwhile to spend time exploring the possibilities:

- reducing or eliminating unnecessary movements between operating points
- reducing operation time
- eliminating performance in two places when one place would be sufficient by modifying the

work slightly or by improving the utilisation of tools and machines

## Simplification

Probably the most important way of improving the essential operation is through simplification. Invariably there are easier ways of performing an operation. The task may be approached in many ways, such as using motion economy and examining various aspects: materials, the operator, design, power, handling, tools, machines and equipment.

### Motion economy

Using the principles of motion economy (see below) often saves time and reduces fatigue.

### Materials

A different material is often easier to work with and can save time. Perhaps a cheaper material is available which will not affect the quality of the finished product, or a lighter or heavier gauge could be used to advantage. The possibility of using waste or rejects should be examined. Another factor is whether the most economical lengths or sizes are being purchased, since cutting may often be avoided by wiser purchasing. This helps reduce losses due to wastage.

### The operator

The suitability of a particular operator is often overlooked. Physical details such as height and weight may interfere with the work. For example, a tall operator may be at a disadvantage and suffer from fatigue quickly if he or she is working in a confined space inside an aircraft. The principles of ergonomics (Chapter 21) should be applied to avoid unnecessary fatigue.

### Design

Unfortunately, designers do not always create the simplest designs. Various short cuts are possible and these small rearrangements produce large savings. Tolerances can often be opened without loss of quality. Standardisation of parts simplifies assembly. Methods of reducing the number of parts in an assembly through redesign are often obvious to the operator.

### Power and handling

Greater use of power for assembly and materials handling is recognised as making work easier. However, this factor is not always applied because of capital problems, lack of interest, dislike of changes, or inconvenience. A careful choice of equipment helps to achieve substantial economies, otherwise the expenditure will cancel out the saving.

### Tools, machines and equipment

Although tools, machines and equipment overlap with power and handling, they are treated separately from the operating viewpoint. A vast number of questions could be raised about these items: positioning, running speeds, location of controls, sequence of use, loose or fixed tools, combination tools, use of jigs and templates, and automatic feed. Imagination and the questioning technique can produce large savings.

## INSTALL AND MAINTAIN THE NEW METHOD

Studying the new system and evolving a new method is only about half the work. Installing the new method requires care, detailed planning and the co-operation of everyone concerned.

## Timing

The magnitude of the change is a major consideration. A small rearrangement is comparatively easy, but when transfers of operators and workshops are involved, the disruption of production is obviously considerable and timing becomes important.

## Planning

Detailed planning includes giving adequate information to all concerned; everyone must support the change wholeheartedly if the scheme is to be successful.

## Reviews

Periodic review of the new method is needed to check and correct any deviations from the procedure. During these reviews, the effects of the change should be noted for future improvements.

Resistance points should be examined closely to find the cause. The supervisor has a heavy responsibility during the period of installation and in maintaining the new method. Acceptance of change and ability to arouse enthusiasm and confidence in employees are the key factors for successful operation of the revised scheme.

# Using motion economy

The principles of motion economy are fundamental to method study. Correctly applied, they can eliminate movements, reduce them or make them easier. Motion economy therefore makes a valuable contribution towards improving performance.

There are no detrimental effects such as increasing boredom and frustration. The tasks become less tiring and less irritating because the employee usually knows better ways but remains silent for various reasons. When output is sufficient, the time saved allows for many improvements. These improvements are in areas such as applying various aspects of motivation (Chapters 11 and 12), modern quality control (Chapter 27), safety measures (Chapter 21), time management (Chapter 8) and training for advancement or job enrichment (Chapter 19).

The principles apply, regardless of job complexity, in the office and on the shop floor. Furthermore, they have many domestic applications in outside activities and domestic situations, especially in the kitchen where many accidents occur through ignorance of motion economy.

## SEVEN PRINCIPLES OF MOTION ECONOMY

### Minimum movements

All materials, tools and equipment should be arranged so that the minimum amount of movement is necessary for their use. The degree of movement needed to carry out an operation was classified by Gilbreth into five groups:

- finger motions only
- finger and wrist movements
- fingers, wrist and forearm
- fingers, wrist, forearm and upper arm
- fingers, wrist, forearm, upper arm and shoulder

Figure 25.4 illustrates the collective normal and maximum groupings. The use of the first three classifications constitutes the *normal working area*. The inclusion of the last two classifications provides the boundary for the *maximum working area*. This will have to be used if all the tools, materials and equipment cannot be accommodated within the normal working area.

The aim is to reduce the movements of the upper arm and shoulder to a minimum. The natural sweep of the arms at each side of the body produces areas in the shape of arcs in the horizontal and vertical planes (Fig. 25.4) and forms the working areas described. Items used more frequently should be placed as close to the assembly as possible. Workplaces should be planned in accordance with the natural arc of working area.

### Simultaneous movements

When different limbs are working at the same time, they should be balanced by synchronising the movements. For example, stretching out both hands at once to pick up a bolt and a nut. This principle is important because balance is achieved, less effort is required as concentration is reduced, and learning is easier. Fatigue is reduced because the natural reaction of a body is to divide exertion evenly between the left and right sides. Thus, when the left hand is moved, the right hand tends to move in a similar fashion.

### Symmetrical movements

Symmetrical movements are closely related to simultaneous movements. To achieve balance, the movements should be performed on the left- and right-hand sides of the body about an imaginary line through the centre of the body. An example of combining simultaneous and symmetrical movements is the range of physical exercises that involve both arms and a swinging motion.

### Natural movements

Natural movements make the best use of the shape and design of the body. Using feet, for instance, is often overlooked. They can be used to perform an operation if they are more suitable than

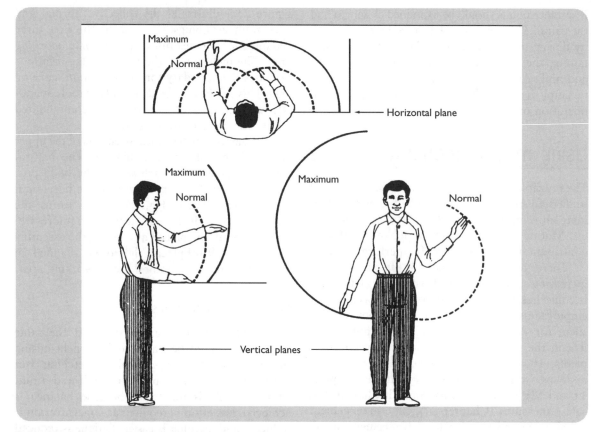

**Figure 25.4** Normal and maximum working areas
The normal working area is covered by movements of the fingers, wrist and forearm, in the horizontal and vertical planes. The natural sweep of the arms forms arcs around the body. The maximum area is covered by bringing in areas of the upper arm and shoulder as well.

hands, or as an additional function when the hands are occupied. A common example is when an assembly is held in a particular position for drilling by the hands, a foot is used to operate the machine.

### Rhythmical movements

A natural rhythm in the cycle of operations should be arranged. Regular repetition of movements develops speed and reduces mental and physical fatigue.

### Habitual movements

Habitual movements are closely associated with rhythmical movements. Precise repetition is habit forming which reduces mental effort. Practice produces a movement that nears a reflex action. Habitual movements are not possible unless conditions such as layout, supply of materials, and placing of tools are standardised. Any slight alteration will upset the habit because extra mental effort is needed to locate the item. Therefore the automatic movement is delayed.

### Continuous movements

Any acute change in direction of a limb causes it to slow down, stop and accelerate back to the original speed. This process involves extra muscle movement and tension. Fatigue is increased compared with smooth, curved movements. Layout should be planned using this principle.

## THE SUPERVISOR AND MOTION ECONOMY

Although a detailed study of an operation may need the services of a specialist, there are often many obvious faults that a supervisor can easily improve. Some of these glaring faults are:

- working in cramped and dangerous positions
- poor siting of tools, materials, machines and equipment, which need extra and awkward movements to use them
- long stretching movements
- using unnecessary force, such as pulling excessively, levering, hammering and ramming
- groping movements which cause eye strain and fatigue
- losing control of the operation temporarily
- unnecessary movements such as changing the position of tools and materials, and walking round to various positions
- lengthy adjustment
- long pauses due to fatigue
- inadequate tools

The supervisor can eliminate many of these faults by using motion economy. The use of small mechanical aids also helps. These may include simple transportation devices such as gravity feed containers and rollers, drop-deliveries into bins, and quick-release clamps.

# Setting time standards

## BSI DEFINITION OF WORK MEASUREMENT

The application of a technique designed to establish the time for a *qualified worker* to carry out a specified *job* at a defined level of performance.

## APPLICATION OF WORK MEASUREMENT

The use of work measurement provides more accurate time standards for the following activities and functions. Two important aspects are the use of a standard time and a typical procedure.

- planning operations
- control systems
- pay systems
- costings
- budgets
- estimates
- stress reduction programmes

## Standard time

Human work may be divided into physical work which is measurable, and mental work which can only be estimated. Machine work must also be considered in work measurement, but this work can be calculated easily and there are no problems of developing appropriate measurement techniques. People vary in their rate of working. Consequently, the time determined by work measurement is the *average* time a number of operators would take to perform the operation without feeling more than healthily tired at the end of each day. This value is known as the *standard time* for a job.

## Procedure

- *Select the work to be measured*: Selection for work measurement is similar to selection for method study. Work should be studied on a priority basis (Fig. 25.5).
- *Record all the relevant information*: All available data on the job should be collected and recorded. Such sources as production schedules, inspection records and drawings, provide useful information.
- *Define the job in detail*: A job analysis should be carefully conducted. This involves breaking down the work into elements or distinct parts which are convenient for observation, measurement and analysis.
- *Measure the work*: The main techniques are time study, synthesis, predetermined motion time systems (PMTS), varifactor synthesis, activity sampling and rated activity sampling.

## TECHNIQUES OF WORK MEASUREMENT

## Time study

This basic technique is a direct observation of the job while it is being performed by the employee. The observer should possess an adequate job breakdown, the ability to estimate the rate of working, and a stopwatch to measure the elements

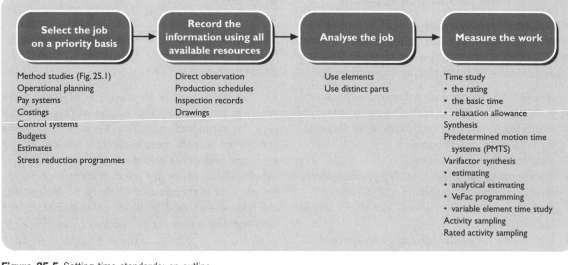

**Figure 25.5** Setting time standards: an outline

accurately. The important features to discuss are the rating, the basic time and the relaxation allowance.

### The rating

The employee's rate of working is given a numerical value. The observer must judge the rate relative to a standard rating scale that runs from 0 to 100, based upon the BSI recommendation. Standard performance is represented by 100 and is defined by the BSI as 'the rate of output which *qualified workers* will naturally achieve without over-exertion, as an average over the working day, provided they know and adhere to the specific method, and provided they are motivated to apply themselves to their work'. Other rating scales use 80 and 133 in place of 100.

### The basic time

Given the rating and the actual time taken to perform an element of the job, the basic time for that element may be calculated. For example, if the observed rating is 90, the observed time is 0.10 min and the standard rating is 100, this would appear as:

$$\text{Basic time} = \frac{90 \times 0.10}{100} = 0.09 \text{ min}$$

### Relaxation allowance

An addition to the basic time is provided to allow for the general physiological and psychological effects of performing the work, and to allow for attention to personal needs. The time allowed varies depending on the nature of the job, and is obviously subjective.

### Synthesis

Many jobs contain some elements that are common to all of them. Consequently, a saving in time study is possible by building up a range of element times which can be used when required in a particular job. A sufficient range of element times might be accumulated to provide the correct time for the whole job, even before the job is performed. Building up a stock of synthetic data may be accelerated by planning a series of studies to cover a wide range of elements. This is a long-term scheme and economic considerations are essential.

### Predetermined motion time systems

Whereas the synthetic data in synthesis are established by observation of the separate elements of a job, the data obtained by predetermined motion time systems (PMTS) are calculated from standard times for basic human motions. These times are classified according to the nature of the motion and local conditions.

The purpose is to remove the factor of human judgement. The essence of the technique is that all work in an industrial environment consists of various combinations of a relatively small number of basic human motions. Times for these motions are measured from highspeed films and scaled to allow for circumstances, such as a heavy weight takes longer to lift than a light weight. A specialist analyses the job to find its basic movements in detail and then computes the times required from special tables to find the total for the job. Any allowances which need to be made are added.

The two main systems are known as work-factor and methods-time measurement (MTM). The work-factor system originated in the USA in 1934. A similar system was later introduced by the Methods-Time Measurement Association.

## Varifactor synthesis: four techniques

### Estimating

The BSI defines estimating as 'a means for assessing the time required to carry out work, based on knowledge and experience of similar types of work, without a detailed breakdown of the work into *elements* and their corresponding times at a defined level of performance'.

### Analytical estimating

Some types of non-repetitive work, such as maintenance jobs, do not lend themselves to complete syntheses of all the elements involved by observation alone. This problem is overcome by analytical estimating which is a development of estimating. In analytical estimating, the time required to perform elements is estimated from knowledge and experience of the elements concerned. The degree of accuracy depends largely upon the ability of the estimator.

### VeFac programming

Formerly known as variable factor programming, VeFac programming was developed by WOFAC Corporation of America. The aim is to reduce and control payroll costs in areas such as clerical work, data processing, drafting, inspection, maintenance, packaging, sales and design. The scope is virtually unlimited. Briefly the steps are collection of the facts, preliminary reporting, developing target times (from WOFAC prime worktime data), establishing work schedules, and periodic reporting. VeFac programming is not a way of speeding up the process, but a way of encouraging employees to use their time more productively.

### Variable element time study

Variable element time study (VETS) was introduced by Dr Whitmore. It is used to set time standards for non-repetitive jobs and is based on calculating average times taken to complete jobs. Rating is employed using four multipliers corresponding to slow (0.5), average (0.8), fast (1.0) and very fast (1.2), rather than the detailed rating scales used in time study. VETS does not give precise measurement, but the times are sufficiently accurate to provide reasonable control of indirect labour (Chapter 29).

## Activity sampling

The work content of some jobs is so varied that normal techniques of work measurement cannot be applied effectively. When a reasonable assessment is required for these jobs, a form of statistical sampling is used which assesses the results of a few samples of work content or individual movements. The samples are selected at random intervals from an appropriate period. Each observation records the work occurring at that instant and is expressed as a percentage of all the observations of that particular activity. This gives an indication of the percentage of time spent on each activity.

## Rated activity sampling

Rated activity sampling is an advanced form of activity sampling. Each work element is rated to determine the work content *in addition* to the percentage of time spent on the activity.

## QUESTIONS

1 Outline a logical sequence for applying method study.

2 Illustrate by examples the main recording techniques in method study.

3 What is meant by the 'questioning technique' in method study?

4 Explain and give examples of four main ways in which an operation could be improved.

5 How can the supervisor ensure that a new method is installed and maintained with the minimum disruption?

6 Discuss methods of reducing operator fatigue.

7 State and explain the seven principles of motion economy.

8 Describe some of the glaring common faults that the supervisor can easily eliminate.

9 Discuss the uses of three timescale charts, including a brief description of each type of chart.

10 What are the objects of work measurement?

11 Explain the term 'standard time' in connection with work measurement.

12 Outline a typical procedure for applying work measurement.

13 Briefly describe the main techniques of work measurement.

14 Give an account of time study including the rating and calculation of the basic time.

15 Outline a typical procedure for setting methods.

16 Setting time standards should follow a strict procedure. Discuss the implications of this statement.

17 Setting time standards may be used for many activities and functions. Outline the main uses for supervision.

---

### CASE STUDY

Dennis has not thought seriously about using work study in his section until the works manager sends for him and says quite bluntly that he is not satisfied with the section's performance levels: 'We have to improve our productivity, Dennis, otherwise we shall all be out of a job now that we're without that cosy contract with Eclipse Engineering'.

On the way back to his section Dennis goes to have a word with Mary, one of his fellow supervisors, 'Just been told in no uncertain terms by the old man about productivity and all that'. Mary looks up in surprise, 'Me too! I was going to come along and see you'.

At that point, another supervisor arrives with the same story.

*Consider the courses of action open to the supervisors. What other approaches could have been used by the works manager?*

Regina Tool Company is in financial difficulties. A lucrative, long-standing order has been cancelled. Reliance on other erratic orders has meant that either the workforce rapidly becomes more flexible and efficient or the plant will be forced to close down.

Andy, the shop steward, has little trust in management and, over the years, many employees have experienced unfair treatment. The company's poor industrial relations reputation is not helping to solve the problem at the general meeting of employees being held by the managing director, who is attempting to convince them of the urgent need for drastic changes.

Andy speaks up: 'We've heard all this before – many times in fact – but we're still here. Why don't you give us some facts and figures? We also hear that you've just given yourselves handsome increases and yet *you* are expecting *us* to take cuts'.

*Consider the managerial philosophy in this company and discuss the alternatives that might have paid off now. What could be done to rectify the immediate situation?*

# 26

# Production control

## Introduction

Production control includes many aspects to provide a comprehensive view of the production area:

- types of production
- production planning
- the broad aspect of production control
- the main aspects of production control
- production delays
- techniques to reduce delays
- the supervisor's role
- production control in the small company
- computer systems
- an example of a computer system

## Types of production

The main factors affecting the type of production are the length of runs, variety of goods produced, spreading fixed costs (those that tend not to change with the length of production runs), and preparation costs. The three types of production are job, batch and flow.

## Job production

All products of the *one-off* type – a bridge, an office block, an ocean liner, a special-purpose machine, or a very large transformer – come under this heading. This is also known as jobbing. A large proportion of small companies and some very large ones are engaged in this type of production, mainly by contract. High calibre engineers, highly

skilled operators and competent supervisors are essential. General-purpose machines are used since there is little scope for standardising the processes. Output planning relies on the customer placing an order; consequently, this may cause idle time between jobs because there are often delays between an enquiry, the tender and the eventual contract.

## Batch production

Batch production is adopted when a range of products are manufactured in quantities that do not justify the continuous flow line method. General-purpose machines are used and scheduled to ensure maximum possible machine utilisation. This principle of machine utilisation, meaning each machine may be performing operations on a number of different components, illustrates the main distinguishing feature between batch and flow production. Figure 26.1 shows the differences between the two types.

In batch production the machines are grouped in types to suit the particular function, which involves specialist supervision, tooling and inspection; in flow production the machines are arranged in strict operational sequence. Each machine performs a particular job at maximum efficiency while the flow line is in operation. A combination of the two types may be seen in many large companies. The majority of products manufactured in quantity come under this heading: ready-made suits, paintbrushes, watches, books, lampshades, mirrors, furniture and plain bearings.

The combination of types is known as *batch/ flow production*. Here the batch production of

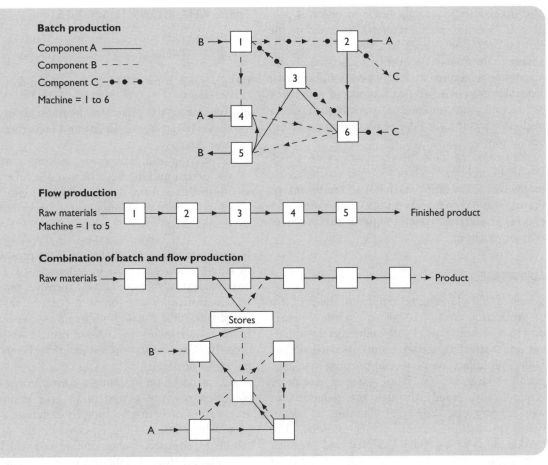

**Figure 26.1** Machine layout, batch and flow production
In flow production the machines are laid out in strict operational sequence whereas in batch production the machines are grouped according to function. Each machine may perform its particular operation on a number of different components.

components feeds a product flow line. For example, in motor car manufacture, the flow line will be fed with batch-produced engines, wheels complete with tyres, and back axle assemblies.

## STOCK ORDER PRODUCTION

To produce an economic batch size, the quantity is often increased above the actual orders received, the balance being placed in stock. Design of the product is intended to satisfy a specific market but companies may modify the product to suit particular requirements. Work-in-progress tends to become excessive in providing queues of work

to maintain high machine utilisation. This often leads to setting up work-in-progress stores, which are controlled in conjunction with scheduling, otherwise overstocking may tie up an excessive amount of working capital (Chapter 28). The control method *just-in-time* (see below) helps to eliminate these storage problems.

# Flow production

In flow production each batch of work is manufactured in strict operational sequence. Figure 26.1 illustrates the principle where machines are aligned (not necessarily in straight lines) in order of production. Speed of manufacture is governed by the slowest operation as each batch or assembly must adhere to the flow line sequence. Consequently, no scheduling is required for each operation, but batch sequences must be scheduled. Compared with batch production, the amount of work-in-progress is negligible and there is little or no queuing between operations.

Examples of flow production goods which usually incorporate batch production assemblies are motor vehicles, washing machines and refrigerators. Petrol, gas and many chemicals are produced by *process production*, which follows a purer form of flow production.

## ADVANTAGES

When careful planning is completed, the problem of production control is not so complex, breakdowns and faulty work are immediately apparent and corrective action is concentrated on the fault. Full utilisation of special-purpose machines produces large savings. Floor space is used more economically, mainly through the reduction of work-in-progress. Effective planning in detail before production commences is essential. The market must be carefully analysed and sounded periodically to ensure adequate sales of the large output levels.

## PROBLEMS

Heavy losses occur when the plant is shut down through labour troubles or lack of materials. Similarly, when a new line is introduced, changeover time is costly and must be reduced to a minimum.

## THREE WELL-KNOWN TECHNIQUES

### Group technology

Group technology (GT) has three main features:

- integrating the phases of manufacturing processes by grouping similar and recurring tasks and designs
- identifying and cataloguing existing component design and methods of manufacture
- using this information (sometimes with some modification) to manufacture existing and new products

It also provides the benefits of flow production to batch production. The installation of GT may be comparatively simple and inexpensive, provided certain principles are followed. Claims say it is possible to reduce lead times by up to 90 per cent, space requirements by 50 per cent, and set-up times by 75 per cent, without incurring heavy capital expenditure.

GT is based on updating a conventional complex design retrieval system to give immediate access to information relating to designing a new part. Thus design time is saved if the system reveals a proposed new or similar part which has been made before. Furthermore, this information is computer-based, carefully classified, coded into family groups, and integrated with the manufacturing process.

The approach involves investment in retraining and reorganising the workforce, introducing a new design retrieval system, and changing methods of manufacture. A simplified diagram of the GT process is shown in Fig. 26.2.

**Figure 26.2** Group technology: simplified diagram

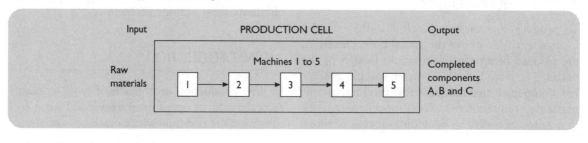

## Advantages

GT provides a relatively simple way of manufacturing more customised products for close-knit market segments. This is an important feature in responding to strong overseas competition. The benefits include adaptations to accommodate work group concepts; more effective supervision; increased job satisfaction; reduced costs in manufacturing, tooling, process planning, total set-up time, and manufacturing lead time; lower investments in work-in-progress, working stocks and buffer stocks; and simplified production control.

### Flexible manufacturing system

Many companies manufacture goods for mature markets that constantly demand product diversification and new products. This situation causes intense competition and the urgent need to automate. Within manufacturing technology are many techniques, the ultimate goal being computer-integrated manufacturing (CIM).

A flexible manufacturing system (FMS) is a computerised manufacturing cell that caters for this flexibility. Flexible machining centres and automatic vehicles or transporters between operations allow the automated system to cope rapidly with design changes and variations on the component mix.

An FMS is controlled by a computer that makes decisions for moving parts and components from machine to machine. The machine centres have 'intelligence' that checks parts, the operational state of machines, tool wear and tool capability. Quality may be monitored automatically by statistical process control (SPC) equipment.

An FMS normally uses robots for routine production since they are versatile, reprogrammable, reliable hence economic, need fewer operators, cause fewer human problems, and do not require training.

### Manufacturing automation protocol

In closed-loop operations, manufacturing automation protocol (MAP) provides communication between administration, assembly points and processes so that information and instructions may pass easily between different types of computer systems. MAP employs rules and procedures to standardise the system.

# Six stages of production planning

### STAGE 1: GATHER RELEVANT INFORMATION

Stage 1 involves gathering information on the product in the form of drawings, specifications from the designers, and drawing office records. When a clear picture is drawn up of all the processes involved, further investigation of work content and reference to past production records provide information which can help when deciding whether to purchase components or assemblies from outside or to produce them internally.

### STAGE 2: ESTABLISH THE PLAN

Stage 2 involves more detailed problems of setting stock lists and parts lists, determining the availability of jigs and tools, preparing supplies of drawings and specifications, together with many general jobs to ensure a complete planned programme is presented to production control.

### STAGE 3: PRODUCE PROCESS LAYOUT INSTRUCTIONS

With the aid of information on existing machines and equipment available for production, it is now possible to produce process layout instruction sheets. An example is shown in Fig. 26.3.

### STAGE 4: PRODUCE DETAILED PROCESS OPERATIONS

Stage 4 involves establishing times for all the operations so that the total time may be calculated for producing the product. All the elements in an operation are listed along with the time allowed. An example is given in Fig. 26.4.

### STAGE 5: DRAW UP A MASTER PLAN

A plan is now drawn up to show the dates when each production stage must be ready and each

**Figure 26.3** Process layout instruction sheet

The table shown contains the following structure:

PROCESS LAYOUT INSTRUCTION

Part name .................... | No. of sheets ....................
Part no. .................... | Sheet no. ....................
Material unit .................... | Drawn by ....................
Time/100 parts .................... | Checked by ....................
Weight/100 parts .................... | Standard order quantity ....................

| Dept. | Operation | Op. no. | Time allowed | Set-up time | Machine | Tools | Special equip/t |
|---|---|---|---|---|---|---|---|
| | | | | | | | |

**Figure 26.4** Detailed process operation sheet

DETAILED PROCESS OPERATION SHEET

Part name .................... | Operation ....................
Part no. .................... | Material/unit ....................
Time allowed .................... | Date ....................

| No. | Element | Time allowed | No. | Element | Time allowed |
|---|---|---|---|---|---|
| | | | | | |

phase completed so that the delivery date agrees with the estimate. The type of chart most suitable for this control function was developed by Henry L. Gantt and is called the *Gantt chart*. Figure 26.5 illustrates a simple target date chart using the Gantt principle. Each part of the plan is subjected to an estimated time which is plotted. The actual time taken is also plotted underneath the estimated or standard time, thus clearly indicating the true position in relation to time and subject.

The Gantt chart is versatile as it can be adapted to any control system where a number of functions are allied to the time factor. There are certain disadvantages, however, particularly in showing interrelationships between activities. More advanced systems involve the use of critical path or network analysis (Chapter 23).

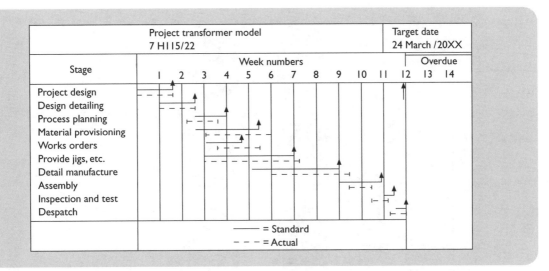

| Stage | Project transformer model 7 H115/22 | | | | | | | | | | | | Target date 24 March /20XX | |
|---|---|---|---|---|---|---|---|---|---|---|---|---|---|---|

**Figure 26.5** Production sheet based on a Gantt chart
This is a simple target date chart using the Gantt principle. As a master schedule it controls the production of a new transformer from initial design through to delivery. Actual production progress is measured against estimated 'standard' times for achieving delivery by the target date.

## Total lead time

Within the master plan is the total lead time (TLT). This begins when materials are ordered, it runs through various production processes, and it ends when finished goods are delivered to the customer. TLT is the sum of many lead times in the process chain and usually includes various storage times as well as actual processing times; storage times may be reduced by using logistics (Chapters 5 and 30).

Within TLT is a forecasting lead time which is usually inevitable because of the delay before the customer actually orders the product. Added to the forecasting lead time is the customer's lead time, calculated from the order date to the delivery date. The time varies according to the type of industry and may be from a few hours to several months.

The forecasting lead time is pure speculation or guesswork within TLT because of market uncertainty. But the ratio of forecasting lead time to customer lead time does give some indication of risk: the smaller the ratio, the smaller the risk.

### The ideal manufacturing situation
To minimise costs, production should be so arranged that the supplier sends a continuous steady flow of materials at a rate suited to the input of the first manufacturing process without delays or storage. Each process is set at a rate to feed the following processes, without delay or storage. At the last processing stage, the output of finished products is immediately packaged and loaded for transportation to the customer. Depending on output requirements, each process is multiplied (say to three machines) to satisfy demand, and the loading of the following processes is treated in the same way. In most situations this ideal is not possible; it is simply a target to aim at by various logistics specialists. Techniques to reduce delays are discussed later on.

## STAGE 6: SELECT PLANT AND EQUIPMENT

When the master plan is completed, it is time to select the plant and equipment or to modify existing configurations. Many factors influence selection:

- type of production
- technological developments
- availability and training of operatives
- physical and environmental constraints
- reputation of suppliers
- compatibility with existing facilities
- maintenance aspects

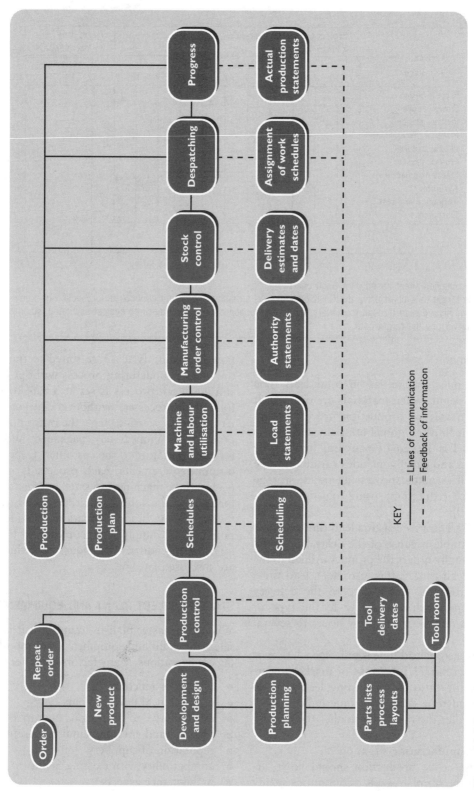

**Figure 26.6** Production planning and control: simplified diagram

The trend towards integrated manufacturing systems involves careful consideration of current rates of change in technologies, the use of computer-aided design (CAD) and computer-aided manufacture (CAM), and market forecasts on which to base capacity requirements, bearing in mind economic aspects. Increasingly important is effective maintenance to avoid costly breakdowns.

# Production control

The purpose of production control is to choose the most *economic method* to manufacture the correct *quantity* at the *right time* and with the *required quality*. It may be defined as the direction of all production activities according to a planned programme and fully utilising available facilities in the most economic way.

Planning and controlling production depend upon many factors peculiar to the particular industry and the products being manufactured. However, basic principles and sequences usually apply and they are discussed when constructing a practical system within a particular company. Figure 26.6 is a simplified chart showing the main aspects of production planning and control.

### THE BROADER CONCEPT OF PRODUCTION CONTROL

Several activities are undertaken outside the production control department which nevertheless form an essential part of this function:

- sales forecasting and sales orders
- specifications and drawings from the drawing office
- financial accounting concerning the purchase of capital equipment, which in turn affects the economic batch size of production and the purchase of materials in certain quantities, depending upon availability of funds and storage space
- capabilities of the toolroom to produce requirements such as jigs, fixtures, special tools and other equipment
- storage of finished goods and partly finished goods

- materials control, which is sometimes treated as a separate activity outside production control

These few activities should indicate sufficiently the breadth of production control in practice. Production problems often originate from services outside the responsibility of the production controller. Therefore, he or she must rely upon the flexibility of the control system to overcome difficulties.

# Six aspects of production control

### SCHEDULING

- Listing all the items required for production, including raw materials, components and sub-assemblies which may be purchased or produced internally.
- Placing them in a convenient sequence for production, considering such problems as time taken to produce, time required on the production line, the production cycle, and allowance for scrap and waste.
- Routeing the materials and assemblies from section to section so that the plan of production illustrates to everyone concerned the whole sequence of operation from commencement to completion of the programme.

### Essential information

Scheduling presents a workable programme of production in workshop language. The sequence of manufacturing and the quantities will depend upon sales orders, economic batch size, manufacturing time and delivery dates. On this basis the information required for effective scheduling includes:

- sales orders
- promised delivery dates
- planning layout
- parts lists
- machine load statements
- labour utilisation estimates
- supply details for tools, equipment, materials, items from sub-contractors, components from suppliers, and jigs and fixtures

| MASTER SCHEDULE | | | | | | | | | | | | | | |
|---|---|---|---|---|---|---|---|---|---|---|---|---|---|---|
| Component Helical spring<br>Component no. 6:8940 | | | | | | Maximum run 7000<br>Minimum run 2000 | | | | | | | | |
| Production | Quarter (in week nos) | | | | | | | | | | | | | |
| | 1 | 2 | 3 | 4 | 5 | 6 | 7 | 8 | 9 | 10 | 11 | 12 | 13 | |
| Scheduled<br>Below schedule<br>Above schedule<br>Total | | | | | | | | | | | | | | |

**Figure 26.7** Master schedule

- scrap and waste statements
- information from the progress section as work proceeds, schedules being revised as feedback from actual progress is compared with estimates
- information on finished goods, storage facilities and despatch

*Types of schedule*

### The master schedule

The master schedule usually provides a weekly or monthly indication of requirements over 3 months, 6 months or 12 months. The schedule indicates plant capacity: orders are entered as they are received and the resultant capacity is calculated for the period. When capacity is filled, orders are either carried forward to the next period or arrangements are made to increase capacity for that period. This immediately shows the current position, the basis for increasing output to accommodate delivery dates, and the overall loading of plant in the factory. Figure 26.7 outlines the main requirements of a master schedule. Production schedules (Fig. 26.16) and workshop schedules (Fig. 26.17) are discussed later.

### MACHINE AND LABOUR UTILISATION

Machine and labour utilisation aims to organise the loading of machines and labour so that idle time is reduced to a minimum and co-ordination is achieved. The activities include keeping accurate records of plant capacity, preparing statements that compare the current loading with the maximum capacity available, and compiling machine and labour records that indicate the actual and possible utilisation.

Information for preparing these records may be obtained from plant records, planning sheets, operation layouts, work study records and previous records of machine and labour utilisation. It provides management with efficiency ratios, production shops with schedules, and feedback of information to scheduling for revision purposes. Examples are shown in Figs 26.8, 26.9 and 26.10.

There are many different display boards; some use discs, others use pegs or rotary devices. Set-up times for these display boards are much shorter and the current situation is more easily seen than from a chart, which needs to be read.

*Ratios of efficiency and effectiveness*

### Labour utilisation

$$\frac{\left(\begin{array}{c}\text{Net machine}\\\text{running time}\end{array}\right)}{\left(\begin{array}{c}\text{Number of}\\\text{operators}\end{array}\right) \times \left(\begin{array}{c}\text{Average hours}\\\text{worked per week}\end{array}\right)} \times 100$$

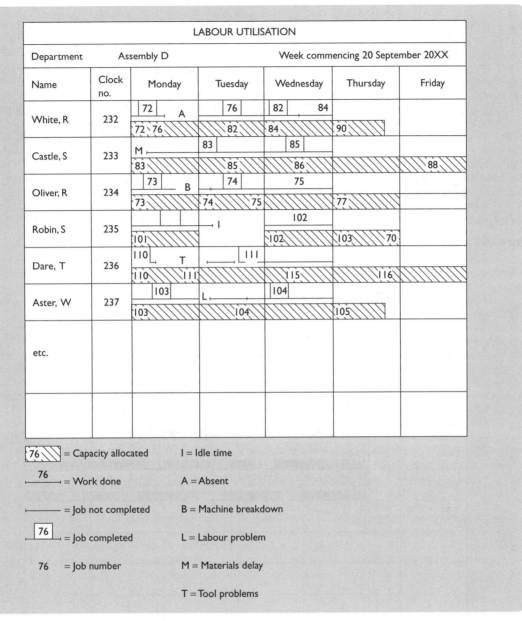

**LABOUR UTILISATION**

| Department | | Assembly D | | Week commencing 20 September 20XX | | |
|---|---|---|---|---|---|---|
| Name | Clock no. | Monday | Tuesday | Wednesday | Thursday | Friday |
| White, R | 232 | 72 A | 76 | 82  84 | | |
| | | 72 ⟍76 ⟍⟍ | ⟍82⟍ | 84⟍⟍ | 90⟍ | |
| Castle, S | 233 | M | 83 | 85 | | |
| | | 83⟍ | 85⟍ | 86⟍ | | 88⟍ |
| Oliver, R | 234 | 73 B | 74 | 75 | | |
| | | 73⟍ | 74⟍ 75 | ⟍ | 77⟍ | |
| Robin, S | 235 | I | | 102 | | |
| | | 101⟍ | | 102⟍ | 103⟍ 70 | |
| Dare, T | 236 | 110 T | 111 | | | |
| | | 110⟍ 111⟍ | | 115⟍ | 116⟍ | ⟍ |
| Aster, W | 237 | 103 L | | 104 | | |
| | | 103⟍ | 104⟍ | | 105⟍ | |
| etc. | | | | | | |
| | | | | | | |

| 76 ⟍⟍ = Capacity allocated | I = Idle time |
|---|---|
| 76 ⊢⊣ = Work done | A = Absent |
| ⊢⊣ = Job not completed | B = Machine breakdown |
| 76 ⊢⊣ = Job completed | L = Labour problem |
| 76 = Job number | M = Materials delay |
| | T = Tool problems |

**Figure 26.8** Labour utilisation shows the current job labour ratio

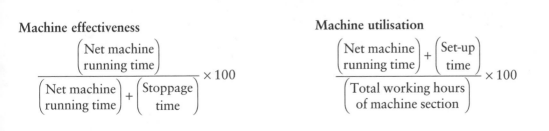

**Machine effectiveness**

$$\frac{\left(\begin{array}{c}\text{Net machine}\\\text{running time}\end{array}\right)}{\left(\begin{array}{c}\text{Net machine}\\\text{running time}\end{array}\right) + \left(\begin{array}{c}\text{Stoppage}\\\text{time}\end{array}\right)} \times 100$$

**Machine utilisation**

$$\frac{\left(\begin{array}{c}\text{Net machine}\\\text{running time}\end{array}\right) + \left(\begin{array}{c}\text{Set-up}\\\text{time}\end{array}\right)}{\left(\begin{array}{c}\text{Total working hours}\\\text{of machine section}\end{array}\right)} \times 100$$

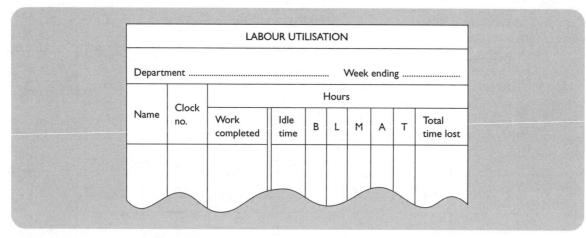

**Figure 26.9** A summary breaks down the total time lost on a job

| | | | | | | | | | |
|---|---|---|---|---|---|---|---|---|---|
| LABOUR UTILISATION | | | | | | | | | |
| Department .............................................. Week ending ......................... | | | | | | | | | |
| Name | Clock no. | Hours | | | | | | | |
| | | Work completed | Idle time | B | L | M | A | T | Total time lost |
| | | | | | | | | | |

**MACHINE LOADING**

| Department | | | | Week commencing | | |
|---|---|---|---|---|---|---|
| Machine | | Monday | Tuesday | Wednesday | Thursday | Friday |
| Type | No. | | | | | |
| Lathe | | 121 / 122 S / 124 / M 126 | | | | |
| | | 121 / 122 / 124 / 126 | | | | |
| Lathe | | 132 / B 133 / 134 / 135 | | | | |
| | | 132 / 133 / 134 / 135 | | | | |
| Lathe | | 136 M / 138 / 138 S | | | | |
| | | 136 / 138 / 139 / 140 / 141 | | | | |
| etc. | | | | | | |

121 ∨ = Machine running time      B = Breakdown

121 ■ = Capacity allocated      M = Material delay

I = Idle time      S = Set-up delay

**Figure 26.10** Machine loading chart

**Table 26.1** Manufacturing order control documents

| Production factor | Paperwork | Operation |
|---|---|---|
| 1 Operator | Labour loading schedule | Operator allocated |
| 2 Machine | Machine loading schedule | Machine allocated |
| 3 Materials and drawings | Material requisition | Issued |
| 4 Tools | Tools requisition | Issued |
| 5 Authority to produce | Works order | Carry out operation |
| 6 Identity | Identity label | Affix to assembly |
| 7 Inspection | Inspection order | Inspection: passed or rejected |
| 8 (a) Move to next operation | Authority to move | Transport |
| (b) Move to scrap | Reject order | Transport |
| 9 Control | All copies of documents | Complete and despatch to control |
| 10 Costing | All copies of documents | Complete and despatch to costing department |
| 11 Pay and bonuses | Works order copy | Complete and despatch to payroll section |

## MANUFACTURING ORDER CONTROL

Manufacturing order control provides documents that give authority to the production shops to produce, according to the schedule and the plan. It controls the issue of paperwork, such as the movement of materials from stores to the first operation point, and from operation to operation until the product is completed. Similar controls are applied to the preparation of tooling, jigs and fixtures, their movement from process to process, commencement of work on each operation, and recording progress of the job through the production shops.

### The procedure

The procedure varies widely depending on the size of the organisation and the type of product. The information normally required to operate the procedure is obtained from process layout sheets, schedules, and details of scrap and shortages. Documents are prepared to cover all the activities connected with manufacturing the product. A typical list of these documents and schedules in their sequence of use is given in Table 26.1.

### Types of manufacturing order

There are three main types:

- Single cards have all the information on the front and act as identity labels.
- Multi-copy orders reduce writing to a minimum.
- Single-copy tear-off orders have perforations dividing each section.

Figure 26.11 gives an example of the single-card type. If the product is manufactured in one department, a job card is usually raised with works orders attached for each operation. When more than one department is involved, a route card travels with the assembly from department to department.

## STOCK CONTROL

Stock control, also known as inventory control, uses clerical procedures to achieve a variety of objectives:

- Material required for production or other uses is available on time in the right quantity and of the right quality.
- Information is provided for financial control.
- Stock is safeguarded.
- Accurate stock records are maintained.

To achieve these purposes there are two main aspects: *materials control* and *stock control proper*. Materials control covers the purchasing and cost of materials, and the organisation of material flow

| MANUFACTURING ORDER | | | | |
|---|---|---|---|---|
| Order no. | Batch no. | Quantity | Part name | Part no. |
| | | | | |

| Materials | Quantity | Date required |
|---|---|---|
| | | |

| Tools | Quantity | Date required |
|---|---|---|
| | | |

| Operator | Clock no. | Machine | No. | Part no. | Quantity | | Standard time | Actual time |
|---|---|---|---|---|---|---|---|---|
| | | | | | Passed | Rejected | | |
| | | | | | | | | |

Signature inspection ............................................................

Signature foreman ............................................................

Date ............................................................

***Figure 26.11*** Manufacturing order card: provides a record from initial order to final inspection

within the company. Stock control proper controls the quantity and quality of materials and components in accordance with the production plan.

## Clerical records

The clerical nature of stock control means it can be carried out in a section other than the stores where the physical movement of stock actually occurs. The records include job analysis sheets, purchase requisitions, manufacturing orders, goods received notes, and material requisitions. A record card for each type of material may contain details such as description of material, part number, location in stores, reordering level, maximum and minimum quantity levels, quantities on order, receipts, issues, balance, any quantity appropriated, and the price.

## Stock checking

Most stock levels are regularly reviewed to dispense with obsolescent and obsolete materials. Physical stock checking, though tedious and time-consuming, is essential to prove the accuracy of the stock records. There are two main ways:

- Annual stocktaking involves suspending the movement of all materials during the count.
- Perpetual inventory, along with continuous stocktaking, avoids the suspension of all material movement.

Perpetual inventory uses a reliable individual who is fully employed checking physical stocks against stock records throughout the year. He or she maintains a register of all the counts and variances. This record is acceptable to the auditors, who must certify its accuracy for entry in the balance sheet under the Companies Act.

## DESPATCHING

Despatching authorises the operator to carry out work in accordance with the standard method by using the allocated tools, drawings and scheduled information. The despatching section is responsible for:

- assigning the work to the workplace or machine
- preparing, assembling and issuing the materials, tools, fixtures and gauges for production
- releasing works orders and production sheets
- co-ordinating the movement of work-in-progress by using a recording procedure

## Methods of despatching

### Decentralised despatching

The orders are issued in a batch to the despatcher or the supervisor in each department. His or her responsibility is to decide upon the most suitable sequence for issuing the orders and to ensure materials, tools and the manufacturing orders arrive on time to each operator or machine. The advantages of this scheme are that the supervisor has more control of production activities within his or her section, there should be more flexibility of operation, and paperwork is considerably reduced. The capabilities of the supervisor or despatcher decide the success of this arrangement. Probably maximum machine utilisation is more difficult to achieve.

### Centralised despatching

Orders are despatched directly to operators or machines from a centralised office. Here records and charts are kept of capacities, any backlog, and loadings of operators and machines. Greater control of production is claimed for this method, which gives more overall flexibility when operating near the optimum level of production. Sometimes it is assumed that the supervisor merely runs the machines to produce in the sequence outlined and therefore is not responsible for all the production aspects of the section. Centralised despatching does have some disadvantages: there is more red tape, there is a duplication of effort, and prompt action is difficult. The supervisor can object to an order if he or she feels justified.

## PROGRESSING

Progressing provides the means for co-ordinating the production programme by revealing and, if possible, eliminating or correcting any deviations from the schedule. Regulating the progress of materials and parts through the various production processes is known as *expediting*. Other names given to this task are progress chasing, stock chasing and follow-up. This difficult task is carried out in the following way. There are two methods of expediting: unit and departmental.

- taking responsibility for all production orders after they have been issued
- co-ordinating the production activities to produce work-in-progress at the correct time at the right place in the right quantity and of the right quality
- investigating and reporting variances from the schedules
- providing alternative routes for production processes when breakdowns or bottlenecks occur
- recording and analysing progress records of production for comparison between planned and actual output at each stage

### Unit expediting

Unit expediting gives the expeditor responsibility for progressing a unit or contract from the beginning through to the final stage of production. Slow-moving runs, complex products and long runs are usually suitable for this method. All the problems connected with the unit are centralised through one person who is fully aware of the whole situation. Unfortunately, this often results in a number of expeditors who are all dealing with one supervisor in each department, which adds to the problems of overall control.

### Departmental expediting

In departmental expediting, one expeditor is responsible for all work passing through a department. It is suitable for fast-moving products but it may cause control problems. To avoid conflict the supervisor must be prepared to pass to the expeditor the responsibility for production progressing.

## Production delays

- *Personnel problems*: absenteeism, labour turnover, disputes, poor selection, lack of training

- *Machines*: breakdowns, poor maintenance, bottlenecks through lack of duplication of vital pieces of equipment, inefficient operation, loading errors or oversights, unsuitable machines
- *Materials*: overdue deliveries, inefficient ordering, poor quality, poor stores handling and transportation
- *Design*: poor design creating production difficulties, unsuitable materials recommended, accuracy required is too high for equipment available, tolerances and allowances too tight without good reason
- *Equipment*: lack of correct tools, jigs and fixtures, delays in deliveries of equipment
- *Planning*: excessive set-up times due to uneconomical batch sizes, poor estimates of work content
- *Inspection*: inadequate, causing excessive scrap at later stages

## Reducing delays

### OPTIMISED PRODUCTION TECHNOLOGY

Optimised production technology (OPT) reduces work-in-progress by removing bottlenecks. It identifies bottlenecks, establishes work schedules that ensure the supply of materials to the appropriate points even though machines may be idle at earlier stages, and integrates the manufacturing system.

### JUST-IN-TIME

Just-in-time (JIT) is a Japanese production control method. It avoids unnecessary time spent on procuring, storing and distributing materials, thus eliminating storage problems and the cost of keeping stock awaiting use. The aim is to plan work at each production stage so that the next stage receives exactly the input required and delivers its output just-in-time for the following stage to commence work, and so on.

The philosophy is to eliminate continuously *non-added-value* (NAV) activities by concentrating on improving quality, materials, flow, flexibility of employees and machines, and making appropriate arrangements with suppliers and distributors.

NAV activities include attempting to eliminate all waste, all delays, and unnecessary time spent on all stages of operations from design to marketing.

Obviously there is a similarity between JIT and traditional work study techniques, budgetary control and quality stock control assurance. The difference is in top management's acceptance of responsibility to change both the attitude of everyone concerned and the fundamentals of the manufacturing process to cope with improvements in lead time and work-in-progress.

Operators are personally responsible for quality and production control. They belong to *cells* (a group of operators) who organise their own work, conduct servicing of equipment, apply quality control, and arrange the timing of workflow between cells.

### Essential requirements

- Relying on suppliers to provide regular, smaller quantities.
- Rapidly transporting materials to production or process stages.
- Creating and keeping a co-operative well-trained workforce.
- Effectively maintaining machines and equipment.
- Coping quickly with breakdowns.
- Applying sensitive control devices.
- Adapting to different machine load times.
- Despatching the finished product quickly.

### AUTONOMATION

A fundamental requirement is to avoid defective materials and work-in-progress entering further production stages. Autonomation theoretically corrects this fault by either relying on operators to check visually or employing automatic check mechanisms. Moreover, careful performance measurement and continuous improvement are essential.

### THE KAWASAKI PRODUCTION SYSTEM

Kawasaki, a very large Japanese company, has overcome some of the difficulties of just-in-time. JIT tends to concentrate on improving lead time and work-in-progress, but usually creates little

improvement in productivity performance. This fault is mainly due to the need for smaller batch sizes and more frequent set-ups. The Kawasaki production system (KPS) designs flexibility into the process to avoid time loss through the small batch sizes.

### The philosophy

The aim of KPS seems old – elimination of waste and continuous improvement – as does the approach – applying simple, inexpensive ideas to solve problems and to achieve precise planning. The philosophy, however, is new. There must be:

- a change in attitudes and practices
- re-education programmes
- enthusiasm and efforts must be continuous
- simple ideas, followed if necessary by hi-tech back-up in this sequence, not the reverse
- a flexible assembly line designed to be non-specific to produce variations in the same product and different products

KPS is therefore not an easy option but success produces outstanding productivity improvements without heavy capital expenditure.

### KAIZEN

A Japanese philosophy, kaizen claims that any working method can be improved if human creativity is allowed to flourish and if there is a flexible organisation to encourage change. The aims are to improve production planning and control as well as reducing costs and production delays by adapting the organisational culture. The concept of continuous improvement is a fundamental requirement which is achievable through suitable company strategy and tactical processes. Kaizen not only applies to production but also to marketing, corporate objectives and the personnel function.

## The supervisor's role

Effective production control assists supervisors by relieving them of the numerous activities associated with this activity. Consequently, supervisors can devote more time to their true role of supervising their sections. Supervisors should give their full support to the individuals who use all their energies to ensure the various factors of production are dealt with correctly. These factors include loading, materials and tools movement, authority to proceed, inspection, costing, pay control, drawings, and progress chasing.

## THE SIZE OF THE COMPANY

Company size has a significant effect on a supervisor's role. In a small company it is not possible to relieve the supervisor of routine production control by using specialists. But the opportunities to do this increase as the company grows. This allows the supervisor to concentrate on directing and ensuring that employees become fully productive. The supervisor's influence should be increased rather than decreased as he or she becomes the vital link between employees and management.

Further growth creates more tasks to be undertaken by the supervisor, especially co-ordinating new activities with existing systems and procedures. Such activities may include more detailed planning and control, costing, inspection, materials control, preparation of details for pay and bonuses, and complex reports.

Successful co-ordination as growth continues is an arduous task and very demanding on the supervisor; it usually requires more education and training. The supervisor's outlook must fully encompass managers' and employees' viewpoints on production; each person's role, tasks, authority and responsibility; the environment; and the organisational and employee cultures.

# Small companies

Organised production control may not exist in the small company. The supervisor controls by keeping most of the relevant activities in his or her head and making arbitrary decisions as problems arise. This lack of method is usually demonstrated by impracticable estimates of delivery dates and prices, and general inefficiency. Chaos quickly develops if the supervisor is sick. As the company grows, the urgency of introducing a production control system becomes more obvious. Often haphazard arrangements are made initially until a logical approach is introduced. The next few sections consider a simple production control system which can be elaborated or rearranged to suit the particular workshop.

## INFORMATION FROM THE OFFICE

The supervisor should receive the following information:

- orders received
- promised delivery dates
- any special information on orders
- revised delivery dates
- urgent orders – delivery required as soon as possible
- materials and equipment received
- promised delivery dates for materials and equipment

## INFORMATION FROM THE WORKSHOP

The supervisor should keep a record of the following matters and report details promptly to the controlling office:

- progress of work through each stage of manufacture
- any breakdown of plant
- shortages of materials, components and assemblies
- any other reasons for stoppages

Transmitting information from the workshop to the office may be conducted in many ways. Written forms of feedback to various control points, such as the cost office, pay section, progress section and the supervisor, are often essential. However, in the very small company they may be dispensed with entirely.

### Forms

**Operator's work ticket**
An operator's work ticket is a simple document used by an operator to record output. When completed it is passed to various sections for calculating pay or for costing. An example is given in Fig. 26.12.

| WORK TICKET | | | |
|---|---|---|---|
| Operator's name ................................................. | | Week commencing ................... | |
| Clock no. .................................................................. | | | |
| Section ...................................................................... | | | |
| Operation | Quantity produced | Total | Checked |
|  |  |  |  |
|  |  |  |  |
|  |  |  |  |
|  |  |  |  |
| Operator's signature ..................................................... | | | |
| Supervisor's signature ............................................... | | Date ......................... | |

*Figure 26.12* Operator's work ticket: used to calculate costs and wages

## Job card

Each job card states the work to be performed by an operator. Job cards are usually completed and collected on a daily basis, and the information is used for making entries in the workshop schedule. Figure 26.13 illustrates the type of card which can be used for this purpose. It may be designed to include details of bonus schemes and any other information required.

## Detachable ticket

A ticket may be designed with a number of perforated sections containing information on each operation. As each operation is completed in sequence, a section is torn off and signed by the operator who places it in a box which is emptied daily. Usually the ticket is tied to the assembly and each section bears the job number, the operation and any other relevant information (Fig. 26.14).

## THE ESTIMATE

The estimate must be based on the production schedule and the capacity of the workshop to provide an adequate delivery date. Although the estimate is closely related to the order, which is dealt with in the office, the supervisor may have to prepare the estimate. The type of form for this purpose would be circulated internally (Fig. 26.15). The costing aspect is covered in Chapter 29.

## THE PRODUCTION SCHEDULE

The production schedule records the progress of each manufacturing order, which is raised when the estimate is accepted. It should be located in a convenient place for easy access. The example in Fig. 26.16 shows the information usually recorded.

## THE WORKSHOP SCHEDULE

The workshop schedule indicates the jobs to be undertaken by the workshop and provides information for the supervisor (or progress chaser) to expedite the work. A refinement of this system would include a weekly summary or an arrears schedule to prepare a revised workshop schedule. Figure 26.17 shows a typical workshop schedule. The information is only intended to indicate the

**JOB CARD**

Job no. ................................................................................ Date job required ........................

Operation .......................................................................... Operation no. ............................

Section ..............................................................................

| Date | Operator's name | Clock no. | Time | | | Passed | Rejected |
|------|-----------------|-----------|------|------|------|--------|----------|
|      |                 |           | Commenced | Finished | Total |        |          |
|      |                 |           |      |      |      |        |          |

**Figure 26.13** Job card: outlines an operator's work, often completed daily

| Job no. | | Operation 5 | Operation 3 | Operation 1 |
|---------|---|-------------|-------------|-------------|
| Operation | Hrs Mins 1 = : 2 = : 3 = : 4 = : 5 = : 6 = : | Op. clock no. .... Job no. ............... Time ................... Date ................... | Op. clock no. .... Job no. ............... Time ................... Date ................... | Op. clock no. .... Job no. ............... Time ................... Date ................... |
| Total time | = : | Operation 6 | Operation 4 | Operation 2 |
| Passed/rejected ................... | | Op. clock no. .... | Op. clock no. .... | Op. clock no. .... |
| Inspector ................... | | Job no. ............... | Job no. ............... | Job no. ............... |
| Storekeeper ................... | | Time ................... | Time ................... | Time ................... |
| Date ................... | | Date ................... | Date ................... | Date ................... |

**Figure 26.14** Job ticket: torn off at perforations on completion of each operation

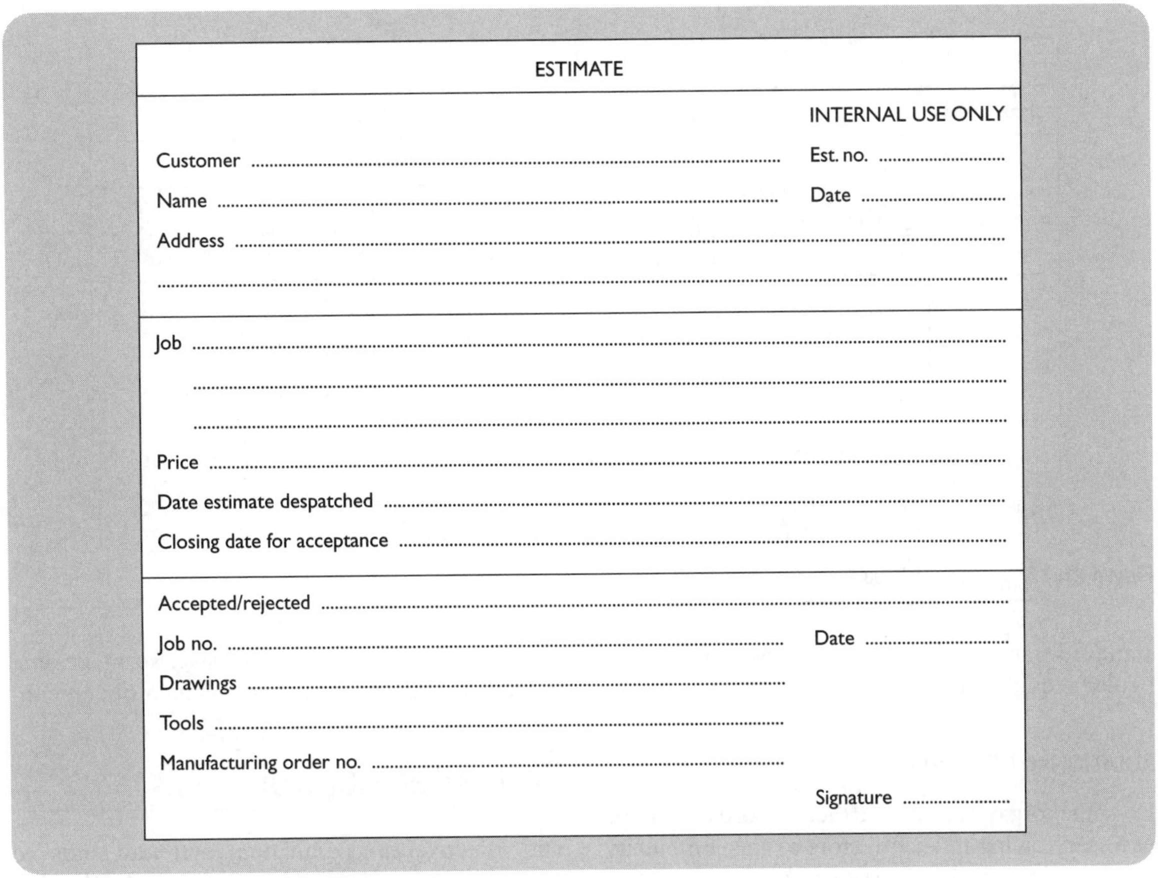

ESTIMATE

INTERNAL USE ONLY

Customer ........................ Est. no. ........................

Name ........................ Date ........................

Address ........................

........................

Job ........................

........................

........................

Price ........................

Date estimate despatched ........................

Closing date for acceptance ........................

Accepted/rejected ........................

Job no. ........................ Date ........................

Drawings ........................

Tools ........................

Manufacturing order no. ........................

Signature ........................

*Figure 26.15* Estimate: for internal circulation

PRODUCTION SCHEDULE

| Manufacturing order no. | Date received | Job description | Job no. | Cost code | Quarter (in week nos) | | | | | | | | | | | | |
|---|---|---|---|---|---|---|---|---|---|---|---|---|---|---|---|---|---|
| | | | | | 1 | 2 | 3 | 4 | 5 | 6 | 7 | 8 | 9 | 10 | 11 | 12 | 13 |

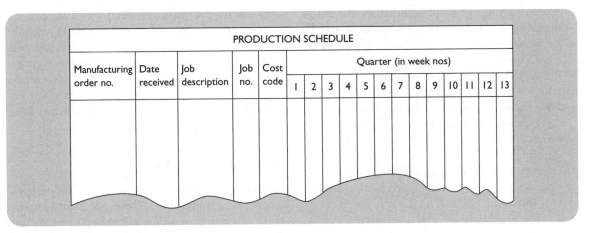

*Figure 26.16* Production schedule

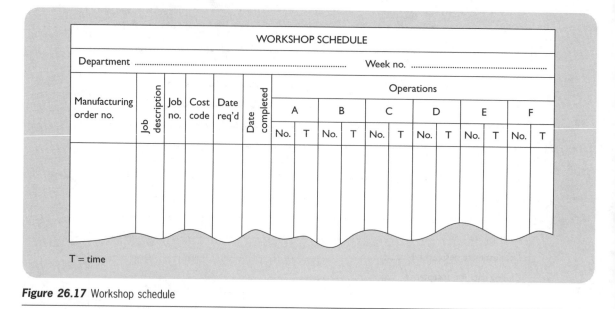

**WORKSHOP SCHEDULE**

Department ............................................................................ Week no. ...............................................................

| Manufacturing order no. | Job description | Job no. | Cost code | Date req'd | Date completed | Operations | | | | | | | | | | | |
|---|---|---|---|---|---|---|---|---|---|---|---|---|---|---|---|---|---|
| | | | | | | A | | B | | C | | D | | E | | F | |
| | | | | | | No. | T | No. | T | No. | T | No. | T | No. | T | No. | T |

T = time

**Figure 26.17** Workshop schedule

standard framework; it may be varied to suit particular requirements.

### ADDITIONAL RECORDS

In some organisations further records may be necessary owing to such factors as the complexity of operations and the size of the stores. When there are many operations and lengthy machining, it may be worthwhile to use loading charts and additional progress sheets. The size of the stores is another example. In some companies the range of materials is small, so visual inspection may be sufficient for reordering, especially if the materials are commonplace and present no problems of delivery delays. In other companies it may be necessary to use stock records, material requisitions and a strictly regulated reordering system.

In conclusion, good sense and a thorough grasp of the particular requirements of the work situation should override stereotyped systems. They are only intended as guides and provide basic principles upon which a sound production control system should be based. The tendency is to create unnecessary paperwork and excessive controls. Each proposed document and each existing document should be stringently tested for its usefulness. Comments such as 'It may be useful' or 'We should really keep a record' do not justify its exist-

ence. Paperwork is very expensive, so make sure to have a definite reason for raising a document.

## Computer control

The effectiveness of manual systems tends to rely upon supervisors and employees who develop experience and use it often without creating any permanent records which can be referred to by others. This reliance upon individuals understandably creates problems. Properly managed manual systems are efficient but limited compared with the benefits offered by a computer. However, according to the experience of many companies, care is essential before adopting a computer system. To appreciate a computer system, one short visit to an appropriate company is better than reading long, complex explanations.

### COMPUTER PACKAGES

Computer packages vary in cost, comprehensiveness and suitability. There are many on the market, each containing a number of programs. Appropriately selected and properly installed, they provide an indispensable resource of considerable power. But they do need competent managers to get the most out of them. Packages cover all the production control activities mentioned earlier. Documentation varies to accommodate computer printers. Sophisticated analysis is easy but must be appropriate to needs. Large amounts of data can be readily processed.

## BENEFITS OF COMPUTERS

Computers can answer many complex questions which are essential for formulating long-term strategies and for day-to-day running of the business. However, accuracy does rely upon the correct information being fed into the computer in the first place. Typical advantages are more accurate data on bills of material, engineering alterations, inventories, goods received and materials movements; reduced work-in-progress; and improved control of many activities.

## COMPUTER KNOWLEDGE

Users need to know the capability of packages, how to use the programs to suit their requirements, and how to operate a display screen. Why and how the computer works is relatively unimportant since programs are designed to be user-friendly, giving clear hints and advice on how to proceed.

Users should also remember legislation on the misuse of computers. The Computer Misuse Act 1990 was mentioned in Chapter 17. Briefly there should be no unauthorised access to computer material, no unauthorised access to commit any ulterior intent, and no unauthorised modification of computer material.

Unfortunately, many managers remain computer illiterate, even in large companies, and some find the change very difficult to accept. But the numbers are dwindling rapidly as more computers are installed and the Internet grows in importance. Perhaps three basic concepts are helpful for the supervisor who has no experience of operating computers: online processing, database systems and batch processing.

### Online processing

Online processing means the user of a terminal may enter information which is used immediately by the computer. Rapid response with appropriate data is displayed and the information is fed into various programs automatically. Thus the user interacts directly with the system and can update and retrieve information immediately.

### A database

Information stored in the computer's memory is called a database. This information may be added to, deleted or modified (updated) by means of a terminal, providing authority is given to the user. Others may view data without changing it. Locating information in a database is easy and versatile – it may be found by asking the appropriate question. A typical example is, Find all the shareholders in France who hold more than one thousand shares in company A.

The information is stored in electronic files, similar to physical information stored in cabinets except computers store them in their memory or on disk. Access is rapid by pressing appropriate keys on the keyboard terminal. The information is stored only once to serve many different purposes. Such database management may be compared with an intelligent filing cabinet, capable of checking, searching and discriminating between all the information it holds to produce a requirement.

A package that handles the information is called a *database management program*. The database stored in the computer's *hard disk* (internal storage) should always be stored on back-up *floppy disks* (external storage). In other words, always make copies since it is fatal to rely on the hard disk alone. Faults and errors do occur, which could mean the loss of vital information.

### Batch processing

Processing operations together as a group is called operating in batch mode. It can be used to run jobs that do not need continuous operators attention, such as printing reports.

# A computer system

A computerised system is shown in Fig. 26.18. It illustrates the main application programs or modules and the information flow between them.

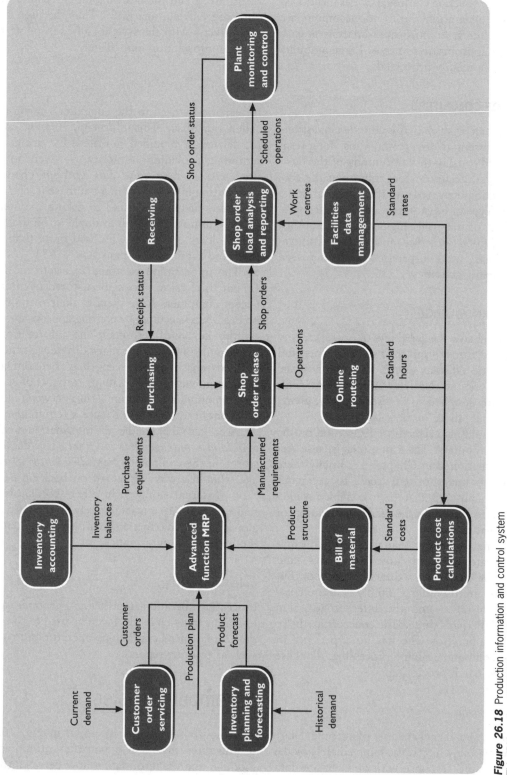

**Figure 26.18** Production information and control system

This IBM system (COPICS) provides management and operating personnel with the architecture and tools needed to develop individual, functional systems that are elements of a dynamic, integrated, online planning and control system for a manufacturing company.

This IBM system is called COPICS (Communications Oriented Production Control System).

## CUSTOMER ORDER SERVICING

Orders are entered in *central control* where the status of orders is checked and any changes are entered. Users may retrieve and display up-to-date information. All data for invoicing is in the database, along with sales statistics as required.

## ENGINEERING AND PRODUCTION DATA CONTROL

Three programs cover bills of material, online routeing and facilities data management. A production definition database provides bills of material or parts lists and any changes in the product due to engineering alteration. Comprehensive data on each item allows design engineers to retrieve and view, to determine usage, and to change procedures as required.

Online routeing describes an item's manufacturing process or routeing which may be used for costing, production planning, shop-order release and progressing. The facilities management program is used to capture and maintain plant resource data and to plan utilisation of plant resources. Engineers use a terminal to create, maintain and retrieve machine and tool data, designate alternative work centres, and identify machines and work centres by cost centre or department.

## COST PLANNING AND CONTROL

Cost accountants may create, maintain and retrieve cost data. The program allows analysis and simulations. Online users can change cost factors, simulate cost changes and review the impact.

## INVENTORY MANAGEMENT: THREE PROGRAMS

- *Inventory accounting* gives a basic inventory status of all items. Thus supervisors and inventory controllers may enter and record material movements and physical counts. Users can receive immediate responses to enquiries on material availability.
- *Inventory planning and forecasting* helps planners to analyse demand, forecast sales, establish order quantities, set reorder points, and calculate safety stock.
- *Material requirements planning (MRP)* allows planners to view the material plan and respond to exceptions. Thus the plan is kept valid at all times.

## SHOP FLOOR MANAGEMENT: THREE PROGRAMS

- *Shop order release* assists in preparing shop documentation, shop-order release, and issue of materials.
- *Shop order load analysis and reporting* starts and finishes dates of operations, calculates loads for machines and times, and maintains plans of workload input and output for work centres.
- *Plant monitoring and control* is of special interest and is detailed below.

### Plant monitoring and control

A set of databases is maintained in the following areas:

- *Employee database*: this includes employee administrative data; work schedules; employee activities and attendance, including overtime, leave and holidays.
- *Shop order database*: this includes release shop order information with routeings, schedules, standards and status.
- *Departmental database*: this includes valid departmental numbers with corresponding work schedules and supervisors.
- *Work centre database*: this includes all valid work centres used by regular and rework operations.
- *Transaction database*: this includes all transactions entered during the shift as feedback data to appropriate programs.

The program provides online functions for departmental supervision, production control, departmental employees, and administration. It captures in real time the shop-floor activity. This includes information needed to meet due dates and to reduce the cost of unnecessary chasing and expediting of parts.

### The departmental supervisor's role

By using the operation's start and finish dates, the departmental supervisor has the information to work on the right jobs while continuing to supervise the department efficiently. On display is the status of employees and jobs currently in process or due to arrive. Therefore the assignment of these jobs is more easily controlled to make full use of the available resources.

### The production control supervisor

Expediting is easier for the production control supervisor as he or she may locate various activities immediately. These activities include locating in-process orders for the required part, reviewing the status of a particular shop order, changing the priority, changing to alternative operations, and perhaps splitting the shop order to relieve a critical situation.

## PURCHASING AND RECEIVING

Purchasing and receiving programs help to ensure materials have the right quality and quantity, and they are available when required. Purchasing data is maintained in supplier and purchase order databases. Buyers are provided with production requirements, comprehensive information on suppliers, including quotation data, previous orders and delivery dates. Requisition and official orders may be created and follow-up is easier. The receiving program assists in reception and inspection control.

## QUESTIONS

1 Explain the importance of production planning to the supervisor.

2 Describe the Gantt chart and draw up a simple example.

3 Give an account of the various stages of planning production.

4 What is the purpose of production control and how is it achieved?

5 Outline the main aspects of production control and illustrate the purpose of each one.

6 Describe the activity of scheduling.

7 Discuss machine and labour utilisation, illustrating some efficiency ratios that may be used to control them.

8 Outline the purpose of manufacturing order control in a production control system.

9 Discuss the two main aspects of stock control.

10 What are the purposes of stock control and how are they achieved?

11 Give a detailed account of the purposes of despatching and expediting in a system of production control.

12 Give an account of the typical causes of production delays, illustrating them wherever possible with examples from your own experience.

13 The supervisor must adopt the right attitude towards the production control department. Explain this statement in detail.

14 Explain the three main types of production and give examples of products manufactured under each type.

15 Explain group technology and list its advantages.

16 Discuss the possible limitations of manual production control systems compared with the probable benefits of computer systems.

17 What is the aim and philosophy of just-in-time working?

18 Outline the essential requirements of just-in-time working.

19 Explain the philosophy of the Kawasaki production system.

20 What are the main techniques available to reduce production delays?

21 Explain the kaizen philosophy.

22 Discuss manufacturing automation protocol.

23 Outline the supervisor's role in modern production control systems.

24 How would you describe the ideal manufacturing system?

25 What is total lead time?

26 How would you attempt to convince employees that aiming for continuous improvement is an essential feature for everyone to follow?

The works director is holding his monthly meeting with the works manager and has ordered the five supervisors to attend. The factory consists of five production stages, the stores is undermanned through high labour turnover, and the personnel department is trying to resolve a bonus problem created by the works director, who is attempting to save money. Each supervisor is ordered to explain why there are production delays. A summary of the answers is given below.

- *Stage 1*: There is insufficient warning of production orders from the sales department. The bonus problem is causing work to rule. Employees refuse to work overtime until the bonus is sorted out.
- *Stage 2*: Employees are all part-time women who are reluctant to work overtime. The machines are overloaded about 50 per cent of the time.
- *Stage 3*: The supervisor at stage 2 does not allow sufficient time for stage 3 to arrange appropriate manning. Insufficient warning of workload causes delays when materials are ordered from the stores.
- *Stage 4*: This department is overmanned. Four skilled versatile operators are often on idle time.
- *Stage 5*: Testing reveals 15 per cent of finished goods have to be returned to stages 3 and 4. No delays occur at this stage.

*Comment on the obvious problems in this factory. Suggest solutions for each stage, bearing in mind the situations at other stages. Consider the overall organisation in this company and any action the works manager and supervisors might contemplate.*

Bill Pritchard, the recently appointed works manager, has heard rumours that some departments are overloaded with work compared with others. Every time he airs this subject at his weekly meetings, he is assured by the supervisors that there are no unfair workloads.

Bill decides to introduce a work distribution chart and instructs the supervisors to complete daily logs as a check on the production control reports.

After four weeks, to Bill's surprise, there are no discrepancies. Expecting at least some mismatch between records, he conducts some spot checks. The first check in one of the suspect sections reveals that a fitter is not performing the task written up in the log. On querying it with him the fitter replies, 'I was told to build up hours on this one. We do it all the time. It's the system'.

Similar cases are found in other sections.

*Consider carefully the choices of action that Bill could take. What are the deeper implications of this discovery?*

# 27

# Total quality control

## Introduction

The philosophy of total quality control (TQC) is to involve *all* employees in attempting to improve continually the product (or service) to satisfy customer requirements. This philosophy depends upon the following criteria from top management. An overview of total quality control is shown in Fig. 27.1.

- A total commitment to TQC and all its implications.
- Recognising that TQC is vital for survival of a business.
- Creating an environment for *all* employees that encourages TQC to flourish.
- Ensuring that TQC is treated as an essential requirement for all stages of production from research and development, through to design, manufacture, performance and reliability of the product (or service).

**Figure 27.1** Total quality control: an overview

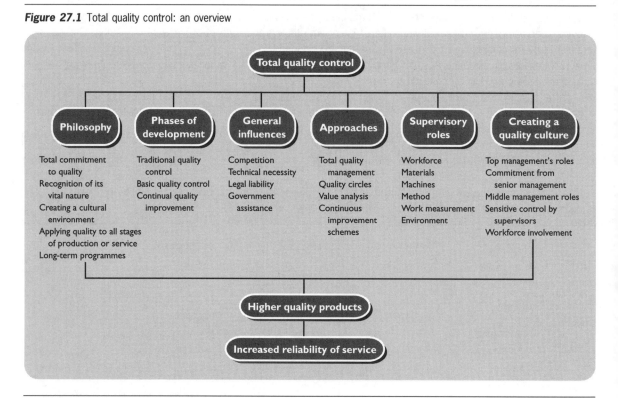

**Total quality control**

| Philosophy | Phases of development | General influences | Approaches | Supervisory roles | Creating a quality culture |
|---|---|---|---|---|---|
| Total commitment to quality | Traditional quality control | Competition | Total quality management | Workforce | Top management's roles |
| Recognition of its vital nature | Basic quality control | Technical necessity | Quality circles | Materials | Commitment from senior management |
| Creating a cultural environment | Continual quality improvement | Legal liability | Value analysis | Machines | Middle management roles |
| Applying quality to all stages of production or service | | Government assistance | Continuous improvement schemes | Method | Sensitive control by supervisors |
| Long-term programmes | | | | Work measurement | Workforce involvement |
| | | | | Environment | |

**Higher quality products**

**Increased reliability of service**

## QUALITY CONTROL: THREE PHASES

### Traditional quality control

Traditional quality control emphasises product input features such as labour, materials, method study, time study, machines and equipment, and the environment. It is based on reducing the unit cost of a product to increase profit, expand the business and satisfy investors. To remain employed, people are forced to perform within the limits set by management, who decides on design and quality requirements.

### Basic quality control

Basic quality control determines standards and specifications of the product, establishes inspection points during manufacture and after completion, and uses certain techniques such as statistical quality control. Employees perform according to set methods and timescales. Trade unions use various pressures to influence methods, times, pay and working conditions.

### Continual quality improvement

This phase commits *everyone* to improving the quality of the product. Commitment involves modern human resource management, a complete change of attitude by top management and employees, creating an appropriate environment, involvement and co-operation from everyone, and appropriate training and development. Such quality control incorporates all aspects of operations, which include effectiveness, productivity and all possible savings. To maintain quality standards means using quality control audits, appropriate education, training and development, statistical quality control, quality circles, and interchanging information on quality between companies. Essentially a long-term programme, it demands considerable enthusiasm and dedication.

## THE QUALITY CULTURE CONCEPT

After World War II various individuals studied quality and how quality programmes could transform productivity and quality levels. Two famous specialists, J.M. Juran and W. Edwards Deming, worked mainly together on these projects and produced a new quality culture concept. Their ideas were not received enthusiastically in the West. However, in Japan they were discussed and accepted. Consequently, Japan's reputation for shoddy goods was quickly changed, largely due to the new culture.

Deming persuaded Japan to bring the customer into the organisation and create close contact with the employee and supplier to work towards continuous improvement. Deming's philosophy maintained that improved performance meant raising the level of the whole system, not the level of employee performance alone. This meant a broader approach to 'quality' by encompassing the customer's requirements and improving performance in the broadest sense.

Juran's ideas included changing management's attitude from accepting quality levels to aiming for higher quality. This change could be achieved by believing a 'breakthrough' to higher quality is desirable and feasible by long-term thinking and continuous development programmes.

## THE UK REPUTATION

Critics claim the UK has secured a reputation for poor quality goods and services, although there are notable exceptions. The major reasons are outlined below, then the next few sections consider essential areas for improvement.

- top management does not perceive or acknowledge the need for high quality
- an inability to implement good ideas and innovation
- a powerful resistance from middle management to change
- a strong emphasis on short-term results and ignoring long-term projects
- the misconception that quality is the province of inspection alone, which implies that inspection is more important than reducing manufacturing faults
- poor job flexibility
- a complacent workforce who does not recognise the idea that the customer comes first

# Improvement: four major influences

## COMPETITION

In Far Eastern countries there has been continued successful development in many activities which is serious for the West. Consequently, a company's reputation for quality products and service is now vital for its survival. Research has shown that managers are responsible for quality failures, not employees. Managers often seem to adopt a complacent attitude. They accept defects as inevitable and make little attempt to improve quality. A negative outlook is also prevalent: wait and see if the customer complains; inspect quality rather than prevent faults; and ignore or fail to seek employees' comments.

### Commitment to quality

The main reason for Japan's success is commitment to quality by everyone in the organisation. Such continuous improvement programmes and the manufacture of standard designs have been the main contribution to this success, *not* using advanced technology and superior product design. In these circumstances market orientation through market research (Chapter 4) is essential to achieve maximum customer satisfaction provided quality coincides with customer requirements.

This form of commitment involves the zero defects (ZD) philosophy, which is commonplace in Japan. ZD means aiming for a 100 per cent quality target and ensuring each job is done correctly first time. Arguably this is not humanly possible because people are fallible. The philosophy, however, is sound and generates enthusiasm and co-operation. Without such high aims any company will have difficulties in competing with a ZD rival.

## TECHNICAL NECESSITY

Manufacturing processes are often made less costly by using interchangeable parts. These may be selected at random and, when assembled, conform to the standards laid down. This practice allows designers to maximise tolerances without interfering with set quality standards. Inspection is adjusted to allow permissible variations from the standard to pass within set limits.

Genichi Taguchi, a Japanese specialist, has devised other methods. These include determining the critical product parameters that cause variability; designing the product to minimise item-to-item variation and performance variation; analysing and eliminating factors that cause output variability; and identifying controllable quality variables, such as machining tolerances and materials.

## LEGAL LIABILITY FOR DEFECTIVE PRODUCTS

### Consumer Protection Act 1987

Part I of the Consumer Protection Act 1987 (CPA) provides effective remedies for consumers who have suffered loss due to defective products. This implements the 1985 EC Directive on Product Liability. A producer of a defective product is strictly liable for the damage caused unless the person or company can rely on one or more defences listed in the act. A product is 'defective' if it fails to operate safely in the associated circumstances. The term 'safely' includes components. A product is considered 'unsafe' if it is a danger to other property apart from risk of death or injury.

The term 'damage' refers to death, personal injury, or loss of or damage to any property, including land. Claims relating to property, however, are not covered by this act since financial or pure economic loss (for the purposes of the CPA) may be recovered under the laws of contract or negligence in appropriate cases.

Under Part II it is a criminal offence to supply consumer goods that do not comply with general safety requirements. Part III replaces existing law on misleading price indications.

### Implications

The need to improve quality control procedures is clearly the main implication, but there are others. More care and caution are essential when drafting advertisements, sales promotion projects, instruction booklets, and any particular safety precautions.

The General Product Safety Regulations 1994 overlap with the Consumer Protection Act 1987 and impose a general safety requirement for products marketed by producers and distributors. The definition of a 'safe product' is complex: one which under normal or reasonably foreseeable conditions of use, including duration, does not present any risk, or only minimal risk, compatible with the usage which is considered as acceptable and consistent with a high level of protection for the safety and health of users. Certain factors must be taken into account to determine whether a product is safe:

- characteristics which include composition, packaging and assembly and maintenance instructions
- effect on other products where it is reasonably foreseeable that it will be used on other products
- presentation, including labelling, instructions for use and disposal, and any other indication or information provided by the producer
- the categories of consumers at serious risk when using the product, particularly children

The regulations are enforced by prohibition notices and other provisions in the 1987 act. Breach of regulations may lead to a fine of up to £5000 and a jail term of up to three months.

## Implications

The regulations obviously impose stringent obligations on producers and distributors. Producers are prohibited from putting unsafe products on the market and must provide relevant information to minimise misuse and highlight any dangers. Distributors must apply due care to ensure compliance with producers' obligations; they must not supply products which are dangerous when they should be aware of the risks; they should participate in monitoring the safety of products on the market; communicate any information on the product risks; and co-operate in any action to avoid those risks.

## GOVERNMENT ASSISTANCE

The importance of higher quality standards was recognised in the government's White Paper (1982).

Four areas were identified which could improve quality: certification schemes involving a national accreditation system and a quality awareness campaign; adopting BSI standards on quality; using the standards when introducing regulations; and encouraging public purchasers to examine products more carefully.

The British Standards Institution introduced BS 5750, a national standard on quality for suppliers and manufacturers. It indicates a cost-effective quality management system and a structured approach. It does not provide any quality standards for a product. There are many specific requirements which can be followed to receive an appropriate certification. BS 5750 is not intended to offer a scheme for total quality management (TQM) since it is not possible to achieve commitment from everyone in an organisation to a continual quality improvement programme.

# Quality: the supervisor's role

The supervisor is powerless to create a total quality environment without full support from the hierarchy. However, even without support the supervisor should at least stress the following basic concepts:

- Foster more responsibility by reminding each employee that he or she is also a customer. This idea stresses the reliance on other employees' efforts compared with relating solely to a remote outside customer.
- Allow as much freedom as possible in working arrangements, consequently the employee will feel more commitment.
- Ensure adequate feedback on quality is received by *all* employees. Discuss the causes of any faults with them.
- Tell superiors why faults are occurring; do not assume they know the reasons.
- Transmit information on quality well up the line whenever the opportunity occurs.
- Discuss the economic aspects of poor quality products with individuals whenever the opportunities occur. Often employees do not appreciate such aspects as possible company insolvency, competition from abroad, and effects on the cost of living and standard of living.

# Basic quality control

Any quality control technique must follow a lead from top management with its committed quality programmes and indoctrination of a quality culture. The techniques have to be introduced when the climate is right. To help attitude change, an employee must be appropriately educated and trained to understand the reasons for changes. Typical techniques are associated with the basic concept of quality control in its various forms. There are three main activities.

## ESTABLISHING STANDARDS AND SPECIFICATIONS

Establishing standards and specifications makes it possible to ensure the product conforms to requirements. The standards are set by top management in conjunction with production engineering, which assesses the feasibility of the proposed standards. The sales department assesses the market requirements. The purchasing department provides information on the standards of material available. The production department then indicates the feasibility of manufacturing at the proposed standards within proposed costs.

### Acceptable standards

Perfect standards in production are costly and difficult to achieve. The basic standard for a product to sell effectively must conform to the consumer's minimum standard at a selling price which is acceptable for that level of quality. Naturally there is an area of acceptability which allows for slight variations that do not drastically change the performance of the product. These variations are caused by chance variables and assignable variables:

- *Chance variables* are inherent in the production processes; examples are machine limitations, material imperfections, limitations of inspection equipment, and human error.
- *Assignable variables* are external influences such as incorrect operation of machines, misuse of equipment, incorrect sequence of operations, worn and faulty machines, worn inspection equipment, and variations in working conditions, including humidity, temperature and vibration.

## INSPECTION

The purpose of inspection is to separate defective goods from those conforming to the standard of accuracy laid down by management. This important aspect of quality control attempts to ensure only goods of adequate quality pass to the consumer and that faults are located in materials, components, work-in-progress or finished goods.

The inspection department often supervises the task of salvaging rejected work, or the disposal of scrap to reduce the possibility of defects returning accidentally (or sometimes intentionally) to the production line. It is also responsible for the general control of all inspection devices.

Inspection provides information for statistical quality control, but setting quality standards is outside its function. Quality standards must be in writing to be measurable, reasonable and understandable. Rigid inspection is uneconomic since it tends to increase scrap by rejecting anything which does not conform exactly to the drawing. Reasonable inspection is flexible and allows a degree of departure from the drawing so long as adequate operation of the product is not impaired and quality standards are maintained. Quality control provides these limits within which inspection can operate effectively.

### Inspection methods

- *Hundred per cent inspection*: This entails the inspection of every single item in a batch or process. It is costly and human error makes it difficult to carry out satisfactorily, so it is usually avoided if possible. Hundred per cent inspection is only justified for large and complex products with critical stages of production which would involve heavy losses if faults were not discovered in the early stages.
- *Sampling method*: The sampling technique involves selecting at random a given number of pieces for inspection. Statistical tables provide the appropriate sample size for the total number involved at a set level of quality. The number of rejects gives a fair indication of the quality level for the whole batch.

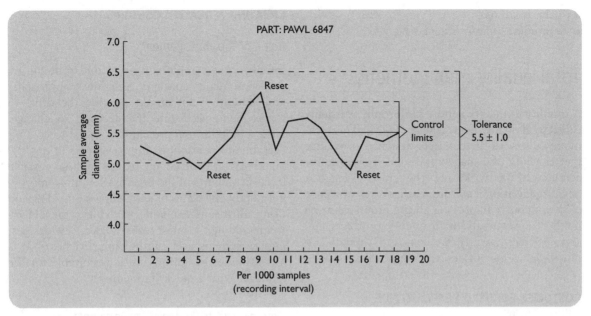

**Figure 27.2** Statistical quality control chart
Control limits are set for each process. Sampling results are plotted on a graph to show trends. Corrective action can then be taken at an early stage, wherever trends indicate that control limits are in danger of being exceeded.

## STATISTICAL QUALITY CONTROL

Statistical quality control uses statistical methods to provide information for supervisors and operators to maintain control of the actual processes. The theory of probability is used to establish a set of control limits for each process by determining the range within which the chance variables are likely to occur. When these limits are exceeded, an immediate indication is given that some action must be taken to correct an assignable variable which forced the process over the specified limits. The physical side of process control involves sampling at regular intervals and plotting results on a chart as quickly as possible to show the current trend. Figure 27.2 shows a typical chart for this purpose.

Control charts of this nature are provided for each process and a running record is maintained. When the plot falls outside the limits, the incident is reported and an immediate investigation follows to find the reason for the deviation. Remedial action is taken to steer the process back to within the specified limits. Experience usually shows when the process is veering away towards the limits and corrective action may be taken earlier. Thus a higher percentage of the product is manufactured within the specified limits.

This emphasis on controlling the process ensures increased quality in the early stages of production. It also means higher machine utilisation in later stages, less possibility of damage to machines, and a reduction in further processing of faulty work. The concept of statistical quality control has been highly simplified here for the purpose of explanation. It can be very successful when correctly applied in suitable circumstances.

# Approaches to quality control

The general theme for all quality control is to adopt a managerial philosophy to counteract complacency and to involve everyone in a commitment to quality improvement in the long term. The main techniques are:

- total quality management
- quality circles

- value analysis
- continuous improvement schemes

# Total quality management

A monitored quality culture philosophy is usually called total quality management (TQM). This technique covers all the concepts designed to change the behaviour of managers and supervisors, and the attitudes of the workforce. The aim is to create a new organisational culture that involves everyone in continuously improving all the processes at all levels. Consequently, high quality products and services emerge which are constantly updated or innovated as part of an evolving process.

## CUSTOMER-FOCUSED PERFORMANCE IMPROVEMENT

The vital aspect of TQM is to create a continuous process of improving performance directly related to customer requirements. This philosophy is in line with TQC as outlined in the introduction. The reliance on employees, supervisors and managers to provide detailed feedback on all customer contacts involving quality is stressed again. Such feedback is the only reliable way to ensure adequate communication.

## QUALITY IMPROVEMENT CONCEPTS

Implementing TQM is a vast project involving all the managerial skills outlined in Chapter 8. These are suitably revised and aligned to cope with quality improvement concepts. The main concepts are:

- comprehensive assessments of the current quality situation
- restructuring the organisation to accommodate the new objectives and the proposed organisational culture
- sound education and training schemes on quality culture for everyone on processes
- organising processes at the input or early phases before production proceeds
- establishing the total involvement of everyone
- controlling through continuous application of improvement techniques

## CREATING A QUALITY CULTURE

### Roles of top management

Initially considerable education and training are needed in quality concepts, techniques, approaches and systems. This should provide the drive to succeed and accelerate the decision to change. Next a long-term approach is essential to commit everyone to continuous improvements in quality. Standards are forced up to the highest possible levels in all parts of the organisation, thus improving all processes. This practice implies providing and using all means available to achieve the objective, including the latest technologies, new designs, quality systems and cultural improvements. It is a continuous evolution and is unsuitable for the manager with a quick-fix mentality.

### Commitment from senior management

Education and training in TQM at this level and below is equally important. Top management's policy objectives must be clear to senior managers when organising for quality improvement by restructuring, defining policies, objectives and values, and compiling a comprehensive quality programme for middle managers. A fundamental need is to concentrate on initial processes rather than wait for results at production stages. Also effective workforce teams must be established, since they determine quality, along with adopting a new organisational culture and improving job flexibility.

### Middle management roles

Interpreting senior management's structural decisions provides ample opportunity to exploit change rapidly through a new favourable climate of co-operation and collaboration. Sufficient sensitivity and a comprehensive understanding of quality culture are needed for successful implementation and support to supervisors.

### Supervisor's roles

The supervisor must supervise processes and pass on the TQM philosophy to the workforce. All processes in the main functions (administration, production, etc.) involve six aspects: the workforce, materials, machines, method, work measurement and the environment.

## The workforce

The supervisor should encourage employees to be quality-minded and conscientious. They ought to be proud of the product and the company. Their enthusiasm must be aroused by dynamic leadership. Most employees are basically conscientious and take pride in their work, so the supervisor should constantly be watchful for undesirable pressures and counteract them.

If the employees are not fully aware of the standards set for each process, they can hardly be expected to aim for high quality. Similarly, they must be fully trained and familiarised with better methods of performing operations. Careful selection is also vital to avoid misplacement and inferior output. Finally, there is the problem of careless people who lack concentration for various reasons. Waste is very costly, so careless people must be consulted immediately and appropriate action taken.

Information received through a computer helps to identify 'quality' more easily. Also it provides appropriate guidelines to an employee on performance related to other employees. An employee's performance may not be obvious to him or her until information on others highlights the situation. The synergistic importance of teamwork and group activity (Chapter 5) is stressed. Employees should identify strongly with each other and the organisation.

## Materials

If materials are reported to be faulty or of the wrong type, the supervisor should investigate and report with recommendations. The cost of production or administration rises if more time is spent on unsuitable materials. Every effort must be made to rectify the situation quickly.

## Machines

If a machine develops a fault, the supervisor must either order the machine to be stopped to avoid excessive waste, or report the defect immediately, depending on the circumstances. Machine servicing and rearrangement of schedules should follow as a natural consequence of control.

## Method

There is always room for improvement in *how* a process is accomplished. Many ways are always open for consideration since employees usually structure their own ideas into their work to some extent.

## Work measurement

Measurement of ongoing performance is fundamental for control. Often there is reliance on the individual; when straightforward management is difficult, individuals can make quite accurate assessments using their intuition. Typical examples in a conscientious quality culture are changes in the sound of a machine, appearance of the process, and a feel of the situation.

## The environment

The effects of changes in conditions should be remembered. Temperature, humidity, draughts, pollution and lighting are typical variances which may cause problems for people and processes.

## THE BUSINESS IMPROVEMENT PROCESS

The business improvement process (BIP) is one approach to TQM which is gaining in popularity and often is known as business process re-engineering or business process redesign. BIP means rethinking and redesigning all the processes to discover and improve the core activities, the product range and logistic operations. This may be achieved in many ways, typically by introducing a radical change in the organisational structure from a tall hierarchical pattern to a flatter pattern which is process-driven. There should be improvements in product delivery time, customer service and profit margins. Such rethinking involves many techniques (including O&M). The concept should be viewed as a continuous activity where an organisation is constantly evolving as ideas, structures and approaches are incorporated. Note that the concept includes all the quality culture aspects of TQM and should not be seen in isolation.

## WORKFORCE INVOLVEMENT

The ultimate effect if management and supervision are successful is a favourable attitude by everyone to quality improvement. Commitment to achieving high quality becomes a culture in itself. There is no extra cost involved and everyone sees quality as their own responsibility. The future of the company is assured. Success may depend on courses for managers and supervisors through TECs (Chapter 6) to teach techniques on how to run employee workshops on improving innovation. The aim is to encourage a flow of ideas to identify threats and opportunities, and implement the necessary changes.

## ASSESSING THE RESULTS OF TQM

Success is usually measured in terms of growth and changes in share price, market share, return on investment and workforce stability. Successful competitive strategy naturally embraces other activities, such as choice of products, production strategy and tactics, selection of particular market segments, and investment policy.

# Quality circles

The Japanese were the first to exploit quality circles (QC) in the early 1960s, although the concept originated in the USA some years earlier. Development elsewhere was very slow until the 1990s, when more attention was paid to the successful application of the technique in Japan.

QC is based on 'motivation by participation': a small group (usually from five to ten people) who are engaged in similar activities meet regularly under the leadership of the supervisor to discuss work problems. Topics may include quality, materials, machines, equipment and safety. The meetings are voluntary and in company time, although once established there is a tendency to meet at other times. The group identifies the problem, analyses it, solves it, and makes recommendations to management. On receiving agreement, the group implements the solution whenever it is feasible.

In the UK there was some success, but many schemes declined. The main reasons for disinterest are incompatibility with organisational culture, uneasy relationships between hierarchical levels at meetings, and difficulty in introducing ideas by using rigid formal systems that resist change.

## INITIAL CONSIDERATIONS

If the decision to install QC comes from top management, the first stage may be to establish a steering committee. Its functions will include financial allocation and cost considerations, responsibility for training, launching the scheme, the appointment of leaders and a facilitator, and co-ordination of the project.

## OBJECTIVES

The main aims are to improve productivity by participation, to improve quality at less cost, to reduce frustration and grievances, to reduce labour turnover, and to push real power down to lower levels in the organisation.

## MEMBERSHIP

There are various forms of group composition. The simple one is where a supervisor decides the idea is worth trying, receives permission from management, and asks for volunteers to make up a group. A more structured group may include an inspector and a quality engineer. A full-scale launch will include a training seminar on QC, a collective decision to attempt the technique, establishing a steering committee to guide and advise, training sessions for circle members, and chairmanship training for the leader.

## TRAINING REQUIREMENTS

Improvements are possible, even with simple approaches. Many brilliant ideas are locked up in employees' heads and remain there for various reasons. No training is necessary because often the solutions already exist. In highly complex situations, however, it is argued that training in some areas is particularly important. These areas usually include problem-solving techniques, use of initiative, brainstorming, Pareto analysis, data gathering, and cause–effect diagrams.

## GENERAL APPROACHES

Obtaining the backing of management is vital, otherwise the outcome may be a lowering of morale accompanied by a demotivating effect. The union should be consulted and direct involvement should be encouraged. During discussion within the group, all members are encouraged to contribute, the subject matter is thoroughly aired, all possible solutions are considered, and a written report is submitted to management. After agreement, implementation by the group must be handled with extreme care, remembering all the human problems which may be involved.

### Low-key approach

The initial reaction from other employees may cause concern, therefore it is worth taking a low-key approach until the outcomes are appreciated. Considerable work is necessary and the meetings are time-consuming. Anything worthwhile, however, takes courage and perseverance before successful results are seen. Previous experiences have shown the need for a trained facilitator, general training for circle members, and contact with other companies who have adopted the technique.

### A typical structured approach

- Allow members to select the programme, perhaps employing brainstorming or individual proposals.
- Draw up a list and vote on the selection of a problem.
- Gather the data and analyse it.
- Establish solutions and determine the most suitable one, possibly setting a target and agreeing a timescale.
- Obtain agreement from management.
- Implement the proposal.
- Check periodically and revise as necessary.

### APPROPRIATE LEVELS

The orthodox sites for QC are on the shop floor, in the office, or on the retail stores floor. Within these sites are found the majority of employees using similar skills and experience. They will easily identify with each other in the work situation, and distinguish similar problems. Individually and collectively they determine ways of overcoming problems and implementing their ideas.

This distinction avoids confusing QC with other forms of group activity, such as works committees, project teams, value analysis groups and joint consultative committees. These groups are composed of employees who do different work and who usually deal with tabled problems or plans. But recalling the definition, it may be argued that groups of supervisors could also form a QC. Indeed France has at least one group of this nature.

### SOME ESSENTIAL POINTS

- Apart from the leader, all QC members should be volunteers performing similar work.
- Select the 'right' circle leader.
- Prepare carefully at all stages of implementation.
- Obtain management commitment.
- Obtain union support and involvement.
- Provide adequate training programmes for QC members.
- Be receptive to co-workers.
- Unless there are exceptional circumstances, QC should be implemented by the members.

### THE SUPERVISOR'S PART

If a simple approach is used, the supervisor must seek management approval and receive full backing. He or she should remember the background to constitutional management and participative supervision, with emphasis on the analytical aspect of the radical framework described in Chapter 2.

If management takes the initiative, the supervisor should insist on adequate training as a leader and for the members of the group. He or she should do everything possible to win the support of employees and the unions. The supervisor's reports to management should coincide with all the requirements outlined in Chapter 16. If there is any debate at management level, he or she should insist on implementation by the members, unless there is a very good reason for denying them this opportunity.

The supervisor should be convinced the concept is sound. In the event of failure the cause should be looked for elsewhere, not simply blaming the concept of QC.

# Value analysis

Value analysis aims to improve the reliability and reduce the cost of an existing product by critically studying the product and its components to assess their function and cost. At the design stage the technique is called value engineering. A psychological questioning attitude is essential when attempting to improve design at lower cost. Success depends upon allocating sufficient time, using imagination, and creating an atmosphere where people feel free to come up with new ideas or suggestions, regardless of how absurd they may seem. Invariably savings occur, either by changing the method of producing a component and redesigning it, or dispensing with it entirely by redesigning other components.

## METHOD

- Select the product for study.
- Define the function of each part, noting its cost and design.
- Determine the various ways of performing the function and how they could be incorporated in a design or designs.
- Cost each design idea and compare it with previous costs: if one is cheaper, continue with the study; if it is more expensive, abandon it and try again.
- Select the optimum design considering cost and reliability.
- Implement the design and review it periodically.

## THE VALUE ANALYST

Usually an engineer, the value analyst needs to be enthusiastic, creative and trained in value engineering. Ideally a multidisciplinary team is chosen to conduct the study. However, the supervisor may also conduct similar studies with a group of employees. Many improvements in quality and reliability have been recorded.

# Continuous improvement schemes

The many approaches to continuous improvement are based on harnessing human creativity. A typical example is the Japanese philosophy kaizen outlined in Chapter 26. All the approaches encourage change by adopting a flexible organisation, providing varying forms of autonomy, and radically reviewing all activities. Approaches such as TQM, business improvement process, re-engineering and empowerment are typically associated with schemes of continuous improvement.

# Service industries

Service industries often use the term 'reliability' instead of 'quality'. Reliance means trust and confidence, safety and dependability. Relating these definitions to transport services, energy supplies, communication (telephones, etc.), health facilities, education, the legal system, repair and delivery services, and financial services clearly emphasises their importance to consumers.

## REPUTATION

Low reliability is a regular topic of newspaper reports. The quoted explanations vary from service to service, but typical causes are poor ethical standards, human fallibility, insufficient funds, poor management, environmental and economic conditions, and government policies. Increased pressure on the government to improve reliability through legislation has been partially successful, but inevitably new areas for improvement become apparent as cases are reported.

The importance of reputation is often overlooked by employees. For example, the term 'service' applies to all aspects of consumer contact as well as the main service offered. This applies at all times when direct and indirect communication occur. One company does not allow the telephone to ring more than three times before someone in the office must answer the call if an employee is absent.

## MEASURING RELIABILITY

In some service industries reliability is conceptual or abstract. Consequently, there are application difficulties in the technical and human fields. Intangible outcomes are sometimes inescapable in the following instances:

- The performance of many professional service occupations is difficult to measure, considering probability and the depth of existing knowledge; typical examples are surgeons, doctors and research scientists.
- Some service activities do not necessarily respond to quantitative techniques.
- Expertise and ethical standards may not respond to testing techniques.
- Revising or setting standards is not a straight-forward process.
- It may be difficult to convince all employees that the customer or potential customer must receive immediate attention, politeness, hospitality and the best possible service.

## FINANCIAL SERVICES ACT 1986

The Financial Services Act 1986 is an important addition to legislation and a good example of the urgent need to protect the customer. It is so complex that implementation has to be undertaken in stages over two years. Practically all types of investment business are affected. Investors are more protected through a framework of organisations which establish and enforce rules of good practice.

Heading the framework is the Securities and Investments Board, under which a number of self-regulatory organisations (SROs) operate. Each SRO sets its own rules based on general principles which amount to anyone who advises on or sells investments must observe high standards of integrity. This includes acting with due skill, care and diligence, and dealing fairly with customers.

An advisor must extract as much information as possible on the client's personal financial situation, identify the person's needs, and give the best possible advice. The meaning of 'best advice' naturally depends on the uniqueness of each case, therefore only guidelines are suggested. Proof of best advice demands careful recording of information from clients and the advice which is offered.

## QUESTIONS

1 What possible reasons are there for the manufacture of poor quality goods in a company?

2 To accomplish market dominance, everyone must feel totally committed. Discuss this statement.

3 What is the difference between total quality management and quality control?

4 Outline the long-term effects of Dr Juran's ideas on quality management.

5 Outline the aims of total quality management.

6 Discuss the main features of a quality culture.

7 What are the supervisor's roles in the creation of a quality culture?

8 What are the possible basic concepts of quality improvement that a supervisor may follow without the full support of senior management?

9 Explain quality circles and offer opinions on why there appears to be disinterest in the concept within the UK.

10 Explain the zero defects concept.

11 Describe the three main activities of quality control.

12 Explain the difference between chance variables and assignable variables in quality control. Give examples of each.

13 What is the purpose of inspection?

14 Discuss the nature and uses of statistical quality control.

15 Discuss the supervisor's responsibilities for quality control.

16 Why is reliability in the service industries difficult to measure?

17 Explain the philosophy of total quality control.

18 Outline the supervisor's roles in total quality control.

19 Explain the three phases of development which emphasise the importance of continual quality improvement.

20 Quality should conform to customer requirements. Discuss this statement.

21 Outline the business improvement process.

A sales representative is paying her usual three-monthly visit to a long-established client who is obviously angry, saying 'I've had enough of your firm. You cause me more and more paperwork. The time I spend on 'phone calls and correspondence is now beyond a joke'.

The representative attempts to placate him. 'I do understand, but it's the computer. They're trying hard to sort things out but it takes time.'

'Look, Linda, I'm not interested in your problems. I've got enough of my own. Your invoices are never right, orders get mixed up and it takes ages for them to deliver the right items.'

'But we're the best in the field – there's no one to touch us.'

'You may think so, but I don't. I'm adding up all the costs now and your company isn't top any more, I can tell you!'

'I'm sorry, Peter. You're a valued customer and I'll have a go at them when I get back next week.'

When the representative returns to the office she is told that the client has cancelled his standing order.

*Was it the computer's fault? Outline the main causes of the problem as you see it and comment on the representative's approach.*

'I can see that we're never going to solve the quality problem until you both appreciate the other's point of view.' The managing director looks wearily at the managers of the sales and production departments and continues, 'We know the sales representatives have to take the blame and we risk losing repeated orders *and* we know the production people have to maintain the performance criteria. You're dependent upon each other and somehow we must figure out a way'.

The production manager is quick to reply: 'In production we are subjected to continual pressure from sales to get the orders out on time, but we have to consider the cost factors as well'.

The sales manager reacts, 'What you do not understand is we're only a small firm. If my reps promise a delivery date for something, customers expect it to be there on time and in top condition. They're not bothered about our problems!'

*What can be done in this situation?*

# 28

# Financial control

## Introduction

The supervisor needs to know the importance of recording and maintaining accurate financial records, and being able to speak intelligently on financial topics to employees. Employees probably have three questions on financial control: Has the company made a profit? What is the dividend likely to be? Is the company sufficiently solvent to stay in business? From the trade union's viewpoint there is the question of a fair share of the profit for employees. From management's viewpoint, financial information is crucial for achieving and maintaining stability.

### ACCOUNTING

Accounting is essential in any form of economic situation. Resources are always scarce in complex economies, consequently financial information in appropriate forms provides vital evidence on the alternatives available. Therefore, accounting in this sense may be defined as collecting, presenting and interpreting economic data. Within this term, *financial accounting* (often called bookkeeping) is used to provide reports to everyone outside an organisation, whereas *managerial (or cost) accounting* copes with the activities within the organisation.

### Limitations of financial accounting

Financial accounting provides historical information, therefore the delay does not allow for immediate control of operations, but lessons may be learned for future activities. Furthermore, the accounts provide information on the *whole* of the company, whereas sensitive control depends upon information on individual sectors of the organisation. However, accounts provide valuable information by using various interpretation techniques to show variations from period to period and analysing the significance of changes to show trends. These aspects are covered later.

### THE GENERAL FINANCIAL POSITION

Financial control provides statements, interpretations and decision making on the general financial position in a company. Cost control (Chapter 29) provides control of processes and operations within the departments by using various techniques or costing systems.

Closely associated with financial control and cost control is administrative control (Chapter 30) which permeates all functions in the organisation and is an important way of improving productivity. There are many systems and procedures operated by administration. Systems include sales, production, accounting, purchasing and distribution. Typical procedures within accounting are bought ledger, sales ledger, payroll, cash book, cash forecasting, share register, fixed assets and stock control.

Managers and supervisors will be involved in all three types of control. This chapter concentrates on managing and supervising for financial control.

### ESSENTIAL FEATURES

Bearing in mind the term 'accounting' and the importance of financial control, this chapter considers the following features:

- management's roles
- the main aspects of financial management
- financial transactions
- problems of financial accounting
- sources of capital
- employment of capital
- forecasting and budgeting
- interpretation of accounts and statements
- information revealed in accounts

# Management's roles

Sensitive control of cash is critical as serious errors may lead to bankruptcy or liquidation of the business. Consequently, there must be effective financial management. Generating sufficient accurate financial information for effectiveness depends upon many principles and practices of financial control. These include:

- careful recording of all financial transactions
- satisfying legal requirements
- decision making on many factors, such as cash flow, the capital structure, acquisition of funds, dividends, degree of liquidity, and investments over all timescales considering mergers and takeovers
- solving economic problems caused by government moves, recession and market changes
- policy making to reduce risk and make profits

## THE FINANCIAL CONTROLLER'S ROLES

The roles of the financial controller are providing financial information for managers to help them decide on the best courses of action, making financial forecasts and plans, recognising deviations from plans and making corrective adjustments. They apply to short-term plans and long-term plans.

### Short-term plans

Short-term plans are formulated by detailed interpretation of long-term plans for control, perhaps on a daily or weekly basis. These calculations indicate shifts in profit, income or expense when deviations are likely. Typical shifts would be raw materials prices, pay changes and output variations. This aspect, known as budgetary control, is covered in the next chapter.

### Long-term plans

Based on policy by senior management, forecasts are prepared for several years ahead, perhaps the next five years. They cover sales, market growth prospects, and new and existing products. Their critical nature should be understood as expansion or contraction programmes hinge on them. The chief accountant forecasts profit, capital employed and cash needs for each year. Management assesses their significance and may adjust prices, sales volume, quality, advertising and sales promotion plans. Management will also consider various financial programmes involving research and development, cost-cutting, concentrating on more profitable lines, diversification, disposing of surplus assets, marketing strategy, overdrafts and loans.

# Main aspects of financial management

Financial accountancy is essentially a *tool* to be used by managers, employees and shareholders. Employees should understand its importance and adhere to financial procedures to accomplish high quality data for management decisions. Indeed all managers should understand *financial accounting* (providing information on historical performance) and *management accounting* (providing information for current performance). Effectiveness depends upon the following aspects:

- the reasons for past performance, through an analysis of previous accounts
- present performance, by examining up-to-date accounts
- future performance planning, by establishing objectives (corporate planning), strategies and tactics
- financial control, by monitoring systems and procedures to ensure that developments coincide with plans

## FINANCIAL POLICY

A successfully managed organisation will have its financial policy integrated with its business policy. Financial policy usually contains written procedures on a variety of topics divided into three main areas:

- *Internal matters* relate to funds employed, types of fund, reserves, dividends to be paid, profits and financial decision-making procedures.
- *National matters* relate to government departments involved in income tax and duty, legislation (Companies Acts), the Stock Exchange, other institutions, health and safety, and green issues.
- *International matters* relate to the European Union, including EC directives and other financial aspects; investments overseas; mergers; green issues; and general co-operation.

## MANAGEMENT INFORMATION SYSTEMS

Sound management information systems (MIS) provide regular, accurate and up-to-date financial information for decision making. They collect, record, collate, analyse and distribute information to managers for background information, for immediate control and for planning. The effectiveness of MIS depends on design to suit the company's requirements. This implies that managers know their wants and are able to specify them, that the design is administratively sound in terms of the techniques employed, that appropriate devices are chosen (manual or computerised), and that general sources of information are established. The systems are usually managed by the administration department. This feature is discussed in Chapter 4 on information technology and in Chapter 30, which includes terminology and the supervisor's role.

## COMPUTERISED FINANCIAL CONTROL

With a complete suite of programs it is possible to manage all financial accounting activities using computers. Reports may be printed, giving the financial position when required to control progress and profitability. Display terminals in appropriate locations provide immediate updates and online processing. Packages are available to:

- analyse current financial situations with previous periods and with budgets
- maintain accounting controls and satisfy auditing needs
- provide strict control over cash flow
- prepare the payroll, sales invoices and accounts payable

Appropriate control programs can provide valuable marketing statistics, market research data, performance of sales representatives, customers' buying trends, and many other sales reports in financial or quantitative terms.

## DYNAMIC EFFECTS

The dynamic nature of business imposes at least three requirements: continual updating and revision of financial plans; accurate forecasts and plans; flexible estimates with built-in controls to revise as circumstances change. This dynamic mechanism must contain arrangements for:

- continuous monitoring
- immediate action when deviations occur
- careful and precise allocation of responsibilities for each financial sector
- provision for major adjustments when daily monitoring fails due to unforeseen changes

# Financial transactions

Money is directly and indirectly paid and received in various business transactions. Among many, typical transactions are sales of products, payment by purchasers, buying materials, paying suppliers and paying employees. Settlements may be paid in cash or deferred as credits or debits to be paid later. Other transactions may not follow a set pattern, such as selling plant and machines no longer required, repaying loans, paying dividends and buying new machines.

## RECORDING FINANCIAL TRANSACTIONS

- *Cash book*: this contains all cash received which is debited (left-hand side) and cash paid which is credited (right-hand side); in large companies there may be a number of cash books to meet different requirements.

- *General or nominal ledger*: this is usually divided into capital and current accounts, loan accounts, investment accounts and other private and confidential accounts.
- *Sales ledger*: this contains all customers' accounts.
- *Bought ledger*: this contains all suppliers' accounts.

Entries in the books of account are made easier by using at least two subsidiary books. Daybooks record sales, purchases, sales returns and purchase returns; journals record miscellaneous transactions. The entries are *posted* to the accounts, but the daybooks do not form part of the double-entry system. To satisfy control and legislative requirements, other records include double entry, profit and loss, balance sheet, cash flow and various accounting ratios.

The totals of debit and credit entries should agree at the end of an accounting period. These totals are drawn up in a trial balance to check on their accuracy. Adjustments are made to rectify any inaccuracies. The final figures are then used to compile financial reports.

## DOUBLE-ENTRY BOOKKEEPING

Double-entry bookkeeping is used to simplify the recording of all transactions. The system is self-checking by recording each transaction twice: one entry on the credit side and one entry on the debit side. Thus the totals of each side should agree. Credit entries on the right-hand side represent all income and receipts; debit entries on the left-hand side show all expenditure on assets or expenses.

## PROFIT AND ACCOUNTS

Although the object of a business may be to provide goods or services for the community, the achievements of a company are based upon its ability to run at a profit.

Owing to sociological change, the amount of profit has become an important factor in managerial policy. The surplus must be sufficient to pay shareholders and to provide adequate sums for replacement of capital equipment and expansion programmes. Excessive profits, however, should be avoided because of the social obligations towards the community to provide quality products at a fair price. Management must also consider the question of high productivity and its part in the national economy, e.g. the need for competitive prices in the export market.

In general it may be said the consumer will only buy within a price range that is considered appropriate for the quality of the goods. This fixes the upper limit of the price range. The supplier will attempt to market a product of his or her choice which provides sufficient return to pay for all expenses and provides a suitable amount of profit.

### Accounting for profit

Three accounts are used to show how profit is determined and used; some examples are given in Figs 28.1 and 28.2. A full set of accounts should indicate two sorts of profit:

- *Trading profit* is calculated by deducting all the costs directly connected with production from the total sales.
- *Net profit* is arrived at by deducting all the indirect expenses from the trading profit; in other words, net profit is the amount remaining after all expenses for a period have been deducted.

### Manufacturing and trading account
The manufacturing and trading account lists all items directly connected with production and contrasts them with sales; this provides the trading profit.

### Profit and loss account
The profit and loss account lists all items not connected with production and contrasts them with the trading profit to provide the net profit. The profit and loss accounts produced for public companies may be a summary of the complete account. There is no need to disclose all the information so long as the provisions of the Companies Acts are met. Many companies, however, issue full accounts to satisfy their obligation to shareholders. A pro forma example is given in Fig. 28.2. To keep the main report concise, any notes are usually given at the end; these notes go into greater detail and provide appropriate explanations.

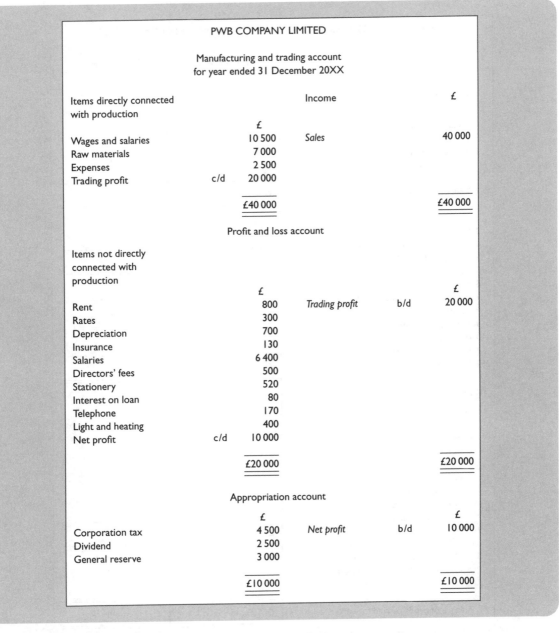

**PWB COMPANY LIMITED**

**Manufacturing and trading account for year ended 31 December 20XX**

| Items directly connected with production | | £ | Income | | £ |
|---|---|---|---|---|---|
| Wages and salaries | | 10 500 | Sales | | 40 000 |
| Raw materials | | 7 000 | | | |
| Expenses | | 2 500 | | | |
| Trading profit | c/d | 20 000 | | | |
| | | £40 000 | | | £40 000 |

**Profit and loss account**

| Items not directly connected with production | | £ | | | £ |
|---|---|---|---|---|---|
| Rent | | 800 | Trading profit | b/d | 20 000 |
| Rates | | 300 | | | |
| Depreciation | | 700 | | | |
| Insurance | | 130 | | | |
| Salaries | | 6 400 | | | |
| Directors' fees | | 500 | | | |
| Stationery | | 520 | | | |
| Interest on loan | | 80 | | | |
| Telephone | | 170 | | | |
| Light and heating | | 400 | | | |
| Net profit | c/d | 10 000 | | | |
| | | £20 000 | | | £20 000 |

**Appropriation account**

| | | £ | | | £ |
|---|---|---|---|---|---|
| Corporation tax | | 4 500 | Net profit | b/d | 10 000 |
| Dividend | | 2 500 | | | |
| General reserve | | 3 000 | | | |
| | | £10 000 | | | £10 000 |

**Figure 28.1** Layout of the annual costs

## Appropriation account

The appropriation account details how the net profit is used in the business. Usually there are three main groups: tax, dividend and general reserve. The general reserve or undistributed profit is retained for replacement of capital equipment or fixed assets and for expansion programmes. The appropriation of profit to reserves is known as ploughing back the profits. How the profit is divided depends upon such factors as the total amount of surplus, commitments towards shareholders and the prudence of the management in establishing adequate reserves for plans.

PROFIT AND LOSS ACCOUNT FOR THE YEAR ENDED 31 DECEMBER 20XX

| | Present year | Previous year |
|---|---|---|
| | £ | £ |
| 1 *Turnover*<br>Deduct:<br>trading and manufacturing<br>expenses<br>wages and salaries<br>materials consumed<br>overhead costs | | |
| 2 *Total expenditure* | £ | £ |
| 3 *Gross profit (1 – 2)*<br>4 Deduct: Depreciation on cost | | |
| 5 *Trading profit (3 – 4)* | £ | £ |
| 6 Income from investments<br>7 Profit before taxation (5 + 6)<br>8 Taxation<br>9 Profit after taxation (7 – 8)<br>10 Minority interests<br>11 Extraordinary items | | |
| 12 Net profit (9 – 10 – 11) | £ | £ |

**Appropriation account**

| | | |
|---|---|---|
| 1 *Net profit*<br>Deduct:<br>dividends<br>transfer to fixed assets<br>   replacements fund<br>transfer to debenture<br>   redemption reserve<br>transfer to preferred share<br>   redemption fund | | |
| 2 *Total appropriations* | £ | £ |
| 3 Profit and loss balance (1 – 2)<br>Add: profit and loss balance from<br>previous year | | |
| *Balance* of profit carried forward | £ | £ |

**Figure 28.2** Pro forma profit and loss account

## THE BALANCE SHEET

The balance sheet is a statement of all the assets and liabilities at a certain date, normally the last day of the financial year. Under the Companies Acts, two formats for a balance sheet may be used: horizontal and vertical. The horizontal format (Fig. 28.3) has been largely superseded by the vertical format (Fig. 28.4). In practice, various items may be shown

**PWB COMPANY LIMITED**

Balance sheet as at 31 December 20XX

| Fixed liabilities | £ | Fixed assets | £ |
|---|---|---|---|
| Capital | 45 000 | Land and buildings | 18 000 |
| General reserve | 5 000 | Plant and machinery | 12 000 |
| Loan | 5 000 | Vans | 4 000 |
| | | Furniture and fittings | 3 000 |
| Current liabilities | | Current assets | |
| Creditors | 4 700 | Stock | 11 500 |
| Bank overdraft | 5 000 | Debtors | 14 500 |
| Tax outstanding | 2 000 | Cash in hand | 3 700 |
| | 66 700 | | 66 700 |

**Figure 28.3** Horizontal format: liabilities on the left, assets on the right

in alternative places. The Companies Acts establish accounting principles or valuation rules to be used when preparing balance sheets, but they may be set aside if they cause any distortion which does not present a true and fair statement. For detailed information and to comply with the strict legal requirements, it is essential to study the complex acts and their examples of various formats.

## THE CASH FLOW STATEMENT

The cash flow statement is a primary report within other financial statements such as the profit and loss account and the balance sheet. All input and output of cash is identified and a report is drawn up to show the effect of the transactions on the company's cash balances. This information is a vital part of assessing the true state of a business since profit is an assessment or an opinion based upon all accounting procedures, whereas the cash balances are facts.

The report is classified between the operating, investing, financing and economic activities. Collectively, it shows the net movement of cash in a particular period. The source and amount of cash flowing in, and its disbursement show the consequent change in the final cash situation, and how

the cash has been used to finance the activities of the business. Thus, the true measure of any increase in shareholder wealth is clearly illustrated. Furthermore, it shows how any borrowings or increases in equity capital are being used for future investment.

Preparation of the report has to take into account the definition of cash flow: an increase or decrease in an amount of cash or cash equivalent resulting from a transaction. Therefore any item which is outside this definition is not a cash flow and should not be included. Cash means cash in hand and deposits repayable on demand from any bank or other financial institution. Cash equivalents mean short-term highly liquid investments which are readily convertible into cash without notice. The headings in the statement are operating activities, returns on investment and servicing of finance, taxation, investing activities, and financing.

# Financial accounting: six problems

## DEBTS

The launching of a product from idea to sale is usually a slow process. This time lag often causes

## BALANCE SHEET AS AT 31 DECEMBER 20XX

| | Present year | Previous year |
|---|---|---|
| **Employment of capital (employment of funds)** | £ | £ |
| 1 Tangible assets<br>    Freehold property<br>    Leasehold propery<br>    Plant, machinery and furniture | | |
| 2 Intangible assets<br>    Research and development<br>    Goodwill | | |
| 3 Investments<br>    Loans to trade<br>    Loans to associated companies | | |
| Total fixed assets (1 + 2 + 3) | | |
| 4 Current assets<br>    Stock<br>    Debtors<br>    Investments<br>    Cash in hand<br>    Cash at bank | | |
| 5 Creditors (due within one year)<br>    Trade creditors<br>    Bank overdraft | | |
| Net current assets – *liabilities* (4 + 5) | | |
| Total assets less current liabilities (1 + 2 + 3) – (4 + 5) | | |
| 6 Creditors (due after one year)<br>    Trade creditors<br>    Bank loans | | |
| 7 Provision for liabilities and charges | | |
| Net assets (6 + 7) | | |
| **Capital employed (sources of funds)**<br>8 Capital and reserves<br>    Called-up share capital<br>    Reserves<br>    Profit and loss account | | |

*Figure 28.4* Pro forma vertical balance sheet

expenditure problems; expenditure may commence with the purchase of various assets, such as buildings, plant and materials, and continue with pay and a variety of other expenses as plans are developed.

## Degree of indebtedness

A considerable period of time may elapse before any income is received, but during this time funds must be found to pay all the debts arising. This degree of indebtedness must be known to maintain financial stability. The accountant's responsibility is to provide accurate evidence to management on this risk. Furthermore, the banks and other financial institutions will require this evidence, together with other information to calculate the risk involved if a loan is needed. Creditworthiness may be established by considering the orders in hand, profits over the years, the value of fixed assets, and other liabilities outstanding.

## DEBTORS

Debtors are often an exasperating problem for small businesses who are having to wait for long periods before receiving payments from outstanding accounts. The problem has been partly resolved by the introduction of legislation. The Late Payment of Commercial Debts (Interest) Act 1998 is designed to protect small businesses from financial losses they suffer because of late payments. There is a statutory right for them to charge interest on overdue accounts.

However, the regulations are complex and advice is essential. The first stage of the act applies to small businesses claiming from large businesses. The second stage (in force by late 2000) applies to small businesses claiming from other small businesses. The final stage (in force by late 2002) applies to large businesses and public sector bodies claiming from each other and from small businesses.

## LEGAL REQUIREMENTS

The accounting requirements of the Companies Acts are intended to protect and safeguard the investor. Every company must keep proper books of account, as laid down in a comprehensive schedule of detailed requirements covering all the important items in the balance sheet, profit and loss account, and cash flow statement. A copy of these statements is sent annually to the Registrar of Companies. They may be seen by any individual on payment of a small fee.

## Auditing

The Companies Acts also state the rights and duties of auditors. A report must be completed which conforms to a stringent list of requirements in the schedule. Auditing must cover all the accounts, including any group accounts. The auditors must possess appropriate qualifications stated in the acts. The accounts must give a true and fair view of the company's activities and state of affairs. They must also be acceptable to the Commissioners of Inland Revenue, who require a copy for taxation calculations.

## MANAGERIAL REQUIREMENTS

Unfortunately, conventional accounting procedures for the preparation of final accounts and records do not provide information in its most suitable form for managers to become more effective. The exercising of managerial skills demands the analysis of complex external economic affairs and internal business activities. The use of cost accountancy, budgetary control and other forms of management accountancy is essential for this purpose. The management accountant needs considerable expertise to provide all relevant information to managers, who may then use their skills with a thorough knowledge of the possible consequences.

## SOCIAL OBLIGATIONS

The modern approach is for a company to recognise there are social obligations to its employees, shareholders, the community and trade unions. Today these obligations tend to be based on the concept of adequate reward for all social groups, rather than the maximisation of profits alone. Probably this change was caused by the reduced influence of shareholders; the increased power of trade unions; and the strengthening of the bond between the company, its employees and consumers.

Another trend is the increased emphasis on long-term stability and growth, in view of the risk undertaken by the shareholder and the overall effect on the community. A person who invests in a company expects an adequate return on the capital invested; how much dividend should be expected is another question. Certainly the investor does not expect management to take extreme risks, unless that person is a gambler who chooses to invest in a company where the dangers of collapse are recognised.

To satisfy these obligations, companies usually produce interim and final accounts which give considerable detail. The annual report is particularly informative as explanations on financial matters are included together with photographs of the products and factories. Many companies allow visitors to tour the premises, and talks are often arranged on specific financial topics.

# Sources of capital

The ways of raising capital depend on the type of business and its reputation. However, there is always the element of risk. This determines whether there will be sufficient profit to repay those who provided the capital and whether a surplus will be available to expand the business.

The sole proprietor business is very restricted because, when the person wishes to start the business, no reputation exists in most cases. Therefore, the sole proprietor must depend upon personal resources and loans from friends and relatives. Sometimes a bank may loan funds if it is convinced the enterprise will be successful.

A similar situation exists with partnerships. As the business develops and appears to be stable and thriving, the opportunity to increase its credit will be established. If creditworthiness is acceptable, suppliers will deliver more goods at longer credit terms. Banks will also allow overdrafts and loans on this basis. Other ways of raising money are to sell property already owned. Indirect methods are to buy assets on hire purchase or hire on a rental scheme.

Continued expansion of the concern often demands large sums of cash, more easily raised by forming a private limited company. Further expansion may mean inviting the public to invest, which involves the issue of shares through conversion to a public limited company. This is conducted by an issuing house or, if the company is very secure and of high reputation, it may make a direct issue to the public. The issuing house will handle all the requirements, including capital gearing (proportion of ordinary and preference shares, and loans), advertising and legal aspects.

## THE STOCK EXCHANGE

The raising of capital through the issue of shares is safeguarded by the Council of the Stock Exchange. This gives the investor the right to sell and buy shares, but the cash is not withdrawn from a company. Only the shares change hands and often they are bought and sold several times over a short period before the share certificate is issued by the company to the eventual holder. The council applies stringent requirements on a company before agreeing to a quotation or giving permission to deal in the particular shares. The Stock Exchange provides a market for stocks and shares which can be bought and sold in a fair and straightforward manner. The prices are determined by supply and demand, not by the Stock Exchange.

## SHARES AND DEBENTURES

The two main types of share are ordinary and preference; debentures are loans not shares. All three form the permanent capital of a company. The ordinary share carries more risk, normally has voting rights, and a dividend is payable but the amount depends upon the prosperity of the business. Before any dividend is payable, both preference shareholders and debenture holders must receive their fixed rate of dividend or interest respectively. Debenture holders are creditors, therefore the fixed interest rate is payable regardless of profit or loss. Further security is possible by issuing a mortgage debenture; this means the loan is secured by a fixed charge on a company's assets.

# Employment of capital

Usually a company is either expanding or contracting. Healthy expansion demands adequate supplies of cash. Careful planning of expenditure is difficult to assess. The requirements are divided into fixed or permanent capital – essentially long-term assets – and circulating or working capital involving short-term activities.

## FIXED CAPITAL

Fixed capital covers land, factory and office buildings, plant and machinery, furniture and fittings, vans and cars. It obviously contributes to profit, so a charge for depreciation is included as an expense in the annual accounts. A prudent requirement is to keep reserves for unexpected occurrences such as legal costs, accidents and damage. Land may appreciate, but most fixed assets need replacing through obsolescence and short-term life.

## CIRCULATING CAPITAL

Current assets continually change their form and are retained for only a short period. Items such as raw materials are bought, pay and expenses are paid, and finished goods are sold. Cash changes its form into goods through various processes and returns to its original form when products are sold, hence the name 'circulating capital'.

## BALANCE OF CAPITAL

It is important to maintain a correct balance between fixed and working capital. Too much cash spent on fixed capital may mean insufficient working capital to make full use of the plant and machines. However, insufficient cash spent on fixed assets may mean surplus cash lying idle or perhaps ineffective use of working capital.

# Forecasting and budgeting

Forecasting financial activities is based upon previous financial records of income and expenditure, and on predictions of the trends in sales, production costs and general expenses. The difficulties of forecasting are aggravated when markets are unstable or when there are no previous records to indicate trends, as with a new business. Forecasting is naturally guesswork, so be prepared for the unexpected. Take precautions and be flexible.

## CASH FORECASTING

Cash forecasting (or budgeting) is critical since many companies fail through cash shortages, not through profitability problems. Furthermore, there is always the danger of being taken over at less than the market value when there are liquidity problems. The purpose of cash flow is to assess the planned output levels and the relevant cost, and to estimate the effects on cash resources. The difficulty is that planning to make a profit does not imply there will be a cash surplus. Therefore sources of short-term finance should be investigated in preparation for emergencies. Typical facilities are bank loans and overdrafts, factoring (institutions offer cash against debtors), hire purchase agreements, and delaying payments to creditors.

## THE FINANCIAL BUDGET

The forecast or estimate is used to plan the financial budget, which is adjusted to make the best use of available cash. These adjustments include decisions on cash requirements or cash investments if there is a surplus, and consideration of the choices of expenditure. Budgeting for cash flow in the form of income and expenditure is essential as an indication of events. However, financial controls must check continually and promptly on the *actual* cash flow to make corrections and revisions as the situation changes.

# Interpretation of accounts and statements

The capability to interpret accounts and statements is essential to control, co-ordinate, and provide trends for planning and forecasting. Basically there is a heavy reliance on collecting and converting data into a more meaningful form for data processing. Information is derived from this processed data and it must be *useful* to the manager. The information should obviously be reliable not only for interpreting statements but also for calculating accounting ratios.

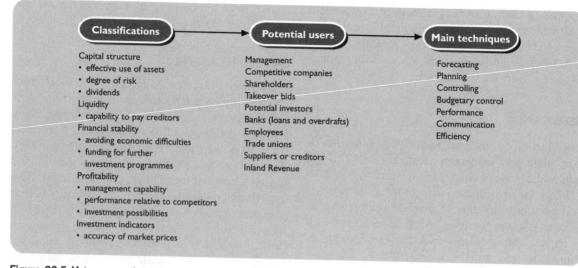

**Figure 28.5** Major accounting ratios: classifications and uses

Unfortunately, apart from the reliability factor, studying accounts may easily create incorrect impressions, but accounting ratios do provide a guide. Furthermore, the Centre for Inter-firm Comparison acts as a data collection point, compares the results of a number of companies that contribute, and indicates achievements and weaknesses.

### THE INVESTOR

Many supervisors and employees are now shareholders in their own companies and in others, consequently there is often a keen interest in control and performance. Also some companies provide profit-sharing schemes and offer favourable schemes to buy their shares. The true financial position of a company and its prospects are usually very difficult to assess. For example, the current value of fixed assets may not be indicated and the progress of research and development schemes is naturally not revealed. Predicting the future of any company is hazardous, but some indication is possible by studying the reputation of the managing director, market trends and the efficiency of the organisation. Hidden factors may still influence appearances. It is easy to be misled, even with inside knowledge.

### ACCOUNTING RATIOS

Accounting ratios are the relationships between various sections in a set of accounts. They should give a clearer analysis of financial information by comparing their variations from period to period, and analysing the significance of the changes. Standards are set from previous information in the company or from information provided by companies in a similar industry. They provide a yardstick against which to measure the changes, allowing people to make comparisons and look for trends.

### RATIO ANALYSIS

The financial position may be assessed by calculating and assessing various ratios but remember the warnings given earlier. Access to the actual accounts for accurate information is unlikely since many businesses operate various schemes. Different books may be kept for publication to shareholders, for the Inland Revenue, and for managing the business. Published accounts always provide the best impression of the financial situation. Figure 28.5 illustrates the analysis and uses of major accounting ratios. Here are some typical ratios.

## MANAGEMENT OF THE CAPITAL STRUCTURE

There are many reasons why capital structure ratios may appear favourable or adverse, so treat them with caution. They tend to show the return to shareholders and the degree of risk to lenders. Usually they need further investigation to determine validity. Some of the reasons are demand problems, shortage of skilled labour or materials, unreliable machines and equipment, and deliberate restrictions on sales.

### Net worth

Net worth represents the value of the assets which would theoretically exist if all were sold for their book values and all liabilities were paid. The aim of most businesses is to increase net worth, or value of the owner's interest, by increasing profit. Net worth is unlikely to represent the true value of the business because the book values of assets will not coincide with actual value if sold. Some assets may appreciate, e.g. land and buildings; other assets may depreciate, e.g. furniture, stock, plant and machinery. Furthermore, the items may not be revalued accurately in the balance sheet.

### Net worth/fixed assets ratio

The net worth/fixed assets ratio shows the owner's or shareholders' stake in the total assets compared with long-term liabilities. Excluding any bank loan, take the capital and general reserve (say £50 000) and divide it by the total assets (say £66 700) to obtain the ratio (here 0.75).

### Stock ratio

A simple calculation for the stock ratio takes the amount of stock that is held and relates it to the purchases needed to satisfy a certain sales level. Divide stock by purchases then multiply by 365 to obtain the number of days. Another common ratio relates sales to stock turnover. This measures the number of times stock is replaced in a period. Take care to use the same basis of comparison for the periods; the stock values may have been quoted in different ways and the sales figures may have been expressed using cost price or selling price. Also there may be seasonal difficulties which distort the ratio.

### Debtor days

Control of debtors' payments may be assessed by calculating the number of days that credit is allowed. But in practice there may be some distortion which can be taken into consideration. Comparing the days with other companies is a useful indication. Divide debtors (say £200 000) by sales (say £250 000) then multiply by 365 days to obtain an average credit period (here 29.2 days).

### Creditor days

Calculated like debtor days, creditor days gives, an indication of short-term financing to control operations. Divide creditors by purchases then multiply by 365 days. The figure provides a trend guide by relating it to previous periods.

## LIQUIDITY (OR SOLVENCY)

Liquidity is important, considering the risk of supplying goods on credit and not receiving payment. New customers are usually vetted before credit is allowed. Credit rating agencies provide this information for a small fee.

### Current ratio (working capital ratio)

The current ratio assesses a company's ability to cover current liabilities by current assets. Divide current assets (say £27 500) by current liabilities (say £11 000), to obtain the ratio (here 2.5). A ratio of between 3 and 2 is usually acceptable but it varies according to the particular industry and the general economic situation. Financial difficulties may cause ratio reduction below generally acceptable levels and increased liquidity problems when debtors (part of current assets) delay payment.

### Quick ratio (liquidity ratio)

Since current assets often include items not convertible into cash for many months (typically stocks) it is more prudent to use quick assets which convert into cash, say within five to six weeks, and compare them with liabilities due in the same period. Take debtors and cash (say £14 500 + £3700) then divide by creditors, bank overdraft, and tax outstanding. (say £4300 + £5000 + £2000) to obtain the ratio (here £18 200 ÷ £11 300 = 1.6).

## FINANCIAL STABILITY

### Gearing ratio

Gearing is the relationship between the value of the owner's or shareholder's investment (equity) and the company's long-term debts. The gearing ratio shows the company's long-term financial stability. If long-term debts are high compared with equity then gearing is high and often causes problems such as difficulty in obtaining short-term credit, paying interest on debts, and tying up assets as security. Low gearing is obviously favoured. Indeed when further capital expenditure is considered, it is important to achieve a balance between short- and long-term funding and availability. Unless long-term funds are sufficient, relying on short-term funds such as further bank overdrafts may cause cash flow problems through higher interest charges and delays in improving profit.

## PROFITABILITY

Profitability indicates managerial capability, allows comparisons with competitors, and shows whether there is an investment possibility. Many ratios are in current use; they are usually associated with net profit, gross profit, capital employed, and taxes. Here are some typical examples.

### Net profit/sales

Net profit/sales varies from industry to industry and from company to company. Divide net profit (say £10 000) by sales (say £40 000) to obtain the ratio (here 0.25).

### Gross profit/sales

Gross profit/sales varies like net profit/sales. Use a similar calculation.

## INVESTMENT INDICATORS

### Earnings per ordinary share

Take net profit after tax and subtract the gross preference dividend (say £50 000 − £5000); now divide this by the number of ordinary shares (say 225 000) to obtain the earnings per ordinary share (here £0.20).

### Price/earnings ratio

Divide the market price (say £2.50) by the earnings per share (£0.20 from the last calculation) to obtain the price/earnings ratio (here 12.5).

### Dividend yield

Dividend yield determines the rate of return on a share based upon its real value, not its nominal value. Take the nominal value of the ordinary share (say £1) and multiply by the actual yield (say 20 per cent); now divide this by the market price per share (say £8) to obtain the dividend yield (here 0.20/8.00 = 0.025 or 2.5 per cent).

### Dividend cover

Dividend cover relates the profit cover for an ordinary share dividend to the amount of profit retained in the company. Take the net profit for the year after tax and subtract the gross preference dividend (say £58 000 − £4000); now divide this by the gross dividend on ordinary shares (say £18 000) to obtain the dividend cover (here 3).

## INFORMATION REVEALED IN ACCOUNTS

Research conducted by the US-based Centre for International Financial Analysis shows wide variation in the *amount* of financial information revealed by different types of company and between different countries. According to the survey, large UK companies disclose more information when compared with equivalent concerns in the EU and the USA, but less than those in Sweden and Singapore. In the UK the Accounting Standards Board is the body responsible for formulating accounting rules. The aims are to avoid confusing financial analysts; to prevent abuse of existing practices where fraudsters have been able to overvalue a company to boost its share price; and to prevent the concealment of adverse currency movements.

## Accounting conventions

- Provide a true and fair view of the financial position at the date of the report.
- Record all transactions at their historic cost – the value at the time of the transaction.
- The business is assumed to continue to an indefinite date, so it is alright to take a long view about ownership of assets.
- Take a prudent view of profit; anticipated profit is not given but an anticipated loss may have some provision in the accounts.
- Calculate profit based on matching sales with the costs of those sales.
- Income and expenditure which spreads over a longer period may 'accrue' by splitting the amounts on a day-to-day basis for calculating an appropriate amount for the set period.

## QUESTIONS

1 Discuss profit and loss and how they affect the business.

2 Outline some of the common risks that a company will have to face.

3 Give your opinion of what a sound financial policy is for a company.

4 What are the objectives of an accounting system?

5 Why is financial control so important?

6 How may capital be raised in a company?

7 What is the purpose of the balance sheet and the profit and loss account?

8 State how you would explain to an employee the problems involved in dividing up profit among shareholders and for other purposes.

9 How would you explain to an employee the need to make a profit?

10 What forms of protection are afforded to shareholders in a public limited company and what facilities are available if an investor wishes to sell shares?

11 What is fixed capital and what is circulating capital?

12 Give a brief account of forecasting and budgeting.

13 Explain net worth.

14 Discuss ratio analysis, outlining the possible problems.

15 What are the main financial accounting topics likely to interest employees?

16 Explain the system of double-entry bookkeeping.

17 Why is cash flow a vital financial activity?

18 What is the purpose of cash forecasting?

19 The supervisor should appreciate that information must be reliable when preparing statements for interpretation of accounts. Explain why this is so important.

20 Many employees are now investors in their own companies. Consider the information a supervisor should possess in discussions on financial matters with employees in these circumstances.

21 Explain the uses of the major accounting ratios.

Poolside Electronics has undergone a difficult period of financial control since the chief accountant suddenly decided to leave. Eventually a replacement arrived but the managing director was alarmed by his initial report. Apparently, many essential controls were missing and procedures needed immediate and drastic revision to avoid possible chaos. The main problem areas were planning, controlling and performance evaluation.

*Suggest the accounting ratios that could be established to overcome these difficulties.*

'The trouble with these budgets is that the finance department sees us as just a mass of figures and nobody up there seems to appreciate the problems *we* have to face. They think that all they've got to do is pull the budget strings and we'll dance the tune!', Ted Noake says harshly, and means every word.

The works manager agrees, 'I know what you mean, Ted. Your section is a difficult one to handle with so many different runs every week. But you know they have to get the figures right otherwise we would have cash flow problems'.

'They'll have bigger cash flow problems if they don't put a little common sense into their planning. All they think about is the past and the future. It's about time we had some plain talking about the *present* between finance and production!'

*Consider how this barrier between the two departments could be overcome.*

# 29

# Cost control

## Introduction

Although financial control (Chapter 28) provides control statements on the general financial position, these statements do not give detailed information on processes and operations. Control at these activity levels relies on cost accounting.

The costing function provides a means of scientific control over *all* expenditure in the company, which is vital for directing its activities, for estimating accurately, and for assisting in establishing the selling price. Neglect of costing and its use places a company in a vulnerable position. Although a company may escape repercussions for a number of years, eventually keener competition from home or abroad will force the issue.

Costing may be regarded as a service or maintenance programme of expenditure. For example, it is wiser with machine maintenance to plan a programme of careful assessment and preventive maintenance than to wait until machines break down, which causes upheavals, delays and heavy losses. The same applies with control of expenditure.

### ADVANTAGES OF COSTING

The expense of effectively running a costing system that checks and provides information for control purposes is negligible compared with the savings and lessened risks that otherwise remain hidden and are difficult to assess. There is a strong need for costing: many companies fail to estimate accurately the cost of a job and therefore may suffer a considerable loss.

The clerical aspect of costing can be time-consuming for supervisors and they may feel the burden is not worthwhile. Clerical assistance is necessary to relieve them of this problem, thus allowing more time for controlling the variances (see below). Although supervisors are mainly concerned with the control aspects of costing, they should understand the *costing environment* within which they operate. Unless they appreciate the type of system or techniques in operation, they may fail to grasp the significance of procedures and activities which seem totally unnecessary.

### DEFINITION OF COSTING

Costing may be defined as collecting, recording, classifying and allocating expenditure to ascertain the cost of products or services for planning and control purposes by indicating points where corrective action is required. These costs may be categorised for control purposes:

- *By type*: Direct costs are identified with a unit of output, whereas indirect costs (or overheads) are associated with administration, marketing activities and production costs which are not directly related to a unit of output.
- *By behaviour*: Fixed costs tend to remain constant but over long periods they vary as extra capital expenditure affects them. These extra costs are known as semi-variable or semi-fixed variable costs and vary in relation to output.

Other categorisations are by function (selling, administration, distribution), by a job or a contract, and by resource such as labour, materials and other expenses.

## MAIN OBJECTIVES

- To provide promptly the cost of each item of expense.
- To summarise and apportion costs, thus giving the total cost of each product or service.
- To provide budgets and standards for control.
- To advise management on costing aspects that affect the selling price and economic production.
- To calculate the profitability of each product or service.
- To provide data for setting prices.
- To provide data for decision making on alternative courses of action.
- To provide data for stock evaluation.

## CURRENT TRENDS

Trends in cost management are concentrating more on identifying and tracing causes of excessive costs; and analysing data for strategic decisions such as product research and design, degree of product variety, investment in technology, and plant layout and location. These trends demand new costing techniques and systems which are being installed in some progressive companies.

## MAIN ASPECTS

The supervisor needs to be familiar with the following aspects to identify the costing systems and procedures, and to understand their importance in controlling processes and operations:

- costing techniques
- cost–profit–volume analysis
- costing methods
- budgetary control
- elements of cost
- allocation and apportionment
- estimating

# Costing techniques

The main techniques for recording and dealing with costing problems are:

- historical costing
- total absorption costing
- standard costing
- marginal costing and integrated techniques

All four techniques are now described, followed by a survey of costing methods – how to find actual costs based upon the type of production – which may be grafted onto any one of them.

# Historical costing

Historical costing records actual costs when or after the expense occurs. The basic costing methods associated with historical costing are *job costing* and *process costing*. Both methods provide essential information but fail to give economic indications of the *expected* performance level of each cost. In other words, a yardstick is not provided against which efficiency can be measured.

# Total absorption costing

Total absorption costing attempts to identify all costs associated with a particular activity or unit of production. Direct labour and material costs are straightforward, but the indirect or overhead costs are difficult. The technique is to treat these indirect costs (or fixed costs) as though they are variable and then attach (or absorb) them to units of production as they are manufactured. Theoretically, by the end of a period, the total fixed costs absorbed should equal the actual total fixed costs.

On the basis of previous experience and provided production remains unchanged, it is obviously possible to relate fixed costs to labour costs or to materials costs, and arrive at a rough formula. This simple approach will not necessarily be a fair apportionment. The personnel department's cost will vary with the number of employees engaged in an activity; insurance will vary in proportion to the capital value; and rent and rates vary with the size of the area. Total absorption costing is arbitrary and it is difficult to apply fairly without applying bias to some activities.

# Standard costing

Standard costing estimates or predetermines the costs of each element, compares them with the actual costs, calculates the variances, and presents management with reports on those items requiring some action to stop any trend away from the standard.

## THE SPHERE OF STANDARD COSTING

Standard costing can be used in most companies regardless of size or type, although it is easier to apply in some industries where the product is standardised and there are long production runs. Standards are based upon prevailing conditions and a particular output level. If these factors change then the standard costs are distorted and must be revised.

## ESTABLISHING STANDARD COSTS

### Direct labour

Setting reasonable standards for labour costs demands the services of work study engineers who can assess the work content and establish suitable times for each operation. Wage rates can then be applied and standard costs calculated. These costs should remain stable until there are alterations in the operational content or changes in pay rates.

### Direct materials

The quantity of material required for an operation is found by compiling a standard material specification. This is based upon drawings, on experience of the particular operation, and allowing for average scrap and waste through cutting. The standard quantity can then be priced by referring to the purchasing officer or a price manual. An allowance should be made for forecasted price changes in the proposed period.

### Overheads

Usually the overhead expenses for each department are found by referring to a budget, which is calculated on such factors as machine hours, direct labour hours or prime cost. These factors are based upon the capacity of the particular department – the costs are divided into fixed and variable.

The capacity of a department is open to a number of interpretations. A choice must be made to ensure standard treatment of all overheads allocated to departments. Supervisors should understand clearly which definition of capacity is being used, otherwise they will not be able to assess the variance accurately and take appropriate action. Here are some interpretations:

- *Maximum theoretical capacity*: if an assumption is made that the department runs without any loss of time.
- *Normal capacity to manufacture*: when normal time losses such as setting up times, idle time and breakdowns are deducted from the maximum theoretical capacity.
- *Normal capacity to manufacture and sell*: a further reduction is made for trade recessions, especially seasonal sales.
- *Short period capacity to sell*: when each year's sales capacity is used as a guide.

## EIGHT ASPECTS OF STANDARD COSTING

### Information on time

The essence of standard costing is to provide management with vital information for effective control. Whether effective control is achieved depends upon two main factors:

- the ability of management to take correct actions
- the ability of the cost accountant to provide the information on time

Time is most important. Delays are expensive when costs are moving sharply away from standards. The supervisor must appreciate the importance of time and ensure cost returns are made promptly.

### Measurement standards

The use of standards is superior to any other form of comparison with actual costs. For instance, comparing the actual costs of one period with those of another period can be misleading. This is because there is no positive indication as to which is the more efficient cost; or if the costs are similar, no indication is given that they are at an effective level.

## Exceptions

Variances from the standard are easily seen by using the *principle of exceptions*. This means presenting management with those costs that are deviating from the standard and omitting or excepting those that are conforming to the plan. Much time is saved since this avoids the need to sort through pages of costs, and so more time can be spent on considering what action should be taken.

## Relevant information

Clerical operation of standard costing is more economic because only information actually used is recorded, otherwise masses of data are produced with no specific purpose in mind.

## Before and after

Standard costing makes it easy to do before and after comparisons on the effects of changes. It is easy to see the consequences of altering types of material, pay rates, bonus schemes, output, and tools or machines.

## Cost consciousness

The inherent process of maintaining a constant watch on standards and revising where necessary encourages management and supervision to become cost conscious and aware of those costs that tend to deviate continually.

## Pinpoint weaknesses

Standard costing provides top management with a reliable indication of the effectiveness of managers and supervisors. Reports on variances, the action taken, and the results in the next period clearly show the weak spots in the organisation. These in turn demand action from top management and the results of this provide a guide to the effectiveness of this level.

## Sound system

The system should not always be condemned if it does not work properly. The supervisor must appreciate that standard costing is sound. But its effectiveness depends upon the individuals running the system. Operators must record details accurately and appropriate decisions need to be taken at each level, up to the board of directors.

# Marginal costing

Marginal cost is the direct costs of labour and materials plus variable overhead expenses, or is the additional cost of producing one more unit or product. The procedure of marginal costing may be shown in tabular form (Fig. 29.1). The relevant terms are:

- *Variable costs*: those costs that tend to vary in relation to output; they include direct labour, material and expenses (i.e. prime cost), variable overheads for the factory, and under some systems the variable element of selling, distribution and administration costs
- *Fixed costs*: all costs that tend to remain constant for a period of time, and within a specified range of output, such as management and supervision costs, depreciation of fixed assets, rent, heating, lighting, power, insurance and subscriptions
- *Sales revenue*: the actual amounts received from selling the products
- *Contribution*: the sales revenue less the total variable costs (the marginal costs) for a product
- *Fund*: the total sum of the contributions

The total fixed costs are finally deducted from the fund to give the net profit. Conventional costing and marginal costing are compared in Fig. 29.1.

## THE THEORY OF MARGINAL COSTING

Provided fixed costs tend to remain static, an increase in production should normally mean a reduced cost per unit. If production is decreased, an increase in cost per unit should be expected. This theory is based on the assumption that all fixed costs are segregated and not affected by fluctuations in output. Therefore, as output rises, the spread of fixed costs is greater and a smaller amount will

Sales revenue − Prime cost and factory overheads = Gross profit − Administration overheads = Net profit

CONVENTIONAL

| Products | £000s | | | | |
|---|---|---|---|---|---|
| | Sales | Prime cost and factory overheads | Gross profit | Administration overheads | Net profit |
| W | 10 | −4 | 6 | −6 | 0 |
| X | 14 | −5 | 9 | −8 | 1 |
| Y | 12 | −4 | 8 | −7 | 1 |
| Z | 8 | −2 | 6 | −5 | 1 |
| Totals | 44 | −15 | 29 | −26 | 3 |

Sales revenue − Marginal costs = Contribution (fund) − Fixed costs = Net profit

MARGINAL

| Products | Sales | Marginal costs | Contribution fund | | Fixed costs | Net profit |
|---|---|---|---|---|---|---|
| W | 10 | −7 | 3 | 10 | −7 | 3 |
| X | 14 | −10 | 4 | | | |
| Y | 12 | −10 | 2 | | | |
| Z | 8 | −7 | 1 | | | |
| Totals | 44 | −34 | 10 | | −7 | 3 |

***Figure 29.1*** Conventional costing versus marginal costing
This illustrates the distortion factor met in conventional costing when attempting a fair apportionment of fixed overheads to cost centres. The marginal costing technique eliminates this factor.

be attached to each unit. As output falls, the load attached to each will be larger.

The term 'attached' does not mean apportioned, but is used here to indicate the portion of fixed costs which will appear when calculating the average cost per unit. In accordance with this theory, the term 'marginal cost' will represent the change in variable costs when producing one unit more or one unit less. This amount of change will be the difference between the two total costs when output changes by one unit.

## MAIN ASPECTS

### *Variable and fixed costs*

Supervisors may assume that variable costs will be constant per unit regardless of fluctuations in output. But they should remember that possible changes may occur because of price alterations for raw materials and components and, if production is increased to a point where overtime is incurred, the rates of pay will be affected and variable costs will rise. In practice, fixed costs also tend to vary over long periods of time as policy decisions involve additional capital expenditure on new factories or extensions of existing premises. Such costs are known as semi-fixed or semi-variable. This aspect does not nullify marginal costing, as many decisions are based upon short-term runs of periods up to a year.

The important aspect is that fixed costs remain the same, irrespective of production level. Even when production stops completely, fixed costs continue. This indicates the critical role played by those who control variable costs. The effectiveness of controlling these variable or marginal costs decides the amount of contribution, which governs the profit margin.

## Contribution and new products

### A proposed new line
The following calculations for proposed new product B are based on apportioning the load of fixed costs according to the sales value of each product. This calculation is misleading because it attempts to split fixed costs among the products, which distorts the situation. In reality the new product will contribute another £500 towards fixed costs and profit. In this case, as the contribution from existing product A already covers fixed costs, the contribution from the new product B directly increases the profit by £500, i.e. by 50 per cent. Here is the misleading approach:

### Product A

| | £ |
|---|---|
| Sales | = 27 000 |
| *Less* Marginal cost | = 20 000 |
| Contribution | = 7 000 |
| *Less* Fixed costs | = 6 000 |
| Profit | = 1000 |

### Proposed product B

| | |
|---|---|
| Sales | = 3 000 |
| *Less* Marginal cost | = 2 500 |
| Contribution | = 500 |
| *Less* Fixed costs | = 600 |
| (apportioned on total sales) | |
| Loss | = 100 |

Here is the marginal costing approach:

| Product | Contribution | Fund | Fixed costs | Profit |
|---|---|---|---|---|
| A | = £7000 | | | |
| B | = £ 500 | £7500 | –£6000 | £1500 |

### Existing lines and proposed change
This example involves a company that manufactures three products. Under certain marketing conditions the company may need to investigate the effect on profitability of reducing its range of products. The current situation is given first, followed by the effect of the proposal to abandon product A and divide the surplus capacity equally among the remaining products, B and C.

*Existing lines*

| | A | B | C | (£000s) |
|---|---|---|---|---|
| Sales | 10 | 10 | 10 | |
| *Less* Marginal costs | 7 | 6 | 5 | |
| Contribution | 3 | 4 | 5 | |
| Fund | | | | = 12 |
| *Less* Fixed costs | | | | = 11 |
| Profit | | | | = 1 |

*Proposed change*

| | A | B | C | |
|---|---|---|---|---|
| Sales | Abandoned | 15 | 15 | (increased proportionately) |
| *Less* Marginal cost | | 9 | 7½ | |
| Contribution | | 6 | 7½ | |
| Fund | | | | = 13½ |
| *Less* Fixed costs | | | | = 11 |
| Profit | | | | = 2½ |

Provided market decisions prompted such a change, the proposal would lead to a substantial increase in profitability. Unfortunately, certain limiting factors mean that a change of product range is seldom straightforward. Typical examples are availability of trained labour, shortage of raw materials, production capacity available, limited cash resources, and the state of the market. These factors must be considered in identifying those products that will make the best use of available resources.

# Cost–profit–volume analysis

The supervisor should be able to understand the further use of the contribution concept in marginal costing through its relationship with cost–profit–volume analysis. The relevant technique is called break-even analysis and it includes calculations to show the change in profitability when output is altered or when the product range is revised, along with the profit/volume ratio.

## THE BREAK-EVEN TECHNIQUE

The break-even technique locates the level of production where sales revenue equals all the costs. Also indicated are the relationships between sales revenue, variable costs, fixed costs, and profit or loss at various levels of output.

## THE BREAK-EVEN POINT

The break-even point is the level of output where neither a profit nor a loss is incurred. Its importance usually lies in its ability to indicate the volume of sales needed to cover the degree of profit required for various purposes, the revision of selling prices to provide sufficient sales revenue to cover estimated profit and establish a particular break-even point, and the variable cost per unit.

## CALCULATION OF THE BREAK-EVEN POINT

*Example 1*

$$\text{Break-even point} = \frac{\text{Fixed costs}}{1 - \dfrac{\text{Variable costs}}{\text{Sales revenue}}}$$

Sales revenue = £10 000
Variable costs = £6 000
Fixed costs = £2 000

$$\text{Break-even point} = \frac{£2000}{1 - \dfrac{6000}{10\,000}}$$

$$= \frac{2000}{2/5}$$

$$= £5000$$

*Example 2*

$$\text{Break-even point} = \frac{\text{Fixed costs}}{\text{Selling price per unit} - \text{Variable cost per unit}}$$

Use the figures from Example 1 and assume a selling price per unit of £1.

Selling price per unit = £1

$$\text{Variable cost per unit} = £1 \times \frac{6000}{10\,000} = £0.60$$

Fixed costs = £2000

$$\text{Break-even point} = \frac{£2000}{1 - 0.60} = £5000$$

## THE BREAK-EVEN CHART

Construction of the break-even chart depends on what information is required. An example is shown in Fig. 29.2. The $x$-axis is used to show output or sales; the $y$-axis indicates the cost. Here are the main features:

- The fixed costs line remains static at £30 000.
- The variable costs line is the total costs less the fixed costs, amounting to £20 000.
- The break-even point is where the variable costs line intersects the sales line.
- The vertical dotted line intersects at the point where output will provide sufficient funds to break even at 50 000 units.

Profit or loss is indicated at any rate of activity. If the output is plotted, the vertical distance between the sales line nd the total costs indicates the profit or loss. Consequently, potential profits or losses are easily seen over a range of volume.

### Limitations

Costs do not behave in such a simple manner. They do not always fit conveniently into fixed and variable groups because they vary for other reasons besides fluctuations in output. The supervisor will know from experience that when attempts are made to increase production, invariably *extra* costs appear, such as overtime and bonuses. This explains why maximum production does not necessarily

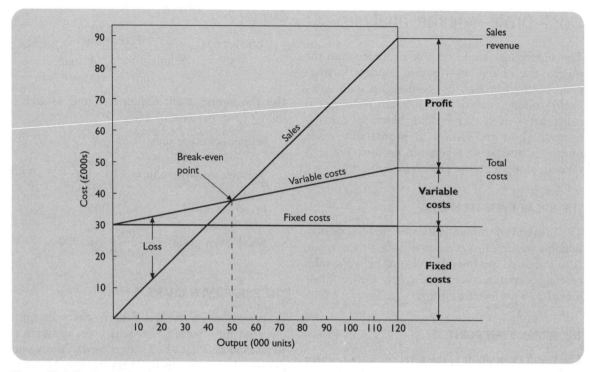

**Figure 29.2** Break-even chart
Here the x-axis shows output and the y-axis shows cost. The x-axis may be required to show output in monetary value, sales in units or as a percentage, or the plant capacity. The dotted line indicates the point in output where sales exactly cover the costs; there is neither profit nor loss.

match with maximum profit. On the marketing side, it is quite common to make price reductions when the company decides to increase sales.

Whatever its disadvantages, the break-even chart clearly shows the relationships between fixed costs, variable costs and sales revenue. Within the relatively narrow limits of production fluctuations, the errors inherent in straight-line graphs are practically eliminated. Thus marginal costing and its techniques can help in solving problems related to levels of production, range of products, pricing of products, and sub-contracting.

### The safety margin

The difference between sales revenue (or budgeted income) and the break-even point (or break-even income) should be as large as possible since changes in sales near the break-even points are difficult to control. A suitable measurement for assessing safety is to calculate the margin as a percentage:

$$\text{Safety margin} = \frac{\text{Budgeted sales} - \text{Break-even sales}}{\text{Budgeted sales}} \times 100$$

Budgeted sales = £500 000

Break-even sales = £410 000

$$\text{Safety margin} = \frac{500\ 000 - 410\ 000}{500\ 000} \times 100$$

$$= 18 \text{ per cent}$$

Keeping a careful check on this margin is essential. The smaller the percentage, the greater the risk.

### Contribution and value added

As illustrated in Fig. 29.2, contribution represents the difference between sales (or income) and variable costs. This portion of sales or income contributes to non-variable or non-assignable costs and it is useful for determining the viability of proposed new products.

Value added is another useful calculation which explains the relationship between income and expenditure, and is suitable for establishing control ratios and some financial incentive schemes. The usual definition of value added is income minus materials and services expenditure. Consequently, it shows the amount of money available for internal costs, such as direct labour, design, disposable profits, rent and rates.

Various control ratios may be calculated, such as value added/staff salaries, value added/ workforce wages, and value added/all salaries and wages. The control features are:

- income that may be increased by selling prices
- costs that may be reduced by cuts in materials and services

## PROFIT/VOLUME RATIO

Profit/volume ratio is a guide to the profitability of the company, which is expressed as a percentage. The formula is:

$$\frac{\text{Sales volume} - \text{Total variable costs}}{\text{Sales value}} \times 100$$

Sales volume $= £10\ 000$

Sales value $= £10\ 000$

Total variable costs $= £6\ 000$

$$\frac{\text{Profit/volume}}{\text{ratio}} = \frac{10\ 000 - 6000}{10\ 000} \times 100$$

$$= 40 \text{ per cent}$$

Note that the formula uses the sales volume (in £) not the actual volume (in units). Also costs are assumed to be two definite groups: fixed costs and variable (marginal) costs; and a linear relationship is used for variable costs. Other relevant information should also be considered when using the profit/ volume ratio. The variable costs may be substituted by the variable cost per unit, and the sales volume may be substituted by the selling price per unit.

Clearly the aim is to increase the profit/volume ratio. This may be achieved by reducing variable costs or by raising the selling price. If various products are sold, the aim is to improve the sales mix by increasing the volume of the products with

a high profit/volume ratio and reducing the volume of those products with a low profit/volume ratio. But remember the safety margin.

## THE PROFIT/VOLUME CHART

The profit/volume chart may be preferred as it indicates more clearly how alterations to volume (or output) affect profit and it illustrates what happens with changes in selling price. An example is shown in Fig. 29.3. The profit/volume chart takes into account any changes in fixed costs and the effect of unit contribution. Here is how to construct it:

1　The horizontal axis indicates volume (or output).
2　The vertical axis indicates fixed costs which are below the zero point and variable costs above the zero point.
3　A selling price line may be drawn from the fixed cost point to the unit contribution point, noting the break-even point on the horizontal axis, and assuming a set selling price. This line will show the profit by multiplying the unit contribution by the difference between the break-even volume and the actual volume.

*Effect A*

| | | |
|---|---|---|
| Fixed costs | $= £20\ 000$ | |
| Variable costs | $= £20\ 000$ | (calculated as £2.00 per unit contribution on selling price $Y$) |
| Selling price | $= Y$ | |
| Profit per unit | $= £2$ | (added for each unit sold above 40 000, the break-even point) |

*Effect B*

| | | |
|---|---|---|
| Fixed costs | $= £25\ 000$ | (up £5000) |
| Variable costs | $= £25\ 000$ | (calculated as £2.25 per unit contribution on selling price $X$) |
| Selling price | $= X$ | |
| Profit per unit | $= £2.25$ | (added for each unit sold above 25 000, the break-even point) |

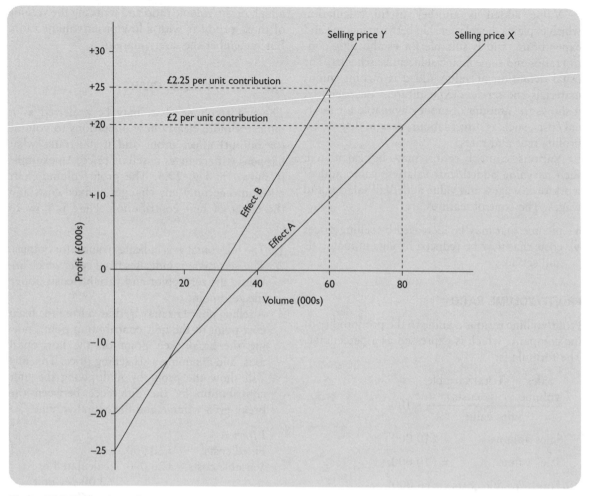

**Figure 29.3** Profit–volume chart
The break-even volume is reduced from 40 000 to 30 000 if the fixed costs rise to £25 000 and if the selling price is increased from X to Y. Note that under selling price Y, the profit will increase faster as output rises (effect B).

# Costing methods

## JOB COSTING

Job costing is the method of costing those jobs which have to be kept separate during production. These non-standard jobs include one-off products, such as a large transformer, a bridge, a ship or an office block. Each job is given a number and all costs connected with it are booked by allo-cating them to that number. All labour charges are allocated from job clock cards, materials from stores requisitions and an appropriate proportion of production overheads. A proportion of selling, distribution, administration and R&D expenses is allocated to give the total cost of the job *when* added to the production cost consisting of total labour, material and overhead costs. These details are shown in the job cost summary (Fig. 29.4).

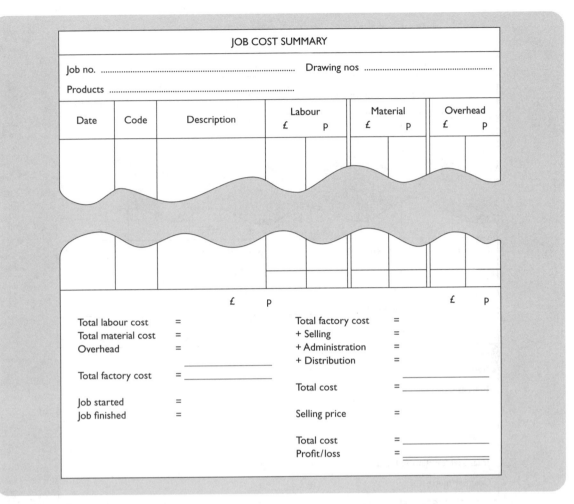

| Date | Code | Description | Labour £ | Labour p | Material £ | Material p | Overhead £ | Overhead p |
|------|------|-------------|----------|----------|------------|------------|------------|------------|

**JOB COST SUMMARY**

Job no. ................................................................ Drawing nos ........................................................

Products ..........................................................................

|  | £ | p |  |  | £ | p |
|--|---|---|--|--|---|---|
| Total labour cost | = | | Total factory cost | = | | |
| Total material cost | = | | + Selling | = | | |
| Overhead | = | | + Administration | = | | |
| | | | + Distribution | = | | |
| Total factory cost | = | | Total cost | = | | |
| Job started | = | | | | | |
| Job finished | = | | Selling price | = | | |
| | | | Total cost | = | | |
| | | | Profit/loss | = | | |

**Figure 29.4** Job cost summary
One-off products are costed separately. The card shows how the total job cost consists of the production cost (labour, materials and overhead) plus an allocated proportion of selling, distribution and administration expenses. R&D may be recorded separately or it may be covered by administration.

## PROCESS COSTING

Process costing is suitable where products are manufactured by set processes which are not isolated to individual jobs, as in job costing. A whole range of items may be produced from the same starting material, simply by changing the process. And the starting material itself may be produced in one or more steps using raw materials or other, more fundamental starting materials. Chemicals, foods, paints and textiles are ideal for process costing.

Control of costs is achieved by ensuring all charges associated with each process are allocated correctly. These charges include labour, materials and overheads, but the transfer cost (the cost from the previous process) is separated in the process cost sheet, thus giving a clear indication of the present process cost. Figure 29.5 shows a typical layout of a process cost sheet.

## OTHER METHODS

- *Terminal costing and contract costing*: these methods are a form of job costing used in the building and construction industries.

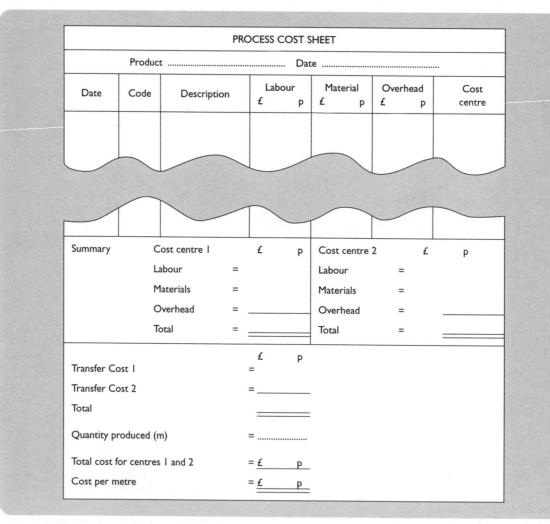

**Figure 29.5** Process cost sheet
Process costing is used when a product passes in sequence through several distinct processes. All charges associated with each process must be allocated correctly. Notice that the transfer cost (from the previous process) is separated, giving a clear indication of the present process cost. The cost per metre is the average cost per metre for the period covered.

- *Batch costing*: this method is used where a number of jobs can be processed together; each batch is costed and the total cost is divided by the number of units in the batch, thus providing an average cost per unit.
- *Unit costing*: this method is suitable if manufacturing is continuous and the units of output are the same, e.g. mining and brewing.
- *Multiple costing*: typically used in the car industry, it combines a number of methods to cost a range of manufactured products; the products are assembled from sub-contracted parts and components made in-house.
- *Operation costing*: large-scale production and repetitive work are suitable for operation costing; the method is based on locating a unit cost for each operation and assessing the effect of waste at each stage of production.
- *Operating costing*: a form of unit costing to locate the cost of a service, such as various types of transport, gas, electricity and water supplies.

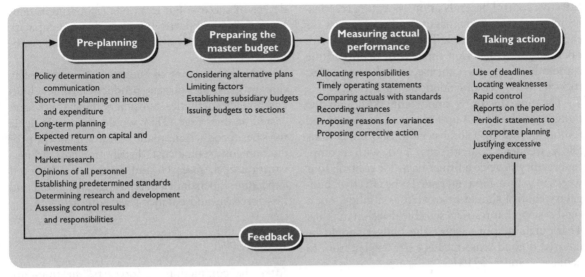

**Figure 29.6** Budgetary control: outline of a typical procedure

# Budgetary control

Budgetary control establishes departmental budgets by pre-planning all the activities within the company and their cost. These form an overall budget, through which co-ordination and control can be achieved. Each budget is determined by the policy planned for the forthcoming period and the expectations of expense based upon previous experience and estimated changes. Co-ordinating all the budgets to maximise profit and maintain a stable business is one of the main difficulties of budgetary control. But the system does have the advantage of setting clear targets for each department, all aligned in the same direction. An essential requirement is the participation of managers and supervisors.

## THE MASTER BUDGET

Pre-planning determines the master budget, which consists of many functional budgets co-ordinated into an action plan. Such pre-planning covers broad policy, daily planning of production, profit and return on investments. Scheduled daily activities are consolidated into weekly, quarterly and annual budgets. These form the process of budgeting and ensure co-ordination of all the functional budgets. Figure 29.6 illustrates a typical procedure for budgetary control.

## THE BUDGET

The budget is a plan with these characteristics:

- agreed by those responsible for the activity
- covers a set period
- expressed in financial or quantitative terms
- relates to the whole organisation (the master budget) or to a functional aspect (distribution, production or administration budget)

## THE CONTROL FEATURE

The system compares financial performance of an activity with its budgeted performance. If actual costs are lower then the *variance* is positive or favourable; if they are higher then the *variance* is negative or adverse. If the variance exceeds agreed limits, an investigation should reveal the reasons and the accountable department or individual. This form of responsibility usually involves a *responsibility centre* which may be:

- a cost centre – such as a maintenance department
- a revenue centre – such as a sales department
- a profit centre – such as a subsidiary company in a large organisation

Effective control depends upon allocating responsibility to competent managers and supervisors for each activity or function. They are provided with operating statements on time, with details of the standard, the actual expense and the variances, together with recommendations for action.

The time factor is important. Although the budget may be drawn up for a year, control is too remote over such a long period. Shorter periods allow frequent comparisons, and with prompt reports they provide a firmer basis for control; four weeks may be a good interval. To be effective, budgetary control should be treated as a guide, not a rigid system that restricts sensible decision making. There are situations where the budget should be ignored if good sense means extra expenditure to achieve a vital objective.

## The human factor

Although the budget may be useful as a statement or plan of the most likely outcome of events, the targets may not necessarily be most appropriate for control purposes. The motivational aspect may demand more than targets set for planning. Then control targets may need to be raised to satisfy people's desires to reach more difficult targets. A typical example is to set targets for salesmen that are above the planned volume of sales, but which offer various forms of reward as a reinforcement to motivation.

## THE PROCEDURE

Co-ordination and control of the budgets may be carried out by a budget controller or budget committee. When studying operating results, the controller would meet with the managing director and senior executives to discuss the circumstances, the current position, and possible courses of action. Changes in policy may then be decided upon.

## Forecasting

Considerable information on the limiting factors, such as the amount of cash available and the determination of sensible estimates, govern the degree of success. For example, estimating a sales budget depends partly upon production capacity and the cost of excessive production over the optimum level.

Actual forecasting of budgets follows the policy that governs sales targets, production of new lines and financial activities. Subsidiary budgets are forecasted at this stage. They would include budgets for sales, production, plant utilisation, stock, production cost, selling cost, distribution cost, administration cost, research and development, capital expenditure, personnel, purchasing, cash, profit and loss forecast, and balance sheet forecast.

## The final plan

After the completion of forecasts, meetings are held to complete the budgets by considering the various plans submitted. The master budget is then completed and issued. When period statements are circulated, the executives responsible for the budgets take appropriate action. The statements and reports from executives are fed back to the controller for discussion relating to the three aspects of policy making, forecasting and budget preparation, thus completing the control cycle.

## THE BUDGETARY PROCESS

The master budget and the budgetary process are equally important since the the budgetary process forces managers and supervisors to prepare for changes as they think ahead, interpret and anticipate. Co-ordination is possible as each department attempts to integrate operational plans with other departments. Thus supervisors visualise operating relationships with each other and aim to improve them.

A comprehensive understanding of the process is essential to avoid misconceptions. Managerial performance and supervisory performance are judged by capability to adhere to the budget and contingency arrangements. Supervisors should understand the process and its importance, and they should co-operate. Unfortunately, many view a budget as another administrative or bureaucratic hindrance.

## INTERRELATIONSHIPS WITH STANDARD COSTING

Certain fundamentals are common to budgetary control and standard costing:

- a pre-planned standard for each item of expense
- measurement of actual costs
- comparison of actual and standard costs
- discovery of reasons for the variances
- recommended courses of action to correct the variances

The practice had developed of relating standard costing to production activities alone, whereas budgetary control is a system applied to *all* activities, including sales, production, stock, plant and buildings, and finance. Although budgetary control and standard costing are interrelated, some industries might have difficulties in introducing standard costing but would be able to operate budgetary control effectively.

## ADVANTAGES OF BUDGETARY CONTROL

1 All the functions of the company are co-ordinated and controlled, indicating clearly to supervisors their responsibility for a particular section of the master budget and the importance of achieving the stated objective.
2 The continuing process of budgetary control gives more accurate indications of trends and eases the problems of forecasting. Signs of change become evident much earlier and management has the opportunity to take full advantage of the situation.
3 The risks of operating and financing the company are reduced. Close control of working capital, including cash in hand, is assured by means of the budget statements. Similarly, all income and expenditure is forecasted and checked as results become available. This enables any deviation to be brought quickly under control.
4 Effective budgetary control is a means of convincing prospective investors of the company's stability when more capital is required for expansion programmes.

5 The system automatically provides performance indicators and an incentive to improve on targets and reduce costs.
6 Strengths and weaknesses are highlighted, together with an indication of how costs behave; this leads to increased effectiveness.
7 Delegation is an essential requirement and reduces the possibility of overloading some managers and supervisors.

## POSSIBLE DISADVANTAGES

1 Effective delegation may be difficult unless responsibilities are carefully defined and checked regularly.
2 The system may tend to become too rigid unless compromises are employed to maintain flexibility, but not to excessive lengths.
3 A high standard of data input is essential within reasonable limits, considering the cost and administration expenses of running the system.
4 The system is not a remedy for inept managers or supervisors.

## RESPONSIBILITY FOR VARIANCES

Assessing supervisory performance is usually based on efficiency aspects – those portions of variances that supervisors may directly influence. Price aspects are subject to external influences outside supervisors' control, e.g. economic conditions and abrupt price changes. Efficiency is normally measured as a ratio of input and output and, understandably, is a relative term. Therefore variances are indicators demanding attention and investigation. They do not provide answers.

### Labour variances

Apart from obvious fluctuations in productivity due to degrees of motivation and disputes, labour costs may be accurately budgeted. Predictable changes can usually be seen well in advance since they often depend on trade union agreements and general pay increases. However, there are some unpredictable features, such as changing the hourly rate to suit emergencies, or placing an employee with a rate of pay that is unrelated to the job.

### Material variances

Acquisition and usage are treated separately. The purchasing manager's responsibility is to buy at economic prices and on favourable terms, whereas the production manager aims to use materials efficiently. In practice the two are interrelated since sudden enforceable change in usage may mean buying at uneconomic rates and increased carriage costs to hasten delivery. Efficiency is usually measured by comparing the bill of materials (a specification of quantities allowed for a number of production units) with the quantities used. Variances may occur due to pilfering, poor handling, imperfections, poor standard of work, methods changes, and machine maintenance problems.

### Variance analysis

Random variances tend to be ignored if they are within reasonable or set limits. Significant variances demand an investigation, but someone must decide what is significant. This decision is often based on judgement, hunches or a feel of the situation. The alternative is to set a percentage deviation from the budget, based on its financial implications. With a machine maintenance budget of £500, 20 per cent is obviously insignificant compared with a 5 per cent deviation from a £500 000 material budget. Nevertheless, analysis might show the material deviation is due to the machine deviation. Analysis usually conforms to cost-benefit examination by applying statistical techniques and problem-solving approaches. These isolate randomness from controllable events and indicate courses of action.

### CASH FLOW EXAMPLE

An important example of budgetary control is cash flow, which demands critical analysis and constant monitoring for the company to remain solvent. The budget shows input and output of cash from capital and revenue sources. It is prepared in conjunction with the budgeted profit and loss account and balance sheet. This includes such features as sales and purchases, interest from investments, disposal of fixed assets, creditors and debtors, and capital expenditure. Any items that have no effect on cash flow, such as asset revaluation and depreciation, are excluded.

Critical control is possible with the aid of a computer, by presenting various scenarios resulting from the budget using 'what if' techniques. Typical examples are the risk of overtrading or undertrading, unforeseen expenses, the initial expense involved in expanding any section before financial gains are made, and buying expensive capital items.

### The supervisor's responsibility

The supervisor should appreciate that everyone has an impact on cash flow to varying extents. All actions involving expense eventually have some effect, but often this is not understood unless cash flow is explained.

When there is insufficient cash for the payroll or to pay suppliers, the company is forced to borrow. Borrowing is expensive and directly reduces profitability. Every small item of expenditure that could be avoided adds up to large sums across the whole organisation. Also there is an essential need to justify all expenditure in terms of timing and quantities.

Although forecasting such expenditure is often difficult, its importance should not be underestimated. Usually some impact is possible by using straightforward calculations and understanding how the organisation operates. The time spent on this activity is worthwhile, especially when associated with general and maintenance forecasting.

### Factoring

Certain options are open to a company facing difficulties with cash flow, mainly overdrafts, resorting to venture capital, and factoring. Factoring is a common and popular solution. A simple definition of factoring is supplying cash in exchange for outstanding customer invoices. Factoring companies offer two main schemes: full service factoring and invoice discounting.

# Elements of cost

The total cost of manufacturing a product is split into elements which may be grouped together for control purposes:

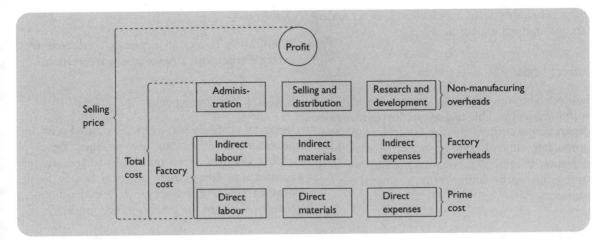

**Figure 29.7** Elements of cost
Elements of cost are based on production factors (factory cost) and non-manufacturing overheads. The relationship between this total cost and the selling price determines the profit or loss.

- *Labour*: to change the form of materials
- *Factory overheads*: utilised by labour such as premises, machines and equipment
- *Overheads*: services of a non-manufacturing nature, such as administration, selling, distribution, R&D

Production consists of two groups of costs known as *prime costs* and *factory overheads*; together they form the *factory cost*. The non-manufacturing overheads are added to the factory cost to form the *total cost*. The difference between total cost and selling price will provide the profit or loss figure. Figure 29.7 illustrates the elements of cost and method grouping to arrive at the profit and selling price.

## PRIME COSTS OF PRODUCTION

A direct cost arises when expenditure can be directly allocated to a product or cost centre (a particular or isolated point of production) instead of being apportioned or shared. This implies that direct responsibility can be traced for that particular cost. If this is not possible then the cost is indirect. If tracing small items such as nuts and bolts would not be worthwhile, they would be treated as indirect materials. The three elements of direct costs are direct labour, direct materials and direct expenses.

### Direct labour

Direct labour refers to those employees who work directly upon the manufacture of the product. Their pay must be justified in relation to the product or unit. Therefore chargehands and supervisors could be included as direct labour, although they are usually classed as indirect labour.

### Direct materials

Direct materials are allocated to the product; in other words, they are all the materials that become part of the product. They include raw materials, partly finished or finished components, and sub-assemblies.

### Direct expenses

Direct expenses are all the expenses (other than labour and materials) which are directly employed on a product or unit. Costs such as tools and drawings would be included, provided the whole charge was absorbed in the processing of that particular product.

### FACTORY OVERHEADS

Factory overheads are all indirect expenses attributed to manufacturing. They are divided into three elements: indirect labour, indirect materials and indirect expenses.

### Indirect labour

Indirect labour is all labour indirectly connected with production. This means employees in service departments, such as quality control, inspection, production control, tooling shops, internal transportation of materials, components and products, stores, the works dining room, maintenance and welfare.

### Indirect materials

Indirect materials include all consumables such as oil, grease, cotton waste, sawdust, cleaning fluids, and small items such as nuts, bolts and screws.

### Indirect expenses

Any remaining costs are indirect expenses; they are usually running expenses such as electricity, gas, water, rent and insurance.

### NON-MANUFACTURING OVERHEADS

Non-manufacturing overheads include all overheads other than factory overheads. They are divided into four elements: administration, selling, distribution, and research and development.

### Administration

Administration covers all those management expenses that are not covered by selling, distribution and production. Among them are the expenses of directing and controlling, and the administration of functions such as finance, accounting, auditing, and secretarial and legal activities.

### Selling

Selling includes all expenses incurred to maintain and develop sales, such as sales promotion, advertising, the sales general office, and the force of sales representatives.

### Distribution

Distribution covers all expenses connected with external transport, storage and warehousing.

### Research and development

Research costs are any items associated with improving and developing the product. Development costs arise when the results of research are applied and create some practical benefit to the product. If a new product is involved, development costs apply until the prototype is completed.

# Allocation and apportionment

Costs are allocated and apportioned according to particular circumstances and the number of different products manufactured by the company.

- *Direct costs* are allocated directly to the product using the most suitable method.
- *Factory overhead costs* are usually recovered in two stages: by allocating (charging) them to departments (or cost centres) and then by recovering (apportioning) them to each product.
- *Non-manufacturing overhead costs* are recovered in a variety of ways depending on circumstances.

### DIRECT COSTS: PRINCIPAL REQUIREMENTS

### Labour control

Any method of allocating labour costs usually includes the following activities and the responsibility rests with the department in parentheses:

- *Engagement of employees*: application forms, wage rates and any revisions (personnel department)
- *Record of attendance*: clock cards or job cards, hours attended daily (time office)
- *Direct hours worked*: based on each product or cost centre from job cards or time sheets, job numbers and hours (supervisor and employee)
- *Calculation of direct labour cost*: based on each product or centre for total costs calculated

*Table 29.1* Material control

| Activity | Form | Responsibility |
|---|---|---|
| 1 Establish stock levels | Authorisation sheet | Accountant, purchasing officer and production manager |
| 2 Cost pricing method | Authorisation sheet | Cost accountant |
| 3 Replenishing stocks | Purchase requisition | Storekeeper |
| 4 Ordering goods | Official order | Purchasing officer |
| 5 Receiving goods | Goods received note | Storekeeper |
| 6 Accepting goods | Inspection note | Inspector |
| 7 Payment for goods | Purchase invoice | Accountant |
| 8 Issuing materials | Materials requisition | Storekeeper |
| 9 Returning materials | Materials returned note | Supervisor |
| 10 Transfers | Materials transfer note | Storekeeper |
| 11 Recording stock | Bin cards<br>Material control cards | Storekeeper and stores clerk |
| 12 Charging materials to product or cost centre | Materials requisition<br>Material returned notes<br>Job cost summaries | Cost clerk |
| 13 Checking stock | Stock check sheets | Stock checker or internal auditor |

and entered on job cost summaries (cost department)

- *Weekly wages calculated*: total hours attended and bonus calculated from clock cards, job cards or time sheets (wages department)

## Material control

Typical procedures for controlling materials are given in Table 29.1, which includes the activity, the appropriate forms and the responsibilities.

## FACTORY OVERHEAD COSTS

Factory overhead costs are usually apportioned to individual departments or cost centres. A cost centre is a point or area where cost control may be applied. This could be a section, a group of machines, an individual or a group of individuals. A supervisor or manager is responsible for each cost centre. In this way the total costs of production and servicing departments may be obtained and idle time is easily calculated. Also an overhead rate may be calculated for each department or cost centre. An average rate for the complete factory is not usually acceptable because responsibility varies.

## Ways of apportioning factory overhead costs

- *Employees' wages*: National Insurance contributions and employers' liability insurance may be charged under this method.
- *Number of employees*: some items which may be fairly apportioned under this method are dining-room costs, pay department expenses, welfare costs and costing expenses.
- *Floor area or cubic capacity*: some examples which apply are lighting, heating, rent, fire insurance and general upkeep.
- *Technical measurement*: where the overhead can be measured within the cost centre, technical measurement provides a fair means of apportioning the charge; examples are lighting overheads from the number of bulbs or kilowatts consumed, heating overheads from the number of radiators, metered water and metered electricity.
- *Value of buildings and plant*: this may be used as a basis for items such as depreciation, insurance and repairs.
- *Direct charges*: a direct charge is sometimes possible when employees are engaged within a cost centre for purposes such as supervising and machinery maintenance.

## Methods of absorbing overheads

Recovery or absorption is straightforward when only one type of product is manufactured. The total factory overhead cost is divided by the number of products manufactured during the period, providing a uniform recovery rate for each product. When a range of products are manufactured, the allocation of a fair charge is more difficult. Job costing and many process costing systems have similar problems. Some of the methods used in these circumstances are prime cost percentage, direct wages percentage, direct material percentage, labour hour rate, and machine hour rate.

### Prime cost percentage

The factory overhead for the period is divided by the prime cost and expressed as a percentage. Expenses are often omitted from the prime cost.

$$\text{Percentage of prime cost} = \frac{\text{Factory overhead}}{\text{Prime cost}} \times 100$$

Period: July 20xx

Factory overhead = £2000

Direct labour     = £3000

Direct material   = £2000

$$\frac{2000}{5000} \times 100 = 40 \text{ per cent}$$

A job with a prime cost of £100 would therefore be charged £40 for the factory overhead cost.

### Direct pay percentage

Direct pay percentage is usually inaccurate, but a higher degree of accuracy is attained when rates of pay, machines, work content, etc., are similar for all the products manufactured.

$$\text{Percentage of direct pay} = \frac{\text{Factory overhead}}{\text{Direct pay}} \times 100$$

Period: July 20xx

Factory overhead = £2000

Direct pay       = £3000

$$\frac{2000}{5000} \times 100 = 66.67 \text{ per cent}$$

A job with a direct pay cost of £100 would therefore be charged £66.67 for factory overhead cost.

### Direct material percentage

Direct material percentage is usually unsuitable where products are manufactured from various materials within a wide price range.

$$\text{Direct material percentage} = \frac{\text{Factory overhead}}{\text{Direct material}} \times 100$$

Period: July 20xx

Factory overhead = £2000

Direct material   = £2000

$$\frac{2000}{2000} \times 100 = 100 \text{ per cent}$$

### Labour hour rate

The labour hour rate is useful where the operator's time is a very important aspect of the work; this is because the calculation is based upon the number of direct labour hours for the job.

$$\text{Direct labour hour rate} = \frac{\text{Factory overhead}}{\text{Direct labour hours}}$$

Period: July 20xx

Factory overhead     = £2000

Direct labour hours = 8000

$$\frac{£2000}{8000 \text{ h}} = £0.25 \text{ h}^{-1}$$

A job that takes 20 hours to complete would therefore have a factory overhead of £5.

### Machine hour rate

Machine hour rate is more accurate where the operating hours of machines are a dominant feature of production.

$$\text{Machine hour rate} = \frac{\text{Factory overhead}}{\text{Machine hours}}$$

Period: July 20xx

Factory overhead = £2000

Machine hours     = 4000

$$\frac{£2000}{4000 \text{ h}} = £0.50 \text{ h}^{-1}$$

A job that takes 20 machine hours to complete would therefore have a factory overhead of £10.

## NON-MANUFACTURING OVERHEAD COSTS

Non-manufacturing overheads are recovered in various ways. Administration costs may be written off as a general expense in the profit and loss account, or apportioned between work-in-progress and cost of sales, or averaged out among all products. Selling and distribution costs are usually written off to the cost of sales account. Research and development costs may be written off over a period of years (similar to fixed costs) and attached to factory overheads, or treated as a direct charge to the particular product, or written off as a general expense in the profit and loss account.

### Overcoming the distortion factor

Overhead costs are increasing in many companies and becoming a higher percentage of total costs. This means that product costs can easily be distorted. Traditionally, non-manufacturing overheads were allocated by using either direct labour or machine hours as a base. To avoid distortion, they are allocated using the activities which cause them to increase. This technique is often called responsibility cost accounting or activity cost accounting. Typical examples are training and labour turnover. Suppose a training centre's overheads are based upon the number of employees in each department serviced, then there will be distortion if one department's staff need more training because of continual technological advancement. Similarly, one department may suffer a higher labour turnover compared with others.

# Estimating

Estimating is quite similar to production planning, where costing also plays an essential part. The need for estimates arises in job production, as outlined in Chapter 26. If a customer has particular requirements which cannot be met by a standard product, then an estimate or quotation needs to be drawn up. Points to consider are reliability of the estimate, the eventual cost, and loading for profit.

## RELIABILITY

Reliability means starting at an earlier stage than production planning. Costly expenses to consider are research, design, drawings and specification preparation. Reference to past records is essential but the future always contains unknown factors which demand an intelligent guess by the specialists involved in forecasting.

## EVENTUAL COST

The actual cost of estimating must also be considered. The person who is responsible for an estimate has a heavy burden as an error may involve the company in a considerable loss which cannot be claimed from the customer in normal circumstances.

The estimator must have a clear idea of the customer's requirements and be able to link them to cost records. Although it is possible to construct an estimate by calculating the direct labour, material and expenses, this tedious and lengthy process can be replaced by concentrating on the total cost of sub-assemblies or components which may be common to a number of jobs. Thus time and effort may be saved.

Naturally some parts will need the full treatment of establishing prime cost. However, the estimator may build up a library of information by using statistical methods to cover a range of costs for a variable. If standard costs are available, they help in assessing the cost of components.

## LOADING FOR PROFIT

Top management is responsible for loading the total cost with a suitable profit margin. Although the estimator may be given a percentage to work with, there are occasions when the loading varies with circumstances. For example, winning a contract is important for prestige, or for lack of other work, or for the desire to discourage the customer because of an overfull order book.

The vital importance of the delivery date is often overlooked by companies. Delay may be costly and frustrating to the customer. Therefore it is usual to include a penalty clause in the contract. This clause operates on a set sum to be paid by the supplier for every day or week that delivery is overdue.

## QUESTIONS

1 Define costing and outline its main objectives.

2 Write accounts of job costing and process costing.

3 Draw a diagram illustrating the main elements of cost and briefly describe each one.

4 Outline a typical procedure for controlling materials.

5 Describe the various ways of apportioning factory overheads.

6 Write an essay on standard costing.

7 What are the purposes and advantages of budgetary control?

8 Describe a simple system of marginal costing.

9 How can costing help the supervisor?

10 When would it be worthwhile to accept an order at less than total cost?

11 Explain how to use the principle of exceptions in connection with standard costing.

12 What is meant by break-even technique? Illustrate your answer with a diagram.

13 Define cash flow and explain its importance in a control procedure.

14 Outline the safety margin in break-even techniques and the need to keep a careful check on it.

15 Explain what is meant by contribution and value added.

16 Draw up a framework to illustrate a typical procedure for budgetary control.

17 Why is pre-planning an essential factor for budgetary control?

18 Explain the use of total absorption costing.

19 Budgeted cash flow demands constant monitoring. Explain this statement.

20 How does the human factor influence budgets in practice?

21 Outline the supervisor's responsibility for cash flow.

22 The supervisor should understand clearly the use of cost–profit–volume analysis. Explain its importance.

23 Outline the uses of the profit/volume ratio.

Redboard needs a quality component because any faults mean a costly dismantling of the product. Storage is limited and regular small deliveries are essential. Usually the company stipulates a six-monthly contract. Two companies are asked to quote for component X at 200 a week. The details are restricted to the following information:

- *Company A*: A small engineering concern, well-established and noted for quality products. The manager is casual and not bothered about a long-term contract. The fitters are skilled and have been with the company for many years; the machinery is old and there is obviously a reliance on the workforce. For component X the manager quoted fixed costs of £900 a week, variable costs of £3.50 per unit, and a profit margin of 8 per cent. These figures would stand for one year.
- *Company B*: A modern small concern with new machines and equipment, an unskilled workforce, an obvious customer-oriented manager, and a stipulated one-year contract with a penalty clause for late deliveries. Fixed costs are £1500 a week, variable costs are £2.50 per unit, and the profit margin is 10 per cent.

*As part of his training, a senior supervisor at Redboard is asked to make a presentation, including prices and comments on the quotations.*

Mark Johnson established a small business thirty years ago. Previously he worked as an engineer for a large electronics firm, found a gap in the market for a complex component and decided to manufacture it himself. The business has been successfully developed into a medium-sized company with 250 employees.

Approaching retiring age, Mark brings his daughter Alison into the business. She studied management with the object of eventually taking over. Alison, straight from university, chooses to spend some time on the shop floor to get the feel of the place. Within a short time it is obvious to her that control is poor although there is little discontent. The company still has no major competitors and employee benefits are high.

She overhears two supervisors: '. . . and I seem to spend most of my time filling in control reports but they don't seem to do any good. It would be much better if we could just get on with the job'.

'Why worry, Colin?', the other replies. 'You're well paid; you have an easy time really; everything goes like clockwork here'.

'And what happens when the old man packs up soon? That girl of his is going to be in dead trouble if she tries to use any management science or whatever they call it here.'

'The management information system is what they call it. Should be renamed the mis-information system!'

Alison withdraws quietly and decides to check up. When she asks the chief accountant about the variances and what happens, he replies, 'We don't do anything but we've got the records if you'd like to see them'.

Her father replies to the same question with, 'It's all there. We know exactly what is going on. I try to discover the sources and reasons, but it's a very complicated system. Hard to say who is really responsible when we have problems, but we get by'.

By now Alison is very worried. 'But what happens if the rumours are true about Rodgers Industries developing a cheaper model?'

*Consider the options now open to Alison. How could the supervisors help her?*

# 30

# The administrative features of productivity

## Introduction

Apart from all the earlier techniques and concepts to improve productivity, there remain certain important features which complete the overall organisational scene. Control of these administration aspects is often not taken seriously. But it should not be ignored or underestimated, especially when related to information technology.

- administration control
- regulated control
- deregulated control
- the office supervisor's role
- managing business information
- cost reduction concepts
- environmental aspects
- creating growth
- supervisory control
- cost reduction checklists
- the administration of maintenance

## Administration control

The administration function (Chapter 4) is unique since it permeates all functions and creates unusual control problems. To illustrate, staff may be dispersed over many different sites and enjoy a different culture which isolates them from other employees.

Within administration, the expanding use of information technology means more essential information can be provided for use by management. Such automation becomes costly if it is not preceded by extensive clerical work study (organisation and methods) to simplify and reorganise jobs, the organisational structure and control mechanisms. Consequently, a company may have regulated control or deregulated control.

## Regulated control

Administration is treated seriously under regulated administrative control since information technology changes have forced senior management to control staff and activities closely. Complex systems are established along with total quality management to achieve effective administration. Human resource management is practised and recognised as being of equal importance to office automation. Within regulated administrative control, it is essential to have an accurate definition of productivity and its application. The ways of measuring productivity are equally important. These aspects are now discussed.

### DEFINITIONS OF PRODUCTIVITY

Productivity is the degree of effectiveness of resources. Put another way, productivity is the degree of accomplishment in two main areas which are assessed by ratios: output over input, and effectiveness over efficiency. Productivity usually refers to operational performance of the workforce, but overall productivity includes *all* employees, supervisors and managers.

Many internal and external factors influence productivity. Internal influences are controllable and can be thought of as either soft or hard. Soft factors include employees, the organisation and work methods. They provide the means for rapid

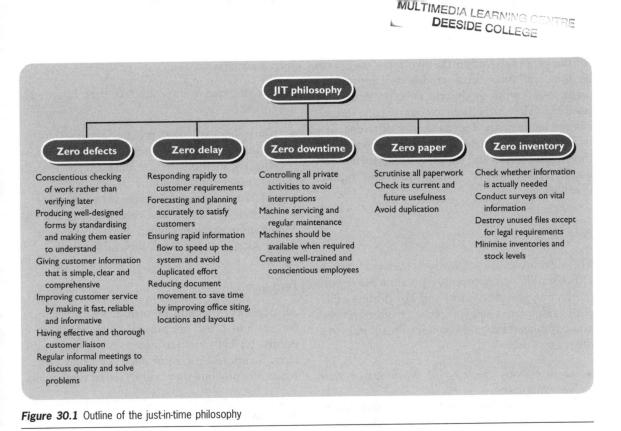

**Figure 30.1** Outline of the just-in-time philosophy

productivity improvement. Hard factors include capital expenditure and technology. They are long term but equally important. External influences, such as political, economic, legislative, and environmental factors, are usually considered to be outside the control of the company.

## MEASURING PRODUCTIVITY

The human factor is of prime importance. This has been recognised by most institutions, including the International Labour Organisation. The key feature is assumed to be collaborative management, so productivity is measured by using labour as the resource factor. Understandably, all other resources affect labour effectiveness. Labour productivity is generally defined as the ratio of employees to output, or man-hours to output; materials productivity is defined as the ratio of cost (or amount) of materials consumed to output; and capital productivity is defined as the ratio of assets employed to output. Measurement of overall productivity must include the effectiveness of all main functions, especially administration. Such effectiveness

in administration is heavily dependent upon managerial philosophy and cost reduction techniques.

## JUST-IN-TIME ADMINISTRATION

Although just-in-time (JIT) is a production control concept (Chapter 26), it can be applied to other functions, especially administration. A typical example is share registration work, which involves large quantities of paper. Using JIT, deliveries of paper can be arranged to coincide with usage and so save expensive storage and financial costs.

The main thrusts of JIT are to improve quality, increase materials flow, ensure employee and machine flexibility, reduce downtime and inventory, and work closely with customers, suppliers and distributors. Figure 30.1 gives an outline of JIT and shows the main improvement areas. The philosophy is to apply five 'zeros':

- zero defects
- zero delay
- zero downtime
- zero paper
- zero inventory

All the proposals within the five zeros may seem obvious, no more than traditional approaches using sound work study and effective marketing practices. They have been recognised by specialists for many years. Inevitably the difference lies with top management; they must adopt these three philosophies and sincerely apply them: total quality, collaborative management and market orientation.

## Zero defects

The obvious cause of waste is defective work. Office staff have a notorious reputation for rework (correcting previous work) and not dealing efficiently with queries and complaints from employees and customers. Probably the seven main improvement areas are:

- conscientious checking of work rather than verifying later
- producing well-designed forms, standardising them, and making them easy to understand
- giving simple, clear and comprehensive information to the customer
- providing a fast, reliable and informative service to the customer
- liaising effectively with the customer
- discussing quality and solving problems at regular informal meetings
- giving a helpful, accurate service to all employees

## Zero delay

Avoiding delays means concentrating on *throughput* of information and paperwork, not on output alone. Throughput implies that customers' needs come first and that everything possible is done to achieve this objective. The main themes are:

- responding rapidly to customer requirements
- accurately forecasting and planning to satisfy the customer
- ensuring rapid information flow to speed up the system and avoid duplicated effort
- reducing document movement to save time by improving layouts, office siting and locations

## Zero downtime

Reduce or remove unproductive time by attending to:

- controlling all the private activities often occurring in offices and arranging for more effective methods of avoiding telephone calls that upset concentration
- machine servicing and regular maintenance
- machine availability when required, e.g. employing more machines where bottlenecks occur
- creating well-trained conscientious staff

## Zero paper

All paperwork should be scrutinised to check its current and future usefulness. Often duplication occurs, typically similar records being kept in different locations. Also some documents may be filed when it is obvious they will never be used again.

## Zero inventory

Check that information is actually needed, not requested just in case. Conduct surveys on alleged needs for vital information. Destroy files that are never used, except those satisfying legal requirements. Minimise inventories and stationery stock levels to avoid the high cost of space and storage.

# Deregulated control

The opposing situation is allegedly far more common. This allows poor control, low productivity and sometimes badly operated computer systems. Under deregulated control, critics claim that effectiveness is ignored, motivation and morale of other employees are adversely affected, the office is treated as a joke, and there is a constant stream of farcical office stories circulating within the organisation.

**OFFICE TALES FROM PERSONAL ACCOUNTS**

- Private individual enterprises selling a variety of items.
- Extended lunch and tea breaks.

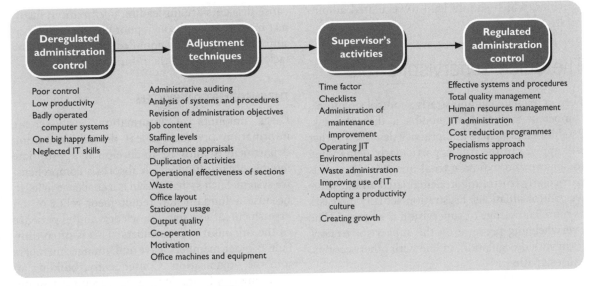

**Figure 30.2** Administrative features of productivity

- Stoppages for drinks and cakes to celebrate birthdays, anniversaries, engagements and new arrivals.
- Private activities, such as knitting, crosswords, reading, arranging outings and sports activities, and telephone calls.
- Drinking sessions during extended lunch breaks.
- Travelling expense claims for meetings to discuss matters that could have been dealt with by a telephone call.
- Flexitime being used for slacking while the office is deserted.
- Private use of stationery and machines.
- The smoking room being used for regular gatherings when smoking is banned in the office.

## NEGLECTING IT SKILLS

A fundamental difficulty with deregulated control is the lack of skills by managers and employees to make full use of information technology (IT). This is a major obstacle that must be overcome for companies to grow, compete and survive. According to surveys, over 6 million employees interact with IT daily but their skills levels are below the satisfactory minimum. Moreover, a disturbing practice is that most IT skills are learned on the job, which encourages bad practices. Apparently, senior

management often does not realise the role of IT and IT skills development in improving profits. Indeed IT is changing rapidly and many managers are relying on trial and error to keep up with developments that will decide survival later.

## ADMINISTRATION AUDITING

An essential requirement for the removal of deregulation is the systematic regular analysis of all the systems and procedures. The aim is to reorganise all administrative resources to achieve administration objectives. This includes managers, supervisors, staff, stationery, finance and budgets.

Using all the techniques and specialists discussed in previous chapters, the auditing team arranges for many studies. These involve job content, staffing levels, performance appraisal, duplication of activities, operational effectiveness of each section, waste, office layout, stationery usage, output quality, co-operation, motivation, office equipment and computers.

The philosophy is to achieve total quality (Chapter 27), which means treating each function as equally important and worthy of equal attention in terms of productivity. Figure 30.2 illustrates the total process to remove deregulated control. This concept follows a set pattern to introduce many adjustment techniques and essential supervisory activities, which should lead to regulated administrative control.

# The office supervisor's role

Even in regulated administrative control situations, competent supervision remains a difficult task. Established principles and practice described earlier still apply, but the role is particularly demanding to achieve and maintain total quality. The task is particularly frustrating in deregulated administrative control situations. Frustration actually increases as more knowledge of supervision is acquired. The overwhelming pressure on the supervisor to conform with deregulation, in line with other sections, causes apathy.

## MEETINGS

If there are formal supervisory meetings, a collective approach to management should be proposed to change from deregulated control to regulated control. The alternative is to arrange informal meetings to persuade management to establish a formal committee, preferably with a management representative. The philosophy of the agenda should be to form a strong group to counter the pressure. Items will be various proposals suggested by committee members to consider ways of combating indifferent top management and how to achieve company survival.

# Managing business information

The administration department may employ a specialist to harness business information in the organisation. This applies particularly in the large concern. Titles vary such as information manager, information advisor, database administrator and information technologist. Alternatively, the administration manager's role will include this responsibility. The vital nature of business information is easily overlooked and its costs are often not related to its value. An examination of most management topics clearly highlights information aspects which may cause complex problems unless managed correctly. Typical examples that may cause disasters are misleading information; incorrect interpretation through poor presentation; oversimplified and undersimplified presentation; and lack of confidence in the information system.

## THE INFORMATION SYSTEM

Large amounts of information easily create information *overload* unless the administration department is 'allowed' to develop an appropriate flexible organisation which absorbs a comprehensive system. Such system design is a challenge in itself, because a fundamental requirement relies on an assessment of existing knowledge and experience of the organisation's members. This is often difficult as older members leave and younger members join the organisation. Consequently, building an economical information system to satisfy requirements is difficult and suffers with the inevitable problems. Herein lies the importance of the supervisor's role and responsibilities, and the vital nature of many features mentioned in previous chapters. These features provide an overview of the whole organisation, which are listed below:

- The effects of IT and integrated systems in the organisation (Chapter 1).
- IT developments on decision making and middle management (Chapter 2).
- Specialism in IT and management science (Chapter 3).
- The administration function: subfunctions, hardware, software, networks, the network manager, network providers, the open systems revolution and integrated systems (Chapter 4).
- Communication: real-time information and statistical presentation of information (Chapter 14).
- Financial control reports and ratios, and MIS on financial accounts (Chapter 28).
- Cost-control ratios and procedures, and control features, especially feedback (Chapter 29).

### Total systems approach

The MIS concept is to provide information for management purposes rather than for routine administrative needs. This concept may include integrating all the subsystems into a large system. Thus a total systems approach is achieved which has many advantages: data are entered once only, all relevant files are immediately and automatically updated, and data are immediately retrievable on a functional basis. Such interfunctional systems ensure co-ordination and encourage co-operation between managers.

## Information

The term 'information' is often interchangeable with 'data'; it is too broad to distinguish between raw information (or raw data) entering a system, the processing stages (or data processing), and the output stages of business information (or business data) for the use of managers and supervisors.

## Informal data

The term 'informal data' is used to cover all data entering a system through various channels such as telephone conversations, lunch break and golf course meetings, and conversations on journeys and in interviews. It also applies to conversations within the organisation which include passing knowledge and experience from one person to another, and avoiding duplicated effort to locate information already available. Although informal data is an important factor for problem solving and decision making, it is difficult to control and it relies upon a specialist in the organisation to recognise duplicated effort.

## Formal data

All written and recorded data are known as formal data when it enters a system. Data are then aggregated, tabulated, charted, or filed manually or electronically for future use.

## THE KNOWLEDGE MANAGER

The tendency in many companies is to reduce the amount of knowledge that managers and employees possess through the adoption of various policies. They include re-engineering (which often replaces specialists), removing older members, outsourcing, drives to cut costs without considering the knowledge aspect, and engaging younger members who have a limited knowledge of business.

To overcome this tendency, some concerns are appointing a knowledge manager to assess the situation, compare it with other companies, and make recommendations. There is a distinct difference between knowledge which is in a person's head and information or data available within a system. Apart from possessing this knowledge, a person with *appropriate* knowledge can use information far more effectively. It is usually much easier to acquire the rudiments of a skill than to apply them successfully on a real project.

Probably a sensible plan is to tap the knowledge in people's heads before they leave. However, expertise in this particular subject is in short supply. Finding a competent knowledge manager who is educated and trained to cope with this problem is a fundamental consideration in progressive companies.

## THE SUPERVISOR'S ROLE

Although the supervisor may not be involved in the administration system of providing business information, it is vital to feed back opinions on the value of information received. This role may include:

- assessing the usefulness of the information received
- determining whether the information is too simplified or too complex for the purpose intended
- presenting evidence that the information is misleading, incomplete or inaccurate
- suggesting how the information could be improved in terms of quality, timeliness and completeness
- questioning the accuracy of a decision considering the information already available, its formal or informal nature, experience and existing knowledge applied, and sources of information
- relying too heavily on the information available and so restricting feedback to ensure change rather than to strengthen an existing weak system
- visualising an ideal information system to satisfy requirements and feeding back the ideas
- questioning an increasing or decreasing reliance on knowledge and experience, as against using information received

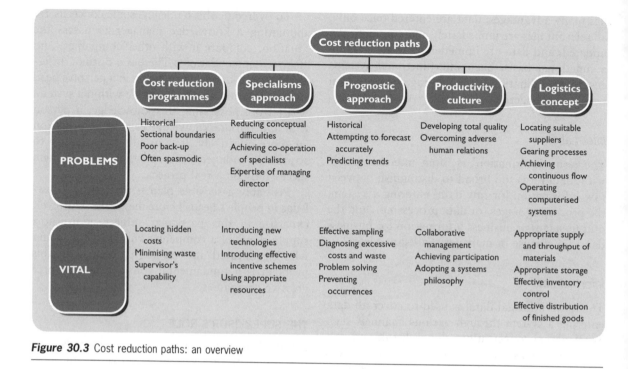

**Figure 30.3** Cost reduction paths: an overview

---

- making a conscious effort to select people who should receive the information, rather than sending it to everyone

### Cybernetic control and feedback

If there is any doubt about the importance of feedback, read the sections on homeostasis (Chapter 9) and cybernetics (Chapter 23). Unfortunately, self-regulation is not always possible in systems since deviations from a required level of performance may have to be observed rather than relying on a computer program. If there is a failure to report back, the controller is powerless to rectify the problem.

# Cost reduction concepts

Measuring productivity accurately usually relies heavily on costing systems that are naturally historical and tend to treat standards as objectives (Chapter 29). The modern approach is to incorporate cost reduction into the costing systems as a continuing updating process of preventive measures in line with total quality control (Chapter 27).

Consequently, complacency due to misinterpretation is avoided, especially where low productivity is hidden in a flourishing new market, or where high productivity in one section masks another section's poor performance. Cost reduction concepts fit into five main categories:

- cost reduction programmes
- the specialisms approach
- the prognostic approach
- productivity culture
- the logistics concept

More than one concept may operate simultaneously in some companies. Figure 30.3 provides an overview of cost reduction paths.

### COST REDUCTION PROGRAMMES

Cost reduction programmes are planned through the costing system, which is naturally historical in nature. Investigations are conducted when costs and waste are considered suspect. Often sectional boundaries in the organisation restrict improvement, so local attempts are made to rectify problems without there being sufficient back-up.

Programmes may be established on an ad hoc basis if senior management is confronted suddenly with poor profits, or they may follow a timetable coinciding with reports. Such arrangements suffer from spasmodic efforts to improve. Sometimes they are inherently wasteful themselves. Work study and work measurement techniques are often used to study existing activities. There is also a reliance on basic control procedures.

To succeed, programmes should be ongoing, well-planned and logical. This is achieved by analysing the effect on revenue and profit contribution in the short-term and the long-term. The justification of costs is important; some costs are obviously essential whereas others may appear to be unnecessary or a luxury until closely examined.

### Hidden costs

Probably the most difficult area is hidden costs, or an apparent need caused deliberately for personal gain, without any real need. Here is how they affect marketing and purchasing.

### Marketing

Take great care when trying to reduce marketing costs. During a recession excessive cutting of advertising and sales promotion may seem prudent, but it could prove disastrous if it 'accelerates the downward spiral of sales.

### Purchasing

There are many ways to reduce purchasing costs. Typical methods are reducing stock levels, making rather than buying or vice versa, competitive bidding, importing at better prices, exclusive buying deals, and co-operative purchasing. Couple them with constant assessment of the market to analyse prices, delivery dates, new products and materials, and quality levels. Finally it may be advantageous to lease rather than buy some items, e.g. cars.

### THE SPECIALISMS APPROACH

The specialisms approach relies on specialists to find the most appropriate resource and to ensure its most economic use. Typical examples are:

- scientific and technological expertise provided by engineers who may make enormous savings through the introduction of new technologies
- effective financial and non-financial incentive schemes recommended by a personnel manager

Effectiveness often depends upon the conceptual capabilities and co-operativeness of specialists, and the expertise of the managing director in achieving co-ordination.

### IMPROVING THE USE OF INFORMATION TECHNOLOGY

The information revolution has changed concepts of the organisation, the work, control and senior management effectiveness. Now automatic control is possible, empowerment can be improved, and the Internet, e-mail, and many other activities are becoming essential requirements for improving productivity and ensuring survival. Information for problem solving and decision making is enhanced through the world's largest library, the Internet, and the advantages of being connected are growing, although there are certain precautions.

### THE PROGNOSTIC APPROACH

The prognostic approach relies on sampling; diagnosing excessive costs and waste; attempting to anticipate, forecast or predict trends or faults; and recommending courses of action to remove the problems and prevent recurrences. It differs from other approaches but still relies on historical information for diagnosis. Common applications are statistical quality control techniques and planned maintenance.

### PRODUCTIVITY CULTURE

Productivity culture accepts the systems philosophy, creates a collaborative management style, and encourages full development of participative techniques. Rapid adaptation to change occurs in all parts of the system. Scientific and technological updating is automatic, along with improving the organisation and developing creative approaches to jobs. A total quality culture and human resource management are fundamental requirements.

## The approach in practice

There are various ways of involving everyone in a productivity culture. Participative concepts may include encouraging employees to adopt a questioning attitude to all procedures, and recognising the possibility of insignificant improvements. They use all the method study techniques, typically abandoning a form which no longer serves any purpose, or modifying a small component. Naturally a reward is essential, in keeping with the saving. Another approach is to question all bureaucratic devices by concentrating on streamlining the organisation and removing any rigid obstacles that hinder activities rather than encourage customer orientation.

## THE LOGISTICS CONCEPT

Taking into consideration the cost reduction concepts already discussed, logistics may be viewed as a total concept of cost reduction which incorporates the flow of goods from the company's supplier, through all the processes in production and marketing, up to and including delivery to customers. Logistics encompasses forecasting, planning, all goods and information flow, and ensures a continuous process of movement and minimum storage. Naturally the application of information technology and operational research are important features.

This concept is a co-ordination activity which attempts to bring together and control all the flow process points, so creating an uninterrupted stream of goods. The activity may start at the storage of goods in a supplier's warehouse, and proceed through a number of subfunctions: the company's reception and movement of goods on arrival; materials control, including stock levels and inventory; manufacturing resource planning; distribution and point of sale, including electronic devices. Many specialists will be employed in logistics, including purchasing, production, marketing and information technology. Each one will have to make an effective contribution, otherwise the concept fails.

Logistics may be applied in any organisation, such as manufacturing, retailing, services and suppliers, because it can be adapted to information flow alone as well as materials flow.

## Essential requirements

There are many basic requirements which often cause problems: locating suppliers who are able to provide a continuous flow of materials at a competitive price, all manufacturing processes geared to input and output quantities at set rates to provide a continuous flow, all functional boundaries and specialists subordinated to the concept of effective flow, a competent logistics manager to control the processes, top managers who fully support the concept, effective computerised systems to provide accurate incoming and outgoing data, and a human resources manager who is able to create and provide competent employees to operate and control data and processes. Such an abbreviated list of essential requirements obviously restricts the effective operation of logistics in practice.

## The philosophy of logistics

Logistics attempts to maintain a competitive edge, satisfy customer wants, and constantly improve quality and cost-effectiveness by using integrated logistics management. This means achieving overall effectiveness by adopting a co-ordinative approach to physical distribution management and materials management, so creating supply chain management. The chain, in total, incorporates the management of all distribution aspects, so it is often known as distribution management (Chapter 4).

## Practical applications

### Supply of materials

Negotiate with suppliers to provide the right materials, at the right price, at the right time, at the right location. This demands an experienced specialist with appropriate authority to negotiate and contract deals.

### Goods inwards

Arrange the immediate throughput of materials to production, after appropriate inspection for quantity and quality. Receive rejects from customers, and deal with the rejects procedure according to logistics requirements for establishing a competent customer service and encouraging good customer relations.

### Storage facilities

Ensure goods are stored safely, easily accessible for stock-checking and delivered rapidly when required.

### Inventory control

Inventory control is a vital feature of logistics management; it ensures that physical stocks agree with records and are reduced to a minimum consistent with requirements. Stocks lying idle, and obsolescent and obsolete stocks, tie up precious amounts of cash.

### Materials control

A vital feature of logistics is adopting a system of materials control which provides accurate information for ordering, monitoring and maintaining appropriate stock levels. By using JIT and manufacturing resource planning (MRP), the logistics manager will be able to provide more recent data more quickly.

### Distribution of finished goods

Distribution ensures that the right quantities of the right product are sent to the right customers. The goods should be transported in the most suitable way, considering possible damage, cost and delivery time. Logistics provides a comparison of various in-house transport methods and outsourcing opportunities, which enables management to decide on the most appropriate distribution method.

# Environmental aspects

The question of environmental protection was discussed in Chapter 21, concerning health and safety. There are, however, many ways of improving productivity by using techniques to reduce costs. Typical examples are recycling, reducing harmful waste, and avoiding pollution by using more economic devices.

## WASTE MINIMISATION

Waste minimisation is increasingly important for various reasons. They include the introduction of new legislation, rising disposal costs, the demand for greener products, improving environmental performance, improving operating efficiency, the safety of employees, possible income from reusable waste, and improving company image.

## THE SUPERVISOR'S PART

At national level most people probably use some service or product improperly. Glaring examples are seen everywhere. They amount to either ignorance or misguided ideas of democratic freedom. Everyone pays indirectly for waste, but few recognise the problem and are prepared to change their ideas.

The supervisor should appreciate the situation and accept the responsibility to minimise waste. He or she ought to develop a searching attitude towards cost, which means something more than inquiring into the possibility of reducing the cost by direct means. Some examples are the use of a time switch to control lighting and heating, buying a more expensive tool which is cheaper in the long run, applying one coat of expensive covering instead of three coats of cheaper covering, replacing an unsuitable machine with a new one which will produce savings eventually. Such changes require expenditure first, with the savings coming later.

More direct ways should not be ignored, such as cutting out shapes from a metal sheet in a more economical way by altering the position of the pattern, or using a cheaper grade of material which does not impair the efficiency of the product.

To summarise, the supervisor can help by:

- impressing on employees the need to reduce waste
- examining all waste to identify the causes
- establishing waste reduction objectives
- developing appropriate controls to prevent waste

# Creating growth

Although cost reduction is important, there is now more emphasis on how to create growth in a company. This obviously depends on company strategy, competent senior management, and the involvement in effectiveness of all employees. Strategic aspects are to maintain continuous organisational improvement programmes and to develop strategic direction

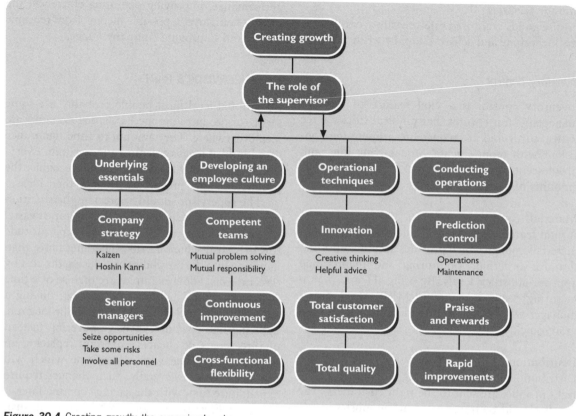

**Figure 30.4** Creating growth: the supervisor's role

by creating new products and seeking new markets. Figure 30.4 indicates the major features. Kaizen and Hoshin Kanri are two Japanese management techniques that take full advantage of environmental changes, the market, employee culture, and new technologies.

### KAIZEN

Kaizen has already been described in Chapters 26 and 27 and is now mentioned again because of its vital importance. It relies heavily on the workforce to devise and implement improvements on the quality of its products or services and the systems and work processes. The concept of continuous improvement is based on competent teams that attend to detail, use modern problem-solving techniques, and endeavour to improve all issues within their remit. Important aspects are mutual responsibility and cross-functional approaches.

### HOSHIN KANRI

Hoshin Kanri is a form of corporate planning by aligning the company and its operating unit (or team) to concentrate on strategic direction. In other words, attempting to break through into new markets and new products, and devising new systems and processes. Various routes are explored by using innovative thought. Opportunities are taken rapidly and with some risk.

## Supervisory control factors

### THE TIME FACTOR

Does the item vary in cost on a regularly occurring or an intermittent basis? Waste may occur because an employee regularly has half a day off each week or there will be cases of epidemics such as influenza or gastroenteritis. An intermittent

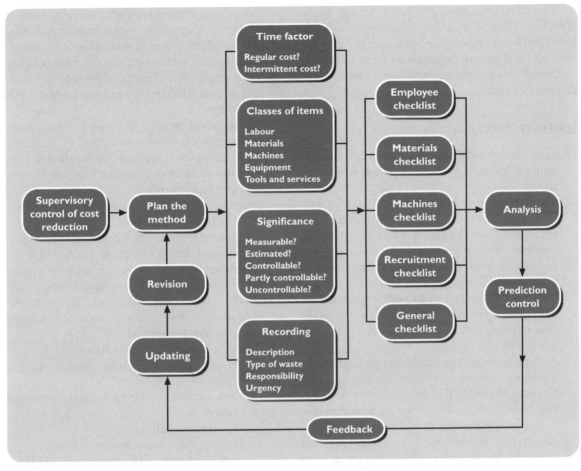

**Figure 30.5** The continuing nature of a cost-control process

example might be absences to attend a race meeting or a football match.

## CLASSES OF ITEMS

Items may be divided into labour, materials, machines, equipment, tools and services.

## SIGNIFICANCE

An item's waste may be measurable or it may have to be estimated. It may be decided that the item is controllable, partly controllable or uncontrollable.

## RECORDING

All factors should be recorded, together with a description of the item or type of waste. The

question of responsibility is also involved. Timeliness of information is important so that action may be taken early.

# Cost reduction checklists

Supervisory control of cost reduction schemes relies on ensuring there is a comprehensive coverage on the probable areas of waste. This may be practised by using checklists periodically. Figure 30.5 shows the continuing nature of supervisory control; the main factors help to create a plan which uses checklists. Prediction control ensures constant revision of the plan based upon the success or failure of the scheme.

The checklists here are not intended to be complete. They provide indications which should be revised by the supervisor according to his or her own knowledge and experience of the particular section. It is essential to revise checklists as circumstances change.

## EMPLOYEE CHECKLIST

1 Skilled employees must be given skilled work, semi-skilled employees semi-skilled work, and so on.
2 The pay should be appropriate to the job. Giving high levels of pay to employees who are performing low levels of tasks is obviously wasteful. The importance of servicing (providing assistance to) highly paid employees is a fundamental requirement.
3 Use the knowledge, skills and experience of employees effectively. Unfortunately, the problems of rising and declining industries make this task extremely difficult.
4 Avoid time wasted by employees through walking about between one operation and another. Examine the ways this factor can be reduced. For example, it is cheaper for an unskilled employee to bring materials to a skilled employee.
5 Aim to cut out idle time completely. Question the schedules, check workflow, and try to close the gaps.
6 Reduce frustration of the employee through poor product design. Search for ideas from employees and ensure adequate rewards for successful improvements.
7 Try to improve training schemes. Poor training produces poor employees.
8 Ensure that financial and non-financial incentives schemes are suitable and operating properly. Unsound incentives have disastrous effects.
9 Keep up to date with motivation techniques. Practice and experiment until better results are achieved. Motivating is an art which demands perseverance.
10 Do not give up if management's attitude is poor. Set an example and demonstrate good practices. Attempt to relieve the adverse pressures by explaining that managers are very busy, they carry a heavy burden of responsibility, and are easily misunderstood. Unfortunately, there is no logical alternative to this approach. Unless there is alignment with managers and attempts to excuse their conduct, the outcome is siding with employees. This is obviously unsound and widens the gap between management and employees.
11 Using inexperienced employees. The danger of accidents, excessive scrap and the effect on other employees is apparent. Such causes as poor selection and lack of suitable employees are outside the supervisor's scope. He or she should complain and try to train the unfortunate individual as soon as possible.
12 Carelessness, apparent laziness, accidents and absenteeism are examples of areas where the supervisor must take positive action after adequate investigation by personnel counselling.
13 Quality being neglected for quantity. An appraisal of the financial incentive scheme and attitudes is essential.
14 Working conditions below standard.
15 Unsuitable tools, machines, equipment and materials.
16 Poor maintenance resulting in breakdowns and frustration.
17 Inadequate instructions.
18 Inadequate induction schemes.
19 Avoidable overtime. This becomes a habit for supervisors and employees unless a firm stand is taken by assessing workloads and setting appropriate standards.
20 Low morale and high labour turnover. This situation is obviously complex and demanding on supervisors and managers.

### Recruitment checklist

Check the following possibilities before any recruitment requests are considered:

- employing a part-timer
- using a temporary employee
- working overtime, so long as this is not excessive and long term
- avoiding the outstanding work or integrating it in another job
- mechanising or automating, and combining with other tasks

- simplifying the job and combining with another job
- job sharing
- contract hire schemes

## MATERIALS CHECKLIST

1 Use the cheapest available that suits the purpose. Make sure the quality of the finished product is not impaired.
2 Not requisitioning sufficient supplies.
3 Inadequate supplies available at the stores.
4 Damaged material through negligence.
5 Salvage may be used in some cases by sorting and selling it to companies.
6 Poor storage facilities may easily soil materials and become shop-worn.
7 Inadequate materials handling may cause damage and delays which may be overcome by closer control.
8 Faulty materials should be reported immediately to the purchasing officer or executive responsible for supplies.
9 Excessive consumption of consumable materials should be investigated. Costs may rise considerably unless such items are strictly controlled. Often small items tend to be used carelessly and are subject to pilfering.
10 To avoid time-wasting and waste, small parts and components should be placed in separate containers.

## MACHINES CHECKLIST

1 Replacement of obsolescent machines with more efficient models.
2 Effective maintenance programmes to minimise breakdowns and ensure their prompt attention.
3 Attending to the effective layout of machines and equipment, especially if procedures are changed.
4 Remove redundant machines.
5 Ensure the economic operation of machines by scheduling to reduce idle time.
6 Use the correct type of model for each operation.
7 Ensure that attachments which save time and accidents are fitted and used.

## GENERAL CHECKLIST

1 Application of work study to simplify, standardise and generally improve methods, and to measure the work content.
2 Work planning and scheduling.
3 Correct use of jigs and tools.
4 Tolerances should be opened to limits which do not affect the quality of the product but allow for savings in its manufacture.
5 Check on housekeeping. Slackness leads to more accidents, increased cleaning costs and loss of materials.
6 Excessive use of services such as lighting, heating, compressed air, water and power.

# Administration of maintenance

The maintenance of plant and machinery is an important productivity factor, especially when associated with just-in-time techniques. Measuring maintenance work by analytical estimating (Chapter 24) is essential if accurate information is to be provided for effective planning and control. Automation, higher precision and heavy investment costs cause a greater cost load when breakdowns occur. The supervisor will easily recognise management's attitude to maintenance by examining the programme below.

## MAINTENANCE IMPROVEMENT PROGRAMME

1 Strong support from management for a long-term investment plan, apart from its direct and indirect production cost.
2 A firm long-term plan to optimise the use of plant and machinery as part of the manufacturing process.
3 Regular maintenance audits of plant and machinery performance to assess the strengths, weaknesses, alternative arrangements and problems. Auditing also clearly indicates improvement areas, creates an awareness of maintenance difficulties, and helps to motivate action.
4 The formulation of policy and tactical plans from audit results.

*The main features*

- Reviewing the organisation regularly.
- Improving the training of employees and maintenance staff.
- Assessing material resources.
- Purchasing new plant and machinery if required to avoid bottlenecks.
- Introducing new working arrangements and maintenance control mechanisms.
- Evaluating maintenance management information regularly by conducting and integrating the analysis of faults, seeking responses from employees, attending to supervisory problems, and assessing the effectiveness of changes.
- Adjusting maintenance based upon the evaluations.

## THE SUPERVISOR'S PART

The supervisor's terms of reference on maintenance determine his or her role and responsibilities. The main decisive situations are:

- operating a technique such as just-in-time
- relying on a maintenance department
- sole responsibility for maintenance
- participating in a maintenance improvement programme

### Just-in-time technique

The vital need for *minimum machine stoppages* has already been noted. The supervisor has a sensitive role to play in ensuring employees who are responsible for machine maintenance receive all the help they need immediately and remain motivated. They are probably backed by the maintenance department in these circumstances. Any difficulties with the human aspect should be reported to management. If there is a delay then steps should be taken to alleviate the problem.

### The maintenance department

The supervisor should provide the department with all the information required and assist in the preparation of sound plans. In the absence of a planned programme, the supervisor should stress the need by supplying appropriate evidence. Invariably the maintenance costs are more than offset by increased output due to a reduction in downtime.

### Supervisory responsibility

Sole responsibility for maintenance is a heavy burden. The supervisor must convince employees that machines should be treated with care. Any carelessness or deliberate negligence should be carefully investigated and the appropriate action taken.

Improved training in maintenance and time spent on planning is always worthwhile. This factor should be stressed to management, along with proposals for machine replacements and additions. Periodic overhaul of machines and equipment is a fundamental requirement and all control records should be kept up to date. There should also be a procedure for reporting and dealing with emergency breakdowns.

### Maintenance improvement: supervisors' roles

- Liaising closely with management by providing all appropriate information which will be helpful.
- Assisting with the establishment of maintenance target levels.
- Suggesting any improvements in procedures, systems, and control mechanisms.
- Proposing any further training and encouraging the co-operation of employees.

## PLANNED OR SCHEDULED MAINTENANCE

Planned or scheduled maintenance is designed to reduce the number of sudden breakdowns of machinery and equipment. The scheme aims to keep plant running continuously during production time by adopting a programme of continuous maintenance which reduces emergency maintenance to a minimum. Accurate maintenance records and effective control procedures help to reduce maintenance costs by making the best use of maintenance staff.

## Preventive maintenance

Preventive maintenance specifies periodic cleaning, servicing, inspection and replacement of parts prone to breakdown. It includes duplication of vital parts which are built into the machines where practicable. An example is two valves or two motors which can be quickly switched from one to the other in the event of a breakdown. Where this system is not possible, provision is made for spares to be immediately available for replacement. Schedules are established for servicing time, consequently maintenance may be conducted without interrupting production. Within this scheme any vital parts are replaced after a specified running time. They are then serviced and prepared for replacement next time the change is due. The advantage is that changeover time can be arranged rather than waiting for a sudden breakdown, which always seems to occur when it is least convenient.

Preventive maintenance must be justified on a cost reduction basis. Economies should be demonstrated, typically by keeping records of previous waste through breakdowns and comparing the situation with forecasts for preventive maintenance. Unfortunately, plant still breaks down at inconvenient times in spite of preventive maintenance. Therefore, keeping a balance of savings is essential. This avoids the tendency for the programme to grow continually in attempts to stop breakdowns completely, which would be uneconomic and practically impossible to achieve.

## Long-term maintenance

Long-term maintenance schemes are usually more sophisticated than preventive maintenance. They include built-in maintenance devices which automatically compensate or provide facilities for switching to duplicated sections when breakdowns occur. A typical example is automatic or semi-automatic lubrication devices to maintain essential moving parts. Protective covers and guards ensure that certain vital parts of a machine are safely sealed from dust and corrosion. Where practicable, permanently sealed units are built into the machine. These units are stringently tested for endurance and are replaced at the end of their recommended life.

## QUESTIONS

1 Outline the main factors that affect productivity.

2 Measurement of overall productivity must include the effectiveness of all main functions. Discuss this statement.

3 Explain the terms 'regulated control' and 'deregulated control' associated with administration control.

4 What is just-in-time administration?

5 Discuss the four main cost reduction concepts.

6 Write an essay on the supervisor's part in reducing waste.

7 Discuss the problem of attitudes towards waste in the factory.

8 As a supervisor, how would you conduct a cost reduction programme?

9 Discuss the ways in which labour costs could be reduced.

10 What methods would you employ to carry out a survey of materials costs in your section?

11 In what ways could you develop a cost-conscious outlook among your colleagues?

12 What arguments would you use to convince an employee that cost reduction is very important?

13 How would you deal with this attitude from an employee who has carelessly broken a tool: 'I can't see that it matters; there are plenty more in the stores and the firm can afford it'?

14 What are the essential requirements for a maintenance improvement programme?

15 Describe ways of improving plant efficiency.

16 Outline a plan for an initial survey of the effectiveness of your department.

17 There is ample opportunity for the supervisor to develop a cost-conscious outlook in employees. Do you agree with this? Explain your answer.

18 Outline the main cost reduction concepts.

19 Discuss the just-in-time philosophy to improve productivity.

20 List the administrative features of productivity and the part the supervisor plays in the sequence of control.

21 Explain logistics and its use in cost reduction schemes.

22 How does a productivity culture differ from a cost reduction programme?

23 Supervisory control of costs relies partly upon the time factor, the significance of the amount of waste, and recording the information. Discuss this view.

24 Discuss the uses of cost reduction checklists.

25 Explain the supervisor's role in encouraging all personnel to generate growth by using creative thinking.

26 Discuss the techniques of Kaizen and Hoshin Kanri.

27 How should a supervisor tap the knowledge acquired by employees during day-to-day activities?

28 The supervisor has a moral responsibility to bear in mind environmental pollution when considering costs. Explain the significance of this view.

29 The supervisor's role should include feeding back opinions on the value of the information received. How should the supervisor gather these opinions?

## CASE STUDY

Meadowland Products was involved in importing toys and marketing them to retail outlets. The rising costs of importing were causing concern since the company was operating on narrow profit margins. A programme of cost reduction was obviously needed but it was proving difficult to choose the best approach in view of the nature of the business. The main features of the organisation were coping with deliveries from overseas, storing the toys in suitable conditions, stock control, selecting and packing for retailers, and distribution on time.

*Suggest a suitable cost reduction approach in these circumstances.*

## CASE STUDY

In the Robson Company a feud has developed between works manager Cliff and maintenance engineer Howard. Howard is responsible to the managing director and seems to be in favour. Cliff is similarly responsible but does not receive the support he expects. He is intent on introducing a planned maintenance programme to avoid the continuing breakdown problems, but Howard will not entertain the idea.

*As a supervisor working for Cliff, how could you assist him with this problem?*

## CASE STUDY

Rose Tints relied heavily on administration to provide a rapid mail order service. In recent months complaints on the service were increasing and regular clients were not reordering. The administration manager retired two months ago and a newcomer was having difficulty coping with his new job. He decided to write a report to the managing director proposing a change from deregulated systems to regulated control; this would be costly to start with but worthwhile eventually. He further suggested appointing a human resource manager and introducing a computerised network.

*Explain the implications of these changes. Justify the high cost considering productivity and customer service.*

# Suggested projects for Part Three

**Project 1**
Conduct a small work study project in your establishment. Outline the procedure to be adopted, record your findings and any resistance from subordinates, give an account of the installation of the new method and any follow-up. Keep a detailed record of your study and include your personal observations.

**Project 2**
Revise the layout of your workshop. Draw up diagrams to show the existing layout and the proposed layout. Include a detailed account of the reasons for your proposals and the probable snags you would expect to encounter during the changeover period.

**Project 3**
Choose two assembly operations and carry out a thorough study of the methods in use. Revise the operations using the principles of method study and motion economy. Write a detailed report on the existing operations and the proposed changes.

**Project 4**
Conduct a survey of the existing production control system in your establishment. Analyse the system and the requirements; redesign a new system using Gantt charts if they are not already employed.

**Project 5**
Study labour and machine utilisation in your company. Draw up the existing scheme and redesign it, or design a new scheme if your company does not have one.

**Project 6**
Study the production system in your company and plan or revise a system of progressing. Illustrate your method with suitable diagrams and explanations.

**Project 7**
Investigate the inspection activities in your establishment and devise a suitable system of quality control. Make an account of the existing arrangements and justify your proposed scheme.

**Project 8**
Conduct a survey of administration control in your company by studying the systems in operation and attempting to determine their effectiveness. If the systems are computerised, assess the comments from VDU operators and supervisors who use the information for day-to-day control.

**Project 9**
Investigate the procedures for quality control in the offices. Pay particular attention to quality failures from administrative records. Try to establish any attempts to improve quality through administrative processes and comment on their success.

**Project 10**
Study the cash flow system in your company over an appropriate period. Determine whether there have been any crises and how they were controlled.

**Project 11**
Examine the employee culture in your establishment. Interview clerks and operators to determine their attitudes towards contributing ideas and their experiences of the outcomes.

# Bibliography

## The classics

Argyris, C. *Organisation and Innovation* (Wiley 1957)

Beer, S. *Cybernetics and Management* (English University Press 1968)

Burns, G. and Stalker, G.M. *The Management of Innovation* (Tavistock 1966)

Carnegie, Dale *The Leader in You* (Pocket Books 1945)

Carnegie, Dale *How to Win Friends* (World's Work 1938)

Cattel, R.H. *Analysis of Personality* (Penguin USA 1965)

Drucker, P.F. *The Practice of Management* (Pan 1955)

Elbourne, F.E. *Fundamentals of Industrial Administration* (Macdonald & Evans 1947)

Fayol, H. *Industrial and General Administration* (Pitman 1949)

Fiedler, F.E. *The Contingency Model* (Holt, Rinehart & Winston 1966)

Follett, M.P. *Dynamic Administration* (Pitman 1941)

Gowers, E. *The Complete Plain Words* (HMSO 1954)

Herzberg, F. *The Motivation to Work* (Wiley 1959)

Katz, D. and Kahn, R.L. *The Social Psychology of Organisations* (Wiley 1966)

Likert, R. *New Patterns of Management* (McGraw-Hill 1961)

McDougall, W. *An Introduction to Social Psychology* (Methuen 1953)

McGregor, D. *The Human Side of Enterprise* (McGraw-Hill 1960)

Maier, N. *Psychology in Industry* (Houghton Mifflin 1946)

Maslow, A.H. *Motivation and Personality* (Harper & Row 1954)

Mintzberg, H. *Nature of Managerial Work* (Harper & Row 1973)

Murrell, K. *Ergonomics* (Chapman & Hall 1965)

Schein, E.H. *Organisational Socialisation* (Winter 1968)

Simon, H.A. *Administrative Behaviour* (Macmillan 1957)

Stammers, R. and Patrick, J. *Psychology of Training* (Routledge 1975)

Stewart, R. *Reality of Management* (Heinemann 1963)

Taylor, F.W. *Scientific Management* (Harper & Row 1911)

Trist, E.L. *Organisational Choice* (Tavistock 1963)

Urwick, L. *The Elements of Administration* (Pitman 1943)

Woodward, J. *Industrial Organisation* (Oxford University Press 1965)

## Modern

Adam-Smith, D. *Human Resource Management* (Pitman 1998)

Anderson, R. *Data Processing* (Pitman 1990)

Appleby, R.C. *Modern Business Administration* (Pitman 1994)

Atkinson, P. *Achieving Results through Time Management* (Pitman 1988)

Bartram, P. *Perfect Business Writing* (Century 1994)

Bennett, R. *Management* (Pitman 1997)

Bennett, R. *Organisational Behaviour* (Pitman 1996)

Bragg, M. *Reinventing Influence* (Pitman 1996)

Brown, A. *Organisational Culture* (Pitman 1998)

Burnes, B. *Managing Change* (FT Management 1995)

Cameron, K.S. and Freeman, S.J. *Cultural Congruence* (JAI Press 1991)

Drucker, P. *The Practice of Management* (Heinemann 1989)

Fisher, K. *Leading Self-directed Work Teams* (McGraw-Hill 1993)

Freemantle, D. *What Customers Like about You* (Brealey 1998)

Freemantle, D. *Incredible Bosses* (McGraw-Hill 1990)

Handy, C.B. *Understanding Organisations* (Penguin 1976)

Handy, C.B. *The Age of Unreason* (Business Books 1989)

Handy, C.B. *The Hungry Spirit* (Hutchinson 1998)

Hargie, O. *Handbook of Communication Skills* (Routledge 1997)

Heller, R. *Culture Shock* (Coronet 1991)

Hollinshead, G. *et al. Employee Relations* (Pitman 1998)

Jennings, D. and Wattam, S. *Decision Making* (Pitman 1998)

Kanter, R.H. *The Change Masters* (Allen & Unwin 1984)

Katzen Bach, J. and Smith, D. *The Wisdom of Teams* (Harvard Business School 1993)

Kinlaw, D. *Coaching* (Gower 1998)

Lockyer, K. and Gordon, J. *Critical Path Analysis* (Pitman 1991)

Mullins, L.J. *Management and Organisation Behaviour* (Pitman 1996)

Murphy, M. *Small Business Management* (Pitman 1996)

Oakland, J.S. *Total Quality Management* (Heinemann 1989)

Pascale, R. *Managing on the Edge* (Viking 1990)

Pedler, M. *et al. Self-development in Organisations* (McGraw-Hill 1990)

Pocock, M.A. and Taylor, A.H. *Financial Planning and Control* (Gower 1989)

Senior, B. *Organisational Change* (Pitman 1997)

Sherwood, D. *Unlock Your Mind* (Gower 1998)

Simon, C. and Naylor-Staples, X. *Effective Communication for Managers* (Cassell 1998)

Walsh, C. *Key Management Ratios* (Pitman 1995)

Walton, M. *Deming Management at Work* (Mercury 1991)

Wellins, R.S., Byham, W.C. and Wilson, J.M. *Empowered Teams* (Jossey Business Management 1991)

Wisniewski, M. *Quantitative Methods for Decision Makers* (Pitman 1997)

Wood, F. *Business Accounting* (Pitman 1989)

## Journal articles

Reddin, W. (1969) Managing organisational change, *Personnel*, July

Denison, D.R. (1984) Bring corporate culture to the bottom line, *Organisational Dynamics*, Autumn

# Index